PUEBLA DE LOS ANGELES

INDUSTRY AND SOCIETY IN A
MEXICAN CITY, 1700-1850

Dellplain Latin American Studies

* indicates a book in the series that is now out of print.

Dellplain Latin American Studies

PUBLISHED IN COOPERATION WITH
THE DEPARTMENT OF GEOGRAPHY
SYRACUSE UNIVERSITY

Editor

David J. Robinson

Editorial Advisory Committee

John K. Chance
Arizona State University

William M. Denevan
University of Wisconsin

W. George Lovell
Queen's University

Robert McCaa
University of Minnesota

Linda Newson
University of London

Publication Design and Cartography

Marcia J. Harrington
Syracuse University

"The Marketplace, Puebla, around 1835" by Agustín Arrieta
Reproduced with permission from the "Colección del Banco Nacional de Mexico", Mexico City

PUEBLA DE LOS ANGELES

INDUSTRY AND SOCIETY IN A
MEXICAN CITY, 1700-1850

Guy P. C. Thomson

Dellplain Latin American Studies, No. 25

Westview Press
Boulder, San Francisco & London

In memory of
Alfredo Portilla-Livingston
Born March 2, 1948
Died October 6, 1988

Dellplain Latin American Studies

This Westview softcover edition is printed on acid-free paper and bound in softcovers that carry the highest rating of the National Association of State Textbook Administrators, in consultation with the Association of American Publishers and the Book Manufacturers' Institute.

Copyright © 1989 by the Department of Geography, Syracuse University

Published in 1989 in the United States of America by Westview Press, Inc., 5500 Central Avenue, Boulder, Colorado 80301, and in the United Kingdom by Westview Press, Inc., 13 Brunswick Centre, London WC1N 1AF, England

Library of Congress Cataloging-in-Publication Data
Thomson, Guy.
    Puebla de los Angeles : industry and society in a Mexican
city,
  1700–1850 / by Guy Thomson.
      p. cm.—(Dellplain Latin american studies; no. 25)
     Includes bibliographical references and index
     ISBN 0-8133-7781-1
     1. Puebla (Mexico)—Industries—History—18th century. 2. Puebla
(Mexico)—Industries—History—19th century. 3. Puebla—Economic
conditions.   4. Puebla (Mexico)—Social conditions. I. Title.
II. Series.
HC138.P78T47 1989
330.972′48—dc20   89-37522
                                                    CIP

Printed and bound in the United States of America

The paper used in this publication meets the requirements of the American National Standard for Permanence of Paper for Printed Library Materials Z39.48-1984.

10   9   8   7   6   5   4   3   2   1

Errata for Guy P.C. Thomson, *Puebla de los Angeles*

Page

23: paragraph 3, line 4 should read 85,615 *cargas,* not 85,65.
67: Table 2.3—Woodwork, 596 (5.6%) should be under Guanajuato, not under Oaxaca.
117: Fig. 3.1—points on graph where values are given as zero should be read as years with no data. Source of data is AAP, Cuentas (1799–1855).
118: Fig. 3.2 should read Quantities of Maize Sold from the Patio and Trojes of Puebla . . .
119: "Row Numbers" should read "Years."
123: line 9 from bottom should read Fig. 3.3; line 5 from bottom should read Fig. 3.2.
124: Fig. 3.3—base of graph should read Years (from 1804 to 1815).
125: line 7 should read Fig. 3.2; lines 7 and 11 from bottom should read Fig. 3.2.
156: Table 4.2—column for 1771, "Total District," 71,366, should be in column of year 1777(1); column 1777(2), "Total City" should read 47,295, not 7,295.
159: Table 4.3 is in error; see correct table below.
174: Table 4.7—West 11 (whole cuartel) values should read: 1821, 620; 1828, 713; 1830, 661; 1834, 520; 1844/46, 822.
183: Table 4.10—in Sources the "b" should read *.
185: Table 4.11—in 1846 column, Food and Drink should be 102 (5.14%), not 10 (25.14%).
212: line 3 of footnotes should read época, not "-poca."
292: line 9 should read Table 8.1, not 8.2.
293: line 12 should read Table 8.2, not 8.3.
300: line 10 should read Table 8.3, not 8.4.
306: Table 9.1—column head should read Tax Categories (1847), not 1947, both pages.
322: Table 9.5—in left column each line should read "Holders of One Stall," "Holders of Two Stalls," etc.; total in each year should read 120.
348: Table A.1—years 1821–28 missing, see over.

TABLE 4.3 PUEBLA AND MEXICO CITY POPULATION, 1740-1848: MORTALITY FROM MAJOR EPIDEMICS

	PUEBLA			MEXICO		
	Whites	Indians (Tributaries)	Total		Whites	Indians (Tributaries)	Total
1735		6,782					
1736				1736		6,786	
1737 EPIDEMIC - Typhoid			54,000 deaths	1737 EPIDEMIC - Typhoid			40,150 deaths
1742	15,000 families		91,000	1742	50,000 families	8,400	98,000
1746			50,366	1748		8,049	
				1750			90,000
				1754		7,262	
1761/62 EPIDEMIC - Smallpox* & *Matlazahuatl*			9,160 deaths	1761/62 EPIDEMIC - Smallpox			14,600 deaths
1764		5,169					
				1772 EPIDEMIC - *Matlazahuatl*			13,000 deaths
1775		4,934				4,400	
1777			56,168				
1779	28,813		53,870				
1779 EPIDEMIC - Smallpox & Measles			18,000 deaths	1779 EPIDEMIC - Smallpox		estimates of 9-20,000 deaths	
1786		5,705					
1793		3,425	56,859		52,706	8,893	130,602
1797/98 EPIDEMIC - Smallpox			10,000 deaths	1797/98 EPIDEMIC - Smallpox			7,143
1800		3,746				9,672	
1801		2,985					
1803			67,800	1803	67,500		137,000
				1810/11			150,000/168,846
				1813			123,907
1813 EPIDEMIC - Yellow fever			7,089-17,000 deaths	1813 EPIDEMIC - Yellow fever			20,385 deaths
1822/23			47,842				165,000
1833 EPIDEMIC - Cholera			5,000 deaths	1833 EPIDEMIC - Cholera			9,619 deaths
1848			71,631				
				1855			200,000

* 80,000 perished in the province of Puebla

TABLE A.1 CONTD.

	1821	1822	1823	1824	1825	1826	1827	1828
TLAXCALA								
San Pablo de Monte	875	380	930	449	430	185	70	218
Santa Inés Zacatelco	135	195	285	571	445.5	411	518	561
Topoyango	275	125	191	180	258	130	275	130
Teolocholco	38	70	75	100	-	-	3	-
Tetlatlaca	263	270	403	125	250	239	310	35
Ixtacuixtla	833	786	1933	2073	1748	1014	1620	1328
Ponotla	-	25	110	115	55	65	-	-
Tlaxcala	-	60	117	500	500	500	-	-
Nativitas	2833	2977	4414	3252	3723	2293	3301	3644
District of Tlaxcala	5252	4888	8458	7365	7409.5	4837	6097	5916
TEPEACA AND TECALI								
Tepeaca	140	75	290	235	550	75	100	100
Nopalucan	150	170	290	218	165	-	-	500
Tecali	85	135	-	10	48	-	43	-
Zicatlacoya	-	-	-	-	-	-	-	-
Acaxete	780	971	908	808	830	180.5	545	554
Districts of Tepeaca and Tecali	1155	1351	1488	1271	1593	255.5	688	1154
PUEBLA - DISTRICT								
Resurrección	1081	874	1303.5	1002	1420	552	12191	439
Huatinchan	55	80	200	78	13	63	22	50
Amazoque	637	717	757	687	823	323	442	368
Totimehuacán	550	596	785	455	324	330	231	437
District of Puebla	2323	2267	3045.5	2222	2580	1268	1914	2294
PUEBLA - CITY								
Cathedral	1027	800	780	1004	1290	1310	1478	1675
San Sebastián	3748	3018	3758	3830	4584	3543	3155	3577
San Marcos	246	174	112.5	118	116	61	275	320
Senor San José	1215.5	999	787	611	920	641	628	645
Santa Cruz	100	151	200	40	53	31	45	95.5
Santo Angel	1080	919	1476	1388	1664.5	499	1285.5	1424
City of Puebla	7416.5	6061	7113.5	7091	8627.5	6085	6866.5	7736.5
CHOLULA AND ATLITXCO								
San Pedro Cholula	2564	2647	3961	2986	3838	2077	2537	2444
San Andrés Cholula	1386	1292	1289	710	1033	923	788	950
Santa Clara Ocoyuca	873	527	898	863	933	590	947	830
Santa Isabel Cholula	95	126	144	320	40	50	18	50
Calpan	90	35	85	95	185	50	130	265
Tianguismanalco	160	130	310	115	180	85	60	190
Curonango	1430	1171	1615	1458	2038	1321	1673	2103
District of Cholula	6598	5928	8302	6547	8247	5096	6153	6832
HUEJOTZINGO								
Huejotzingo	4062	2960	5343	3744	4242	3475	3407	3501
Chaucingo	130	80	90	90	50	70	40	20
San Martín	416	685	740	812	655	607	465	590
	4608	3725	6173	4646	4947	4152	3912	4111
Total	27352.5	24220	34580	29142	33404	21693.5	25630.5	28043.5

Source: AOP, Libros de Diezmos, Trigo, Vols. I-III.

Contents

Part I   Crisis and Instability in a Provincial Economy: Puebla 1700-1830

Part II Puebla in the Protectionist Era

Tables

Figures

Abbreviations

AEA	*Anuario de Estudios Americanos*
CDIHE	*Colección de Documentos Inéditos para la Historia de España*
BSNGE	*Boletín de la Sociedad Nacional de Geografía e Estadística*
CIHS-	Centro de Investigaciones Históricas y Sociales - Instituto de Ciencias
ICUAP	Universidad Autónoma de Puebla
DHCAM	*Documentos para la historia del crédito agrícola en México*
HMex	*Historia Mexicana*
HAHR	*Hispanic American Historical Review*
IESHR	*Indian Economic and Social History Review*
INAH-DIH	Instituto Nacional de Antropología e Historia - Departamento de Investigaciones Históricas
JGSWFL	*Jahrbuch für Geschichte von Staat, Wirtschaft und Gesellschaft Lateinamerikas*
RHA	*Revista de Historia de América*
TAms	*The Americas*
WMQ	*William and Mary Quarterly*

Values, Weights and Measures

a) Money

Mexican Currency	Contemporary equivalent values
1 peso = 8 reales	5 pesos = 1 Pound Sterling
1 real = 4 cuartillas	1 peso = 5 French Francs
1 real = 8 tlacos	1 peso = 1 U.S. Dollar
1 real = 12 granos	

b) Weights

1 libra = 1 English lb. approx. = 16 onzas = 0.46 kilos
1 arroba = 25 libras = 11.5 kilos
1 quintal (hundredweight) = 4 arrobas = 100 lbs. = 45 kilos
1 tercio = 1 "carga de acémila" (mule load) = 7 arrobas = 175 lbs =
    80.5 kilos
1 fanega = 1.5 English bushels = approx. 65 kilos of maize
1 carga = 2 fanegas = 14 arrobas = 400 lbs.

c) Linear measures

1 League = 2.6 English miles
1 Castilian yard (*vara*) = 36 English Inches = 0.836 meters
"Largo de Manta" of 1 piece of *manta* = 32 yards = 26.75 meters

---

Sources: Francisco Telles Guerrero, *De Reales y Granos*, pp. 87; Reinhard Liehr, *Ayuntamiento y Oligarquía*, Vol. 2, pp. 51-52; Manuel Carrera Stampa, "The Evolution of Weights and Measures in New Spain", *HAHR*, Vol. XXIX, 1949, pp. 2-24; Jan Bazant, "Industria algodonera poblana de 1803-1843 en números", *HMex*, Vol. XIV, 1964, pp.142; Enrique Florescano, *Precios del maíz*, pp.73-76.

Acknowledgments

In the preparation of this book many debts have been incurred. Malcolm Deas provided the original stimulus and guidance as my thesis supervisor. Without periodic proddings from David Brading, Brian Hamnett, Edward Countryman and Alistair Hennessy, the study most probably would have remained unpublished as a doctoral dissertation. I received added encouragement from David J. Robinson, John Coatsworth, Juan Carlos Garavalgia, Juan Carlos Grosso, and Mary Kay Vaughan. Anthony MacFarlane and Brian Hamnett read and suggested improvements to much of the text. I am particularly grateful to Anthony McFarlane as an exemplary colleague: for his interest, encouragement and companionship. Lastly, Louise Campbell provided critical support on the occasions when the project of recasting an imperfect sculpture seemed impossible.

I acknowledge the generous financial support of the Department of Education and Science, The London School of Economics, the British Academy, the University of Warwick, The British Council, C.O.N.A.C.Y.T. (Mexico), and the Mexican Ministry of Foreign Affairs. Warwick University Research and Innovations Fund paid for the typing of the manuscript, a task expertly executed by Caroline Hansen, Vera Collett, Caroline Carr and Kay Rainsley.

In Mexico, my debts are too numerous to list fully. Moisés González Navarro provided excellent supervision during my first acquaintance with archival research. Fellow researchers, Fernando Díaz y Díaz, Aristides Medina Rubio, Julie Hirchberg, Marcos Vivanco, and Blanca Lara provided companionship during long days in the archives. The "compañeros de la comuna" and the Portilla family allowed me to share their homes in Mexico City. Enrique Florescano and Alejandra Moreno Toscano provided, in the Centro de Estudios Históricos (I.N.A.H.), a stimulating and critical forum for first airing the results of the research. Alfonso Vélez Pliego, then Director of the Faculty of Philosophy at the Universidad Autónoma de Puebla, generously proportioned unlimited microfilm facilities. Finally, the staff of the following libraries, archives and museums provided the environment for research: the Archivo de Indias (Seville), the Archivo General de la Nación (Mexico), the British Library, the Public Record Office, the Archivo del Ayuntamiento de Puebla, the Archivo General de Notarías de Puebla, the Archivo de la Catedral de Puebla, the Biblioteca Nacional (Mexico), the Hemeroteca Nacional (Mexico), the Biblioteca Lafragua (Puebla), Biblioteca Palafoxiano (Puebla), the Museo Bello, the Museo del Estado de Puebla, the Centro de Estudios Históricos (Puebla), the Institute of Latin American Studies Library (Austin, Texas) and the Bodleian.

Guy P.C. Thomson
Warwick

Introduction

From soon after its foundation in 1532 until the early twentieth century, Puebla de los Angeles was Mexico's second city. Throughout this time this city, eighty miles to the east of the capital, was the country's major center of manufacturing, specializing in cotton textiles but also producing hats, soap, candles, confectionery, glass, porcelain and pottery, paper, leather goods and ironware. Puebla was also a large city by American standards, with a population which fluctuated between 45,000 and 80,000, rivalling if not exceeding that of most Spanish American capitals, during the 1700-1850 period.[1]

The city of Puebla de los Angeles is the principal subject of study. Spatial narrowness and the regional historian's obsession with place has, it is hoped, been compensated, by the breadth of thematic focus - encompassing social, economic and political history - and by looking at the history of the city within a regional context and in comparative perspective. Research for this study began at a time when Mexican regional historical research was in its infancy. It is now in its childhood and this study suffers from some of the defects of a precocious and uninhibited infancy. Were a study of the region of Puebla to be begun now, the student would be well advised not to take on more than one of the subjects which occupy the ten chapters which follow. Notable historiographical advances have been made in all of the main areas covered, the understanding of which has been taken beyond the conclusions reached in this study.[2] Any merit in this study therefore lies in its broad scope, its long time period (bestriding the conventional division between "colony" and "nation") and its search,

---

[1] Louisa Schell Hoberman and Susan Migden Socolow (Eds.), *Cities and Society in Colonial Latin America*. Albuquerque, 1986, p. 5.

[2] For the results of recent research on the Puebla region see: Centro de Investigaciones Históricas y Sociales (CIHS), Instituto de Ciéncias, Universidad Autónoma de Puebla, *Puebla en en siglo XIX: Contribución al estudio de su historia*. Puebla, 1983; CIHS, *Puebla de la Colonia a la Revolución*. Puebla, 1987; Juan Carlos Grosso, *Estructura productiva y fuerza de trabajo. Puebla, 1830-1890*. Puebla, 1984; Francisco Telles G., *De Reales y granos. Las finanzas y el abasto de la Puebla de los Angeles, 1820-1840*. Puebla, 1986; Alberto Carabarín, *El trabajo y los trabajadores del obraje en la ciudad de Puebla, 1700-1710*. Puebla, 1984; Carlos Contreras, *La ciudad de Puebla. Estancamiento y modernidad de un perfíl urbano en el siglo XIX*. Puebla, 1986; and Jay Kinsbruner, *Petty Capitalism in Spanish America: The Pulperos of Puebla, Mexico City, Caracas, and Buenos Aires*. Boulder, 1986.

inevitably a preliminary one, for interrelations between the variety of subjects covered.

From the beginning, the set of questions which animated the research for this study were similar, in some respects, to those which preoccupied Bourbon administrators and mercantilists during the late colonial period. Surely, in an empire governed upon mercantilist principles, a colonial city whose economy was based upon the production of goods directly competitive with those of the metropolis was an anomaly, if not an affront ? That the second city of New Spain, for over two hundred years, had been able to satisfy much of the colony's demand for basic manufactures, was evidence of Spain's industrial backwardness, a state Spain's talented administrators were intent upon overcoming. Puebla's industries highlighted the failure of the imperial economy to move beyond mere bullionism and a largely "passive" trade to a more dynamic colonial trade which would hasten Spain's own industrialization. Indeed, Viceroy Count Revillagigedo (1789-94) saw the industrialization of New Spain as the principal threat to the integrity of the Empire:

> ...no debe perderse de vista que esto es una colonia que debe depender de su matriz de España, y debe corresponder a ella con algunas utilidades por los beneficios que recibe de su protección, y así se necesita gran tino para combinar esta dependencia y que se haga mútuo y recíproco el interés, la cual desavia en el momento que no necesitase aún de las manufacturas y sus frutos.[3]

Similar, though more confident, colonialist sentiments were voiced by Henry Ward, the first British Minister to Mexico during the 1820s. He argued that Mexican industry could only compete with the European if protected by high import tariffs. These, however, would represent a "tax" upon the rest of the population. It would be much better for Mexico not to attempt to compete but to concentrate upon mining and agriculture, in which she enjoyed obvious natural advantages.[4]

Thus Puebla as a subject originally appealed as an anomaly, a ready made counterfactual hypothesis, a city which specialized in what a colonial entrepot was not supposed to be doing: substituting imports and shielding itself from the impact of colonial trade. It seemed that a detailed study of a region over the period of transition from colony to independent nationhood would permit an empirical verification of the largely untested (at the time of research) hypotheses concerning the impact of Bourbon trade liberalization during the eighteenth century and the degree of external economic

---

[3] Conde de Revillagigedo, *Instrucciones que los Virreyes de Nueva España dejan a sus sucesores.* Mexico, 1873, Vol. II, p.136.

[4] Henry Ward, *Mexico in 1828*. London, 1829, Vol.II, pp. 74-82.

dependence of Latin American countries after Independence.[5] It is hoped that the resulting monograph will be of interest to students concerned with the economic impact of Spanish colonialism, with the effect in America of Bourbon mercantilist and liberal policies, with the effects of Britain's early industrialization on a manufacturing city at the "periphery" or with the Latin American responses to the early stages of "neo-colonialism" and "informal imperialism".

While guided by these problems, the study has only partially been fashioned by this concern with relations between a colonial city and the "external sector". It is easy to overstress the importance of the external connection. This, after all, was Mexico before its railway age when natural geographical obstacles and rudimentary transport and communications played a key part in fashioning regional economies by setting restraints upon overseas and even inter-regional economic relations. Quite as important as the city's economic relations with Europe, were its economic ties with other cities and regions of New Spain and its centrality within the province of Puebla itself. After all, the Intendancy of Puebla (later the State, under federalism, or Department, under centralism)) was both extensive and not sparsely populated, at least by Spanish standards. In 1803, Humboldt compared its land area to that of Aragon and noted that its population exceeded that of Catalonia.[6] The relations between the city and this wider provincial society are quite as important to understand if any judgement is to be made about the city's competitiveness with other Mexican cities and regions or the extent of the region's "dependency" in relation to the more developed economies of the United States and Europe.

Despite the thematic breadth of this study, its primary focus is economic. The actors who receive most attention are the city's merchants, manufacturers and artisans. And the part of their lives which the study examines is their work, be it buying, selling, producing, assembling, borrowing, investing, setting up machinery or gathering workers under a single roof to operate machines.

The long time span of the study might seem at first unmanageable, but it has an important purpose. Throughout the entire 1700-1850 period of study, the urban and regional economy of Puebla remained a shadow of what it had been during the "golden age", lasting for a century after the city's foundation in 1532. During its first prosperous century, the city and its immediate region became Spanish America's principal producer of woollen cloth and New Spain's breadbasket. Manufactured and agricultural goods reached markets extending to the northernmost settlements of New Spain and as far south as Peru. The city possessed a merchant body which

---

5 Stanley J. Stein and Barbara H. Stein, *The Colonial Heritage of Latin America*. New York, 1970; and D. C. M. Platt, *Latin America and British Trade 1806-1914*. London, 1972.

6 Alejandro Humboldt, *Ensayo Político sobre el Reino de la Nueva España*. Mexico, 1966, pp. 157-161.

rivalled that of the viceregal capital, serving as the inland port of Mexico's Atlantic trade.[7] And during the seventeenth century Puebla's population approached that of the capital. Economic conditions would never again be so good. One aim of the study was to trace how *poblanos* perceived their region's glorious past and to observe what measures they took to prevent further decline and to achieve a degree of reconstruction.

It was therefore necessary to look into the eighteenth century in order to understand the pathology of relative economic decline. For Puebla, rather like Boston, the eighteenth century was one of "variable instability".[8] There were brief periods of growth, longer periods of acute depression, within a longue durée of population stagnation (caused by emigration to other regions), progressive marginalization from the principal trade routes, and the loss of extra-regional markets for agricultural and manufactured goods.[9] So while other regions of New Spain underwent sustained, broadly based and sometimes spectacular (in the case of the Guadalajara basin and the Bajío) economic growth, Puebla slipped back ever-further in the provincial economic stakes. The only area of growth during the eighteenth century was around cotton cloth and shawl production and this appears to have been more a response to agricultural depression, poverty and unemployment than a sign of economic dynamism or a harbinger of industrial transformation.

This, then, is a study of a regional economy over a period of fairly continual economic instability and political crisis. In the latter part of the period (1810-1850), the Mexican economy lost the relative dynamism and high productivity which it had enjoyed over the second half of the

---

7 As an eighteenth-century chronicler observed: "...era [Puebla] como almacén o bodega a donde venían a parar la mayor parte de géneros de Europa y de aquí se difundían a las provincias comarcanas que acudían a la Ciudad de los Angeles a proveerse de lo que en cada una de ellas se necesitaba. Duró esto hasta los principios de este nuestro siglo...", Mariano Fernández Echeverría, *Historia de la Fundación de la Ciudad de la Puebla de los Angeles*. Puebla, 1963, Vol. I, p. 296. On Puebla's commercial centrality during the seventeenth century see also: Pierre Chaunu, *Seville et l'Atlantique 1504-1650 Deuxiéme Parte. Partie Interpretative Ports-Routes-Trafics*, Vol. VIII, 1959, p. 714; and José F. de la Peña, *Oligarquía y propiedad en Nueva España, 1550-1624*. Mexico, 1983.

8 This term is used by to describe the uneven performance of Boston during the eighteenth century (also past its "golden age") in the face of competition from New York and Philadelphia, currency insufficiency and colonial, Indian and revolutionary wars. See G.B. Warden, "Inequality and Instability in Eighteenth Century Boston: A Reappraisal", *Journal of Inter-disciplinary History*, Vol. VI, 1976, pp. 585-620.

9 Juan Carlos Garavaglia and Juan Carlos Grosso, "La región de Puebla/Tlaxcala y la economía novohispana (1670-1821)", *Historia Mexicana*, Vol. 35, 1986, pp. 549-600.

eighteenth century.[10] The economic stagnation and political instability which marked the half-century following the outbreak of the revolutions of Independence in 1810 were unpropitious conditions for fostering an indigenous industrial revolution or the Rostovian "take-off". Yet the modern machines and revolutionary forms of industrial organization, which so revolutionized British society during this period, were introduced to Mexico between 1835 and the 1850s. And they were concentrated in Puebla, enabling the city to reassert its industrial lead in Mexico. Yet by 1850, no illusions existed, even in Puebla, that modern machinery and the factory system had substantially altered Mexican economy and society, which remained overwhelmingly pre-industrial, with modern or artisan industry confined to a few highland cities in the center and south of the country.

The introduction of modern industrial technology served therefore a restorative rather than a revolutionary purpose. Given the constraints upon export-led, agricultural or mining growth (the path which Mexico eventually took out of economic stagnation) before the coming of the railways, it is hard to imagine any other way by which Puebla might have achieved economic reconstruction than through the mechanization of its traditional staple industry; cotton textiles. Industrial modernization behind protectionist tariffs, lifted the city from the depths of post-colonial decay during the 1820s to a state of tangible prosperity by the 1850s.

It might be assumed that economic stagnation and the failure of industrial modernization to lead to "industrial revolution", left Mexican society suspended, unchanged, in a petrified state during the first half the nineteenth century. Such was not the case. Economic stagnation and periodic economic crises were accompanied by substantial social changes which, on occasions, posed a serious challenge to the social order. These social changes are far more difficult to pin-point than their portentous European counterparts because of the restorative and piecemeal character of economic change. The political articulation of social changes was muted for the same reasons, the popular movements of the period becoming submerged beneath the military struggles. The study has attempted, however, to uncover some of the social history of the period.

As in Philadelphia and New York (in many respects Puebla's industrial cousins, from where Puebla industrialists acquired many of the skills and the machinery when establishing their factories), a clear division had emerged between master artisans and journeymen well before the onset of the new technology.[11] During the later eighteenth century, increasing

---

[10] John Coatsworth, "Obstacles to Economic Growth in Nineteenth Century Mexico", *American Historical Review*, Vol. 83, 1978, pp. 80-100.

[11] David Montgomery, "The Working Class of the Pre-Industrial City, 1780-1830", *Labor History*, Vol. 9, 1968, pp. 3-32; Sharon V Salinger, "Artisans, Journeymen, and the Transformation of Labor in Late Eighteenth-Century Philadelphia", *William and Mary Quarterly*, Vol. 40, 1983, pp. 62-84; Gary Nash, *The Urban*

European competition led to a decline in the effectiveness of the guilds as a means of maintaining an approximate equality of wealth among artisans within the same craft, while the decline of the apprenticeship system and the growth of larger units of production undermined the artisan household as the principal productive unit.[12] After Independence, political factionalism in Puebla fed upon this division of wealth and interest between the better established and wealthier artisans and the mass of irregularly employed journeymen. Periods of artisan militancy in Puebla during the 1820s and early 1830s coincided with the upsurge of artisan radicalism in Philadelphia and New York (and in Mexico City and Lima), assuming a less articulate though no less threatening form.[13] Thereafter, while overt class politics became submerged under ethnic politics in the United States cities, Mexico's artisan radicalism disappeared beneath the politics of protectionism and the accompanying military conflicts.

The social history of this period in Mexico has, to date, been confined to tracing (generally from census records) changes in the occupational structure, the organization of production, in the household as an economic unit, in residential patterns and work habits.[14] Work has barely begun on the broader cultural and political world of the non-elite population. This

Crucible:Social Change, Political Consciousness and the Origins of the American Revolution. Cambridge (Mass.) 1979, pp. 233-63 and 312-38; Bruce Laurie, *Working People of Philadelphia, 1800-1850*. Philadelphia, 1980, pp. 3-30; and Sean Wilentz *Chants, Democratic New York City and the Rise of the American Working Class, 1788-1850*. New York, 1984, pp. 23-60.

12   For these developments in Mexico City, see: Jorge González Angulo Aguirre, *Artesanado y ciudad a finales del siglo XVIII*. Mexico, 1983; and Felipe Castro Gutiérrez, *La Extinción de la Artesanía Gremial*. Mexico, 1986.

13   Laurie, *Working People*, pp. 85-104; Wilentz, *Chants, Democratic New York*, pp. 219-254. For militant artisans in Santiago de Chile, before they were regimented into Diego Portales' militias: L. A. Romero, *La Sociedad de la Igualdad: Los artesanos de Santiago de Chile y sus primeras experiencias políticas, 1820-1851*. Buenos Aires, 1978, pp. 38-40; for merchant-led protectionist radicalism in Lima during the late 1820s to mid 1830s: Paul Gootenburg, "The Social Origins of Protectionism and Free Trade in Nineteenth-Century Lima", *JLAS*, 1982, pp. 334-5; and for Mexico City artisan radicalism: Luis Alberto de la Garza, "Reformismo y Contra Revolución: La Caída de la Primera República Federal en México", mimeographed paper, Mexico, 1987.

14   For social history based largely upon the population census, see chapters by Adriana López Monjardín and María Dolores Morales in Alejandra Moreno Toscano (Ed.), *Ciudad de México: Ensayo de Construcción de una Historia*. Mexico, 1978; Silvia M. Arrom, *The Women of Mexico City, 1790-1857*. Stanford, 1985; John K Chance and William B. Taylor, "Estate and Class in a Colonial City: Oaxaca in 1792", *CSSH*, Vol. 19, 1977, pp. 454-87; and Patricia Seed, "Social Dimensions of Race: Mexico City, 1753", *HAHR*, 62, 1982, pp. 569-606.

study only touches upon these themes which are currently being researched in greater depth by Mexican historians.[15]

Apart from analyzing the causes of economic stagnation and crisis and charting entrepreneurial responses and social consequences, this study also has a political dimension. Politics and political economy provide keys to understanding the intersection between social and economic history. An abundant pamphlet literature permitted the elaboration of a subjective element to the study. This made it possible to advance beyond mere speculation about subsistence, insecurity and the pursuit of profit, to looking at the visions which animated people and to understanding the actions they took to advance their causes.

Much of the pamphlet literature is concerned with the role of the state in the economy. The form and substance of the Mexican state changed substantially during the 1700-1850 period. The study observes the emergence, apogee, decline and abolition of a guild system embracing most of Puebla's industries. Wholesale and retail trade underwent parallel phases of increasing restriction until the 1760s, followed by liberalization. The food supply of the city, from being closely controlled and supervised by the municipal government, was gradually freed after 1810. The government of the city also grew more uniform. From having been, at the beginning of the period, a complex interweaving of different ethnic jurisdictions under autonomous governors, it had become a single, unified municipality by the early nineteenth century.[16] Finally, on the level of provincial government, Habsburg administrative pragmatism gave way to Bourbon centralizing uniformity, culminating in independent statehood. The first thirty years of republican government, saw Puebla veer between the extremes of centralism and federalism. In the realm of ideas, *poblanos* over a century and a half passed from the corpus mysticum, to mercantilism, to physiocracy, to Smithean and Saint Simonean liberalism, to extreme autarkic protectionism. Not one of these systems of thought was either fully or generally embraced, or, for that matter, conclusively abandoned. These themes provide the ideological and institutional syntax of the study.

The apparent victory of economic liberalism (the abolition of most of the corporate institutions and privileges which permeated life during the colonial period) by 1821, and the establishment thereafter of representative institutions modelled on ideals of egalitarian republicanism, disguised underlying continuities. Many crafts continued, after the abolition of the

---

[15] A tantalising start has been made by Alejandra Moreno Toscano, "Los trabajadores y el proyecto de industrialización, 1810-1867", in Enrique Florescano et al., *La Clase Obrera en la Historia de México, de la colonia al imperio*. Vol. I, Mexico, 1981, pp. 302-350; and Frederick J. Shaw, Jr., Poverty and Politics in Mexico City, 1824-54, Ph.D. dissertation, University of Florida, 1975. Luis Alberto de la Garza (Ciencias Políticas, UNAM) is working on popular politics in Mexico City and Puebla during the first half of the nineteenth century.

[16] Hugo Leicht, *Las Calles de Puebla*. Puebla, 1967, pp. 178-79.

guilds in 1813, to organize an informal guild structure and the guild procession at Corpus Christi was observed as late as the 1860s.[17] The municipal government continued to intervene in the economy to favour the "common good", to set the "just price", as well as to protect or advance the particular economic interests of the conciliar group. State and national politics remained an elite affair, dominated in Puebla by patricians, clerics and the occasional spokesman for the artisans (more often a merchant or shopkeeper than a craftsman). Genuine popular politics were distrusted, quickly suppressed or diverted into fruitless military campaigning. Thus liberal reforms and constitutional republicanism modified but did not seriously undermine many of the more traditional features of urban society and politics.

The ideological manifestation of this underlying continuity of corporatist attitudes and forms was protectionism, the province's main contribution to Mexican national politics over the period. Protectionism became a religion in Puebla during the thirty years following Independence. It served as a doctrine for combatting economic liberalism which many feared would undermine the entire social edifice. It provided a coherent diagnosis of present ills, a path to salvation and a sentiment which, on occasions (particularly accompanying foreign wars and blockades), amounted to a collective hysteria. Thus, protectionism offered a cement, a passion, which could bind together divergent elements in provincial society, endowing politics with a sense of common purpose. It provided an area of common political ground in a hierarchical and crisis stricken urban society which was facing the novelties of representative republican politics and the introduction of modern industrial technology with some ambivalence. And it presented a formula by which regional interest groups throughout the Republic could agree upon a national project with prospects of immediate achievements and rewards. Against this, liberalism's promise of distant gains after a prolonged disruption of urban society, could hardly compete.

---

[17] Descriptions of guild processions: in 1809, showing loyalty to Ferdinand VII, José García Quiñones, *Descripción de las demostraciones con que la muy Noble y muy Leal Ciudad de la Puebla de los Angeles, Segunda de este Reyno de Nueva España.* Puebla, 1809; in 1825, celebrating the First Federal Republic, Eduardo Gómez Haro, *Puebla y sus Gobernadores.* Puebla, 1915, pp. 80-81; and in 1865, honoring the arrival of Prince Maximilian Habsburg: Anon., *Puebla en Cifras.* Mexico, 1944, p. 39.

PART I

✢ ✢ ✢

CRISIS AND INSTABILITY IN
A PROVINCIAL ECONOMY:
PUEBLA 1700-1830

✢ ✢ ✢

Chapter 1

THE ECONOMY OF THE PUEBLA REGION IN THE EIGHTEENTH AND EARLY NINETEENTH CENTURIES

C olonial Mexico was the sum of its regional economies. Mexico City, in spite of its privileged status as viceregal capital, its dominance of overseas trade and its demographic primacy, probably exercised less direct influence beyond the valley of Mexico than had its Aztec predecessor. New Spain's physical geography, combined with the generous regional scattering of the sources of wealth, encouraged, from the beginning of European settlement, a centrifugalism, economic localism and administrative and intellectual parochialism which became the most marked features of colonial life. Provincial societies acquired a high degree of autonomy and the dominance of provincial centers by the viceregal capital, asserted by a recent scholar of late colonial Mexico City, is not borne out in the growing corpus of regional studies.[1]

---

[1] "Mexico City occupied a primary position in the economy of the colony at large, dominating much economic activity in the provinces....[serving] as the residence of most families which made great fortunes..in the provinces.", John E. Kicza, *Colonial Entrepreneurs; Families and Business in Bourbon Mexico City.* Albuquerque, 1983, p. 227. Recent economic studies of other regions: P. J. Bakewell, *Silver Mining and Society in Colonial Mexico: Zacatecas 1546-1700 .* Cambridge, 1971; D. A. Brading, *Miners and Merchants in Bourbon Mexico, 1763-1810.* Cambridge, 1971 (In Guanajuato, the economic ties with Mexico City were stronger than with non-mining regions); D A Brading, *Haciendas and Ranchos in the Mexican Bajío: León, 1700-1860.* Cambridge, 1978; John K. Chance, *Race and Class in Colonial Oaxaca.* Stanford, 1978; Manuela Cristina García Bernal, *La Sociedad de Yucatán, 1700-1750.* Seville, 1972; Charles H. Harris III, *The Sánchez Navarro: A Socio-Economic Study of a Coahuilan Latifundio, 1846-1853.* Chicago, 1964, and *A Mexican Family Empire: the Latifundio of the Sánchez Navarros* (these studies reveal the inter-dependence of Northern and Central Mexico, rather than the dominance of the former by the latter); Richard Lindley, *Haciendas and Economic Development Guadalajara, Mexico at Independence.* Texas, 1983; Claude Morin,

Among the regional centers of New Spain, the Puebla region was of outstanding importance. From soon after its foundation Puebla de los Angeles not only enjoyed a high degree of autonomy but also grew to challenge Mexico's claim to be the political and economic center of New Spain.[2]   Indeed, there were moments in the seventeenth century when consideration was given to transferring the colony's capital from its insalubrious, flood and riot-prone island site to the healthier, more open and spacious and peaceful "Angelópolis" eighty miles to the east.[3]

For a century following the Conquest, Puebla's development as an agricultural, manufacturing and trading center was unbroken and unmatched.[4] However, with the abolition of inter-colonial trade and the onset of the mining depression in the mid-seventeenth century, Puebla's early advantages began to slip away so that by the eighteenth century Puebla was recognized as the sick man among Mexico's provinces.[5] The region's economy over the century and a half examined in this study veered between stagnation and crisis with only brief, windfall periods of prosperity made possible, as often, by crises elsewhere - Atlantic wars and blockades, and international trade recessions - as by any secular improvement in the province's trading position. The paradox which confronts us is how a province endowed with such abundant natural resources and so well placed to take advantage of them , traversed by New Spain's principal trade axes - the Mexico - Veracruz - Antequera triangle - proved unable, except for short periods, to secure at least stability, even if sustained prosperity proved

Michoacán en la Nueva España del Siglo XVIII: Crecimiento y Desigualdad en una Economía Colonial. Mexico, 1979; and Eric Van Young, *Hacienda and Market in Eighteenth-Century Mexico: The Rural Economy of the Guadalajara Region, 1675-1820.* Berkeley, 1981.

2   For Mexico-Puebla rivalry during the seventeenth century see: José F. de la Peña *Oligarquía y propiedad en Nueva España, 1550-1624.* Mexico, 1983, pp. 163-171; Jonathan Israel, *Race,Class and Politics in Colonial Mexico, 1610-1670.* Oxford, 1975; and Manuel Alvarado Morales, *La Ciudad de México ante la fundación de la Armada de Barlovento, 1635-1643.* Mexico, 1983.

3   W. Michael Mathes, "To Save a City: the *desague* of Mexico Huehuetoca, 1607", *The Americas,* Vol. 26, 1970, p. 419-438; Thomas Gage, *The English American. A New Survey of the West Indies,* 1648. Guatemala City, pp.51-52; and, Francisco Clavijero, "Breve descripción de la Provincia de México de la Companía de Jesús", in Mariano Cuevas, *Tesoros Documentales de México, Siglo XVIII,* Mexico, 1944, pp. 324-327.

4   Guadalupe Albi-Romero, "La sociedad de Puebla de los Angeles en el Siglo XVI", *Jahrbuch für Geschichte von Staat,* 1970, Vol. 7, pp. 17-145; and, Francois Chevalier, *Land and Society in Colonial Mexico, The Great Hacienda.* Berkeley, 1970.

5   Juan Carlos Garavaglia and Juan Carlos Grosso, "La Región de Puebla-Tlaxcala y la Economía Novohispana (1670-1821)", *Historia Mexicana,* Vol. XXXV, 1986, pp. 549-600.

illusory. The prolific petitioning and pamphleteering which issued from the city's presses, making Puebla Mexico's most articulate province over the thirty years following Independence, show that this was a paradox which preoccupied contemporaries. The city's Golden Age (1550-1650), and the short periods when it seemed that it had been recovered (during, for instance, the bubble of activity accompanying the Napoleonic Wars), exercised a powerful influence upon the imagination and political and commercial behavior of the province's leaders and entrepreneurs.

The essential precondition for the existence of an autonomist provincial mentality was an appreciation of an abundance of natural resources and the knowledge that these had once, and might once again, be successfully tapped. We must therefore begin by looking briefly at Puebla's natural endowments.

The City and its Region

The Mexican plateau is a sequence of basins separated from each other by volcanic ridges and mountain barriers of considerable density. The Puebla basin is the easternmost of these. It is made up of a series of interconnected plains and valleys, at altitudes of between 1,600 and 2,600 meters, extending ninety miles east-west and eighty miles north-south, bounded by the Sierra Nevada in the west, the Sierra Mixteca in the south and the Sierra Madre Oriental to the east and north. The Puebla region is also the most extensive and meteorologically and ecologically the most varied of the great basins of the Mexican plateau. Here the relation between mountainside and valley bottom is more favorable for agriculture than in any other temperate region of settlement within central and southeastern Mexico. The principal market towns and agricultural valleys could all be reached from the provincial capital along cart roads within one or two days. Although the central valley of Puebla is at a higher altitude than the neighboring valley of Mexico, and more exposed to the prevailing winds, particularly the northerlies (*nortes*) , humid in summer and often frost-bearing in winter and spring, and the desiccating southerly "*viento de Mixteca*", commentators over the centuries agree that this region has the most benign climate of the entire Mexican plateau.[6] Only pockets within the relief shadow of the Sierra Madre, between Perote and San Salvador el Seco, lack adequate rainfall to support arable farming. Large areas of the province are naturally irrigated by streams running off Mexico's four largest volcanos. Other parts, such as the Acatzingo-Tehuacan valley, are irrigated through an ingenious system of *galerías filtrantes* of Pre-Columbian origin,

---

[6] Enrique Juan Palacios, *Puebla y su territorio*. Puebla, 1917, Vol. I, p. 140.

4

which carry water from springs at the base of the limestone hills to fields in the center of valleys which otherwise would be arid and unproductive.[7]

Puebla de los Angeles was founded in 1532 when, at a time of humanist ascendancy, Viceroy Mendoza was seeking to bring some order to the freebooting society of conquistadores. Available *encomiendas* had already been granted and the Franciscan order had established a dense network of monasteries in this region leaving little political space for the growing number of Spanish farmers, artisans and vagrants attracted to these fertile valleys. Puebla de los Angeles was originally conceived as a "social experiment" designed to ease the settlement of these community-less Spaniards who, after receiving some help in becoming established from local Indian communities, would live off the fruits of their own labor and enterprise, rather from Indian tribute and labor service. It was hoped that the city would become a model for immigrant Spaniards who would imitate Puebla's industrious *vecinos* and learn that nothing could be gained in New Spain without hard work and self reliance. Puebla would also provide the seat for a diocese extending over much of southeastern Mexico.[8]

The city was granted extensive privileges which, combined with the valley's ideal location for the early development of pastoral and arable farming, and the opportunities in transport and trade, made Puebla one of the most attractive regions of settlement for immigrants from other parts of New Spain as from the Peninsular. Few other central places in Spanish America could have been freer than Puebla over the first century of its foundation: exemption from *alcabala* and *almojarifazgo* for one hundred years, all other taxes for thirty years, virtual self-government by a council elected from among the vecinos with no special privileges being accorded to *encomenderos* , a dispensation from the prying offices of *alcalde mayor* and *corregidor* and a healthy distance from the authoritarian administration of Viceroy Mendoza.[9] These privileges contributed to Puebla becoming Spanish America's foremost manufacturing city, and in New Spain, a

7 Enno Seele,"Galerías filtrantes en el Estado de Puebla", *Comunicaciones* , Vol. VII, 1973, pp. 141-4.

8 For the foundation and early history of Puebla: Pedro López de Villaseñor, *Cartilla Vieja de la Nobilísima Ciudad de Puebla*. Mexico,1961; Mariano Fernández de Echeverría y Veytia, *Historia de la Fundación de la Ciudad de la Puebla de los Angeles en la Nueva España, su Descripción y Presente Estado*. Puebla, 1963, 2 vols; Francois Chevalier, "La Signification Sociale de la Fondation de Puebla de los Angeles", *Revista de Historia de América*, Vol. XXIII, June, 1947, pp. 105-130; Julia Hirchberg, "La Fundación de Puebla de los Angeles - Mito y Realidad", *Historia Mexicana*, 1978, pp. 185-223; and her "Social Experiments in New Spain: A Prosopographical Study of the Early Settlement at Puebla de los Angeles, 1531-1534", *Hispanic American Historical Review*, Vol. 59, 1979, pp. 1-33.

9 Pedro López de Villaseñor, *Cartilla Vieja*, pp.65-66; and Albi-Romero, *Sociedad de Puebla*, p. 126.

5

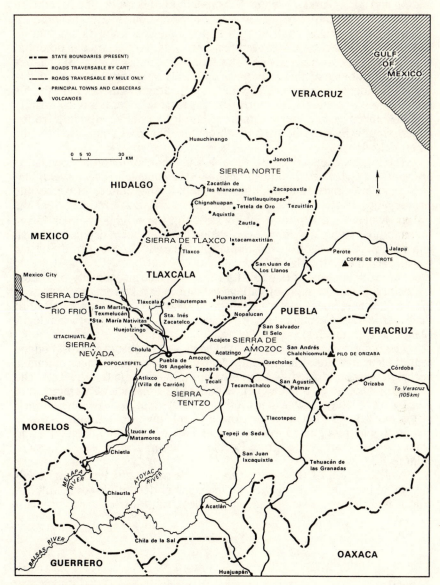

Figure 1.1 The Puebla Region

trading and administrative center second only to Mexico.[10] The foundation of Puebla may therefore be seen as a subtle expression of Royal absolutism: the granting of extensive privileges to a town of commoners, amounting almost to republican self-government, in order to curtail the potential autonomy of *encomenderos* and the religious orders, as well as to counter-balance the power of the viceregal capital. The full implications of this became evident a century later when, as Jonathan Israel shows, Puebla interests challenged the authority of successive viceroys and the city became, under Bishop Palafox, the test case for a process of secularization which would, by the mid eighteenth century, have affected most of the viceroyalty.[11]

The First Audiencia chose a sensible and durable site for the foundation of the city: a fertile, level and well-ventilated savanna left vacant after a Pre-Conquest war between neighboring Indian city states, close to the convergence of the Atoyac and San Francisco rivers, headwaters of the Balsas system [12] In spite of the existence of the originally much larger Indian city of Cholula nearby, Puebla soon became the undisputed political and economic center of the entire plateau region lying between the Sierra Nevada and the Sierra Madre Oriental.

On the southeastern flank of La Malinche volcano, the city of Puebla stands at the apex of a fan of valleys extending in all directions, except to the north where the Bloque de Tlaxcala separates the central valley of Puebla from the plateau region of Apizaco, Huamantla and San Juan de los Llanos (see Figure 1.1).

The political boundaries of the Intendency of Puebla lay far beyond the central plateau region. Like the Intendencies of Mexico and Oaxaca, Puebla occupied territory extending from the Gulf to the Pacific (Figure 1.2). The colonial bishopric of Puebla even included the Province of Veracruz and tithes were received from as far south as Tabasco. In 1849, the tenuousness of the natural links between the northern and southern extremities of the province was recognized as a political fact when Tlapa, Igualapa and Ometepec were amputated from Puebla to join the new State of Guerrero (Figure 1.3)

A description of the agricultural region must start within the city's municipal boundaries. Here, among the ruins of declining Indian *barrios*, wheat, maize, lucerne, temperate vegetables, fruit, flowers, dairy products

---

[10] Albi-Romero, "La sociedad de Puebla", pp. 138-144.

[11] Jonathan Israel, *Race, Class and Politics*, pp. 192-247.

[12] At Conquest the site had long been a no-man's land on the frontier between the warring states of Tlaxcala, Totimehuacán-Cuautinchán and Cholula. See Antonio Carrión, *Historia de la Ciudad de Puebla de los Angeles*. Puebla, 1970, Vol. 1., p. 19.

Figure 1.2 The Intendancy of Puebla in 1800

8

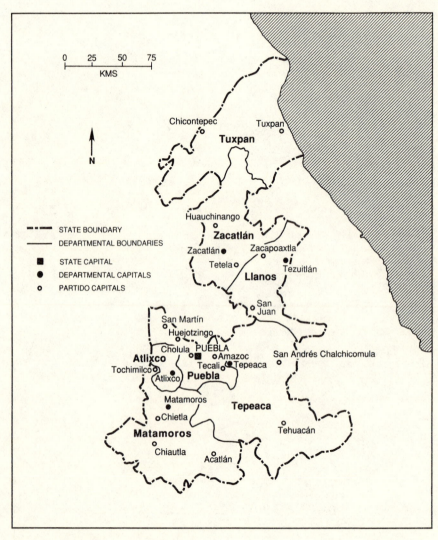

Figure 1.3 The State of Puebla in 1850

and maguey (for *pulque*) were produced intensively for the urban market.[13] In contrast to much of the central Puebla region, there was little land concentration within the municipality. Only four estates were designated as haciendas, and these were smaller than haciendas elsewhere in the valley.[14] Otherwise, the municipality was a patchwork of numerous (over 150) ranchos, orchards, gardens and smaller plots, generally owner occupied, but sometimes rented from surrounding villages, Indian *barrios*, religious corporations or from the *propios* of the municipality.[15] Land use extended beyond agriculture to flour milling (there were 12 mills within the municipality), lime, stone and clay quarrying, as well as extensive grazing upon the ejidos. Puebla was a key point on the extensive networks of transhumance/livestock trade of sheep, mules and horses, between the pastoral *tierradentro* and the agricultural south-east of New Spain.[16]

Running east from the city, an unbroken valley stretches for almost one hundred kilometers to the edge of the Sierra Madre, narrow at first but broadening into the fertile and well-watered valley of San Andrés Chalchicomula at the foot of Citlaltepetl (volcano of Orizaba). Along this axis, a relay of market towns: Amozoc, Tepeaca, Acatzingo, Quechula, San Agustín Palmar and San Andrés Chalchicomula concentrate the agricultural surpluses (principally of maize, wheat, and vegetables), for the markets of Puebla and the tierra caliente of Veracruz. At Tepeaca, from Pre-Conquest times the principal market center of the region, the valley forks to the southeast, leading through the market towns of Tecamachalco and Tlacotepec, broadening into the valley of Tehuacán before giving way to the tangled topography of the Sierra Madre of Veracruz and the Sierra Mixteca. Tehuacán shared with San András Chalchicomula in the supply of the *tierra caliente* and the Caribbean and was also well placed (on the *camino real*) to

---

13 Among the varied market gardening in the environs of the city, Mariano Fernández de Echeverría y Veytia described in 1781 the custom of planting *maguey* among the ruins of former barrios: "...en el barrio de Santiago hay muchos millares de ellos (magueyales) y su producto hace a sus habitantes indios, que son los dueños de ellos, los mas ricos de la Ciudad en su esfera", *Historia*, Vol. I, pp. 280-4.

14 AAP, Expedientes sobre Empedrados y Estadística, Vol. 175, f. 187, "Noticia de Haciendas del Labor, Ranchos y Molinos...1829; and Roberto Veléz Pliego, "Proprietarios y producción. La economía agrícola del municipio de Puebla a fines del Porfiriato", CIHS Puebla, *De La Colonia a la Revolución*. Puebla, 1987, pp. 285-326.

15 AAP, Cabildo, Vol. 103 f. 223,"Lista de Fincas Rústicas en la Municipalidad de Puebla de los Angeles", 1835.

16 It was estimated that before the wars of Independence, 25-30,000 mules and 15-20,000 horses from "*tierradentro*" were grazed on Puebla's ejidos and sold in the great July horse fair. Much of this livestock was then sold through the *repartimiento* trade to the peasant communities of south-eastern Mexico. See Francisco Javier de la Peña, "Notas", p. 149; and D. A. Brading, *Haciendas and Ranchos*. Cambridge, 1978, p. 79.

supply Oaxaca, Chiapas and Guatemala with wheat and maize in years of scarcity.[17] Tehuacán and San Andrés, indeed, looked as much to beyond the region for markets as they did to the provincial capital.

Southeast from Puebla de los Angeles extends the most arid, sparsely populated and hilly part of the province: the Sierra de Tentzo and the Mixteca Baja de Puebla. Here, among the nopal cactus of a declining cochineal industry, large flocks of sheep and goats were grazed in summer, to be moved south in winter to the remote Pacific region of the province.[18] To the west of these bare limestone hills, a sequence of fertile and intensively cultivated valleys, resembling a continuous oasis, runs due south from Puebla, eventually to disappear into the Mixteca after Acatlán. This chain of valleys commences at the southern boundaries of the provincial capital in the fertile wheat and maize producing districts of Totimehuacán, Valsequillo and Cholula, descending in altitude to the warmer wheat, flower and vegetable growing valley of Atlixco, forever irrigated from streams running off the Sierra Nevada, descending further through the sub-tropical sugar-producing valleys of Izucar, Chietla, Chiautla and Acatlán. This valley chain also produced commodities much prized in the markets of the cold plateaus further north: pomegranates, peanuts, cumin, chick peas, aniseed, saffron, avocados, dates and melons.[19]

To the west and northwest of the city of Puebla, the old camino real to Mexico City leads through valleys which historically have been, and remain, the demographic core and agricultural heartland of the province, running sixty kilometers to the foothills of the Sierra de Río Frio, famous in the nineteenth century for its bandits. The districts of Cholula, Huejotzingo and San Martín Texmelucan, well-watered from surrounding limestone and volcanic massifs, extremely fertile due to their volcanic soil, well-sheltered

---

17 José Antonio de Villa-Señor y Sánchez, *Teatro Americano. Descripción General de los Reynos y Provincias de la Nueva España, y sus Jurisdicciones.* Mexico, 1746-48, Vol. I, p. 350. During the great maize famine of the mid 1780s the farmers of San Andrés and Tehuacán appear to have done very well, exporting their surpluses to other parts of the region and beyond. See Enrique Florescano and Rodolfo Pastor, *La Crisis,* pp. 485-6 and 509-20.

18 35,000 goats were fattened and slaughtered in Tehuacán in 1802. Vicente Nieto *Descripción y Plano de la Provincia de Tehuacán de las Granadas* (1791). Puebla, 1960, p. 14; and for transhumance: Ursula Ewald, *Estudios sobre la hacienda colonial en México. Las propiedades rurales del Colegio Espíritu Santo en Puebla.* Wiesbaden, 1976, pp. 127-8.

19 For vivid descriptions of the valley of Atlixco, the most famous valley in all of New Spain, see: Alonso Ponce, "Relación Breve y Verdadura de algunas cosas de las muchas que sucedían en la Provincias de la Nueva España", CDIHE MVIII, 1972, 135-43; and Thomas Gage, *op.cit.,* p. 118. For Manuel Flon's description of the subtropical valleys further south: Isabel Gil and Enrique Florescano, (eds.), *Descripciones Económicas. Provincias del Sur y Sureste.* Mexico, 1976, p. 180.

from the frost-bearing northerlies, contained the most valuable agricultural estates of the area. These small estates, which had grown up among the lands of declining Indian communities from the late sixteenth century, produced temperate fruit and vegetables, wheat, maize and *pulque* for the provincial capital, for the valley of Mexico in its years of scarcity and for Spanish settlements and garrisons in the Caribbean.[20] Cholula itself, once the metropolitan center of the region, by the end of the colonial period was renowned, apart from its drunkenness, for its intensive vegetable production (including asparagus), magueys and flowers.[21]

Finally, completing the circle, to the north of the city the extremely fertile wheat growing valley of Nativitas, the only bright spot in the region's agricultural development during the eighteenth century, extends to the hilly and largely pastoral Bloque de Tlaxcala and the Malinche, where much of the wool was produced for the textile *obrajes* of Huamantla, Santa Ana Chiautempan, Cholula and Puebla. Beyond this barrier, a sequence of maize, barley and pulque producing *bolsones* --Huamantla, Nopalucan, Tlaxco, San Juan de los Llanos, Cuyoaco and Chignahuapan -- leads into the labarynthine topography of the Sierra Norte de Puebla. Here the districts of Tezuitlán, Tlatlauqui, Zacapoastla, Tetela and Zacatlán commence in the pine forests of *tierra fria* , promptly descend through the fruit and maize growing valleys of the *tierra templada*, dropping precipitously into the coffee and sugar growing foothills of the *tierra cálida* finally to reach their political boundaries with Veracruz and Hidalgo in the rolling cattle raising lowland savannas and forests of the *tierra caliente*. This vast region was only loosely integrated with the economy of the central valleys, its agricultural and mineral resources remaining largely unexploited until well beyond the period covered by this study.[22]

Such are the parameters of the agricultural region of Puebla. Its impressive natural advantages had three important consequences for the agricultural history of the province which will be discussed more fully later in the study. First, Puebla was the first region of New Spain to come under the plough, its fertility and the opportunities it offered becoming famous

---

[20] Ursula Ewald, "The Von Thünen Principle and Agricultural Zonation in Colonial Mexico", *Journal of Historical Geography*, Vol. III, 1977, pp. 122-33.

[21] Francisco Ajofrín, *Diario de viaje a la América septentrional en el siglo XVII*. Madrid, 1958, p. 202; and Mariano Fernández, *Historia*, Vol. I. pp. 290-1.

[22] Horst Pietschmann found that *alcaldes mayores* of these northern districts reported some of the lowest volumes of trade through *repartimiento* in the province, suggesting a weak commercial linkage with the center. There were, however, exceptions with the villages of the district of Zacatlán sending between 60 and 80 cargas of eggs to Mexico City and Puebla each week, mainly produced through repartimiento. Horst Pietschmann, "El comercio de repartimientos de los alcaldes mayores y corregidores en la región de Puebla-Tlaxcala en el siglo XVIII", *Comunicaciones*, 7, 1973, pp. 127-9; Gil and Florescano, *Descripciones*, p. 177; and Florescano and Pastor, *La Crisis*, Vol. II, p. 567.

over the sixteenth century among migrants from the arid regions of western and southern Spain, which provided the bulk of Puebla's settlers. Thus, from soon after the Conquest, Puebla became New Spain's first diversified region of settlement based upon small estate agriculture, balanced by trade and manufacturing, producing for a rapidly expanding regional, but, more importantly, extra-regional and overseas markets. Puebla was to New Spain in the sixteenth and early seventeenth centuries what the Bajío became in the later seventeenth century and what Guadalajara became in the eighteenth century.[23]

The second consequence of Puebla's "natural abundance", as frequently noticed by travellers as it was lamented by farmers, was that food prices were markedly lower in the valley of Puebla than in the valley of Mexico.[24] Puebla thus fulfilled Adam Smith's basic requirements for the "natural" development of towns and manufacturing.[25] The third consequence of Puebla's meteorological and hydrological advantages is that complete harvest failures caused by frosts or drought have been less common in Puebla than in regions further east. Consequently subsistence crises were less marked in the Puebla region than in, say, the valley of Mexico or the Bajío. If the harvest failed in the north of the province due to a late frost borne by northerlies, the valleys of Tehuacán and Atlixco, where frosts were unknown, could always serve as surplus granaries. As suggested, these natural advantages were by no means regarded universally, as blessings. As Enrique Florescano has shown for the valley of Chalco, the maize hacienda thrived only in periods of food shortage and high prices.[26]

The Puebla region's imposing agricultural potential was complemented by abundant mineral resources suited to most basic industries. In the

---

23 Chevalier, *Land and Society*, pp. 53-54, 59-7; Albi-Romero, "Sociedad de Puebla", p. 96; and for glowing descriptions of the valley see the letters in Enrique Otte, "Cartas privadas de Puebla del siglo XVI", *Jahrbuch für Geschichte von Staat*, Vol. III, 1966, pp. 10-87; and J. Lockhart and E. Otte, *Letters and People of the Spanish Indies*. Cambridge, 1976, pp. 117-119; 123-131; 135-45.

24 There is abundant literary evidence to show that basic food prices in Puebla were much lower than in the capital. Agustín de Vetancurt. *Tratado de la Ciudad de México, y las grandezas que la ilustre después que la fundaron Españoles*. Mexico, 1698, pp. 46-47; José María García "Apuntes sobre la Ciudad de Puebla", *BSMGE* 1st series, Vol. X, p. 112, *Calendario Cumplido*. Puebla, 1840, pp. 21-22; "Geografía. Ciudad de Puebla", *La Guirnalda. Semanario de Historia, Geografía, etc.* Mexico, 1844, Vol. I, pp. 51-52; Jesús Hermosa, *Manual de Geografía y Estadística de la República Mexicana* Paris, 1857, p. 139.

25 Adam Smith, *The Wealth of Nations*. London, 1970 (Edn.), pp. 496-520.

26 The 1785-6 agricultural crisis was felt less severely in Puebla than in any other region of settlement in central Mexico: Florescano and Pastor (eds.), *La Crisis*, Mexico, 1981, Vol. II, pp. 490-534; and, Enrique Florescano, *Precios del maíz y crisis agrícolas en México*. Mexico, 1969, pp. 182-197.

immediate environs of the city the following minerals are found: onyx for glazing church windows; red, black and white clay for tile, brick, pottery and porcelain manufacture; hard limestone and chalk for building and sculpture; flint for glass making and high quality *tequesquite* (quicklime or glass wort) for soap, glass and majolica manufacture. Slightly further afield, high grade iron ore was found at Huamantla, lead and copper at Tezuitlán and gold at Tetela. Only silver was not found in abundance within Puebla's section of the Sierra Madre, a fact of great significance to the economic history of the province as later chapters will show. The provincial capital's considerable locational advantages as an agricultural and industrial center were confirmed by the relative abundance, for the Mexican plateau, of water power from the Atoyac and San Francisco rivers, used for driving machinery to mill flour, full cloth, grind flint and lime, and mint coin. From the 1830s it was the Atoyac which drove the first modern textile mills and powered the machinery at Mexico's first modern iron works at Panzacola in neighboring Tlaxcala. Water power gave Puebla's entrepreneurs a head start over their rivals in Mexico, Querétaro and Guadalajara.[27]

---

[27] For the natural advantages of Puebla's location for the development of industry see: for early flour milling: Fausto Marín Tamayo, *Huexotitla La Propiedad Privada del Molino Activo Mas Antiguo de América*. Puebla, 1959, p. 10, and Miguel Zerán Zapata, *La Puebla de los Angeles en el Siglo XVII*. Mexico, 1945, p. 46; sheep-rearing and woollens: (as early as 1556, the Bishopric of Tlaxcala, Puebla, was producing 85-90,000 *arrobas* of wool, i.e. 2,1125,000-2,250,000 lbs.); Guadalupe Albi, "La sociedad de Puebla", p. 96; Jan Bazant, "Evolución de la industria textil poblana (1554-1845)", *Historia Mexicana*, Vol. 13, 1962, pp. 473-56; silk and cochineal dye: Jan Bazant "Evolución", pp. 477-8; Antonio Vázquez de Espinosa, *Descripción de la Nueva España en el siglo XVI. Mexico*, 1944, pp. 87-88; Woodrow Borah, *Silk Raising in Colonial Mexico*. Berkeley, 1943, p. 43; Hugo Leicht, *Calles de Puebla*. Puebla, 1967, p. 276, and Mariano Fernández y Echeverría, *Historia de la Fundación*, p. 299-300; and Francisco Paso y Troncoso, *Epistolario de la Nueva España*. Mexico, 1939-1942, Vol. 16, pp. 5-21; fruit and preserves: (of which large quantities were sent to Peru), Alonso Ponce, "Relación breve y verdadura", *CDIHE*, Vol. 57, 1872, pp. 135-143; Thomas Gage, *The English American*, p. 52-62; and Woodrow Borah, *Early Trade and Navigation between Mexico and Peru*, Iberoamericana No. 38, Berkeley, 1954, p. 83; glass and pottery: *Academia Mexicana de Arte Popular.Alferería Poblana*. Mexico, 1954; Fernández de Echeverría, *Historia de la fundación*, Vol. 1, p. 304, and Efraín Castro Morales, "Origen de algunas artistas y artesanos europeos de la región de Puebla-Tlaxcala", *Comunicaciones*, No. 7, 1973, p. 118; early tanning: Pedro López de Villaseñor, *Cartilla Vieja*, p. 64, and Hugo Leicht, *Calles*, pp. 258-9.

Agricultural Production and its Problems

Soy la quietud en los Reynos
de los campos la cosecha
abasto de los poblados,
de los Ricos la grandeza
el consuelo de los Pobres
y el adorno de la mesa
Tu eres causa de mil malas
Motivo de mil tragedias... [28]

At first renowned as a sheep raising and cochineal producing region, fostering America's first woollen broadcloth industry, by the 1550s Puebla had become firmly established as New Spain's major wheat producer. This lead was probably retained throughout the entire colonial period, in spite of the growth of wheat production in the valley of Toluca and the Bajío in the seventeenth century and in the valley of Guadalajara in the eighteenth. The physiocratic verse reproduced above, written in Madrid but published in Puebla in 1797, illustrates the importance placed upon wheat as the fount of public wealth. For the province of Puebla, wheat was the region's principal and most enduring agricultural staple throughout the period covered by this study. For the Church, wheat provided the backbone of the tithe. For the municipality of Puebla, the tax on flour (*el derecho de tres cuartillas*) entering the city from the surrounding mills was the chief single source of municipal funds. And for the farmers, millers, sifters, packers, barrel-makers, brokers, crown purveyance officials, merchants and muleteers who managed the production, processing and consignment of the crop, wheat was their livelihood.

If flour was the Puebla's chief export (the city possessed a milling capacity of 14 flour mills, unrivalled in Spanish America) this staple was also directly responsible for many of the region's most entrenched economic and social problems.[29] During the 18th century, Puebla's large estate sector was characterized by a rapid turnover in ownership, chronic indebtedness, severe labor scarcity and indiscipline and a speculative mentality among farmers and merchants investing in agriculture. All of these ills were observed by contemporaries and put down to the instability of wheat prices and the volatility of extra-regional demand for flour. The physiocratic Intendant, Manuel Flon, saw the mismanagement of wheat farming as both a symptom and a cause of many of the wider problems facing the province. An examination of the problems facing wheat

---

[28] *Nueva relación en que se refiere la disputa que tuvo el trigo con el Dinero*, Puebla, 1797.

[29] The milling capacity of Puebla remained stable over the entire period. 14 were counted in 1698 and in 1852. Miguel Zerón Zapata, *La Puebla*, p. 46, and Juan del Valle, *Guía de Forasteros*. Puebla, 1852, p. 197.

agriculture and the flour trade over the eighteenth century will therefore provide clues to understanding the broader character of the regional economy. In particular, it will help account for the diversification of the provincial economy into manufacturing, necessary both for the commercial survival of merchants as for subsistence of the rural and urban poor. It will also help explain the skepticism so prevalent among poblanos about any likely long term benefits from any closer association with the international market. Finally, the volatility of flour exports and the competition faced in the Caribbean, especially from American merchants from Philadelphia and Baltimore, provided the economic rationale for protectionism.

Flour was not the region's only agricultural staple. Puebla specialized in the production of broad panoply of temperate foodstuffs. *Tocinería* products (soap, ham, tallow, and lard) rivalled flour in value among the goods sent beyond the region. The city's tanneries, cloth factories and forges (producing ironware from stirrups to balconies) also supplied an extra-regional demand. The province's producers served broadly three markets:

i) the regional market and that of the Mexican southeast in the neighboring provinces of Mexico, Veracruz and Oaxaca.

ii) the mining and hacienda districts of the provinces of the interior, known as *tierradentro*, to the north and northwest of Mexico City.

iii) an overseas market of the Spanish garrisons and shipping in the Caribbean and the Pacific, as well settlements on *tierra firme* reached by sea: chiefly the Yucatán, Florida and the Captaincies General of Caracas and Guatemala.

The "golden age" of Puebla's agriculture was in the sixteenth and early seventeenth century when producers enjoyed high prices and expanding demand in all of these markets. If tithe revenues are taken as a loose guide to the value of agricultural production, then Puebla diocese's lead over Mexico, its closest rival, was maintained until well into the eighteenth century.[30] As early as the 1630s, however, Puebla's initial comparative advantages were being eroded with the development of other regions of agricultural production in New Spain and with growing official restrictions upon inter-colonial trade, commencing with the prohibition in 1634 of trade with Peru, for long one of Puebla's principal markets. The problems facing

---

[30] In the 1640s the Puebla of Bishop Palafox "...was twice as rich [in tithes] as the archbishopric of Mexico and several times richer than most of the other bishoprics." This ratio was maintained at least until the 1670s. Israel, *Race,Class and Politics*, p. 219, and, Francois Chevalier, *Land and Society*, p. 260. Puebla's lead over other Mexican bishoprics in tithe yield was still apparent in the 1720s, see Garavaglia and Grosso, "La Región de Puebla", pp. 557-8.

Puebla's agricultural sector over the later seventeenth and eighteenth centuries are reflected in the records of the Bishopric's tithe receipts.

Over the last quarter of the seventeenth and the first quarter of the eighteenth centuries, Puebla's tithes, apart from a brief recovery in the 1690s, languished at around half the level they had attained over the late sixteenth and early seventeenth centuries.[31] By the third quarter of the eighteenth century Puebla's tithe yield had recovered but the diocese's lead among the other tithe districts of New Spain, sustained until the 1720s, had long since been lost to the dioceses of Mexico and Michoacan.[32] Puebla's tithe revenues continued to recover over the final three decades of the eighteenth century but at a rate only commensurate with the price inflation which John Coatsworth has suggested accompanied New Spain's recovery in silver mining.[33] Official statistics gathered by Humboldt show that, between 1770 and 1790, Puebla's tithe revenues grew at a considerably slower rate than those of the dioceses of Mexico and Guadalajara, lagged behind those of Michoacán and Oaxaca and only exceeded those of

---

[31] From 1645 until the beginning of the last third of the 17th century Puebla's tithes were yielding around 150,000 pesos. Between 1674 and 1690, tithe receipts dropped to around 100,000 pesos a year. Tithes then recovered to contemporary estimates of between 200,000 and 300,000 pesos during the 1690s, a decade of great prosperity. Between 1708 and 1725 Puebla's tithes rarely reached half the level they had attained a century earlier. Elias Trabulse, *Fluctuaciones económicas en Oaxaca durante el siglo XVIII*. Mexico, 1979, p. 17; and Aristides Medina, *La iglesia y la producción agrícola en Puebla, 1540-1795*. Mexico, 1984, pp. 171-229. A sense of the opulence of the Puebla bishopric in the late 1690s is conveyed by Gemelli Carrerri's account of his visit to Puebla. He reported the bishopric to be enjoying revenues of 300,000 pesos: "the government is profitable because many rich merchants live there. The reader, by the numbers of monasteries so rich and well provided, may judge of the greatness, magnificence and wealth of the city. The bishop, when I went to take my leave of him, made me a present worth fifty pieces of eight [pesos]." Dr. John Francis Gemelli Carrerri, *A Voyage round the World*. London, 1752, p. 519-520.

[32] Aristides Medina found no records of total tithe receipts for the period 1726-48, precisely the period during which contemporaries bewailed the general economic decline. This was period a period of severe depression in the mining industry. Trabulse, observing Oaxaca's depressed tithe receipts, points to the close correlation between the tithe and mining production curves. From 1748 to 1770 tithes recovered, averaging around 180,000 pesos annually, increasing to 300,000 pesos during the 1770s and 350,000 pesos during the 1780s. *BAGN* (lst Series), Vol. I, p. 195.

[33] John H. Coatsworth, "The Mexican Mining Industry in the Eighteeenth Century", in Nils Jacobsen, and Hans-Jurgen Puhle (eds.) *The Economies of Mexico and Peru During the Late Colonial Period*. Berlin, 1986, pp. 26-45.

Durango, a province which suffered severer problems of famine and epidemic disease than Puebla faced during the mid-1780s.[34]

How can Puebla's poor agricultural performance be explained when other regions, such as the Bajío and Guadalajara basin were experiencing such spectacular growth ? On the face of it, ever more frequent Atlantic wars offered Puebla's farmers, food processors and merchants expanding opportunities for developing an export market for flour and ships' stores in the Caribbean . In wartime, garrisons would be strengthened and supplies from metropolitan Spain interrupted, obliging administrators to turn to American sources of supply. No other region was better placed than Puebla to take advantage of this. Moreover, an elaborate administrative apparatus - the *proveeduría de víveres* - had existed in Puebla from the establishment of the Manila galleon and the *Armada de Barlovento* in the mid-seventeenth century, to finance and organize the region's exports. Few regions of Spanish America could boast an overseas market for temperate agricultural goods. What, after all, was enriching the cities of Philadelphia, New York and Baltimore over the eighteenth century ? Why was Puebla unable to use this market as a boon to compensate for the loss of the market of the *tierradentro* ?

The problems facing Puebla's commercial agriculture in general, and wheat farming and flour trade, in particular, have no single cause. An explanation can be found by examining developments in each of the three market areas, just mentioned. Perhaps the main cause of Puebla's agricultural decline, and certainly the one upon which contemporary chroniclers place the greatest weight was the loss of the valuable market of Mexico City and the *tierradentro*, first to the Bajío and, later, to the province of Guadalajara. From the mid-sixteenth century until the later seventeenth century, Puebla's flour, candles and soap had complemented the city's textiles in supplying the city of Zacatecas, attracting scarce silver in return.[35] By the turn of the eighteenth century, however, Puebla's millers were unable to compete with those of the Bajío even in the Mexico City market, while the market of *tierradentro* had been lost altogether, providing instead the foundation for Guadalajara's eighteenth-century prosperity.[36] As we shall see, the loss of the market for agricultural goods in the interior was in part compensated by the development of the cotton textile industry. But textiles also faced increasing competition over the eighteenth century and contemporaries saw the loss of Puebla's ability to exchange agricultural and manufactured goods with the silver of the mining districts, whether in the *tierradentro* of New Spain or in Peru, as the principal cause of the

---

[34] *BAGN* (lst Series) Vol. I, p. 195, and Michael Swann, *Tierra Adentro: Settlement and Society in Colonial Durango*. Boulder, 1982, pp. 125-139.

[35] P. J. Bakewell, *Silver and Society in Colonial Mexico, Zacatecas 1546-1700*. Cambridge, 1971, pp. 64, 75, 237.

[36] Francisco Clavijero, "Descripción", p. 327.

region's decline, symbolized by the removal of the city's silver mint and the headquarters of the mercury monopoly during the 1730s.[37]

The provincial and southeastern market provided little compensation for the loss of the market of the interior. The demographic stagnation of the province over the eighteenth century meant that the maize and meat consumption of the city of Puebla declined while flour consumption grew only slightly: from 30,416 *cargas* in 1698 to 52,951 *cargas* in 1802, modest if compared with Guadalajara's increase in flour consumption from 5,000 *cargas* in 1766 to 15,000 *cargas* in 1804.[38] The port of Veracruz consumed 11,000 cargas of Puebla's flour annually in the early 1770s but no other population center of southeast Mexico could match this.[39] Antequera de Oaxaca consumed 9,244 *cargas* of wheat flour in 1828, of which Puebla's mills contributed only 2,140 *cargas*.[40] The regional market was simply too slender to support Puebla's estate sector which had achieved its capacity during the early colonial period in response to extensive extra-regional and overseas markets.

This leaves us with the overseas market. The most valuable market here was Havana which consumed around 35,000 cargas of flour annually at the turn of the nineteenth century.[41] However, the Cuban market was only accessible to Puebla producers when war had interrupted the supply from Spain and when trade with neutrals (generally the United States) was forbidden. Over the seventeenth and eighteenth centuries, it seems that Puebla's producers received the lion's share of crown purveyance orders through the *comercio de víveres*, both in the Pacific and in the Caribbean.[42]

---

[37] For a broad and penetrating explanation of Puebla's economic decline, nothing can rival Juan Villa Sánchez, *Puebla Sagrada y Profana* (1746), republished in Puebla in 1835 by Francisco Javier de la Peña and republished again in 1967, pp. 69-90.

[38] Miguel Zerón Zapata, *La Puebla*, p. 46, *Jornal de Veracruz*, Vol. I, March-June 1806, p. 145; and Eric Van Young, *Hacienda and Market*, p. 60.

[39] AGI Mexico, Audiencia Vol. 2485, "Cuenta del Proveedor de Víveres de 1771 a 1776."

[40] *Voz de la Patria*. Mexico, VI, 10 Nov. 1830, Suplemento 30.

[41] During the early 1790s Puebla's mills were contributing well over one half of Havana's needs. Humboldt, *Ensayo*, p. 261; and AGN, Intendencias Vol. 734, f. 103.

[42] The earliest mention of the *comercio de víveres* is found in Toribio Motolinia's chronicle of the 1540s: "Va el camino del puerto a México por medio de esta Ciudad [de los Angeles]...cuando las recuas son de vuelta, cargan de harina y tocino y bizcocho para matalotaje de las naos", quoted in Hugo Leicht, *Calles*, p. 40. For the records of the Crown purveyance trade to the Caribbean and the Pacific between 1641 and 1755, see AAP, Vols. 151-153. These have recently been analysed by Garavaglia and Grosso, "La Región de Puebla/Tlaxcala", pp. 574-80.. See also Bibiano Torres Ramírez, *La Armada de Barlovento*. Seville, 1981, and Manuel Alvarado Morales, *La ciudad de México ante la fundación de la Armada de Barlovento, 1635-1643*. Mexico, 1983.

This was, however, an unstable, as it was an "unnatural", market since demand depended upon the vagaries of Spanish shipping and military involvement. Between wars, Puebla's wheat farmers and flour millers had to make do with assembling orders from a combination of less substantial sources: Spanish shipping in the Pacific, the return trade with Venezuela, the Spanish population of Campeche and the Yucatán, and return fleets leaving from Veracruz. Venezuelan demand was most irregular due to the preference of the Caracas Company for Castilian flour.[43] The irregular Pacific market was more easily supplied from the diocese of Michoacán, once Acapulco became New Spain's principal Pacific port. From mid-century, American coastal shipping encroached ever more daringly upon Caribbean *tierra firme* markets, including Campeche and the Yucatán. Thus Puebla farmers grew increasingly dependent upon chance demand accompanying Spanish involvement in Atlantic wars. Yet, however substantial this wartime demand was in the short term, it could not serve adequately as an anchor for securing any sustained profitability of Puebla's estate agriculture. This became even less possible from the late 1760s, when North American flour merchants began to challenge the monopoly Castilian and Puebla flour had hitherto enjoyed in the Caribbean.[44]

In hindsight, it would have been wise for Puebla farmers, in the interests of their own solvency, to have refused to serve as the surplus larder for Spanish settlements and garrisons in the Caribbean. It is clear from James Lewis's work that the hectic activities of Crown officials, merchants, local administrators and farmers which followed the strengthening of garrisons and interruption of food supplies from Spain in

---

[43] The War of Spanish Succession had obliged Venezuela to seek alternative sources for its wheat than Castile, initiating a pattern of inter-colonial trade in which Puebla's flour and other goods (hats, soap, glass and cloth) supplemented silver in the return trade for Venzuela's cocoa. Castilian flour was, however, preferred in Venezuela where, with the formation of the Guipuizcoan company (1728), and with Castilian pressure, all importation of Puebla flour ceased. Imports of Puebla flour were possible once more with *comercio libre* (permitted with Venezuela in 1778) but, by this time, the staples in New Spain's trade with Venezuela - the exchange of silver for cocoa - were reorienting towards the metropolis. Inter-colonial trade responded sluggishly to *comercio libre*. Arcila Farías, *El Comercio entre Nueva España y Venezuela*. Mexico, 1950, pp. 93-94.

[44] For the entry of Anglo-American merchants into the Spanish Caribbean market: James A. Lewis, "Nueva España y los esfuerzos para abastecer La Habana, 1779-1803", *Anuario de Estudios Americanos*, Vol. 33, 1976, pp. 501-26; and his "Anglo American entrepreneurs in Havana: the background and significance of the expulsion of 1784-1785"; and Linda K. Salvucci, "Anglo-American merchants and stratagems for success in Spanish imperial markets, 1783-1807", in Jacques A. Barbier and Alan J. Kuethe (eds.), *The North American role in the Spanish Imperial economy 1760-1819*. Manchester, 1984, pp. 122-133; and John Coatsworth,"American trade with European colonies in the Caribbean and South America, 1790-1812", *WMQ*, Vol. XXIV, 1967, pp. 243-65.

wartime, served only to deepen the problems facing Puebla's agriculture.[45] Yet, because wars interrupted Castilian supplies so frequently and because Spain permitted neutral trade only for short periods, the valley of Puebla was obliged to respond to this irregular, but often immense, demand.

The potential scale of overseas demand for Puebla's foodstuffs over the eighteenth century was probably of a greater order than in any other period of the region's history. This can be illustrated by looking at Crown purveyance orders accompanying Spanish wartime involvement. In wartime the normally lethargic *comercio de víveres* would suddenly become a much larger operation as orders were placed with farmers, millers, sifters, merchants, *tocineros* and manufacturers. During a four year period leading up to and during the War of Jenkin's Ear, at least 64,000 *cargas* of flour were remitted to the Armada de Barlovento by Puebla millers and flour merchants through the *asentista* (holder of the *proveeduría de víveres*).[46] During the Seven Years War the proveeduría in Puebla spent 787,270 pesos (102,337 pesos a year) mainly on flour for Havana, Veracruz and the Armada de Barlovento.[47] Between 1771 and 1776, 1,207,29 pesos (201,337 pesos a year) were spent, again, largely on flour for the Caribbean.[48] During the Anglo-Spanish war of 1779-82 the much larger amount of 6,037,388 pesos (2,012,462 pesos a year) was spent on flour, ham, lard and biscuits for the supply of garrisons in Veracruz, Havana, New Orleans, Florida ,Guatemala and Campeche, the largest single item being 31,454 *cargas* of flour, valued at 869,431 pesos, sent from Puebla to Havana.[49] During the war with Britain in the early 1790s, the Puebla *proveeduría* had an annual contract to supply Havana with 18,000 cargas of flour, well over half the total consumption of the city.[50] Thus. in wartime, the *comercio de víveres* clearly offered farmers and merchants spectacular opportunities and high prices. However, peace often brought lean years,

---

45 James A. Lewis, "Nueva España y los esfuerzos", pp. 501-26. The Crown directed efforts to stimulate commercial agriculture in the cultivation of the socially and strategically useful crops. Hemp and linen were also unsuccessful during the same period. Ramón María Serrera Contreras, *Lino y Cañamo en Nueva España (1777-1800)*. Seville, 1974, pp. 267-284.

46 Garavaglia and Grosso,"La Región de Puebla/Tlaxcala", pp. 577-8.

47 Luis Chávez Orozco, *Mercedes y Pensiones, Limosnas y Salarios en la Real Hacienda de Nueva España*. Mexico, 1945, p. 38.

48 In 1774, Miguel Antonio de Zavaleta, the *proveedor* in Puebla, sent biscuits, beans, lentils and ham valued at 40,000 pesos to Acapulco and 8,805 cargas of flour valued at 84,977 pesos to Veracruz. AGI México, Audiencia, Vol. 2485, "Cuenta del Proveedor de Víveres...".

49 BL. Ms. 9770 K5, "Estado de los caudales, víveres, y demás efectos que se han gastado en los destinos que se expresa desde que se declar de Guerra, en este Reyno, hasta 30 de Mayo de 1782 años".

50 AGN, Intendencias, Vol. 734, f. 103.

such as occurred during the 1740s, and again, after the Seven Years War. During these recessions, some of the most acute observations were made about the problems facing Puebla's agriculture, often by bishops preoccupied by declining tithe revenues.[51]

The consequence of a volatile overseas and depressed domestic market was a highly unstable price level for wheat. At the start of the eighteenth century 9 pesos/carga was considered a fair price for good wheat. During the 1740s prices as low as 2 1/4 pesos/carga were recorded among general lament on general economic and moral decline.[52] In the late 1760s, as a result of the decline of Caribbean demand following the Seven Years War, Bishop Fabián y Fuero observed that wheat that used to sell at 8 to 12 pesos/carga now sold for only 5 pesos.[53] Prices improved from the mid-1770s with increased demand from the Caribbean garrisons but in peace-time prices would always slump. Intendant, Manuel Flon observed after the Peace of Amiens that "Nunca se han visto mas baratos [los trigos] como se han vendido este año, hasta el precio de 5 pesos....resultando de esto el abandono de las fincas y el atraso de la agricultura, que solo podrá precaverse en parte con la salida de harina para la Habana, y demás islas de Barlovento."[54] Wheat prices recovered over the revolutionary period only to slump again after Independence when prices of 6 to 8 pesos/carga were reported, it being recognized that 12 pesos was the minimum necessary to cover production costs.[55] The laments of wheat-growers and flour-merchants continued throughout the subsequent decades.[56] Indeed, only with the coming of the railroad would the cereal agriculture of the central valley of Puebla find a way out of a cyclical pattern characterized by long periods of depression punctuated by short interludes of commercially acceptable prices.[57]

---

[51] Often cited are the agricultural observations of Bishop Francisco Fabián y Fuero, *Colección de Providencias Diocesanos del Obispado de la Puebla de los Angeles.* Puebla, 1770.

[52] Enrique Palacios, *Puebla y su Territorio*, Vol. II, p. 469 (citing the chronicler, Bermúdez de Castro).

[53] Luis Navarro García, "La Sociedad Rural de México en el Siglo XVIII", *Anales de la Universidad Hispalense*, Vol. XXIV, No.1, 1963, p. 49.

[54] AGN, Archivo Histórico de Hacienda, Vol. 917-3; Manuel Flon, 13 January 1804.

[55] *El Caduceo*, Puebla, Vol. III, No. 5, 5 July 1824.

[56] See pp. 138-140 for the pressures for restoration of the wheat assize during the slump of the mid-1830s.

[57] For the recovery of Puebla's cereal agriculture see the two essays by Roberto Vélez Pliego, "Rentabilidad y productividad en una hacienda mexicana: Hacienda y Molino de Santa Cruz", CIHS, *Puebla en el siglo XIX*, pp. 289-314, and "Proprietarios y producción. La economía agrícola del municipio de Puebla a fines del Porfiriato", CIHS, *Puebla de la colonia a la revolución*, pp. 285-326.

The recovery of the Caribbean market for temperate foodstuffs during the 1770s brought a temporary reprieve to Puebla's farmers. A regular system of Crown purveyance was once more established with the growth in Spanish military presence and the rapid growth of the city of Havana.[58] Indeed, after half a century of depression, the early 1770s were reported to be boom years for the province.[59]

By the end of the decade the first effects of the shift in Spanish economic policy, from an anachronistic mercantilism to the more fashionable physiocracy, were being felt. This was in response to the sluggish response of Puebla agriculture to official promptings to increase supply of flour to the Caribbean during the late 1770s. Between 1776 and 1779 Puebla was expected to send 14,000 cargas of flour to Havana annually. In most years, however, only between 8-10,000 *cargas* were actually received. Lewis describes the insurmountable obstacles facing the *proveeduría* in this decade: shortage of pack mules and carts, the absence of storage facilities in Veracruz, the profiteering of Veracruz merchants holding back flour, quite apart from the grumblings and unreliability of Puebla's farmers, who demanded payment in advance, only to complain when prices rose.[60] In 1782 the Crown granted complete freedom to wheat-farming, flour-milling and the sale of wheat and flour, and instructed *alcaldes mayores* to encourage farmers to plant wheat and to remove all obstacles to its trade between jurisdictions.[61] Two years later all flour sent to the Islas de Barlovento was declared free from *alcabala*.[62] Puebla flour merchants could now, for the first time since the restrictions were placed on inter-colonial trade in the 1630s, trade freely with the Caribbean. Lewis points out, however, that the speculative mentality of flour merchants grew rather than diminished after *comercio libre*.[63] The Bourbon commercial

---

[58] Havana's population grew from around 36,000 in the 1760s to over 50,000 during the 1790s, reaching (by Humboldt's probably exaggerated estimate) 80,000 by 1803, ranking as Spanish America's second city after Mexico. Hoberman and Socolow, *Cities and Society*, p. 5. By the early 19th century Havana consumed around 35,000 cargas of flour annually, to Mexico City's 127,333 cargas and Puebla's 52,000 cargas. Paris consumed 506,666 cargas in 1803. Humboldt, *Ensayo*, p. 261.

[59] "Es cierto que desde el año de 1771 hasta el de 78 en la Nueva España se esperimentó la edad de oro, semillas en abundancia, ninguna epidemia, finalmente el público logró una paz octaviana, que caracteriza a estos años", J. A. Alzate, *Gacetas de Literatura de México*. Puebla, 1831, Vol. II, p. 281.

[60] James A. Lewis, "Nueva España y los Esfuerzos", pp. 101-26.

[61] Eduardo Arcila Farías, *Reformas económicas del siglo XVIII en Nueva España*. Mexico, 1974, Vol. I, p. 137.

[62] AGN, Reales Cédulas, Vol. 129, f. 31.

[63] James Lewis, "Nueva España y los Esfuerzos", pp. 125-6.

reforms resolved none of the problems facing the region's commercial agriculture and flour exports, indeed these intensified.

The change in spirit within imperial trade policy was given a particular immediacy in Puebla with the appointment of Manuel Flon as Intendant in 1786. Leaving a successful military career, Flon developed a keen interest in the problems of Puebla's agriculture. Soon after his appointment he visited the wheat-growing district of Cholula and wrote a scorching indictment of farming methods, labor practices and ecclesiastical mortmain, highlighting the structural problems facing farmers throughout the region.[64] His prescriptions for the maladies of Puebla's agriculture were often repeated over the subsequent two decades. Flon's interest in agriculture went beyond physiocratic ideal to Georgic practice. By the early 1800s, he had acquired a wheat estate, a flour mill and had built a *casa del campo* close to the city.[65] This forty-two room palace stood among wheat fields and orchards and was linked to the city by a *paseo* planted with plane trees. Next to the house Flon constructed a boating lake, "donde navegaban canoas grandes y barquichuelos bellamente construidos con sus piececitas de artillería."[66] Few Puebla farmers, however, experienced Flon's personal success or shared his liberal convictions in matters of political economy, in spite of the increasing wartime demand over this period.

Export figures published in the *Gaceta de México* and the *Jornal de Veracruz* show the imposing expansion of flour exports from Veracruz over the first half of the 1790s, peaking in 1793 when 12,908 *cargas* of flour left Veracruz.[67] In this year, 85,65 *cargas* of flour entered the city of Puebla from the surrounding mills, a figure only exceeded in 1799 and 1802.[68] However, war with France obliged Spain to concede permission to neutral powers to trade with the Caribbean for the second time, between 1793-7 (the first was between 1778-1784).[69] But Puebla appears to have succeeded in sharing the market with North American competitors until Britain's entry into the war, since New Spain's flour exports remained buoyant. We have no export figures for the critical 1797-1801 period, but all evidence suggests that with the granting of a third permission to neutrals (between 1798-99), Puebla's stake in the Caribbean market was all but substituted by supplies from the United States. This brought a chorus of

---

64 AGN, Intendencias, Vol. 48, Manuel Flon to Viceroy, 12 May 1790.

65 In 1801 Flon owned the hacienda of San Baltazar Torija (Cuautinchán) and the Molino de San Antonio (Cholula). ACP, Diezmos de Trigo, 1801-1828. For a sketch of Flon's career: *BAGN*, Vol. XVI, 1945, pp. 285-86.

66 Hugo Leicht, *Calles*, pp. 387-8.

67 *Gacetas de México. Compendio de Noticias de Nueva España desde principios del año de 1784.* Mexico, 1784-1797.

68 AAP, Cuentas, 1793, 1799 and 1802.

69 Javier Ortíz de la Tabla, *Comercio exterior de Veracruz, 1778-1821: crisis de dependencia.* Seville, 1978, p. 325.

complaints from Puebla's officials, city councillors, millers and merchants.[70] Permission to neutrals was promptly rescinded in 1799, permitting Puebla's flour and *tocinería* products to regain an impressive hold on the Caribbean market over the decade before the Hidalgo revolt (apart from a short but very marked slump between 1805-07 when permission was once more granted for neutrals to trade). After 1810, flour and *tocinería* exports to the Caribbean plummeted, never again to recover.[71] By 1826 the British Minister, Henry Ward, could observe that Americans faced little challenge in the Caribbean flour-market and he saw little chance of Mexicans regaining their position before the road between Veracruz and Puebla was improved.[72]

Viceroy Revillagigedo had made the same observation in 1793, believing that poor husbandry and high transport costs would always prevent Mexico's flour from competing with American flour in the Caribbean.[73] *Poblanos* on the spot, however, could not afford such complacency. They had to wrestle with the problems of this tantalizingly attractive but frequently elusive overseas market for their province's staple products. Their conflicting diagnoses of what lay at the root of Puebla's agricultural problem and their divergent remedies are worth briefly outlining for they represent the two principal strands in Puebla's political economy which we shall observe reappearing in different contexts and at different times throughout the study.

There was one area of common agreement in Puebla: that North American merchants should be excluded from the Caribbean market. The *comercio de neutrales*, argued one prominent merchant, Dionysio Fernández Pérez, in 1798, had reduced Puebla's agriculture to ruins, with "el extranjero haciéndose felíz a costa de nuestra destrucción ".[74] Beyond this point of unanimity, local interests diverged into broadly two positions. The first might be labelled "liberal physiocracy" most clearly seen in Manuel Flon's prescriptions for Puebla's agriculture: the reduction of the debt burden of estates in ecclesiastical mortmain, the reduction of tithes and taxes, improved labor conditions for Indians and the abolition of debtors' prisons on haciendas and the removal of fiscal obstacles to inter-regional

---

[70] AGN, Industria y Comercio, Vol. 20, fs. 139 and 145-157.

[71] Miguel Lerdo de Tejada, *Comercio Exterior de Mexico*. Mexico, 1967, *Balanzas del comercio maritimo, 1796-1854*.

[72] Ward, *Mexico in 1828*, Vol. II, p. 15.

[73] BAGN lst series, Vol. II, pp. 46-7. Humboldt made the same observation in 1803:"It is the difficulty of this descent which raises the carriage of flour from Mexico to Vercruz, and prevents it to this day from competing in Europe with the flour of Philadelphia", Humboldt, *Political Essay on the Kingdom of New Spain*. London, 1811, Vol. I, p. 58.

[74] AGN, Industria y Comercio,Vol. 20, f. 45.

trade.[75] Like most liberal diagnoses in this period, causes were confused with symptoms. The underlying causes of the problems of Puebla's agriculture were threefold.

(i) There were too many small estates in competition with each other for a stagnant regional market. In short : overcapacity.[76]

(ii) Throughout the eighteenth and early nineteenth centuries, farmers complained of labor scarcity. This was a consequence of the demographic stagnation of the central region and the reluctance of villagers to work on estates, accounting for the coercion used on Puebla estates by farmers in no position to pay high wages.[77] Harsh treatment of labor and pressure by landowners upon diminishing village labor supply further impelled villagers to migrate beyond the region, rendering the labor shortage more acute.[78]

(iii) Rudimentary transport and poor communication between Puebla and her extra-regional and overseas markets, gave a firm advantage to her seaport competitors, Baltimore and Philadelphia.[79]

---

[75] The fullest exposition of Flon's ideas on agriculture is found in his indictement of estate agriculture in the district of Cholula: AGN, Intendencias Vol.48, Manuel Flon to Viceroy Conde Revillagigedo, 12 May 1790. For Flon's ideas on land redistribution and the emancipation of Indian labour: AGN, AHH, Vol. 917, Manuel Flon to Viceroy, 14 April 1804, and, AAP Cabildo, Vol. 78, Flon to Ayuntamiento, 22 April 1809.

[76] Ursula Ewald argues that this marked feature of Puebla rural society - the large number of small estates - was a consequence, not of the Crown's policy to limit the formation of *latifundia*, but of the early and intense commercial interest in this region, serving to intensify competition among settlers for land. *Estudios sobre la Hacienda Colonial en México. Las Propiedades Rurales del Colegio Espíritu Santo en Puebla*. Wiesbaden, 1976, p. 15.

[77] This was one of the principal reasons given for the failure of experiments in linen and hemp agriculture, Ramón María Serrera Contreras, *Lino y Cáñamo*, p. 279.

[78] For problems of labor recruitment and harsh labor conditions on Tlaxcala's haciendas: Claude Morin, *Michoacán en la Nueva España del Siglo XVIII*, p. 250; and James D. Riley, "Landlords, Labourers and Royal Government: The Administration of Labor in Tlaxcala, 1680-1750", in Elsa Cecilia Frost, Michael C. Meyer and Josefina Zoraida Vázquez (Eds.), *El trabajo y los trabajadores en la historia de México*. Mexico, 1979, pp. 221-41. For resentment of debtors' prisons and harsh labor conditions: Juan E Hernández y Dávalos, *Colección de Documentos para la Historia de la Guerra de Independencia de México, 1808-1821*. Mexico, 1877-82, Vol. V, p. 552, and Brian Hamnett, *Roots of Insurgency: Mexican Regions, 1750-1824*. Cambridge, 1986, pp. 85-6.

[79] Contemporaries often complained of the shortage of draft animals, the unreliability of brokers and muleteers, the insecurity and poor state of the roads, not to mention the inadequate storage facilities in Veracruz. For an example of a typical complaint: INAH, Microfilm Collection, *Proveedor de víveres* to Manuel Flon, 17 Feb. 1796,

In view of these obstacles, the set of interests opposed to "liberal physiocracy" appears as more pragmatic and attuned to the times. This second position, which can be called "corporate-traditionalist", favored the defence and strengthening of Church wealth, seen as the backbone of Puebla's agriculture, the maintenance of price assizes (*posturas*) on staples such as wheat, and the establishment of corporate privileges for flour brokers. This position was embraced by farmers, flour merchants, brokers and ecclesiastics and found representation among a majority of Puebla city council, which remained very much a farmer-merchant club.[80] The "corporate-traditionalists" demanded solutions, however, which were discordant with the liberal tenor of official policy. The *Consolidación de Vales Reales* between 1805-09 , the abolition of all price controls, guilds and monopolies in 1813 and the rejection by the *cabildo* of projects from flour brokers for a monopoly of flour exports in 1803 and 1817, effectively scuppered any hopes of a return to traditional corporate solutions.[81] Nevertheless, liberal policies continued to be resisted and corporate solutions sought until well into the nineteenth century.[82]

Structures and Trends in Land Ownership

In the face of price instability one might expect to find a consolidation of estates, in an attempt to control supply, as occurred in the neighboring valley of Chalco over the mid-eighteenth century.[83] This did not happen in Puebla. Tax records and *hacienda* listings suggest that in the principal wheat-growing jurisdictions of Atlixco, Huejotzingo and Cholula, the number of estates remained quite stable over the century. Tlaxcala presents a more erratic picture with a wide fluctuation in the number of estates under cultivation. And the figures for Tepeaca, Puebla's largest and wealthiest cereal producing district, reveal a growth in the number of estates over the second half of the eighteenth century, a reflection of this district's more

---

"Sobre que se hagan responsables los arrieros de las cargas que llevan y den razón y cuenta de ellas; and, James Lewis, "Nueva España y los esfuerzos", pp. 112-3, and Ramón Serrera, *op. cit.*, p. 279.

80 Reinhard Liehr, *Ayuntamiento y oligarquía en Puebla, 1787-1810*. Mexico, 1976, Vol. I, pp. lll-121.

81 Between 1805 and 1809 Puebla's holders of church mortgages - principally rural estate owners - contributed 2,153,614 pesos to the 12,750.000 pesos raised in all of New Spain. Asunción Lavrín, "The Execution of the Laws of Consolidación in New Spain: Economic Aims and Results"", *HAHR*, Vol. 53, 1973, p. 36. For the corporate projects of flour brokers: AAP, Expedientes sobre Corredores de Lonja, 1628-1866 Vol. 225 fs. 28-29, 68-72.

82 See Chapter 3.

83 Florescano, *Precios del maíz*, p. 185.

TABLE 1.1 HACIENDAS AND RANCHOS IN PUEBLA AND TLAXCALA

	1632	1675	1698	1712	1716	1741	1744	1759	1773	1779	1785	1791	1803
Atlixco	90	-	72	-	-	-	62	-	-	-	-	85	100
Huejotzingo	-	-	76	-	-	-	76	-	-	-	-	67	75
Tepeaca	-	-	-	-	-	-	279	-	-	-	-	294	370
Cholula	-	-	58	-	-	-	58	-	-	-	-	51	58
Tlaxcala	-	268	-	184	240	-	-	-	-	160	287	*239	-
Chalco (Haciendas only)	-	-	-	-	-	57	46	43	37	-	-	-	-

Sources: 1632: Chevalier, *Land and Society*, p. 64; 1698: Zerón Zapata, p. 46; 1744: Villaseñor y Sánchez, in Enrique Palacios, *Puebla y su territorio*, pp. 468-473; 1791: AGN, Padrones, Vol. 22, 25, 17 and 38, and AGN, Historia, Vol. 73, Expdte. 4; 1803: *Jornal de Veracruz*, Vol. 1, March-June, 1806, pp. 129-228. Tlaxcala, Trautman, p. 136; and Chalco, Florescano, *Precios*, pp. 185-187. *Only 223 estates were registered for tax purposes in this year of the 287 listed. See Juan Carlos Garavaglia and Juan Carlos Grosso, "Consideraciones sobre las alcabalas de Nueva España", CIHS, 1984, p. 48.

favorable economic and demographic performance than was experienced by the depressed districts of the center-west of the province.

Rather than consolidate estates, evidence from Tlaxcala and Atlixco suggests that landowners often left their estates fallow when prices were low and, in years when prices were more acceptable, the best irrigated land would either be farmed directly, or, as was increasingly the practice over the eighteenth century, land would be sub-let to speculative flour millers and merchants.[84] This practice probably explains why the number of estates listed as under cultivation in Tlaxcala fluctuated over the century (see Table 1.1).

Research to date upon eighteenth-century Tlaxcala presents a contradictory picture of enduring demographic stagnation (the population of the province stayed at around 60,000 for the entire century, falling towards the end), especially among the Indian population, at the same time that there emerged a commercially dynamic cotton textile industry.[85] Moreover, the province experienced periods (generally short, to be sure,) of agricultural prosperity, centered upon the wheat-producing district of Nativitas. The location of Nativitas, whose estates were developed during the later seventeenth century with the draining of the flood plains of the river Atoyac, and its tributary the Zahuapán, close to the milling centers of Puebla and the *camino real*, made it a favorite place for speculative wheat farming by *poblanos* for the extra-regional market.[86] The recent research of Juan Carlos Garavaglia and Juan Carlos Grosso on the *alcabala* tax shows Tlaxcala to have suffered a dramatic and sustained decline in alcabala revenue from the mid 1780s to the early nineteenth century, linked, it seems, to a crisis in the cotton textile industry but probably accelerated by demographic decline and emigration as well as by the difficulties facing commercial, especially wheat, agriculture.[87]

---

[84] For descriptions by contemporaries of eighteenth-century farming practices in the Puebla-Tlaxcala region: Luis Navarro Garcia, "La sociedad rural de México en el Siglo XVIII", *Anales de la Universidad Hispalense*, Vol. XXIII, 1963, p. 49, and, Wolfgang Trautman, *Las transformaciones en el paisaje cultural de Tlaxcala durante la época colonial*. Wiesbaden, 1981, pp. 140-98.

[85] Claude Morin, *Santa Inés Zacatelco (1646-1812) Contribución a la Demografía Histórica del México Colonial*. Mexico, 1973; and, Brian Hamnett, *Roots of Insurgency*, pp. 9-11, 35-40.

[86] The healthy performance of the wheat-growing district of Nativitas (a zone which produced high quality wheat for extra-regional demand), when other branches of Tlaxcala's economy were in decline, may be deduced from the wealth of its tithe farmer during the 1780s and 1790s, Estevan Munuera, and the bouyancy of tithe receipts between 1805 and 1828. AOP, Documentos de Diezmos (Cuadernos y Hojas Sueltas). Remates 1783-1801 and Diezmos de Trigo (1805-1828), BSMGE 1st series, Vol. II, "Estadística de la Municipalidad de Nativitas", p. 254-6.

[87] Juan Garavaglia and Juan Carlos Grosso, "Consideraciones sobre las alcabalas de Nueva España", Unpublished mimeograph, Mexico, 1984, pp. 40-57, and for the

Two lists of Tlaxcala's estates (*haciendas, ranchos, molinos* and *ventas*) made in 1712 and 1791, demonstrate that there was no significant trend in concentration of ownership over the century, a strategy which might have been expected in order to confront an unstable market. (See Table 1.2) In 1791, only two proprietors owned more than two *haciendas*; both in the arid district of Apizaco where concentration of ownership greatly exceeded that in any other district. A comparison of the lists also suggests that the commercial cultivation of haciendas fluctuated more than that of *ranchos*, the number registered of the latter remaining broadly the same in 1712 as in 1791. *Ranchos* perhaps found the task of weathering periods of recession, such as the 1710s clearly were, more easy than haciendas. Moreover, it can be observed that estate ownership in the flat, cereal-growing, peripheral districts of Nativitas (wheat), Tlaxco (wheat, barley and *pulque*) and Huamantla (maize and barley) fluctuated substantially more than in the hillier, poorer, more pastoral and "proto-industrial" central districts of Hueyotlipa, Apizaco, Tlaxcala, Iztaquistla and Chiautempan. A final observation can be made: the lack of continuity of ownership within the same family over this eighty-year period. The only district with any substantial degree of continuity was Chiautempan, the center of the region's *obraje*-based woollen textile industry, where five of the seventeen proprietors names in 1712 were still in possession of sixteen of the district's twenty seven estates in 1791, after Apizaco the highest concentration of ownership in Tlaxcala.[88] Only one name in the important cereal-producing districts of Huamantla and Nativitas recurs in the 1712 and 1791 lists.

---

decline of the textile industry in the face of increased European imports, following *comercio libre*, see Morin, *Michoacán*, p. 125-6.

[88] Isabel González Sánchez, *Haciendas y Ranchos de Tlaxcala en 1712*. Mexico, 1969.

TABLE 1.2 TLAXCALA'S ESTATES REGISTERED FOR TAX PURPOSE (UNDER CULTIVATION): 1712 AND 1791

	Proprietors		Haciendas		Ranchos		Total estates (incl.molinos,ventas & casas del campo -obrajes)	
	1712	1791	1712	1791	1712	1791	1712	1791
Nativitas	34	35	22	33	15	9	37	43
Apizaco	10	10	8	10	11	8	19	19
Huamantla	34	35	23	41	21	14	44	56
Tlaxcala*	37	42	21	26	16	24	37	50
Chiautempan	26	27	8	13	20	21	28	34
Tlaxco	13	32	12	25	7	9	19	36
Total	154	181	94	148	90	85	184	239

Source: Isabel González Sánchez, *Haciendas y Ranchos de Tlaxcala en 1712*, Mexico, 1969; and AGN, Historia, Vol. 73, Expte. 4.

Discontinuity of ownership is hardly surprising when the degree of debt burden, under which most of Tlaxcala's estates were laboring in 1712, is taken into account. In that year Tlaxcala's 184 estates were valued at 1,777,979 pesos and their owners owed 1,124,308 pesos, 63 percent of their value, in mortgages, requiring annual interest payments of around 56,000 pesos. And the predicament of Tlaxcala's farmers must have been rendered particularly acute by their traditional dependence upon the increasingly unstable extra-regional market (little of Tlaxcala's wheat was consumed internally).[89]

Elsewhere in the center west of the province, a similar pattern appears to have held: the survival of an agrarian structure typified by a large number of small (compared to other regions) estates, no observable consolidation of estates into latifundia, heavy indebtedness of farmers to Church creditors, a rapid turnover of estate ownership, irregular demesne production between long periods of estates being left fallow, and, a drift towards rental agreements towards the end of the eighteenth century to accommodate speculative wheat farming for the volatile Caribbean market. These structural characteristics and trends are well illustrated by the dire

---

[89] Of the 10,000 cargas of wheat harvested in mid-nineteenth century Nativitas,9,600 were dispatched beyond the province, mainly to the Sierras of Hidalgo and Puebla, and to the coastal lowlands of Veracruz. In 1849, over 60,000 cargas of wheat were harvested in Tlaxcala, of which only 12,000 cargas were consumed locally, the remaining 48, 000 leaving the state, 13,000 milled and 35,000 in grain. BSMGE 1st series, Vol. I, p. 107,Vol. II, p. 254.

predicament of the prodigiously fertile and potentially highly productive district of Atlixco.

In a perceptive preamble to the military census of the district of Atlixco in 1791, Ignacioo Maneyro observed urban society in the once opulent Villa de Carrión to be in the depths of decay while the wheat-based rural economy edged towards a precipice. As in Tlaxcala, estates were small and landownership dispersed. In that year the district's 86 estates belonged to 46 owners, of whom only the Carmelite Order of Puebla possessed more than two haciendas.[90] Between them Atlixco's landowners owned 6,000 oxen and many hundred threshing horses. A deceptive prosperity had briefly returned to the valley with the liberalization of inter-colonial trade and elimination of fiscal obstacles to the flour trade. The 1791 harvest, over half of which was sent beyond the province, approached 37,000 cargas raised from only forty of the valley's wheat estates. This equalled the harvests of Atlixco's Golden Age in the early seventeenth century and exceeded Havana's annual flour consumption.[91] Such conditions, Maneyro commented, enabled estate owners to live "very decently, and defray the mortgages of over 1,400,000 pesos which burden their estates more than any others in the Kingdom." He added, however, that wheat production in the valley was hazardous in spite of an eternally warm climate, excellent irrigation and inexhaustible soil fertility which permitted some of the highest yields in New Spain and the possibility of raising two harvests annually. The valley's humidity demanded frequent weeding of fields, greatly adding to labor costs, and, in some years, excessive humidity destroyed harvests. Good years, therefore, had to compensate for bad and Atlixco's wheat farmers had traditionally been granted the privilege of selling their grain at one peso/carga above the *postura* in recognition of higher production costs and risks, as well as of its incomparable quality.[92]

Such an agricultural system, especially one so heavily burdened with Church mortgages, required at the very least, a stable market and predictable prices, conditions which appear to have held during the 1780s and early 1790s. Thereafter, Spanish involvement in the Napoleonic wars in 1795 and the granting of permission to American "neutrals" to supply Havana removed such conditions. By 1795, so critical was the predicament of Atlixco's landowners, that they were obliged to default on interest payments amounting to 80,000 pesos.[93] Thereafter, under stop-go

---

90 Ignacio Maneyro,"Descripción de la Villa de Carrión en la Valle de Atlixco...1791", AGN, Padrones, Vol. 25, fs. 1-3.

91 Chevalier, *Land and Society*, p. 64. The entire province of Guadalajara produced 43,000 cargas of wheat in 1802, rising to 54,287 in 1804. Humboldt, *Ensayo*, p. 261, and BL, Ms. 20896 Add. 171557 f. 39.

92 AGN, Padrones, Vol. 25, f. 1.

93 AGI, Indiferente General 2438, (1794-5),"Expediente del Gremio de Labradores de la Villa de Carrión."

wartime conditions of demand, speculatory wheat growers concentrated their investment in the districts closer to Puebla, Atlixco growing ever more marginalized and depressed. On top of this came the *Real Consolidación* decree which forced the wheat farmers of the valley to come to terms with their indebtedness, many of them abandoning business. The "free trade" decree followed in 1813, finally removing Atlixco's privileged wheat *postura*. By the mid-1820s, more than twenty of Atlixco's formerly productive wheat estates lay abandoned.[94]

The 1790s and 1800s were by no means a period of irredeemable agricultural crisis or decline everywhere in the province. Indeed, in the depressed years following Independence, the 1800s were remembered as a boom period which contemporaries grafted onto earlier periods of prosperity, often choosing to forget the intervening century of decline. And it was over these pre-war years that the foundations of several of Puebla's principal fortunes were laid. These successful careers were made, however, by people with their main interests and investments beyond agriculture; in trade, manufacturing and bureaucracy, people often of recent immigrant stock. Unencumbered by the debts under which Creoles labored, these energetic immigrants, mostly from northern Spain, seemed more prepared to take risks and better able to adapt to unstable market and political conditions.[95]

Over the Napoleonic war "boom" no group of landowners, in any of Puebla's principal agricultural zones, succeeded in recovering their former prosperity. By the mid-1790's one thing had become clear: estate agriculture on its own, however skilled the husbandry, was an inadequate base for sustained business success. We need therefore to look beyond agriculture, to trade and manufacturing, in order to understand the complex repercussions of Puebla's long term regional economic decline as well as short term effects of Spanish involvement in the Napoleonic wars.

---

94 *El Caduceo*, Vol. II , No. 20, 10 July 1824, p. 37.
95 Examples of immigrant careers may be found on pp. 75-82.

Industry in the Eighteenth Century

Las fábricas en que se emplean los vecinos (tenidos por los mas hábiles e ingeniosos de toda esta Nueva España, y con razón) son los delicados tejidos de lana, algodón de la China; hermosa, delicada y limpia loza, o barro aún más fino que el de Talavera; cristal y vidrio; todo género de armas finas y de fuego, que corren de gran fama en todo el reino por su delicado temple y primorosa hechura. Pero sobre todas estas fábricas, las más rica, pingüe y opulenta es la del jabón, pues se surte de aqui casi todo el Reino....En las demás artes y manufacturas son tan diestros que con razón y propiedad puede llamarse esta ciudad la Barcelona de la América...[96]

Puebla was the first region in the New World to acquire a broad base of industries, introduced by European artisans, using European technology and producing for the settler population. The province's agricultural and industrial histories possess a similar pattern and periodization, responding to the market changes caused by fluctuations in silver production and extra-regional competitive factors. Puebla's early industries, of which the most notable was woollen broadcloth, like wheat agriculture, enjoyed a "golden age" until the abolition of inter-colonial trade and the onset of the mining depression. Then followed a long twilight of decline and retrenchment over the later seventeenth and the first half of the eighteenth centuries, prompting the growth of a guild system. Over the second half of the eighteenth century, certain industries, most notably cotton textiles, experienced renewed growth but within a context of unprecedented instability resulting from Atlantic war and the onset of the Industrial Revolution in Europe.

Had New Spain in 1800 been at the dawn of industrial revolution, it would be tempting to use the term "proto-industrialization" to describe the social processes, commercial practices and product specialization which made domestic and small workshop manufacturing so conspicuous a part of urban and rural life in Puebla over the eighteenth century.[97] To do so, however, would be to overestimate the importance of a sector which, however successful in attracting capital and, after 1830, even the most modern technology, would not be instrumental in transforming Mexico from being a predominantly rural and agricultural society until beyond the middle of the twentieth century. Varied and commercially dynamic industries were present in the central valley of the province throughout the colonial period but, in 1800, Puebla was not a "proto-industrial" or, even less, an "industrializing" region.

Despite the passing of the "golden age" of Puebla's manufacturing, the central region of the province was, nevertheless, one of the most

---

[96] Francisco de Ajofrín, "Viaje", *Real Academia de la Historia*, Vol. XIII, 1957, p. 47.

[97] For some of the first results of this fast growing research area: Peter Kriedte, Hans Medick and Jurgen Schlumbohm, *Industry before Industrialisation: Rural Industry and the Genesis of Capitalism*. Cambridge, 1981.

industrialized parts of America at the beginning of the nineteenth century, comparable to eastern Pennsylvania and parts of New England. With agriculture seemingly irredeemably depressed and with no mining frontier, it was only to be expected that the new ideology of modern industry would prove attractive to contemporaries. Especially during the depressed decades following Independence, many enterprising *poblanos* saw in the machine, a way out of Puebla's cyclical pattern of economic stagnation, punctuated by short periods of fitful growth, followed by renewed depression. The panacea of industrialization held a fascination for the post-Independence generation. During the 1820s and 1830s, clerics, merchants, shopkeepers, artisans and manufacturers, albeit for reasons of self-interest, considered themselves responsible for maintaining the cohesion of a provincial society threatened by severe economic dislocation, population decline, unemployment, poverty and public disorder. It seemed that industrialization offered solutions to all of these problems.

For the moment, we must examine the colonial history of manufacturing more closely, for here we can find explanations of why industry exercised such a fascination and also why the expectations of the more ambitious industrial entrepreneurs of the 1830s and 1840s came to so little. Two variables must be borne in mind when assessing the market conditions facing colonial manufacturing in the Puebla region: the state of the external sector, and, competition from other manufacturing regions in New Spain. Governing both variables was the state of mining production, the motor of Mexico's internal and overseas trade throughout the colonial period and the nineteenth century.

The position of colonial manufacturing in relation to the external sector, on the face of it, should not have been an unfavorable one. Geography afforded a high degree of protection adding onerous inland freight costs to a fiscally burdened Atlantic trade which, throughout the colonial period, had favored high value and low volume goods.[98] Mexicans were therefore able to produce most basic articles of consumption competitively given this import handicap. As a result, within the economy of New Spain as a whole, manufacturing occupied a rank which surprised and irritated Bourbon administrators such as Viceroy Count Revillagigedo, who sought to increase the mother country's stake in the colony's supply of manufactures, in line with mercantilist theory.[99] He recognized tax

---

[98] D. A. Brading, *Miners and Merchants in Bourbon Mexico 1763-1810*. Cambridge, 1971, pp. 95-8.

[99] On the eve of the revolution of 1810, the secretary of the Consulado of Veracruz, in calculating the total annual production of the economy of New Spain, estimated that manufacturing accounted for 38% (72,386,000 pesos), agriculture 47% (89,285,000 pesos) and mining 15% (28,45,000 pesos). Fernando Rosenzweig points out that Quiróz exaggerated the stake held by manufacturing by including raw material values which properly should belong to agriculture. He adjusts industry's share to

impediments and high carriage costs, combined with the unwillingness of Spanish producers to send goods which appealed to Mexican tastes, as the principal obstacles to increasing imports from the metropolis, mentioning silk-cotton shawls (rebozos) and saddlery, both Puebla specialties, as two valuable import "plums" ignored by Spanish importers and industrialists.[100]

Against these factors, which should have afforded a high degree of protection to the Mexican market, there was a countervailing factor which rendered the market peculiarly vulnerable to import penetration. This was New Spain's obsession --the colony's fatal flaw in Humboldt's view-- with silver mining.[101] The high level of silver production during the half century preceding the Hidalgo revolt, and the high price level created by the silver boom, however much they may have served as motors for internal circuits of trade, served even more to attract investment to the external sector. This, combined with the Bourbon liberalization of Atlantic trade, served to increase pressure from imports, highly competitive with Puebla's staples: cotton and woollen cloth, leather goods, glass, pottery, soap, candles and ironwork. The principal mercantile groups in New Spain could not ignore these expanding opportunities in overseas trade, indeed the exchange of silver for imported European manufactures became their raison d'être.[102] As the eighteenth century proceeded, New Spain's manufacturers and artisans had therefore to accommodate themselves within a financial and commercial environment at worst opposed, and at best indifferent to their interests.

Sustained commitment to manufacturing by prominent merchants occurred only when the external sector was in crisis, either as a result of war or international financial crisis and trade recession. Under such circumstances, the hemorrhage of silver slowed to a trickle and pressure from imports slackened. European merchants returned home or, along with Mexican merchants, looked for alternative areas of investment. Industry temporarily flourished.[103] But such conjunctures, frequent as they were during the 1750-1850 period, were never of sufficient duration to encourage merchants to entertain ideas of an autonomous industrial sector permanently shielded from external competition or to commit themselves to

---

29% and agriculture's to 56%. Fernando Rosenzweig, "La economía novohispana al comenzar el siglo XIX", *Ciencias Políticas y Sociales*, Vol. IX, 1963, p. 480.

[100] BAGN lst series, Vol. I, 1930, pp. 203-4, and Vol. II, p. 198.

[101] Humboldt, *Political Essay*, Vol. V, p. 404-7.

[102] For New Spain's mercantile practices: Brading, *Miners and Merchants*, pp. 95-104; Morin, *Michoacán en la Nueva España*, pp. 141-208; and John Kicza, *Colonial Entrepreneurs*, pp. 43-133.

[103] Humboldt noted this phenonenon: "Cuando sucede estar así estancado el comercio exterior, se despierta por un momento la industria mexicana...", Humboldt, *Ensayo Político*, p. 230.

sustained investment in manufacturing. Thus Mexican producers had frequently to adapt to unsteady commercial backing and uncertain market conditions. External instability impressed itself deeply upon the structure of Puebla's manufacturing and on the mood of the region's political economy both of which, by the turn of the nineteenth century, exhibited a responsiveness, as well as a resistance, to external pressures and crises.

Puebla's manufacturers and artisans faced competition not only from Europe but from other American manufacturing regions. The interplay of external and internal competitive factors is best illustrated by examining the fortunes of the region's two principal colonial staples: woollen broadcloth and cotton *manta*.

The spectacular rise and fall of colonial Spanish America's only high quality woollen broadcloth industry appears to have coincided with the first great cycles of silver production in Mexico and Peru.[104] It is fair to assume that the city's other staples: metalwork, glass, majolica pottery, leatherwork and *tocinería* products obeyed similar market factors and that the state of Puebla's manufacturing depended upon the ability of its artisans and merchant-manufacturers to place their goods upon the principal commercial circuits through which coin and manufactured goods were exchanged.[105] Thus the peak of Puebla's colonial development coincided with the summit of Mexico's silver mining boom in the late sixteenth, early seventeenth centuries.

The chroniclers cite the abolition of inter-colonial trade in 1634 as the turning point, signalling the passing of Puebla's "golden age." It is likely, however, that this merely compounded other factors which already were reducing demand for Puebla's costly woollen broadcloth. From a peak of 40 units in the 1570s, the number of woollen broadcloth *obrajes* fell to 35 in 1604, and to 22 in 1622.[106] By 1634, Peru, Puebla's principal overseas market, had become progressively less accessible as a result of the growth of the Andean textile industry, the decline of the Veracruz-Huatulco route (upon which Puebla had been strategically located and along which had passed much of the trade between Europe, New Spain and Peru), and the reorientation of Peruvian trade towards the Cartagena route and the Philippines.[107] Although there is evidence that the prohibition upon inter-

---

[104] Alberto Carabarín Gracia, "Auge y declinación de los obrajes en Puebla: tres enfoques historiográficos", Unpublished paper given at the LASA Conference, Universidad Metropolitana, Mexico City, 1983, pp. 14-18.

[105] In the 1630s, Thomas Gage reported the Puebla mint to be coining "half the silver which cometh from Sacatecas", Gage, *A New Survey*, p. 37; Villa Sánchez, *Puebla Sagrada*, pp. 86-7; and Leicht, *Calles de Puebla*, p. 5.

[106] Romero, "La Sociedad", p. 136, Zerón y Zapata, *La Puebla*, p. 38, and Leicht, *Calles de Puebla*, pp. 276-9.

[107] For the growth of manufacturing in Peru and Ecuador: "Memoria de Miguel Sánchez de la Parra", (1584). CDIHE Madrid, 1892, pp. 278-9; J. L. Phelan *The Kingdom of Quito in the Seventeenth Century*. Madison, 1967, and Javier Ortíz de la Tabla,

colonial trade was more honored in the breach in Puebla, it seems certain that by the 1630s, South America as a volume market had been lost.[108] Thereafter, Puebla's goods would be confined to the Mexican market and the irregular demand, through the *comercio de víveres*, from Spanish shipping and garrisons in the North Pacific and the Caribbean.

Over the later seventeenth and eighteenth centuries Puebla's woollen cloth industry faced growing overseas competition. Spain's own state-sponsored woollen industry sought a colonial market, and imports from the metropolis, combined with British goods entering New Spain through the asiento, had effectively destroyed Puebla's fine woollen broadcloth industry by the 1740's.[109] Of the 22 *obrajes* of fine cloth in 1622, only 10 "*obrajes, obradores* and *trapiches*" producing inferior cloth remained in 1700, falling to six in 1710, and to a mere two in 1794, producing rough blankets and friezes.[110] The coarser woollen cloth industry which remained also faced growing competition, but from within New Spain. Puebla's early comparative advantages, based upon the central valley becoming New Spain's first sheep-raising region and the existence of a Pre-Conquest cochineal industry, gradually slipped away as cochineal production shifted south and as sheep-raising shifted north, giving a crucial price advantage to Querétaro's *obrajeros* who provided the bulk of the colony's ordinary woollen cloth over the eighteenth century.[111] By 1800 wool was twice as expensive in Puebla as in Saltillo or Guadalajara. This ratio still held after Independence when, in the early 1820s, wool was selling in Puebla at prices of between 42 to 56 reales/arroba, in contrast to 14-30 reales/arroba in Querétaro, San Luis Potosí and Aguascalientes.[112]

"El obraje colonial ecuatoriano. Aproximación a su estudio", *Revista de Indias*, Nos. 149-150, 1977, pp. 471-542; and for the decline of the Huatulco trade, Borah, "Early Colonial Trade".

[108] For resistance in New Spain to the prohibition on inter-colonial trade: Israel, *Race, Class and Politics*, pp. 29, 191, 196-197; and Alvarado Morales, *La Ciudad de México*, pp. 55-70.

[109] Bazant, "Evolución de la industria textil", p. 489, and for a synthesis of the chroniclers' explanations for the decline of the woollen industry: Garavaglia and Grosso, "La Región de Puebla-Tlaxcala", pp. 566-8 and 580-4.

[110] AAP, Gremios, Vol. 224, fs. 176-225; AGNP, Judicial Miscellaneous, Obraje inspection in 1710 and 1759, and AGN, Historia, Vol. 74, fs. 406-455.

[111] John Super, "Querétaro Obrajes. Industry and Society in Provincial Mexico, 1600-1810, *HAHR*, Vol. 56, 1976, pp. 197-216; and R. E. Greenleaf, "The Obraje in the Late Mexican Colony", *The Americas*, Vol. XXIII, 1967, pp. 227-50.

[112] For wool prices: Saltillo (1786, 1792, 1802-3, 1842-45), Charles Harris, *A Mexican Family*, pp. 89, 238; Querétaro (1793. 1826 and 1844) Humboldt, *Ensayo*, p. 452; Ward, *Mexico*, pp. 183, 349, and *BSMGE* lst series, Vol. II, p. 20; Guadalajara (1803) BM, Ms 20896 Add. 171,557; Puebla (1800-1822) AAP, Abastos, Vols. 88-89, and AAP RPP, Censos, Vol. 41, f. 411, and Vol. 42, f. 37.

By 1700, in spite of the loss of its in initial comparative advantages, the city nevertheless conserved most of the industries upon which its early reputation had been founded. The masters of the principal crafts (fine pottery, tanning, saddlery, hat making, iron work) formed into guild corporations so as to confront, more effectively, the decline of demand. Puebla also acquired new industries, most notably, *manta* and *rebozo* weaving, supplying the regional, extra-regional and overseas markets during the eighteenth century.

Cotton-spinning and weaving had been important industries in the central valley of Puebla at the time of the Conquest but appear to have sustained a prolonged decline over the sixteenth and seventeenth centuries. Only towards the end of the seventeenth century did creole and mestizo artisans take up cotton weaving, an industry, Jan Bazant has argued, they had hitherto shunned.[113] The growth of creole-mestizo cotton textile weaving was a phenomenon common to most regions of central and southeastern Mexico over the eighteenth century. Oaxaca, Mexico, Valladolid and Guadalajara had all acquired important textile industries by the last third of the century.[114] The Puebla industry, however, appears to have emerged half a century earlier than elsewhere. It also became commercially the most dynamic of New Spain's provincial textile industries. How, then, can the early growth and subsequent development of Puebla's cotton textile industry be explained?

A definitive answer to this question must await much deeper research into the region's demography and the development of the internal market of New Spain during the eighteenth century. Some tentative and preliminary suggestions may, however, be made. The most fruitful areas of inquiry would appear to be, first, the contradictory phenonemon of the demographic recovery of the central valley of Puebla within a context of economic decline. Here, "cottage" industry developed as a necessary source of subsistence, especially for the non-Indian population. The second area of explanation lies in the emergence of a regional mercantile group dedicated to financing and managing the cotton textile industry. These developments, when seen within the wider context of the growth of the internal market of New Spain, the recovery of silver mining, the introduction of more modern weaving technology and the Bourbon fiscal

---

[113] Bazant, "Evolución", pp. 493-501.

[114] Guy Thomson, "The Cotton Textile Industry in Puebla during the Eighteenth and Early Nineteenth Centuries", in Jacobsen and Puhle, (Eds.), *The Economies*, pp. 169-202; Carmen Aguirre Anaya and Alberto Carabarín García, "Formas artesanales y fabriles de los textiles de algodón en la ciudad de Puebla, siglos XVIII y XIX", CIHS, *Puebla De la Colonia*, pp. 25-54; Jorge González Angulo and Roberto Sandoval, "Los Trabajadores Industriales de Nueva España, 1750-1810", in Enrique Florescano et al., *La Clase Obrera*, pp. 173-238; and Manuel Miño Grijalva, "Espacio económico e industria textil, los trabajadores de Nueva España: 1780-1810", *Historia Mexicana*, Vol. 32, 1982, pp. 524-553.

inducements to encourage cotton agriculture in the Gulf region, provide compelling explanations. An added factor of importance was Puebla's central location, on the two principal routes from the *tierra caliente* of Veracruz and Oaxaca, where since Pre-Colombian times much of Mexico's cotton had been grown. Finally, the shift of mercantile investment from the remote Indian districts of the Sierra Mixteca, where much of the colony's cotton manta had traditionally been produced through repartimiento, to the more accessible and now relatively more densely populated plateau districts, undoubtedly favored Puebla as a rational location for the development of creole-mestizo cotton weaving.[115]

An impending Malthusian crisis over the first third of the eighteenth century perhaps accounts, more than any other single factor, for the origins and early development of the industry in the central valley of Puebla. Chapter Four will examine the demographic background more fully. Suffice it here to observe that the rapid recovery of the Indian population from the mid-seventeenth century until the catastrophic epidemic of 1737, accompanied by the sustained growth of the creole and mestizo populations, coincided with a period of secular economic decline, affecting Puebla's traditional manufacturing and agricultural staples. This conjuncture threatened a crisis of subsistence to which the labor- intensive cotton textile industry offered a palliative. Once the industry had become established, at first perhaps to satisfy only the regional market, then commercial capital was attracted to it and its full potential realized. For much of the eighteenth century, Puebla became New Spain's principal producer of cotton cloth, *manta trigueña poblana* reaching markets as far north as Chihuahua and Coahuila.

A contemporary description of the city of Puebla in 1744, at a time when the decline in the region's economy had reached its nadir, provides evidence for this explanation for the industry's growth, as well as insight into its developing commercial structure. Fray Juan Villa Sánchez observed a city abandoned by its more enterprising merchants and woollen clothiers, locked in the clutches of a body of rentiers who farmed the *alcabala*, Crown monopolies and revenues of local government, noticing that the tax yield had risen in inverse ratio to the visible economic decline of the city. He described a city of widows and young girls, unable to find spouses, driven to the spinning wheel. The streets teemed with ragged beggars, women abandoned to their fate, artisans desperate to sell their wares and petty criminals.[116] Over this period Puebla also became the most riot-prone city of New Spain, a position hitherto occupied by the viceregal capital.[117]

---

[115] This argument is developed more fully in Thomson, "The Cotton Textile Industry", pp. 170-78.

[116] Villa Sánchez, *Puebla Sagrada*, pp. 69-90.

[117] Eugenio Aguareles, "Una conmoción popular en el México virreinal", *AEA*, Vol. 7, 1950, pp. 125-161.

Amidst this poverty and disorder, Villa Sánchez pinpointed the principal elements of the commercial and productive structure of a newly established industry which has remained Puebla's staple until the present day. Villa Sanchez' description is more eloquent than any paraphrasing:

> A los tejídos de algodón ministra ingente porción de cargas de este fruto que viene a esta ciudad de la costa del Sur y jurisdicciones de Teutila, Cosamaloapan, Tuxtla y otras; sirve al comercio en greña, a los encomenderos que lo reciben, a los muchos tenderos que lo menudean, y de aquí pasa a las manos de la gente más miserable; es la última apelación de la pobreza el hilado de algodón; es el mesquino socorredor, especialmente de pobres doncellas y viudas, que puestas de sol a sol a la rueda de un torno, que es el de su corta fortuna en aquel diuturno trabajo, logran escasamente el estipendio, más para enfermar que para matar el hambre; es el signo evidente, es la demostración palpable de la mucha pobreza que hay en La Puebla, no se pasa por calle alguna donde no se oiga el repique general (no de fiesta, sino de gran trabajo) de los bastones o cañas con que azotan el algodón; y las onzas que hilará una pobre mujer en el día le vendrán a rendir el precio de un real de plata. De estas miserables manos pasa a la de los tejedores, o de mantas que suplen el lienzo para camisas, o de paños de reboso o del que llaman chapaneco para forros y otros semejantes: también es cortísimo y no correspondiente al trabajo la ganancia de este oficio. De estos pasan los géneros a los comerciantes, que remiten muchas porciones de ellos a tierra adentro y otras partes para provisión de varias ciudades, pueblos y haciendas.[118]

Villa Sánchez was observing the industry at a turning point. A permanent body of wholesale merchants specializing in dealing in raw cotton and marketing finished cloth beyond the region was becoming established in Puebla for the first time.

The great woollen clothiers of sixteenth and early seventeenth-century Puebla had themselves managed the supply of raw material, production and marketing of cloth to markets as far distant as Peru.[119] The more modest cotton weaver, if he sought access to the extra-regional market, had perforce to use the services of merchants. Mercantile involvement in the industry can be observed in the early 1740's when *veracruzano* merchants were seen diverting their investment from foreign trade into financing cotton agriculture for the expanding highland industry, with Atlantic trade interrupted by the War of Austrian succession (1739-48).[120] Peace having been restored, demand from Spain's own expanding cotton textile industry made sustained investment in cotton agriculture now profitable.

---

[118] Villa Sánchez, *op. cit.*, p. 71-2

[119] Guadalupe Albi, "La Sociedad", pp. 17-145.

[120] Enrique Florescano and Luis Chávez Orozco, *Agricultura e industria textil de Veracruz: siglo XIX*. Jalapa, 1965, p. 117.

At first, the system of *repartimiento* was used, based upon the exchange of raw cotton for manufactured goods at annual cotton fairs in the growing districts, administered by *alcaldes mayores* who acted as intermediaries between merchants and the largely Indian (in Veracruz) and mulatto/negro (in the Pacific region of Puebla) cotton growing communities.[121] Later in the century, as a result of the growth in internal and overseas demand for raw cotton, and the abolition of *repartimiento* trade in 1786, merchants became more directly involved in cotton agriculture. In wartime, when the blocking of imports precipitated sudden price rises, the principal merchants of the city (Tiburcio Uriarte, Joaquín Haro y Portillo, Dionisio Fernández Pérez, etc.) would turn from foreign trade to investment in the *veracruzano* cotton trade. By the end of the eighteenth century, a handful of wholesalers enjoyed a veritable cotton monopoly. Customs records show that in the final three months of 1799, eight Puebla wholesalers supplied 60 percent of all the cotton supplied to dealers and weavers throughout the entire west-center of the region (the geographical core of the cotton weaving industry).[122] This monopoly would play a crucial role in the transformation of the industry during the 1830s and 1840s and would also determine the limits of that transformation.

If the supply of this prized raw material attracted mercantile interest, so also did the marketing of the finished product: the thirty yard cotton *manta* piece. Still in 1744 Villa-Sánchez records that the wholesale raw cotton and finished cotton cloth dealers were almost all outsiders ("ultrones"), who did not know the city.[123] Over the second half of the eighteenth century, however, the trade in Puebla's *ropa de tierra* (cloth produced in the colony) became a much less improvised affair. Successful in finding markets even in the far north of the country, indeed, wherever there was silver, the merchants who specialized in Puebla's cloth grew to rival import wholesalers in wealth and status. They settled around the inns to the northeast of the plaza mayor, where dealers and muleteers would stay on route to the *tierradentro*. Indeed, the Calle de Mesones became the center of the trade. By 1803 Manuel Flon counted 28 *almacenes de ropa de tierra*.[124] These merchants were later remembered by the chronicler, Francisco Javier de la Peña: Juan Luis Palacios, "riquísimo comerciante español de lienzos

---

121 An example of *repartimiento* trade in cotton: Joseph Díaz de Blea, Puebla merchant, paid 1,500 pesos in a bill of exchange to Cayetano Bravo, alcalde mayor of Cosomaloapan, for 118 1/4 cargas of cotton. The bill could be exchanged for goods at the Jalapa trade fair. AGNP, Judicial Miscellaneous 1759. Other sources for repartimiento cotton production: INAH Microfilm Collection AJP, Roll.38; AGN, Industria y Comercio, Vol. 1, fs. 360-81.

122 AJP (1800) Puebla Aduana to Manuel Flon, 20 April 1800.

123 Villa Sánchez, *Puebla Sagrada*, p. 87.

124 Manuel Flon, "Descripción, p. 146.

de algodón," who donated 20,000 pesos to each of Puebla's four hospitals and 10,000 pesos to the prison, and Roque de la Peña and Fernando Gutiérrez de Nansa, "montañeses ricos," who each gave 12,000 pesos to embellish the parish church of Señor San José. Puebla's weavers brought their *mantas* and *rebozos* to the counters of these merchants.[125]

Through their ability to advance credit to weavers, Puebla's cloth merchants extended their influence beyond the weaving barrios of the capital to the entire central region of the province during the second half of the eighteenth century. The scale of the cotton textile industry by the last decade of the eighteenth century was impressive. Manuel Flon counted 1,170 looms in the city alone in 1794 while neighboring Tlaxcala contained 950 looms.[126] The 1791 census of four city parishes shows that well over 20% of the population was employed in textile manufacture.[127] Although Puebla's merchants, like India's merchants in the same period, favored a cash relationship over a putting-out system, the independence of the weaver was progressively curtailed as merchants grew to control the supply of both raw and spun cotton.[128] In the next chapter we shall assess the social implications for the weaver of this concentration of wealth and control among the cloth merchants. For the moment, we must examine the state of the industry on the eve of the economic crisis accompanying Independence. We must also offer an explanation of why, if merchants were so fully in control of this valuable industry from the mid-eighteenth century, were they so averse to any significant technological innovation before the 1830s?

Puebla's cotton textile industry reached the peak of its colonial development, in terms of pure volume, during the five years preceding the Peace of Amiens. This period would be long remembered, when even "los tejedores estaban vestidos de terciopelo y rasos, tachonadas de hebillas y botones de oro y plata, y las hilanderas con enaguas de muselina de cinco pesos la vara...".[129] But, as we have seen with Puebla's trade in flour and foodstuffs, the 1797-1802 period was an exceptional interlude of prosperity disguising an underlying secular decline in Puebla's competitive position vis-a-vis other Mexican regions and, more significantly when we are considering textiles, with an industrializing Europe.

---

[125] Francisco Javier de la Peña, "Notas", pp. 173.

[126] AGN, Historia, Vol. 74, fs. 407-55, "Razón de Fábricas....", (1794) and AGN, Alcabalas, Vol. 37.

[127] Analysed in Chapter 2.

[128] See for example K. N. Chaudhuri, "The Structure of the Indian Textile Industry in the 17th and 18th Centuries", *The Indian Economic and Social History Review*, Vol. XI, 1974, pp. 131-181.

[129] Estevan de Antuñano, *Ampliación, aclaración y corección a los principales puntos del manifiesto sobre el algodón manufacturado y en greña*. Puebla 1833, repr. ed. Mexico, 1955, p. 72.

By the turn of the nineteenth century, Puebla's principal Mexican competitor was Guadalajara. By 1802, Guadalajara's production of cotton *mantas* and *rebozos* was valued at 1,620,423 pesos, almost equalling that of Puebla. In the following year, Guadalajara exceeded Puebla's production which had commenced a sudden decline as a result of the resumption of cloth imports following the Peace of Amiens.[130]

However galling was this competition from "upstart" Guadalajara, ultimately it was overseas competition which caused Puebla's textile merchants and cotton weavers the greatest anxiety. The complementarity rather than competitiveness of Puebla's textiles with imported cloth from Europe may be observed from the records of textile entries to Mexico City's custom's house, shown in Table 1.3. In peacetime, between 1785 and 1792, entries of Puebla and European cloth remained stable, particularly the former. During the war with France and Britain, between 1793 and 1801, while entries of European cloth dropped markedly, there was not the increase in Puebla cloth entries (to make up the deficit), which might have been expected. There is no observable substitution effect and the slight increase in entries of Puebla cloth did not begin to compensate for the shortfall in European cloth. The reason is simple. The Puebla industry specialized in ordinary cotton *manta* s very little of which was consumed in Mexico City, the colony's principal market for fine cloth.[131] Most of Puebla's manta passed through Mexico City to the mining towns and hacienda districts of *tierradentro*, markets satisfied increasingly by Guadalajara's production. Thus Puebla's textile industry failed to take advantage of the opportunity offered by the substantial decline in fine cloth imports during a period of almost a decade.

The return of peace in 1802 removed impediments to Spanish imports which now entered the luxury-starved Mexican market in unprecedented quantities. Table 1-3 shows that Puebla's *manta* remissions inland continued to hold up well for a further four years. It seems, therefore, that the protectionism of the colonial system was sufficient to permit the survival of Puebla's manta industry, although diversification into, for instance, cotton prints, appears not to have been a serious option, presumably because of the Catalan lead and greater competitiveness in this line. Mexican war-time experiments with large scale calico printing were short-lived.[132]

---

[130]   BL, Ms 20896, Add. 17,557; and Humboldt, *Ensayo Político*, p. 451.

[131]   Entries to the Mexico City customs house are recordes in the *Correo Semanario Político Mercantil*, Vols. I-III.

[132]   Manuel Miño Grijalva, "El Camino hacia la Fábrica en Nueva España: El Caso de la Fábrica de Francisco de Iglesias, 1801-1810", *Historia Mexicana*, Vol. 46, 1984, pp. 135-47.

TABLE 1.3 ENTRIES OF EUROPEAN AND PUEBLA CLOTH
TO THE MEXICO CITY CUSTOMS HOUSE 1785-1812

	Year	Entry of Puebla Cloth (in *tercios*)		Entry of European Cloth (in *tercios*)	
Peace	1785	4384		12800	
	1786	4013		8258	
	1787	4732		6662	
	1788	4811		7872	
	1789	ND		6244	
	1790	4879		8015	
	1791	5206		8270	
	1792	6158		7315	
War with France	1793	6046		6420	
	1794	6426		5477	
	1795	6938		5019	
Peace	1796	6917		6571	
	1797	6980		2188	
War with Great Britain	1798	6576		1624	Neutral
	1799	7517		3323	Trade
	1800	7097		2942	
	1801	7626		2725	
Peace	1802	5672		9446	
	1803	6334		12842	
War with Great Britain	1804	6482		6433	
	1805	6401		3358	
	1806	ND		ND	Neutral
	1807	ND		ND	Trade
French Invasion	1808	ND		ND	
	1809	4768		5120	
	1810	1452	(Jan-June)	3388	(Jan-June)
Mexican Wars	1810	786	(Aug-Dec)	1455	(Aug-Dec)
	1811	603	(Mar-July)	2413	(Mar-July)

ND = No data available
One *tercio* = 175 lbs.

Sources: 1785-1805, *Gaceta de México*, Vols. I-XIII; 1809-1811, *Correo Semanario
Político Mercantil*, Vols. 1-3.

The shock for both Mexican and Spanish textile manufacturers and dealers came not in 1802, when merchants optimistically anticipated the resumption of normal trading relations within a protected colonial market, but after 1805, with the renewal of war with Great Britain. Faced once more with a blockade of the American market and the cessation of bullion remissions to Europe the Crown, in desperation, granted neutral powers access to the colonial market between 1805 and 1807. Figures for textile imports through Veracruz show the virtual substitution of Peninsular by Asian and "American" (United States and, presumably, British) goods between 1806 and 1808, with cheap cottons, especially Asian prints, predominating over the more expensive linens, silks and woollens. In earlier trading concessions to neutrals, cotton goods had been specifically excluded.[133] This time they were permitted. The disastrous impact upon Puebla's cotton textile industry of the arrival of cheap and attractively colored cottons on the Mexican market, for the first time, can be only surmised. Unfortunately, Mexico City customs figures are lacking for the crucial years between 1805 and 1809. When figures resume in 1809, it is clear that the hold of Puebla *manta* in the markets of the interior had diminished (Table 1.3). And after 1810 it slipped away altogether.

Wartime instability and declining internal and external competitiveness are perhaps sufficient explanations for the absence of any concerted attempts to modernize or "transform" the cotton textile industry over the final decades of colonial rule. These conditions encouraged a speculative mentality among merchants, similar to the behavior observed with wheat agriculture. Cotton gins were established at Orizaba and Tlacotalpan, which promised to greatly reduce carriage costs since raw cotton had traditionally been transported to Puebla unseeded and still on the stem. This was because of Puebla's cheaper and more abundant labor supply. Cotton merchants failed, however, to prepare the ground among Puebla's spinners who rejected the ginned cotton, preferring hand stripped and caned cotton with its fibres intact, as it responded better to their spinning wheels.[134] All attempts before Independence at establishing cotton ginning plants in Veracruz failed because of resistance from Puebla.

There appears to have been no effort in Puebla to address this problem and we are persuaded by the opinion of José Maria Quirós, the secretary of the Consulado of Veracruz, that little could be done to improve efficiency at the spinning stage (so necessary for the future competitiveness of the industry) so long as raw cotton dealers continued to see an advantage in exploiting the dependence and poverty of spinning women. He observed that merchants lacked any incentive to introduce technical innovations in

---

[133] Miguel Lerdo de Tejada, *Comercio exterior*, "Balanzas, 1802-1812".

[134] Florescano and Chávez Orozco, *Agricultura e Industria*, p. 244, and Tomás Quiróz, "Artes", *El Jornal de Veracruz*, Vol. II, pp. 229-30.

spinning since they continued to profit from the almost gratuitous services of a large female urban and rural proletariat. Puebla was fast becoming a city of widows and spinsters over the last years before and during the wars of Independence, obliged to spin in order to survive. Puebla's cotton weavers' guild was also strongly opposed to the mechanization of spinning, claiming that the good reputation of Puebla's *rebozos* and *manta* was in part due to the caning of the cotton by the spinners.[135] Any mechanization of spinning they feared would further diminish the weavers' stake in the industry. So, before Independence, Puebla's cloth merchants were not ready to sacrifice their long-established control over the spinners for the uncertainties and costs of mechanization. Nor would they risk further antagonizing the cotton weavers, anxious to retain a vestigial autonomy. That confrontation would await the 1830s. Given the instability of wartime demand, accompanied (one suspects) by declining profits, merchants preferred the limited fixed capital costs and labor flexibility of the traditional system.

By 1810, the disintegration of Puebla's cotton cloth industry, the province's principal industrial staple for over a century, was already well advanced. Cotton growers in Veracruz called in vain for steadier mercantile investment.[136] This had fallen off as a result of the decline in cotton prices between 1803 and 1810, itself a consequence of the collapse in demand for colonial and Peninsular manufactures.[137] As early as 1803, the affairs of the cotton weavers' guild had fallen into complete disarray, as illegal and unsupervised production grew to exceed that of the guild masters and officials.[138] Finally, Puebla's *manta* lost its good reputation in the markets of the interior as quality and commercial reliability declined with the onset of the wars of Independence.[139] Cotton weavers migrated to the interior or joined the insurgent or royalist armies in their hundreds.

---

[135] *El Jornal de Veracruz*, Vol. II, pp. 230-2; and González Angulo and Sandoval, "Los trabajadores", pp. 212-3.

[136] The price of raw cotton in Veracruz fell from 24 reales/arroba in 1798-1802 to 12 reales/arroba in 1810. AGN Industria y Comercio, Vol. I , f. 404; and Robert Potash, *El Banco de Avío de México. El fomento de la industria, 1821-1846*. Mexico, 1959, p. 20.

[137] El Costeño, "Fomento la fábrica de algodón", in *Diario de México*, Vol. VI, 1807, pp. 270-2, 375-76.

[138] This is examined at greater length in Chapter 3.

[139] Javier de la Peña, "Notas", p. 153.

Credit and the Provincial Economy, 1800-1830

La provincia de Puebla es entre todas las de esta Nueva España la que ha resentido el fatal golpe de la insurreción...Consumida la industria, se evaporó el numerario...Las familias se vieron dispersas, la opinión extrabiada, las propiedades invadidas, avandonada la agricultura, y moribundo el comercio.[140]

The Napoleonic wars, the ensuing Mexican war of Independence and the end of Spanish rule in 1821 had far-reaching effects upon the provincial economy which resounded over the subsequent decades. Indeed they set the agenda for much of the political economy, economic policy and entrepreneurial behavior which are the subject matter of Part Two of this study. The Napoleonic wars brought a short, illusory but unforgettable spell of prosperity. The wars of Independence coincided with, perhaps caused, the beginning of two decades of economic crisis.

An explanation for Puebla slipping from the economic stagnation or "variable instability" which had characterized the provincial economy during the 18th century, into the crisis of the 1810-1835 period, can be found by examining four broad areas of change. First, the Wars of Independence, by causing a sudden fall in mining production, disrupted the market for the region's manufactures in *tierradentro*. The short term crisis occasioned by the insurgency heralded the onset of a prolonged depression in the mining industry to endure well beyond the period covered in this study. This historic depression, coupled with the abolition of the municipal *abastos* of the provincial capitals of Central Mexico, and the collapse of the Spanish mercantile structure, removed the principal mechanisms by which inter-regional trade was conducted. The exchange of silver and livestock with manufactures, the key to Puebla's access to the market of the interior, was therefore seriously undermined.[141]

The second area of change was, as has already been shown, beginning to make itself felt long before Independence: the collapse of Spanish colonial mercantile monopoly. From 1821, Puebla's staple industries (textiles, flour, soap, pottery, glass) faced much more direct competition from the industrializing world, particularly Great Britain. This, combined with the partial substitution of Spanish by British, French and German import merchants by the mid-1820s, who settled away from Mexico City and Puebla, and showed little interest in financing local manufactures,

---

[140] AGN Consulados, Vol. 463, fs. 1-9, "Representación de la Junta recaudadora del préstamo forzoso", 11 April, 1815.

[141] For long distance exchange between the North and the Southeast, and the disruption caused to it by the wars and the abolition of the *abastos*, see Harris, *A Mexican Family Empire*, pp. 91-93; and Guy Thomson, "Traditional and Modern Manufacturing in Mexico, 1821-50", in Reinhard Liehr (Ed.), *La formación de economías latinoamericanas y los intereses económicas europeas en la época de Bolívar, 1800-1850*, Bibliotheca Ibero-Americana, No. 33. Berlin, 1989, pp.67-69.

posed a major threat to Puebla's economic lifeblood.[142] The Spanish commercial monopoly and mercantile practices had always provided a degree of protection for American manufactures, favoring the development of inter-regional along side colonial trade. At Independence, the Puebla region faced the rapidly developing international economy much more directly than every before.

The third (and long anticipated) area of change in Puebla's economic predicament was the loss of protected market for the region's flour and manufactures in the Caribbean with the decline in Spanish naval power in that area. This effectively ended Mexican exports and left the country much more exposed to contraband imports which she was poorly equipped to resist. The home market in the Mexican southeast was, therefore, also threatened. The loss of the Caribbean market and the decline of the market of the Mexican southeast, now that regions such as the Yucatan, Tabasco and even Veracruz could acquire their flour, temperate goods and manufactures more cheaply from abroad than from the Mexican tableland, removed an important area of commercial speculation which had attracted merchants to Puebla even during the relatively depressed 18th century.

Finally, the market of the Puebla region itself tumbled from stagnation into crisis as a result of growing unemployment, emigration, population decline and general poverty, a consequence of all the factors mentioned, as of the secular trends explored in this and later chapters.

Puebla's decline is clearly reflected in the records of mortgage loans (censos) to manufacturing, trade and agriculture between 1800 and 1830.[143] By dividing these thirty years into five year periods and by distinguishing Church from private loans, it is possible to observe different rates of decline over time and between the three sectors. The obligation to register all notarized mortgage contracts with the "Public Registry of Property" make this a reliable source for estimating changes in the credit market, one which has been more thoroughly exploited by Greenow for the province of Guadalajara.[144] In contrast with most other primary sources,

---

[142] As one British merchant put it,"San Luis and Aguascalientes are the best places for business and the city of Mexico has become the worst." UG Ms., Wylie Papers, Vol. 1, 1 June 1830, Wylie (San Luis Potosí) to Cooke (Manchester).

[143] "Industry" refers to all artisan and small factory production, including flour mills, bakeries and brickworks. "Agriculture", refers to haciendas, ranchos and sugar mills. "Commerce", refers to wholesale and retail businesses exclusively, not to manufacturing concerns which retailed their products, such as wax chandleries, which are included with "industry".

[144] Linda Greenow, *Credit and Socioeconomic Change in Colonial Mexico: Loans and Mortgages in Guadalajara, 1720-1820*. Boulder, Colorado, 1983; and her "Spatial Dimensions of the Credit Market in Eighteenth-Century New Galicia", in David J Robinson (Ed.), *Social Fabric and Spatial Structures in Colonial Latin America*. Ann Arbor, 1979, pp. 227-279. Further details of the Guadalajara register are to be

this source has the particular advantage of remaining undisturbed by the momentous political changes of the epoch, thus helping to overcome the historiographical discontinuity which so unnaturally separates the colonial from the republican periods. What, then, do these records show?

At first, as Table 1.4 demonstrates, the figures for the 1801-05 quinquennium reflect the scale of the short war-time boom experienced in Puebla, as in other parts of America, as a result of the disruption of transatlantic trade. During these five years, one third of all the loans were registered, and more than one third of all the credit for the entire thirty year period was dispensed.[145] In fact, there were only two years (before the Peace of Amiens) during which the domestic market was protected by war, with Puebla's position in the Caribbean market relatively unchallenged by competitors. The figures are therefore all the more remarkable. Industry received more than one half of all credit. Loans went to flour millers, bakers, weavers, chandlers, *tocineros*, tanners, potters, iron founders, and bell makers. Many of these loans came from leading merchants involved normally in the import trade (José Bernardo Aspiroz, Pedro Paso y Troncoso, Tiburcio Uriarte, Gaspar de Echavarri, Juan Jorge Rizo) now investing in domestic production.[146] Only 8 of the 32 loans came from corporate bodies: six from the Church and two from Indian communities.[147]

Commerce followed industry in importance as a focus of investment between 1801-05. Loans went principally to cotton cloth dealers, livestock (especially mule) dealers, mercers and retailers of dry goods. The principal lenders were again, wholesale importers and cotton merchants: Tiburcio Uriarte, Juan Palacios, José Tello, Juan Jorge Rizo and Francisco Pereyra. All but 2 of the 32 loans to commerce were from private sources, Church bodies preferring to invest in the less profitable but less risky agriculture.

The second sub-period, from 1806 to 1810, witnessed a dramatic decline in the number and value of loans to all three sectors. The number of loans halved and the amount invested was reduced by four fifths of the

---

found in David J. Robinson and Linda Greenow, *Catálogo del Registro Público de la Propiedad de Guadalajara: Libros de Hipotecas, 1586-1820*. Guadalajara, 1986.

[145] Loans for the purchase of urban or rural property or for the redemption of mortgages are excluded from these estimates, which refer only to loans for the day-to-day running of businesses and estates or the stocking of shops and workshops. The direct impact of the *Real Consolidación* decree of 1805, ordering the redemption of all loans mortaged with chantries, chaplaincies and pious works, is not therefore reflected in these figures.

[146] AGNP, RPP, Vol. 38, fs. 132, 171, 215, 314, 412.

[147] Corporate (Church or Indian community) capital investment was concentrated almost exclusively in flour milling and *tocinería*, on security of landed estates, these two branches of industry absorbing 80% of all loans to industry between 1801 and 1805, illustrating the importance of the Caribbean market, the chief outlet for these goods.

TABLE 1.4 LOANS TO INDUSTRY, COMMERCE AND AGRICULTURE 1800-1830

	INDUSTRY			COMMERCE			AGRICULTURE			TOTAL		
	Loans	Value of	Average	Loans	Value of	Average	Loans	Value of	Average	Loans	Value of	Average
1801-1805	37	358,729	9,965	32	174,154	5,442	21	150,406	7,162	90	683,289	9,592
1806-1810	17	61,846	3,638	12	40,009	3,334	10	41,038	4,104	39	142,894	3,664
1811-1815	16	43,703	2,732	16	172,548	10,784	21	169,193	8,057	53	385,444	7,272
1816-1820	10	30,687	3,070	17	67,873	3,992	3	3,382	2,460	30	105,942	3,531
1821-1825	20	54,960	2,748	27	82,952	3,072	15	72,348	4,823	62	210,260	2,391
1826-1830	7	20,966	2,995	4	27,123	6,781	12	49,065	4,088	23	127,154	5,528
Total	107	570,902	5,386	108	564,659	5,228	82	489,433	5,969	297	1,624,995	5,471

Loans from Private sources

	INDUSTRY			COMMERCE			AGRICULTURE			TOTAL		
	Loans	Value of	Average	Loans	Value of	Average	Loans	Value of	Average	Loans	Value of	Average
1801-1805	28	218,589	7,807	30	169,404	5,647	14	100,406	7,172	72	488,399	6,783
1806-1810	15	56,497	3,766	12	40,009	3,334	5	15,902	3,180	32	112,409	3,513
1811-1815	7	21,903	3,129	14	156,648	11,182	13	95,475	7,344	34	274,027	8,060
1816-1820	10	30,697	3,070	17	67,873	3,992	2	3,382	1,691	29	101,952	3,516
1821-1825	10	21,823	2,182	10	30,952	3,095	7	28,866	4,095	27	81,642	3,024
1826-1830	1	1,166	-	4	27,123	6,781	3	23,000	7,666	8	51,289	6,411

Loans from Church Bodies and Indian Communities

	INDUSTRY			COMMERCE			AGRICULTURE			TOTAL		
	Loans	Value of	Average	Loans	Value of	Average	Loans	Value of	Average	Loans	Value of	Average
1801-1805	8	140,140	17,517	2	4,750	2,375	7	50,000	7,143	17	194,890	11,464
1806-1810	2	5,349	2,674	-	-	-	5	25,136	5,027	7	30,485	4,355
1811-1815	9	27,800	2,422	2	16,000	8,000	8	73,717	9,215	19	111,518	5,869
1816-1820	-	-	-	-	-	-	1	4,100	-	1	4,100	-
1821-1825	10	33,136	3,313	17	51,000	3,059	8	43,482	5,435	35	127,618	3,646
1826-1830	6	19,800	3,300	-	-	-	9	26,064	2,896	15	45,864	3,058

Source: AGNP, RPP, Censos, Vols. 38-42

credit received during the previous quinquennium. The Church collapsed as a source of credit, illustrating the severity of the impact of the *Real Consolidación* decree.[148] Prominent merchants--Rizo, Tello, Uriarte, Pereyra--continued to lend to trade and industry but loans were smaller and the merchants fewer in number. The disintegration of Puebla's Spanish wholesale body had commenced.

Over the later 18th century, as a result of the *comercio libre* reforms and the abolition of the trade fair at Jalapa, the merchant body of Puebla had substantially recovered the position it had enjoyed during the earlier colonial period. At the height of the war boom in 1802, Manual Flon had the Commercial Regiment restored to its full complement of 300 men, as originally laid down in 1742, but reduced by Viceroy Revillagigedo in 1793.[149] Puebla's wholesale merchant body then commenced a sharp decline, with many Spanish merchants returning to the Peninsula well before the outbreak of the revolutions. By 1807, of the 52 dealers in European cloth resident in the city in 1803, only 32 remained. And of the 28 dealers in domestically produced cloth, only 18 remained in business.[150]

If it was the external instability occasioned by the Napoleonic wars which was the decisive factor conditioning the provincial economy before 1810, after that date, internal factors assumed a growing importance. Prominent among these were insurgency, extraordinary taxation, forced military recruitment, mule embargoes by insurgents and loyalists, epidemics and agricultural crises. Some reflection of the disruption caused by these events can be found in the mortgage records, as well as the tithe, customs, tax and food price records, to be examined more closely in Chapter 3.

The trend with mortgage loans was cyclical. At first, between 1811 and 1815, there was an appreciable recovery of Church and private investment, an apparent reversal of the previous five years. Then between 1816 and 1820, private investment halved and Church loans dried up altogether. Between 1821 and 1825, Church lending recovered while private lending continued to decline. Finally, between 1826 and 1830, both Church and private lending collapsed almost entirely.

The recovery of the credit market between 1811 and 1815 comes as a surprise since this was the height of the insurgency during which extensive areas of the province were occupied by rebels, harvests were laid waste, commerce with the interior and the coast was interrupted, the food supply of the city was in crisis, the population was decimated by the 1812-3

---

[148] The *libros de censos* show 13 estate owners, merchants and manufacturers agreeing to pay over a quarter of million pesos to the Real Junta de Consolidación, the value of the redemption of Church mortgages on their properties. AGNP, RPP, Censos, Vol. 39 fs. 24, 29, 42, 51, 54, 79, 89, 94, 95, 103, 107, 162; and Vol. 40, f. 10.

[149] AGN, AHH, Vol. 663, Expte.4, f. 20.

[150] Florescano and Gil, *Descripciones económicas*, p. 162; and AGN, Consulados, Vol. 463, Exp.3 (1807).

epidemic, while the departure of Spanish merchants, with their capital, became a flood. A closer examination of the mortgage loans reveals, however, that investments were being made precisely as a response to the crisis. The upturn in investment should not, therefore, be taken as a sign of recovery, but of adjustment to upheaval.

Loans to·agriculture were often to make good damage caused by insurgents or to finance speculative wheat growing.[151] Loans to industry were confined to a far narrower range of activities than before the war with a concentration of investment in war-related industries: iron foundries (weapons), brickworks (for the city walls), tanning (saddlery), printing (propaganda), with staples such as flour milling, tocinería and was chandlery absorbing the remaining investment. Loans to commerce continued the pre-war pattern of investment by wholesalers to finance the purchase of imports by Puebla retailers, with one notable difference. The names of the great merchants of the pre-war period--Rizo, Uriarte, Echavarri, Tello, Palacios--have disappeared from the records, with newcomers prominent: Gregorio Mujica, José Domingo Couto (*veracruzanos*), Nicolas Fernández del Campo (*montañés*), Francisco Puig (*catalan*). By 1815, the *junta* charged with raising a forced loan reported that the great merchants of pre-war years:

> Tiburcio Uriarte, Fernando Nanza, José Aguirre, Francisco Bazo y otros, desesperados de progresar aquí y amenazados de inevitables pérdidas han marchado a la Peninsula con sus gruesas y flóridos caudales. Los que nos han quedado cada día se empobrecen mas...[152]

The claim that the war had impoverished the merchant body, coming as it did from a *junta* seeking a reduction in forced taxation, should be treated with some caution. The war undoubtedly opened as well as closed many commercial opportunities. The traditional, monopolistic trading system was modified, and lesser merchants found more room for maneuver. But the mining depression, the outflow of bullion and coin, the disintegration of the merchants' guilds, the cheapening of imports and the increase in contraband, all must have increased competition and cut into merchants profit margins, while heavy taxation over the decade following the renewal of war with Britain in 1805 cut into their stock of capital.[153]

---

[151] AGNP, RPP, Censos, Vol. 40, fs. 130, 132, 332. The records of wheat tithes reveal damage by Insurgents occuring between 1811 and 1816 in the districts of Amazoc, Huejotzingo, Cholula and Nativitas. AOP, Diezmos de Trigo, 1805-1828, 3 Vols.

[152] AGN, AHH, Consulados, Vol. 727, 11 April 1815.

[153] Outflow of bullion: A single *conducta* carrying five million pesos left Puebla for Veracruz in 1814, accompanied by 87 coaches, 7, 000 mules, and 500 passengers, Antonio Carrión, *Historia de la Ciudad de Puebla* (1897) Puebla, 1970, Vol. II p. 157; Ortíz de la Tabla estimates that 32,180, 282 pesos left the country legally

If the merchant body in 1820 contained fewer men of great wealth, it was no smaller than in 1807. Indeed, the number of businesses retailing cloth had grown by one, to 38, with a decline only in the number of establishments dealing exclusively in domestically produced cloth. The number of wholesale warehouses only declined from 15 in 1807 to 13 in 1820.[154] Fortunes could be consolidated over the decade by avoiding too narrow a specialization and by developing broad portfolios of interests. So merchants such as Joaquín Haro y Portillo branched from dealing in imported and domestic cloth into *tocinería* and flour-milling, while the two import merchants, Estevan de Antuñano and Francisco Puig, diversified into dealing in raw cotton and financing cotton and woollen cloth weaving.[155]

The most conspicuous change brought by war to Puebla's merchant body was the transformation in membership. Of the 34 dealers in European cloth resident in Puebla in 1807, only 9 remained in 1820. Dealers in domestically produced cloth show a higher survival rate: 7 of the 18 dealers of 1807 were still in business in 1820.[156] This change in personnel was a consequence of the return to Spain of *peninsulares* and the arrival of merchants from other regions, particularly from Veracruz. So by 1820, Puebla's merchant body was broadly the same size as it had been before the wars, but it was now more creole, more involved with local and regional

---

between 1813 and 1816, *Comercio Exterior de Veracruz 1778-1821*. Seville 1978, p. 352. The British consul in Veracruz reported in 1824 that 140, 000,000 pesos had left the country since 1810, R. A. Humphreys, *British Consular Reports on Latin America 1824-26*. London, 1940, pp. 302-3. Disintegration of the *consulados* and the cheapening of imports: Ortíz de la Tabla, *Comercio exterior*, pp. 266-67; Humphreys, *British Consular Reports*, pp. 300-330; extraordinary war taxation: I have estimated that between 1805 and 1819, at least 1,875,120 pesos were raised from wealthier citizens, commerce and religious corporations in Puebla for sustaining the Royalist cause, over and above the 2,300,000 pesos raised through the *Real Consolidación* (From the Bishopric: 177,000 pesos between 1805 and 1811 for the Spanish Army in the Peninsular, 295,226 pesos between 1811 and 1814 for the viceregal government; 300,000 pesos raised by Manuel Flon between 1810-11; 526,179 pesos contributed by notable citizens between 1810-13, Antonio Carrión, *Historia*, Vol. II, pp. 72-3; 200,000 raised through a forced loan in 1815; 25,000 pesos spent annually between 1810 and 1816 on the regiment of volunteers; and 226,715 pesos spent between 1814 and 1819 on maintaining the Royalist infantry and cavalry force in the city: AAP, Militar, Vol. 118, f. 26 and Cabildo, Vol. 89, f. 251.) The representation against the forced loan of 1815 claimed that *poblanos* had been contributing over 1,500,000 pesos annually over the previous five years. This was probably an exaggeration.

[154] AGN, AHH, Consulados, Vol. 463, Expte. 3, and AAP, Militar, Vol. 119, Expte. 1319.

[155] See Chapter 2 for merchants' careers.

[156] AAP, Militar, Vol. 119, Expte. 1319.

54

activities than with extra-regional and overseas business, and was certainly less opulent.[157]

The mortgage records for the period 1816-20 show a marked decline in private, and a complete collapse of Church lending. The sector to suffer most was agriculture where lending ceased almost entirely. Already in a parlous state before the wars, the problems now facing Puebla's agriculture now seemed insuperable since access to the lucrative Caribbean market was barred after 1811. The insurgency, although never able to hold the central valley of Puebla for long or mount an attack on the provincial capital, nevertheless had a profound impact upon the valley's agriculture. During the height of the rebellion of Miguel Hidalgo and José María Morelos, widespread damage was caused to sugar cane and cereal harvests in the districts of Izucar, Chietla, Atlixco, Cholula, Huejotzingo, Nativitas and Tlaxcala. Even after the defeat of Morelos, estates continued to be sacked, the wheat tithe records for 1814-15 registering several incidents in these districts.[158] During the period 1811-15 much of the province was occupied by rebel bands with the central valley effectively hemmed to the north, south and east.[159]

Although merchants were able to negotiate safe passage for their goods through insurgent lines, Puebla's deputy to the Cortes pointed out in June 1814 that increased carriage costs resulting from these unofficial levies, combined with the frequent embargo of mules, were disrupting Puebla's supply of raw materials and access to markets.[160] The authenticity of this claim is confirmed by complaints from farmers and the municipal officials encharged with the city's food supply. *Alhóndiga* officials believed that this disruption, rather than meteorological factors, was responsible for the excessively high food prices of 1815-16.[161] Farmers complained of severe labor shortage caused by military recruitment, the storming and release of prisoners from debtors jails upon haciendas and the general breakdown of order whereby "every credit, every payment, every debt and every real

157 An index of the greater austerity of the Puebla elite after the wars of Independence is the decline in number of licensed privately owned coaches, falling from 145 in 1807 to a mere 7 in 1821. The number of licensed coaches (principally for let, not privately owned) rose to between 20 and 30 during the 1820s, 30 and 40 during the 1830s, 40 and 50 during the 1840s, peaking at 64 coaches in 1854 before the Revolution of Ayutla led, once more, to a drastic disminuition. AAP, Pensiones Municipales, 1807-1821, Vol. 158, Expte. 1595.

158 AOP, Diezmos de Trigo, 1805-28

159 For a full account of the wars of Independence in the province of Puebla see Antonio Carrión, *Historia*, Vol. II pp. 52-252; Eduardo Gómez Haro, *La Ciudad de Puebla y la Guerra de Independencia*. Puebla, 1910; and the recent masterly study of Hamnett, *Roots of Insurgency*, pp. 150-177.

160 Hernández y Dávalos, *Documentos*, Vol.V, pp. 550-3.

161 AAP, Cabildo, Vol. 85, f. 160.

easily becomes illusory." Many farmers abandoned their estates to take refuge in the provincial capital.[162]

The decline of agriculture over the decade of the wars is confirmed by the records. After 1811, flour and *tocinería* products disappear from the list of Veracruz's exports.[163] The records of the Bishopric's wheat tithes over the 1805-1828 period (see Figure 1.4) show wheat production (estimated from the wheat diezmo multiplied by ten) rising to a peak between 1805 and 1810, averaging 35,000 cargas a year during this last short export cycle for Puebla's flour. Production then dropped precipitously between 1810 and 1815, climbing slowly thereafter as flour found easier access to the extra-regional market, once the violent period of the wars was over. Figure 1.4 reveals that there was a clear tendency for wheat production to concentrate and increase within the boundaries of the municipality of Puebla, over the decade. Conversely, production in the more exposed and remote jurisdictions remained depressed until the 1820s. Looking at the city's overall flour consumption (see Figure 3.4) and taking this as an index of both local and overseas demand, then wheat and flour production over the entire period running from 1810 to the mid-1830s was depressed. The only part of agriculture to depart from the general picture of stagnation and decline was stock rearing, as a consequence of the abolition of the *abasto de carnes* and consequent decline in extra-regional supply.[164]

In the early 1820s, contemporaries diagnosed the same three causes of agricultural decline as during the eighteenth century: low prices, labor scarcity and estate indebtedness. There was no shortage of ideas for how estate agriculture might be redeemed, but after so long in the doldrums, and facing such depressed or inaccessible regional and extra-regional markets, little confidence existed in the possibility of recovery until the coming of the railway.[165] Thus, landowners remained a shadowy and unassertive political force in the thirty years following Independence, in contrast to the more articulate merchants, artisans and manufacturers who devised Puebla's protectionist political economy, organized the protectionist lobby and sought to reconstruct and transform the urban economy.

---

[162] For attacks on hacienda jails (*tlapixqueras*), Hernández y Dávalos, Vol. V, p. 552; and for the breakdown of order in the countryside, Hamnett, *Roots of Insurgency*, pp. 150-177.

[163] Miguel Lerdo de Tejada, *Comercio Exterior*, "Balanzas".

[164] AAP, Rastros, Vol. 90, fs. 42-44; and AAP, Matadero, Vol. 226.

[165] During the 1820s hacendados pleaded insolvency as a result of the destruction caused by the insurgency. They complained especially about the loss of control over village labour forces, the essential pre-condition for successful estate agriculture, and apparently lost during the upheaval of the wars. See *El Caduceo*, Vol. II, No. 10, p. 37; Vol. III, No. 2, p. 5; and Vol. 5, No. 37, p. 156. For the state government's response: AAP, Decretos y Ordenes, Vol. 55, f. 55, "Providencias para el arreglo de los operarios del campo", 4 September 1824.

56

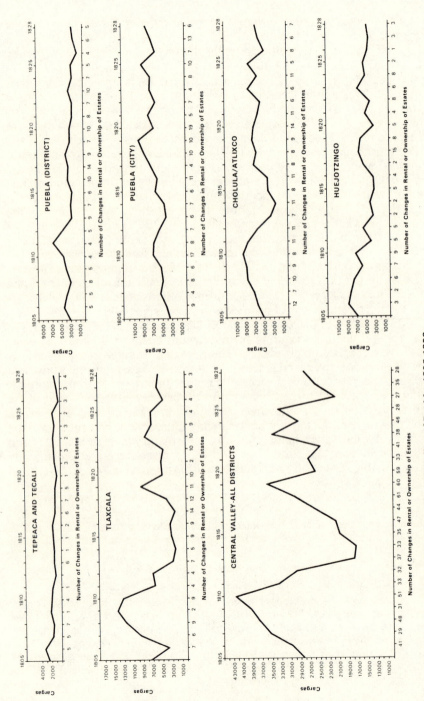

Figure 1.4 Wheat Tithes in the Central Valley of Puebla, 1805-1828

The first five years of Independence saw a recovery in the credit market. Loans to commerce, industry and agriculture increased markedly over the previous quinquennium. A notable feature of these years is the recovery of the Church as a lender. Moreover, Church bodies are found lending beyond agriculture, their customary patch, to manufacturing and, almost without precedent, to commerce. This may be explained by the delay in the re-emergence of a body of wholesale merchants to replace the repatriated *peninsulares*, the colony's great lenders.[166] The Church, however impoverished by the *Consolidación* and the wars, at least received a regular, albeit declining, income from rents on its urban properties and interest on mortgages.[167] Thus Church credit served as an important bridge between the collapse of the *peninsular*-dominated wholesale body of the 1810s and the emergence of a more cosmopolitan group during the 1830s.

The slump in foreign trade in the immediate aftermath of Independence was accompanied by a perceptible, though short-lived, bubble of activity within certain industries benefitting from the slackening of pressure from imports and from tariff protection conceded by Iturbide's government.[168] This, of course, had been a familiar pattern during the Colony and one to be repeated on a more imposing scale during the 1830s.

It is interesting to observe the behavior of two wholesalers --the *veracruzano* Estevan de Antuñano and the Catalan Francisco Puig-- investing in industry during this trade slump. Both men had arrived in Puebla during the 1810s as wholesale dealers in imported goods, Puig becoming an important lender to the retail trade, Antuñano working in partnership with his future rival, the Genoese merchant, Andrés Vallarino.[169] Both served in the Commercial Regiment during the wars of Independence, contributed to Patriotic loans and attained aldermanships on the *cabildo*. Both became controversial figures since they went beyond the customary limits of mercantile involvement in industry (lending and

---

[166] The British consul in Veracruz saw the shortage of coin as the principal obstacle to the growth of trade with Mexico in the early 1820s while Henry Ward, the British Minister, blamed the reluctance of the Spanish to relinquish their hold on the country, combined with a lack of confidence in, and knowledge of, the Mexican market, accounting for the hesitancy of Euopean merchants in stepping into the peninsulares' shoes. See Humphreys, *British Consular Reports*, pp. 318-9; and Ward, *Mexico*, Vol. I, p. 442.

[167] Church bodies owned 1383 of the 2564 domestic dwellings in Puebla, of which a proportionately higher number of dwellings fell into the higher tax categories. See AAP, Padrón de Casas, 1825.

[168] AGNP, RRP, Censos, Vol. 41, fs. 376, 41, 44; Vol. 42, fs. 24, 37,70,79, 114, 117, 150, 152, 345, 424.

[169] AGNP, RPP, Censos, Vol. 41, fs. 14, 17, 226, 227, 334; and Miguel A. Quintana, *Estevan de Antuñano, Fundador de la Industria Textil en Puebla*. Mexico, 1957, Vol. I, p. 11.

marketing) by installing modern machinery, thereby directly controlling the productive process.

Francisco Puig took advantage of the favorable conditions facing the region's woollen industry over the late 1810s and early 1820s.[170] Woollen cloth manufacture throughout the country was becoming a more localized affair with *obrajes* springing up in Aguascalientes, Zacatecas, Durango, San Luis Potosí and Coahuila, with the old centers of cloth production in the Bajío, notably Querétaro, declining. The south-east of Mexico also benefitted, helped by the growth of sheep raising in the Puebla-Veracruz region, following the abolition of the *abastos*. In 1820 Puig, alert to these conditions and aware, as a merchant, of the relaxation of pressure from imports, introduced Puebla's first modern spindles and entered production of *entrefino* cloth, coarse serge and blankets in a large two storey building, known as "Casa Puig" or "El Chito Cohetero," overlooking the Parián, the city's cloth market.[171] The factory remained in production until 1850, long after Puig's death from cholera in 1833, under the management of his widow, becoming an important supplier of both cotton and woollen yarn to weavers, as well as marketing their cloth.

At Independence, Antuñano was already well established in the trade in raw cotton from Veracruz. In 1821, in response to Emperor Iturbide's decree prohibiting imports of cotton yarn, Antuñano established modern cotton spinning machinery in his own house in the weaver's quarter ("el barrio alto de San Francisco"), the factory to be called "La Educación de los Niños." The factory was still in operation in 1823 but production appears to have ceased in the following year, perhaps as a consequence of the more liberal tariff of the First Federal republic.[172] Antuñano re-emerged as the city's pioneering textile industrialist in the early 1830s.

The early 1820s were an unpropitious moment for embarking upon a strategy of import substitution industrialization. For a short period Mexican policy makers put their faith in liberal economic policies, opening the doors to foreign merchants, in a vain attempt to attract foreign loans and bring about economic recovery. For Puebla, these policies had disastrous consequences, sending the province's already troubled economy reeling into deeper crisis.[173]

By the mid-1820s the full implications of liberal trade policy and the economic changes accompanying Independence became evident, as a mercantile structure based upon British dominance of the external sector fell into place. Between 1824 and 1827 imports recovered, rising significantly

---

170 Loans to woollen obrajes, AGNP, RPP, Censos, Vol. 41, fs. 411, 414; and Vol.42, f. 37.

171 AAP, Tierras y Aguas, Vol. 47, f. 6.

172 Bazant, "Evolución", pp. 508-9.

173 Inés Herrera Canales, *El Comercio Exterior de México, 1821-75*. Mexico, 1977, p. 27.

above the level they had maintained during the quarter century before Independence.[174] Textiles, although occupying a smaller share of the total value imports than between 1806-1818, when they had averaged 85%, still lead imports in value, amounting to between 64 and 70 percent of imports between 1824 and 1827.[175] More significant, as far as Puebla's cloth merchants, weavers and spinners were concerned, was the unprecedented increase in the volume of textile imports, now that textile prices had fallen substantially from pre-Independence levels. And the proportion of cheap cottons (competitive with Puebla's *manta*) to dearer cloth had also increased markedly.[176] Mexico's cotton spinners and weavers had never before faced such stiff competition from imports, demonstrated by the vigorous petitions from the traditional centers of cloth production throughout Mexico and Central America. In Puebla, employment in cloth weaving declined sharply during the 1820s, with weavers vociferous in their demands for tariff protection.[177]

Pressure from imports was felt far beyond textiles, across the entire structure of Puebla's industry.[178] The records of mortgage loans for the period 1826-30 reveal the gravity of the crisis facing the urban economy. Lending to industry and commerce collapsed while agricultural credit was greatly reduced. Church lending fell by three fifths and private credit, by over one third, compared with the previous quinquennium.

Conclusion

This chapter began setting out the theme of autonomy. Inexhaustable soil fertility, abundant natural resources, a benign climate, a central location, political autonomy, and an adequate population enabled the first European settlers and subsequent generations to establish and sustain a broadly based regional economy, serving as well, extra-regional and overseas markets. Until the early seventeenth century autonomy was a reality: Puebla had become its own metropolis, succeeding in attracting and retaining, in return for its agricultural and industrial exports, the colony's most valuable commodity: silver. Bishop Palafox's completion of the gold-encrusted cathedral in the mid-seventeenth century symbolized the achievement of this diversified and assertive provincial settler society. Yet this event also signalled the end of Puebla's "golden age." Thereafter, autonomy became an aspiration, less and less a reality.

---

[174] Ortiz de la Tabla, *Comercio Exterior*, p. 325.

[175] Lerdo de Tejada, *Comercio Exterior (balanzas 1824-27)*.

[176] This is examined more closely in Chapter 6.

[177] Javier de la Peña, "Notas", pp. 161-2.

[178] Pressure for protection from these industries is examined more fully in Chapter 5.

The chapter has demonstrated how, during the second half of the seventeenth, the eighteenth and early nineteenth centuries, the province, in the face of mounting competition from other Mexican regions and from overseas, lost the broadly-based prosperity which it had enjoyed during the first century of colonization. Of course, a land-based settler society, supplemented by industry and trade, survived. But great fortunes were no longer to be made by specialization in any single activity, rather, great wealth was achieved only by a skillful combination of trade, agriculture and industry. Puebla continued to attract European immigrants, especially during the second half of the eighteenth century. A few swiftly made their fortunes. But, in general, opportunities both for immigrants as for *poblanos* were distinctly more limited during the eighteenth and early nineteenth centuries, than settlers letters reveal them to have been during the sixteenth century.[179] In part, this was because Puebla, by the later colonial period, was an old region of settlement, with available arable land already occupied. But there are also other, more compelling reasons for Puebla's loss of dynamism. These are found in the demographic, social and economic structure of the city and its region, which must now be explored in greater detail.

---

[179] For instance in Otte and Lockhart, *Letters and People*, p. 142.

Chapter 2

THE SOCIAL STRUCTURE OF PUEBLA IN THE LATE EIGHTEENTH AND EARLY NINETEENTH CENTURIES

No appropriate or accessible model of social structure is available for historians of colonial urban Spanish America. Was Puebla still organized in accord with Aquinean corporate principles, introduced from Spain, at the time of its foundation? Certainly Puebla in 1800 possessed an archaic institutional and associational structure. There was an abundance of exclusive and semi-autonomous corporate associations to which most urban dwellers formally owed their primary allegiance: cabildos (for the Indian *barrios* as well as the Spanish *casco*), craft guilds, retail corporations, convents, confraternities, *comunidades de indios*, *maestranzas*, etc.. The minute regulations and ordinances of these corporations were intended to demarcate the legal, social, economic and cultural context of the members lives. Considerable respect and privilege were granted to old families, descended from the founders or from families who had contributed to the "golden age" of the city during the first century of its foundation. Great importance still continued to be placed upon noble titles and honors. Indeed, Puebla's nominations for nobility outnumbered those of any other province of New Spain in the last years of colonial rule.[1] Race also remained an important principle of social organization, seemingly adding a further element of rigidity and prescription to the city's social structure. People were expected to know to which racial group they belonged, to be aware of the rights and obligations pertaining to that group, as of its place within the caste hierarchy which the Spanish hoped would give some form and stability to a colonial society. So, on the face of it, Puebla in 1800 appeared as a traditional society, organized into overlapping estates and corporations, as yet unmodified by the changes which were leading to class societies elsewhere in the Atlantic world.

---

[1] Doris M. Ladd, *The Mexican Nobility at Independence*. Texas, 1976, pp. 178-81.

Yet, on closer scrutiny, it is clear urban society in Puebla had long outgrown these formal corporate boundaries. In many respects, the Puebla of 1800 was quite modern. It was only through a combination of administrative oversight and the Creole fondness for clinging to privileges and institutions which had long been abolished or become redundant in Europe that the city retained an archaic institutional structure. The mercantile profession had by now long been accorded the highest prestige, with successful immigrant merchants, even from modest Peninsular backgrounds, able to marry into Puebla's oldest and most honored families. Puebla's "*Gremio de Labradores*" no longer enjoyed unquestioned prestige and respect. Landownership, as observed in Chapter 1, unless combined with some more profitable activity, no longer provided the key to success which it had offered during the sixteenth and much of the seventeenth centuries. Artisans more often honored guild ordinances in the breach and guild masters complained that they no longer received the support of the cabildo in their attempts to command the obedience of *rinconeros* and unexamined artisans. And the once separate juridical and political world of the Indian population had long been eroded, as a result of mestizaje and the movement of Spaniards, negroes and mulattos into their barrios.[2]

In 1800, Puebla de los Angeles contained a highly fluid society in which the importance of wealth far outweighed that of corporate privilege, custom or prescription in allocating social status and political influence. The stability of urban society over a prolonged period of economic crisis probably owed more to the high rate of emigration than to people living in conformity with ideals and ordinances of corporate institutions. This chapter describes the shape of urban society and proposes a necessarily loose model of social stratification.

Race, Occupation and Marriage in the Census of 1791

Puebla was a multiracial city containing the wide diversity of occupations common to all of New Spain's provincial capitals: clergy, bureaucracy, professionals, absentee estate owners, merchants, manufacturers, muleteers, artisans, shopkeepers, street and market sellers, domestic servants, porters and messengers, day-laborers, out-workers and keepers of households. In 1777 the 71, 366 people who lived in Puebla city and district professed to belong to the following ethnic groupings:

---

2 Reinhard Liehr, "Die Soziale Stellung der Indianer von Puebla am Ende der Zweiten Halfte des 18 Jahrhunderts", *JGSWGLA*, Vol. 8, 1971, pp. 74-125; and, Fausto Marín-Tamayo, *La división racial en Puebla de los Angeles*. Puebla, 1960.

European and Creole (white)	18,369
Castizo	2,416
Mestizo	10,942
Negro	31
Mulatto	2,899
Indian	24,039
Other Castes	12,670 [3]

Whites thus made up one quarter of the district's population, the mixed castes two fifths and Indians just over one third. Since 1681, the share of whites had declined from 28% to 26%, of the castes from 50% to 40% while that of Indians had increased from 21% to 34%.[4] The proportions for the population of the province as a whole, numbering 506,670 in 1793, were whites comprising one tenth, the castes one seventh and Indians almost three quarters.[5]

Before proposing a general model of social stratification appropriate to the Puebla case, it is useful at this point to examine the racial and occupational structure of the city and selected rural districts revealed in the 1791 military census. Were the returns from this census complete, then it would have been possible to make a bolder analysis of social class at this stage. Unfortunately the returns for only four of the city's six parishes exist and the census for rural areas omits the majority Indian population. Missing are the returns for Puebla's largely Spanish and mestizo central parishes of Sàgrario and San José. This source, therefore, throws light upon the social structure of the peripheral *barrios* where a large proportion of the city's artisans lived and worked. An overview of social structure must await the next section.

The four parishes of San Marcos, San Sebastián, Santo Angel Analco and Santa Cruz, extending over the western and eastern flanks of the city contained a third of the city's population in 1791 (See Figure 2.1). Table 2.1, disaggregates the population of these parishes and the rural districts of Huejotzingo, Tepeaca and San Juan de los Llanos according to race. The urban parishes housed the administratively autonomous Indian *barrios* accounting for their disproportionate share of the city's Indian population. The castes were also well represented and, as would be expected, whites were much less well-represented than in the central parishes. In the three rural districts Indians made up an even larger share of the population than in

---

[3] AGI, Audiencia de México, Vol. 2578.

[4] Peter Gerhard, "Un censo de la diócesis de Puebla en 1681", *Historia Mexicana*, Vol.. 30, 1980-81, pp. 530-60.

[5] Conde José Gómez de Cortina,"Población en el Departamento de Puebla", *BSNGE*, Vol. 1 , Mexico, 1839.

64

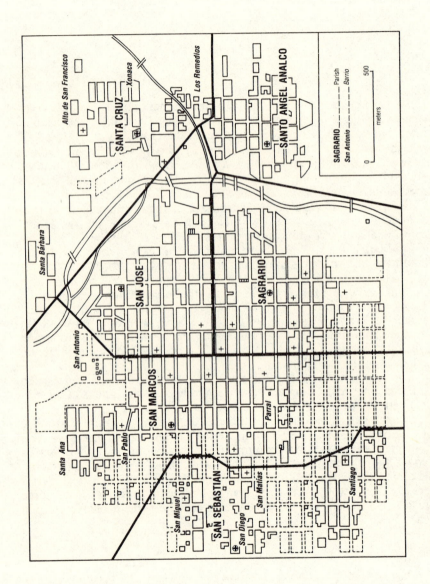

Figure 2.1 Parishes of Puebla in 1791

all but one Puebla's peripheral parishes. Thus, the further a traveller journeyed from the central square of Puebla de los Angeles, the more Indian the province became.

TABLE 2.1 RACIAL DISTRIBUTION OF POPULATION IN PUEBLA PARISHES AND DISTRICTS IN 1791

	Spanish	%	Castes	%	Indians	%	Total
District of Puebla	19,532	35	17,391	(31)	18,940	(34)	55,863*
Parish of San Sebastián	357	(10)	396	(12)	2,598	(78)	3,330
Parish of San Marcos	2,550	(35)	2,554	(35)	2,103	(29)	7,207
Parish of Santo Angel	1,164	(22)	1,902	(36)	2,190	(42)	5,256
Parish of Santa Cruz	1,231	(34)	944	(26)	1,424	(40)	3,599
Huejotzingo	2,196	(10)	4,200	(19)	16,212	(71)	22,608
Tepeaca	10,250	(14)	12,072	(17)	50,140	(69)	72,538
San Juan de los LLanos	2,886	(7)	5,345	(13)	33,697	(80)	41,928

*This total does not include priests, nuns or monks, numbering 996.
Source: AGN, Padrones, Vols. 22, 2738; and AAP, Vols. 128-129.

Intermarriage between members of different racial groups was not uncommon although Table 2.2 reveals that three of the four principal racial groups, Spaniards, mestizos and Indians, preferred marrying with other members of their caste. Only mulattos and negroes married more often beyond their caste, a pattern common to other cities in New Spain.[6] Indians were the most endogamous racial group, followed by Spaniards, mestizos and mulattos and negroes. Caste endogamy was more common in the west than the east of the city, 93% of San Sebastián's Indians marrying within their caste, 85% of San Marcos' Spaniards marrying within theirs. Santo Angel and Santa Cruz, racially more balanced parishes, had correspondingly higher rates of inter-racial marriage. However, all racial groups in these Puebla parishes were significantly more endogamous than their counterparts in Antequera de Oaxaca suggesting that the city of Puebla was far from being the racial melting pot which Chance shows Antequera to have been by the end of the eighteenth century.[7] The degree to which the high rates of emigration beyond the region contributed to Puebla's relatively conservative marriage pattern can only be surmised.

Turning to the occupational structure of the four city parishes and three rural districts (represented in Table 2.3), four broad characteristics stand out. First, a suprisingly small proportion of the non-Indian population was engaged directly in agriculture: less than a third of the population of

---

[6] John Chance, *Race and Class in Colonial Oaxaca*. Stanford, 1978, pp. 164-172.
[7] *Ibid.*, pp. 184-5.

TABLE 2.2 MARRIAGE BY RACIAL GROUP IN FOUR PARISHES OF PUEBLA, 1791

Marriage Partners	San Sebastián	San Marcos	Santo Angel	Santa Cruz	Total
Español-Española	47	349	143	120	659
Español-Mestiza	12	103	48	30	193
Español-India	7	8	13	11	39
Español-Mulata	2	11	5	4	22
Mestizo-Española	5	75	45	36	161
Mestizo-Mestiza	18	262	140	100	520
Mestizo-India	10	32	24	26	92
Mestizo-Mulata	0	8	11	8	27
Indio-Española	8	16	8	11	43
Indio-Mestiza	28	62	67	44	201
Indio-India	495	387	313	252	1447
Indio-Mulato	2	2	3	3	10
Mulato-Española	1	7	4	7	19
Mulato-Mestiza	4	27	23	11	65
Mulato-India	2	4	2	1	9
Mulato-Mulata	2	12	6	11	31
Total marriages	643	1365	855	675	3538

Source: Lier, *Ayuntamiento y oligarquía*, Vol. 1, p. 82.

TABLE 2.3 OCCUPATIONAL STRUCTURE OF 4 PUEBLA CITY PARISHES AND 3 RURAL DISTRICTS IN 1791, WITH COMPARISONS FROM ANTEQUERA DE OAXACA AND GUANAJUATO

	Puebla Indian		Puebla Non-Ind.		Huejotzingo Non-Ind.		Tepeaca Non-Ind.		San Juan de losLlanos Non-Ind.		Oaxaca Non-Ind.		Guanajuato (excl.tributary Indians)	
	No.	%	No.	%	No.	%	No.	%	No.	%	No.	%	No.	%
DEALING	27	1.3	177	7.3	89	7.1	476	12.6	192	13.6	346	10.3	681	6.4
FOOD & DRINK	283	14	120	5	29	2.3	117	3	24	1.7	176	5	364	3.4
TEXTILES	226	11.2	669	27.4	411	32.8	598	15.8	37	2.6	1083	30.3	-	-
DRESS	157	7.7	312	12.8	48	3.8	167	4.4	27	1.9			590	5.5
METALWORK	70	3.5	162	6.6	24	1.9	109	2.8	35	2.5	583[a]	16.5	-	-
WOODWORK	71	3.5	40	1.6	30	2.4	47	1.2	20	1.4	596[b]	5.6	-	-
LEATHERWORK	103	5.1	153	6.3	38	3	95	2.5	33	2.3	87	2.5	-	-
MINING	-	-	-	-	-	-	-	-	-	-	14	0.4	5,057	47
BUILDING	384	19	29	1.2	11	0.9	22	0.6	1	-	91	2.6	-	-
REFINING	-	-	-	-	-	-	-	-	-	-	-	-	792	7.6
OTHER INDUSTRY	147	7.3	278	11.4	10	0.8	22	0.6	125	8.9	54	1.5	271[c]	2.5
ARTS & ENTERTAINMT.	43	2.1	18	0.7	165	13.2					30	0.8	96	0.9
TRANSPORT							793	20.9	39	2.8				
SERVICES	185	9.1	204	8.4							58	1.6	283	2.6
UNEMPLOYED	-	-	-	-	22	1.8	70	1.8	1	-	34[d]	1	517[d]	4.9
AGRICULTURE	318	15.7	86	3.5	363	29	1240	32.8	850	60	207	5.8	686	6.4
GOVERNMENT, PROFESSIONAL, CHURCH	8	0.4	191	7.8	13	1	32	0.8	25	1.7	665	19	235	2.7
TOTAL	2022		2439		1253		3788		1409		3541		10,679	

Sources: AGN, Padrones, Vols. 20, 27, & 38; AAP, Padrones, Vols. 128-9; and Chance, *Race and Class*, p. 148; and Brading, *Miners and Merchants*, p. 250
[a]Includes metal, wood,wax and pottery;
[b]Includes wood, metal, construction and pottery;
[c]Includes fuel, candles, soap and lime;
[d]Miscellaneous.

Huejotzingo and Tepeaca, and just over 3% of Puebla's peripheral parishes, compared to 6% of Antequera's non-Indian population.[8] In the province of Puebla, agricultural labor and farming generally was an Indian activity. So 15% of the Indian population of the four urban parishes were engaged in agriculture, mainly working as laborers in the wheat fields, flour mills and orchards surrounding the city.

A second distinctive feature of Puebla's occupational structure was the large number of non-Indians engaged in domestic manufacturing, as much in rural areas as in the provincial capital. Textiles led over other crafts: 28% of non-Indians in Puebla and 33 percent of the same group in Huejotzingo worked in the textile industry, mainly as weavers of cotton cloth. While the core of the industry lay in the center-west, cotton weaving had also assumed a governing importance in the center-east, employing 17 percent of Tepeaca's non-Indians. Tailoring was also an important employer of non-Indians in the city and central valley. Little weaving went on north of the central valley, emphasizing the marked concentration of Hispano-mestizo "proto-industrial" activity in the villages and towns of the central valley, along the principal trade route carrying Veracruz' cotton and tobacco to Puebla, and on to the *tierradentro*.

Specialization in transportation was the third distinctive feature of the region's non-Indian occupational structure. Carting, muleteering and porterage were particularly common occupations in the east of the city, especially in the parish of Santa Cruz, and throughout the entire district of Tepeaca, where almost 20% of males were so employed. Here we see the key importance of the Veracruz road as a source of employment for the province's Hispano-mestizo population.

Trade was the fourth area in which non-Indians specialized. Here, urban Indians were only sparsely represented and the extent to which rural Indians engaged in trade cannot be discerned from the census. The high propensity for non-Indians to migrate within and beyond the region - a subject we examine more closely in the next chapter - is more easily understood when their occupational specialization is taken into account. Agriculture, the Liberal solution for the problem of unemployment among the city's artisans, occupied relatively few Spaniards and mestizos in the 1790s. The three most common occupations for non-Indians at this time - textiles and clothing, transport and commerce - were all easily transferable and transportable.

A closer examination of the occupational structure of the four urban parishes reveals an appreciable degree of caste specialization, although less marked than that which Brading observed in the mining city of Guanajuato.[9] Table 2.4 shows a clear concentration of Indians and mulattos within the most arduous and lowest paid (though not necessarily the least

---

[8]   *Ibid.*, p. 148.

[9]   D. A. Brading, *Miners and Merchants*, pp. 257-60.

TABLE 2.4 OCCUPATIONAL STRUCTURE OF FOUR PUEBLA PARISHES IN 1791 BY RACIAL GROUP.

	Spaniard (European & Creole)		Mestizo (includes Castizos)		Mulato (includes negros)		Indians	
	No.	%	No.	%	No.	%	No.	%
DEALING	150	11.7	16	1.6	3	1.8	9	0.4
FOOD&DRINK	45	3.5	74	7.6	11	6.5	325	15.5
TEXTILES	341	26.6	300	30.8	33	19.4	226	10.8
DRESS	74	5.8	195	20	33	19.4	168	8
METALWORK	110	8.6	48	4.9	15	8.8	71	3.4
LEATHERWORK	39	3	96	9.9	15	8.8	103	5
WOODWORK	20	1.6	16	1.6	5	2.9	69	3.3
BUILDING	7	0.5	20	2	2	1.2	384	18.3
OTHER INDUSTRY	173	13.5	90	9.2	13	7.6	170	8.1
TRANSPORT & SERVICES	65	5.1	78	8	36	21.2	171	8.2
ARTS & ENTERTAINMENT	9	0.7	10	1	-	-	43	2
AGRICULTURE	65	5.1	21	2.1	2	1.1	349	16.6
ADMIN/PROF/ CHURCH/MILIT	183	14.3	10	1	2	1.1	10	0.5
Total	1281		974		170		2098	

Source: AAP, Padrones, Vols. 128-129.

skilled) occupations: cotton spinning, work in bakeries and flour mills, construction, porterage and agriculture. These groups were also over-represented in the less prestigious crafts: hat making, shoemaking and earthenware. As to be expected, Indians and mulattos were poorly represented in non-productive and high status occupations such as bureaucracy, clergy, military, liberal professions and trade. Spaniards, conversely, monopolized these categories and were only thinly represented within unskilled occupations. Mestizos, like Indians and mulattos, were under-represented in commerce, the professions and the bureaucracy. But like Spaniards, mestizos were under-represented in the unskilled manual categories. Where most mestizos and all the other races met, worked together and intermarried (and where race does not seem to have been the main influence in the allocation of employment) was in the intermediate, skilled and semi-skilled occupations: cotton weaving, woollen cloth manufacture, tailoring, cigar-making, iron work, and confectionery. Thus, what Seed has observed for Mexico City in 1773, also holds true for Puebla in the 1790s: "Artisans were less obviously racially stereotyped than any other occupation".[10]

For the moment, the observation can be made that the social structure of these four parishes, if not exactly egalitarian, at least does not accord with the two class model used by contemporaries to describe urban society. First, the patrician element was only sparsely represented, being largely concentrated in the central parishes (missing from the census). There was a handful of Peninsular merchants, creole clergy and owners of estates and flour mills living beyond the built up area of the city. Apart from a few priests, monks and the occasional European merchant, very few members of the elite lived in these four parishes. Just over 2% of families in the parishes of Analco and Santa Cruz, mostly Spaniards, employed servants. This contrasts strongly with 41% of families in a block in center of the city employing servants in 1821.[11] And, although there were many artisans in these parishes, there were very few master craftsmen who had apprentices residing with them, again mainly Spaniards, or who operated large workshops. Most men in these four parishes were employed in skilled or semi-skilled crafts, many in services and day laboring, and, only very few in high status occupations.

Yet, this largely artisan society was cut across by racial divisions, embraced or imposed as a result of the Spanish obsession with *limpieza de sangre* and with the maintenance of a stable and hierarchical colonial social order. Race does appear to have had an important impact upon social stratification, particularly at the two extremes of the social hierarchy.

---

[10] Patricia Seed, "Social Dimensions of Race: Mexico City, 1753," *HAHR*, Vol. 62, 1982, p. 584.

[11] AAP, Padrones, Vols. 128-9 (1791); and AAP, Hacienda Municipal, Diversos Años, Vol. 103 (1832).

Spaniards and Indians tended towards endogamy. And race appears to have been important in allocating the more lucrative and leisured jobs to Spaniards and the more arduous and unpleasant ones to Indians. However, between these two extremes, race appears to have favored Spaniards and mestizos only in cotton weaving and tailoring, hardly lucrative occupations, beyond which the extraordinary diversity of occupations was apportioned fairly evenly among the races. The whole discussion about racial factors in stratification is highly problematic. This is particularly true for these parishes which, until the eighteenth century, had been almost exclusively an Indian domain, corresponding, juridically at least, to the Spanish ideal of two separate republics and social orders. By the end of the eighteenth century, little remained of Indian political autonomy, which had survived only for the convenience of tribute collection. It is clear from the subordinate occupational position of Indians, that any economic or social autonomy which they might once have enjoyed, had been extinguished by the end of the colonial era.

Social Stratification in Puebla in the Late Colonial Period

How was urban and provincial society ordered hierarchically? How useful are these racial categories for describing hierarchical social ordering ? What factors apart from race were important in social stratification? What general models of social structure can be usefully applied to an eighteenth century Spanish American provincial society? To date, little research has been done to advance our understanding of social structure beyond the analysis of racial and occupational terminology offered by the population census. Historians have recognized the need to take account of more subjective factors, such as contemporary perceptions of race or the honor accorded to particular occupations, and to advance beyond census data to parish, notarial and probate records, before firmer conclusions about social structure can be reached. But very little has yet emerged which takes our understanding of social structure beyond simply intuitive assumptions about stratification applied to the racial and occupational categories found in censuses.[12] Thus the recent vigorous historical debate over "race or class?" ended in stalemate, and Seed's work on Mexico City, correlating census

---

12 This study makes no claim to any "quantum" historiographical advance, particularly since no research was carried out in parish archives, and permission to work in the Puebla judicial archives (containing probate records, an essential source for the historian of stratification) was denied. If there is any innovation it has been to combine qualitative data about the status and productivity of particular occupational categories, drawn from property and income-tax, notarial and scarce probate records, with census data to provide a more solid, though still largely speculative, understanding of social class in Puebla.

with parish records, remains the only substantial advance in our understanding of the class structure of at least one colonial Spanish American city.[13]

Contemporary descriptions of colonial urban social structure emphasize the great gulf which separated the rich from the poor, presenting a picture of highly polarized, dualistic social order.[14] Historians have tended to work with this basic assumption of social dualism. Seed adopts a marxist classification and divides the Mexico City of 1753 into two classes: a "dominant class", which owned the "means of production", and a "laboring class", composed of those living solely off the product of their labor. The dominant class was made up of "residual elites", composed of the religious, civil and military bureaucracy, rural property owners, manufacturers and mineowners; the "owners of the means of distribution", composed of merchants and property-owning shopkeepers; and the managers and overseers employed by the latter groups. The laboring class included everyone who made a living from their manual labor, be they propertied artisans or property-less day-laborers.[15] Frederick Shaw also sees Mexico City (of the 1840's) as a two-class society with a "patrician" 20 percent of the population living decently, separated by an immense gulf from the "plebe" or *populacho*, composed of "journeymen artisans, unskilled laborers, street peddlers, and domestic servants and their families, earning a subsistence income or less..[16] Chance and Taylor favor a three-class model in their study of Oaxaca in the 1790s, observing a "well-developed middle layer of professional and skilled occupations" bridging the gap between elite and masses.[17] None of these studies, however, offers adequate evidence to substantiate either a subjective view of class, based upon contemporary attitudes and perceptions, or, an objective evaluation of socio-economic status based upon a measurement of property and income. We will now attempt to advance a definition of social class in Puebla by drawing upon evidence from a wider distribution of sources.

---

[13] The debate, sparked off by the article of John K. Chance and William B. Taylor, "Estate and Class in a Colonial City: Oaxaca," *CSSH*, Vol. 19, 1977, pp. 454-87, has been synthesised by Fred Bronner, "Urban Society in Colonial Spanish America: Research Trends", *LARR*, Vol. 31, 1986, pp. 30-31.

[14] "Mexico is the country of inequality. Nowhere does there exist such a fearful difference in the distribution of fortune..." wrote Alexander von Humboldt in 1803, *Political Essay on the Kingdom of New Spain*, Vol. II, p. 184.

[15] Patricia Seed,"Social Dimensions", p. 578.

[16] Frederick Shaw, *Poverty and Politics in Mexico City, 1824-54*, Unpublished PhD. dissertation.. University of Florida, 1975, p. 39; and his, "The Artisan in Mexico City (1824-1853) ", in Elsa Cecilia Frost, et al. *El Trabajo*, pp. 414-18.

[17] Chance and Taylor, "Estate and Class", p. 472.

Was late colonial Puebla the two-class society which the Intendant, Manuel Flon, described in 1803 ?

La mayor parte de estos habitantes vive de su industria y trabajo corporal, dedicados los mas al hilado de algodónes que apenas logran su muy escasa subsistencia, de modo que componiendo una mitad de la población el Estado eclesiástico, los empleados en tribunales y oficinas, los ricos y hacendados, los mercaderes y artesanos de crédito, puede asegurarse que el resto de gentes no alcanza otro arbitrio ni recurso honesto que el del turno y el algodón.[18]

Where Flon differed with his contemporaries (as with recent interpretations of late colonial society) was in rating the numerical balance between the two classes as being roughly equal. Flon was as impressed by the sheer scale of the superordinate class, as he was shocked by the poverty of the "plebe".[19]

Although one is persuaded by the generous proportions and functional complexity which Flon ascribed to the Puebla upper class (contemporary descriptions usually rate this class as much smaller), his general model is unsatisfactory and (deliberately) simplistic. More serviceable, for the purpose of this study, is a four-class model of socio-economic stratification, somewhat more complex than that adopted by Chance and Taylor. The classes which have been discerned are:

I)   THE ELITE
II) THE MIDDLE CLASS
III) "LA PLEBE"
IV) THE UNDERCLASS

The criteria which have been used for delineating these classes - income, property, honor, prestige, political influence - we shall introduce as the analysis proceeds. For the moment, this will take the form of a delineation of categories of people involved directly or indirectly in Puebla's business life. An explanation of how this pattern of social stratification emerged must await an account of the uses made by different social groups of guild, municipal and clerical institutions, the subject of the next chapter.

---

18 AGN, AHH, Consulado, Vol. 917-23, 13 Jan 1804, Manuel Flon to Sres Priores y Consules del Real Consulado de Veracruz; and, *El Jornal de Veracruz*, Vol. II, p. 146.

19 The neo-classical terms "*plebe*" and "*patricio*" acquired a more common usage at the end of the eighteenth century, the "*plebe*" in Puebla referring to people who hitherto had been identified by their caste. In 1822, the editor of *El Farol* defined the "*plebe*": "cuyo nombre conviene por ahora – casi todos los individuales de las castas". *El Farol*, Puebla, No. 19, 3 March 1822, p. 165.

I) THE ELITE

Urban society in Puebla over the late-eighteenth and early nineteenth centuries had at its summit a peninsular and creole elite, composed of senior Crown and ecclesiastical officials, professionals, wealthy wholesale merchants and landowners, all of whom routinely developed economic interests beyond their primary specialization, often in industry. This elite comprised probably less than one hundred families.[20] This was a patrician group, whose position rested upon the recent acquisition of wealth, the growth in importance of the military orders and privileges, and the professionalization of the colonial bureaucracy under the later Bourbons. It also comprised a small hereditary element, holding entails, noble titles and other corporate privileges.[21] Admission to the elite was probably more easily achieved among recent immigrants to the region than by mobility from lower social categories.[22] Elite families owned large two or three-storey houses, often with two or three patios, within a few blocks of the main square.[23] Apart from their residences, they would often own properties and businesses elsewhere in the city as well rural estates. A mark of elite status would be the ownership of a coach, of which there were 145 in private ownership in 1807. Only the intendant, Manuel Flon, owned more than one coach.[24] Elite families would generally have between three and five servants residing within the household: a cook, a coachman, household servants, and only very rarely, a slave.

---

[20] This is, of course, an approximate estimate based upon tracing the recurrence of names of prominent families in the records of forced loans during the wars of Independence, the property census, and the census of coach owners.

[21] Liehr states that there were only three members of the high nobility in Puebla in 1800, although members of lower, military orders were more numerous. He also records that "A fines del siglo XVIII vivían en Puebla muchos hidalgos empobrecidos que trabajaban a menudo en profesiones poco apreciadas",. *Ayuntamiento y Oligarquía*, Vol. 1, p. 64. Doris Ladd notes the exceptionally high rate of nominations for titles of nobility of *poblanos*, compared with subjects from other regions of New Spain, in the last years of Spanish rule, *The Mexican Nobility*, pp. 178-181.

[22] Liehr shows how, between the 1787 and 1808, immigrants from the northern provinces of the Peninsular, chiefly merchants, acquired increasing weight on the city council, at the expense of local landed interests. Liehr, *Ayuntamiento y Oligarquía*, Vol. I, pp. 111-121.

[23] A sense of the size of elite houses can be ascertained from reading a population census. Information is recorded spatially, as the census taker moved from one room to another in each dwelling. The recording of an elite dwelling, often housing several families living in single "entresuelo" rooms below the principal family's apartments, could take up several pages in a census. For a description of typical elite dwellings: Liehr, *Ayuntamiento y Oligarquía*, Vol. I, p. 56.

[24] AAP, Pensiones Municipales, 1807-1832, Vol. 158 Expte. 1595; and Liehr, *Ayuntamiento y Oligarquía*, Vol. I, p. 55.

If not exempted by special privilege from military service, members of the elite could preserve a patrician decorum by joining an order of *maestranza* , by serving the Crown in the Royal Cavalry, or in the older Commercial Regiment, rather than in the more plebeian militias established by the Bourbons in the 1760s.[25] Established elite families perpetuated their wealth and political influence through entailing their estates and by owning "perpetual" aldermanships on the cabildo, which were passed on from father to son.ʾ The political aspirations of newcomers to the elite, who lacked patrician antecedents, were accommodated by the sale of offices, the increase of elected cabildo positions and by the increasing availability of military positions during the last decades of colonial rule.[26] As important to the elite as were these ties with local government and the military, was the maintenance of firm family connections with the secular church and religious orders. Church bodies controlled the lion's share of urban real estate, a large proportion of the province's capital stock in urban and rural mortgages, as well as directly owning many estates and businesses, while receiving revenues from loans and properties, from pious endowments, from tithes and parish dues. A few case studies of elite families will illustrate the range and the depth of their interests

The possession of a flour mill distinguished the most influential group within Puebla's elite. The most ubiquitous family name in this group over the first half of the nineteenth century was Haro y Tamariz. The family's success illustrates the apparent ease by which an energetic immigrant could gain admission to the Puebla elite and assume, almost immediately, a position of provincial leadership. The Basque merchant, Joaquín de Haro y Portillo, arrived in Puebla in the 1790s and soon contracted marriage with the daughter of one of Puebla's few holders of an entail, José Ignacio Tamariz y Carmona, owner of the Mayorazgo flour mill, a bakery, and estate in Tepeaca, as well as properties in Puebla itself, all of which Haro inherited on the death of Tamariz in 1808. [27]

Haro had a keen eye for making judicious investments during the unstable Napoleonic and Independence periods. When Manuel Flon temporarily suspended the municipal meat monopoly in 1800, Haro and fellow Basque merchant, José Bernardo Aspiroz, entered this lucrative albeit risky business.[28] As a result of ties established through the city meat

25 A city chronicler described the merchants, landowners, bakers and professionals who formed a cavalry squadron after the deposition of Ferdinand VII as "voluntarios patricios nobles", Pedro López de Villaseñor Cartilla Vieja p. 372; and for the noble aspirations of cavalrymen and army officers: Liehr, *Ayuntamiento y Oligarquía*, Vol. I, pp. 62-3.

26 *Ibid.*, pp. 99-111.

27 Reinhard Liehr, *Stadtrat und Stadtische Oberschicht Von Puebla am Ende der Kolonialzeit (1787-1810)*. Wiesbaden, 1971, pp. 197 and 200.

28 AAP, Abastos, Vol. 88 f. 168; and Liehr, *Stadtrat*, p. 197.

supply from the *tierradentro*, the principal market for Puebla's textiles, and through the flour trade with the *tierra caliente* of Veracruz, the main source of Puebla's raw cotton, by 1807 Haro had become one of Puebla's principal raw cotton dealers and wholesalers of locally produced cotton cloth.[29] He was elected alderman to city council each year between 1800 and 1806 and was admitted to the Commercial regiment as a sergeant major.[30] The death of his father-in-law coincided with the *Consolidación* decree, leaving Haro with 80,000 pesos of debts owed to the *Real Hacienda*. This he agreed to repay at the manageable annual rate of 4,000 pesos, with no interest, until the debt was payed off.[31] Within a decade of his arrival, Haro had amassed a fortune almost unmatched in the Puebla of his time which, under less extraordinary circumstances would have taken a lifetime to achieve. Haro learnt to profit from the instability brought on by war.

Joaquín de Haro y Portillo rounded off his investment in Puebla's principal staple commodities when he acquired two *tocinerías* from the *montañes* merchant, Roque de la Peña, in 1806, adding a further *tocinería* to his portfolio in the early 1810s.[32] By 1822 Joaquín owned almost one quarter of all the pigs kept in the city for slaughter.[33] A prominent contributor to Royalist finances over the wars of Independence, Haro was elected to represent the province of Puebla in the Cortes in Spain in 1820. He died in 1825, having made an important contribution, as leader of the provincial militia, to the victorious federal cause in the previous year.[34] His five sons all achieved prominence following Independence, in politics and modern industry.[35]

The only flour-milling family to rival the Haro y Tamariz in its breadth of impact upon late colonial and early republican Puebla was the Furlong, descended from an Irish refugee, James Furlong who, fleeing persecution in Belfast, settled in Puebla in the 1760s. He married Ana Malpica in 1772, the daughter of a long-established soap manufacturing family.[36] At his death in 1802 he left four flour mills - Guadalupe, Batán, Amatlán and Enmedio - and extensive urban property to his nine sons. Three entered the Church; Tomás becoming rector of the orphanage of San Cristobal and *mayordomo* of the Santa Rosa and Santa Inés convents, Apolinio serving as chaplain and *mayordomo* of Puebla's wealthiest convent, La Concepción,

---

29 AGN, AHH, Consulados, Vol. 463 Expte. 3.

30 AAP, Cabildo, Vols. 69-74; Leicht, *Calles*, p. 186.

31 AGNP, RPP, Censos, Vol. 39 f. 95; and Liehr, Ayuntamiento, Vol. II, p. 75.

32 AGNP, RPP, Vol. 39, fs. 51-54, and Vol. 42, f. 243.

33 For Haro's activities in *tocinería*, see page 144.

34 AAP, Cabildo, Vol. 89 f. 251; and Leicht, *Calles*, p. 186.

35 See Index for Luis Haro and Joaquín Haro y Tamariz.

36 Leicht, *Calles*, pp. 130, 164, and 223-4.

and Joaquín, taking charge of the oratory of San Felipe Neri, also an important property holder in Puebla and contributor to the building of the first *Hospicio de Pobres* (public work house). The other sons followed their father into milling and baking, some diversifying into modern industry over the 1830s and 1840s. All six entered politics, at least at the municipal level, occupying the posts of alderman and mayor, with Patricio and Cosme attaining prominence in state and national politics, both serving as governors of the State.[37]

The untimely death from cholera of the State governor, Patricio Furlong, in 1833 required his executors to draw up a detailed inventory of his estate which provides a rare insight into the habits, tastes and business activities of a member of the Puebla elite. General Don Patricio Furlong resided in spacious dwelling adjoining his flour mill, Huexotitlán, amidst a large acreage of fertile, irrigated, wheat and alfalfa producing land. Thirty seven Indians were employed in the mill, residing in an adjoining *calpan*, and were indebted to the amount of 1,080 pesos. Patricio's house was richly furnished with European furniture, including a German piano valued at 300 pesos, the walls adorned with crystal mirrors and religious iconography, as well as a framed map of the Mexican republic. His library contained nearly 120 works in over 300 volumes, ranging from classical, French revolutionary and pre-hispanic American history, constitutional law and educational theory, military history and manuals of military strategy, the works of Feijóo, Humboldt and other figures of the Enlightenment, including practical, agricultural, industrial and scientific publications, and much contemporary political literature, including Francisco García's radical *Plan de Zacatecas*, betraying Furlong's liberal political convictions. The house contained a small armory of sixteen firearms and seventy bayonets. The family owned two ornate coaches and several carts to carry flour to bakeries in the city. From the balance of the estate it is evident that Patricio's flour mill borrowed heavily from religious institutions managed by his brothers.[38] Such privileged access to credit, which was critically scarce during this period, helps to explain how the Furlong brothers achieved such dominance of milling and baking. For much of the period between 1810 and 1830, they owned almost one third of Puebla's flour mills and one fifth of the city's bakeries.[39]

The Furlongs' rivals in milling and baking were the García de Huesca, also of recent immigrant stock. Pedro García y Huesca arrived in Puebla during the 1760s, becoming so successful as a baker that he was able to acquire the Huexotitlán flour mill in 1774, after having become its principal

---

[37] *Ibid.*, pp. 164-6.

[38] AGNP, Miscellaneous Judicial Estate of Patricio Furlong, 1833.

[39] See Index for further refernces to their role.

creditor.[40] A decade later, Pedro added the Molino de Santo Domingo to his estate, Puebla's most productive flour mill, purchased from the Dominican order. This mill is commandingly situated on the river Atoyac at the point selected in 1830 for the construction of Mexico's first operating modern cotton spinning mill.[41] By 1800 Pedro and his three sons, José, Matias and Vicente, owned three flour mills and several ranchos and haciendas in the immediate vicinity of Puebla and in the sugar producing valley of Izucar, thirty miles to the south. They were a family of great borrowers. By farming their wheat fields around Puebla intensively and steadily, thus adding to the collateral value of their estates, they were able to raise some of the largest loans registered in *libros de censos* over the unstable and capital-scarce first twenty years of the nineteenth century.[42] They invested these loans in cereal farming, speculative grain purchases, the financing of *tocinerías* and the purchase of bakeries.

During the wars of Independence, all three brothers served as officers in the Patriotic regiment, contributed to patriotic loans and, for several years, occupied the municipal posts of mayor and alderman. Over this decade José García de Huesca regularly supplied, on his own account, over 10% of the city's annual supply of flour and was able to bid for lucrative extra-regional contracts of the kind celebrated in May 1815 with a Panamian merchant, who paid 46,549 pesos in *géneros de Castilla* in exchange for 1,000 *tercios* of flour from the Santo Domingo mill. By 1817, José, Matias and Vicente all owned city bakeries, Matias García and Patricio Furlong being charged in that year, by the council's tribunal of fair trading, for plotting to defraud the public by charging "unjustly" high prices, illustrating the oligopolistic position enjoyed by these two families in milling and baking.[43] The fruits of wartime speculation were revealed in 1827 when, at the height of phobia against the Spanish, an inventory of Captain José García de Huesca's estate was published in *El Patriota*, valued at well over half a million pesos.[44]

Haro y Tamariz, Furlong and García y Huesca, although perhaps the most prominent, formed part a much larger circle of Puebla's mill-owning families. The example of the intendant Manuel Flon's investment in wheat growing and milling, in disregard of official injunction against high royal officials engaging in private economic pursuits, has already been

---

[40] Fausto Marín-Tamayo, Huexotitla: *La Propiedad Privada del Molino Activo Más Antiguo de America.* Puebla, 1959, p. 26; and Liehr, *Stadtrat*, p. 196; and AOP, Diezmos de Trigo, Vol. 1.

[41] AGNP, RPP Censos,Vol. 38, fs. 19, 22, 51, 59, 61, 169; and Vol. 39, fls. 109, 187, 226; Vol. 40, fs. 357, 379.

[42] AAP,Cuentas - Garitas, Vol. 32; and AGNP, RPP, Censos, Vol. 40, f. 357.

[43] AAP, Panaderías, Vol. 87, fs. 42-47.

[44] *El Patriota*, Vol.III, No. 8, 13 June 1827, p. 29.

mentioned.[45] In the wheat tithe records can be found the names of many of the most prominent post-Independence families: Mangino, Munuera, Mujica y Osorio, Calderón, Couto, Olaguibel, Reyes and Alday. These merchants and public officials took over wheat estates and flour mills for short periods between 1805 and 1828, in order to plant when prices were high and the promise of high returns great.[46] Since most estates and mills were heavily encumbered with Church mortgages, ready cash but little capital was needed to take over an estate and the rate of turnover was extraordinarily high.[47] The turnover rate for flour-mills was higher even than that for wheat estates, an average of four of the region's twenty flour mills changing hands annually. The rate of turnover for mills and haciendas was appreciably higher in the city and district of Puebla than in outlying districts.[48] The example of two public officials who made their fortunes through such speculation further illustrates the key importance of the control of the production and commercialization of wheat in the allocation of wealth and political power in Puebla over this period.

Estevan de Munuera used his collectorship of the ecclesiastical tithe of Puebla's richest agricultural districts - Nativitas, Atlixco and Izucar - to assemble an imposing estate by the beginning of the nineteenth century.[49] This comprised an hacienda in Cholula, several *tocinerías* and two flour mills in Puebla, as well as extensive urban real estate.[50] Munuera served as *alcalde* on the city council during the 1790s, becoming prominent in the "*milicia activa*" during the wars of Independence, reaching the rank of Colonel of Cavalry. He served as interim governor of the State after the successful federalist revolution, spearheaded by the states of Puebla and Jalisco, against Iturbide's empire in 1824.[51]

Rafael Mangino, administrator of the royal *alcabala* and treasurer of various pious funds, acquired the strategically located Topoyango flour mill where much of Nativitas' important wheat harvest was milled. His marriage to María Josefa de Mendivil y Ovando, the daughter of an important and long-established landowning family (the last Puebla family to be ennobled in the late colonial period), brought with it extensive urban

---

[45] See p. 23.

[46] See Table 2.5, and AOP, Diezmos de Trigo,Vols. I-III.

[47] Between 1805 and 1828 of the 293 haciendas, molinos and ranchos from which the Cathedral collected wheat tithes directly, there were often as many as forty to fifty changes in ownership or tenancy annually, peaks in turnover accompaning price rises and preceding increases in wheat production, illustrating the speculative character of wheat farming over this unstable period.

[48] See Figure 1-4, p. 55.

[49] AOP, Diezmos, "Libros en que se firmen los recibos....1780".

[50] Leicht, *Calles*, p. 424; and Liehr, *Stadtrat*, p. 198.

[51] Leicht, *Calles*, p. 424.

property. In 1800 he was reported to be constructing "una posesión de casas de los tratos de panadería, tocinería, mesón, calera y dos hornos de fabricar cal", demonstrating that Mangino was responding energetically to the brief boom accompanying the Napoleonic wars. Rafael died in 1806. His son was listed as the most important private house owner in the city in 1832, owning fifteen substantial properties. Rafael junior inherited his father's financial skills, serving as finance minister in various governments over the 1820s and 1830s.[52] This strategically important post, and the Ovando family tie which he shared with Estevan de Antuñano (the city's foremost textile entrepreneur), were to have historic consequences for Puebla.[53]

If these profiles of prominent elite families reveal that wheat contributed centrally to their fortunes, they also show that *tocinería*, Puebla's other staple commodity, often accompanied wheat growing and milling in their portfolios. This broad pattern of investment, characteristic of Puebla's wealthiest families, is illustrated by the fortunes of several families for whom *tocinería* appears to have been a central line of business. The inventory of the estate of the merchant-manufacturer, Tomás Méndez de Granilla, lists a retail dry goods store, a substantial two-storey dwelling containing a flour warehouse, a flour-sifting establishment, two *tocinerías*, two indigo dye houses apart from eight houses from which he collected rent. His assets included 23,000 pesos in credits to flour millers, 23,057 in cash among total assets amounting to 237,994 pesos, against modest liabilities of only 13,000 pesos.[54] This healthy balance and the date of the inventory (1779), illustrate vividly the scale of the external demand for flour and *tocinería* products resulting from Spanish participation in the American war of Independence.

The estate of another merchant-*tocinero*, Captain José Bernardo Aspiroz, illustrates the hazards as well as the opportunities of business during the Napoleonic wars, and the fragility of even the broadest investment strategies. Prominent in the militia and city alderman for several years, during which he acquired almost a monopoly in the city's meat supply, at his death in 1810, Aspiroz owned two tanneries, three *tocinerías*, and collected rents from six private houses. Temporary wartime demand had encouraged him to extend credit amounting to over 150,000 pesos to shopkeepers, mineowners and merchants as far a field as Tehuantepec and Guanajuato and to run up debts of his own with import merchants and chaplaincies amounting to 136,000 pesos. Although his estate showed a balance in his favor of 99,000 pesos, his widow held out little hope of

52 AAP, Padrón General de Tiendas (1832)", and Leicht, *Calles*, p. 373.
53 Ladd, *The Mexican Nobility*, p. 18; and Leicht, *Calles*, pp. 353-55.
54 AGNP, Judicial Miscellaneous: Estate of Tomás Méndez de la Granilla, 1779.

being able to collect these debts or repay his liabilities once the insurgency had commenced.[55]

A final example of an elite family reveals the extent to which wealth could be successfully conserved, indeed increased, over the upheaval of the wars of Independence. The inventory of the estate of Cayetano María Torres Torija is a good example of a *tocinero*-landowner of more modest means than either Méndez Granilla or Aspiroz but still firmly established within the wealthiest layer of Puebla society.[56] Although resident in Puebla, Torres owned a permanent seat on Tlaxcala's cabildo and served during the wars of Independence in Tlaxcala's cavalry squadron, established to protect landed estates, of which Torres owned three, from insurgents.[57] At his death in 1824, Torres left his business in a healthy state with assets of almost 100,000 pesos against liabilities of only 18,000 pesos.[58] Accounts kept between 1814 and 1817, reveal a profitable enterprise producing soap, pork and lard for the local market and that of the south-east.[59] While soap production was his main line of business, Torres took advantage of the opportunity provided by the abolition of the Puebla *abasto*, selling 2,384 sheep and cattle in the city from his estates over these years. Overall earnings came to 45,206 pesos against costs of 21,407 pesos demonstrate the impressive profits which could be made during the insurgency from supplying the local and the regional market, just as Bernardo Aspiroz's indebtedness reveals dangers of dealing in the extra-regional and overseas market after 1807.[60]

These, then, are some examples of Puebla's wealthiest social group. Merchants are clearly prominent, several of Peninsular birth. The overall

---

55 AGNP, Judicial Miscellaneous: Estate of José Bernardo Aspiroz, 1810.

56 Members of the Torija family, into which, it may be presumed, the Tlaxcala landowning family of Torres married, had operated *tocinerías* and *trapiches* in Puebla since the seventeenth century, continuing to do so until the mid-nineteenth century. See Leicht, *Calles*, pp. 41 and 45.

57 AGNP, Judicial Miscellaneous: Estate of Cayetano María de Torres Torija, 1824.

58 Few entrepreneurs or landowners, in the depressed conditions of the mid-1820s, were able to raise a loan of 10,000 pesos, as Torres did shortly before his death. AGNP, RPP, Censos, Vol. 42 f. 217.

59 Between November 1814 and April 1817, Torres sent 25 consignments of soap, valued at 25,662 pesos, to 48 towns and villages in the intendancies of Puebla, Oaxaca and Mexico. The soap was dispatched by mule, every two to three months, in loads of up to 150 *arrobas*, divided into 20-30 batches, generally sold wholesale to small town shopkeepers.

60 The inventory of his estate reveals that Torres was able to pay the medical and funeral expenses of his father, pay off all outstanding debts, provide an allowance for two brothers and two cousins, a dowry for a sister, monthly allowances for a maiden aunt and two other female members of the family, continue the rental of the family coach and pay the salaries of the servants of the house.

picture is of this elite is somewhat skewed since few of the people mentioned were from old Puebla families, enjoyed noble status (beyond the standard *hidalguía* accorded to the Basques) or had inherited entails. Several, however, married into families whose permanence among the Puebla elite had been established for several generations by means of entails, perpetual positions on council, specialization in particular lines of business, property ownership, as well, no doubt, as by less tangible factors such the honor and prestige accorded to inherited wealth and status. Deeper research into marriage patterns than has been possible in this study would no doubt indicate the extent of the overlapping between new and old wealth and of mobility into and out of the elite.

II) THE MIDDLE CLASS

Ranked below the elite was a broadly-based middle class made up of the middle and lower ranking clergy, Crown officials and professionals, lesser merchants and shopkeepers, owner-managers and managers of *obrajes*, *tocinerías* and bakeries, *artesanos de crédito*, struggling owners of rural estates and the vestiges of the Indian nobility. While, in 1823, members of the elite reported daily incomes of between 40 and 80 reales and, as we have seen, might own estates valued at well over 100,000 pesos, Puebla's middle class families were more likely to earn between fifteen and thirty reales a day and to possess estates valued at anything between 2,000 and 40,000 pesos. The assessment for an abortive income tax (see Table 2.5) in 1823 showed owner-managers of potteries, glass factories, hat factories, bakeries, wax chandleries and *tocinerías* as earning between sixteen and thirty two reales a day, incomes on a par with a skilled manager (*dependiente*) of a retail store and comparable with the salary level Lindley found for a comparable social group in Guadalajara in the same period.[61] What distinguished this middle class from the elite was that, apart from rarely owning more than one business, heads of families were much more likely to be directly involved in managing their businesses. But was this middle group merely a managerial class dependent, in one way or another, on the patronage or direct economic control of the social elite ? Or did Puebla, America's principal manufacturing city, contain a "bourgeoisie" in possession of a degree of economic, political and cultural autonomy ?

---

[61] See Table 2.6. The salary of a skilled manager (*dependiente*) of a "casa de comercio" in 1825 was advertised at 1, 000 pesos per annum. *El Caduceo*, Vol. 5, No. 1, 1 April 1824, p. 4. Richard Lindley found that the slaries of Guadalajara clergymen, military men and bureaucrats fell between 100 and 1,000 pesos per annum, mentioning the specific cases of a clergyman receiving 600 pesos p. a., a teacher 20 pesos a month and a captain of the army 35 pesos a month. Richard Lindley, *Haciendas and Economic Development. Guadalajara, Mexico at Independence*. Austin, 1983, pp. 16 and 125.

TABLE 2.5 DAILY WAGES IN PUEBLA IN 1823 (in *reales*/day)

Male Occupations		Female Occupations	
THE ELITE			
3 Merchants	16, 40 and 80 c		
THE MIDDLE CLASS			
2 Tocineros	16		
Master chandler	16		
Master hatmaker	28.5		
Master potter	16		
3 Master glassmakers	32		
"LA PLEBE"			
Doctor	4	Keeper of Bread shop	4
Shopkeeper	8	Small shopkeeper	2.5
Cashier in *tocinería*	2-3	Confectioner	4
Cashier in chandler shop	6		
4 Apprentices in chandler's shop	3-4		
Confectioner	6		
Foreman (*mayordomo*) of bakery	3		
Chocolate maker	8		
Chandler	3		
Refreshment stall-keeper	2.5		
Master cotton weavers	2-3		
Master calico printer	3		
Keeper of hat shop	4		
22 Hatmakers	2.5-3.5		
2 Tailors	3 & 8		
Sculptor	4		
Carpenter and coppersmith	4		
Muleteer and blacksmith	3		
THE UNDERCLASS			
Keeper of bread stall	1	Chocolate maker	1
6 Journeymen in *tocinería*	2	*Atolera*	0.5
4 Journeymen in chandler's shop	2	*Tortillera*	0.5
Domestic servant	1	Ribbon Weaver	1
Biscuit maker	1	Cotton Spinner	0.5-1
4 Cotton weavers	1	Buttonhole maker	2
3 Cotton spinners	0.5	Seamstress	0.5-1
Calico printer	1	Washerwoman	0.5
Hatmaker	1		
2 Servants in hat factory	0.5		
Tailor	1		
10 Potters & 1 Bricklayer	0.5-1		
Singer	1		
Shoemaker	1		
2 Carpenters	1&2		
3 Cooper, blacksmith, tin beater	1		
Muleteer	2		
Carrier	1		
10 Glassmaker	2		
2 Farm laborers	0.5-1		
Coachman	2		

Source: AAP, Padrones, Vol. 133

This is an intriguing but elusive question. Class, after all, is in part a subjective phenomenon, created as much by attitudes and conventions as by measurable differences in wealth. The paucity of literary sources and contemporary descriptions, coupled with the apparent uniformity of religious and institutional life and the closed nature of politics, limit the possibility of exploring the mental and subjective world of the eighteenth and early nineteenth centuries. Chapters 4 and 5 will, however, suggest the existence of a class factor in politics, with a putative middle class becoming more vocal during the 1830s, after the first ten years of "aristocratic" republican government. For the moment, notwithstanding the limitations of a static and wealth-based class analysis, it is nevertheless useful to pose the question.

Did this city founded for "commoners", which for three centuries had drawn its wealth principally from manufacturing contain a class which did not simply imitate the behavior and aspire to the status of the elite but sought instead to dignify a style of life which necessarily involved at least the supervision of, if not direct involvement in, manual labor? Albi shows how the principal woollen clothiers of the later sixteenth and early seventeenth centuries successfully challenged the group of *encomenderos* and heirs to the original *vecinos* who hitherto had monopolized municipal office.[62]   These, however, were merchant-manufacturers of very substantial wealth who would have stood out conspicuously from among the mass of artisans, and even from the select group of *"artesanos de crédito"*: masters of those crafts which traditionally were accorded a particular honor for producing commodities of great value and requiring great skill (silk spinning and weaving, silver and gold work, and passamanery). But what of the more modest owners of *obrajes* producing rough woollen cloth, the owner-managers of *tocinerías*, bakeries, hat factories, potteries, glass factories, retail stores, mule transport and grain dealing businesses ? Did they form self-conscious and self-confident urban middle class? Unfortunately, this question must remain a largely rhetorical one, since our knowledge of contemporary social attitudes is inadequate to provide a satisfactory answer. The following profiles of families within this "middle group" suggest, however, some lines for future enquiry.

Beyond the clergy, bureaucracy and professionals, numbering several hundred in the early nineteenth century, a proportion of whom would have considered themselves as belonging to the elite, the most numerous and conspicuous group within Puebla's middle class were the owner-managers of bakeries and *tocinerías* and the owners and managers of retail cloth and dry goods stores. Between 1746 and 1852 the number of *tocinerías* fluctuated from 19 in 1796 to a peak of 50 in 1835. The number of bakeries fluctuated between 19 in 1803 and 29 in 1820. The number of retail cloth businesses flutuated between 38 in 1820 and 68 in 1846. The

---

[62] Guadalupe Albi, "La Sociedad".

number of *tiendas mestizas* fluctuated from 73 in 1814 to 91 in 1846.[63] Any of these businesses, if well managed or in "good times", could maintain its owners family in relative decency and comfort. It was from this group that much of the capital and entrepreneurship was drawn during the broadly based attempt at industrial transformation during the 1830s and 1840s.

Until 1813 bakers and *tocineros* belonged to exclusive corporations, prospective entrants to which were required to demonstrate sufficient capital (4,000 pesos in the case the Bakers' guild) and potential production capacity (the use of at least 6 *tercios* of flour a day or around 30 pig carcasses a week) to sustain fiscal and other obligations (supplying horses for the militia) which the city demanded from them in return for the guild privileges and ordinances which the municipality would enforce. These barriers to entry tended to confine these trades to the better off. *Tocineros*, bakers, tanners , retail merchants and prominent manufacturers were well represented on city council, occupied the higher ranks of the urban militia or served in the Commercial Regiment, were often accorded the honor of serving as *alcaldes del barrio* (justices of the peace) and took precedence in religious processions.[64] Some profiles of this "urban yeomanry" will illustrate the character of this important intermediate class.

As we have seen, the ownership of *tocinerías* was common among the urban elite, but often only as one element within broad portfolios of investments often encompassing trade, manufacturing and agriculture, extending into politics. Most *tocineros*, however, did not own rural estates or engage in other lines of businesses, and would normally possess assets of between 10,000 and 50,000 pesos, at best, half those of an elite family. In a competitive business involving considerable capital investment and the supervision of often as many as ten or more workers, the owner's residence in and direct management of a *tocinería* was considered desirable. Owner-managers of *tocinerías* in 1823 claimed that they earned 16 reales a day in contrast to the two to six reales earned by cashiers, shop keepers, soap-cutters, pig-tenders and slaughterers.[65] Inventories of the estates of Pedro Fernández Durán, Doña María Nicolasa Villar and Manuel de Izarduy illustrate the scale and character of owner-manager *tocinería* businesses.

---

[63] See pp. 314-15.

[64] The *tocineros* that Liehr lists as holders also of municipal offices, tended also to be landholders and should be included among the elite. They, of course, would have been useful mouthpieces for *tocineros* belonging to this middling category. Similarly, after Independence, only the most prominent *tocineros* entered the *cabildo*: the Calderón, Rodríguez and Domínguez families returning aldermen and mayors during the 1820s and early 1830s. See Liehr, *Stadtrat,* pp. 195-201. And also AAP, Cabildo, Vols, 90-101. For the hierarchical organization of a procession, see José García Quiñones, *Descripción de las Demostraciones.*

[65] See Table 2.6, and, AGNP, Judicial Miscellaneous, Estate of Torres Torija, 1824.

All three were active in guild affairs over the third quarter of the eighteenth century. Pedro Fernández Durán, Captain in the urban militia, acted for the guild in 1760 when thirty three *trapiches* (clandestine, small-scale *tocinerías*), mostly operated by women, were ordered to be shut down.[66] At his death in 1782, he left assets of 14,887 pesos and a balance of 9,932 pesos. His nephew, Juan Durán, also active in the guild, operated the *tocinería* until it failed in the crisis of 1802-3.[67] Similar continuity of production, prominence in guild affairs and departure from the business as a result of the crisis accompanying the resumption of Atlantic trade, following the Peace of Amiens, may be observed with the Izarduy business.[68] At his death in 1790, Manuel de Izarduy left an estate worth 37,532 pesos with a balance of 21,949 pesos in favor of his widow who operated the *tocinería* until 1802.[69] Finally, the inventory of the estate of María Nicolasa Villar at her death in 1784, valued at 53,106 pesos, with a balance of 36,685 pesos, demonstrates the imposing value of a single *tocinería* business in an era of high overseas demand.[70] The role of the guild in attempting to hedge its members against the instability of external demand by restricting production to the privileged few is examined in the next chapter.

While elite families, such as the Furlong and García de Huesca, were able to combine bread-baking with flour mill and agricultural estate ownership, most bakers found management of a single bakery a sufficient match for their resources. The proportion of bakeries which formed part of larger businesses or were operated as partnerships seems, however, to have been greater than in *tocinería*. Entry into baking could be by rental of a going concern, by the formation of a company or by the outright purchase of a bakery with the building housing it. The rental of a bakery could cost anything between 700 and 1000 pesos a year.[71] For this modest outlay a baker could expect a turnover of anything from 200 to 600 pesos a month.[72] Partnerships in bread-baking were fairly common. One such venture was the partnership between Joaquín Ramírez, baker, and Sebastián Pérez Cornejo, flour miller who together invested 14,000 pesos in a bakery

---

[66] AAP, Tocinerías, Vol. 232, f. 103; and Vol. 233, f. 90, and AGNP, Judicial Miscellaneous, Papers covering purge on *trapiches* in 1760.

[67] AGNP, Judicial Miscellaneous, Estate of Fernández Durán, 1782.

[68] AAP, Tocinerías, Vol. 233 f. 255.

[69] AGNP, Judicial Miscellaneous, Estate of Izarduy, 1790.

[70] AGNP, Judicial Miscellaneous, Estate of Villar, 1784.

[71] Bakery rentals: AGNP, PN, No. 5 (1841-2) f. 88; PN, No. 6 (1843) f. 10; PN, No. 7 (1851), f. 43.

[72] AAP, Militar Vol. 118, f. 276.

over five years, dividing the net profits of 18,466 pesos equally until the company's liquidation in 1827.[73]

The outright purchase of bakeries with their buildings was less common than rental agreements or a simple transfer of the use of ovens and equipment from one baker to another.[74] This was because bakeries were often housed in large and costly two-storey buildings in the center of the city.[75] The inventory of the estate of José Kern illustrates the comfortable status of an independent and successful owner-manager of a bakery.[76] Along with many other bakers he rented land close to the city for growing wheat during the wars of Independence.[77] At his death in 1816, Kern's bakery was valued at 27,789 pesos, excluding the building, 17,529 pesos of which comprised credits lent out to millers and farmers. A significant feature of the inventories of Kern's and other bakeries is the amount of effective cash held: Kern died with with 6,640 pesos in the till. The liquidity of bakers accounts for their ability to engage in speculative investment in wheat agriculture and also for their bearing the brunt of municipal taxation over the decade of the wars of Independence.[78] This liquidity might also account for the successful marriage of Kern's daughter to the future governor of the State, flour-miller and baker, Patricio Furlong. Liquidity was also a necessary attribute of a successful retail merchant, a "middle class" group who are examined more closely in Chapter 9.

If *tocinería*, bread-baking and the retail trade constituted the core business activities of Puebla's middle class, as well as forming an important speculative arena for the elite, what gave this city its peculiar character was the substantial number of manufacturers and master craftsmen. Since the sixteenth century, Puebla had been renowned as much for its more

---

[73] AGNP, PN, No. 8 (1827), fs. 100-105.

[74] The fixed capital value of bakeries (excluding the building) was quite small, ranging from 400 to 2,000 pesos in three examples in inventories: AGNP, PN, No. 5 (1842) fs. 8-9; and Judicial Miscellaneous, Estate of José Kern, 1816; and Inventory of La Panadería Francesa, 1855.

[75] The *montañés* import merchant, Fernando Gutiérrez de Nanza, paid 16,000 pesos for a bakery building, when he chose to diversify from the stagnant foreign trade sector into financing wheat farming and baking in 1800. AGNP, RPP Censos, Vol. 38, f. 16, and Vol. 40, f. 232.

[76] AGNP, Judicial Miscellaneous, Estate of José Kern, 1816.

[77] Other bakers figure as important wheat producers on land close to the city during the wars of independence: José María Yllescas and Gertrudis Espindola. AOP, Diezmos de Trigo, Vols. 1-3.

[78] From 1775 until the end of the period, the council raised three quarters of a real on each *carga* of flour entering the city. During the wars of Independence, an additional tax - "la pensión de algos" - (10% of bakers' sales) was raised to fund extraordinary war costs. This yielded around 11, 000 pesos a year between 1814 and 1818. AAP, Militar, Vol. 118, f. 276.

specialized and skilled industries as for its basic staples in textiles, soap and flour. The most prominent skilled industries were decorated silk shawl-making, ironwork (locks, stirrups, spurs, etc.) copper-work (bells, cauldrons, etc.), leatherwork (decorated saddlery and bridlery), decorated felt hats, passamanery, majolica pottery and glassmaking. Only a handful of families in each of these crafts can be considered to have belonged to the middle class. These were the families whose enterprises produced on a larger scale, employed more workers, used more capital, and made higher profits than the smaller units in their respective crafts.

What kinds of people operated such enterprises ? The chronicler Javier de la Peña, wrote in 1835 of two wealthy artisans he remembered from his youth in the 1800s:

...yo conocí a dos maestros, un sombrerero llamado Don Manuel Cadena y otro tejedor de lienzos de algodón, Don José Aguilar, con toquillas de onzas de oro en los sombreros, botones de las mismas y escudos en sus vestuarios, sillas de montar magníficas con fustes guarnecidos de plata maciza, y el ruedo de higas de las anqueras de la propia; sus mujeres estaban ricamente adornadas, y rivalizaban con las señoras de primera clase, etc., sus casas eran espaciosas y muy curiosamente adornadas; en la sala habia hermosas arañas de plata, y no pocos utensilios de servicio, siendo tan común el uso de este metal, que en algunas acesorías de oficiales honrados, se le daba agua a la persona decente que la pedía en el 'jarro de plata'...[79]

A similar fondness for decoration, religious iconography and silver tableware can be observed in the inventory of Don José García de Aragón, master silk shawl weaver. Shortly before his death in 1781 García had been inspector of the silk weavers' guild.[80] The inventory shows him to have been entirely free from indebtedness to merchants with assets of 5,707 pesos against debits, largely from funeral expenses, of 1,079 pesos. He contracted his own spinners, using cocoa beans from Guayaquil as remuneration (this was a period of critical currency shortage when *tocinerías* were stamping soap for use as money).[81] He worked two looms

---

[79] Francisco Javier de la Peña, "Notas", p. 146. With such considerable property, Manuel Cadena was able to borrow 12,400 pesos from a wholesale merchant in 1807, a service to which very few artisans could turn AGNP, RPP, Censos, Vol. 39, f. 91. In 1822 Cadena's son was operating his father's hat factory.employing 22 *oficiales*. By 1832 he was the owner of 16 houses in the city from which he collected rents. Chapter 5 shows him as an important figure in post-Independence popular politics. AAP, Padrones, Vol. 133, fs. 151-8; and AAP, Padrón General de Casas (1832).

[80] AGNP, Judicial Miscellaneous, Estate of García de Aragon, 1781.

[81] The circulation of printed soap - known as *señales or pintaderas* - released by *trapiches* (smaller *tocinerías*), was forbidden by the *Tribunal de Fiel Ejecutoría* in 1781. AGNP, Judicial Miscellaneous (1781)

and would have employed as many as five or six *oficiales* and apprentices. He also operated a press for dyeing his own yarn, his stock of indigo being his most valuable possession. Loans to grandmother and grandchildren suggest that he was a bastion of his family, as the possession of a small armory of weapons, numerous brass instruments and uniforms show him to have been active in the militia.

Specialized weavers, such as García de Aragón, were afforded an appreciably higher status than the weavers of ordinary cotton cloth (*manta*). This was because they possessed a powerful and restrictive guild, controlled all stages of production, and produced a valuable product. In 1823 master *manta* weavers received only three reales a day, *oficiales* a mere one real for a day at the loom and spinners a standard half real for a day at the spindle. Master silk shawl weavers probably received between 15 and 30 reales a day. Such a weaver was Don Francisco Armenta, the son of an important eighteenth-century silk weaver, who employed twelve *oficiales* in his workshop in 1833. Inventories of cloth retail stores in the 1830s and 1840s list "*rebozos de Armenta*" as valued at 10 pesos each while ordinary cotton *rebozos* were worth only nine pesos the dozen.[82]

Information on the status of master potters and glass manufacturers is sparse. Their enterprises were often housed, like bakeries, in fine two-storey buildings, often exuberantly decorated with geometrically arranged ceramic tiles, with a *retablo* over the entrance, serving to advertise the products inside.[83] Inventories reveal that glass and pottery factories bear comparison with *tocinerías* and bakeries in the value of equipment, but by the 1820s it was much less common for potters and glass manufacturers to own the buildings in which their factories were housed.[84] Lacking property to serve as collateral, these businesses rarely appear as borrowers in the notarial archives. More common than mortgage loans were rental agreements and business partnerships, generally between two masters or between a merchant and a master. From the 1830s, joint-stock ventures involving several shareholders became more common.[85]

Unlike bakers and *tocineros*, pottery and glass manufacturers do not appear to have served on the *cabildo* before 1821, although it is possible that during the heyday of Puebla's majolica industry over the seventeenth century, certain masters were so honored. In 1821, Lieutenant Mariano Santiago Alvarez, manufacturer of glass and pottery, was elected alderman and chosen to represent the master potters on the *Junta de Artesanos*.[86] The

---

82   For the status of *rebozo* weavers, see Guy Thomson, "The Cotton Textile Industry in Puebla", pp. 188-94.

83   Leicht, *Calles*, p. 385.

84   AAP, Padrón de Tiendas, 1825.

85   For partnerships in glass manufacture: AGNP, PN, No. 7 (1824), 24 March 1824; and PN, No. 4 (1835), 8 January 1835. See Chapter 7 for joint stock ventures.

86   AAP, Cabildo Vols. 90 and 93.

advent of artisans to the cabildo was made possible by the abolition of permanent aldermanships, the extension of suffrage and the introduction of popular elections for municipal officers, with special instructions from Spain that artisans should be directly represented. Again, at the height of federalist and republican fervor in 1824, artisans were elected to the cabildo as aldermen: Juan Carrillo, descendent from a long line of Puebla potters, whose father had been *alcalde del barrio* in the parish of Analco, and inspector of the guild shortly before its abolition; Juan José Ascué, likewise from a long-established mulatto iron-working family; and Juan Vargas Machuca, a master shoemaker.[87] All these men owned urban property and the degree to which they represented the wider artisan, largely property-less, class was a matter fiercely debated at the time.

Two final examples of prominent masters from the iron-working industry will serve to complete this glimpse of the artisan "patriciate". The inventory of the estate of Don Roque Jacinto de Yllescas, master iron-founder from the parish of Analco, reveals an even greater exuberance than was evident in the descriptions of the Cadena, Aguilar and García de Aragón households.[88] At his death in 1783, Yllescas' estate was valued at 21,717 pesos, with debts of only 427 pesos (much of this the cost of *pulque* served at his funeral). The modest value of his estate was belied by the opulence of his household furnishings and the luxury of his personal wardrobe: carved cedar tables, desks and chairs, sixteen chests, three wardrobes, three painted screens, three painted bedsteads, 57 paintings and engravings of saints, numerous mirrors, crucifixes, statuettes of saints, and an array of Chinese, European and Puebla glass and porcelain, a quantity of silver tableware, a library containing 96 volumes of mainly religious literature, a chaise (*forlón*) valued at 300 pesos, a wardrobe containing 14 jackets, dresscoats, some of them embroidered and with silver buttons, a cannon and an armory of firearms and sabres. Of his seven houses valued at 14,703 pesos, four contained forges, with the principal foundry, which had been under his direction, containing a stock of machetes, knives, hoes, plowshares, axes, stirrups, chains, locks, and iron bars valued at 3,134 pesos.

Yllescas' iron-working business was clearly a complex enterprise supplying iron goods, as his credit records show, to blacksmiths, military detachments, haciendas and mining camps throughout the region and beyond. Roque Yllescas headed the leading iron-founding family, established for at least three generations, in Puebla's principal metal-working parish, Santo Angel Analco. He was not only a leading light in the militia and the iron-founders' guild, but the patron and benefactor of the parish, providing Analco with fresh water, rebuilding the bridge connecting the parish with the main section of the city, adorning the parish church with

---

[87]   AAP, Padrón de Casas, 1832.

[88]   AGNP, Judicial Miscellaneous Estate of Roque de Yllescas, 1783.

decorative ironwork, embellishing its plaza, founding a religious confraternity for iron-founders and covenanting a *Casa de Hospeduría*, attached to the parish church.[89]

Roque Yllescas was not the wealthiest iron founder in Analco parish. In 1793, Juan Ignacio Morales died leaving 70,000 pesos, the value of four houses with forges in the Plazuela de Analco, and four houses elsewhere in the city, including a splendid specimen of domestic architecture, the Casa de Alfenique, now the State museum. He is listed in the 1791 census as a Spanish widower, living with his seven children and two Indian servants.[90] The Yllescas and Morales formed the core of a cluster of respectable metal-working families, mostly of mixed race, residing in the parish of Analco and conspicuous in the 1791 census for possessing servants and apprentices: the *mulatto* Ascué and Crespín families, iron-founders who dominated guild affairs over the second half of the eighteenth century; the *castizo* Sánchez family, manufacturers of arquebuses; the *mestizo* Antolín family, gilders; the Spanish-*castizo* Murillo family, bellmakers.[91] The Murillo, Ascué, Morales, Crespín and Yllescas were still working their forges in Analco *barrio* forty years later.[92]

III) "LA PLEBE"

Set apart from the middle class was a much larger group of craftsmen and shopkeepers of lesser means. Occupationally, this class overlapped with the middle class. Many worked in the same trades and crafts but were dependent upon, or in competition with, the larger businesses of manufacturers and leading retailers. Artisans and shopkeepers of the "meaner sort" (to adopt the term used in the British American colonies) operated workshops and stores with much smaller stocks and less capital than did the businesses of the "middling sort".[93] They rarely owned

---

[89] Leicht, *Calles*, p. 258.

[90] AAP, Padrones, Vol. 128 f. 180.

[91] AAP, Padrones, Vol. 128 Expte. 1388. Juan Murillo, maker of bells and copper cualdrons, cast the bronze bust of Miguel Bravo, a popular local insurgent leader, located in the Plazuela del Parral. He represented his trade in the municipal *Junta de Artesanos* in 1821 and owned his own house, valued at 1, 420 pesos in 1832. See Leicht, *Calles*, p. 303, and Padrón General de Casas (1832).

[92] AAP, Padrón General de 1830 , Cuarteles 3 and 4.

[93] Richard Hofstadter observes the habit, in the British American colonies, of referring to "the better sort" ,"the middling sort" and the "meaner sort": *America at 1750 A Social Portrait*. New York, 1973, p. 133. The distinction which can be drawn between British colonies, and New Spain is that, in the former, the "better sort" was less wealthy and numerous, the "middling sort" occupied a much more dominant stake , while the "meaner sort" was a minority. In contrast, in Spanish colonial society, the "better sort" enjoyed a far more preponderant share of power and wealth, the "middling sort" was a less autonomous and important class, while the "meaner sort" comprised a powerless and property-less majority. A comparison between late

property, and thus are rarely found in the notarial records raising mortgage loans. They appear, however, in the tax records; in the lowest tax categories where there number is under-represented, since many people in this class operated semi-clandestine businesses.

Businesses in this class made full use of family labor. They rarely employed more than one or two assistants or officials from beyond the family, and often were prevented by guild ordinances from doing so. The elite and the middle class used their political influence in the cabildo, or their control of guild affairs, to limit the scale of operation and commercial success of this class. The recurrent struggle between the *tocineros* and the owners of the much smaller *trapiches* is an example of this.[94] In the income-tax assessment of 1823, a band of daily earnings of between three and eight reales corresponds to this group, setting them apart from the most numerous category, including most women, who earned less than two reales a day.[95] They are further distinguishable from the middle class by the fact that, when work was available, they labored full time at their counters and crafts, rather than placing their businesses in the hands of assistants or managers, a common practice among wealthier craftsmen and manufacturers and seemingly the norm among owners of bakeries and *tocinerías*. This, then, was truly a toiling class, but also one which aspired to maintain its independence and to achieve a "decency", even if "respectability" proved elusive, due to poverty and discrimination from the wealthy and more powerful.

This class attracted great attention after Independence, following its sudden enfranchisement, first with constitutional experiments in Spain and later with the federalist revolution in Mexico in 1824. The American minister at this time, who had close links with Mexican politicians who were becoming practiced at organizing the "plebe", commented that:

> The laboring man of the cities and towns includes all castes and colors; they are industrious and orderly, and view with interest what is passing around them. Most of them can read, and in the large cities, papers and pamphlets are handed about in the streets; and sold at a cheap rate to the people.[96]

This was the class most directly hurt, first by the technological changes transforming the manufacturing system elsewhere in the Atlantic world (and soon to be introduced into Mexico), and also by the economic disruption accompanying Independence. From early in the eighteenth century, it had

eighteenth-century society in Mexico City and Philadelphia has been ventured by G. P. C. Thomson, "The Americas: Philadelphia and Mexico City.," *History Today*, Vol. 34, 1984, pp. 29-35.

94 See pp. 140-46.

95 See Table 2.6.

96 Joel Poinsett, *Notes on Mexico Made in 1822*. New York, 1969 p. 121.

proved to be a restless class, with migration to Mexico City a common route taken by artisans and shopkeepers dissatisfied with their lot in Puebla.[97] This "safety valve" perhaps made it a less "dangerous" class than it might otherwise have been.

Working in a craft which involved the continual use of a manual skill disqualified a man from holding municipal office before Independence.[98] This veto against artisans serving on the cabildo, in strong contrast to their prominence in local politics in the British and even the Portuguese American colonies, was a grievance deeply felt in Puebla's first open municipal elections in 1821, as the following passage from an artisan's broadsheet reveals:

> Dura todavía la memoria de la humilación en que este Ilustre Ayuntamiento tuvo – los artesanos en aquellos tiempos bárbaros en que los pesos se adquiria el derecho de gobernar los pueblos por medio de baras [municipal staffs of office] bendibles y renunciables. Para eterno oprobio de aquella edad de hierro veimos a los dos immortales Coras, los Magones, los Zendejas y otros Artistas ilustres, confundidos y adocenados con los Doradores, Tintoreros y Almonederos: y si aquellos a pesar de la nobleza de su profesión, se vieron tan mal parados, que sería de los otros?[99]

So, even Puebla's most prestigious and honorable artisans (the individuals listed here were painters) were denied access to municipal office before Independence. And even after 1821, with the *ayuntamiento* now open to anyone, very few artisans or small shop keepers sought or achieved positions on council or in state politics, entrusting their mandate to men from the middle class or the elite, especially to the clergy, to merchants, and to prosperous shopkeepers, who for patronage and ideological affinity, sought to represent artisan interests.[100]

Before Independence, artisans were also barred from entry to the commissioned ranks of the urban militia or from service in the Commercial Regiment where a merchant complained in 1816 of having to serve next to artisans, "miserable que por su clase, e indecencia de sus casas y alimentos no pueden desahogar esa carga."[101] A census of Puebla's twelve newly-established militia companies, made in 1767, listed 1,044 men serving in the ranks and non-commissioned categories; 784 Spaniards, 80 mestizos,

97 See pp. 155-164.
98 Liehr, *Ayuntamiento y Oligarquía*, Vol. I, p. 54.
99 Anon. (Presbítero Antonio María de la Rosa, Cura de Santo Angel Analco), *Exito del Proceso Formado a Manuel López de Guerrero*. Puebla, 1822, p. 2.
100 See Chapter 5.
101 AAP, Cabildo, Vol. 85, April 27 1816.

179 *pardos* and one *negro*.[102] This body of men represented a substantial proportion of Puebla's working age men of non-Indian descent (only men between the ages of 16 and 36 were selected). The largest occupational cohort in the militia worked in textiles: 185 men were listed as cotton weavers, serving mainly in the ranks, although a few *rebozo* weavers and one passamanerist (religious garment maker) served as corporals and sergeants. All the other sergeants and corporals were from the following occupations: *tocinería*, baking, tanning, silverwork, arms manufacture and barber-surgery. Military ranking therefore reflected and reenforced the social division between the middle class and the "plebe": on the one hand were the owners or managers of larger enterprises, along with artisans in the more prestigious crafts producing highly valued luxuries, who occupied the higher ranks, on the other, were the masters producing more basic goods in small workshops, or *oficiales* working for others, who provided the soldiery.

Metal workers followed *textileros*, comprising 20 percent of the militia, and tailoring came third, occupying 18 percent. The diversity of relatively skilled crafts represented in the ranks of the militia -fine pottery, carpentry, shoemaking, armory, iron-founding, cauldron-making, glass-making, gilding, silk-weaving, passamanery, broadcloth-weaving and carriage-making - suggests strongly that the militia was the preserve of the "decent", middle-ranking artisanry, and not of the poorest artisans. This is confirmed by the fact that low status occupations - baking, candle manufacture from tallow, pottery, brick-making and bricklaying, stone masonry, hat-making, spinning and carding - are all significantly under-represented in the census. The mass of the poorer urban population was composed of tribute-paying Indians, who were exempt from military service, or, of castes, who were too poor to afford the uniforms, musical instruments and weapons, effectively disqualifying them from serving in the militia.[103]

Thus, in the militia records can be found a stratum of urban society composed of modestly respectable artisans. This class stood above the mass of the poor population and, in the militia at least, deferred to a class of wealthier manufacturers and artisans of the more prestigious trades who occupied the higher ranks. The incorporation of this class of artisan within the militia from the 1760s presaged a deeper involvement of Puebla's

---

[102] AAP, Militar, Vol. 87.

[103] Indians were not liable for military service, nor were negroes, free or enslaved, since they were forbidden from carrying arms. See Christon I. Archer, *The Army in Bourbon Mexico. 1760-1821*. Alburquerque, 1977, pp. 11, and 231.

artisanate in military affairs from the outbreak of the wars of Independence.[104]

IV) THE UNDERCLASS

The lowest class in urban society, often referred to as "*el populacho*" (the unruly section of the "plebe"), was probably the most numerous. Judging from the indignant references of European and North American travellers to this class, it was proportionately larger, more unruly, less well-clothed, more diseased, than the poor to which they were accustomed in their own countries.[105] In the travelogue, a section on the *léperos* of Mexico became an obligation.[106] They also became the stock in trade of the *costumbrista* columnist and lithographer.[107] Poinsett, the American minister, observed this class to be composed of:

> ...beggars, idlers, drones...that prey upon the community and who, having nothing to lose, are ready to swell the city of popular ferment, or lend their aid in favor of imperial tyranny [he is writing in 1822]. .In Mexico, these people have been kept in subjection by the strong of the vice regal government; but it is to be feared, that they will henceforward be found the ready tool of every faction.[108]

Beyond the sensational reputation of this class, which reflects more the nervous state of mind of people of property, what can be said about its socio-economic character ? People belonging to this class owned very little property, worked irregularly at their crafts and trades and received low incomes (rarely over two reales a day, the standard subsistence income

---

104 Archer points out that, at the turn of the nineteenth century, Puebla, already the most militarised province in the colony, was contributing a disproportionately greater number of recruits to the Regiment of New Spain, equal to those from the viceregal capital: Archer, *The Army*, p. 234.

105 For descriptions of Puebla in the 1820s: Joel Poinsett, *Notes*, pp. 38-41; W Bullock, *Six Months' Residence and Travel in Mexico*. London, 1824, pp. 79-110; Mark Beaufoy, *Mexican Illustrations*. London, 1828, pp. 121-22; and Henry Ward, *Mexico*, Vol. II, pp. 267-69, 274-78.

106 Joel Poinsett, *Notes*, pp. 49 ,63, 77; Ward, *Mexico*, Vol. II, pp. 267-37; Charles J. Latrobe, *The Rambler in Mexico*. New York, 1847, p. 118; Frances Calderón de la Barca, *Life in Mexico* London, 1970 (Edn.), pp. 63-66-75; Moreno Toscano, *Ciudad de México Ensayo de Construcción*, pp. 17-19.

107 "El Populacho de México", *El Museo Mexicano*, 1844, Vol. III, p. 450. This class figures prominently in the works of Manuel Payno, *El Fistol del Diablo*. Mexico, 1967, and *Los Bandididos de Río Frio*. Mexico, 1968; See also: "Soldiers and Proletarians", engraved by Moritz Rugendas, in Carl Sartorius, *Mexico about 1850*, p. 129.; and for a striking portrait of a "lépero poblano", Manuel Payno, "Viaje", pp. 165-6.

108 Poinsett, *Notes*, p. 121.

throughout the eighteenth and nineteenth centuries).[109] This level of income required that all who could work in a family (including children) dedicate themselves to a service which would contribute to a family income adequate for sustaining life. Apart from their poverty and low incomes, what also characterized people in this class was their dependence upon others for employment. Most of the people in the three classes we have already described operated businesses which they owned or at least managed independently. Many in this fourth class were tied to others by credit or worked directly for them in domestic service or as day-laborers. The product of their labor was rarely their own. The exception to this would be the small scale street and market sellers, porters and artisans working beyond the boundaries of the guild system. Such people, however, suffered irregularity of income and employment, as well as persecution from guild and municipal officials, conditions which were hardly compensated by their relative independence.[110]

Occupationally, the "underclass" fell into two broad categories: the self-employed, and those who worked for others as day-laborers or on longer contracts. The self-employed generally depended upon merchants and manufacturers, both for providing their raw materials (usually through a cash or credit rather than a putting-out arrangement), as for purchasing the finished products of spun wool, cotton or silk, woven cloth, hats, stitched shoes, stitched, finished and embroidered clothes for tailors, etc.. The condition of these artisans depended upon the degree of mercantile encroachment as well the state of the market for their products. In the cotton textile industry, as a result of increasing competition from abroad, as from other regions of New Spain, particularly after *comercio libre*, the status of cotton spinners, always low, declined still further, while that of cotton weavers, once firmly established among the respectable guild artisanate, wavered on the boundaries between the "plebe" and the underclass. During the early 1790s Cholula's spinners earned less than was necessary for even an individual's subsistence.[111] Cotton weavers in the outlying towns of Tlaxcala and Huejotzingo, by now fully subjected to Puebla cloth merchants, barely earned two reales a day: the wage of an agricultural peon. By 1822, in the depths of the post war depression, Puebla's own cotton cloth weavers, once proud members of the *Gremio del Arte Mayor de la Seda* which had exercised jurisdiction over the entire

---

[109] See Table 2.5; *El Invitador*, Puebla, Vol. 1, No. 37, 25 August 1826, p. 175; Isabel González Sánchez, "Sistemas de trabajo, salarios y situación de los trabajadores agrícolas, 1750-1810", in Florescano, *La clase obrera*, pp. 150-172.

[110] For examples of official persecution see Chapter 3 and Appendix. 1.

[111] For conditions of weavers and spinners in Cholula: Luis Chávez Orozco, *El crédito agrícola*, p. vi; and AAP, Gremios, Vol. 234, fs. 260-267.

province, were earning barely more than one real a day, and cotton spinners, only half a real.[112]

In such times of hardship for the self-employed, deserted by their merchant backers, those in direct employment - the other main category within this lowest class - might perhaps have considered themselves fortunate. The principal areas of direct employment were day labor in building and agriculture, unskilled labor in the larger workshops and factories (obrajes, bakeries, tocinerías, potteries and flour mills), household service and employment in carrying and transport. Indians figured prominently in all of these categories in 1791.[113] Work in bakeries, because of the heat and unsociable work hours, was perhaps the least desirable and lowest status urban occupation. Owners of bakeries depended upon criminals sent from the courts for their supply of labor, who would work off their sentences at the kneading table and the ovens.[114] Bakers also frequently tied their workers to their employment by indebting them and restricting their movement beyond the workplace.[115] The income-tax records of 1823 indicate a clear differentiation in workshop employment. On the one hand, apprentices and oficiales, who might entertain the hope of one day becoming masters, earned between two and four reales a day, and, on the other, simple day-laborers rarely earned more than one real a day.[116] This differentiation between the more skilled artisan and the jornalero is evident in a census of workshops made in 1821 which listed administrators and skilled categories separately from day laborers and children. Table 2.6 suggests that the opportunities for "career mobility" were nil for workers in flour milling, tocinería, hat-making and woollen cloth manufacture, while in pottery, glass and wax candle-making, something of the graduated hierarchy between master, oficial and apprentice, which presumed a degree of career mobility, remained. What this meant in terms of wages and living standards in such a period of economic crisis, when Puebla's potteries, and many businesses in most other industries, were going bankrupt, is, of course, uncertain.

Finally, women were an important element within Puebla's lower class. Women's employment was concentrated in low paid, labor-intensive and home based occupations, rarely revealed in the census unless a widow or spinster headed a family. Of the thirty three widows heading families or living alone in a single block of the north of the city in 1821, fourteen were cotton spinners, seven were seamstresses, eight took in laundry, while the

---

[112] Thomson, "The Cotton Textile Industry", p. 189.

[113] AAP, Padrones, Vols. 128-9.

[114] This practice continued into the republican period. As late as 1849, a court in Puebla condemned two prisoners to two years labor in a bakery: AJP, 3 December 1849, Trial of Antonio Rivera and Juan de la Cruz Coral.

[115] For an example see: AAP, Panaderías, Vol.87, fs.82-89.

[116] See Table 2.6

TABLE 2.6   THE LABOR FORCE OF SELECTED MANUFACTURING
UNITS IN PUEBLA, 1821

	Administrators & skilled categories (*maestros & oficiales*)	Jornaleros Adults	Jornaleros Children
FLOUR MILLS			
Huexotitlán	2	30	7
La Teja	1	18	8
Cristo	5	21	-
Mayorazgo	1	21	9
POTTERIES			
Calle del Espejo	15	-	6
Calle de San Pablo de los Naturales	17	-	5
Calle de Sayas	11	-	1
Lozería de Alvarez	11	-	1
Lozería de Trillanes	9	-	-
Lozería de Carrillo	8	-	7
Calle de Espíndola	9	-	5
Calle de Alfaro	8	-	6
TOCINERIA			
Calle de Cholula	1	4	-
GLASS FACTORY			
Calle de la Santísima	10	3	-
CERERIA (wax candles)			
Calle de la Carnicería	6	-	-
VELERIA (tallow candles)			
Calle de la Santísima	6	9	-
SOMBRERERIA			
Taller de José Cadena	3	22	-
OBRAJE DE LANA			
Pablo González	6	18	-

Source: AAP, Hacienda Municipal, Varios, Diversos Años, Vols. 109 & 113; and
Padrones Vol. 113.

other four worked at tortilla-making, confectionery, milk-selling and begging.[117] . Women were vital to the textile and clothing industries. They predominated in the lower ranks of commerce, keeping small shops and market stalls and street-selling. And women outnumbered men in household service. From the income-tax records of 1823 it is clear that women rarely earned more than half a real a day, although higher incomes of up to four reales were attainable, particularly in retailing. In 1823, women, especially cotton-spinners, were exempted, more frequently than men, from payment of the income-tax because of "poverty", insolvency or "for being burdened with family".[118]

Conclusion

The intention of this chapter has been to draft an impressionistic map of the city's social structure to serve as a frame of reference for the rest of the study. Puebla was clearly no two-class society, with a great empty gulf between elite and masses. Rather it was a city containing a large middle sector, with its economic core composed of manufacturers, artisans and shopkeepers, living decently and enjoying considerable political influence. This class, aided by the capital of the elite and Church institutions, and the labor of the poor, was responsible for sustaining Puebla's character as a manufacturing and commercial city, commanding extensive extra-regional markets. Beneath, lay a tier of people - a plebeian artisan class - engaged in similar occupations to those of the middle class, aspiring to achieve its independence and respectability, but failing in the face economic uncertainty and instability which threatened to submerge its members within the city's large "underclass"

The accuracy of this model of social stratification is unavoidably limited. The social boundaries separating groups are blurred by the necessity of drawing data from several points within at least a fifty year period. Over this time, Puebla's social and institutional structure was changing in response to unprecedented economic and political instability. Entire groups of people - the cotton cloth weavers being the most conspicuous example - were finding their status in urban society altered, generally downwards, except in short periods of wartime boom. The social historian thus has only blunted arrows to aim at a moving target. But, this is still early in the story. "Class", as has often been pointed out, is a social relationship that "must be understood historically in action.[119] Chapters 3 and 5 focus, in part, on the political relations between the putative social

---

[117] AAP, Padrones, Vol. 134, fs. 65-75.

[118] AAP, Padrones, Vol. 133, "Contribución Directa".

[119] E.P. Thompson, *The Making of the English Working Class*. London, 1965, pp. 9-10.

classes outlined in this chapter, enabling this social analysis to be put to the test.

Chapter 3

THE POLITICAL ECONOMY OF THE PUEBLA REGION: FROM CORPORATISM TO PROTECTIONISM, 1700-1850

New Spain differed from, say New England, in the high degree of regulation of most aspects of economic life. Foreign trade was largely monopolized by the *proveeduría de víveres* and by exclusive groups of merchants belonging to *consulados de comercio*, of which there were three by the end of the eighteenth century: in Mexico City, Veracruz and Guadalajara. This privileged access to foreign trade by *consulado* merchants and the near monopoly of silver coin, Mexico's chief export, which it gave them, also ensured their precedence at the regional trade fairs at Jalapa, Lagos and Saltillo, where imported goods were distributed and Mexican goods (*efectos de tierra*) exchanged. This enabled *consulado* merchants to dominate inter-regional as well as foreign trade. Long distance, as indeed local and regional, trade was further restricted by the exclusive privileges granted to individuals for the supply of key commodities of basic consumption, of high revenue potential or of strategic necessity: meat, tobacco, salt, ice, quicksilver (used in silver production), gunpowder, playing cards, etc.[1] Regional and local trade was less restricted to privileged groups but no less closely regulated. Maize farmers and dealers supplying the larger provincial cities were expected to sell only through the municipal granary (*alhóndiga*) at prices fixed each day. Sheep and cattle-dealers could only sell through the municipal slaughter house (*rastro*) or licensed convents and only on contract from the lessee of the municipal meat supply monopoly (*abastecedor de carnes*). All goods brought into the city, which had not already been contracted by retailers,

---

[1] For eighteenth-century economic regulations: Eduardo Arcila Farías *Reformas económicas*. Caracas, 1962. 2 Vols; Brading, *Miners and Merchants*; Morin, *Michoacán en la Nueva España*; and Joaquín Real Díaz, *Las Ferias de Jalapa*, Seville, 1959.

houses (*garitas*)were constructed at the points where main roads entered the cities and harsh penalties were exacted upon anyone found forestalling and regrating before goods entered the market.[2]

Services were also closely regulated. All retail stores had to be licensed by the city council whose fair price tribunal (*Tribunal de Fiel Ejecutoría*) had the power to fix the prices of most goods of basic consumption, to inspect and close down premises which did not accord with municipal health, labor and price regulations. Brokers, hoteliers, wine and *pulque* tavern-keepers, muleteers, carters, coachmen, porters and water carriers also required licenses, the control over the issuing of which became an important source of political influence among the poor.[3] A close watch was kept upon usury, with a maximum interest level of 5 percent enforced until inflation and scarcity of coin, accompanying the wars of Independence, caused interest rates to spiral upwards.[4] Finally, minute regulations and restrictions surrounded most productive activity, the craft guilds counting on the *Tribunal de Fiel Ejecutoría* to enforce observance of their ordinances. Only the Indian population was theoretically exempt from any restrictions upon what they produced or sold, although in practice Spanish corporate institutions succeeded in curtailing this freedom.

The Colonial Experience of Corporatism in Puebla

At the turn of the nineteenth century, the entire fabric of Puebla's trade, services and manufacturing was permeated by such regulations, privileges and monopolies.[5] Yet, within a decade, the Cortés of Cadiz had abolished all restrictions upon trade and exchange. The abruptness of the free trade law of 1813 in fact disguises a more gradual process going back well into the eighteenth century. Moreover, 1813 was no means the end of corporate, municipal and state intervention in the economy. The abundant corporatist and interventionalist features of Puebla's economy in the eighteenth and early nineteenth century were an assemblage of ad hoc sets of ordinances and regulations, which had accrued over the first two centuries of colonial life, each designed to fulfill a particular purpose corresponding to the particular time when they were first introduced. They reflected the heterogeneous nature of colonial society and were a result of the interplay of the competing and conflicting interests to which the colonial

2 For food supply and local trade regulations: Irene Vázquez de Warman, "El pósito y la alhóndiga en la Nueva España," *Historia Mexicana*, Vol. 17, 1967, pp. 395-426; Florescano, *Precios del Maíz*, pp. 43-84; and Bakewell, *Silver Mining and Society*, pp. 58-73.

3 Moreno Toscano, *Ciudad de México: Ensayo de Construcción*, pp. 18-19.

4 Morin, *Michoacán*, pp. 184-5.

5 Liehr, *Ayuntamiento y Oligarquía*, Vol. II, pp. 36-56.

state was exposed. There are, however, certain clearly discernable general characteristics which should first be mentioned.

The first was the peculiar status of the Indian population, the largest racial group within the city and forming a majority within the province. In their economic lives, Spanish America's Indians, from the mid sixteenth century, were among the least regulated people in the western world. By virtue of being the original inhabitants of the continent, the Spanish Crown conceded to its Indian subjects the right to produce freely and sell whatever they liked and granted them complete freedom from tithes and sales taxes and exemption from the ordinances of the guilds and monopolies which regulated the economic lives of the white and mixed population. In return, Indians had to pay an annual tribute. Indians were, of course, subject for much of the colonial period, to strict sumptuary regulations and restrictions upon place of residence. Moreover, institutions such as the labor *repartimiento* (designed to regulate and ration the use of Indian labor), and the *repartimiento de comercio* (designed to prevent the intrusion of non-Indian merchants into Indian communities) served severely to limit the supposed economic freedom of Indians. But ideally and legally, Indians were free economic men, in marked contrast to almost everyone else in colonial society. And in the city of Puebla, they comprised over one third of the population, to whom most of the economic regulations examined in this chapter did not apply.

A second general feature of colonial economic regulation was the priority given to revenue yielding privileges and monopolies, in order to finance all levels of civil administration from municipal to metropolitan government. The introduction of the tobacco monopoly during the eighteenth century is a good example. Conversely, corporate privileges which either failed to yield significant revenues or threatened Peninsular industrial or commercial interests would often not receive official support and sometimes faced the opposition of the colonial administration. The half-hearted official backing for the enforcement of the ordinances of the craft guilds is a good example of this.

A final general characteristic of colonial corporatism was the willingness of the Crown to concede economic privileges to groups of settlers whose economic livelihood would otherwise have not been viable in the face of competition from lower social categories or from the indigenous population. Examples of this may be observed in the the price assize on wheat, designed to maintain the commercial viability of estate agriculture, the support given to *tocineros* in their campaigns to root out competitors, the maintenance of a public maize granary (*alhóndiga*) and a capital fund (*pósito*) to enable owners of maize estates to compete in the market place with smaller maize producers. What these privileges had in common was the affirmation they gave to a hierarchical colonial social order which public officials generally agreed was both desirable and necessary in order to guarantee the respect of the masses for the "decency" of the elite, thus ensuring social stability.

Hardly surprisingly, as a result of two centuries of economic intervention obeying these three general sets of motives, among many others, the resulting pattern of corporate privileges, institutions and economic regulations was both complex and contradictory. It is best understood by examining, in some detail, particular areas of experience.

The Guilds

For reasons which will now be obvious, the colonial environment was not ideal for fostering effective guild institutions. Nowhere in America can a "guild system", in which all the crafts became incorporated into guilds whose ordinances received unreserved legal backing from the State, be said to have emerged.[6] The social and economic climate of America was altogether too exposed for the sheltered requirements of the craft guild. The freedom of Indians to practice any craft, the competition which Spanish artisans faced in every skill from among the colored castes, the continuing influx of European immigrants, the ambiguous territorial jurisdiction of the colony's principal cities, the privileged position of merchants in colonial economic and social life, all tended to reduce the effectiveness of guilds in controlling entry to and in establishing jurisdiction over their crafts. Nevertheless, guilds did emerge in the larger colonial cities. And they served to enable groups of artisans to carve out and hold onto often an important share of production within their respective crafts. By the early eighteenth century, Puebla's guilds were among America's most active and most developed. They performed an important service in maintaining the commercial viability, the stylistic conformity and the social and racial exclusiveness of several crafts over a prolonged period of economic stagnation and instability. They contributed to the pattern of social differentiation within certain crafts which has been observed in last chapter,

---

6 For an excellent discussion of the general problem: Lyman Johnson "Artisans" in Hoberman and Socolow, *Cities and Society*, pp. 230-4; Guilds in New Spain: Liehr, *Ayuntamiento y Oligarquía* Vol. I, pp. 22-36; Francisco del Barrio Lorenzot, *Ordenanzas de gremios de la Nueva España* Mexico, 1920; Dorothy Tanck de Estrada, "La abolición de los gremios", in Celia Frost et al., *El trabajo y los trabajadores*, pp. 311-331; Jorge González Angulo Aguirre, *Artesanado y ciudad a finales del siglo XVIII*, Mexico, 1983; Felipe Castro Gutiérrez, *La Extinción de la Artesanía Gremial*, Mexico, 1986; and Manuel Carrera Stampa, *Los gremios mexicanos. La Organización Gremial en Nueva España, 1521-1821*, Mexico, 1954. For studies of Guatemala see: Hector Humberto Samayoa Guevara, *Los Gremios de Artesanos en la Ciudad de Guatemala 1524-1821*. Guatemala, 1962; And in Buenos Aires: Lyman L Johnson, "The Artisans of Buenos Aires during the Viceroyalty, 1776-1810", Ph.D. dissertation, University of Connecticut, 1974; and his "The Silversmiths of Buenos Aires: A Case Study in the Failure of Corporate Social Organisation", *JLAS*, Vol. 8, 1976, pp. 181-213.

leaving Puebla at Independence with a caste of independent master manufacturers who had dominated guild affairs. Thereafter, these men contributed importantly to the emergence of the protectionist coalition, ensuring the survival of industries which might otherwise have succumbed to foreign competition.

Puebla's guilds emerged during the last quarter of the seventeenth century, in response to the contraction of the market for the city's manufacturing staples, resulting from the prohibition upon inter-colonial trade and the down-turn in silver production. The establishment of the guild of broadcloth weavers in 1676 signalled the start of a process of incorporation lasting until abolition itself in 1813.[7] By 1730 the following guilds held regular elections for the posts of *alcalde* and *veedor*: shoemakers, tailors and hosiers, dyers, saddlers and harness-makers, carpenters and turners, weavers of broad and short cloth, silk weavers, white potters, red potters, hat makers and cappers, coachmakers, schoolmasters, iron founders, blacksmiths, sword-makers and armorers, tin and silver beaters, knife-makers and wax-chandlers and confectioners.[8]

Although some were more specific than others, guild ordinances shared a common tenor. All forbad anyone to practice the respective craft without examination before elected guild officers, generally a mayor and two inspectors. Ordinances sometimes prohibited blacks and mulatos or Indians (quite illegally) from practicing a craft.[9] Ordinances prescribed in varying detail the materials, techniques, finishing and decoration of manufactures. They often specified the maximum scale of production and placed limits upon the number officials and apprentices which a master might employ. To guard against mercantile encroachment, they forbad the sale of products by anyone not master of the guild, or anywhere but from his or her licensed shop (*tienda pública*). Custom and, from 1784, law allowed widows to continue the craft of their deceased husbands, provided it accorded with the "decorum of their sex".[10] Guild inspectors were empowered to patrol workshops, streets and marketplaces to inspect the goods of guild masters and officials, hawkers and market stall-holders to enforce ordinances. Goods from Spain or from other parts of New Spain could not be prohibited but their origin had to be made clear to buyers and they could be inspected by guild officers and withdrawn from sale if faulty. Ordinances usually spelt out the corporate, religious and ceremonial duties

---

7 Silvio Zavala, *Ordenanzas del Trabajo, Siglos XVI y XVII*. Mexico, 1947, pp. 200-213.

8 For guild elections: AAP, Gremios, Vol. 223, fs. 236-242; Vol. 233, fs. 3-56; and AGNP, Miscellaneous Guild Papers (hereafter MGP).

9 The guild of shoemakers was particularly active in attempting to stamp out competition among the castes and the Indian population: AGNP, MGP (Affairs of the Gremio de Zapateros, 1736-60).

10 AAP, Panaderías, Vol. 230 f. 256.

of guild members. Terms of apprenticeship, costs and content of examinations, fines and punishments (ranging from a few pesos for absence from guild assembly to two hundred lashes or ten years' exile for fraudulent work or sale of goods without examination) were often specified with precision in the ordinances.[11]

Legal backing in the enforcement of guild ordinances, as with most other aspects of economic regulation, was provided by the city council's *Tribunal de Fiel Ejecutoría*, composed of an alcalde, two *consejales* and a notary, with two aldermen elected to it every three months. This body was charged with reviewing the level of prices of most consumer products to ensure the "just price" and to avoid unfair gains by merchants; with periodically setting price assizes (*posturas*) of commodities of basic consumption such as wheat; with preventing illegal buying and selling of goods by regraters (*regatones*) before they arrived to market, and with detecting secret meetings and trading cartels of artisans and merchants. The "*Fiel*" collected the half annate tax (*media annata*) charged upon guild examinations, which provided its principal source of income. In spite of this, Liehr argues that the *Fiel* was generally indifferent to the decline of the guilds over the late eighteenth century.[12]

Ideally, Guilds aspired to guarantee the ordered and fair promotion of officials to masterships, to promote equality of wealth among masters, to protect the various stages and processes of production from outside encroachment, particularly by merchants, and to guarantee quality of product for the consumer at just prices. In practice most guilds fell short of most, if not all, of these ideals. Some examples of guild litigation will illustrate the purpose they fulfilled and help explain how they survived for so long in spite of having ceased to achieve the ideals of their ordinances.

One of the principal developments within Puebla's crafts over the eighteenth century was the encroachment by merchants upon the autonomy which guild masters sought for their crafts. The intensity of this pressure would fluctuate in unison with the fortunes of the external sector. When war interrupted foreign trade and held up imports, merchants sought investment domestically and intensified their commercial control over the crafts. The strategy adopted was generally to form an agreement with a disaffected guild master and to use his knowledge of the art and influence among unexamined guild officials and outworkers to finance a productive structure which could compete favorably with the workshops of dominant guild masters who kept more strictly to the ideal of guild autonomy. Such mercantile encroachment was evident in the hat making industry from early in the eighteenth century.

---

[11] Guild of Iron and Lock workers' ordinances (1748): AAP, Gremios, Vol. 226 fs. 244-252; Woollen clothiers: Zavala, *Ordenanzas*, p. 200-13; Schoolmasters: AAP, Vol. 176, fs. 1-2; Tanners, Shoemakers, Joiners, Sculptors, Tailors, Pasamanerists, Saddlers, Silk Spinners and Weavers, Hat makers: AAP, Vol. 11 fs. 4-196.

[12] Liehr, *Ayuntamiento y Oligarquía*, Vol. II, pp. 36-44.

The affairs of the hat maker's guild throughout the century reveal a struggle by a handful (six or seven) of guild masters, operating large, commercially autonomous workshops to maintain their control over guild affairs, and to resist the practice of lesser masters who supervised hat making in the homes of unexamined outworkers. Low quality hats made against ordinance (or so the guild maintained) were then sold directly to merchants at prices which threatened to undercut the hats made in the large workshops. For most of the century masters operating the large workshops dominated guild affairs although on occasions, either a compromise was reached during a trade recession by which all guild masters would combine to stamp out illegal production, or more rarely and generally in periods of expansion, lesser masters temporarily gained control of guild affairs and succeeded in legitimising mercantile intrusion by applying ordinances less strictly.[13] The result of this tug of war within the hat makers' guild, lasting over a century, was that, far from moving towards the guild's ideal of greater equality among masters, hat making became ever more polarized between a handful of large workshops employing anything up to twenty officials and apprentices, and the majority of workshops, employing less than four officials.

The affairs of the silk-weavers' guild over the eighteenth century show a similar tendency to divide into two caucuses as a result of growing mercantile involvement. Cotton *manta* and indigo dyed silk-cotton shawls (*rebozos*) - Puebla's eighteenth century industrial staples - were produced in smaller workshops than those current in hat making. The 1733 ordinances permitted a maximum of only two looms which imposed a modest scale of production upon master weavers.[14] To maintain their status, it was therefore necessary for masters to retain control over all the processes of production and marketing. The ordinances also reveal that the guild aspired to exercise authority beyond the city to the entire center-west of the region, where the industry was developing so prodigiously over the first half of the eighteenth century.

The activities of the silk weavers' guild were directed at two potential threats to the masters' autonomy and status. The first challenge came from beyond the guild in the attempt by merchants to control raw material supply, particularly spun cotton, and to finance weaving among unexamined officials. This was long struggle in which merchants were ultimately victorious by successfully encouraging cotton spinning and weaving in

---

13 AGNP, MGA, Affairs of the Guild of Hatmakers (1703-68). This conflict is examined more closely in G. P. C. Thomson, "Economy and Society in Puebla de los Angeles, 1800-1850", unpublished D.Phil., University. of Oxford, 1978, pp. 347-351.

14 AAP, Gremios, Vol. 234, fs. 29-50.

rural areas where the guild proved unable to exercise greater control.[15] The consequence was a secular lowering of status of cotton-weavers over the second half of the eighteenth century as the profits from dealing in raw, spun and finished cotton cloth went increasingly to merchants rather than independent cotton-weavers. The guild attempted on several occasions to reassert its authority but succeeded in doing so only for short periods, when merchants had temporarily abandoned the industry, as in 1802, following the Peace of Amiens.[16]

The second challenge came from within the guild and led ultimately to secession and the formation of a cotton-weavers' guild, independent of the silk weavers in 1797. Here guild affairs show silk masters intent upon maintaining the distinction between the less prestigious cotton weaving and the more prestigious *Arte Mayor de la Seda*.[17] A rigorous examination had to be taken before a weaver could pass into the hallowed company of the kind of *rebozo* weavers described in the last chapter. As with hat making, although the guild lost control over cotton weaving, it nevertheless succeeded in preserving the autonomy and exclusiveness of a small caste of fairly wealthy *rebozo* weavers who maintained the viability of the industry after Independence. Manta weaving, however, became a subsistence industry almost entirely subject to mercantile control. This marriage of commerce with craft possessed, however, strong elements of reciprocal interest which were to serve as the basis for the industry's recovery in the 1830s, contributing a popular element to protectionist politics.[18]

The records of the tanner's guild over the eighteenth century reveal how a few master tanners, by enforcing the strict application of guild ordinances, succeeded in controlling an industry, which along with *tocinería*, flour-milling and baking, furnished the wealth of some of Puebla's principal families. The key to the guild's control of the industry was its monopoly of the sale and distribution of a vital chemical, sulphate of copper (*cacalote*), used in the tanning of hides. No pelt could be sold in the city without having been treated in with this chemical. In 1738, the guild strengthened it hold over the tanning industry by gaining a monopoly over the purchase of hides from the municipal slaughter house, itself the city's only source of meat.[19] The activities of the guild over the eighteenth century were dedicated to the enforcement of its monopoly of *cacalote*, with

---

15 For the Puebla guild's loss of control over weavers in Cholula and Tlaxcala : AAP, Gremios, Vol. 234, fs. 86-117, 233-8, 260-7.

16 AAP, Gremios, Vol. 234, fs. 268-78.

17 Guild proceedings against cotton weaver weaving silk: AAP, Gremios, Vol. 234, f. 168, and AGNP, MGA, Affairs of the Silk Weavers' Guild (1740-1776).

18 AAP, Gremios, Vol. 226, fs. 98-100, 139-140.

19 AGNP, MGA, Affairs of the Tanners' Guild (1738).

evidence of litigation in 1707, 1714, 1740, 1751, 1774, 1796 and 1797.[20] For much of the century three generations of a single family, the Bermúdez de Castro, occupied the *alcaldía* and *veeduría* of the tanners' guild.[21]

The tanners' gain was the shoemakers' and saddlers' loss for they, perforce, were obliged to buy their pelts from this small monopoly. The shoemakers' guild was one of Puebla's largest, containing 27 masters in 1736 and 23 in 1811.[22] It was a poor guild, dependent for its raw material upon the often faulty hides supplied by the tanners.[23] It was so poor in 1736 and 1740 that its masters were unable to raise the necessary sum for providing an angel for the Corpus Christi procession.[24] Poverty made the master shoemakers particularly assiduous in rooting out illegal practices and persecuting non-Spanish shoemakers, and inspections of illicit premises often taking place amidst considerable violence.[25]

The affairs of the shoemakers' guild offer vivid insight into the racial and social tensions among Puebla's lower class artisans and the status boundaries which the guilds attempted, largely unsuccessfully, to maintain between the castes. An inspection of all shoemaking premises in 1797, by the *alcalde* and *veedores*, in the company of the *Síndico Personero del Común* and the entire *Tribunal de Fiel Ejecutoría*, reveals the considerable corporate muscle which could still be brought to bear in the enforcement of guild ordinances. But the response to the demand that an offending shoemaker with a stall in the main square comply with ordinances also reveals the contempt felt towards the guilds among unexamined artisans. Rather than submit to guild ordinances Antonio Rosas exclaimed that "he would prefer to close his workshop and go to Mexico, and false manufactures he would make for that Public."[26] Thus, guild exclusiveness should be seen as one of the several factors contributing to emigration over this period.

The affairs of the guild of fine potters were less violent though no less contentious than the struggle of Puebla's shoemakers' guild to maintain control of the craft. Behind the success of a remarkable group of master potters, whose names are still borne by many of Puebla's streets, was the rigid enforcement, for over a century, of the ordinances of 1671. These

---

20 AAP, Gremios, Vol. 26, fs. 113,121,138,164,187.

21 AAP,Gremios, Vol. 233, fs. 3-56.

22 AAP, Gremios, Vol. 233, fs. 3-56; and AGNP, MGA Affairs of the Shoemakers' Guild (1811)

23 AGNP, MGA Affairs of the Shoemakers' Guild (1724-1736), and AAP, Gremios, Vol. 234, fs. 391-3.

24 Each guild was expected to provide a papier-maché angel to lead their section of the guild procession. AGNP, MGA Affairs of the Shoemakers' Guild (1736 and 1740).

25 AGNP, MGA Affairs of the Shoemakers' Guild (1736, 1741 & 1748).

26 AAP, Gremios, Vol. 234, f. 330.

specified that all fine pottery in Puebla should be produced in accord with the techniques and styles developed from Arab models in Talavera, Spain.[27] For over a century the Zayas, Espindola, Micieses, Alfaro, Aguilar, Talavera, Morgado, and Pliego, controlled guild affairs and dominated an industry which, although undergoing cycles of expansion and contraction (forty six enterprises in the late seventeenth century falling to twelve factories during the 1730s-60s, recovering to sixteen in 1794, falling to less than half this number in 1804), provided remarkable stability for this almost endogamous core of families.[28] Freedom to depart from the Talavera style was granted in 1782 in the face of a revolt by masters wanting to work in the Chinese style, a privilege hitherto restricted to a single master potter, Diego Espindola.[29] Greater stylistic freedom, combined with the interruption to imports from the Peninsular caused by war, encouraged a period of growth in the industry before a severe recession set in after 1802.

While space forbids close scrutiny of the affairs of the other guilds, election records reveal that during the period of economic contraction, from the late seventeenth century to the mid eighteenth century, the guilds ensured an impressive continuity and stability for a core of families within each craft. In the iron working industry, the names Arrutía, Yllescas, Ascué and Palomino recur over the entire century; in the wax chandlers' guild Medina, Muñoz, Bertel and De la Cruz fill the records for the 1720s to the 1760s; the Pérez family held the *alcaldía* and *veeduría* of the dyers' guild over the same period. In the carpenters' guild, a single individual, José Carillo (a turner), was inspector for every year between 1732 and 1754, while Ignacio Maldonado occupied the same position in the saddlers' guild between 1736 and 1761. The Portillo and Morgado families controlled guild office in the broadcloth weavers' guild between 1731 and 1761. These were all small guilds of between four and ten masters.[30]

In the second half of the 18th century, the guilds faced mounting problems which so reduced their effectiveness that, by their abolition in 1813, they were in no position to put up a defence. The principal problem facing the guilds was the economic recovery and expansion occurring throughout New Spain as a result of the *comercio libre* reforms and the recovery of silver mining. Guilds were at their most effective in periods of economic stagnation. From the 1770s, but especially over the 1790s and 1800s, when peace permitted, imports of cheaper and stylistically more

---

27 AAP, Gremios, Vol. 227, fs. 137-142.

28 For the affairs of the Fine Potters' Guild, AAP, Gremios, Vol. 227, fs. 52-275; AGN, Historia, Vol. 74, fs. 407-55; and *El Jornal de Veracruz* Vol. I, 1806, p. 146.

29 AAP, Gremios, Vol. 227, fs. 249-60.

30 For a fuller examination of the activities of the guilds: G. P. C. Thomson "Economy and Society", pp. 344-84.

sophisticated manufactured goods grew at an unprecedented rate.[31] The realization must have dawned upon many artisans and master-manufacturers that the ordinances of the guilds could do very little to protect them in the face of what threatened to become overwhelming competition, and that what was needed was much more direct encouragement and protection from government. The transmutation of a guild to a protectionist mentality was no sudden progeny of Independence but was fostered over the half century before Independence in response to increasing competition from overseas.

If the expanding external sector posed problems for Puebla's crafts in peacetime, the long periods of Spanish involvement in war with Britain and then France offered conditions no more favorable for the guilds. Mercantile investment was promptly transferred from imports to speculation in domestic manufacturing so that the guilds faced mounting internal indiscipline and an unprecedented challenge from unexamined artisans, backed by merchants. In late 1790s, with the domestic market temporarily protected by Atlantic war, the guilds are found to be fighting a desperate rear guard action. In 1797, the cotton-weavers were granted their own guild in a vain attempt to bring some order to what had become an unregulated free for all.[32] In the same year, the fine pottery guild complained of the flight of guild masters, officials and apprentices to work for higher wages in unlicensed premises.[33] The guilds of bridle-makers, iron-founders, hat-makers, faced similar problems from unexamined artisans producing in unlicensed premises.[34] Insubordination, drunkenness and general labor indiscipline, combined with a drift of officials from larger licensed to smaller unlicensed unit were the subject of a bitter complaint by Puebla's woollen-weavers' guild to the Viceroy in 1800.[35]

With the signing of the Peace of Amiens, many of the artisans who had been drawn fleetingly into hectic productive activity over the five years of war, faced the immediate prospect of unemployment or emigration to the viceregal capital. To them, guild restrictions, examination fees, prying guild inspections, draconian punishments such as the confiscation of tools or the public burning of looms, must have seemed doubly oppressive. What little legitimacy the guilds still retained was lost over the last decade of their life. Some sense of the opprobrium in which the guilds were held is conveyed in this passage from an artisan broadsheet of 1822:

> Las elecciones anuales de Alcalde y Veedor, los exámenes para poner talleres públicos, el Angel de viernes santo y otro mil socaliñas, al paso que los

---

31 For the growth of imports following *comercio libre*, Ortíz de la Tabla, *Comercio exterior*.

32 AAP, Gremios, Vol. 226, f. 55.

33 AAP, Gremios, Vol. 227, f. 277.

34 AAP, Gremios, Vol. 234, fs. 330-41, and Vol. 226, f. 187.

35 AGN, Industria y Comercio, Vol. 8, fs. 264-66.

112

empobrecían, los exasperaban por la celebre comisón llamada Fiel Ejecutoría,
cuyas boletas para...el Angel....se pusieron aún en el año pasado con la
amenaza de carcel y multa antes de saber la contumacia del Alcalde.[36]

Until their abolition, municipal and viceregal authorities continued to
offer rhetorical support for the guilds. After all, guilds, and the people they
represented, provided an important source of revenue and guild officers and
masters represented an influential group within a potentially unruly sector of
urban society. In practice, though, municipal enforcement of guild
ordinances was, at best, half-hearted, while senior administrators were
outspoken in their opposition to guilds, Puebla's Intendant Manuel Flon
being a notable example.[37] Since the reign of Charles III, the Spanish state
had encouraged the spread of scientific knowledge and technical literature
through economic and patriotic societies. Such public encroachment into
the hitherto private and exclusive domain of the craft guilds made the
"mysteries" of the guilds increasingly redundant and anachronistic. The
Gaceta de Mexico, the *Diario de México*, Antonio Alzate's *Gaceta de
Literatura de México*, and publications of the newly established *Consulado
de Veracruz*, such as the *Jornal de Veracruz* contained by the 1800s an
abundance of technical and practical information for artisans and
manufacturers. In Puebla itself, the private library of the enlightened
Intendant and the libraries of the *Real Seminario Palafoxiano* and the
Academia de Bellas Artes, opened in 1814, contained extensive holdings of
translations of French and British works on applied science and practical
knowledge, to which merchants, manufacturers and artisans would have
had access.[38] By the mid 1820s a reading room for artisans had been
established by the State government and technical publications proliferated
over the early Independence period.[39] The guilds could not hope to

---

[36] Antonio María de la Rosa, *Exito del Proceso*, p. 3.

[37] In 1799 Flon claimed that Puebla's guilds represented only a small number of
unscrupulous masters, long accustomed to exploiting their ancient ordinances to
further their own interests at most artisans'expense. He cited the example of the
guild of iron founders whose sole preoccupation was that an unexamined oficial
should not have a business of his own. AGN, Industria y Comercio, Vol. 23, fs.
173, 178.

[38] For Manuel Flon's influence see:Liehr, *Ayuntamiento y Oligarquía*, Vol. II, p. 128-
29. The library of the Academia de Bellas Artes is now kept in the Biblioteca
Lafragua of UAP. It contains an imposing quantity of eighteenth and early-
nineteenth century French and British applied scientific and industrial literature,
mostly in Spanish translation.

[39] For a letter from a cotton spinner requesting that the artisans' reading room be open
in the evening, work at the wheel not permitting any escape during the day, *El
Caduceo*, Vol. 5, No.3, May 1825, p. 136. Antonio Alzate's *Gaceta de Literatura*
(3 Vols., 1792), despite of its title, a mainly technical and scientific journal, was
republished in Puebla in 1831. A publication specifically for artisans, with many

compete with the State in the provision of up to date technical knowledge. Such an aspiration would, anyway, have gone against the current emphasis upon free access of the individual to knowledge, and, above all, the freedom to apply that knowledge.

Although the decree formally abolishing the guilds came in 1813, Puebla's *Fiel de Ejecutoría* appears to have ignored it, continuing to collect *media annata* taxes on guild elections and examinations until 1819.[40] The restoration of the monarchy in 1814 was followed by an annulment of the decree of abolition. Final abolition came only with Liberal revolution in Spain in 1820.[41] By then, Puebla's guilds had long since ceased effectively to serve the interests of the crafts they claimed to represent. Thus, at Independence, Puebla's artisans stood as "free and equal citizens", swiftly becoming the city's most articulate and vociferous political constituency.

This outline of guild affairs has uncovered some of the processes which explain the social divisions between Puebla's artisans, sketched out in the last chapter. On the one hand, it is clear that the guilds permitted the emergence and survival of a commercially autonomous artisan "patriciate", in the face of growing merchant intrusion into the crafts over the course of the eighteenth century. This they achieved by monopolizing guild offices, controlling entry to the guild, hindering promotion to masterships, limiting production beyond the guild, supervising the sale of goods to the public, and, resisting attempts by outsiders to profit from the marketing of raw materials or finished products. As guardians of the enforcement of their ordinances, the guilds had failed in all of these areas (except that of hindering promotions to masterships) by the end of the eighteenth century. Yet, even a piecemeal exercise of these privileges was sufficient to enable a small numbers of businesses in each craft to attain a leading position and to sustain this over several generations. Many of these businesses weathered the crisis of Independence and their owners contributed importantly to the construction of a protectionist coalition during the 1820s and 1830s.

The other part of the social structure which guild affairs have thrown light upon are the lesser artisans: officials and apprentices awaiting examination in restrictive guilds, such as the Tailors and Hosiers, which systematically blocked promotion, through examination, to masterships; mere employees without guild rights laboring in the workshops of the artisan "patriciate"; unexamined and unlicensed artisans working beyond the guild, financed by merchant intermediaries, and persecuted by guild officers

---

Puebla subscriptions, was the *Semanario Artístico*, published in Mexico City in the early 1840s.

40 By 1819, Puebla's guilds owed the council's *Fiel de Ejecutoría* 995 pesos in unpaid *media annata*, accounting perhaps for the *Fiel's* unpopularity at this time. AAP, Fondos Municipales, Vol. 185, fs. 11-17.

41 Carrera Stampa, *Los Gremios*, p. 275, and Tanck de Estrada "La Abolición", pp. 311-331.

and the municipal *"Fiel"*; and Indians producing competing goods on a smaller scale in the peripheral barrios of the city.[42] It was these people who felt, more directly, the effects of the hectic upturns and downturns in the demand for manufactures, resulting from the vagaries of Atlantic trade and of domestic factors such as epidemics, harvest failures and currency instability. It was people from this group, referred to collectively as *"populacho"*, who flocked to the *barrio de los poblanos* in Mexico City or joined the armies during the wars of Independence.

The Freeing of the Urban Food Supply

The importance of keeping a large city, composed mainly of poor people, fed at fair and acceptable prices accounts for why the ordinances regulating food supply were the most important and consistently applied set of economic regulations. The corporations which enjoyed the privileges accorded by these ordinances contained some of the some of wealthiest and most influential people in the province. It is not surprising, therefore, that deregulation of the city's food supply was the most contentious and drawn out area of economic reform, contrasting with the relative ease of the abolition of the guilds. A brief account of the deregulation of the supply of maize, bread, and meat of the city is essential if we are to more fully understand the rise of protectionism as the dominant ideology among the elite during the three decades following Independence.

I) MAIZE

It was argued in Chapter 1 that, throughout the colonial period, the valley of Puebla appeared to have escaped the full ravages of the subsistence crises which so often afflicted neighboring Mexico City. In proportion to its population, Puebla's immediate agricultural hinterland was far larger than Mexico's. Indeed the valley of Puebla often served as a source of both current and emergency maize and wheat supply for the less well endowed and more densely populated valley of Mexico. As a result of this "natural" abundance, the prices of most basic commodities were lower in Puebla than in the capital. Nevertheless, Puebla's municipal authorities were concerned that cyclical harvest failures and the depressed state of commercial agriculture would leave the city short of food and judged that some kind of corporate inducement was necessary to secure a steady supply.

A public granary (*alhóndiga*), with a reserve (*pósito*) for emergencies, was first established in Puebla in 1626, in response to the sudden influx of refugees to the city following the great flood, food shortages and riots in

---

[42] AGNP, MGA, "Expediente instruído por el Maestro Barranco Sobre que en el Gremio de Sastres no haya Maestro de Trasas" (1805).

Mexico City, when many considered that Puebla might become the viceregal capital. The ordinances were identical to those of Mexico City, themselves modeled on those of Seville, Burgos and Toledo.[43] At first designed for supplying all cereals, from 1666 the *alhóndiga* was used exclusively for storing and marketing maize.

From 1666 until its closure in 1843, the following system for maize sales, with occasional variations, was followed. Maize farmers of substance (henceforth referred to as *labradores*) deposited their maize under cover in storage rooms (trojes), known as "*adentro*", where it was held until they instructed *alhóndiga* officials to sell it. This had to be within a maximum of twenty days of being brought into the city. If the public was unsupplied, granary officials did not have to await permission from the *labradores* before selling, and could sell at their discretion. The *alhóndiga* offered this storage service for *labradores* because most of Puebla's maize came from estates at a considerable distance (mostly in the districts of San Juan de los Llanos and Tepeaca) and in such quantities that it would often not be sold on the day of arrival. Small farmers (*pegujaleros*) and muleteers (*arrieros*), who transported maize from Indian villages on their own account, sold the grain directly from the patio of the building, known as "afuera", on the day it was brought in. The distinction between the *trojes* ("*adentro*") and the patio ("*afuera*") was at once spatial, economic and social. Wealthier maize farmers, selling large quantities of maize in the city, qualified for the services of the *trojes* while peasants, small farmers and petty merchants and muleteers were confined to the exposed patio. Grain was sold from 10 a.m. to 5 p.m. at a price fixed at the level of the first free sales of the day. Sale for resale was not permitted.[44] A tax of one real a *carga* was charged on all entries, to be used for administering the *alhóndiga* and keeping the buildings in good repair.

The council kept its own maize store, the *pósito*, within the *trojes* of the *alhóndiga*. Maize for the *pósito* ideally was purchased in periods of low prices, to be released onto the market either when prices were high (in the hope of depressing them) or, in periods of maize shortage (in order to stimulate maize entries from the region's *labradores*).[45] Maize farmers who were sufficiently well-capitalized to possess barns, habitually held back maize for as long as possible to attain the highest price. In event of a complete maize famine, *alhóndiga* officials were empowered to order

---

[43] AAP, Alhóndiga, 1623-1723 Vol. 109, Expte. 1186; and Liehr, *Ayuntamiento y Oligarquía,* Vol. II pp. 44-7.

[44] For the early history and functioning of the alhóndiga: *Puebla en el Virreinato, Documento Anónimo*. Puebla, 1965, pp. 127-8.

[45] The *pósito* was held partly responsible for the avoidance of famine in Puebla during the "años de hambre" between 1785-7. Leicht, *Calles de Puebla*, p. 296 and AGN, Intendencias, Vol. 59 f. 41.

labradores to release their hoards, even to send out wagons to requisition grain, a desperate measure taken only under conditions of extreme scarcity.

The purpose of the *alhóndiga* was to guarantee a steady supply of maize, the principal diet of a majority of the urban population, at acceptable prices. Manuel Flon, as a physiocrat opposed to economic regulations, nevertheless favored the retention of the *alhóndiga* and the *pósito*, being aware of the strategy among *labradores* of keeping the city in short supply. In 1800, as a result of spiralling maize prices and rumors of abuses, Flon commissioned the councillor, Joaquín de Haro y Portillo, to carry out an inspection of the *alhóndiga*. Haro's findings revealed serious contravention of the ordinances (revised in 1787 after the great famine of 1785-86) and resulted in the first of a series of unsuccessful attempts to reform the institution culminating in its closure in 1843.[46]

Haro y Portillo reported that high prices were less a consequence of the anticipated poor harvest than of systematic abuse of *alhóndiga* ordinances. He reported that patio sellers (small farmers and muleteers) were being prevented from selling except between 12 a.m. and 3 p.m. when their weights and measures were removed. For the rest of the day the *labradores* enjoyed an exclusive right to sell at prices in excess of those received by the patio sellers, "...a practice so harmful to your Public, whose bankruptcy I leave for your consideration." After patio selling had been suspended, the *alcalde* would at first hold back the *labradores'* good maize, selling only maize "so blighted and mildewy... a proceeding so contrary to humanity that I am moved to tears".[47] Moreover, *alhóndiga* officials were receiving commissions (*encomiendas*) for selling the *labradores'* maize, strictly against ordinance. In short, Haro's report showed that the *alhóndiga* was serving principally as the *labradores* maize market, at the expense of the *pegujalero* and the muleteer.

The city council responded swiftly, forbidding the taking of commissions, ordering the stocks belonging to *labradores* to be put on sale each day at two pesos a *carga* less than the price allowed for patio sellers who were to be permitted to sell throughout the day, and into the evening, should they choose.[48] The reforms shifted the balance of advantage firmly in favor of the small farmers and muleteers who sold their maize daily in the patio and against the normally privileged *labradores* who hitherto had sold their maize in their own time (when the price was right) from the "*trojes*". These reforms would have unforseen and adverse consequences for the maize supply of the city during the troubled years which were approaching.

A bad harvest in 1807 marked the beginning of secular price rise which was to continue, apart from brief falls in 1813 and 1818 until the early

---

46 AAP, Cabildo, Vol. 69, f. 195 and Alhóndiga, Vol. 112, "Visitas a la Alhóndiga de Puebla por el Tribunal de Fiel Ejecutoría."

47 AAP, Alhóndiga, Vol. 112, f. 138.

48 AAP, Alhóndiga, Vol.112, f. 139.

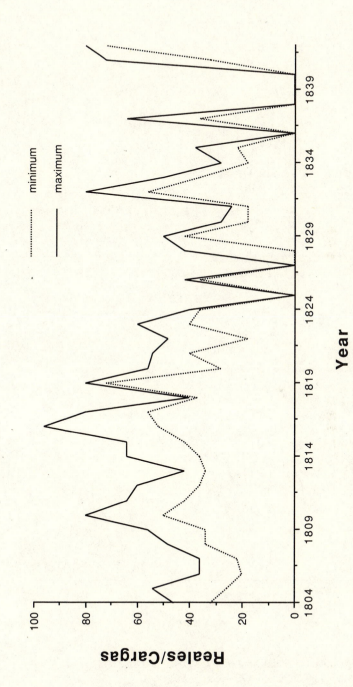

Figure 3.1 Maximum and Minimum Prices for Maize, Puebla, 1804-1842

118

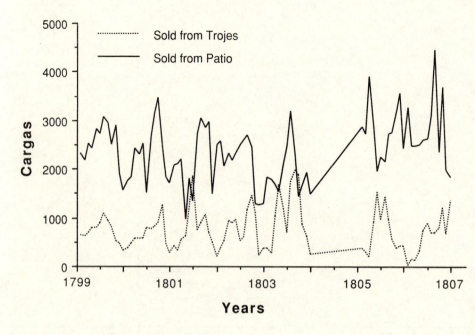

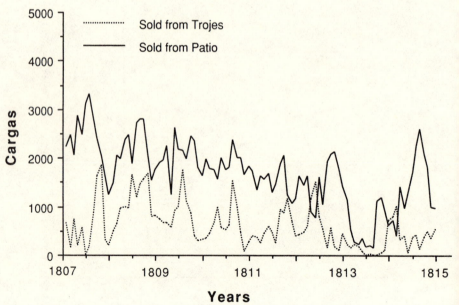

Figure 3.2 Quantities of Maize Sold from the Pósito and Trojes of the
Alhóndiga of Puebla, 1799-1831

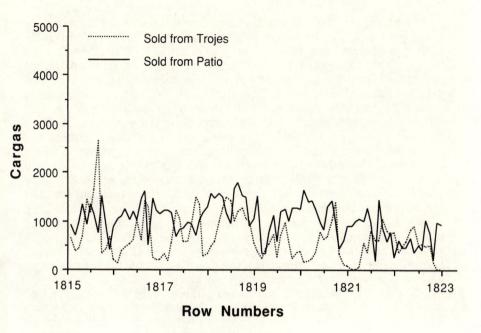

Row Numbers

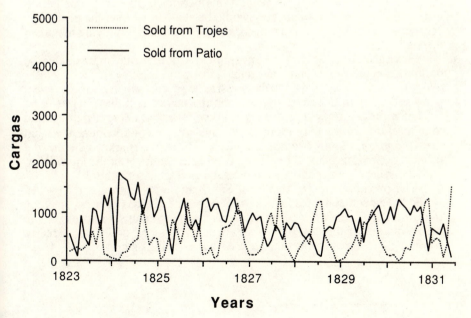

Years

1820s, making any hasty abolition of the alhondiga politically impracticable (see Figure 3.1). An inspection of the *alhóndiga* in 1807 revealed that the problems had not been resolved by the reforms of 1800. José Joaquín Goytía, appointed *alcalde de alhóndiga* in that year, observed that discipline within the *alhóndiga* had broken down, while maize selling in the city had deteriorated into a free for all. The reforms of 1800, which discriminated against *labradores*, combined with six years of low maize prices, had resulted in a marked reduction in maize remissions to the city by *labradores*. Such was the "caprice and absolute license" of the small farmers and muleteers, who had been favored by the reforms, that they not only had the run of the *alhóndiga* but of the streets and plazas of the city where they sold in absolute freedom, often at prices far in excess of the maximum price which the *alcalde* set for each day . The *labradores*, dependent for their maize sales upon the trojes of the *alhóndiga*, found the public already supplied and faced the prospect of their maize rotting in storage.[49] The *alhóndiga* reforms of 1800 appear to have engineered a "Chayonov effect", with the small farmers and muleteers who marketed village maize, taking full advantage of their cost advantage over the more capital intensive cereal haciendas in supplying the urban maize market.

The extent to which the *labradores* had seen their share of *alhóndiga* sales and the urban maize market slip may be observed in Figure 3.2 which shows *troje* sales falling steadily between 1803 and 1807 while sales from the patio increased steeply over the same period. Prices over this period were significantly lower than they would be at any time over the next thirty years, also accounting for the reticence of *labradores* in supplying the urban market

Goytía recommended in his report to Council that maize sales be prohibited in the streets and main square, that patio sales be subject to closer controls by the alcalde, that the daily assize be strictly adhered to (to prevent patio sellers from undercutting maize in the *trojes*) and that the *pósito* be stocked more regularly from the trojes in order to raise depressed prices and to induce *labradores* to remit maize.[50] In short, Goytía recommended that the *alhóndiga* should become the city's sole maize market wherein the balance of privilege should be shifted firmly back in favor of the *labradores*, with the sellers of the patio once more subjected to closer control.

The owners of maize estates of San Juan de los Llanos and Tepeaca would have been delighted had Goytía's recommendations been accepted by the Council. They were being offered an almost exclusive access to the maize market of the city on a plate. But the Council could not agree to confining the sale of maize to the *alhóndiga*, asserting that:

---

[49] AAP, Alhóndiga, Vol.113, fs. 199-206.
[50] *Ibid.*

The establishment of the *alhóndiga* does not exclude the liberty of any individual to sell grain and goods of basic necessity but [it exists] to proportion a *pósito* which assures, as much as it is possible the natural subsistence of the neighborhood.[51]

The substance of Goytía's recommendation was therefore rejected, illustrating the extent to which agricultural interests had lost ground in Puebla city council, now largely dominated by merchants and manufacturers, more concerned with the interests of urban consumers than with shoring up beleaguered *"cuerpos de labradores"* in districts quite remote from the city. From the rhetoric of the above, councillors were clearly imbued with liberal economic principles of the day. But introducing liberal reforms to institutions which had traditionally favored the interests of particular corporate groupings was, in the face of the deteriorating conditions facing commercial agriculture, a risky business, as the next four years would show.

Between 1809 and 1811, central Mexico suffered the most serious harvest failures since the great agricultural crisis of 1785-86. In 1786-87, Manuel Flon, the Bishop and Council had successfully pooled their resources and ingenuity to avoid, in the city of Puebla at least, the hunger which afflicted much of central Mexico. In 1809-1811, the authorities were less well-prepared.

Over the first decade of the nineteenth century, lower than average maize prices, allied to the competition *labradores* were facing in the urban maize supply, appear to have resulted in a decline in commercial maize farming and a run-down of stocks. It is also possible that maize growers were turning to wheat in response to almost unprecedented export demand for flour in the years leading up to the Hidalgo revolt. Even the Council was caught off guard, *pósito* purchases having been minimal in 1808 and *pósito* sales in 1809 and 1810 being quite inadequate to restrain a spiralling price rise.[52] The *alhóndiga* building itself was reported to be in an advanced state of disrepair: the roof leaked, much of the woodwork had rotted and maize often lay sodden and unprotected behind unlocked doors at night.[53]

Late frosts followed by prolonged drought caused the complete loss of the 1809 harvest.[54] Over the first six months of 1810, the Council agreed to apply strong measures against regrating and speculation and ordered that the sale of maize should be restricted to the *alhóndiga* and the main square.[55] Such was the scarcity of maize by May that the Council ordered

---

[51] AAP, Alhóndiga, Vol.113, f. 181.

[52] AAP, Alhóndiga, Vol.114, fs. 27-56.

[53] AAP, Alhóndiga, Vol.112, f. 148.

[54] AAP, Alhóndiga, Vol.113, f. 186.

[55] AAP, Alhóndiga, Vol.113, f. 180.

the *alhóndiga* to cease sales to *tocinerías*.[56] By June the situation had reached a crisis point. Maize speculators, disregarding the Council's orders, continued their regrating of maize beyond the main square and the *alhóndiga*, stocks could not be sold and were rotting and the *labradores* had ceased remissions altogether.[57] Fear of general hunger and social unrest then prompted the Council to take the extreme measure of declaring the *alhóndiga* to be the city's exclusive maize market. Complete freedom from tax and for selling would be permitted, but only within the *alhóndiga* building which would remain open until 8 p.m.. Discrimination in favor of either *labradores* or patio sellers would cease.[58]

This attempt to restore the monopoly in maize supply to the *alhóndiga*, a position it had never really enjoyed, failed. Regrating continued unabated throughout 1810 and 1811 and *alhóndiga* sales continued to fall. By August 1810 the *alhóndiga* was entirely empty prompting the alcalde to order maize to be extracted from the *tocinería* belonging to the Tepeaca landowner Mariano Calderón, one of the largest maize consumers in the city. Very little maize was found there, mostly mixed with barley and oats in preparation for feeding to pigs, and not worth the labor of sorting out. Then, mysteriously, from Tepeaca (whose farmers a few months earlier had declared themselves without a grain of maize)

clean maize of high quality began to arrive from the rancho de Santa María, in carts belonging to the city, bringing relief to the Public, the price was put at ten pesos (80 reales, one of the highest prices registered over the 1804-1843 period), and then many more wagons began to come to supply the Public...[59]

Here then is the proof that the extraordinary prices throughout 1810 were not solely the result of the poor harvest of 1809. The *alhóndiga*'s renewed stock was quickly run down and between September and December. When the extent of the failure of the 1810 maize harvest was appreciated, the Council panicked, spending much of the 50,000 pesos donated by the Intendant on the remaining poor and blighted maize from Tepeaca, even taking the extreme measure of placing an order for 1,500 cargas with a Guatemalan hacienda.[60]

The extraordinary measures taken by the Council to keep the city supplied over this and the following year, and their failure to halt the price rise or ease the supply of maize to an increasingly impoverished and disease afflicted population, reveal the limits of corporate institutions in mitigating the cruel workings of the urban maize market. In January 1811 the Viceroy

---

56   AAP. Alhóndiga, Vol.113, f. 188.
57   AAP, Alhóndiga, Vol.113, f. 196.
58   AAP, Alhóndiga, Vol.113, fs. 189-195.
59   AAP, Alhóndiga, Vol.114, fs. 27-56.
60   AAP, Cuentas (1810).

gave the Council permission to raise 100,000 pesos from a tax on *aguardiente* for the purpose of buying maize for the *pósito*.[61] Because of the insurgency cutting the city off from the sugar and *aguardiente*-producing districts of Izucar, Chietla and Chiautla, this sum could not be raised over 1811. The expensive and poor quality maize bought for the *pósito* in December 1810 could not be sold, rotted and had eventually to be thrown away.[62] A mass desertion of the city during 1811 by men joining the Royalist and Insurgent armies, must have slightly reduced pressure upon the food supply. But Puebla's poor suffered unprecedented hardship and hunger in 1811 which was recognized as a major contributing factor to the high mortality during the yellow fever epidemic of 1812-13.[63]

Only by early 1812, after an improved but still poor harvest in November-December 1811, had the Council received sufficient *aguardiente* revenue to be able to restock the *pósito*. This it did with great haste, little sense and with financially disastrous effects. The purchase of over 17,000 cargas of maize for the *pósito*, amounting to almost a quarter of the city's annual consumption, had the immediate effect of pushing up prices, accounting for their high level through to the excellent harvest of November 1812. Rather than sell the *pósito* maize, *alhóndiga* officials decided, fatefully, to hold onto it in order to see how the 1812 harvest would turn out. Unfortunately the *alhóndiga* buildings were not up to the task of storing such an immense quantity of maize over a hot summer. The *trojes* were filled to overflowing, the walls of the building began to split open and pigeons and worms were reported to be consuming its contents.[64] With the excellent harvest of 1812 it became impossible to sell the now deteriorated maize of the *pósito* in the city. At great financial loss, 13,000 cargas of the *pósito* maize was eventually sold to Mexico City, and the rest either sold to *tocinerías* or thrown away.[65] Prices as well as consumption slumped over 1813, the year of the terrible epidemic.

This three-year crisis in the city's maize supply is observable in Figure 3.2. From June 1809 until October 1812, both minimum and maximum maize prices remained far above the mean for the entire 1804-1842 period. The decline of maize sold by muleteers and peasants from the patio commenced in 1807, dropping precipitously to only one fifth of the 1806 level by 1813 (Figure 3.3). Maize sales by *labradores* from the *trojes*, after a brief recovery in 1808, began a steep decline in 1809, falling to one sixth of the 1808 level by 1813. From July 1812 through to November 1813 sales by *labradores* from the *trojes* all but ceased while patio sales slumped for a shorter period, between February and August 1813.

---

[61] AAP, Cabildo, Vol.80 f.31, and AGNP, RPP, Vol. 40, f. 5.

[62] AAP, Cabildo, Vol. 81, 7 April 1812.

[63] See Chapter 4.

[64] AAP, Cabildo, Vol. 81, 7 April 1812.

[65] AAP, Alhóndiga, Vol. 114, fs. 27-56.

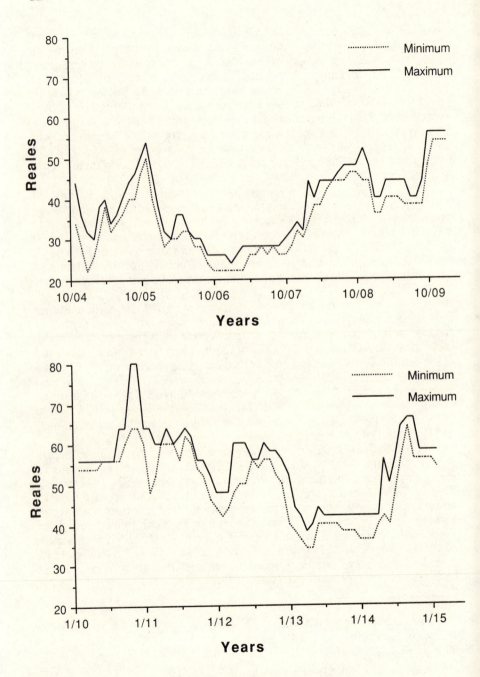

Figure 3.3 Monthly Maize Prices at the Alhóndiga, Puebla, 1804-1814

The sharp variations in monthly maize sales from the *alhóndiga*, with sales generally low in the early months of the year, rising steeply by June and peaking in September and October, is explained by the harvest calendar and monthly price movements. Prices were generally at their highest when maize was at its most scarce over the months before the November harvest. Prices were at their lowest when maize was abundant through December into the new year. From Figure 3.3 it can be observed that, in a minority of years, sales from both the *trojes* and the patio moved quite closely in unison with each other (1799, 1800, 1806, 1808-1811, 1815, 1819, 1825 and 1829). But in most years, peaks in sales from the *trojes* often coincided with troughs in sales from the patio and vice-versa. *Troje* sales in all but very few years were closely bunched over the four or five months before the November harvest with relatively little sold in the other months. In contrast, patio sales, although following the same seasonal pattern, showed less overall variation and tended to peak slightly earlier than the troje sales, in mid-summer, thus often missing the autumn months with the highest prices. By September and October the maize stocks of villages and small farmers had been run down and the advantage passed to the *labradores* who had stored up maize in their barns. This was the time hallowed strategy which the *alhóndiga* was designed to countervail.[66]

Between 1814 and 1817 the city faced a further protracted crisis in maize supply, prolonging the Council's dilemma of what to do with the *alhóndiga*. In June 1814 , taking note of the flight of landowners to the provincial capital and fearing harvest failures in the insurgency-devastated hacienda districts of the plateau, the Council instructed villages in the *tierra caliente* to plant extra maize [67] Figure 3.1 reveals that maize prices rose steadily from February 1814, remaining well above the mean throughout 1815, 1816 and 1817. The high prices over these years were a result of bad weather causing poor harvests compounded by the requisitioning of carriage-mules by troops, a new system of tolls on main roads and extraordinary wartime taxation. From Figure 3.3, which distinguishes monthly sales from the *trojes* from sales from the patio, it seems clear that the latter, dependent as they were upon mule transport, suffered disproportionately from wartime disruption to provincial transport. Figure 3.3 also shows that after a prolonged slump between 1811 and 1814, between 1815 and 1817 estate agriculture had recovered its place in the urban market. Over three years of high prices, for the first time in the century sales from the *trojes* in several months exceeded patio sales, especially in the months of high maize prices, shortly before the harvest. This suggests that the *labradores* found wartime fiscal and military conditions less damaging than their frequent complaints would suggest, and

---

[66] For the classic study of this mechanism: Florescano, *Precios del Maíz*, pp. 88-110.
[67] AAP, Cabildo, Vol. 83, 17 June 1814.

less disruptive than did their *pegujalero* and *arriero* competitors. It was observed in Chapter 1 how wheat agriculture, reflected in rising tithes, also recovered substantially after 1814.[68]

An inspection of the *alhóndiga* by a Council syndic in 1816 confirms that the *labradores* had reestablished their hold over the *alhóndiga*. In his report he accused the alcalde of using the *pósito* merely to benefit the labradores, at the expense of the public. *Labradores* would only allow their maize to be sold at the times of the day when the stocks of the patio had been sold and prices were high. At this moment, the alcalde, instead of putting the *pósito* on sale, thus deflating prices, withdrew it instead, encouraging prices to further rise. Thus:

> far from being a break on the prices of maize of the *labradores* in benefit to the Public, the *pósito* was a mere gift to them, or at least it enabled them to keep their funds in order. It served no other purpose than what the *labradores* normally resorted to, to prejudice the pockets of the common people... [69]

By October 1816 maize was in such short supply that the Council instructed all *subdelegados* of districts to report on the existence of maize stocks in their districts.[70] Following the harvest in November, with the poor of the city facing severe hunger, the Council ordered maize in the district of San Andrés Chalchicomula to be brought to the city forthwith.[71] The harvest was insufficient to prevent prices rising to a historic peak of over 95 reales the *carga* in January and February of 1817, falling over the second half of the year as stocks were run down with the promise of a bumper harvest. Over 1818, for the first time since 1808, maize prices fell below the mean. A decade of crisis in the supply of the city's most essential food was over.

The fall in maize prices in 1818 was to be a brief interlude preceding the final prolonged price rise of colonial Mexico. Since the catastrophic harvests of 1809-1810, high maize prices in Puebla had been more a result of the disruption caused by war, ineffective management of the food supply and market speculation than of particularly bad weather. The ten-year cycle of meteorological crisis which Florescano has observed for the valley of Mexico, returned in 1818 to destroy the maize harvest and send prices once more spiralling upwards.[72] For once, the alcalde of the *alhóndiga* was well prepared, stocking the *pósito* early in 1819, releasing it when prices rose in the months before the harvest, encouraging farmers to bring in their stored maize, thus averting a potentially serious shortage. With the profits from *pósito* sales, the alcalde was able to restock with good Atlixco maize in

---

68   See Figure 1-4.
69   AAP, Alhóndiga, Vol.112, f. 160.
70   AAP, Cabildo, Vol. 85, 2 October 1816.
71   AAP, Cabildo, Vol. 85, 11 December 1816.
72   Florescano, *Precios del Maíz*, pp. 112-139.

early 1820, ready for a further shortage predicted by the Intendant Ciriaco de Llano, which did not materialize.[73] This is one of the few examples of the *pósito* serving the function for which it had been designed. To be effective, however, cash had to be available at the moment that the alcalde judged it prudent to buy. In 1818-19 the alcalde had spent over 55,000 pesos on *pósito* maize. This was a potential drain on municipal funds since *pósito* outlays were rarely recouped. After Independence cash was even scarcer and, although the *alhóndiga* and municipal supervision of the city's maize supply soldiered on until the final closure of the building in 1843, its effectiveness after 1821 was always limited by cash restraints.

Why didn't the provincial and municipal authorities grasp the chance which Independence offered for the abolition of a costly and usually ineffective institution? Practically every other corporate institution, monopoly and set of special privileges had been abolished. Why should the Council still be expected to maintain a building largely for the convenience of maize farmers far away in the districts of Tepeaca and San Juan de los Llanos? A reply verging on cynicism was given to this question in a report from a commission charged in 1839 with exploring the possibility of the closure of the *alhóndiga*. After thorough research into the past and present performance of the institution the commission advised that the *alhóndiga* be retained. It admitted that municipal funds were inadequate to guarantee the ideal function of the *pósito* as a moderator of price rises in years of scarcity or as bait to entice *labradores* to bring their stored maize into the city for sale. Their report concluded, with stark frankness, that:

> In good harvest years everyone speculates and the *alhóndiga* sees little activity, but in years of bad harvests, speculators are few and monopolize sales. Certainly you [the Council] lack the resources to remedy such unfortunate occurrences, but perhaps the Public will be persuaded that the crisis was not your responsibility and not move their lips to complain; but if you auction the *alhóndiga*, the Public is not composed of philosophers, and if left to follow their senses, they will attribute the cause of the evil to you, and your name will be execrated as the author of their ruin and of the *Banco de Beneficencia* [a bank for funding the *Hospicio de Pobres* which had foundered during the copper money crisis of 1837], in which your hopes of averting the hunger which presently threatens them was founded.

The commission advised that the sale of the *alhóndiga* would not "convenience the public good" and should be retained to ensure "the honor and decorum" of the council.[74]

---

73 AAP, Cuentas, Vol. 50, and Cabildo, Vol. 89, 4 Feb. 1820.

74 AAP, Cabildo, Vol. 106, 22 May 1839; and AAP, Alhóndiga, Vol. 114, fs. 234-241.

The retention of the *alhóndiga* should therefore be understood against the climate of tension and uncertainty which prevailed in a city undergoing economic decline, with a large hungry, poor and unemployed population, among whom on several occasions since 1820 order had seemed close to breaking down. Thus successive and municipal administrations after Independence sought to create the impression that they were taking measures to confront grain speculation and to ease the supply of the most basic element in the diet of the city's poor.

The first post-Independence proclamation regulating to maize supply was issued in August 1822, in anticipation of harvest failure resulting from late frosts and drought. It was circulated to all the villages and haciendas of the State. The order *(bando)* established the principle, made explicit for the first time since the free trade decree of 1813, that maize brought to the city could be sold anywhere and at any price. Maize sold in the *alhóndiga* would still be expected to pay a customary due of one real/carga but otherwise there would be no restrictions or privileges except that farmers selling from the *trojes* would be expected to sell their maize at two reales/carga less than the price set for the day and applying to the sellers of the *patio*. The order also promised that mules carrying grain would be exempted from requisition by the military. In spite of these assurances, maize was critically scarce in the city over the winter and spring of 1822-23 with mule embargoes by troops a common complaint.[75] The Council was obliged to spend over 50,000 pesos of its scarce funds for stocking the *pósito*, the last period in which this institution was put to effective use.[76]

For a decade following the agricultural crisis of 1822-23, maize prices remained consistently below the mean (see Figure 3.1) and few problems faced the city's food supply. In 1830 the Conservative state government moved the *alhóndiga* to a handsome and spacious new home in the ex-Colegio de San Luis and in 1831 the *alhóndiga's* ordinances were revised. Recognizing the inadequacy of municipal finances (which had fallen steadily over the 1820s) for sustaining an effective *pósito*, the Council granted the alcalde the right to offer farmers sureties of up to 1,000 pesos at the toll gates of the city if, at any time, sufficient maize for the city's supply was not forthcoming.[77] This authority did not prove sufficient to confront the two major agricultural crises which afflicted the population during the 1830s.

The first maize shortage cruelly accompanied the cholera epidemic of 1833. Anticipating the failure of the harvest, in September 1832 prices spiralled from 48 to 80 reales the *carga* within a few days, as stocks became exhausted and speculators held back grain. Owners of *tocinerías* were ordered to sell their maize to the public, the Bishop instructed tithe

---

75 AAP, Cabildo, Vol. 91, f. 67; Vol. 92, fs. 163 and 221.

76 AAP, Alhóndiga, Vol. 114, f. 108; and Cabildo, Vol. 91, f. 470.

77 AAP, Alhóndiga, Vol. 114.

colecturías to release their grain, and the Governor of the State provided 10,000 pesos from his own pocket for buying maize.[78] These measures failed to compensate for a severe shortage of maize during 1832 and 1833, made more critical by mule embargoes by troops accompanying the Liberal revolution, extraction of grain to Mexico City, grain hoarding and speculation.[79] The guarantees offered by the alcalde of the *alhóndiga* were insufficient to attract maize entries from *labradores* and the city suffered from hunger as well as epidemic during 1833. Prices during the mid 1830s then slumped, Francisco Javier de la Peña reporting in 1835 that population decline and the development of agriculture within the immediate environs of the city had so depressed prices that "the more distant farmers are finding it difficult to cost".[80] Crisis returned after a poor harvest in 1838 and now currency devaluation and the circulation of debased copper was given as the cause of severe maize shortages and hunger.[81]

The commission charged with assessing the continued viability of the *alhóndiga* recommended in 1839 that it should be retained, if only to convince the public that the authorities were taking some measures, albeit largely unsuccessful, to avert recurrent shortages. The commission also suggested some reforms. Funding for the *alhóndiga* should be increased by doubling the tax on sales of maize. The *pósito* should be revived and funded from the tax on wheat and meat entries. The alcalde should be a man of substance and should be allowed to offer a surety to farmers of 2,000 pesos against possible losses.[82] These recommendations were accepted but proved no more effective than earlier reforms in guaranteeing the city's maize supply over this or the subsequent crisis in 1841-42.[83] This crisis, the last to be documented in the *alhóndiga*'s records, followed the failure of the 1841 harvest and was intensified by disruption to trade accompanying the withdrawal of copper money from circulation.

The ineffective management of the 1842 crisis represents the last attempt by the Council to intervene in the city's maize supply. Councillors feared a repetition of the riots of December 1841 occasioned by the withdrawal of copper money. Shortage of maize obliged the forty retail *maizerías*, which had grown to supply the bulk of the city's maize in normal years, to close their doors. The maize supply fell into the clutches of a small number of monopolists, well-informed of the loss of the harvests.[84] The Bishop could not come to the public's aid so depleted were the *colecturías*

---

78 AAP, Cabildo, Vol. 101, 18 Sept 1832, and fs. 359,362.
79 AAP, Cabildo, Vol. 102, 10 Feb 1833.
80 Javier de la Peña, "Notas", p. 139.
81 AAP, Cabildo, Vol. 106, 22 May 1839; Vol. 108, 1 December 1841.
82 AAP, Alhóndiga, Vol. 114, fs. 234-241.
83 AAP, Cabildo, Vol. 108, 1 December 1841.
84 AAP, Cabildo, Vol. 111, 8 December 1844.

since the abolition of compulsory payment of tithes in 1833.[85] To save face, the Council instructed the *alhóndiga* to establish its last *pósito* in January 1842 when prices had risen above 80 reales the carga, anxiously observing that "the public is directing its anger against us for not guaranteeing the value of their reales or providing them with their dinners".[86]

The *alhóndiga* passed an unhappy last three years of active life under the management of the incompetent and corrupt alcalde, Manuel Buen Abad. Apart from personally embezzling 3,629 *cargas* of maize in 1845 (two thirds of all maize entries to the *alhóndiga* in that year), the institution had grown to serve as little more than an ally to an insidious group of maize monopolists who had entrenched themselves during the copper money crisis. After a report on his conduct, Buen Abad was dismissed from his post and the right of the *alcalde* to establish a *pósito* or to advance sureties of 2,000 pesos of public funds to farmers was removed.[87] Deprived of the means to serve its minimum function of contracting maize at times of abject scarcity, let alone guaranteeing the sales of farmers, the *alhóndiga* foundered. The buildings went on sale in August 1848 after their undignified use as a dormitory for American troops in March of that year.[88]

The final abolition of the *alhóndiga* coincided with a marked recovery in commercial agriculture and spectacular urban population growth. These conditions, absent since before 1800, appear to have been more effective than any municipal regulations in guaranteeing a more stable urban maize supply. After 1845, until the end of the period covered in this study no further evidence was found of the chronic maize speculation which had routinely accompanied maize shortages, nor was any more concern expressed by the Council of potentially socially disruptive high prices. The monopoly which had emerged over the copper money crisis appears to have dissolved. In 1852 Puebla was supplied from fifty two *maizerías*, evenly distributed throughout the city.[89]

II) THE ABOLITION OF THE MUNICIPAL BEEF AND MUTTON SUPPLY.

Puebla in 1804 consumed considerably less beef and mutton than in 1698. In 1698, 6,000 cattle and 60,000 sheep were slaughtered in the city; in 1804 only 789 cattle and 35,964 sheep.[90] The decline in the consumption of meat reflects both the changing ethnic composition of the population (Indians were not avid consumers of meat and the number of non-Indians

---

85   AAP, Cabildo, Vol. 108, f. 237.

86   AAP, Cabildo, Vol. 108, 9 August 1841; and Vol. 109, 19 January 1842.

87   AAP, Cabildo, Vol. 112, 15 October 1845.

88   AAP, Cabildo, Vol. 114, 4 March and 7 August 1848.

89   Juan Del Valle, *Guía*, pp. 147-8.

90   Zerón Zapata, *La Puebla*, p. 44, and Manuel Flon, *Descripción*, p. 145.

had decreased) but above all, the decline of the Puebla region as a livestock producer.

The supply of beef and mutton for much of the colonial period was either under strict municipal control or leased to an *abastecedor* who would pay the council an annual rent for what was effectively a monopoly in the supply of beef and mutton. Certain convents, the Bishop, and a few local livestock farmers were permitted to introduce cattle and sheep for their own needs. The municipal *abasto* was auctioned every three years and went to the bidder who could offer the public the greatest weight of meat per real. Once chosen, he had to contribute 2,000 pesos annually to municipal funds, he was sworn to supply the public with all the meat they required and he alone was responsible for any losses incurred to stock "from disease, tempest, fog, rockfalls or theft". He was not allowed to possess any military or religious *fuero*, which would limit his accountability under civil courts. The *matadero* and *carnicería* under his jurisdiction were subject to regular municipal inspections to ensure hygiene and fair prices. He was obliged to supply "good and fat" bulls for the "fiestas de toros" held in the main square, though he retained the carcasses. The *Ordenanzas de carnicería* of 1705 specified the precise details for slaughtering, butchering and selling, in gory detail.[91]

The job of *abastecedor* was a risky but potentially very lucrative one. Most of Puebla's beef and mutton was purchased in the provinces of the *tierradentro* and the journey to Puebla was fraught with hazards. The *abastecedor* depended upon the cooperation of the city councils of the main livestock regions - México, Valladolid, San Luis Potosí, Querétaro, Guadalajara and Durango - who would organize auctions where annual contracts were made with *estancieros* and price guarantees (*posturas*) offered. He would then employ his own shepherds to bring the herds and flocks from the *tierradentro*. He had free use of the *ejidos* around the city but had to compete for inadequate grazing with horse and mule dealers who used Puebla as the principal depot for supplying the Mexican southeast with draft animals. The acreage available for grazing had been greatly reduced over the eighteenth century as a result of unrestricted clay mining by the city's potteries and brickworks. He could maintain his own police force to protect livestock and enforce his monopoly in the supply of meat.

The purpose of the Council's *abasto*, apart from providing revenue for the municipality, was to guarantee for the consumer a steady supply of healthy meat and to guard against private monopoly. The system when operating smoothly kept the public well supplied with meat at low prices.[92] Additionally, the *abasto* kept alive important economic ties between Puebla

---

91 Liehr, *Ayuntamiento y Oligarquía*, Vol. II, pp. 53-5; Leicht, *Calles* , pp. 199-200, 371-2; and AAP, Abastos, Vol. 88, f. 184.

92 During the decade before abolition of the *abasto*, mutton prices varied .51 kilo/real and .60 kilo/real and beef prices between 1.61 kilos/real and 1.95 kilos/real. The median maize price was 3.06 kilos/real.

and the *tierradentro*, the main market for the city's manufactured goods. Letter of exchange were used in transactions between the *abastecedor* and *estancieros* of the interior provinces, which they could redeem in the purchase of goods from Puebla's workshops and wholesalers. In turn, the owners of *obrajes* and tanneries also benefitted from access to pelts and hides which might not have been available in such abundance had the city to rely only upon the supply of the province itself. Thus Puebla remained an important producer of woollen cloth and leather goods long after ceasing to be an important livestock producer. Finally, the regional specialization encouraged by the *abasto* released land in Puebla for arable production, particularly wheat, in great demand at the end of the eighteenth century for the export market. But the system also had its disadvantages. Local livestock producers tended to be discriminated against in favor of dealing with the "great families" of the interior. A distant source of supply was exposed to more hazards than a local one. Finally the *abasto* gave great power to, and placed an immense responsibility upon, a single individual who, either through incompetence or dishonesty, could bring great harm to the public. In the last decade of its life, everything which possibly could go wrong with the institution, did go wrong. The decline and abolition of the municipal *abasto* offers a particularly vivid example of the torrid transition from a regulated to a "free" urban food supply.

In 1796 and 1797 a serious drought desiccated New Spain's northern pasture lands, greatly reducing the size of herds and so weakening animals that their transit to Puebla became impossible. One *estanciero* after another withdrew from contracts and declared their inability to guarantee a price for the following year.[93] In 1798 the outgoing *abastecedor* reported that because of high prices, purchases from the *abasto* had slumped, clandestine introductions of meat had increased and salaries of shepherds and herdsmen were long overdue. Come the end of the year he was unable to auction his post.[94] In 1799 the Council was obliged to take on the direct running of the abasto, establishing a *Junta de abasto* to operate the monopoly. In the first year of direct Council management the *Junta* made a loss of 23,132 pesos and was obliged to raise a loan of 40,000 pesos from the Bishop to cover debts and to invest in the *tierradentro* for the supply of the following year.[95] The Intendant, Manuel Flon, who presided over Council deliberations, then decided that matters had gone far enough. He declared that the entire system of meat *abasto* was "ponderous" and inefficient and ordered the meat supply of the city to be freed for an experimental period, to see whether "the public might be better supplied from local farmers."[96]

---

[93] AAP, Abastos, Vol. 88, f. 170.

[94] AAP, Abastos, Vol. 89, fs. 39-41.

[95] AAP, Abastos, Vol.88, fs. 100-1.

[96] AAP, Abastos, Vol.88, f. 202.

Flon was particularly concerned by how the *abasto*, by favoring the stockraisers of the *tierradentro*, discouraged local enterprise, at a time when, given the sorry state of the province's agriculture, encouragement was desperately needed. He particularly suspected those few privileged manufacturers in Puebla, who had gained preferential access to the hides and fleeces, often reselling them at a great profit. He observed how the wealthy tanner and *tocinero* Bernardo de Aspiróz, councillor in charge of the *abasto* in 1800, used the meat supply to his own advantage. How might the provincial economy benefit, Flon asked, if the orders which Aspiróz had placed in the *tierradentro* for 15,000 head of sheep, had been placed instead with sheep raisers in Tepeaca, the Mixteca or Tlaxcala? Accordingly, in March 1800, Flon granted freedom to "all stockmen who want to dedicate themselves to this traffic, to introduce to the city all the sheep and cattle they wish to sell from the Public butchers or from their own counters providing they recognize the Royal dues and the alcabala."[97]

For a decade after freedom was first granted to the sale of meat, the Council continued to act as price sounder and contractor in the *tierradentro* as well as the principal supplier of mutton and beef to the city. In 1805, the imposition of a new tax upon meat sales, to contribute towards the cost of renewing work upon the Huejoteca drainage dyke for the valley of Mexico, made necessary the reintroduction of a monopoly *abasto*. It was placed under the overzealous and imprudent management of Miguel Verazas.[98] Local livestock producers were instructed to sell only through a limited number of licensed butchers where the tax would be collected.

This proved to be easier said than done. Having tasted freedom between 1800 and 1805 suppliers greatly resented this sudden reimposition of control. Attempts by the Council to stamp out illegal meat suppliers (*capoteros*), were resisted with considerable violence and appear to have met with little success.[99] By October 1810, it was reported that 200 of the 500 sheep consumed in the city each week were introduced illegally.[100] Under such conditions it had become an impossible task for the *abastecedor* to estimate how much should be spent each year in the *tierradentro* to keep

---

[97] AAP, Abastos, Vol.88, f. 168.

[98] AAP, Abastos, Vol.89, fs. 2, 25,27,50,79,80.

[99] The *guardia de abasto*'s attempt to shut down Señor Camarón's butcher's counter in September 1808 was met by a small force led by a mounted Señor Camarón, armed with a blunderbuss, a sabre and a *mojarra* (broad short knife), who shouted "Ningunos Soplones Carajos tienen que registrar mi casa, y assi ya se puedan mudar!", AAP, Abastos, Vol. 168, fs. 212-14, 280.

[100] The *abastecedor* complained bitterly that the religious orders were abusing their privilege, by selling meat from their limosna hatches, properly destined for the poor, to the general public, AAP, Abastos, Vol. 169, fs. 20-9. This privilege, and the right Indians had of introducing livestock "for their fiestas", were abolished in June 1810. AAP, Abastos, Vol. 169, f. 12.

the city supplied. As a result, the *abasto* made large losses: in 1807, when livestock contracted from the interior outstripped local demand, in 1808, when a drought decimated herds already purchased for the city, and, finally, in 1811-12 when 24,000 pesos of the 60,000 invested in the interior was lost as a result of Insurgency.[101] This coincided with the decree of the Cortés conceding complete freedom of commerce. By this time local production had increased sufficiently to enable the Council to relinquish its direct responsibility for keeping the city supplied with meat.

Over the last three years of the *abasto* local farmers increased their holdings of livestock and partially substituted the traditional source of supply from the *latifundia* of the interior. Whereas in 1809 only 6,598 of the 29,455 sheep sold in the city were raised in the province, by 1812 only 2,962 of the 17,187 sheep entering the city were not Puebla bred.[102] The granting of freedom, judging from the customs revenues, was followed by an increase in meat entries to the city between 1813-1816. Customs revenues (and consumption ?) then declined steadily until 1821.[103] The city's meat consumption had fallen dramatically compared with pre-war years. In 1817, roughly 10,000 sheep and 480 cattle were consumed in the city compared to 35-40,000 sheep and 1,000 cattle which regularly were consumed before 1810. By 1821, the city consumed only half the 1817 figure though by 1824 sales had recovered to a level of two bulls and eighty four sheep a day (624 and 26,208 a year respectively).[104] There were twenty four licensed butchers in 1817, twenty nine in 1824, growing steadily over the 1830s and 1840s to reach thirty seven by 1852. A few complaints of fraud and sale of "evil-smelling" meat were heard soon after freedom was granted, but after 1818, when butchers were obliged to display the weight per real of their meat on large boards outside their shops, there appears to have been no major cause for Council anxiety.[105] Meat after all was a luxury and not an item consumed by the poor or by the city's large Indian population.

The abolition of the *abasto* presented none of the political risks which faced the Council when, on so many occasions, it decided against the closure of the *alhóndiga*, particularly since, in the last years, the *abasto* had become such a drain upon municipal funds. The freeing of the meat supply and the abolition of the *abasto* were unpopular among those few merchants and manufacturers who had found it useful in lubricating the channels of inter-regional trade and in providing an exclusive source of scarce raw

---

[101] AAP, Rastros, Vol. 90, fs. 42-4.

[102] AAP, Matadero, Vol. 226.

[103] Customs reveneues of 1,847 pesos were paid on entries of sheep and cattle to the city in 1813, increasing to a peak of 2,271 pesos in 1816, falling sharply to 1,012 pesos in 1821, AAP, Rastros, Vol. 90, f. 112.

[104] AAP, Rastros,Vol. 90, fs. 161-7.

[105] AAP, Rastros, Vol. 90, f. 169.

materials. But end of the *abasto* was undoubtedly popular among a much larger number of local and provincial stockmen and dealers who welcomed the sudden increase in local demand for livestock in the otherwise depressed agricultural conditions of the 1810s and 1820s. The abolition of the *abasto* thus offers perhaps the only example of how a liberal economic reform directly contributed to a marked expansion of production and exchange, to the benefit of local and provincial interests and less privileged social groups.

III) THE CORPORATIST ALTERNATIVE: RESISTANCE TO THE FREEING OF THE BREAD SUPPLY OF THE CITY, 1813-1851

At the turn of the nineteenth century, of all basic foodstuffs, bread was the most regulated in its price and quality, as in the labor conditions under which it was produced. Wheat farmers, millers and bakers constituted a powerful economic group in Puebla, persuading the Council to supervise the production and sale of bread. In spite of population decline during the eighteenth century, the quantity of flour consumed by the city increased from 30,416 cargas in 1698 to 52,951 cargas in 1802, while maize consumption remained largely static over the same period (36,500 cargas in 1698 and 36,677 cargas in 1802).[106] Between 1799 and 1855 wheat flour entries never fell below 43,000 cargas annually (See Figure 3.4). Thus wheat flour contributed more to the *poblanos* diet than any other single commodity. Puebla's urban Indians were also important consumers of bread, particularly *semitas*, buns made from bran and unbleached flour, still produced in the *barrios* to the east of the city.

The *Tribunal de Fiel Ejecutoría* granted licenses to bakers to open businesses, sounded wheat prices from farms and mills three times a year, fixing the assize (*postura*) of wheat and regularly inspected bakeries, checking weights, quality and labor conditions. Baking was confined to an exclusive corporation of a maximum of twenty bakers and had a privileged status among the city's guilds. Bakers took precedence in guild processions, occupied the higher ranks in the urban militia for which they provided many of the horses. But entry to the profession required no demonstration of craft skills or arduous examination, merely a proof of sufficient capital (a minimum of 4,000 pesos) and potential turnover (a daily consumption of six *tercios* of flour).[107]

The wheat assize was the central matter of controversy in the Council's policy towards the baking profession and the wheat supply of the city. As

---

[106] Zerón Zapata, *La Puebla*, p. 46, and Flon, *Descripción*, p. 145.

[107] Liehr, *Ayuntamiento y Oligarquía*, Vol. I, p. 33.

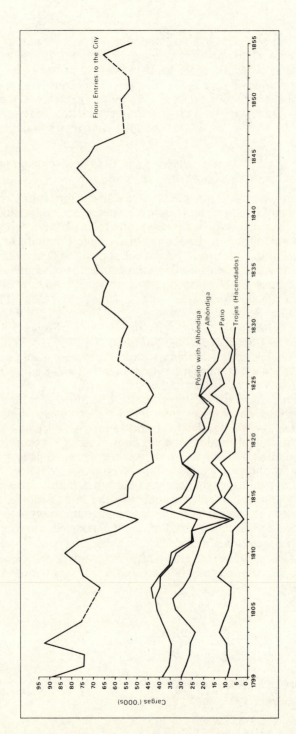

Figure 3.4 Cereals in Puebla, 1799-1855

early as 1767, the wheat assize had been temporarily abolished in an attempt to prevent collusion between bakers, farmers and councillors who would receive bribes during the sounding period (*calicata*) when the price for the subsequent four months was being fixed. However, the unstable conditions facing wheat agriculture during the last half century before Independence prompted the restoration of the assize on several occasions (1769, 1777, 1789 and 1802). The principal purpose of the Puebla wheat assize was to provide a basis for profitability in a beleaguered agricultural sector facing an erratic external market. The aim was to set prices in slump years above their "natural", free market level, in order that farmers receive a "just" price, sufficient to keep them in business.[108] The Puebla assize stands in strong contrast to the wheat assizes of Mexico City and Buenos Aires which were set by councils representing consumer interests and opposed to the monopolizing tendencies of farmers acting in concert with millers and bakers to force prices above their "natural" and "just" levels.[109]

In January 1813 Puebla's wheat assize was finally abolished and complete freedom was granted to the manufacture and sale of bread. A set of regulations issued in the following year show, however, that the Council was not prepared to leave the city's wheat supply and baking profession completely unregulated. Farmers were prohibited from "holding back, hiding, hoarding and regrating" on penalty of a fine of 2,000 pesos. Bakers were free to sell at prices they chose but these had to be displayed clearly on a board outside their shops and must reflect no more than "a just and moderate gain". Bread rolls could only be sold in even numbered quantities, not in odd numbers or with an extra piece thrown in (the "baker's dozen"), to ensure fair competition. Cartels and reselling of wheat by millers, sifters and bakers were prohibited, as were "companies and confederations" of farmers, bakers and millers. A permit from the *Fiel Ejecutoría* was still required before opening a bakery. The *Fiel* would retain its tutelary role, inspecting bakeries regularly and keeping a book of transgressions. The Intendant reserved the right to reestablish the assize.[110]

A four year wheat price rise, following the abolition of the assize, raised concerns about the wheat supply falling into the hands of a group of grain speculators and there were calls for its restoration echoing over the

---

[108] The retention of the wheat assize in Puebla, so long after physiocratic consellings from Spain had counselled its abolition, may be explained by the continuing representation of landholding interests in municipal government, in spite of the rise of merchants(whose interests any way, as we have seen, overlapped closely with the estate owning sector, because of the flour trade). Liehr, *Ayuntamiento*, Vol. II, pp. 66-74.

[109] Lyman Johnson, "The Entrepreneurial Reorganisation of an Artisan Trade: The Bakers of Buenos Aires, 1770-820", *The Americas*, Vol. 37, 1980-81, pp. 139-160; and María del Carmen Calvento Martínez., "Intereses parrticulares y política de abastecimiento en México", *Revista de Indias*, Vol. 36, 1976, pp. 159-160.

[110] AAP, Panaderías, Vol. 87, f. 43, and Cabildo, Vol. 84, 28 November 1814.

subsequent twenty years.[111] The last of these, in 1835, will shortly be examined more closely. The abolition of guild privileges and barriers to entry to the profession brought important changes to baking over the 1810s and 1820s. The number of bakers expanded from twenty in 1813 to thirty six a year later, numbers shrinking to twenty nine in 1817, remaining at this capacity over the 1820s and 1830s.. Two bakers with important flour milling interests, whose families between them owned one fifth of all bakeries, were prosecuted in 1817 for fraudulent under-weight sales and "unjust" prices. The same two families, the García de Huesca and the Furlong, appear to have been behind "a plot to tyrannize the Public" and push up prices in 1824, culminating in a short-lived reassertion of price control by the Council.[112] Thus, freedom, rather than leading to a greater equality of wealth among bakers resulting from greater competition, appears instead to have permitted the consolidation of a core of powerful families for whom baking was merely a part of wider enterprises, often including flour milling.

A decade now passed during which few complaints were heard from baker, council or public about the price of bread. The baking profession retained the same size in 1835 as it had in 1825 and the same families were prominent: García, Furlong, Caámano, Olaguibel and Ramírez. However, many bakers by the mid 1830s were concerned about declining sales, falling prices and unfair competition from those bakeries (one suspects of the kind owned by the Furlong family) which formed part of larger businesses, often including flour mills and wheat estates. This was a period of severe shortage of silver coin, resulting in the emission of copper money, a source of particular anxiety in a profession which provided such a basic item of consumption. In September 1835, a group of bakers petitioned the Council for a return of the wheat assize existing until 1813, drawing attention to the general disorganization of the trade and warning of the harm to the public which would arise from its breakdown.[113]

The basis of their argument was that a wheat assize - in Puebla an assize which would necessarily raise rather than lower wheat prices - would provide the bedrock of value which would enable the long-depressed provincial economy to recover. By establishing a stable, controlled and centrally enforced minimum priced for wheat, a virtuous chain of reactions would be set in motion. With more certain prices, investment would once again be directed towards agriculture, provincial trade would recover, money in circulation would increase, industry would revive, labor would be employed, wealth would be more evenly distributed, political conflicts would be mollified, and so on. Here was De Quesnay's *Tableau Economique* at work on the minds of a group of bakers in what, after all,

---

[111] AAP, Cabildo, Vol. 84, 7 January 1815

[112] AAP, Panaderías, Vol. 87, fs. 42-7,104; Cabildo, Vol. 93, fs. 101,145-47.

[113] AAP, Cabildo, Vol. 104, 25 September 1835.

was Mexico's most important wheat-growing province. The bakers for whom the return of the assize had a particular appeal were those whose bakeries represented their sole livelihood and who managed their own businesses. They were particularly concerned by the growing inequalities of wealth and asked the Council why bakers should be so much poorer than other merchants ?[114]

The Council promptly established a commission to examine the bakers' petition. The Commission's report fully supported the bakers' argument and, indeed, elaborated upon it. A four monthly assize would guarantee a moderate gain to the baker, a less adulterated and better quality bread for the public, fewer bakers would suffer bankruptcies, more would be in position to advance credit to farmers, who would be able to operate their estates more effectively in response to a more stable and attractive urban market. And, not least, municipal funds would benefit. The system of regulation through periodic promulgation of bands, the commission argued, had failed: "The Bands ruin only the honorable man who carries them out, while others take advantage of them in their disobedience."[115]

The Council, in spite of the presence of four bakers upon it (Calderón, Morales, Manzano and Olaguibel), decided, after several long and heated debates, against accepting the Commission's recommendations, on grounds that the restoration of the assize would be harmful to the "public good". They admitted that bakers would benefit but feared that prices would held artificially high and that the public would be harmed. Since freedom had been granted, the city had never been so abundantly supplied from so many retail outlets (there were 137 bakeries and *vendajes de pan* in 1835).[116] The Council decided in favor of the continuation of the policy of periodically issuing bands and inspecting bakeries.

Had the petition of Puebla's bakers and the report of the Commission been accepted, and the wheat assize restored and enforced, the history of the subsequent twenty years might have been very different. Agriculture and food processing would have attracted more investment and less money would have gone into risky ventures, involving the introduction of a new technology, producing expensive goods for an uncertain market. Puebla's precocious attempt at early industrialization might not have occurred.

The debates of 1835-36 over the restoration of the assize mark an important watershed in the disintegration of a narrow corporatist mentality and the emergence of a more broadly based protectionist coalition in Puebla. They reveal a constructive, albeit unimaginative, response to economic depression from an influential section of the urban elite. For wheat farmers, millers and bakers, the restoration of the assize offered a much less strenuous path to economic recovery than the industrial investments which

---

[114] AAP, Cabildo, Vol. 104, 16 May 1836.

[115] *Ibid.*

[116] AAP, Cabildo, Vol. 104, 31 August 1836.

many chose to make between 1837 and 1842. Joaquín and Cayetano Ramírez, bakers in 1835, had become spinning factory owners by 1839. Diego Ibarra, Baltasar Furlong, Mariano Carranza and Manuel Caámano, also bakers in 1835, had joined the Ramírez brothers as industrialists by the early 1840s. Several flour mill owners, possessing water powered buildings ripe for conversion took similar decisions: Cosme Furlong, Manuel Rangel and Luis Haro.

In spite of the failure of bakers to restore the wheat assize as the fount of value in the provincial economy of Puebla, baking and flour milling, although undergoing a decline in the number of enterprises, attracted investment and prospered over the 1840s with the recovery prices, urban demand and the market of the Mexican south-east. Baking continued to be subject to regularly reissued municipal bands and inspections, and bakers kept a close eye upon each other, drawing the Council's attention to fraud and "contraband" activities among fellow bakers on several occasions.[117] Figure 3.4 shows that the amount of flour entering the city between 1836 and 1846 often reached pre-Independence levels. In the 1847 tax assessment twenty two bakers and ten flour sifters and packers, along with wholesale merchants and spinning factory owners, were the highest assessed businesses in the city. Thus, to be a baker in Puebla in 1850 was no less prestigious or lucrative than it had been in 1800, in spite of the abolition of the guild and the assize.[118]

Tocinería: from Guild to Protectionism, 1757-1852.

From the sixteenth century until the late nineteenth century, Puebla was Mexico's main center of pork treatment (*tocinería*). The city's specialization in *tocinería* was fostered as a result of the abundance and high quality of the local quicklime (*tequesquite*) used in soap manufacture and the curing of ham, the relative cheapness of barley and maize used for fattening pigs, and the geographical and commercial advantages which were examined in Chapter 1.[119] The industry's heyday was during the first half of the eighteenth century, the city's consumption of pigs doubling from 40,000 in 1698 to 80,000 in 1746, when fifty *tocinerias* were active.[120] Throughout

---

117 AAP, *Panaderías*, Vol. 82, fs. 103-16.

118 The barrage of indignation from Puebla's flour millers and sifters, following the introduction of 3,000 barrels of US flour to Veracruz in September 1851, is evidence of the recovery of the Puebla flour trade, *Iniciativa que la H. Legislatura del Estado de Puebla lleva al Congreso General que no se apruebe el pryecto de ley relativo a permutar la introducción de Harinas por el Puerto de Veracruz*. Puebla, 1851.

119 Mariano Fernández de Echeverría y Veytía, *Historia*, Vol. I, p. 302.

120 Juan Villa Sánchez, *Puebla Sagrada*, p. 70; and Leicht, *Calles*, p. 40.

the later colonial period, until the end of the period covered in this study, *tocinería* shared a triumvirate, along with flour milling and textiles, at the head of the city's manufacturing industry.

From the fattened pig of *tierra fría*, bred in the districts of Tepeaca, San Juan de los Llanos and Huamantla, came many of the basic essentials of life: pork meat (the meat most commonly consumed by the city's poor); ham, *cecina* and sausage (*longaniza*) for the *tierra caliente* and the Caribbean; soap for the Caribbean and much of New Spain and Central America; lard used for cooking throughout Mexico where olive oil was scarce and hardly used; and tallow, for the candles of the poor.[121] The high value of a fattened pig ready for slaughter, between seventeen and twenty pesos was common during the eighteenth century, the same price as a mule, twice that of a horse or an ox, inevitably confined the business to the well off. The restrictive municipal licensing policy for *tocinerías* limiting their number to fifty, the requirement that prospective entrants to the business show sufficient capital, the limits upon the time that animals could be held in the city before slaughter, requiring at least access to, but preferably possession of, a rural estate, all tended to reenforce the privileged nature of the profession.

After bread baking, *tocinería* was the most closely regulated of the city's economic activities. The central abuse which the Council sought to extirpate was the rearing and fattening of pigs within city bounds, considered dangerous to citizens' health and offensive to principles of good urban government (*buena policía*). This offence, committed chiefly by smaller concerns, known as *chiqueros* or *trapiches*, was the most common cause of Council prosecution between 1658 and 1702.[122] Over the first half of the eighteenth century such abuses appear to have been overlooked, perhaps because the prodigious expansion of the industry permitted the *tocinería* and the *trapiche* to exist side by side. Over this period soap was well established on the lists of goods exchanged with Venezuela's cocoa, and, it seems that much of the Spanish Caribbean was supplied from Puebla's factories until the middle of the eighteenth century.[123]

During the second half of the eighteenth century, the fortunes of Puebla's *tocinerías*, as with wheat agriculture, flour milling and other industries, were closely tuned to the vagaries of Spain's military involvement and the interruption this brought to Puebla's Caribbean market and to Atlantic trade. Over this period, Puebla's *tocinerías* faced a secular

---

[121] At the end of the seventeenth century, Puebla was consuming 40,000 pigs annually. In 1804 Puebla consumed 40,000 pigs to Mexico City's 50,600 in 1791. This was recorded as a bad year for Puebla's *tocinerías*, consumption rising to between 80 and 90,000 in 1808-9. Mariano Fernández, *Historia*, Vol. I, pp. 302-3; Leicht, *Calles*, p. 40; Flon, *Descripción*, p. 145; and Kicza, *Colonial Entrepreneurs*, p. 196.

[122] AAP, Tocinerías, Vol. 232, fs. 94, 106, 113, 144, 119, 166, 231, 237.

[123] Arcila Farías, *Comercio*, pp. 96-103.

decline in extra-regional and overseas demand in the face of competition from other centers of population within New Spain as from the Peninsular and, towards the end of the century, from the United States. To compensate for the deteriorating competitive position of *tocinería*, a guild was formed, the *Gremio de Tratantes de Ganado de Cerdo*, receiving ordinances in the 1757.[124] The *tocineros* became Puebla's most active guild over the half century before freedom was granted to the business in 1813. As in the seventeenth century, litigation concentrated on the "illegal" activities of *trapiches*, now regarded by *tocineros* as dangerous competitors in a shrinking market place. The Council was prepared to grant the guild considerable corporate weight for two reasons: *tocinerías* became an important source of municipal funds and *tocineros* or families with interests in *tocinería* succeeded in gaining solid representation on Council, a position they retained until the end of the period covered in this study.[125]

This close relationship between the *tocinería* business and the local and provincial administration was first evident during the Seven Years War which interrupted Caribbean demand for temperate foodstuffs. In the face of declining demand, the guild in 1757 ordered a general inspection of all premises. Several businesses found to be violating ordinances were ordered to be closed, an order which appears at first to have been ignored.[126] In 1759 members of the guild were ordered to pay a municipal tax towards the cost of maintaining the urban militia which had been put on a war footing with the intensification of the conflicts in the Caribbean.[127] In the following year, the guild, now an important contributor to municipal funds, was more successful in confronting competition from the *trapiches*. The Council accepted the argument put forward by Roque de la Peña and Pedro Alvarez, representing the guild, that the poor quality of the *trapiches* product was hazardous to the public health. Thirty-eight *trapiches*, many of them operated by women, were ordered to be closed within three days. In the face of a public uproar, thirteen *trapiches* were reprieved and thirteen others permitted to register as "medios casas", paying a reduced municipal due, while the remaining twelve were ordered to remain closed indefinitely.[128]

The reform ensured a decade of stability for the industry: there were 26 tocinerías in Puebla in 1759 and 28 in 1771. The 1770s then brought a further phase of spectacular growth to the industry, the number of *tocinerías* increasing to 45 by 1775 and to 49 by the end of the Anglo-American

---

[124] Liehr, *Ayuntamiento y Oligarquía*, Vol. I, p. 75, note 86.

[125] Liehr, *Stadtrat*, pp. 195-201.

[126] AGNP, Miscellaneous Judicial Proceedings of the Gremio de Tratantes en Ganado de Cerda (1759), AAP, Tocinería, Vol. 232, f. 269; and Vol. 233, fs. 1, 83.

[127] AGNP, Miscellaneous Judicial, Proceedings of the Guild of Tocineros (1759)

[128] *Ibid.*

war.[129] The decline in demand, once peace was made in 1782, brought a renewed onslaught upon the smaller enterprises on several occasions until early 1790s. Pedro Álvarez, who remained *alcalde* of the guild over this period succeeded in closing down all *trapiches* and *medios casas* in 1791, forbidding, in the following year, the granting of new licenses to anyone seeking to enter the profession.[130] By 1796 only 19 of the 49 tocinerías existing at the peak of overseas demand in 1781, remained in production.[131]

Spanish involvement in the Napoleonic wars from 1793 was not accompanied by the normally expected wartime increase in demand for temperate foodstuffs. This was because of competition from the United States through the *comercio de neutrales*. Only with the prohibition of neutral trade in 1800 did Puebla's *tocineros* encounter a relatively protected Caribbean market, the industry expanding impressively from 24 units in 1801 to 35 *tocinerías* in 1804.[132] The signing of peace brought this investment surge to an end. In 1803 the guild declared many of its members to be bankrupt while others were closing down due an increase in the price of stock and the low price assize for soap and candles which prevented them from covering their costs of production.[133] Under these conditions of hectic upturns and downturns in demand, there was little the guild could do for its members beyond pleading for the assize to be increased.[134] Certain enterprises, however, were in a far stronger position to confront this instability than others, even to profit from it.

An example of a *tocinero* who seemed to thrive on instability was Mariano Calderón. Owner of maize estates in Tepeaca, Calderón acquired in 1802 a *tocinería* and three houses from Ignacio Carmín y Cervantes for 20,000 pesos.[135] He accommodated himself swiftly to guild affairs, obtaining fines and closure orders for two *tocinerías* in 1803, that of José Cárdenas, allegedly for producing inferior lard, and Pedro Bringas, for

---

129 Don Antonio Barcina y Zárate's *tocinerías* are a good example of a business which prospered as a result of the increased overseas demand accompanying the Anglo-American War. In 1797 he left his two *tocinerías* and a fine house (recently remodeled by Puebla's great late eighteenth-century architect, Maestro Mayor Antonio de Santa María Inchauurrigui), valued at 48,675 pesos, to his nephew, Gregorio Porras. See Leicht, *Calles*, pp. 262-280, and AGNP, PN, No. 5 (1797).

130 AGNP, Judicial Miscellaneous, Proceedings of the Guild of Tocineros, 1781, and AAP, Tocinerías, Vol. 233, fs. 232-51.

131 AAP, Militar, Vol. 116, f. 23.

132 Loans to tocinerías: AGNP, RPP, Censos, Vol. 38, fs. 110, 116, 119, 156; AAP, Militar, Vol. 116, fs. 289-306; and Liehr, Ayuntamiento, Vol. I, p. 24.

133 AAP, Tocinerías, Vol. 233, f. 268.

134 AAP, Tocinerías, Vol. 233, fs. 218, 286.

135 AGNP, RPP, Censos, Vol. 38, f. 119.

operating an unlicensed *trapiche*.[136] Calderón's influence was also behind a renewed onslaught on *trapiches* in 1809.[137] By the end of the wars of Independence, through to the 1850s, the Calderón family dominated the *tocinería* industry.

In the three years preceding the Hidalgo revolt the industry returned briefly to its ancient splendor. In 1808 and 1809, between eighty and ninety thousand pigs entered the city in each year, double the number of 1804. In 1809, 38,588 lbs of soap, valued at 144,772 pesos left the port of Veracruz for the Caribbean market.[138]

Instability of demand over the last forty years of the colonial period resulted in a more frequent turnover of enterprises, the disappearance from the lists of proprietors of the great *tocinero* families whose businesses had been established early in the eighteenth century (Bringas, Izarduy, Espino-Barrios, De la Peña, Barcena, Malpica and Durán). Instability also appears to have favored the concentration of ownership in the hands of small number of families who grew to dominate the industry. This last point can be clearly observed in a survey of stock held in the city's *trapiches* and *tocinerías* in 1820. Of the thirty four enterprises, more than one third were owned by the Calderón, Rodríguez and Domínguez families, who owned 30 percent of all the pigs held in the city. A single enterprise belonging to Joaquín de Haro y Tamariz contained one third of the city's pigs ready for slaughter.[139]

The war did less harm to *tocinería* than to other industries because, until the late 1820s, competition from imports was much less acute. Importers still concentrated on high-value, low-volume goods. Nevertheless, with export shrinking and ceasing altogether after 1826, the number of *tocinerías* and *trapiches* declined from 50 in 1805, to 34 in 1820 and 1825. The closure of 11 *trapiches* in 1825, a year in which the *tocineros* José Maldonado and Francisco Calderón were serving as *alcaldes ordinarios* suggests that smaller enterprises were no less vulnerable from punitive Cabildo inspections than before the guild was abolished and freedom of manufacture granted. In 1825 four families: the Calderón, Rodríguez, Domínguez and Gómez had grown to dominate the industry, owning 12 *tocinerías* between them, almost half the establishments.[140]

Over the late 1820s and the early 1830s, the industry entered the leanest period since slump of 1803-05. Soap exports ceased after 1826 and foreign soap and tallow, mainly from the United States, assumed a growing importance in the domestic market. In 1831 the owners of *tocinerías*

---

136 AAP, Tocinerías, Vol. 233, fs. 233,.300-301.

137 Leicht, *Calles*, p. 40.

138 Javier de La Peña, "Notas", p. 149, and Miguel Lerdo de Tejada, *Comercio Exterior*, "Balanzas 1808-1809".

139 In 1822, 2375 pigs were housed in 34 *tocinerías* :AAP, Tocinerías, Vol. 234.

140 AAP, Padrón de Tiendas, 1825.

petitioned the State congress for an import prohibition on *tocinería* products.[141] They claimed to be speaking on behalf of the pig breeders, the carpenters "who were employed exclusively in making soap boxes", the cashiers of the pious works who required punctual payment of interest on mortgages lent to *tocinerías* and the muleteers who transported the finished products. The Liberal revolution of 1832 delayed any swift response to this plea but with the return of the Conservatives in 1834, an import prohibition was conceded on all foreign lard, ham and soap in February.[142] Puebla's *tocineros* also faced internal competition. Francisco Javier de La Peña claimed that "four or six monopolists" (was he referring to Calderón, Rodríguez, Domínguez, et al.?), by importing twelve to sixteen thousand inferior pigs from the *tierradentro*, and by producing cheap and insanitary soap and lard, were ruining the pig breeders of the districts San Juan de los Llanos, Huamantla and San Andres Chalchicomula (many of whom owned *tocinerías* in Puebla).[143]

The prohibition, which seems to have applied both to goods (including livestock) from abroad as from other states, brought a swift and impressive recovery to the industry. By 1835, 50 *tocinerías* were in production in Puebla, of which 43 were rated in the first class tax category, in contrast to only 25 first class businesses registered in 1825.[144] This is a stark illustration of the dynamic impact upon the local economy of an import prohibition, rendered more effective in these years by the slump in foreign trade. That tocinería had once more become a highly profitable industry is supported by the return to the business of two prominent Puebla merchant-tocinero families; Francisco Javier de la Peña, a leading Conservative, and Joaquín de Haro y Tamariz, Governor of the State in 1828 and 1841, both owning *tocinerías* in 1835.[145]

Over the subsequent seventeen years, tocinería appears to have enjoyed a steady prosperity, inferred by a stable ownership pattern. The Calderón family, who entered the business in 1801, still possessed four houses in 1852; the Domínguez family, entering the business in 1820, remained in tocinería in 1852, as did the De la Peña (entering in 1771), the Abelleyra (1825), the Gómez (1820), the Hernández (1835), the Cabrera (1835) and the Breton (1835).[146] The old dialogue between the *tocinería* and the *trapiche* continued but assumed a very different form. Instead a closed corporation of·*tocineros* uniting to use all the legal and illegal means to root

---

[141] *Representación que los comerciantes del giro de tocinería han elevado al Honorable Congreso de este Estado*. Puebla, 1831.

[142] AAP, Leyes y Decretos, Vol. 6, p. 37.

[143] Javier de la Peña, "Notas", p. 149.

[144] AAP, Padrón de Tiendas, 1835.

[145] *Ibid*.

[146] del Valle, *Guía de Forasteros*, p. 141-2.

out competition from the smaller producers, individual tocineros appear to have taken advantage of the protected market to render the *trapiches* dependent upon their larger houses. Thus the decline in number of *tocinerías*, from 50 in 1835, to 33 in in 1846, to 24 in 1852 does not reflect a contraction of the industry so much as the transfer of production, on the part of the more efficient or persistent businesses, from larger to smaller units. Over the same period, the number of *trapiches* increased from 3 in 1835, to 28 in 1846, to 63 in 1852. There was a strong fiscal incentive for this shift, since the smallest enterprises were not taxed. So while in 1835 all but 7 *tocinerías* were listed in the first tax class, by 1847, 27 of the 35 *tocinerías* were listed in the fourth and fifth tax categories, with no first class establishments at all.[147] Juan del Valle commented in 1852 that Puebla's 63 *trapiches* were "dependent on the *tocinerías*", which would employ one or two operatives to extract lard and tallow and cut soap away from the main *tocinería* building.[148]

The emphasis upon quality control and health safety, which *tocineros* had used before 1835 to justify their pressure upon Council to close the *trapiches*, no longer was a concern once the *tocineros* had succeeded in controlling this sector and were themselves departing from the rules. After 1835, the *tocineros*, once the most politically articulate body of entrepreneurs in the city, became the most silent. There is no better illustration of the consequences of protectionism. The relatively exposed market before the prohibition of 1835 had witnessed successive struggles between politically influential larger producers and clandestine "small fry". The prohibition created an economic space, shielded from overseas and extra-regional competition, within which old enemies, the *tocinerías* and the *trapiches*, could rationalize production and minimize their tax burden. Here, then, is a glimpse at the political, as well as the economic, adhesive values of protectionism, a matter to be explored much more fully in the second part of this study.

Conclusion

By Independence, the abundance of economic regulations and corporate privileges which had existed at the turn of the nineteenth century, had mostly been abolished. The 1813 decree, granting freedom to all to produce or sell whatever and wherever they chose, was no sudden forced march from a corporate to a liberal political economy. After the first century of its foundation, when Puebla had been one of the least regulated provincial capitals in the Indies, the city accumulated a body of ad hoc corporate privileges and economic regulations - guilds, monopolies, price

---

[147] AAP, Padrón de Tiendas, 1847.
[148] del Valle, *Guía de Forasteros*, p. 142.

controls - designed to favor principally the Hispanic population. They illustrate the willingness of the colonial state to underwrite a hierarchical urban social order and to protect a provincial economy over a period of prolonged recession. But at no time during the colonial period was the urban economy of Puebla systematically regulated. At the end of the eighteenth century, life was far harder for the guildless artisans of Mexico City, among whom Puebla enjoyed the reputation for providing a freer and less regulated environment.[149] Paradoxically, the proliferation in Puebla's guilds, monopolies and economic regulations during the 18th century, coincided with the growth in influence of merchants whose unregulated activities (particularly after *comercio libre*), worked as a solvent upon the effectiveness of economic groups - such as artisans - holding corporate privileges. By the end of the colonial period merchants had grown to assume a preponderant influence within the Cabildo, perhaps accounting for the swift and unlamented abandonment of corporate privileges and economic controls.

During the eighteenth and early nineteenth centuries, the ordinances of the guilds (when enforced by the Cabildo) served to bolster the interests of certain economic groups: guild artisans, bakers and *tocineros*. The craft guilds aspired to, but never attained (in contrast to the bakers and *tocineros*), corporate control over their crafts. It seems clear that the purpose of the craft guild in Puebla was to defend a significant share of production for the benefit of a small number of leading artisans in each craft, against the challenge of smaller scale producers, often backed by merchants. Thus Puebla's guilds (some and by no means all) succeeded in preserving productive structure, free from mercantile control, which might otherwise have succumbed once Spanish capital took flight and foreign competition intensified, after 1810. Furthermore, the existence of a large body of respected and articulate artisans, many of whom had played a leading role in guild affairs, added weight to Puebla's protectionist lobby during the decades following Independence. Protectionism, as was suggested earlier, was the re-articulation of the corporate mentality, nurtured by the guilds, on the level of state and national politics.

This chapter has also examined the measures taken by the cabildo to supervise the city's food supply with the purpose of ensuring a balance - on the basis of the "just price"- between the interests of urban consumers and the marketers and producers of food. In baking and *tocinería*, the abolition of price and corporate controls in 1813 was swiftly followed by a concentration of ownership, with a few families becoming dominant in each industry. Thereafter, it is clear that both bakers and *tocineros* succeeded in concerting sufficient direct political influence to compensate for their loss of corporate privileges. True, bakers failed to persuade the *cabildo* to re-establish the wheat assize as the fount of value in the provincial economy, a measure which, if implemented, might have led the Puebla economy along a

---

[149] Carrera Stampa, *Los Gremios Mexicanos*, p. 267.

very different path from the one it was to follow during the 1830s and 1840s. This notwithstanding, the bakers, flour millers, flour sifters and flour merchants remained a powerful economic group, matched only by the wholesale cloth merchants and textile factory owners by the early 1850s. The *tocineros* found, in the import prohibition they achieved in 1834, a solution to the joint challenge from imports and small-scale *trapiche* production which they had faced since the mid 18th century. No longer having to compete with better quality imports, the *tocinerías* went into business with the *trapiches*, their former rivals, which proliferated in number over the 1840s.

The most long lasting corporate institution was the *alhóndiga*. Because of maize shortages, caused as much by political as by meteorological factors, the cabildo was obliged to continue attempting to balance the interests of the impoverished urban consumer with those of maize farmers, who hoarded grain in order to sell at times of high prices. However, the *alhóndiga* and the *pósito* appear to have done little to moderate the intensity of price rises: They served more, perhaps, as a means for forestalling criticism of the cabildo during politically embarrassing periods of maize shortage. such as between 1841-42. The maintenance of the *alhóndiga* until the mid 1840s, when the alcalde's pilfering finally ruined its reputation, enabled the *cabildo* to demonstrate that it served broader interests than those of the merchants, shopkeepers and manufacturers who comprised the council chamber and to show that it cared for the welfare of the city's poorest consumers. The reasons for the *cabildo*'s prudence will become clear in the next two chapter which look, among other things, at the social and political disorders of the first fifteen years of Independence.

Chapter 4

THE POPULATION OF PUEBLA, 1700-1833

Over half a million people inhabited the Intendancy of Puebla in 1793, making it the most populated after Mexico. After Guanajuato, Puebla was also New Spain's most densely populated province. Only Guanajuato and Zacatecas had smaller surface areas. In 1803 Humboldt compared Puebla's land area to that of Aragon and noted that its population exceeded that of Catalonia. A French geographer (delving into the 1793 census in the Mexican National Archives in 1865) was surprised to find only 55,010 whites residing in a region which he judged perfect for white settlement: "el país más bello, el más puro, el más productivo y el más elevado del Anahuac". After three hundred years of colonization, Spaniards and Creoles comprised only 10 percent of the population, the mixed races 15 percent, and the Indians, numbering 373,752, made up almost three quarters. Only Oaxaca had a smaller non-Indian population than Puebla, 11 percent of a population of 411,000 in 1793.[1]

The small size of the white population, in a province for so long settled by Europeans, was indeed a sign that Puebla was no longer the magnet to Spanish settlers which the region had been over the sixteenth and early seventeenth centuries. The pole of attraction for immigrants had long since passed to the provinces of the *tierradentro* where, by 1793, non-Indians everywhere represented well over one half of the population.[2] The apparently fragile demographic hold of Puebla's whites was a result of two phenomena which this chapter will seek to clarify. The first was the high rate of emigration beyond the region, chiefly to Mexico City and the interior provinces. The second was that overall population growth was kept in check by high levels of mortality from epidemics which recurred with

---

[1] Alexander von Humboldt, *Ensayo Político*, pp. 51, 104-6, 157-161, and De Jourdanet, "De la Estadística de México," *BSMGE*, lst Series, Vol. 11, 1965, p. 243.

[2] Humboldt, *Ensayo Político*, p. 51

unprecedented frequency between the great typhoid outbreak of 1737 and the first cholera of 1833.

The Demographic Decline of the Provincial Capital and the Center-west During the Eighteenth Century

An examination of Puebla's sluggish demographic performance over the eighteenth and early nineteenth centuries offers both a commentary upon as well as an explanation for the province's economic stagnation. Table 4.1 shows changes in Puebla's population between the ecclesiastical census of 1681 and the national census of 1873. Over this period of almost two hundred years Puebla's population grew by less than two thirds with average annual growth of around 1.1 percent. Before 1793 and after 1824 the average growth rate slightly exceeded this while between these dates, and probably well into the 1830s, the population of the province remained static or in decline.

In 1681 the center west of the province (including the districts of Puebla, Amazoc, Totomehuacán, Cholula, Huejotzingo, Atlixco and Tochimilco, see Figure 4.1 for the regions) contained almost half of its total population and three quarters of all non-Indians, 90 percent of whom resided within the boundaries of the city of Puebla. By 1743 the share of the center west had increased to almost 60 percent of the total population of the province, while this region's share of the non-Indian population had increased to around 80 percent, more than three quarters of whom resided within the capital. It was during this period of sustained recovery of the Indian population and continued growth of the non-Indian population - unbroken by severe epidemics - that conditions became propitious for the early development of the cotton textile industry.

The typhoid epidemic of 1737 appears as a great watershed in Puebla's demographic history. Thereafter a remarkable shift in the regional demographic and racial balance occurred. Between 1743 and 1793, the center-west's share of the province's population declined from 56 to 30 percent of the total while its share of the non-Indian population plummeted from 80 to 42 percent, only a third of whom still resided in the provincial capital. A remarkable scattering of the non-Indian population appears to have occurred bringing a general redistribution of the population within the province as a whole. Without research in parish records, a full understanding of this historic demographic shift is not possible. However, Table 4.1, combined with other evidence, offer some important clues.

The north's share of overall population (including the districts of San Juan de los Llanos, Tezuitlán, Tlatlauqui, Zacapoastla, Tetela, Zacatlan, Huauchinango and Huayacotla) remained at around 18 percent between 1681 and 1793. However, the north's share of non-Indians increased from 10 to 20 percent reflecting a process of white and mestizo colonization which would have important repercussions in the nineteenth century when

TABLE 4.1 POPULATION DISTRIBUTION IN THE PROVINCE OF PUEBLA, 1681-1873

Zones	1681 Total	1681 Non-Indian	1743 Total	1743 Non-Indian	1793 Total	1793 Non-Indian
North	43,440	7,850	87,375	5,405	156,456	26,768
Center/W	116,735	59,805	154,975	87,455	149,487	54,515
Center/E	29,740	3,340	33,790	8,125	72,538	22,322
South/W	25,470	5,960	34,655	4,900	56,077	17,436
South/E	27,940	1,970	46,444	3,350	72,096	7,744
Total	243,325	78,925	357,239	109,235	506,654	128,785

	1824	1869	1873
North	163,929	201,470	202,986
Center/W	129,025	160,853	178,788
Center/E	69,170	69,798	77,116
South/W	59,960	94,481	95,694
South/E	85,432	116,325	111,479
Total	507,516	642,927	666,063

ZONES:
North: San Juan de los LLanos, Zacapoastla, Tezuitlán, Tlatlauqui, Tetela, Huauchinango, Huayacotla.
Center/W: Puebla, Amozoque, Totomehuacán, Cholula, Huejotzingo, Atlixco, Tochimilco.
Center/E: Tepeaca, Tecamachalco.
South/W: Izucar, Chietla, Chiautla, Acatlan.
South/E: Tepeji, Tecali, Tehuacan.

Sources: 1681: Peter Gerhard, "Un Censo;" 1743: José Antonio Villaseñor y Sánchez, *Teatro Mexicano*; 1793 and 1869: BSMGE, 2nd Series, Vol. II, p. 360; 1824: *Memoria presentada al congreso primero constitucional de Puebla*, Puebla, 1826; 1873: Emiliano Busto, *Estadística de la Repúblic Mexicana.*

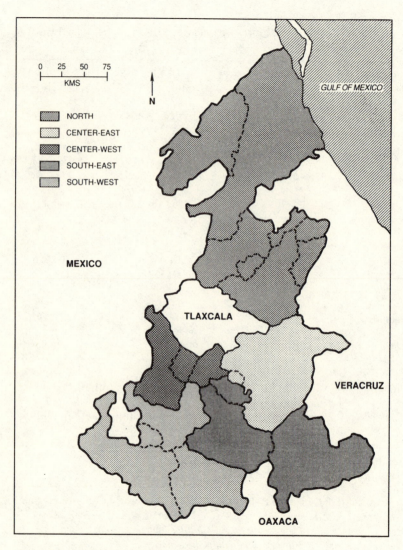

Figure 4.1 Regions of the Province of Puebla

this area assumed the leading edge of the province's economic development and often provided its political leadership. Its share of overall population increased from 17 to 32 percent between 1793 and 1824, when its population exceeded (by 35,000) that of the ancient demographic core of the center-west, a position maintained over the nineteenth century. The growth in number of cattle and sugar estates in this region, particularly in the *tierra caliente* of Huayacotla and Tezuitlán, from 59 in 1791 to 206 in 1804, is further evidence of the expansion of the northern rural economy, and of hispano-mestizo society, in what had hitherto been a largely Indian and commercially unproductive backwater.[3]

The north was not the only sub-region not to have shared the demographic stagnation of the center-west after 1743. The center-east's share of the provinces's population (including the districts of Tecamachalco and Tepeaca) fell from 12 to 9 percent between 1681 and 1743, but then recovered to 14 percent in 1793. More significantly, non-Indians share of the Tepeaca's population increased from 11 to 30 percent between 1681 and 1793. The number of small estates in the center east was also increasing at the end of the eighteenth century, from 121 ranchos in 1791 to 203 ranchos in 1804.[4] The south-east (including the districts of Tepeji, Tecali and Tehuacán) and south-west's (including the districts of Izucar, Chietla, Chiautla and Acatlán) share both of overall population, as of non-Indian population, was also increasing over the eighteenth century. The growth of the white and mestizo population of the district of Acatlán is particularly noticeable, the number of ranchos here increasing from 16 to 43 between 1791 and 1804.[5] The sub-regional picture therefore is not so dismal as the overall figures suggest, since in each sub-region of the province, except the center-west, the non-Indian population can be observed gaining ground while their overall population appears to have benefitted at the expense of the center-west.[6]

The province of Tlaxcala shared the center-west's demographic stagnation. This was to be expected since Puebla's neighbor formed an integral part of the economy of the center-west. Tlaxcala's Indian

---

3 For the increase in number of ranches: (1791) AGN, Padrones Vols. 22, 25, 27, 38; and AGN, Historia, Vol. 73 Expte. 4, (1804), *Jornal de Veracruz*, Vol. I, 1806, pp 129-228.

4 *Ibid.*

5 *Ibid.*

6 During the second half of the eighteenth century, the growth rate of New Spain's Indian population was higher in the sparsely populated margins of the viceroyalty, where land was more abundant, than in the core. This observation fits the Puebla case well, the more extensive northern and southern districts enjoying a higher rate of growth than the more crowded and great estate dominated central districts. Delfina E. López Sarrelangue, "Población indígena de la Nueva España en el siglo XVIII," *Historia Mexicana*, Vol. XII, 1963, pp. 516-30.

154

population suffered disproportionately from epidemics, there being 8,000 fewer Tlaxcalteco Indians in 1801 than there had been in 1681. Trautmann has observed the phenomenon of village abandonment which accompanied this decline. Tlaxcala's non-Indians increased only modestly over the century: from 12,460 in 1681 to 16,270 in 1793. Thereafter, Tlaxcala's population remained static until well into the nineteenth century.[7] What, then, accounts for the relative stagnation of the center-west, including Tlaxcala, from time immemorial the demographic and economic core of south eastern Mexico? Tentative answers can be found in three substantial parish studies.[8]

The parishes studied by Malvido, Calvo and Morin, fall within (or immediately adjoin in the case of Acatzingo) the center-west zone: San Andrés Cholula, three miles to the west of the provincial capital, Acatzingo, twenty miles to the east, and Santa Iñes Zacatelco, fifteen miles to the north west. All three predominantly Indian parishes are in rich, well-watered, agricultural areas which experienced sustained and impressive population growth between 1650 and the epidemic of 1737. For the three parishes this epidemic was a watershed between a long and uninterrupted period of demographic recovery and an unstable century over which serious epidemics became more frequent. The three parishes barely maintained or lost population between 1737 and 1810. The records of births show that the Indian population maintained the high fertility responsible for its recovery before 1737 but, thereafter, higher mortality in frequent epidemics and high rates of emigration kept overall population stagnant or in decline.

The non-Indian population of these rural parishes did not share the poor performance of the Indian population. In Zacatelco, Morin shows that in 1724 non-Indians numbered only 142 living within twenty one households among 6,700 Indians. This tiny non-Indian population was characterized by impermanence and mobility as if, "uncomfortable among a demographically aggressive Indian community." By 1795 the non-Indian population was much more firmly established. It now stood at 569, occupying 100 households, among a smaller number of Indians than in 1724. The higher mortality rate of Indians compared to non-Indians between 1783 and 1821 is revealed in the ratio of births to deaths: Indians 108:100, non-Indians 225: 100. Consequently, non-Indian families were significantly larger than Indian families.[9] It was within these non-Indian households that domestic manufacturing took root and was sustained over

---

[7] Wolfgang Trautman, *Las Transformaciones*, pp. 66-120, 260.

[8] Claude Morin, *Santa Iñés Zacatelco (1642-1812). Contribución a la Demografía Histórica del México Colonial*. Mexico, 1973; Thomas Calvo, *Acatzingo: Demografía de una Parroquia Mexicana*. Mexico, 1973; Elsa Malvido "Factores de despoblación y reposición de la población de Cholula (1641-1810)", *Historia Mexicana*, Vol. 23, 1973, pp. 52-110.

[9] Morin, *Santa Iñés*, p. 65.

the eighteenth century. The district of Nativitas (containing Santa Iñés Zacatelco) housed over three quarters of Tlaxcala's 4,000 looms in the early 1780s, rivalling the city of Puebla.[10]

Lower mortality among non-Indians did not lead, however, to the rates of population growth that might have been expected, in either Zacatelco or Acatzingo. This was because emigration from both parishes was chronic, Calvo estimating that 20 percent of the non-Indian population of Acatzingo (not a textile center) emigrated annually between 1742 and 1791.[11] Morin estimates that at least 8,000 Indians and non-Indians left Zacatelco between 1736 and 1796.[12] Manufacturing districts were more successful in retaining their population with Nativitas and Chiautempan, Tlaxcala's cotton and woollen weaving centers, being net gainers of non-Indian migrants over the second half of the eighteenth century.[13] However, in the center-west overall, the non-Indian population declined over the eighteenth century, largely, it seems, as a result of migration to other parts of the province or beyond.

The first port of call for migrants would probably have been the provincial capital. It might be expected, therefore, to find Puebla's population swelling over the eighteenth century. This was not the case. Instead, Puebla's overall population veered between stagnation and decline while the decline of the city's non-Indian population was more marked than that of the center-west as a whole. How can this be explained ? Did migrants simply pause in Puebla, before proceeding to the more dynamic peripheries of the province or to *tierradentro*? Or did they merely serve to top up an urban population increasingly prone to high mortality from epidemic disease? Evidence for answering these questions is sparse but a brief account of the demographic history of the provincial capital suggests its inhospitality to migrants, as evidence from the viceregal capital reveals the magnetic attractions of that city for migrant *poblanos*.

Over the eighteenth century, in spite of its demographic decline, Puebla de los Angeles was the greatest population concentration in south eastern Mexico. In 1681 its population stood at 67,765, of whom only 14,500 were Indians (34,095 "castes" and 19,170 whites).[14] Between 1650 and the 1737 epidemic the Indian population of the city grew steadily, doubling

---

10 Garavaglia and Grosso, "Consideraciones", p. 45.

11 Calvo, *Acatzingo*, p. 73.

12 Morin, *Zacatelco*, p. 58.

13 Trautman, *Las Transformaciones*, p. 106.

14 Peter Gerhard, "Un censo", p. 532; the Cathedral chapter estimated that there were 69,800 communicants in the city in 1678, José Muñoz Pérez, "Una descripción comparativa de las ciudades americanas", *Estudios Geográficos*, Vol. 15, 1954, p. 120.

TABLE 4.2 POPULATION OF THE CITY OF PUEBLA 1678-1791 BY PARISH

Parish	Ecclesiastical 1678	Civil 1743	Ecclesiastical 1746	Municipal 1771	Civil 1777 (i)	Ecclesiastical 1777 (ii)	Ecclesiastical 1779	Civil 1791
Sagrario	37,000	-	27,097	-	25,427	24,533	25,428	
San Jose	15,000	-	12,965	-	9,260	7,157	7,883	
Santo Angel	8,000	-	5,511	6,119	4,802	1,684	4,746	5,256
San Sebastian	4,600	-	2,898	-	3,791	3,784	3,446	3,330
Santa Cruz	3,200	-	1,905	-	5,362	2,534	5,312	3,599
San Marcos	(incl. in Sagrario and San José)	-	(incl. in Sagrario and San José)	-	7,526	7,603	7,055	7,207
TOTAL CITY	69,800	-	50,366	-	56,168	7,295	53,870	56,859
TOTAL DISTRICT	-	91,000	-	71,366	-	-	66,484	60,733

Sources: 1678 Juan Villa Sánchez, *Puebla Sagrada y Profana* (1146) p. 65. These figures are based upon the Bishop's assessment of the numbers of communicants in the city. They do not therefore include children below the age of first communion; 1743 Jose Antonio Villaseñor y Sánchez. 1746 Juan Villa Sánchez. p. 65. 1771. AAP, Padrón del Curato de Sto Angel (1771).1777. (i) AGN, Historia, Vol. 73, Exp. 5, 24 Dec. 1777. (ii) AGI, Mexico, Audiencia, Vol. 2578. 1779 Franz Tichy, "Siedlung und Bevolkerung." 1791. AAP, Padrones. Vol. 128-129.

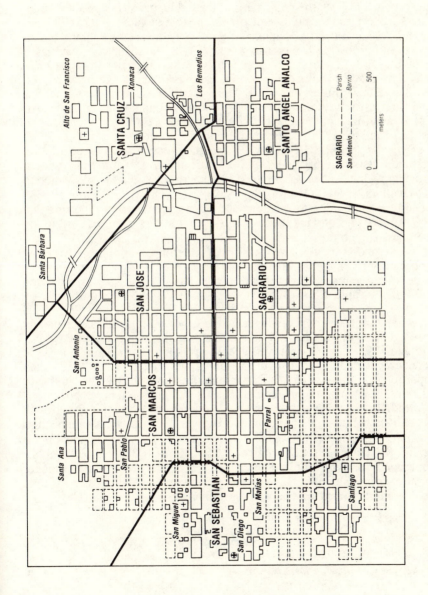

Figure 4.2 Puebla's Parishes and Barrios

between between 1700 and 1735.[15] As a result of the epidemic of 1737, however, the city's Indian population had slipped back by 1743 to only slightly more than in 1681. An estimated 54,000 people from all castes died in the city in 1737-38, the population of the Indian parishes of Santo Angel Analco, San Sebastián and Santa Cruz falling to two thirds of its 1678 level by 1746.[16] The non-Indian population grew at a slower rate than the Indian population before 1737, increasing from 53,365 in 1681 to an estimated 75,000 by 1743. The latter figure appears to reflect its size before the 1737 epidemic for by 1746 the city's population overall stood at a mere 50,366 (See Table 4.2 and Figure 4.2). Here is the first sign that Puebla's population growth, continual since the city's foundation in 1532, had become reversed. Not until the end of the nineteenth century would the level reached before the 1737 epidemic be regained.

Over the second half of the eighteenth century the city's population fluctuated between 50 and 60,000, until the 1813 epidemic which, combined with a deepening of the economic crisis, caused the population to fall to well under 50,000 during the 1820s.[17] The cholera epidemic of 1833 reduced the population to less than 40,000, a contemporary reporting that "sus numerosos barrios casi han desaparecido por una serie de calamidades, y no presentan mas de soledad y ruinas....".[18]

What accounts for the failure of Puebla's population to grow significantly over the eighteenth century ? Was it high mortality from frequent epidemics ? High rates of emigration ? Unhealthy urban living conditions ? Table 4.3 shows that, over the 1737-1833 period, mortality during major epidemics was higher in Puebla than in Mexico City. This was evident in the typhoid epidemic of 1737, when deaths in Puebla greatly exceeded those in Mexico City, in the three smallpox epidemics of 1761-2, 1779 and 1797-8, when deaths in Puebla approached or exceeded those in the viceregal capital, and in the yellow fever epidemic of 1813 when proportionately more *poblanos* then *capitalinos* died. Only in the cholera of 1833 was the scourge of epidemic disease more lightly felt in Puebla.

Studies of the impact of epidemics upon rates of population growth have shown, however, that populations recover their size and continue their growth remarkably swiftly following epidemics.[19] Thus the the doubling of Mexico City's population between 1750 and 1838, while Puebla's population remained static, cannot be explained solely by the latter's higher mortality from epidemics. Indeed, there is strong evidence to suggest that, in non-epidemic years, Puebla was a healthier place than Mexico City.

---

15 Gunter Vollmer, "La evolución cuantitativa de la población indígena en la región de Puebla (1570-1810)," *Historia Mex cana*, Vol. XXIII, 1973, p. 46.

16 Villa Sánchez, *Puebla Sagrada*, p. 65.

17 AAP, Padrones, Vols. 30-38 (1821 Census for the city of Puebla).

18 De la Peña, "Notas", p. 133.

19 E. A. Wrigley, *Population in History*. London, 1969, pp. 6-74.

TABLE 4.3 PUEBLA AND MEXICO CITY POPULATION, 1740-1848: MORTALITY FROM MAJOR EPIDEMICS

PUEBLA

Year	Whites	Indians (Tributaries)	Total
1735			
1736		6,782	
1737 EPIDEMIC			54,000
1742	15,000 families	1748	91,000
1746	50,366		8,049
1750	90,000		
1754	7,262		
1761/62 EPIDEMIC - Smallpox and *Matlazahuatl*			9,160
1764		5,169	
1775			4,400
1775	56,168	4,934	
1779	28,813	53,870	
1779 EPIDEMIC - Smallpox & Measles			18,000
1786		5,705	
1793		3,425	56,859
1797/98 EPIDEMIC - Smallpox			10,000
1800	3,746	9,672	
1801	2,985		
1803	67,800		
1813	123,907		
1813 EPIDEMIC - Yellow fever			7,089-17,000
1822/23	47,842	165,000	
1833 EPIDEMIC - Cholera			5,000
1848	71,631		

MEXICO

Year	Whites	Indians (Tributaries)	Total
1736	6,786		
1737 EPIDEMIC			40,150
1742	50,000 families	8,400	98,000
1761/62 EPIDEMIC - Smallpox			14,600
1772 EPIDEMIC - *Matlazahuatl*		1	3,000 deaths
1779 EPIDEMIC - Smallpox			estimates of 9-20,000
1793	52,706	8,893	130,602
1797/98 EPIDEMIC - Smallpox			7,143
1803	67,500		137,000
1810/11			150,000/168,846
1813 EPIDEMIC-Yellow fever			20,385
1833 EPIDEMIC - Cholera			9,619
1855			200,000

This is demonstrated by the twice yearly recordings of births and deaths made by Mexico City and Puebla *ayuntamientos* during the 1830s and 1840s. Table 4.4 shows the ratio of births over deaths in Puebla to have been, on average, significantly higher than in Mexico City. This, of course, might be explained by the loss of Puebla's population through emigration, the city's emigrants dying elsewhere. Mexico City, a net gainer of immigrants, saw its death-rate correspondingly increased. But Puebla's average monthly excess of births over deaths, amounting to 53, is still impressive when put against the much larger city's average monthly excess of births over deaths: six. And the figures for Puebla correspond to the period of the late 1830s and 1840s when the pace of emigration might be expected to have slackened, as a result of the city's economic recovery. Of course, neither city could boast an urban environment of comparable health to that of Philadelphia. Pennsylvania's capital had a comparable population to Mexico, yet enjoyed a monthly excess of births over deaths averaging 229 during the 1820s. But then, the Philadelphia of Dr Benjamin Rush, freed at last of the scourge of yellow fever, was reputed to be be healthiest city in the United States.[20]

Even if it is true that Puebla was a healthier place than Mexico's disease-ridden capital, the critical variable affecting the demographic performance both of Puebla and Mexico City was almost certainly the rate of migration. Once economic prospects in Puebla improved from the late 1830s, its population recovered very rapidly. Was this simply due to the retention of people who otherwise would have migrated ? Or did economic recovery encourage greater fertility, as contemporaries argued ?[21] The period of Puebla's recovery was one of economic stagnation in the capital, its population increasing only slowly during the 1830s and 1840s. Frederick Shaw observes that continual immigration was necessary to compensate for Mexico City's normal excess of deaths over births.[22] Looked at this way, it is remarkable that Puebla succeeded in maintaining a fairly stable population over the eighteenth century, given the high mortality from epidemics and the hemorrhage of population from migration from which the provincial capital and the center-west appear to have suffered so disproportionately.

So it seems certain that out-migration rather than epidemic disease or high average death rates accounts for the stagnation of Puebla's population over the eighteenth and early nineteenth centuries. Over this period the provincial capital served more as a funnel through which migrants passed to

---

[20] G. P. C. Thomson, "Mexico and Philadelphia", p. 33; *American Journal of Medical Sciences*, Philadelphia, November 1831, pp. 12,26.

[21] For Puebla's demographic performance after 1833, see Chapter 10.

[22] Frederick Shaw, "Poverty and Politics", p. 170.

TABLE 4.4 PUEBLA AND MEXICO: BIRTHS AND DEATHS, 1820-1849

		PUEBLA			MEXICO		
		Born	Died	Net Change	Born	Died	Net Change
1820/21	(9 months)	1932	1103	+829	-	-	-
1831/32	(9 months)	1885	1148	737	-	-	-
1838	12 months)	2669	1765	+904	-	-	-
1839	(12 months)	2322	1760	+562	6639	5638	+1001
1840	(12 months)	2506	2487	+19 smallpox)	6524	8154	-1630
1841	(12 months)	-	-	-	6860	5249	+1611
1842	(12 months)	-	-	-	6656	5904	+752
1843	(12 months)	-	-	-	7120	6244	+876
1844	(12 months)	-	-	-	7113	5950	+1163
1845	(12 months)	-	-	-	7542	5772	1770
1847	(12 months)	2829	2658	+171 (epidemics US invasion)	-	-	-
1848	(12 months)	2757	2598	+159 (epidemics US invasion)	-	-	-
1849	(9 months)	2640	1379	+1261	-	-	-

Total: Born 19,540
      Died 14,898

Net Change +4,642

Average: over 87 months:
      Born 224/month
      Died 171/month

Increase 53.35/month

Total: Born 48, 454:
      Died 42,911

Net Change +5,543

Average: over 84 months:
      Born 577/month
      Died 510/month

Increase 66/month

Sources: Puebla: 1820/21, *La Abeja Poblana*, Puebla, 1820, No. 15, 1821, No. 33 1831/49
AAP, Cabildo, Vols. 100-117; Mexico: Frederick Shaw, Poverty and Politics in
Mexico City 1824-54, unpublished Ph.D. Dissertation, Univ. of Florida, 1975, p.
370

lands of greater opportunity in *tierradentro*, than a final settling place.[23] In the peripheral parish of Santo Angel Analco only 7 percent of the adult population were born outside of the city in 1791. This contrasts with immigrants comprising 38 percent of a random sample of families inhabiting Mexico City's northern barrios in 1811. In 1822 34 percent of the city of Guadalajara's population were listed as born outside of Jalisco's capital.[24] Over 25 percent of the Mexico City sample were from the center-west of Puebla, mostly from the provincial capital. *Poblanos* formed by far the largest regional contingent of immigrants in the capital. They were the only immigrant group to inhabit a *barrio* of the viceregal capital named after their region of origin, the "barrio de los poblanos", observed to be in existence at least as early as the 1740s.[25] Michael Scardville found *poblanos* to be disproportionately well-represented in the record of police arrests in the viceregal capital between 1794 and 1807, with *poblanos* three times as likely to be arrested as migrants from any other region of New Spain.[26] It was during this period that a repertory of disparaging adages

---

[23] Of the 235 adult migrants (84 women and 151 men) among Analco's total population of 5,256, most were agricultural workers, weavers, merchants, muleteers and vagabonds from the neighboring districts of the mesa central, especially Tlaxcala. Indians and Spaniards predominated over the castes. A significant proportion of the Indians were caciques: 24 among the 84 Indian migrants. All but 6 of the 75 Spanish migrants were creoles. See AAP, Padrones, Vol. 128, Expte. 1388.

[24] Alejandra Moreno Toscano and Carlos Aguirre, "Migraciones hacia la ciudad de México durante el siglo XIX. Perspectivas de investigación," INAH-DEH *Investigaciones sobre la Historia de la Ciudad de México*. Mexico, 1974, Vol. I, p. 5; and Sherburne F. Cook, "Las Migraciones en la Historia de la Población Mexicana," in Bernardo García et al., *Historia y Sociedad en el mundo de habla hispana*. Mexico, 1970, p. 361.

[25] Moreno and Aguirre, "Migraciones", pp. 7-9.

[26] Michael Scardaville, "Crime and the Urban Poor: Mexico City in the Late Colonial Period", Unpublished.Ph.D. Dissertation,University of Florida, 1978, pp. 59, 86-87.

TABLE 4.5 POPULATION OF THE PARISH OF SANTO ANGEL CUSTODIO (ANALCO), 1771-91

	1771			1777			1791		
	Men	*Women*	*Total*	*Men*	*Women*	*Total*	*Men*	*Women*	*Total*
Spanish	653	758	1411	685	872	1557	551	613	1164
Mestizo	792	898	1690	567	755	1322	727	971	1698
Mulato/Pardo	101	96	197	111	59	170	109	95	204
Indian	1566	1253	2819	1107	1152	2259	1110	1080	2190
TOTAL	3112	3005	6117	2470	2838	5308	2497	2759	5256

Sources: 1771: AAP, Padrones, Vol. 10 "Padrón General del Curato de Sto. Angel (1771)"; 1777: Gálvez Census, AGI, Mexico Audiencia, Vol. 2578; 1791: AAP, Padrones, Vol. 128

about *poblanos* became current in the capital, still with some echo today.[27]

A closer scrutiny of Puebla's population in 1791 adds weight to the conviction that Puebla was failing to retain its population over the later eighteenth century. Between 1771 and 1791 the population of the parish of Analco (see Table 4.5) declined by 14 percent with a progressive imbalance between men and women, a condition which had become common throughout much of the city by the 1820s. This was particularly marked among the 16 to 50 year-old group, in which women outnumbered men by a ratio of 100:85, implying a severe wastage of the male population, characteristic of a society facing war or undergoing selective out-migration.[28] Widows also increased in Analco, from 274 in 1771 to 416 in 1791, among a smaller female population. In the other three parishes enumerated in 1791, imbalanced sex ratios among people of working age were also markedly greater than in their overall population:

---

[27] In 1767 Francisco Ajofrín observed the relation between "poblanos diestros" and "poblanos, falaces embusteros y trapacistas". Later Francisco Clavijero, the Jesuit historian and native of Puebla, commented from his exile in Italy, "todos los talentos de aquella gente para las artes y todos sus esfuerzos no bastan para procurarse el sustento y así se aplican muchos a robar y estafar cuanto puedan". Puebla stereotypes appear in the anti-Spanish newspaper *El Cardillo* in 1828 when a Spanish shopkeeper was described as "más ladrón que caro, que San Dimás y de un lépero del Barrio Alto de Puebla", and a Spanish comedian as "más ladrón que ha parido poblana" ("the most mischievous man that a Puebla woman ever spawned"). By the 1840s, with economic recovery, the image of the poblano was more positive. The popular *Calendario Cumplido* claimed that "Los naturales de Puebla tienen excelentes disposiciones para las artes, para la milicia y para las ciencias. Son agiles, vivos y bien dispuestos. Era refrán entre nuestros padres que si todos los hombres tiene cinco sentidos, los poblanos tenían siete...". *La Guirnalda* asserted in 1844 that "los poblanos son laboriosos, agiles, muy dados al manejo de las armas y de un valor a toda prueba, por estas razones las tropas de Puebla son unas de las mejores de la República." Puebla women of the lower classes were considered in the capital to be profane "femmes de rien" whose "China Poblana" dress, which left the ankles bare, was not permitted even at a costume ball in 1842, as Frances Calderón de la Barca discovered to her chagrin (she was persuaded not to wear this only after visits from the Ministers of War, the Interior, and finally, from the President himself). Francisco Ajofrín, "Viaje"; Francisco Clavijero, "Descripción", p. 393; *El Cardillo*, Mexico, 1828, No. 14, p. 4; No. 30, p. 6; *Calendario Cumplido*. Mexico, 1840, p. 24; *La Guirnalda*, Mexico, 1844, Vol. I, pp. 51-2; Frances Calderón de la Barca, *Life in Mexico*, pp. 76-7.

[28] Shaw, "Poverty and Politics", p. 170.

SEX RATIOS IN FOUR PARISHES, PUEBLA, 1791[29]

	Ages 16-50	Total population
Santo Angel Analco	100:85	100:95
San Marcos	100:84	100:90
Santa Cruz	100:90	100:98
San Sebastián	100:90	100:96

In the Parish of San Marcos, the principal cotton-spinning and weaving quarter, the sex imbalance among the 16 to 40 age group was a ratio of 100:83. Moreover 748 widows were living in the parish, almost 20 percent of the total female population. The age-sex pyramid for San Marcos (Figure 4.3) illustrates this disproportion between men and women and the poor representation of males in the 17 to 25 age category. The census for San Marcos, unfortunately lacks information on individuals' place of birth, so that hypotheses concerning high rates of in and out migration cannot be further explored without recourse to parish records. But the high concentration of population in the 26 to 40 year age category, amounting to some 36 percent of the parish (compared to 22 percent in the other three parishes) is most likely explained by the large number of immigrants. It was also probably the large migrant population of San Marcos, combined with large scale emigration of males, which brought the average size of family of this parish down to well below the level of the other three parishes:

FAMILY SIZE IN FOUR PUEBLA PARISHES, 1791[30]

	No. of families	Population	Average size
San Marcos	2,465	7,207	2.92
Analco	1,431	5,256	3.67
Santa Cruz	921	3,599	3.90
San Sebastián	926	3,330	3.59

The unusual age structure, imbalanced sex ratio and small average family size of the parish of San Marcos, apart from suggesting an impermanent population accustomed to migration, also reflect the productive structure of the cotton textile industry which depended upon the intensive labor of women at the preparation and spinning stages. The early 1790s was a

---

[29]   AAP, Padrones, Vols. 128-29.
[30]   *Ibid.*

166

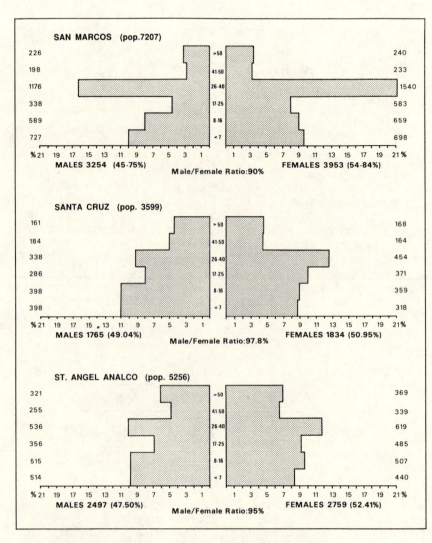

Figure 4.3 Age-sex Pyramids for Selected Parishes, Puebla, 1791

period of severe recession in the textile industry. This further accounts, perhaps, for the demographic peculiarities of this parish, particularly the shortage of men, weavers forming the largest contingent of Puebla's migrants to Mexico City.[31] The combined age-sex pyramid of the four parishes (Figure 4.4) is remarkably similar to that of the city of Durango in the same year whose population Swann shows to have been wasted over the previous fifteen years by epidemics, famine and emigration.[32]

From the fragmentary evidence, it seems clear that the population of the city of Puebla and the center-west of the region possessed certain entrenched characteristics by the turn of the nineteenth century. The rich agricultural valleys of the center-west, although they supported communities of undoubted fertility, no longer provided a sufficiently attractive economic environment to quell the flight of population. The high density of population of the center-west, relative to the other parts of the province, and its predominantly Indian character, appear to have rendered it, after a period of sustained growth between 1650 and 1737, peculiarly vulnerable to the frequent epidemics which afflicted central Mexico with heightened and merciless intensity between 1737 and 1833. Finally, the population of the city itself not only singularly failed to keep pace with the growth of other provincial capitals over the eighteenth century but fared worse even than other districts in the depressed center-west of the province, providing only temporary refuge for the flood of migrants passing through it.

Epidemic Disease and Demographic Crisis, 1791-1833

Between 1791 and 1821 the population of the city of Puebla declined by almost 20% (from 56,859 to less than 46,000). While continued emigration undoubtedly contributed to this, the most serious epidemic suffered by the city since 1737 must also be held partly responsible.[33] In the epidemic of "malignant fevers" (thought to be either yellow fever or typhoid), which afflicted the city between December 1812 and July 1813,

---

31 See report on the state of the industry by Bishop Victoriano López Gonzalo in 1786, Enrique Florescano and Rodolfo Pastor, *La Crisis Agrícola*, Vol. II, pp. 490-534.

32 Michael Swann, *Tierra Adentro*, pp. 87-139, 330-32.

33 Faustino Rodríguez, responsible for Puebla's Cuartel No.3, described the symptoms of the disease to the Intendant, Ciriaco de Llano, which he asserted were identical to the yellow fever (Tifo Heteroides) exprienced in Philadelphia, Havana, Veracruz, Cadiz and Seville in 1800 and in Málaga in 1803-4: AGN, Epidemias, Vol. 13, f. 208.

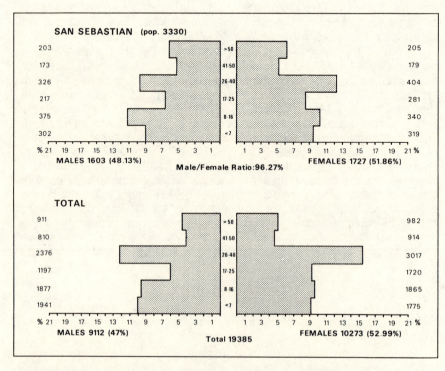

Figure 4.4 Age-sex Pyramids of San Sebastián Parish and Puebla City, 1791

48,726 people fell ill of whom 7,425 died.[34] The chronicler, Francisco Javier de la Peña insists that 20,000 people died in the city in 1813, claiming also that 13-14,000 men joined the royalist and insurgent armies or migrated to Mexico City. This migration and deaths from the 1813 epidemic left a gap in the demographic structure of the city which had not been filled by the time cholera struck the city in 1833, leaving Puebla with a population of less than 40,000, about the level of its population two centuries earlier.[35] While he exaggerates the mortality from the 1813 epidemic, de la Peña is correct in asserting that the combination of high mortality from the epidemic, military recruitment and continuing emigration, left a demographic imbalance which delayed population recovery until the late 1830s.

This accelerated demographic decline was a symptom of a much wider crisis affecting Puebla over the quarter century following the Hidalgo revolt of 1810. The principal element in this crisis was the contraction of most of Puebla's industries in the face of foreign competition and the loss of extra-regional markets. This was a crisis of regional dimensions since many of Puebla's industries were as much rural as they were urban, as in the case of cotton and woollen textiles, or were linked directly to Puebla's main agricultural staples: milling, with wheat agriculture, and *tocinería*, with the production of barley and maize. So industrial decline and the disintegration of Puebla's merchant body during the wars of Independence exacerbated the problems facing the region's commercial agriculture and deepened the secular decline facing the population not only of the capital but of the entire central region of the province. The social problems accompanying economic and demographic decline became more acute with the breakdown of the colonial state: unemployment, vagabondage, prostitution, mounting crime and civil disorder in the city, banditry in its environs and along the principal routes linking the province with its neighbors. All excited anxious commentary among contemporaries and provoked shock among foreign visitors to the city.[36] Examination of the political response to the crisis must await Chapter 5. The remaining part of this chapter will examine more

---

34 *Estado Instructivo que presenta la Junta de Sanidad.* Puebla, October 29, 1813. In Mexico City, 20,385 died from a population of 123,907,as a result of the epidemic, a mortality of 16.5 %: AGN, Epidemias, Vol. 13, f. 247.

35 De la Peña, "Notas", pp. 132-3.

36 Edward Thornton Tayloe, deputy to the United States Minister, reported in 1825 that:
In Puebla there is more misery, more deformed human beings
and less neatness than I have yet witnessed; and I am told
there is more fanaticism in Puebla than in any other part of
Mexico. In the Alameda we saw few well-dressed people
and no pretty women.
C Harvey Gardiner, *Mexico, 1825-1828,The Journal and Correspondence of Edward Thornton Tayloe.* Chapel Hill, 1949, pp. 38-9.

closely the impact of economic and demographic crisis upon the "social ecology" of the city, focussing upon changes in the spatial distribution of population, in the demographic balance between the sexes and in occupational specialization, between the 1791, 1821, 1828, 1830 and 1834 censuses.

The 1813 epidemic struck the poorer, peripheral and largely Indian quarters to the west and east of the city with particular severity. Here mortality was considerably higher than in the central quarters. This is evident from mortality figures recorded by parish shown in Table 4.6. Although the central parishes of San José, San Marcos and Sagrario contained almost 80 percent of Puebla's population, they suffered only 71% of deaths registered by parish priests. In contrast the peripheral parishes of San Sebastián, Santo Angel Analco and Santa Cruz, with only 20 percent of the population, suffered almost 30% of deaths.

The discriminatory character of the epidemic, both socially and spatially, may be explained by two factors, beyond the conditions of overcrowding which the *Junta de Sanidad* gave as reason for high mortality among the poor of certain peripheral barrios.[37] The first was the reduced resistance to disease which resulted from three years of dearth caused by high maize prices between 1810 and 1813. This was the only period over the first half of the nineteenth century, apart from a few months accompanying the withdrawal of copper money during the early 1840s, during which it was reported that the poor in Puebla faced severe undernourishment. Evidence for this can be seen in the alarm expressed by the ecclesiastical, municipal and provincial authorities and the extraordinary measures they took to keep the city supplied with basic provisions.[38]

The second factor explaining high mortality among the poor living on the edge of the city has to do with the way the disease arrived. As in Mexico City, the arrival of the disease in Puebla coincided with heavy campaigning against insurgents in Atlixco and Izucar. Royalist troops returning to the city, and lodging in its barrios, were among the first to suffer.[39] The *Junta de Sanidad* also recognized another source of propagation: from the baggage traffic (mainly of cotton and tobacco) from the *tierra caliente* of Veracruz and Oaxaca. This was customarily unpacked on the edge of the city, from where the cotton was distributed to the women of the peripheral *barrios* and villages to be caned, de-seeded and spun.[40] The fact that Indians, who generally performed these tasks, suffered a disproportionate

37 AGN, Epidemias, Vol. 13, f. 206.
38 AAP, Alhóndiga, Vol. 113 fs. 27-56, 114, 220-21; Cabildo, Vol. 81, 7 April 1812.
39 M. Bustamante, "La situación epidemiológica de México en el Siglo XIX", in Enrique Florescano and Elsa Malvido, *Ensayos sobre La Historia de las Epidemias en México*. Mexico, 1982, Vol. II, pp. 456-7; Leicht, *Calles*.
40 AAP, Sanidad, Vol. 79 fs. 72-74.

TABLE 4.6 DEATHS FROM "FEVERS" DURING THE 1812-13 EPIDEMIC

		Parish of San Marcos				Parish of Santa Cruz	Parish of Señor San José	Parish of Santo Angel Analco	Parish of San Sebastian	Parish of Sagrario	Provisional Hospital of San Francisco		Total
		S*	M*	I*	T*						Male	Female	
1812	September	9	6	25	40	-	-	-	-	54	-	-	-
	October	30	45	85	160	-	23	-	-	48	-	-	-
	November	50	49	130	229	-	26	20	15	-	47	-	-
	December	39	44	93	176	-	34	40	75	110	61	92	-
1813	January	23	15	59	97	-	145	103	131	180	178	164	-
	February	12	3	36	51	-	208	82	126	381	131	102	-
	March	6	1	29	34	-	245	100	45	439	139	110	-
	April	7	2	6	15	-	216	60	16	231	64	26	-
	May	4	1	5	10	-	64	30	15	188	21	-	-
	June	6	1	7	14	-	73	16	18	168	28	-	-
	July	-	4	6	10	-	24	11	9	114	15	-	-
	August	-	-	-	-	-	36	-	12	101	-	-	-
	September	-	-	-	-	-	10	10	-	84	-	-	-
		188	171	482	841	468[a]	1104	678[b]	462	2145	637	494	6829[c]

Sources: AAP, Sanidad, Vol. 89, fs. 1-22: [a]Composed of 165 men, 193 women and 100 children; [b]Includes an estimated 200 deaths not recorded by parish priest. [c]Of these, 1378 were buried in the new cemetery of San Javier: 586 Spaniards and Mestizos. 576 Indians, 37 Negros and Mulatos and 179 children. S* Spanish; M* Mestizo; I* Indian; T* Total

mortality, adds weight to the conviction that it was baggage from the *tierra caliente* which was the source of the disease. It is almost certain that the disease, which reached epidemic proportions so swiftly, was yellow fever, transmitted by lowland mosquitoes travelling inland on baggage trains. The breed of mosquito which carries yellow fever in fact rarely propagates above one thousand feet, the disease being endemic in the Caribbean basin and occasionally appearing as far north as Philadelphia over the eighteenth and early nineteenth centuries.[41] The abnormally warm and humid conditions over the winter of 1812-13 in Puebla must have favored its propagation on the normally temperate and yellow fever free plateau.

Of course, the epidemic of 1812-13 was not the only cause of the population decline occurring between the 1791 and 1821 censuses. The demographic decline of Puebla's peripheral parishes was a secular phenonemon beginning in the early eighteenth century and merely accelerating after 1810. The merging of the two eastern parishes of Santa Cruz and Santo Angel, and the grafting of the parish of San Sebastián onto the parish of San Marcos, resulting from the decline in communicants, occurred, in fact, in 1809, three years before the epidemic. [42] Between 1791 and 1821, the population of Santa Cruz declined by 20 percent (from 3,599 to 2,917), Santo Angel by 46% (from 5,256 to 2,841) and San Sebastián by 60 percent (from 3,330 to 1,300).[43]

Whereas Santa Cruz and Santo Angel Analco succeeded in recovering their populations during the 1820's, the decline of San Sebastián, Puebla's last remaining area of largely autonomous Indian barrios, continued until well in to the 1830s. No doubt there are complex cultural explanations behind the demographic decline of barrios which were first established shortly after the foundation by Indians involved in the city's construction.[44] Evidence, constituting principally occupational data from population censuses, offers some explanation of this parish's decline. The census of 1791 for the parish of San Sebastian (which included the barrios of San Miguel, Santiago, San Martín, San Sebastian, Guadalupe and Parral) reveals a clear specialization among skilled and unskilled occupations linked to the building trade: bricklaying, stonemasonry, carpentry, joinery and metal work (including gilding). Many of those working in building related crafts would have periodically been employed by the master builder, José Antonio Santa Maria Inchaurrigui, Puebla's most popular architect at the

---

41   *Black's Medical Dictionary.* London, 1958, pp. 1011-2.

42   Leicht, *Calles,* p. 401.

43   AAP, Padrones, Vol. 128, Expediente.1387. The figure for the parish of San Sebastián's population in 1821 is only an approximation since the count for *Cuartel* 'L' (containing the barrio de San Miguel) is missing. The figure was reached by combining the population of *Cuartel* 'O' (barrio de Santiago) - 620-with a section of *Cuartel* 'N' (Barrios de San Martín, Guadalupe and Parral) -680.

44   Zerón Zapata, *La Puebla,* p. 29.

turn of the century, still resident in the parish in 1821.[45] Day laboring in city and countryside, market gardening, fruit selling and carrying, work in bakeries and *tocinerías* and shoemaking, were also important sources of employment.

Apart from being 95 percent Indian, the social structure of the parish was much more egalitarian than any of the other four peripheral parishes enumerated in 1791. There were few master craftsmen listed and only four artisans employed apprentices, of whom there were only seven in the entire parish. Only 21 of the 836 families residing in the parish in 1791 employed servants. Thirteen of these families were headed by Spaniards; mostly landowners, mill owners, overseers, merchants, notaries, medics and ecclesiastics, who lived apart from the Indian barrios, on neighboring haciendas within municipal boundaries. The main features of San Sebastian's employment structure were its concentration in the building trades and in casual and menial labor in town and countryside. This narrow specialization.in occupations noted for their instability, in contrast to the more diversified occupational structure of Santa Cruz and Santo Angel, perhaps accounts for the greater extent and duration of the demographic and economic decline of Puebla's western barrios.

The demographic decline of the Barrio de Santiago illustrates the extent of the depopulation affecting the western part of the city. Of the 416 households enumerated in 1791, only 108 remained in 1813 after the epidemic. In these households there lived only 115 able bodied men of whom 25 were unemployed and 16 were working in occupations distinct from those in which they had been trained, mainly in agriculture and in selling pulque.[46] By 1822 the *barrio* had recovered slightly, now with a population of 620 within 148 households, (no larger than many single *manzanas* (blocks) in the center of the city). 177 men with occupations were listed as were 37 widows heading families. In the neighboring barrios of Parral, San Diego and San Matías, of the 926 families listed in 1791, only 300 remained by 1821. With 68 widows and women outnumbering men by ratio of 100 to 68, these *barrios* were clearly sharing fully in Santiago's decline.[47]

---

[45] AAP, Padrones, Vol. 113, Cuartel 'N'; Leicht, *Calles*, p. 452.

[46] AAP, Padrones, Vol. 129 fs. 223-228.

[47] AAP, Padrones, Vol. 133 fs. 1-38.

TABLE 4.7 POPULATION CHANGE IN PUEBLA, 1821-1846

1830 Cuartel Divisions	1821	1828	1830	1834	1844/46
NORTH San Marcos and Señor San José					
14 (whole cuartel)	624	-	882	542	-
15 (whole cuartel)	5665	-	6364	-	-
6 (manzanas 1,3,4)	1158	-	-	694	1645
6 (whole cuartel)	-	-	2558	1355	2881
CENTER San Marcos and Sagrario					
16 (whole cuartel)	7867	6705	6842	-	-
9 (13 of 18 manzanas)	5402	-	5023	-	5462
9 (9 of 18 manzanas)	4011	-	3566	3061	3674
1 (whole cuartel)	3390	3984	3916	-	3074
5 (whole cuartel)	5002	-	4264	2773	4384
5 (8 of 17 manzanas)	3608	-	3490	2157	3457
SOUTH San Marcos and Sagrario					
10 (whole cuartel)	-	5665	5533	-	-
10 (16 of 24 manzanas)	5393	4997	-	-	-
2 (whole cuartel)	1673	1505	1423	-	1755
WEST San Sebastián					
13 (8 of 25 manzanas)	2048	-	-	1487	-
13 (whole cuartel)	-	-	2465	2031	-
12 (whole cuartel)	-	761	1183	-	810
11 (whole cuartel)	6207	1366	1520	822	
EAST Santa Cruz and Analco					
8 (whole cuartel)	1878	-	1966	-	2704
7 (whole cuartel)	1308	1572	1383	-	2037
4 (whole cuartel)		1986	1749		1179
	2917 ⎰			3819 ⎰	
3 (whole cuartel)		1505			2569

Source: AAP Padrones, Vols. 130-148.

Independence brought no respite to Puebla's beleaguered western barrios. Although Santiago's population recovered modestly from 620 in 1821 to 713 in 1828, by 1830 it had fallen again to 661, dropping further after the cholera epidemic to a mere 520 (See Table 4.7). In 1835 a chronicler could observe that:

> la plazuela del famoso barrio de Santiago, que antes estaba muy poblada de buenas casas de maestros y oficiales albañiles en el día se halla arruinadísima.[48]

Santiago's population recovered slowly over the subsequent decade to stand at 822 by 1846.

Compared to the Indian barrios of San Sebastian, the *barrios* of Santa Cruz and Santo Angel on the eastern flank of the city suffered less catastrophically from demographic and economic decline. They contained a population drawn from a broader spectrum of racial groups and social classes possessing a wider range of occupational skills. Social and occupational diversity, and a greater proximity to the commercial core of the city, appear to have facilitated the weathering of period of severe economic and demographic crisis accompanying the wars of Independence. Tables 4.8 and 4.9 show that between 1791 and 1821, while certain industries declined (textiles, leather and construction) others remained stable (metal work and clothing) while others even expanded: brickworks in Santa Cruz and pottery in Santo Angel, taking advantage of freer access to quarrying on the city's *ejidos*.

Notwithstanding the less acute character of the economic and demographic decline in the west of the city, the 1821 census provides evidence for the ravages of war, epidemic disease and emigration caused by adverse economic circumstances. In Santo Angel Analco, of the 1,431 households existing in 1791, only 726 remained in 1821. Of these, 150 households were headed by widows with no apparent means of support than their own labor. At Independence, women outnumbered men in Analco by over two to one. Santa Cruz suffered less acutely from demographic decline between 1791 and 1821, the number of families falling from 921 to 668. In 1821 men and women were more evenly matched although there were 169 widows in the quarter of whom over 140 headed families which they were obliged to support, mainly from spinning cotton and wool.[49] The denomination "widow" seems by 1821 to have become a euphemism for being abandoned by a husband serving in the army and not intending to return or by one who had migrated from the city.

---

[48] De la Peña, "Notas", p. 135.

[49] Of 123 families in manzana 15 of *Cuartel* 'C' (parish of Santa Cruz) in 1821, 43 were headed by widows of whom 23 were spinners, and the others, corn millers, seamstresses or without specified occupations. AAP, Hacienda Municipal, Vol. 104, Padrón del Cuartel 'C'.

TABLE 4.8 MALE OCCUPATIONAL STRUCTURE IN
SANTA CRUZ PARISH, 1791-1846

	1791		1821		1830		1846[a]	
	No.	*%*	*No.*	*%*	*No.*	*%*	*No.*	*%*
Dealing and Retail	40	3.9	46	5.8	59	7.4	92	7.0
Food and Drink	58	5.6	40	5.1	46	5.8	75	5.7
Textiles	314	30.4	174	22.1	155	19.4	461	35.2
Dress	163	15.7	92	11.7	115	14.4		
Metal	40	3.9	24	3.0	33	4.1	44	3.4
Building	127	12.3	148	18.7	68	8.5	115	8.8
Leather	13	1.3	55	7.0	61	7.6	83	6.3
Woodwork	13	1.3	14	1.8	28	3.5	24	1.8
Other Industries (including Glass and Pottery)	91	8.8	49	6.2	57	7.1	85	6.5
Transport and Services	80	7.7	53	6.7	93	11.6	156	11.9
Arts	9	0.9	3	0.4	3	0.4	5	0.4
Agriculture	63	6.1	69	8.8	60	7.5	149	11.4
Administrative	25	2.4	21	2.7	23	2.9	22	1.7
Total	1036		788		801		1311	

Source: AAP, Padrones Vols. 128-148

[a]Cuarteles 7 and 8, including the whole of colonial parish of Santa Cruz and the
northern margin of the parish of Analco. Figures from Juan Carlos Grosso and
Carlos Contreras, "La Estructura Ocupacional...", p. 155

TABLE 4.9   MALE OCCUPATIONAL STRUCTURE:
SANTO ANGEL CUSTODIO (ANALCO) 1791-1853

	1791		1822		1846[a]	
	No.	*%*	*No.*	*%*	*No.*	*%*
Dealing and Trade	34	3.3	33	4.2		
					131	15.8
Food and Drink	193	13.5	81	10.5		
Textiles	149	14.5	99	12.9		
					243	29.3
Dress	83	8.1	89	11.5		
Metal	90	8.8	84	10.9	60	7.2
Building	39	3.8	45	5.8	65	7.8
Leather	108	10.5	56	7.3	67	8.1
Woodwork	15	1.5	6	0.8	25	3.0
Other Industry (including Glass and Pottery)	82	8.0	91	11.5	105	12.7
Transport and Services	82	8.0	64	8.3	62	7.5
Arts	24	2.3	20	2.6	-	
Agriculture	165	16.1	84	10.9	61	7.3
Administrative	18	1.8	19	2.5	11	1.3
Total	1028		771		830	

Source: AAP, Padrones, Vols. 128-148, and Grosso and Contreras
Cruz, "La Estructura Ocupacional...", p. 155)
[a]Cuarteles 3 and 4 covering a slightly smaller area than the
colonial parish

Over the 1820s the population of Santa Cruz grew only slowly while Analco saw its sex balance quickly restored and its population grow by almost 25 percent between 1821 and 1834. Thereafter Analco's population stabilized while Santa Cruz's grew by 35 percent over the 1830s and 1840s. By 1846, Santa Cruz's population had surpassed the level of 1791. The explanation for the impressive demographic recovery of Puebla's eastern parishes over a period when population elsewhere in the city was either stagnant or in decline must await research in parish records. It clearly had much to do with the swift recovery of Analco's male population by the late 1820's. This, along with Santa Cruz's balanced sex ratios, would have provided a firmer base of potential fertility, conducive to demographic recovery. The occupational diversity of these *barrios* and the resilience of staple industries in the face of foreign competition and economic decline during the 1810s and 1820s also helped preserve the traditional social and occupational fabric which, in the western barrios, seems to have been permanently damaged by the crisis. This traditional artisan structure then could serve as a basis for growth over the period of economic recovery during the late 1830s and 1840s.

We now turn to the central part of the city, missing from the 1791 census but enumerated both in 1821 and 1830. Few *cuarteles* in the center of the city (see Figure 4.5 for these subdivisions) could match the demographic performance of the eastern *barrios* over the quarter century following Independence but no central *cuartel* suffered depopulation comparable to the western *barrios*. To facilitate demographic and occupational analysis, the central *cuarteles*, which had been redefined in 1830 (Figure 4.6), falling within the parishes of San Marcos, San José and Sagrario, have been divided into three bands: the North (*cuarteles* 14, 15 and 6, the Center (*cuarteles* 16, 9, 1 and 5), and, the South (*cuarteles* 10 and 2). (see Figure 4.7). This area lost 11 percent of its population between 1791 and 1821, while its share of overall population increased from 80 percent (44,174) in 1791 to 85 percent (39,365) in 1821.

The demographic decline of the three central parishes between 1791 and 1821 was substantial but less precipitous than that of either the eastern or western margins of the city. This area, especially its core around the *plaza mayor*, was, of course, the commercial and administrative hub, not only of the city, but of the entire province. Not even the prolonged and severe economic crisis of the 1810s and 1820s altered this fact. Here resided the bulk of Puebla's wealthy mercantile and landowning families and most prominent military men, public officials, professionals and clergy. Services were, accordingly, concentrated in these quarters: household servants, cooks, washerwomen, seamstresses and coachmen. Commerce, large and small, also crowded into these central *cuarteles*, along with the services it required: brokers, shop-workers, cashiers and managers, messengers and carriers, hoteliers, packing and transport agents, smiths and muleteers. Industry was also well-represented, both the larger units - the majolica and glass factories, most bakeries and *tocinerías*, and the tobacco factories - as well as domestic and small workshop manufacturing:

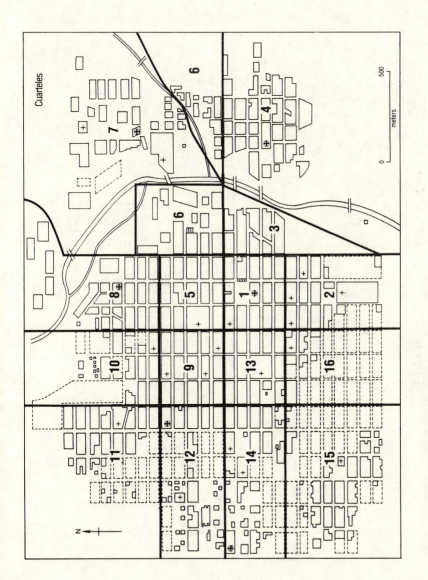

Figure 4.5 Cuarteles Designated by Manuel Flon in 1796

180

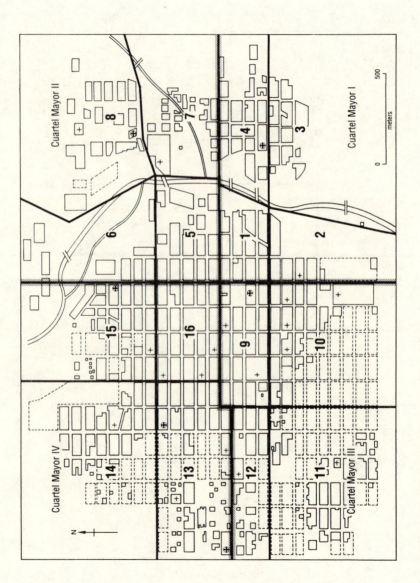

Figure 4.6 Urban Subdivisions in 1830

181

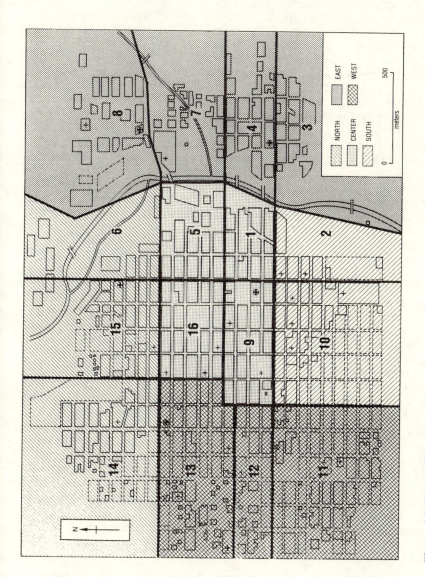

Figure 4.7 Zones of Central Puebla

weaving, tailoring, hat making, metal, wood and leather work, wax candle manufacture and confectionery, with certain streets, or sometimes whole *cuarteles,* specializing in particular trades.

We have observed that mortality during the 1813 epidemic was less in the central quarters of the city than in the western or eastern *barrios.* 4,090 people, or around 10 percent of the population died (not including those sent for treatment to the provisional hospital of San Javier in the *barrio* of San Sebastian). But emigration rather than disease appears to have been the main factor accounting for the demographic decline of the central *cuarteles* after 1791. In the 1821 census for the central *cuarteles,* we find the highest concentration of widows and the greatest imbalance between the sexes of anywhere in the city, especially in *cuarteles* 8, 13, 16 and 14 (See Figure 4.5 and Table 4.10). And, in contrast to Santo Angel and Santa Cruz, this demographic imbalance persisted in several central *cuarteles* during the 1820s and 1830s, accounting for their continuing demographic stagnation or decline.

Between 1821 and 1830 the population of the city as a whole grew by only 5 percent. Considering that there were no serious epidemics over the decade and given the abundant food supply at low prices, this growth rate is low indeed, confirming that the city was continuing to expel its population and that the shortage of men was preventing a normal rate of reproduction.[50] In the North, Center and South, the population of all but three *cuarteles* declined over the 1820s. The population of *cuarteles* 14 and 15 in the North, containing the cotton-weaving *barrios* of La Merced, San Antonio, San Pablo and Santa Ana, grew by over 15 percent over these nine years, in spite of the crisis facing the industry, particularly cotton spinning. This, it is suspected, was a result of immigration from the center-west of the province, traditionally drawn to these *barrios.* Central *cuartel* 1 also grew by 15 percent during the 1820s. In contrast to *cuarteles* 14 and 15, this was a wealthy district with a concentration of government, the university, several wholesale houses, a myriad of retail establishments and the residences of several wealthy families, all offering service employment not available in the peripheral barrios. Single, female immigrants were drawn to such a *cuartel* for household service. This perhaps explains the excess of women to men in 1828 in a ratio of 100 to 68, one of the most uneven in the city. Such a social structure was unlikely to reproduce itself without immigration, the population of the *cuartel* in fact declining by 20 percent between 1830 and 1846.

The population of the other three *cuarteles* of the Center declined at varying rates during the 1820s: *cuartel* 5 by 15 percent, *cuartel* 16 by 13 percent and *cuartel* 9 by 11 percent. In all three districts the ratio of women

---

50 The *Junta de Sanidad* records show that smallpox threatened on three occasions - in 1825, 1827 and 1829 - to assume epidemic proportions but, each time, vaccination campaigns prevented this. "Fevers" occasionally affected the peripheral *barrios* but never in epidemic proportions. AAP, Sanidad, Vol. 79.

TABLE 4.10 MASCULINITY INDEX IN PUEBLA BY ZONE, 1821-1844

Year	1821			1830			1844		
ZONE	LOW	HIGH	AVG.	LOW	HIGH	AVG.	LOW	HIGH	AVG.
North	(Cuarteles 8/10/11)			(Cuarteles 14/15)			(Cuartel 16)		
	77%	181%	84%	74%	93%	91%	-	-	96%
Center	(Cuarteles 5/9/13/1)			(Cuarteles 1/5/9/16)			(Cuarteles 1/5)		
	75%	99%	90%	76%	84%	81%	81%	97%	88%
South	(Cuarteles 16/2)			(Cuarteles 2/10)			(Cuartel 2)		
	59%*	71%	-	82%	84%	84%	-	-	84%
West	(Cuarteles 14/15)			(Cuarteles 11/12/13)					
	68%	86%	73%	83%	101%	94%	-	-	-
East	(Cuarteles 6/7/4/3)			(Cuarteles 4/7/8)			(Cuarteles 3/4/7/8)		
	73%	108%	85%	94%	97%	95%	80%	97%	87%

Source: AAP Padrones Vols. 130-148. [a]Masculinity index = ratio of men to women as percentage; [b]this refers only to the population over the age of twelve

to men became substantially more skewed over the decade. *Cuartel* 16 housed 837 widows in 1830, representing 21 percent of its female population, women outnumbering men by ratio of 100 to 78. In this *cuartel* there was a marked decline in employment in textiles, clothing and commerce over the decade and an increase only in government and domestic service. Cotton-weaving also decreased in *cuartel* 9 although clothing, cobbling, retailing and domestic service expanded slightly (See Table 4.11). In *cuartel* 5, employment shifted markedly from textiles to the military and the services, to be expected since this district housed the city's principal garrison. The overall picture for population and occupations in the Center was of demographic decline, a progressive imbalance in the ratio between the sexes, and a shift away from secondary to tertiary activities, with a marked decline in the textile industry and an increase in military service for men and domestic service for women.

Turning to the two *cuarteles* in the South, population decline over the 1820s was also marked: by 15 percent in *cuartel* 2 and 7 percent in *cuartel* 10. In these districts the occupational structure was extremely varied with no single occupation predominating. Government, military, church, domestic service and agriculture, particularly market gardening, all increased over the decade while the wide range of crafts underwent a marked decline. The military was particularly attractive to the men of this *cuartel*, 527 serving in the army in 1828, the census enumerator explaining the imbalance between the sexes in both *cuarteles* (*cuartel* 10: 100 women to 67 men, *cuartel* 2: 100 women to 62 men) thus:

> Aunque constan muchas mujeres casadas y no aparecen maridos, es con respecto a que, o se hallan ausentes, o con militares de Regimientos de linea.[51]

The imbalance between the sexes was further skewed by the existence of 98 nuns in *cuartel* 10 and 95 nuns in *cuartel* 2. Nunneries were great employers of domestic servants, the convent of Santa Inés housing 39 female domestics serving its 30 nuns and novices.[52]

Puebla's demographic decline had become a matter of serious public concern by the early 1830s. Two municipal syndics reviewing the census returns in March 1831 were shocked by what they found. Not only had the city's population declined by 12,000 since the census of 1828 but women now outnumbered men in a ratio of 100 to 75.[53] They listed the causes of this sudden decline: recruitment for the public militia, political disorders concentrated upon the provincial capital, the decline of demand for Puebla's manufactures, the expulsion of the Spanish, the disappearance of those

---

51   AAP, Padrones, Vol. 136, "Padrón de Cuartel 2º Menor de 3º Mayor".

52   AAP, Padrones, Vol. 129, f. 253.

53   AAP, Cabildo, Vol. 94, 11 April 1826.

TABLE 4.11 MALE OCCUPATIONAL STRUCTURE OF
CUARTEL 9, 1821-1846

	1821		1830[a]		1846	
	No.	%	No.	%	No.	%
Dealing and Retail	291	17.51	354	15.37	370	18.67
Food and Drink	104	6.25	143	6.2	10	25.14
Textiles	106	5.99	333	14.45	154	7.77
Dress	111	6.67			119	6.0
Metalwork	79	4.74	78	3.38	72	3.63
Building	46	2.76	80	3.47	41	2.06
Leatherwork	103	6.23	141	6.12	97	4.89
Woodwork	58	3.48	62	2.69	105	5.30
Other Industries (including Pottery & Glass)	71	4.26	79	3.43	38	1.91
Transport and Services	175	10.52	555	24.09	343	17.33
Arts	43	2.58	81	3.51	72	3.63
Agriculture	37	2.22	28	1.21	32	1.61
Administrative	440	26.45	369	16.0	441	22.27
Total	1664		2303		1981	

Source: AAP, Padrones, Vols. 130-148

[a]Includes female employment. Figures taken from Grosso and
Contreras Cruz, "La Estructura Ocupacional...", p. 152.

merchants who formerly had supported the textile industry, the flight from the city of indebted artisans escaping their creditors. The underlying cause the syndics pointed to was the disintegration of the domestic system which traditionally had sustained Puebla's crafts. But they also blamed a despotic government, heavy taxes, the arbitrary administration of justice and the lack of individual guarantees. The social consequences were everywhere evident: generalized "infidelity of consorts", the decline of the institution of marriage, unprotected women abandoned to their fate, and rampant prostitution. Economic decline thus begot moral decline. And moral decline seemed to point to demographic catastrophe. The two syndics, along with many other leading *poblanos* in the early 1830s, saw as the only solution to economic, demographic and moral decay, the erection of prohibitive tariffs to protect industry and encourage the reconstitution of the domestic system of manufactures.[54]

If the demographic decline of Puebla by 1830 was seen by contemporaries as the result of bad government and economic decline, the cholera epidemic which afflicted the city in 1833 was interpreted by some as a sign of divine retribution for the city which had spearheaded the Liberal and anti-clerical revolution of 1832. Cholera claimed at least 3,000 victims between June and November 1833.[55] Although Puebla suffered less severely from the epidemic than either Mexico City or Guadalajara, cholera coincided with an intensification in the national conflict between Liberals and Conservatives with Puebla at its epicenter.[56] The city suffered four sieges between 1832-34. These caused great damage to outlying settlements and peripheral barrios, the demographic decline between 1830 and 1834 being more precipitous than in any period since the 1813 epidemic. In the *barrios* of the North (particularly exposed to sieges and favored by Santa Anna for their loyalty to the Liberal cause) population fell by 38 percent in cuartel 14 and 54 percent in *cuartel 6*. In the Center, *cuartel* 9 lost 14 percent and *cuartel* 5, 35 percent of their populations. In the western *barrios, cuartel* 13 lost 18 percent of it population while the beleaguered

---

[54] AAP, Cabildo, Vol. 100, 9 August 1831.

[55] AAP, Sanidad, Vol. 81, fs. 257-62; Panteones; Vol. 82, f. 152; Cabildo, Vol. 104, 22 November 1833; and Leicht, *Calles*, p. 231.

[56] At the height of the epidemic in Puebla, during September 1833, 60-80 people were buried daily in the municipal cemetry (burials in churches and churchyards within the city had been prohibited). In Mexico City, during August,300-400 burials took place daily in Santiago Tlatelolco. In Guadalajara, a smaller city than Puebla,daily levels of mortality exceeded 100 at the peak of the epidemic in July and August. Over 14,000 people died in Mexico City from cholera in 1833. Francisco Javier de la Peña estimated, perhaps with some exaggeration, that 5-6,000 perished from cholera in Puebla in 1833. AAP, Panteones, Vol. 82 f. 152,"Lista General de los Sepultados en Santiago Tlatelolco Mexico, 1833; Lilia Oliver, "La pandemia del colera morbum. El caso de Guadalajara, Jalisco en 1833", in Florescano and Malvido, Ensayos, Vol. II, pp. 462, 574; de la Peña, "Notas", p. 133.

Barrio de Santiago saw its already wasted population diminish by a further 21 percent

By 1835, the chronicler Francisco Javier de la Peña estimated that Puebla's population had fallen well below 40,000, observing that, although building was going on in the center of the city, "its numerous barrios have almost disappeared as a result of a series of calamities and now present little more than solitude and ruins".[57] At the height of Santa Anna's siege of the city in December 1832, another contemporary observed the poverty which lay behind the cold demographic and occupational statistics which this chapter has drawn upon:

> Si Ud. diera una ojeada por los barrios de esta capital vería retratado el dolor y la miseria pues hay familias que solo hacen una miserable comida cada 24 horas, por la viudéz, la orfandad y la falta de trabajo, espuestas las mujeres por su necesidad a mil contingencias y los hombres a mil desgracias...encontrara Ud. la más espantosa desdicha; pues apenas se ven familas vestidas y la mayoría que no vale un peso la ropa que se cubren, y los semblantes pálidos, tristes y enfermizos por los malos alimentos y en sus casas no se encuentra un triste petate en que reclinarse.[58]

Conclusion

In the mid 1830s, Puebla's population stood at its lowest level in two centuries. The underlying cause of this demographic collapse was the economic decline of the city as a broadly based agricultural, commercial and industrial center. The moral consequences of population decline were a source of grave anxiety in Puebla during the early 1830s. Not only was the city beset by a high level of crime, but in the civil wars of this period Puebla attracted a unfairly large share of violent and protracted military activity, as the next chapter shows. Furthermore, foreigners, desperately needed for funding and providing the technology necessary for economic recovery, stayed away from Puebla which became renowned for its "fanaticism", xenophobia and criminal element. It seems that only the safety valve of emigration made these conflicts containable.

Many *poblanos* had long been aware that the only way of reviving the region's prodigious economic resources was through a concerted and well enforced set of protectionist policies. The moral crisis which faced the city during the early 1830s made this doubly pressing. The emergence of a protectionist consensus by the late 1830s, the subject of the next chapter, took almost two decades to achieve.

---

[57] De la Peña, "Notas", pp. 132-3.

[58] Un Ciudadano, *Carta al Señor Presidente que debe leer toda la Gente*. Puebla, 1832.

PART II

✣ ✣ ✣

PUEBLA IN THE PROTECTIONIST ERA

✣ ✣ ✣

Chapter 5

POLITICS AND PUBLIC ORDER IN A PERIOD OF ECONOMIC DEPRESSION, 1820-1835

T he physical deterioration of the city and the decline of its population would not have been a matter of such serious public concern had contemporaries seen an alternative to urban life in agriculture or mining. A few Liberal ideologists believed, indeed, that these alternatives did exist. They argued that artisans should become farmers and that industry should be left to the countries which enjoyed the advantages of easy communications, home grown technology and cheap fuel. Mexico, possessing none of these, was best suited to producing precious metals and agricultural goods. Industry had only survived because of isolation, Spanish protectionism and coercive labor conditions. Independence provided the chance to escape from these restrictions and to follow Mexico's natural advantages.[1] These ideas held little currency among Liberals or Conservatives in Puebla. Contemporaries were deeply concerned by the seeming disintegration of urban society, were acutely aware of its economic causes and vigorously proposed their various solutions.

It was the narrowness of the economic options open to poblanos, resulting from the absence of a mining sector and the depressed state of agriculture, which gave the politics of the region a basis for consensus lacking in other parts of Mexico over the first decades of Independence. Poblanos differed on such things as the necessary degree of tariff protection, the desirability of the presence of foreign merchants, the virtues of mechanization, the extent of state and municipal intervention in fomenting industrial projects, the role of the Church in the economy, and, fiscal and monetary policy. But few poblanos believed that laissez faire

---

[1] These arguments were pursued at length in the Liberal papers *El Observador Mexicano* (1827-30) and *El Indicador de la Federación* (1833-34) and are examined by Charles Hale, *Mexican Liberalism in the Age of Mora.* New Haven, 1966, pp. 248-9; and Jesús Reyes Heroles, *El Liberalismo Mexicano.* Mexico, 1974, Vol. III, pp. 419-538.

economic policies would permit the provinces's traditional staples - wheat and textiles - once more to become engines of growth, or that the province had much to gain from closer contact with the international market. For most poblanos during the half century following independence, protectionism seemed to offer the only available escape from deindustrialization and currency hemorrhage which unregulated foreign trade seemed to threaten.

In spite of the broad basis for consensus around protectionist economic policies, Puebla was nevertheless a politically fragmented city at Independence. Given the severity of the economic depression, it would not be expected to be otherwise. This chapter explores certain aspects and episodes in the city's political history over the first fifteen years of Independence.

Institutions and Agencies

Political independence in 1821 brought Mexico suddenly much closer to the international economy. As the Spanish commercial monopoly finally collapsed, direct trade was possible for the first time with the non-Spanish world. Independence also brought with it the opportunity to develop effective institutions on the provincial level through which to advance regional economic interests, something which had not been possible until the very last years of Spanish rule, Puebla having been repeatedly denied its own Consulado de Comercio.[2]

For much of the colonial period, the two most influential bodies in the province of Puebla were the cabildo of Puebla de los Angeles and the secular church headed by the Bishop. A third, and theoretically supreme (though in practice limited) focus of authority was the office of alcalde mayor (becoming the gobernador-militar in the mid-18th century), the agent of the Crown on the provincial level, who presided over the local tribunal of the Royal Audiencia of Mexico, supervised tax collecting, commanded the provincial militia and held the right to preside in cabildo sessions.

Throughout the colonial period, the cabildo, had represented the interests of circumscribed social groupings. For much of the sixteenth century, the descendants of the city's founders and encomenderos, had monopolized office. By the beginning of the seventeenth century, however, hacienda and obraje owners and long distance merchants had achieved dominance of the cabildo.[3] For much of the eighteenth century, long-established poblano families prevailed on Council, representing generally

---

2 The establishment of a Sociedad Económica de Amigos del País was considered in 1814, but this was prevented by the instability of the wars. AAP, Cabildo Vol. 83, April 1814, AGN, Consulados, Vol. 221, Expediente 6 (1789).

3 José Francisco de la Peña, *Oligarquía*, pp. 162-180; and Guadalupe Albi, "La Sociedad" p. 76.

rural interests. Then, towards the end of the century, recently-arrived Peninsular merchants and manufacturers acquired a weight on the cabildo as a result of the reduction in number of inheritable aldermanships and the increase in elected positions.[4] Artisans, and people who worked with their hands, were excluded from office until 1820, contrasting with the practice of admitting artisans to municipal office in the Portuguese and English American colonies.[5]

Thus, at Independence Puebla inherited a narrow political arena. Popular political participation was limited to sporadic riots, uncommon from the mid-eighteenth century, and to the cargo system and cabildos of the city's peripheral Indian barrios. These barrios had all but lost their autonomy and corporate and ethnic identity by Independence, their cabildos serving for little more than tribute collection.[6]

With popular cabildo elections in 1820, resulting from the re-establishment of the 1812 Constitution, the social composition of the Puebla *ayuntamiento* moved markedly in favor of urban middle groups: merchants, shopkeepers, manufacturers and prominent artisans. The Puebla cabildo did not, however, become a substantially more representative, effective or influential institution after Independence. This was for three main reasons. The first was that Puebla's cabildo - and town councils generally throughout Spanish America - had seen its authority and autonomy diminish since the establishment of the Intendant system in 1786. This had been particularly the case under Puebla's energetic intendant, Manuel Flon (1787-1811), and his successor, Ciriaco del Llano.[7] This centralizing trend continued after Independence.[8] Secondly, municipal finances underwent a steady diminution from the beginning of the wars of Independence, greatly limiting the range of action of local government (see Table 5-1). Finally, interests groups increasingly dealt directly through state and national

4   Liehr, Ayuntamiento, Vol. I, pp. 11-121.

5   Gary Nash, *The Urban Crucible*. Princeton, 1979, p. 35; and Charles Boxer, *Portuguese Society in the Tropics; the Municipal Councils of Goa, Macao and Luanda,1500-1800*. Wisconsin, 1965. All restrictions upon *cabildo* membership - barring gender - were finally removed in 1820 with the introduction of popular but indirect elections.

6   Liehr, "Die Soziale Stelklung".

7   Before Manuel Flon was appointed as Intendant in 1787, the Puebla *cabildo* had rarely faced intervention from the *alcalde-mayor/gobernador* militar. Flon chose immediately to exercise a more direct influence in cabildo debates, he intervened in cabildo elections, initiated urban reform projects, presided over the *Tribunal de Fiel Ejecutoria* and personally supervised the control of public order through the Junta de Policía and the *alcaldes del barrio*. See Liehr, *Ayuntamiento*, Vol. II, pp. 97-141.

8   For an indictement of the progressive encroachment upon municipal autonomy since Independence, particularly by the city prefects during periods of Conservative administration (1830-32, 1837-44) see: *Esposición que el Ayuntamiento de la la Capital de Puebla dirige a la Excma. Asamblea del Departamento pidiendo su pronta reorganización*. Puebla, 1844.

TABLE 5.1 INCOME AND EXPENDITURE OF THE AYUNTAMIENTO OF PUEBLA, 1800-1850

Year	Income	Expenditure	Year	Income	Expenditure
1800	29,930	24,248	1826	29,713	29,713
1801	28,420	-	1827	31,416	31,416
1802	38,109	46,551	1828	31,036	31,036
1803	34,502	-	1829	31,442	31,442
1804	46,720	31,117	1830	29,762	29,762
1805	51,347	31,650	1831	-	33,148
1806	59,077	34,942	1832	35,878	35,878
1807	14,496 (34,163)*	18,528	1833	19,363	19,363
1808	94,490 (36,113)*	71,461	1834	13,450	13,972
1809	59,393 (44,241)*	59,393 (47,530)*	1835	35,026	35,026
1810	55,180 (45,187)*	55,180 (45,622)*	1836	36,252	31,684
1811	48,079	48,079	1837	-	-
1812	43,193	43,193	1838	32,169	31,733
1813	30,037	30,037	1839	36,447	36,128
1814	53,786	53,786	1840	40,704	43,572
1815	41,984	41,984	1841	47,031	51,695
1816	45,913	45,913	1842	45,012	45,332
1817	41,233	41,233	1843	41,628	41,769
1818	34,948	34,948	1844	40,193	39,936
1819	38,674	38,674	1845	45,942	45,942
1820	39,925	39,925	1846	61,550	59,883
1821	34,471	34,471	1847	45,650	45,430
1822	32,553	32,553	1848	56,686	56,233
1823	23,007	23,007	1849	48,295	46,911
1824	27,054	27,054	1850	46,322	46,279
1825	30,095	30,095			

Source: AAP, Libros de Cuentas. *Here my calculations differ from those of Reinhard Liehr, whose figures are placed in brackets, *Ayuntamiento y Oligarquía*, Vol. II, p. 22.

institutions, bypassing local government, while the mass of the urban population failed - or were not permitted - to take advantage of the greatly extended suffrage in putting forward popular candidates in local elections.

The decline in authority of the cabildo over the last decades of colonial rule was a consequence not only Manuel Flon's encroachments upon its autonomy but also of the declining prestige of municipal office in the face of the growing popularity of the military profession for the privileges and status which it afforded.[9] The attractions of the military, for patrician and plebeian alike, grew enormously during the wars of Independence. After Independence, most state governors held military rank and possessed some degree of military acumen or influence among the troops, Generals José María Calderón, Patricio and Cosme Furlong being the most prominent. Most of Puebla's military governors, however, engaged actively in business, few following an exclusively military career.[10] Thus, the military career, and the use of force to which it gave legitimate access, became an integral, even the essential, component of provincial politics from 1810. The defence and furtherance of the economic interests of dominant groups within the province owed certainly as much to the canon and the sword, as to the activities of poblanos working through more peaceful channels such as the state and national congresses. This was first demonstrated by the successful federalist revolution in 1824, led by the provincial militia of Puebla and Guadalajara.[11]

If the cabildo saw its authority diminish as a result of the "militarization of politics" and the proliferation of state and federal representative institutions, it also failed to increase its influence among the mass of the urban population, the anticipated consequence of popular cabildo elections.

---

[9] Liehr, *Oligarquía*, Vol. I, p. 118-9.

[10] General José María Calderón, Governor in 1823 and 1825, owned arable estates in Tlaxcala and Tepeaca. The careers of the Furlongs have already been mentioned. Leicht, *Calles*, pp. 166-9, 289.

[11] Because of its proximity to the capital and strategic location on Mexico's principal trade artery, Puebla figured prominently in the bloody political struggles during the half century following Independence, undergoing eight protracted sieges. A *pronunciamiento* in a more remote provincial capital, such as Morelia or Guadalajara, might go unaccompanied by political change on the national level. Such an event in Puebla would often swiftly be followed by the fall of Mexico City and a change in national government. Similarly, political initiatives or coup d'états in the capital generally sought prompt confirmation from its neighbour. Thus the politics of Mexico City and Puebla were rarely out of step. They were the only major provincial capitals not to be taken by the Insurgents during the wars of Independence. The capitulation of Puebla's Royalist garrison to Agustín de Iturbide in July 1821 was the turning point of the Independence movement, being followed shortly by the fall of Mexico City. Puebla's defection from Iturbide's empire in February 1823 prompted the succesful federalist revolution. Puebla figured prominently in the radical Liberal uprisings in 1828 and 1832, in the Conservative movement of 1834-35 and the anti-centralist insurrection of 1844.

In fact, its influence among the poor of the city, and among artisans, probably declined due to the whittling away of many of the cabildo's traditional functions and because the supervision and control of Council elections passed to the State government. The abolition of food supply monopolies, municipal price controls, municipal supervision of selling and the guilds, removed from Council important areas of influence among the poorer sections of the population it did not directly represent. As traditional corporate and municipally supervised institutions dissolved, a political "free market" emerged, in which the prizes went to the highest bidder, more likely to be a popular general, a priest or a party demagogue than a modest alderman or alcalde.[12] Thus, Puebla's cabildo grew to represent middle-ranking retailing and manufacturing interests of the central quarters of the city with the mass of the urban population benefitting only in so far that Council would tend to represent the urban consumer over the rural producer, as Chapter 3 suggested.

The army was not the only body to emerge at Independence with its power enhanced. The Church was probably the most influential body in the politics of Puebla before the Laws of Reform undermined this clerical stronghold. The regular orders, who, under normal circumstances, were dedicated to spiritual exercises, education, welfare, and administering their properties, would take to politics with a vengeance when their immunities and properties were threatened by Liberal legislation.[13] More important in the day to day conduct of politics were the secular clergy who, since the secularization of the parishes of the religious orders in the seventeenth century under Bishop Palafox, had acquired a political influence among all sections of Mexican society, unmatched even by the expanded Bourbon state. The influence of the Puebla clergy may be observed from the top to the bottom of the ecclesiastical hierarchy, with bishops acting as spokesmen for the entire province (often on matters far beyond the ecclesiastical domain), to priests representing urban and rural districts in state and national congresses, and, on the level of the parish, involving themselves

---

12 The political identity of Puebla's barrios, as of the capital's, was by no means annihilated as a result of the loss of their political autonomy. They remained important for the organisation elections and the militia and often petitioned collectively in matters of common interest, Frederick Shaw,"Poverty and Politics", p. 81;and Gómez Haro, *Puebla y sus Gobernadores*. Puebla, 1915, p. 43.

13 The regular orders gave critical support to Bishop Antonio Pérez' opposition to the Madrid decrees of September 1820 and to his adherence to the Plan de Iguala in June 1821. The first copies of the Plan were printed on the press of the convent of La Concordia in February 1821 by Cura Joaquín Furlong. Later, in May 1834, the San Agustín and Santo Domingo monasteries organised a coup d'état, along with part of the city garrison, against the Liberal state government of General Cosme Furlong. Carrión, *Historia*, Vol. II, pp. 322-3, and Michael Costeloe, *La Primera República Federal*. Mexico, 1974, p. 427.

in censorship, the supervision of elections and the maintenance of law and order during periods of civil war and revolution.[14]

Elections and Political Control

Until 1820 the city of Puebla responded to the adverse circumstances of the wars of Independence with a constant, if at times grudging, display of loyalty to the Crown. There was no Puebla counterpart to the "Guadalupes" of Mexico City, and although certain "angelinos" lent notable support to the insurgency, no rule of terror of the kind described by Timothy Anna was considered necessary to keep order in this depressed and all but disintegrating provincial capital.[15] As was suggested in the last chapter, the "political" response of poblanos to the crisis of Independence was migration or enlistment in the patriotic or insurgent armies.

The revolution in Spain in 1820, and the re-establishment of the Cadiz constitution of 1812, radically changed the political atmosphere in Puebla. It was hoped that provincial interests would now be properly represented in the metropolis and grievances swiftly alleviated. But Spain was fatally slow in accommodating American provincial interests. The Council and the junta electoral were obliged to petition twice, in July and September, before the province of Puebla was granted the right to organize its own Diputación Provincial.[16] By the time the Puebla Diputación had been elected - composed largely of priests, lawyers and a few landowners - the Cortés was long over and the undesirable implications of the Madrid decrees had already been appreciated in Puebla.[17] Particularly unpopular within powerful clerical circles, as among the population at large, were the decrees

---

[14] For the careers of prominent Puebla bishops - Francisco Fabian y Fuero (1764-73), Manuel Ignacio González de Campillo (1803-13), Antonio Joaquín Pérez Martínez (1814-29) and Francisco Pablo Vázquez (1831-47), see Leicht, *Calles*, and Carrión, *Historia.*.

[15] Brian Hamnett, *The Roots of Insurgency. Mexican Regions, 1750-1824.* Cambridge, 1986, pp. 141, 150-177; and Timothy Anna, *The Fall of Royal Government in Mexico City.* Nebraska, 1978, pp. 64-97.

[16] *Representación que hace a S.M. las Cortés el Ayuntamiento de la Puebla de los Angeles para que en esta ciudad, cabeza de provincia, se establezca Diputación provincial, como la dispone la Constitución.* Puebla, 9 July 1820; *Representación que hace al soberano congreso de Cortés la junta electoral de la provincia de Puebla....para que en ella se establezca la Diputación Provincial conforme al artículo 325 de la Constitución* Puebla, 18 September 1820.

[17] Ten deputies were elected from Puebla in December 1820 and January 1821 for the Madrid assembly: five priests, two lawyers, and three landowning military men. *La Abeja Poblana*, Puebla, No.16, 15 March 1821.

reducing ecclesiastical immunity, suppressing monastic and hospital orders and prohibiting novitiates in nunneries.[18]

Following the reactivation of the insurgency in February 1821 with the Plan de Iguala and with growing signs of discontent within the city and province, the Puebla elite grew anxious about its impotence vis-a-vis metropolitan Spain and vulnerability in the face of an anticipated popular uprising.[19] The political initiative passed to the Puebla clergy, in particular, Bishop Antonio Pérez. It was felt that only a man with his influence could guarantee the security of Spanish lives and property in Puebla. Rather than risk further popular disorder by arming an angry and probably disloyal population for the defence of the city against Iturbide's approaching army, Intendant Ciriaco del Llano sued for an armistice on July 17, 1821. On July 30th, the cabildo and a "junta de comerciantes" agreed to a full capitulation and to the entry of the Army of Three Guarantees to the city.[20]

Independence immediately reduced the distance over which poblanos had to project their interests. But decision making was now concentrated in Mexico City, Puebla's traditional rival. Although Iturbide's regime was in part a poblano creation (the Iguala movement receiving financial and political support from Bishop Antonio Pérez) the Emperor faced conflicting pressures from other regions of Mexico which he failed to conciliate, provoking the successful federalist revolution of 1823-24. In 1822 Iturbide promised Puebla's Diputación Provincial of Puebla a redress of regional grievances. The unpopular 20% tax on retail trade was abolished, farmers were freed from payment of alcabalas on their crops and livestock, and the city of Puebla was at last granted its own Consulado, to be financed from the avería tax, now to be paid in Puebla instead of Veracruz.[21] All but the last of these decrees was greeted rapturously, the establishment of the Consulado immediately provoking great popular resentment.[22] Although the demands of Puebla's farmers, merchants and shopkeepers had been

---

[18] Farriss, *Crown and Clergy*, pp. 246-7.

[19] Puebla became an unruly place during the wars of Independence. Banditry became common in the environs of the city. The violent inter-barrio wars, held on Sundays and festival days, for a time successfully extirpated by Manuel Flon, revived. Spanish troops were often harrassed while patrolling the outer barrios. On April 11, 1821, there was a mass rising of the barrio population, led by parish priests, and intended to prevent the arrest of Bishop Pérez. AAP, Cabildo, Vol. 90, 5 April 1821, *La Abeja Poblana* Nos. 11, 20, 21, 30,32; No. 5, 1821; and Carrión, *Historia*, Vol. II, p. 213.

[20] AAP, Cabildo, Vol. 90, fs. 53-6, 27 and 30 July 1821.

[21] Robert S Smith, "The Puebla Consulado, 1821-1824," *Revista de Historia de América*, Vol. 21, 1946, pp. 150-61; Robert S Smith and José Ramírez Flores, *Los consulados de comerciantes de Nueva España*. Mexico, 1976; Carlos García, *Manifiesto del Nuevo Consulado de Puebla*, Puebla, 1821.

[22] "Filalethes" *Intereses de la Puebla Bien Intendidos* Puebla, 1821, and *Alcance al Papel Volante Titulado: Intereses de la Puebla....* Puebla, 1821.

met, the province's artisans and manufacturers had, as yet, received nothing.

The request for a Consulado had been a constant in Puebla's petitions to higher authorities over the late colonial period.[23] Why then was Puebla's first "universidad de mercaderes" so unpopular and so short-lived? The year of Independence was an inauspicious time for establishing a privileged mercantile corporation. Since the restoration of the 1812 Constitution, poblanos had acquired at least a taste for the idea of popular sovereignty and equality before the law. A closed, non-elected corporation conflicted with these freshly embraced, and still untried, principles. Moreover, it is suspected that Puebla's artisans and retailers had grown accustomed, since well before independence, to a fairly uncluttered legal environment for their activities, especially since the abolition of the guilds and the establishment of "free trade" in 1813. Thus a commercial tribunal for collecting old debts proved both ineffective and unpopular in Puebla of the early 1820s, as the records of the tribunal confirm.[24] Furthermore, Puebla lacked, at this time, a strong body of import merchants who might have sustained and defended the institution, most Spanish merchants having returned to the Peninsular. The Consulados of Mexico, Veracruz and Guadalajara had represented, principally, Peninsular wholesale merchants and that entire commercial and social structure had disintegrated over the decade of the wars. So the abolition of the Puebla Consulado in July 1824, one of the first acts of the Free and Sovereign State of Puebla, faced little opposition.[25] Finally, the principal reason for Puebla's long-standing desire for its own *consulado*: resentment of dependence on the Consulado of Mexico, was now removed with Puebla's acquisition of the right to adjudicate commercial disputes locally.

A far more pressing problem, and one which would resound over the subsequent three decades, was the crisis facing Puebla's cotton spinners and weavers. This soon became and remained the central issue of debate in provincial politics. The first tariff of the Empire in December 1821 had placed only a modest, 25 ad valorem, duty on imports of ordinary cotton cloth leaving Puebla's *manta* uncompetitive even with finer British cotton goods. To make matters worse for Puebla's weavers, the importation of raw cotton and cotton yarn up to number 60 was prohibited, depriving

---

[23] AAP, Asuntos Varios, Vol. 209 fs. 143-54, "Instrucciones que el Ayuntamiento Constitucional.

[24] The records of Puebla's short-lived *Consulado* are to be found in the AGNP, Miscellaneous Judicial. The Puebla *Consulado*'s first act of debt collection occured in September 1821 when José Miguel Roxas , Puebla weaver, was instructed to pay 122 pesos owed by Francisco Maldonado, muleteer, to Martín Prépero of Tustlahuacan (Oaxaca), the value of cotton. AGNP, Consulado 1821 "Cuaderno de Demandas Verbales del Nacional Tribunal del Consulado

[25] *El Caduceo*, Vol. II, No. 25, 25 July 1824, p. 105.

weavers of cheaper imported yarn.[26] Resentment of the tariff among the city's artisans compounded the anger and disillusion which many felt about the conduct and results of elections since the re-establishment of the Constitution in 1820.

Insight into the intensity of popular electoral grievances may be found in the *Abeja Poblana*, Puebla's first newspaper, edited by the liberal clergyman, Juan Nepomuceno Troncoso. The *Abeja* denounced the first popular Council elections of December 1820 on grounds that they had not been held on a festival day, as the Constitution specified. Worse, the Intendant, Ciriaco del Llano, had controlled nominations and imposed candidates while using the militia to intimidate voters.[27] The practice of elite or executive control of nominations continued after Independence and the elections for the constituent national assembly to draft a new constitution provoked further discord in Puebla.

Iturbide chose a corporate model for the constituent assembly, convoked in late 1821. Mexicans were divided into eleven classes, each being assigned a number of deputies in proportion to their relative importance: Clergy (18 deputies), Hacendados (10), Miners (10), Artisans (10), Merchants (10), Army and Navy (9), Bureaucracy (24), Men of Letters and Professionals (24), Titled Nobility (2), "Pueblo" (9).[28] Puebla was invited to contribute fourteen deputies to the "Cortés Constituyentes": one cleric, a military man, a man of letters, one artisan and ten others from any class. An argument over the selection of the artisan representative provoked the first major public controversy of independent Puebla.

In January 1822, many Puebla artisans became incensed that Francisco Puig, Catalan merchant and owner of a woollen weaving factory, had been selected to represent the city's artisans. An anonymous pamphlet, written in the form of a dialogue between a weaver and shoemaker, argued that Puig, being neither artisan nor Mexican, could not satisfactorily represent the interests of Puebla's artisans. Far better that they be represented by a master of weaving such as Mariano Alatriste from the textile barrio of Santa Cruz, a pillar of the woollen weavers' guild before the wars, a great provider of employment to orphans and widows and an excellent "alcalde del cuartel"[29]

The fiscal of the ayuntamiento judged the tone of the pamphlet to be insulting, seditious and in violation of the Three Guarantees of the Plan de

26 Luis Córdova (ed.), *Del Centralismo Proteccionista al Regimen Liberal, 1837-1872*. Mexico, 1976, p. 29.

27 *La Abeja Poblana*, No. 6, 4 January 1821.

28 *Noticioso Poblano Puebla*, No. 2, 19 November 1821, pp. 10-11.

29 Anon. *Para estos lances sirve la imprenta. Dialogo, Un Zapatero y Un Tejedor*. Puebla, 1822.

Iguala.[30] On February 10 the pamphlet was banned, and after a brief trial (at which Estevan de Antuñano, who had also recently become a factory owner, was one of six jurors), Manuel López Guerrero, the author of the pamphlet, was sentenced to six years in prison for sedition.[31]

The prosecution had accused Guerrero and his "agents" of distributing six hundred copies of "El Diálogo", free of charge, from house to house:

> para estender as su espiritu reboltoso e inquietador, y como ... la mayor parte de los artesanos carece de aquella crítica, maduréz y reflexión que solo es dado a los sabios, de ay es el disgusto (aunque infundado) que ..se ha despertado en muchos.[32]

In López Guerrero's defence, the priest, Antonio María de la Rosa, agreed that Puig was not an artisan but an entrepreneur who was seeking a monopoly in the production of woollen cloth which would leave many artisans without work. He pointed out, furthermore, that the pamphlet was not distributed free of charge but was priced at half a real, the normal for such publications. De la Rosa described the well-attended demonstrations of support following López Guerrero's arrest and testified to his good character,"Es un hombre modesto, cortés y oficioso que ha sabido conciliarse el aprecio cordial de la clases altas y el amor de sus iguales.[33]

Not all Puebla artisans were behind López Guerrero. One defender of Puig testified to his patriotism ("es un Hispano-Americano"), to his knowledge of weaving and spoke of the extensive credit he had advanced to poor artisans. Even Mariano Alatriste, whom Puig's opponent had put forward as a rival candidate, confirmed that Puig knew much of the art of weaving though he cautiously added that "no se le ha visto desenrollar un cadejo de lana"[34] Another observer, a lawyer, pointed out that the cause of the dispute lay as much in an opposition to factory production among unemployed artisans as to any antagonism to Puig personally or to any

---

[30] One of the Three Guarantees was of the union between European and American Spaniards. Guerrero's use of the term "Gachupín for the Catalan Puig was judged to be in violation of the spirit of the Plan de Iguala. Guerrero had claimed that:
> tal caballero no sabe ni a'n cardar un cadejo de lana;
> que si tal supiera pudiera llamársele artesano, y solamente
> es comerciante que por su dinero es dueño de Obraje que
> siempre ha sido gobernado por otros.

Anon. *Para estos lances*, p. 1-2.

[31] Antonio María de la Rosa, *Exito del Proceso Formado a Don Manuel López Guerrero*. Puebla, 1822.

[32] *Ibid.*

[33] *bid.* pp. 2-6.

[34] "R.H." *El Tejedor y El Zapatero. Puebla*, 9 February 1822.

technical consideration disqualifying him from representing artisans.[35] Whether López Guerrero had his harsh sentence reduced is uncertain. What is known is that he received no sympathy from the nine prominent artisans, representing cotton weavers, shoemakers, ironsmiths, saddlers, carriage builders, tailors, carpenters and hat makers, who spoke out in Puig's defence, claiming that he had been elected unanimously by all the guilds of the city in a public meeting.[36]

What appears to have been at the root of the Puig controversy was the widening social gulf between the mass of artisans and the artisan "patriciate", observed in Chapters 2 and 3, exacerbated by the recent introduction of modern industrial technology and organization by merchants such as Puig and Antuñano in the early 1820s. The masters who had secured and defended Puig's election were representative of the "patrician" artisanate, producers either of luxury goods, such as silk cotton shawls and carriages, or owners of large workshops producing on a grand scale, such as José Cadena, hat manufacturer.[37] These were the people who, before Independence, had dominated the guild hierarchy and who still, as the Puig case shows, would use the residual corporate obligations of the guilds to their own advantage, despite their formal abolition. Moreover, these artisans depended upon the social elite for patronage since they were often producers of luxuries or, as property owners, were likely candidates for credit from merchants such as Puig. They were therefore more naturally deferent towards the elite and shared its view of the virtues and necessity of a hierarchical society. The elite, in turn, depended upon artisans such as José Cadena, whose large labor forces, extensive economic ties with outworkers, and ownership of rented property, gave them a firm influence among poorer artisans, guaranteeing that they were regularly returned to the *juntas electorales*. These patrician artisans thus helped preserve the stability of a society undergoing the substantial political and economic changes resulting from Independence. But, as the Puig case also shows, such men could not claim to be representing everyone.

The language used in the Puig controversy suggest that a section of the artisanate felt a bitter sense of betrayal and exclusion after the first year of

---

35 Lic. Francisco Nepomuceno Estévez Ravanillo, *Vindicación de Señor de Cortés Francisco de Paula Puig por la parte en que lo injuria el Dialogo entre el Tejedor y el Zapatero*. Puebla, 6 February 1822.

36 *Satisfacción que los artesanos de esta Ciudad abajo suscritos dan a Señor su diputado Don Francisco de Paula Puig, por las expresiones que vierte el Dialogo del Tejedor y el Zapatero*. Puebla, 11 February 1822.

37 José Cadena had been selected as a "vecino honrado" to help with nocturnal rounds to conserve peace and "public security" during the tense months of March and April 1821, along with Francisco Puig, Estevan de Antuñano and many other prominent merchants, manufacturers and artisans. In 1839 he was elected alderman and in 1841 14 of Puebla's 79 electoral sections chose him as their primary elector. *Lista de los vecinos honrados que se ha nombrado el ilustre ayuntamiento*. Puebla, 1821; and AAP, Leyes y Decretos, Vol. 9, f. 61.

constitutional democracy and the first months of independent nationhood. These were the same workers who were excluded from, or persecuted and unrepresented by the guilds: workers in declining trades, non-examined *oficiales* still hounded by guild officers, cigar-makers pursued by the *estanco*, residents of the depressed and neglected outer barrios, spinners and weavers facing the onset of mechanization. The degree of political awareness and resentment among the poorer artisanate was fully appreciated by the elite at the time. This surely accounts for the Council's prompt prosecution of the "seditious" López Guerrero. The elite's fear of any form of popular political expression was further illustrated by the grateful approval shown by thirty eight merchants, in broadsheet form, to the priest of the Barrio de Analco, Lic. José María de la Llave, for having confiscated and incinerated seditious books and pamphlets while "pacifying" the barrios of Los Remedios and San Baltasar over the period of elections.[38]

Thus, the warning in 1821 from "a citizen of Puebla" that the privileged classes would appropriate the constitutional machinery and create a legislature which amounted to no more than "an assembly of notables" proved prophetic.[39] In 1822, the poor of the city did not have one of their own to represent them although the Council did appoint an "advocate for the poor", to represent them in commercial, civil and criminal disputes. Meanwhile, the elite soothed itself in the belief that:

la plebe aspira nunca a mandar sino a ser mandada con rectitud; no quiere goberna , sino disfrutar las ventajas de un buen gobierno; jamás piensa en ser legisladora, sino en que se le den buenas leyes, reduciendo toda su ambición a una libertad bien arreglada y la abundancia de víveres.[40]

A reply to such elite complacency came from an anonymous Mexico City artisan:

"Ya se ve, que dicen que nosotros somos tontos y no sabemos elegir, porque cualquiera nos engaña. Pobrecitos, cuanto nos cuidan ! Dios se los pague; pero sepan que ya no somos los mismos que agora diez años ! Muy bien sabemos donde nos aprieta el zapato, y a quien debemos elegir ! Mas de qué nos sirve, si aunque conozcamos cuatro o seis señores abogados curas, no hemos de elegir

---

[38] BNM, Lafragua Folleto No. 19, untitled pamphlet signed by 38 merhants, 22 March, 1822. José María de la Llave represented Puebla in the federal congress in 1825-6. It seems that any kind of popular festivity at this time was treated as "sedition", accounting for the violent suppression of the harmless Independence celebrations held on October 7th 1821. "E.D.L.", Realizado en Puebla el importante voto de un ciudadano Puebla, 13 October 1821.

[39] "Un Ciudadano de Puebla", *Representación al futuro congreso representativo*. Puebla, 1821.

[40] *El Farol*, Puebla, No. 19, 3 March 1822, p. 165.

mas que uno, y los demas desecharlos para ajustar con sastres, zapateros, albañiles, no esta malo el trueque?[41]

Much effort also went into more subtle propaganda than the pious assertion that the poor preferred to be led. This often came in the form of printed didactic dialogues, circulated among artisans and designed to persuade the newly-enfranchised popular classes to elect leaders who met with the approval of the elite. A series of such dialogues, between a master weaver, his *compadre* and an oficial were published in Puebla in 1820. The message was that artisans' votes should go to a philanthropic and established figure who had served as an *alcalde del barrio*, found employment for the idle of the barrio, dressed himself and his family in national cloth, encouraged children to attend school, maintained tranquility on his nocturnal rounds, etc.. If on election day, the *oficiales* and *jornaleros* of Puebla could find such a candidate, they should vote for him "sea catalan o indio", making sure that "no haya pulquito [*pulque*] porque todo se ir á la trampa."[42] This last piece of paternal advice to the innocent voter, admonishment about the dangers of drink, was a thread running through much the popular literature of the period.[43] So in 1820-21, the parish priest of Analco concerted his campaign against subversive literature and political disorder with:

---

41 Crítica del Hombre Libre. *Dialogo entre un religioso y su Pilguanejo*. Mexico, 1821.

42 El Tejedor y Su Compadre, *Plática familar entre estos y un aprendiz*. Puebla, 1820 p. 4. Nos. 1-8 of "El Tejedor y Su Compadre" are reprinted in José Miguel Quintana, *Las Artes Gráficas en Puebla*. Mexico, 1960.

43 That drink was viewed as a disinhibitor, and thus, potentially politically disruptive, can be appreciated from a dialogue between a merchant and a weaver printed in 1833. The weaver described the decline of his compadre (and former political boss) to a merchant who was successfully convincing the weaver of the merits of a new mechanised industrial order. This passage thus symbolises the bankrupcty of the old order of the artisan textile industry:

Oh, señor, what a good man my compadre was ! Everyone,
even the rich and powerful, loved him dearly; they even
made him juez de manzana, and, as he was good looking, he
took me around day and night serenading, chasing
drunkards and thieves; he was brave, very brave, my
compadre; but the poor man, from the moment that God
took away my comadre and for the misfortune of taking to
the bottle, abandoned his work, and became poor; and then,
what a battle he gave us in the vecindad; then they put him
behind bars because one night he went around shouting
"Viva........!" who knows for whom ?

Dialogo entre un comerciante y un Tejedor, Puebla, 1833, in Estevan de Antuñano, *Aclaración, ampliación y corección*, p. 33.

misiones contra el pulque y el pulquero, contra las tinas, los cajetes, las almuerceras, y lo que es todavia mas, contra los señores borrachos, que como entonces no eramos ciudadanos ni pedacitos de rei, nos veia con poco respeto este buen este buen señor.[44]

Tariffs, Taxes and Tensions, 1822-30

If the poor of Puebla failed to attain direct representation in 1822, their interests did not go entirely unattended. While there was a general hostility among the elite to any unrestricted exercise of popular sovereignty, their existed, nevertheless, a general conviction, within the same class, that the better off had a responsibility for the welfare of the less privileged. This attitude sprang from inherited corporate traditions and was reinforced and given added urgency by the deepening of the crisis facing manufacturing, the generalized poverty in Puebla of the early 1820s and the mounting threat to public order.[45]

The first impulse among the elite was to see to its own safety and early in 1822, Puebla's merchants, fearing a popular uprising, established a militia regiment, modelled on the colonial *regimiento de comercio*.[46] Once safe in the possession of their property, Puebla's leaders turned their attention to the city's broader economic interests, threatened increasingly by imports. By mid 1822, after several petitions from the city's cotton weavers, the Council and *diputación provincial* concerted pressure upon the

---

[44] "El Poblano en Méjico escribiendo a sus paisanos", *El Farol*, Puebla, No. 17, 17 February, 1822.

[45] Municipal drinking and sanitary regulations reveal an official alarm at the growth of illegal drinking, gaming and dancing establishments, and the increase in prostitution, brawling, theft, murder and banditry. If General José Antonio de Echavarri's regulations of 1823 are to be believed, order was close to breaking down. He prefaced his Bando de Policía with a list of the kinds of people to whom it was to apply:

el desnaturalizado asesino, el ladrón infame, el vago
corrompido y la turba de hombres imorales infestando la
provincia por todas partes.

For this and other decrees: AAP, Leyes y Decretos, Vols. 1-15.

[46] Estevan de Antuñano, with other wholesale merchants and cloth dealers, formed the regiment. It was originally conceived as a defence force for their own businesses","which had come under attack on various occasions since 1820 (particularly those owned by Spaniards). The regiment soon acquired political significance, playing an important part in the federalist movement of 1823-4 and remaining a guarantor of moderate Liberal, provincial interests until its abolition by the Conservative administration of 1830-32. During the 1820s the militia regiment served as a vehicle for the Yorkino (Liberal) party, providing some check to the overbearing influence of the Puebla clergy and Conservative elite. Eduardo Gómez Haro, *Puebla y sus Gobernadores*, p. 18.

Constituyent Congress for import prohibitions, not only on ordinary cotton cloth but on pottery, soap, shoes, made up clothes, worked beeswax, hats: the city's manufacturing staples. Puebla's cotton weavers also petitioned the national congress directly and were rewarded in January 1823 with an absolute prohibition on the importation of ordinary woollen and cotton cloth. Imports of ordinary pottery, ham, lard, tallow, soap, shoes and glass were also prohibited.[47]

The prohibition was a pyrrhic victory for Puebla's protectionist lobby. In the following month, leading figures in Puebla, with the backing of the militia regiment and the city's barrios, adhered to Antonio López de Santa Anna's "Plan de Casamata" and pronounced for federalism. This was the first encounter in a long and torrid relationship between the city and the caudillo of Mango de Clavo.[48] The fragmentation of the national political order during 1823, leading to the fall of the First Empire, ended any possibility, in the short term, of a peaceful reconstruction of the textile industry behind a tariff barrier. The market was flooded with cheap foreign textiles and the predicament of Puebla's artisans further deteriorated.[49]

The first congress of the new federal republic, headed by General Guadalupe Victoria, passed a new tariff in May 1824. Import prohibitions were retained on silk-cotton shawls (rebozos), ordinary woollen cloth, aguardiente de caña, flour, sugar and raw cotton but, to the horror of poblanos, removed from ordinary cotton cloth. This extraordinary exclusion, (considering the concerted pressure for inclusion of cotton textiles in the prohibition from Puebla, the state most instrumental in securing the federal revolution of 1824), is explained by the important, indeed vital, contribution import dues on cottons made to federal revenues.[50] Despite growing pressure from Puebla and other

---

47 AAP, Cabildo Vol. 91, Pt. II, fs. 145, 149; and "Representaciones dirigidas por la Exma. Diputación Provincial de Puebla a S.M.I. y al Soberano Congreso Constituyente, pidiendo la restricción de la libertad del comercio en los artículos que sostienen a la industria fabríl de esta provincia Puebla,8 June and 1 October 1822, Dictamen de la Comisión de Legislación de la Junta Nacional Instituyente del Imperio mexicano sobre la instancia del gremio de tejedores de la ciudad de Puebla: voto particular del Señor (Manuel) Ortíz de la Torre y varias intervenciones relacionadas", 21 January 1823, *Diario de la Junta Nacional Instituyente del Imperio Mexicano*, Mexico, 1823, Vol. I, p. 12; and *Gaceta del Gobierno Imperial de México*, Vol. I, No. 1, 23 January 1823, p. 65.

48 Gómez Haro, *Puebla*, pp. 37-43; and *Acta de la Federación del estado Libre de la Puebla de los Angeles*. Puebla, 1823.

49 The Puebla Diputación asserted that, whereas in 1807 and 1808 6,400,000 pesos circulated between the province of Puebla and its neighbours, in the cotton textile industry alone, by August 1823 scarcely 60,000 pesos were in circulation. *Representación que la diputación provincial de Puebla hizo al Soberano Congreso en 13 de agosto de 1823*. Mexico, 1823.

50 Customs revenues contributed well over one half of federal income in most years between 1825 and 1835. In 1826, ordinary cotton cloth formed 32% of then total

manufacturing states over the mid 1820s, the federal government would not sacrifice this valuable and fairly dependable source of revenue. Thus, cotton cloth was, again, omitted from the list of prohibitions in the new 1827 tariff. Imported cotton cloth was sold on the Mexican market at a tariff and sales tax disadvantage of over 50% but still succeeded in competing very favorably with domestic cloth.

The federal constitution forbad the states from establishing their own tariffs although they were granted freedom to set the level of sales taxes. Denied the most powerful instrument for protecting the cotton textile industry in an import prohibition, the Puebla state congress was confined to the use of limited fiscal instruments and direct financial inducements. In 1826 and 1827 all livestock and raw cotton entering the state were freed from alcabala.[51] The revised 1827 tariff extended the exemption from sales tax to all domestically produced linens, woollens, cottons and silks throughout the Federation.[52] But the reduction or elimination of sales taxes, while undoubtedly popular with merchants, artisans and farmers, was conceded reluctantly by state governments who depended, almost exclusively, upon this source of revenue. Experiments with direct taxes over the 1820s, to repair the deficit, were short-lived and unsuccessful.[53] Moreover, the reduction in sales taxes did not necessarily achieve the object of increasing demand. As one critic had pointed out as early as 1821, "la minoración de alcabalas ha sido hasta ahora mas útil a los Capitalistas que a los pobres Consumidores, que compran las cosas tan caras o mas que antes".[54]

The Puebla state government thus possessed a narrow set of fiscal options over the 1820s. Denied access to customs revenues, it was obliged

---

value of imports, rising to 46% in 1827. No government until that late 1830s felt able to sacrifice this vital source of income. Daniel Cosío Villegas, *Historia de la política aduanal*. Mexico, 1932 Table V, "Ingresos Federales, 1822-56"; Miguel Lerdo de Tejada, *El Comercio Exterior*, Graphs 33&34; and Francisco Arrillaga, *Memoria sobre reformas del Arancel mercantíl*. Mexico, 1824.

[51] *Colección de Leyes y Decretos. 1826, 1827 y 1828.* Puebla, 1829, No.178, p.130, AAP, Leyes y Decretos, Vol. 4, f. 133. Cotton *manta* produced in the State had been free from alacabala since 1820. When in 1826 cloth dealers in San Andrés Chalchicomula were found to have been paying *alcabalas* on Puebla cloth, they were granted restrospective repayment by the State treasury. *El Invitador Puebla*, No. 61, 2October 1823, p. 242; No. 81, 6 December 1826, p. 221; No.102, pp. 406-7.

[52] Robert Potash, *El Banco de Avío*, pp. 47-57. Puebla deputies succeeded in increasing the customs valuation on imported cotton cloth from 2 to 4 reales a yard in 1826, permitting some degree, however inadequate, of protection for the city's manufacturing staple. PRO, MSS.FO.(Domestic Various), Henry Ward to Canning, 1826.

[53] *Colección de los Decretos y Ordenes mas importantes.* Puebla, 1827, No. 47, Memoria presentada al congreso de Puebla de los Angeles Puebla, 1827; and AAP, Leyes y Decretos (1829) Tax laws of 29 May, 21 August and 26 August, 1829.

[54] *El Farol*, December 1821.

to raise revenues from sources which, given the depressed state of the economy, yielded very little. The frustration was intensified by the knowledge that the federal policy of maximizing customs revenues was contributing directly to the reduction of state revenues from other sources through the harm imports were causing to domestic production and employment.

Measures adopted by the state government to provide direct support for manufacturing were no more successful than fiscal policies. On various occasions during the 1820s the state congress approved funds to enable artisans to study modern industrial techniques abroad, to finance the importation of modern machinery, granting monopoly franchises to artisans willing to pioneer their use.[55] These ventures met with little success as a result of shortage of funds, disagreement about the desirability of exclusive privileges and divisions among merchants about the viability of leaving the task of industrial recovery in the hands of artists and artisans.[56] It should also be stressed that the general economic environment at this time was extremely unpropitious for the recovery of Puebla's traditional industries or for the implantation of new ones. Social and political tensions were also growing over the 1820's, causing further distraction from the tasks of economic recovery.

Tensions came to a head in Puebla following the revolution of La Acordada in Mexico City in November 1828. This brought radical Liberals, under Vicente Guerrero and Lorenzo de Zavala, to power for the first time. Puebla found itself at the epicenter of the national struggle between Liberals and Conservatives and between radical Liberals and the moderates, a unenviable position it would retain until the French Intervention. This was in part for geographical reasons but also because the city offered substantial resources to both sides. Conservatives sought support among Puebla's powerful ecclesiastical hierarchy and numerous convents. Liberals were interested in recruiting Puebla's angry and unemployed artisans into their forces. But Puebla should not only be seen as a hapless victim of external meddling in the province's affairs. The events of 1828-1835 demonstrate

---

55 For the experiences in the United States of the cotton weavers, Vicente Enríquez and Francisco Sayas, and, in Europe, of the renowned artist, José Manso y Jaramillo, *El Caduceo*, Vol. I, No. 20, 20 April 1824, p. 77; Vol. II, No. 10, p. 22, No. 16, p. 65; Lucas Alamán, *The Present State of Mexico*. London, 1825, p. 121, AGN, Pasaportes Vol. 9, 2 April 1826; *El Invitador* Vol. I, 28 June 1826, p. 45; *Colección de Leyes y Decretos* (1826 ,27, y 28) No.121, p. 91; No.137, p. 103; José Miguel Quintana, *Las Artes Gráficas en Puebla*, Mexico, 1960, pp. 31-32; Juan del Valle, *Guía*, pp. 157-8, and Leicht, *Calles*, p. 226.

56 The State government made available two lots of 500 pesos to be distributed among poor weavers in 1827 and 1828. These would not have gone far among the city's 1,000-1,500 weavers. *Colección de Leyes y Decretos*, No. 40 p. 160, No. 146, p. 105 and No. 208, p 210. For debates among Puebla's legislators on these matters: *El Caduceo*, Vol. I, No. 53, p. 209, Vol. II, No. 5, p. 17, No.6, p. 21, No.10, p.37.

that the city contained explosive internal tensions while the later 1830's revealed the extraordinary capacity of the province's leaders to persuade governments in Mexico City to adhere to economic policies broadly in harmony with Puebla interests.

The "Sacking of the Parián" - an anti-foreign rampage through the central commercial district of Mexico City - following the revolution of La Acordada, had immediate repercussions in Puebla. Throughout 1828, as a result of the decision of the Puebla state government not to enforce the decree (of December 1827) expelling the Spanish population, Puebla had become a haven for Spanish refugees from other states.[57] While the Puebla elite desired to keep to the letter of the Three Guarantees of the Plan de Iguala (much in the spirit of the Puig case), popular feeling was altogether different. This became evident in December 1828 when two serious riots broke out in Puebla. The first occurred on December 12th. Following a service in the College of Guadalupe, a large crowd sacked "the major part of their (the Spanish) commercial houses".[58] The second happened on Christmas day following the robbery (by mutinous troops) of over ten million pesos leaving the city by mule, destined for Veracruz. This triggered a rising among "la plebe" led by shopkeepers and artisans ("los pulqueros, los vendedores del Parián y todos los de la plaza del mercado") who marched to the point where the mutinous troops were dividing the spoils, succeeding in sharing the plunder.[59] On returning to the city, the crowd sacked and looted two large commercial houses belonging to prominent Spanish merchants. The disorder lasted eight days.[60]

The December riots in Puebla were of a scale and duration unmatched since the riots of the early eighteenth century. Previous disorders had originated in the barrios of the city among the poorer section of the population, were often guided by parish priests, had rarely caused damage to private property (though public symbols such as prison doors were sometimes damaged) and had always involved people seeking redress of specific grievances.[61] These riots commenced in the center of the city, involved people of intermediate social status (shop and stall keepers) who possessed no clear motive beyond loot and self-enrichment. They occurred soon after the sacking of the Parián in the capital and were part of the same breakdown of order accompanying a major political upheaval, an impending war with Spain and an accentuation of animosity towards foreigners, particularly Spaniards. The French minister at this time, Michel Cochelet, considered Puebla to be the most virulently anti-foreign cities in the

---

57 Romeo Flores Caballero, *La contra-revolución en la independencia*. Mexico, 1969, p. 137; and AGN, Gobernación, Vol. 66 fs. 21-30.

58 Carrión, *Historia*, Vol. II, p. 262.

59 *Ibid.*.

60 Gómez Haro, *Puebla*, p. 119.

61 For earlier riots: in 1729, Pedro López de Villaseñor, *Cartilla Vieja*, p. 472, and in 1744, Eugenio Aguareles, "Una Conmoción Popular".

Republic.[62] This can be explained by a combination of religious intolerance and the common belief that foreign merchants were the root cause of Puebla's economic problems.[63]

The Guerrero government pandered to these popular sentiments by strengthening the regime of import prohibitions, by introducing a radical income tax and by banning foreigners from dealing in retail trade. This sudden switch of fiscal policy from a reliance on customs revenues as the main source of federal income, to the direct taxation of the propertied classes, presented a possible solution to the dilemma facing the Puebla state government (that of declining revenues from a flat rate income tax and fixed duties on imports). In May 1829 the federal congress approved a new tariff which prohibited the importation of ordinary cotton cloth. The influence of poblano deputies in securing this appears to have been decisive, having succeeded in securing a majority on the congressional sub-committee which had drafted the law.[64] The short fall in customs revenues resulting from the prohibition would be made up by an anticipated massive increase in direct taxation.

Pressure to exclude foreigners from practicing in the retail trade grew over 1829. The act banning them was approved by the federal congress early in 1830, again owing much to the militancy of Puebla deputies most of whom, the French Consul-General observed, were priests, "they [the *poblanos*] being generally the most animated against foreigners, all of whom they treat as heretics who want to overturn the social order of their country." A *poblano* cleric, Señor Alpuche, was the president of the chamber of deputies and his apocalyptic and xenophobic speeches had helped win over congress.[65]

Popular though these reforms undoubtedly were among wide, and hitherto unrepresented, sectors of urban society, they could not long be tolerated by the Mexican elite which had only temporarily lost the initiative. The successful revolution led by General Anastasio Bustamante in December 1829 inaugurated two years of centralist and Conservative government during which Guerrero's radical reforms were reversed. Over this period, Puebla grew ever more socially and politically polarized. Yet, at the same time, economic policies were pioneered which would have a

---

62   "This is the town where the people's hostility to foreigners is carried to the highest degree. A hat which my wife was wearing on the journey.caused a tumult, and would have compromised our safety, had we not found refuge in a shop." Michel Cochelet, "Souvenirs d'un voyage de Mexico a New York par M. Cochelet en 1830", *Extrait d'un Bulletin de la Societé de Geographie*. Paris, 1845.

63   R W H Hardy asserted in 1829 that "Querétaro and la Puebla de los Angeles are said to be the most fanatical towns in the Republic." *Travels in the Interior of Mexico*. London, 1829, p. 503.

64   Potash, *El Banco*, p. 57.

65   ADF, Mexico, *Correspondence Consulaire Commerciale*. Mexico Vol. II, 17 January 1830, f. 154.

catalytic impact upon the city's manufacturing base, leading, by the late 1830s, to a general economic recovery. Discussion of these policies, which amounted to a revival of eighteenth-century Hispanic mercantilism, is left to the next chapter. For the moment, we must conclude this chapter with an account of Puebla's "años de infamia."

"Los Años de Infamia", 1830-34

The short period of radical reform and heightened xenophobia of the late 1820s had important consequences in Puebla. Well over two hundred Spaniards were expelled from the city under the second decree of exclusion of August 1829, among whom were many clerics, merchants, bureaucrats and military men who had been prominent in provincial politics since Independence.[66] Their departure created a certain space in Puebla's politics into which new men with new ideas could now move. With other foreign merchants hit by the effects of a severe commercial recession commencing in 1826 and deterred by anti-foreign sentiment and legislation, many poblano creoles found their commercial positions and potential political influence considerably enhanced. In 1833 the merchant, turned manufacturer, Estevan de Antuñano, described the emergence, during the 1828-32 period, of a broad coalition of merchants, shopkeepers and artisans - a new political generation - which he saw as a painful but necessary blow to the old order.[67]

President Anastasio Bustamante correctly saw Puebla as a potentially weak link in the reassertion of Conservative centralism. The city which had pioneered the federal revolution of 1823-4 had always shown strong sympathies for the maverick *veracruzano* leader and hero of the war of 1829, General Santa Anna, still a federalist and a protaganist of the Liberal cause. Bustamante therefore imposed a close confident as governor of Puebla, the ruthless and authoritarian Col. Juan José Andrade. Andrade immediately removed from office and imprisoned Puebla's leading "Yorkinos", including Guerrero's governor, Patricio Furlong. He then dissolved the urban militia, since 1823 the guarantor of federalist and Yorkino interests.[68] Within weeks he had established a reign of terror under his police chief Basilio Palacios who censored Liberal publications, forbade Yorkinos from meeting together and established a system of

---

[66] Gómez Haro lists the 216 Spaniards given their passports in Puebla in 1829, *Puebla*, pp. 110-2; and AGN, Españoles, Vol. 5, 25 August 1829.

[67] Estevan de Antuñano, *Ampliación, aclaración y corección a los principales puntos del Manifiesto sobre el Algodón*. Puebla, 1833, p. 54.

[68] *Manifiesto que el Batallón Nacional de Puebla, No.21 hace a toda la Nación sobre la conducta que ha observado respecto al pronunciamiento del ejercito de Reserva.* Puebla, 1830.

domestic espionage using household servants who would report on the conversations, amities and activities of Yorkinos to the Prefecture.[69]

By the middle of 1831 Bustamante, Andrade and Palacios had become much hated figures in Puebla, a city for centuries accustomed to greater autonomy from the capital. Andrade had raised the voting age from 18 to 25 years and increased the property qualification for those entitled to stand for office.[70] Popular resentment of this political disenfranchisement is conveyed in a description of the peripheral barrios of the city in 1832:

> los artesanos que día y noche se fatigan para elaborar sus manufacturas, se ven
> despreciados porque no tienen protección, se afligen y se abandonan cuando
> consideran que mientras ellos se desvelan y les quitan a sus hijos una parte de
> sus sustentos para pagar sus diputados, ven en estos el olvido del pacto social
> y que nada se adelanta en el bien común.[71]

Basilio Palacios' ruthless campaign to stamp out vagrancy and crime was also unpopular. And particularly abhorrent was Andrade's policy of carrying out exemplary punishments in public places, aimed at deterring crime and rebellion. In September 1830, three popular veterans of the Insurgency - Juan Nepomuceno Rosains, Cristobal Fernández and Francisco Victoria (brother of Guadalupe Victoria) - were executed in the Plazuela de Señor San José, the center of the weavers' quarter, for their part in a Yorkino conspiracy to overthrow the Andrade state government.[72]

The unpopularity of the Andrade regime, among both elite and masses, made Puebla an obvious target for Santa Anna's Liberal revolution commencing in January 1832. Over the summer of 1832 Santa Anna's sister, María Francisca, dispatched agents who organized political cells in the barrios of Puebla and Mexico City. These were expected to coordinate popular uprisings to coincide with the approach of Santa Anna's army.[73] These measures proved successful in Puebla, but were never put to the test in Mexico City. On October 4th 1832, Santa Anna's force, numbering some 4,000, including Patricio Furlong with Puebla's disbanded militia, defeated a defence force hastily assembled by Andrade. Andrade's rearguard faced great harassment from the civilian population as it retreated through the barrios of the city.[74] The hated police chief, Basilio Palacios was captured by the crowd ("el populacho") in flight, the *poblano* historian

---

69 Gómez Haro, *Puebla*, p. 120, and Leicht, *Calles*, p. 165.

70 *Colección de Leyes y Decretos* (1830, 1831, No. 62, p. 73.

71 "Un Ciudadano", *Carta al Señor Presidente*, Puebla, 1832

72 Carrión, *Historia*, Vol. II, pp. 191-2; Gómez Haro, *Puebla*. p. 132-135.

73 Gómez Haro, *Puebla*, pp. 136-7.

74 *Entrada del General Santa Anna a la ciudad de Puebla*. Mexico, 1832.

Gómez Haro recording that "lo mató de una manera odiosa, pues llegó la barbarie al estremo de apalear y mutilar el cadaver."[75]

After the fall of Puebla, Patricio Furlong was reinstated as governor to complete the term of office he was elected to serve in 1829. The militia was reestablished and Yorkinos were brought back into the administration. The result of months of campaigning had been a pact between the contending armies, Santa Anna and Bustamante signing an armistice at the Rancho de Zavaleta, near Puebla, in January 1833.[76] Possibly Santa Anna realized that, having incorporated such popular elements in his army, the revolution was acquiring radical social overtones which he felt unable to constrain. Certainly, the pamphlet literature issuing from Mexico City after the fall of Puebla suggests that the defenders of the capital were living in fear of a general popular insurrection as Santa Anna's army approached.[77] The new president, Manuel Gómez Pedraza and his minister, Valentín Gómez Farías, decided against continuing the radical, populist policies of the Guerrero administration. The progressive income tax, the prohibition on ordinary cotton textile imports and restrictions upon foreign merchants were not resumed. Only a short lived issue of copper money, to compensate for the shortage of silver medium, appealed to popular urban sentiments. Instead, Gómez Farías pressed ahead with policies aimed at nationalizing church property and secularizing education, policies deeply offensive to Puebla's peculiar brand of clerical radicalism. The majority of Puebla's poor population had customarily held their religious leaders, especially the Bishop, in high esteem.

Living conditions deteriorated markedly in these years. Employment in the textile industry slumped as a result of trade liberalization, bringing massive cloth imports.[78] The city underwent three protracted sieges during

[75] Gómez Haro, *Puebla*, p. 139.

[76] Carrión, *Historia*, Vol. II, pp. 169-71.

[77] Those organising the defence of Mexico City against Santa Anna stressed that his army was composed almost entirely of:

> 14,000 de la plebe poblana..Su caballería es de bosal, montada por colegiales y sastres,.su artillería es de campaña; o pedreros, propia para asustar faldas y nada mas...La plebe mexicana no es tan fanática, ni tan tonta como la poblana: que no adora a San Sebastián de Aparicio [a popular saint with his shrine in Puebla's weaving barrio de Santa Cruz], y luego sale a buscar que se le aparece robar y matar....nuestro pueblo es docil y respetador de las autoridades enérgicas.

J. M. B.O auxiliamos al gobierno, la patria val al infierno. Mexico, 1832, *Militares a rendirese porque Santa Anna triunfó*. Mexico, 1832.

[78] de Antuñano described Puebla as weaving barrios and villages in 1833:

> ...años hace, que en los barrios de la Merced y San Antonio, no se oye el ruido vital de los telares y urdideras, y años hace, que los del Alto y Santiago, antes poblados de

212

the eighteen months of Liberal administration (in December 1832, July 1833, and between 30 May and 31 July 1834), causing widespread suffering and destruction especially to barrios on the edge of the city.[79] Three years of grain shortage and high maize prices caused by mule embargoes by troops, extraction of cereals to Mexico City and grain hoarding and speculation, added to the sufferings of the city's poor. On top of this came the cholera epidemic of 1832-33, which took with it the governor, Patricio Furlong. The governorship passed to Cosme Furlong who possessed none of the prudence and moderation of his brother. One of his first actions was to exile Bishop Pablo Vázquez, several priests and prominent Conservatives for a period of twelve years to a distance of at least thirty leagues.[80] The poor of Puebla had not only lost their spiritual leader, but also the figure upon whom they relied in adverse circumstances (food shortages, sieges, etc.).

Facing these reverses, it must have seemed to Puebla's barrio dwellers that they had gained nothing from their support of Santa Anna and participation in the Revolution of 1832. As a result of continuing hardship, the political awareness and sympathies of Puebla's poor changed radically over 1833 and 1834. Seemingly in conflict with the city's traditionally Liberal-federalist sympathies, there was widespread support in May 1834 for a *pronunciamiento* of the main garrison against the religious reforms and for the successful retaking of the city by Conservative forces under General Luis Quintanar. He had been sent by Santa Anna, who himself had recently abandoned the Liberal-federalist camp. The infatuation of the poblano "plebe" with Santa Anna would continue until the early 1840s.

The exiled Bishop, priests and Conservative leaders returned in May to be greeted by large crowds and "apocalyptic" bell ringing.[81] The religious reforms were immediately repealed and elections in October brought many poblano clergymen and Conservatives back into the state and federal assemblies.[82] The foundations were being laid for a decade of relative

---

tejedores e hilanderas, están reducidos a escombros.
Cholula, Huejotzingo, Tlaxcala, Santa Ana, y otros muchos,
cuentan larga —poca desde su desolación.
Manifiesto de Algodón. Puebla, 1833, p. 32.

[79] Siege of December 1832: Anon., *Toma de Puebla y Glorias de la Patria*. Mexico, 1832 ; *Resurrección de la Columna de la Constitución Federal*. Mexico, 1832. Siege of July 1833: Anon., *Noticias Extraordinarias de los ultimos sucesos de Puebla*. Mexico, 1833; *Extraordinaria de Puebla y Temixco !!Viva la Federación!!*. Mexico 1833, *Extraordinario Violento*. Mexico 1833. Siege of May/July 1834: Vicente Riva Palacios, *México a través de los Siglos*. Mexico, (1887-9), Vol. IV, p. 348.

[80] Carrión records that the expulsion of the Bishop "produced a general alarm in the city", *Historia*, Vol. II, pp. 269-71.

[81] Leicht, *Calles*, pp. 168-9.

[82] *La Estrella Poblana*, Puebla, Vol. I, Nos. 31, 36, 37.

political consensus in Puebla, under the aegis of conservative-centralism and protectionism .

By June 1835 the change in political temper in Puebla was demonstrated when the Council and many barrios proclaimed support for Santa Anna's Plan de Orizaba, calling for the replacement of the 1824 federal constitution by a centralist republic.[83] The petition from the Barrio del Carmen was typical of "acts of adhesion" from nine barrios, backed by 1,385 signatures. The 198 signatories from the Barrio del Carmen pleaded for constitutional reform, stating that they had kept silence until now but that they were no longer prepared to remain victims of factions. They begged that Puebla be allowed to return:

> al ser con que la naturaleza distinguió, y que poniendo en uso los dones preciosos con que por fortuna fué dotada, recobre su comercio, sus artes y su industria, y nos veamos libres del ataque que constantamente da nuestros intereses el estranjero con el monopolio de manufactura estranjera.[84]

The petition contained a clear economic diagnosis and prescription which economic circumstances over the next decade would translate into an orthodoxy.

Puebla's barrios repeated their mass petitions for an end to the federal system in December 1837.[85] By then, after two years of peace, the city bore little resemblance to the Puebla of stormy years between 1828 and 1834. Joint stock companies were being formed, machinery ordered, buildings converted, foreign technicians employed and men and women taken on in their hundreds to man the new factories in a wave of business optimism which was to last almost five years. Spaniards flocked back to the city and, for a time, the issues over which men fought and died before 1834 - centralism or federalism, aristocracy or democracy, protection or free trade, foreign or national, religious or secular, army or militia - became submerged under a new consensus: industrial progress.

There were voices of dissent but, for a time, the restoration of the prohibition on cotton cloth imports in early 1838 provided a balm which smoothed over divergent interests. By 1842, the view of Puebla from the capital had changed from that of a city of fanatical sans-culottes to one of peace and progress:

> Puebla, que antes estaba dividida en partidos, en lo que siempre se contaba con gente dispuesta para las revoluciones, cuyos vecinos en la mayoría del pueblo son naturalmente, belicosos y con grandes disposiciones para la guerra, hoy presenta a la vista de viajeros una población pacifica, dedicada a trabajo, unida

---

[83] AAP, Cabildo, Vol. 102, f. 282-87, 310.

[84] AAP, Cabildo, Vol. 102, f. 265.

[85] AAP, Cabildo, Vol. 106, 27 December 1837.

por intereses, y opuesta a todo de lo que puede alterar de cualquiera manera su verdadera felicidad que disfruta.[86]

Conclusion

The purpose of this chapter was not to draw any firm conclusions on the substance of post-independence politics in the city of Puebla. The coverage has been too general and ephemeral to be able to say much about ideologies, parties or popular participation. These limitations notwithstanding, it has been possible to observe the following broad characteristics of the city's political life during the first fifteen years of Independence.

By Independence, traditional corporate institutions and attitudes, such as those represented by the merchants' consulado and the craft guilds, no longer commanded general legitimacy in Puebla. This explains the swift demise of Puebla's first consulado and the disorder surrounding the elections for the *Congreso Contituyente*, based upon a corporate model of participation. In Puebla, both were widely seen as attempts by those already in positions of power to maintain their dominance and to block any popular participation. Although the elite succeeded in appropriating the new constitutional machinery and controlling nominations, using allies from among the artisan patriciate, this was at the expense of widespread popular resentment and threatened disorder. The federal revolution of 1823-24, and formal adherence to classical constitutional democracy on the American model, temporarily resolved the crisis of legitimacy faced during Iturbide's empire. Federalism, however, although securing four years of domestic peace, was an unsatisfactory formula as long as the relations between the states and the federation, on practical matters such tariff and fiscal policy, remained ill-defined. Indeed, federalism was a luxury which at this time Mexico could ill-afford. Culminating in the "populist" federalism of Vicente Guerrero and Lorenzo Zavala, the consequence was a Conservative backed military coup d'état under Anastasio Bustamante, inaugurating in Puebla an odious and oppressive centralism of a kind never before experienced.

The return of liberal federalism following the fall of the Andrade regime, although at first welcomed by most poblanos, brought neither peace nor consensus to Puebla. The ill-timed anti-clerical reforms of Gómez Farías reversed Puebla's hitherto consistent support for federalism. General Santa Anna's historic change of heart, from federalism to centralism, can in part be explained by the change of political temper of the city upon which he based so much of his support. Apart from a general revulsion in Puebla towards Gómez Farías' religious reforms, there were other perhaps more compelling reasons why poblanos in the mid 1830's were eschewing federalism. A new and self-confident political economy

---

[86] *Calendario Galván.* Mexico, 1842.

was taking shape and a renewed "spirit of association" could be observed among the city's merchants. Both required a more direct influence upon decisions in the capital than the loose arrangements of the 1824 federal constitution allowed. Puebla's protectionist political economy and the economic conditions which nurtured it must now be examined.

Chapter 6

PROTECTIONISM AND THE ONSET OF PUEBLA'S INDUSTRIAL RECOVERY

Protectionist ideas were popular and protectionist policies common throughout much of Latin America over the post-Independence decades, as they were indeed in Europe over the same period. At first, however, economic liberalism seemed to policy makers to be a progressive and rational substitute for colonial restrictions and Adam Smith informed most of the first tariffs of the newly-independent states. Within a short time, however, particularly in those countries whose colonial economies had depended upon mining production - Mexico, Colombia, Bolivia and Peru - people began to regard liberal political economy more critically. By the late 1820s, the decline in mineral production, the unchecked influx of European imports, the haemorrhage of specie overseas, the growing trade imbalance, the "*clamores*" of artisans engaged in domestic production, the encroachment of foreign wholesale merchants into retail trade and the crafts, all tended to encourage protectionist sentiments.

For most countries with protectionist tariffs over the first half of the nineteenth century, the purpose was not isolation from foreign trade but rather, the control and taxing of imports in order to reduce trade deficits, to raise revenues, and, only as a secondary consideration, to protect or encourage domestic manufacturing. At certain times, however, pressure grew for tariff prohibitions either to protect ailing traditional industries or to encourage new ones. But absolute import prohibitions were granted only exceptionally and for short periods: in Peru (1826-33 and 1848-52) and Bolivia (under General Belzú, 1848-55).[1] Import prohibitions were never achieved in Colombia despite impressive though rarely successful

---

[1] Paul Gootenburg, "The Social Origins"; and Leon E. Bieber, "Bolivia 1825-1850: aislamiento internacional y economía nacional"; Reinhard Liehr (ed.), *La formación de economías Latinoamericanas y los intereses económicas Europeos en la época de Bolívar, 1800-1850*. Bibliotheca Ibero-Americana, No.33. Berlin, 1989.

investment in modern industry.[2] Ecuador made an exception in an otherwise liberal tariff by prohibiting woollen cloth imports in 1829 and again in 1832.[3] Only in Mexico did a prohibitionist tarriff policy endure for longer than a decade (the prohibition on ordinary cotton cloth lasted from 1838 to 1854). And in Mexico, it seems clear that from the establishment of a loan bank for industry in 1830 (*El Banco de Avío*) until the American war, prohibitionist tariffs had a developmentalist as well as a fiscal purpose, however unsuccessful this "neo-mercantilism" may ultimately have been.

Puebla's Predilection for Protectionism

The contribution of Puebla to the onset and survival of the "protectionist era" in Mexico was substantial, perhaps crucial. No other region projected such articulate protectionist propoganda or maintained such persistent political pressure in favor of a protectionist and autonomist model of economic development. The reasons for this have been implicit earlier in the study but need, nevertheless, to be reiterated in the light of the political and social crisis observed in the last two chapters. During the mid-1830s, protectionist pamphleteering increased in abundance and lucidity, providing a subjective commentary on the prolonged economic and political crisis afflicting central and southern Mexico. This was a critical moment during which the ideas, the policies and the actions which would characterize the "protectionist era" came together. What were the principal elements of the protectionist amalgam and why do we find Puebla at the vanguard of Mexican protectionism?

First, Puebla possessed a manufacturing tradition. The region's staple industries were no mere adjuncts to agricultural, commercial or mining specialization but formed the very core of the provincial economy. Those seeking protectionist policies, publicising the cause and investing in new industrial processes during the 1830s were conscious of Puebla's industrial past and references to it, often exaggerated, frequently surface in their writings. Since protectionist ideas tended to be more pragmatic and empirical than their liberal counterparts, this observable industrial tradition was clearly an advantage, just as liberals faced a handicap in only being able to project into an uncertain future. And prominent protectionist, generally practical men of business, could observe in Puebla's economic history commerciable commodities which protectionist policies might revive as

---

[2] Frank Safford, "Commercial Crisis and Economic Ideology in New Granada, 1825-1850"; Liehr, *La Formación*; and Anthony MacFarlane, "The transition from colonialism in Colombia, 1819-1875", in C Abel and C Lewis (eds.), *Latin America: Economic Imperialism and the State*. London, 1985, pp. 111-113.

[3] Francisco Salazar, *Actas del Primer Congreso Constituyente de Ecuador*. Quito, 1893.

valuable staples. Elsewhere in Latin America, it was perhaps the absence of such a tradition of commodity production of industrial staples, except in circumscribed and often isolated areas, which accounts for the lack of resolution and continuity in protectionist thought. Merchants simply saw no long term commercial potential in the commodities to be shielded from foreign competition.[4]

A good example of a practical protectionist polemicist is Pedro Azcué y Zalvide, a Puebla cloth dealer, state and federal deputy, and spokesman for Puebla's handloom weavers during the 1830s. He was tantalized by idea of regaining Puebla's past industrial prosperity, writing in 1835 that:

> Puebla solo sostenía el año de 1815, muy cerca de 30,000 personas en las manufacturas de algodón; y el producto de sus esportaciones llegó a la considerable suma de 6,000,000 de pesos; hoy se encuentra en menos de dos tercios de su antigua población, destruidos completamente sus suburbios; y acrecentando al número de mendigos y andrajosos; su comercio esta reducido al cambio de cobre; y disminuidas las ventas de su mercado a la sesta ó séptima parte de lo que fueron antes.[5]

He was convinced that only with a complete prohibition of imports of cotton cloth would Puebla's prosperity be recovered.

Apart from this historical sense of past grandeur, (and it is interesting to note that Fray Juan Villa Sánchez' classic portrayal of the Puebla of 1746, in a comparable state of decay from past industrial prosperity, was republished in Puebla in 1835), there was clear understanding of why Puebla possessed a manufacturing tradition and what factors had favored or harmed the city's industries. It was well known, for instance, that the Napoleonic wars, by interrupting Atlantic trade, had afforded unprecedented protection, stimulating a short boom at the turn of the nineteenth century:

> ...los felices años (1805-1808)...presentando (Puebla) el aspecto más brillante, porque no habia comercio libre ultramarino; pero muy activo con esta ciudad y las poblaciones del interior. Anualmente estaban en las calles de Mesones y otros dos o tres, de cuatro o seis millones de pesos, y todo se quedaba en manos de nuestros tejedores, sombrereros, silleros, plateros, herreros,

---

4 For the lack of commercial viability of "wage goods", such as cotton cloth, and the insurmountable obstacles facing industrialization in coastal Peru in this period: Paul E. Gootenburg, "Artisans and Merchants: the Making of an Open Economy in Lima, Peru, 1830 to 1860". Unpublished M. Phil. thesis, Oxford University, 1981; and his "The Social Origins", pp. 339-40.

5 Pedro Azcué y Zalvide, *Observaciones contra la libertad del comercio exterior o sea contestación al Diario del Gobierno Federal*. Puebla, 1835, in Luis Córdova, *Protección*, p. 175.

vidrieros, coleros, etc por lo que esta hermosa ciudad tenia una población de 70-80 mil habitantes, todos tranquilos, obedientes y felices.[6]

The French bockade of Mexico's ports between 1837 and 1839 was observed to have had the same effect.[7]

Thus Puebla's long history as a manufacturing society gave local protectionist thought a practical character which made it difficult to contest. There was a contempt for the way economic policy had been entrusted to "simples colegiales" who had not experienced pre-war prosperity and knew nothing of the realities of economic life.[8]

Apart from the sensitivity of Puebla's economy to a volatile external sector, the province's symbiotic economic relationship to the mineral rich *tierradentro* was also appreciated. Posessing no mines, the Puebla region was obliged to export goods to other parts of Mexico or abroad if it was to attract coin. This accounts for the enthusiasm of merchant-manufacturers such as Estevan de Antuñano for the recovery of the market of the silver-rich tierradentro.[9] It also perhaps explains the absence of moral outrage, indeed the general rejoicing, when silver *conductas* were robbed, as occured in 1828.[10] This was considered a legitimate crime since this was coin which, if kept in circulation, would help solve Puebla's problem of unemployment. Indeed it was much later (in 1915) recognized by the Puebla historian, Eduardo Gómez Haro, that the plunder from the robbery of the *conducta*, and the sacking of Spanish commercial houses which followed it, "has been the origen of some of the fortunes which exist and have existed in Puebla".[11]

The currency question also explains the hostility felt in Puebla towards merchants solely involved in "passive trade" - the exchange of imported goods for silver - and also, the desire to exclude foreigners from retailing imports. "Passive trade" was treated by protectionist polemicists as no better than robbery. The merchants who were most admired were those

[6] Francisco Javier de la Peña in *El Amigo de la Religión, Agricultura, Política , Comercio , Ciencias y Artes*. Puebla, 1839, Vol. I p. 58.

[7] El Regenerador Oaxaca, 29 April 1844, in Estevan de Antuñano, *Reflecciones sobre el Bloqueo y el Erario de México*. Mexico, 1838.

[8] Leonardo Tamariz, *Pacificación de la República*. Puebla, 1858, p. 2

[9] Estevan de Antuñano, *Primer Asunto de la Patria, el algodón. Manifiesto sobre el algodón manufacturado y en greña*. Puebla, 1833.

[10] The political sensitivity in Mexico to silver *conductas* leaving the country from the Real del Monte during the 1830s is discussed in Robert Randall, *Real del Monte. A British Mining Venture in Mexico*, Texas, 1972, p. 194.

[11] Gómez Haro, *Puebla*, p. 119.

who put their cash into circulation by investing in local enterprise.[12] The fiscal sacrifice of import prohibitions was justified on grounds that the manufacturing which it encouraged would permit the transformation of "passive trade" into a much more dynamic process. By 1844, it could be observed that as a result of the establishment of a mechanized cotton spinning industry, an achievement which would have been impossible without import prohibitions, "solamente Puebla evita que el estranjero se lleve 11,000 pesos diarios."[13]

But *poblano* protectionist thought was no crude bullionism, tinged with xenophobia. Protectionist arguments showed a subtle understanding of the effects of the "mining constitution" of Mexico's economy upon other economic sectors. One anonymous polemicist, writing in 1836, presented Mexico's economic dilemma with particular acuteness. He was especially concerned with the harm caused by the steady drain overseas of silver specie since the start of the Wars of Independence. This, he observed, had led to a fall in agricultural prices, a drop in demand for manufactured goods, a general shortage of coin, the rapid growth of usury and an increase in interest rates. The consequence was a generalized economic depression. He blamed liberal economic policies and the failure to understand the place of silver mining and exports within Mexico's economy. "Our economy is entirely different from that of other countries," he asserted, "we are an exception to the general rule ... this our economists have entirely forgotten"[14]

He went on to argue that in other countries, from where the economic theories, which Mexicans so gullibly had adopted, had emanated, wages and prices had always been set in acordance with the value of basic foodstuffs and clothing. In Mexico, to the contrary, the quantity of silver mined and in circulation had set wages and prices. As a consequence, wages and prices were higher in Mexico than in non-mining countries, by ratio of three to one. This made Mexico a very attractive market for imports, so attractive was Mexican silver to foreign merchants. The result was that pressure from imports was unremitting, even during the depressed years following Independence. And, local manufactures found it impossible to compete, given the high labor and raw material costs.

The solution lay in protective tariffs, a strictly supervised issue of a paper currency, guaranteed by a "bank of landowners"," and a regulation by which foreign goods would be sold at at a price determined by the discount between the local value of money and the international value of

---

12 For invectives against "passive trade" and "agiotismo", see: Pedro de Azcué y Zalvide, *Observaciones contra la libertad del comercio*, pp. 172-4; and *El Cardillo de los Agiotistas*. Mexico, 1837, No. 1 p. 3.

13 *Calendario de López*. Mexico, 1844.

14 Anon. *Algunas consideraciones económicas (sobre protección a la industria)*. Mexico, 1836.

gold and silver. Thereby, Mexico would remain a producer of precious metals but also could become again a manufacturing and agricultural country. The flaw in this project lay, of course, in the election of Mexico's crisis stricken agricultural sector as the fount and guarantor of value. Chapters 1 and 3 have shown how ill-suited was Puebla's agriculture, locked in ecclesiastical mortmain and facing stagnant prices, for performing this daunting task.

In the Puebla of the early 1830s, industry not agriculture, seemed to offer the only viable sector for reconstituting a "fount and guarantor" of value. Indeed, it was observed in Chapter 3 how a proposal for the restoration of the wheat assize, in effect a subsidy to wheat agriculture designed to regenerate the entire provincial economy, was specifically rejected. In 1830, the establishment of fully mechanized industry had been placed at the forefront of the national economic agenda with the establishment of the *Banco de Avío para el Fomento de la Industria*.[15] *Poblano* entrepreneurs were some of the first to respond to the call to establish *juntas de industria* and to bid for loans from the bank.[16] But while there was unanimity in Puebla about the desirability of industrial recovery, there were widespread differences about the means to that end.

The main bone of contention was over the degree to which labor saving machinery should be applied to Puebla's traditional industries. Here the dispute was between those who saw the recovery of employment as the priority and those who were principally concerned with the recovery in profitability of industry. In 1829, *poblano* pressure had been responsible for the defeat of a congressional project for introducing steel looms throughout the Republic to consume British yarn. The "Godoy Project" was seen by almost everyone in Puebla as a threat to their interests. It threatened Puebla's lead as the chief textile manufacturing region since steel looms would be distributed throughout the Republic. It threatened to destroy the control Puebla's merchants had over the supply of yarn to weavers and the marketing of their cloth. It threatened the residual autonomy of Puebla's weavers and their influence upon cotton spinners.[17]

The *Banco de Avío*, although it was popular among many of Puebla's merchants and fledgling industrialists, faced vociferous opposition from Pedro de Azcué y Zalvide, self-appointed representative of the city's artisans. He feared that the flood of cloth imports which would follow the removal of the import prohibition (revenue from cotton cloth imports were needed to fund the bank) would inflict the final death blow to Puebla's cotton textile industry, greatly increasing the problems of unemployment

---

[15] Potash, *El Banco de Avío*, pp. 69-98.

[16] *Registro Oficial*, Mexico, 1831, Vol. III pp. 214-5; and Miguel Quintana, *Estevan de Antuñano Fundador de la Industria Textíl en Puebla*. Mexico, 1957, pp. 61-75.

[17] Potash, *El Banco de Avío*, pp. 57-63.

and public order.[18] He drew the parallel of the plight of Saxony's weavers faced with British cloth imports following the collapse of the Continental System.

The chief propogandist favoring mechanization was Puebla's principal textile entrepreneur: Estevan de Antuñano. Aware that most of Puebla's artisans viewed machines with deep distrust, he waged a formidable pamphlet campaign defending industrial modernization, often adopting the popular *poblano* idiom, distributing his pamphlets free of charge and sometimes using the socratic form of a dialogue between an enlightened and benificent merchant and a suspicious, though gullible, artisan (usually a cotton weaver). He wrote over sixty pamphlets, many of them lengthy, the longest exceeding eighty pages.[19] He was particularly skillful at playing off different groups of artisans.

Those who had most to lose from mechanization were the cotton spinners. In Antuñano's opinion, they had no reason for concern. Nor had the handloom weavers. Both would be served by the modernization of the textile industry. In February 1834, Antunaño opposed the Puebla legislature's call for the reestablishment of the import prohibition on cloth and yarn. He argued that this should come only after the new factories had commenced production. His justification for opposing what had been Puebla's most persistent request since 1821 was that any prohibition would harm the interests of Puebla's handloom weavers. They had grown accustomed to imported yarn which they found to be cleaner, cheaper and more abundant. Any early return to prohibition would, Antuñano maintained, lead to discontent among Puebla's weavers, "their interests are now entirely opposed to those of the women spinners".[20] Much more important was to complete the construction and equipping of the new factories, partly financed from customs revenues funnelled through the *Banco de Avío* (explaining why Antuñano, with his factory still not completed, opposed any prompt restoration of the prohibition).

Once the factories had entered production, then prohibitions should be restored and customs revenues sacrificed. Women spinners would find employment in the new factories. Weavers would now buy local factory yarn and be guaranteed sale of their products across the factory counters. Weavers and spinners might now accumulate savings enabling them to buy

18 Pedro de Azcué y Zalvide, *Contestación a los Editores del Sol.* Mexico, 1831; and *Registro Oficial*, Vol. VI pp. 11, 61, 86, 146.

19 Many are reproduced in Quintana, *Estevan de Antuñano.* For a full checklist of Antuñano's writings, see José Miguel Quintana, "Biografías y Bibliografías de Economistas Mexicanas", *Suplemento del Boletín Bibliográfico de la Secretaría de Hacienda y Crédito Público*. Mexico, June 1955, pp. 1-2.

20 Estevan de Antuñano, *Discurso analítico de algunos puntos de moral y economía política de Méjico con relación a su agricultura cereal o sea pensamientos para un plan para animar la industria mejicana.* Puebla, 1834, in Quintana, *ibid*, Vol. I p. 260; and Potash, *El Banco de Avío*, p. 131.

machines themselves. A chain of virtuous economic, political and moral consequences would follow. Cotton agriculture in the lowlands would flourish, the ancient ties of economic reciprocity between Veracruz and Puebla would be reestablished, idleness and unemployment would disappear, revolution become unknown.[21]

Not everyone in Puebla was so sanguine about the benefits of mechanization. Two influential Conservative propogandists, Pedro de Azcué and Francisco Javier de la Peña, warned against the introduction of machinery, "for the old looms and spinning wheels fed many: these machines very few. Machines might in time be useful but at present extremely prejudicial".[22] And there was a general popular suspicion of, and hostility towards, the foreign technicians who had come to Puebla to mount the new machinery. Antuñano chose to house his British and New England artisans on his estate near the new factory rather than in the city and he instructed that they only visit the city accompanied by armed guards.[23] In spite of Antuñano's claim that handloom weavers were favorable to the mechanization of spinning, it is clear that they were deeply suspicious of the new factory owners who they feared would soon introduce power looms into their spinning premises. Antuñano attempted to placate the weavers by agreeing in 1839 to limit the number of power looms being introduced to his factory, *La Constancia*.[24] But such pledges could hardly have convinced Puebla's weavers, long accustomed to the fickleness of merchants.[25]

The merchants investing in modern machinery had a useful ally in the well known artisan, José Manso y Jaramillo. Manso was a talented painter, architect and specialist in glass manufacture who had been sent to Europe during the 1820s to study lithography and industrial techniques with instructions to return with models and machines. He was a founder member of the School of Design in 1814 and, by 1830, had established Puebla's first industrial museum (largely, it seems, to provide a home for foreign machines which had not yet found a use in Puebla).[26] In 1835 he

21 Estevan de Antuñano, *Manifiesto sobre el Algodón*, Puebla, 1833.

22 Pedro de Azcué y Zalvide, *Observaciones contra la libertad del comercio exterior*. Puebla, 1835; and de la Peña, "Notas", pp. 162-7.

23 José Miguel Quintana asserts that Antuñano himself suffered an assassination attempt in 1832, and in the following year, during Santa Anna's siege of the city, he underwent a period of detention for threatening the ruin of the spinners and weavers. See *Estevan de Antuñano*, Vol. I p. 47.

24 Estevan de Antuñano, *Economía política en México*, 1 June 1839, Puebla.

25 *Representación que los tejedores de algodón, vecinos de Puebla, dirigen al Gobierno del Departamento*. Puebla, 1840.

26 Manso was a prominent and highly respected figure in Puebla during the 1810s and 20s. He escaped military service during the insurgency (with which he, like many artists in Puebla, sympathised) by becoming a "psalmist" in the cathedral. Here he

published a pamphlet entitled "Apuntes Artísticos de un Artesano de Puebla", in the form of a dialogue between a lucid, urbane and agressive patrician and a sceptical, stubborn and conservative artisan, permitting a full airing of the debate over the merits of mechanization. Manso's purpose was to allay artisans' fears about unemployment. He demonstrated that over half the labor force employed in traditional cotton textiles at the height of its prosperity would still be employed in the mechanized industry, even if production were limited to serving only the provincial market. The other half would immediately find employment in businesses benefitting from the mechanization of textiles: construction, handloom-weaving, hat making, glass, pottery, iron and copper. He warned against nostalgic longing for a return to a golden age which had never been. During the Napoleonic War boom, weavers and spinners may have been able to afford to dress in velvet and fustian cloth, but the consumer had suffered. Mechanization, in contrast, would reduce prices and increase competitiveness, bringing general prosperity. Manso concluded by reassuring the artisan that he would not be abandoned by the merchant once merchants became manufacturers. This point was addressed to the weavers who had grown accustomed since Independence to receiving imported yarn from merchants on credit. Manso assured the weaver that with a prohibition on yarn and cloth imports permitting the mechanization of cotton spinning, merchants and manufacturers would be falling over each other to establish ties with Puebla's weavers.[27] For a time, this proved prophetic, as Chapter 7 will shortly demonstrate.

Such are some of the staple arguments of *poblano* protectionism. Now the economic conditions which made protectionism a viable project must be examined more closely. The most important of these was, without doubt, the deepening of the recession facing Mexico's external trade during the 1830s.

Crisis and Instability in Mexico's External Sector

The critical factor accounting for the renewal of merchants' interest in manufacturing, and for their decision to invest directly in modern industrial technology, was the exacerbation of the crisis facing Mexico's external

---

designed the present magnificent tabernacle. In 1824 he refurbished the *alhóndiga* building as the State Congress. Manso's industrial museum was housed in the State College and was destroyed by an explosion of a gunpowder factory in 1833. In 1843 Manuel Payno was shocked to find this once famous *poblano* artist to be living in poverty - a sign, perhaps, of the passing of an age during which the skilled artisan had been valued more highly. *El Museo Mexicano*, Vol. III pp. 256-57; and Manuel Payno, "Un Viaje a Veracruz en 1843", *El Museo Mexicano*, Vol. III p. 144.

[27] 'J.M.' *Apuntes Artísticos de un Artesano de Puebla*. Mexico, 1835.

sector during the 1830s. Since Independence, the value and volume of Mexico's foreign trade had fluctuated almost as wildly as during the 1790s and 1800s. Imports, at first slow to respond to the end of Spanish rule, climbed rapidly to a peak between 1825 and 1827. This was followed by a two year slump accompanying the British financial crisis and the Acordada revolution in Mexico City. Trade then recovered under Bustamante to reach a further peak over 1830 and 1831 as a result of tariff liberalization and a renewed British bid to replace the Spanish as Mexico's import merchants and silver bankers. Currency deficiency and political instability disappointed British merchants' hopes and trade once more slumped in 1832-33, recovering during 1834-35 to another peak, followed by a protracted slump lasting well into the 1840s.[28]

The short trade recovery of 1834-35 was almost entirely due to a marked increase in coastal trade from the United States. American merchants were taking up the slack left by the return of European merchants. Trade with Britain and France steadily declined as the 1830s proceeded. After 1835, imports from the United States also fell precipitously, remaining stagnant until the late 1840s. This was a result of the financial crash in the US in 1837, anti-American sentiment and discrimination against US merchants following the war with Texas, but above all of the reorientation of of the US economy from overseas to internal trade during the late 1830s and 1840s. Mexico (and other Latin American countries, particularly Colombia) shared with the United States in this tactical retreat from international trade.[29] Mexico's foreign trade fell off generally over the late 1830s and early 1840s for a variety of reasons: mining depression and currency shortage, the deflationary effect of Bustamante's attempt to reschedule the national debt (serving to draw funds away from trade into government loans), the reestablishment of import prohibitions after 1836 (raw cotton imports were prohibited in 1836, cotton yarn in 1837 and cotton cloth in 1838), and not least, the French blockade of Mexico's ports between 1838-39.[30] Not since the years before the Peace of Amiens had competition from imports been so relaxed.

How did Puebla's merchants, propogandists and politicians respond to this instability and uncertainty ?

---

28 For figures on British, French and United States trade with Mexico see: Miguel Lerdo de Tejada, *Comercio Exterior*, Graphs 38 & 41; and BL, State Papers, "Return relating to trade with Mexico from 1820 to 1841".

29 Brantz Meyer, *Mexico as it was and as it is*. Philadelphia, 1841, p. 123. United States trade with Colombia shows a similar pattern: growth until 1837, followed by a deep recession until the late 1840s, William Paul McGreevey, *Economic History of Colombia, 1845-1930*. Cambridge, 1971, pp. 36-37.

30 Leland. H. Jenks, *The Migration of British Capital to 1875*. London, 1971, pp. 111-2; and Jan Bazant, *Historia de la deuda exterior de México, 1823-1946*. Mexico, 1968, pp. 51-61; and Brantz Meyer, *Mexico as it was*, p. 129, and Potash, *El Banco de Avío*, pp. 189-96.

The Currency Problem of the Mexican South-east and the Copper Money Debate

Proximity to Veracruz and the absence of its own mines, had long fostered an awareness in Puebla of the pressing need to attract and maintain a sufficient level of circulating medium to serve provincial requirements. Merchants and shopkeepers had grown accustomed to substitutes for hard currency, using tokens, cocoa beans and even stamped soap for small transactions and letters of exchange for long distance trade.[31] But silver, both as a commodity and as a medium of exchange, because of its international acceptability, was the most sought-after currency in Puebla. The time (before the 1740s) when Puebla had its own mint and mercury exchange, symbolising its centrality to New Spain's commercial circuits, was still remembered in the 1830s.[32] The recovery of such autonomy and centrality, and particularly the reestablishment of its own mint, were among Puebla's principal protectionist aspirations.

By the early 1830s, the shortage of silver coin in the center and the south of the country had become critical. There were three reasons for this. The first was that, since Independence, for reasons of security, efficiency and "federalism", most silver was minted close to the mines in the north-west center and north of the country. Guanajuato, Durango, Zacatecas and San Luis Potosí became Mexico's prinicipal minting centers. Between 1833 and 1838, while national coinage rates remained fairly stable, those of the Mexico City mint plummeted.[33]

The second reason for the demonetarization of the center and southeast was the centrifugal scattering of the country's foreign merchant body. As a result of the decentralization of mintage and of the disintegration of the centralized colonial political order, foreign merchants as often chose to do business away from Mexico City, the center of mintage and emporium of foreign trade before 1821. Thus by the early 1830s, the centers of foreign trade were as much San Luis Potosí, Aguascalientes and Guadalajara as they were Mexico City.[34] In one sense, the foreign merchants established in these peripheral locations were no different from their colonial counterparts, since they were still engaged in the exchange of European

---

[31] For a discussion of currency shortage in the late colony, see Morin, *Michoacan*, pp. 178-87.

[32] Villa Sánchez, *Puebla Sagrada y Profana*, p. 81-82

[33] Lerdo de Tejada, *El Comercio Exterior*, Table No. 54; and Manuel Orozco y Berra, *Apuntes para la Historia de la Moneda y Acuñacion desde antes la Conquista*. Mexico, 1880, p. 141.

[34] The British merchant James Wylie, with an import business in San Luis Potosí wrote in 1830 that "San Luis and Aguascalientes are the best places for business and the city of Mexico has become the worst." University of Glasgow, MSS Collection, Wylie Papers, Vol. I, 1 June 1830, Wylie to Cooke (Manchester).

manufactured goods for silver. But the spatial and political context of their activity contrasts starkly with the state of affairs before Independence.

When commercial wealth had been concentrated in the capital, apart from serving as the engine of the mining economy and the import trade, merchant capital had lubricated the great north-south networks of exchange, which Puebla's artisans and manufacturers saw as the key to their prosperity. Once merchants settled in peripheral locations, adopting trade routes which bypassed the Mexico City-Puebla-Veracruz axis, using ports such as Tampico and San Blas, such ancillary investments were not so attractive nor readily available, even if the tight credit policies of merchants in the 1830s had permitted them.[35] Thus the long-distance trade between pastoral and mineral north and the manufacturing and grain-producing center and south east underwent a marked decline, if Charles Harris' account of the Coahuila case is representative of broader trends.[36]

The third reason for the south-east's currency shortage was, of course, the secular decline in national silver production, with the center sharing disproportionately in this.[37] A temporary solution lay in the issue of a copper currency. From Guerrero's government in 1829 until the abolition of the federal constitution in 1837, copper currency was issued in ever increasing quantities from the Mexico City mint. By 1837 there were at least 4,000,000 copper pesos in circulation in Mexico City and Puebla alone.[38] During the 1840s, many people in Puebla believed that copper money had made an important contribution to the onset of industrial recovery.[39] And as late as the 1850s, Puebla protectionists maintained that the withdrawal of copper money, more than anything else, had brought a halt to industrial growth, leaving the provincial economy once more exposed to the hectic fluctuations of international trade.[40] It is impossible

---

[35] In April 1831 Wylie urged his agent in Tampico to remit money to England without delay so as not to incur unecessary interest on loans held in Manchester. In February of the following year he forbade his factors in the Interior from advancing credit to customers urging them to accept only cash or else to remit goods to England where there were rumors of the failure of an English house which had been dealing in Mexico. UG, MSS Wylie Papers, Vol. I fs. 38, 413.

[36] Harris, *A Mexican Family*, pp. 91-93.

[37] Between 1790 and 1810 Mexico's silver mines had yielded well over 20 million pesos annually. During the 1830s production averaged around 11 million, only rising above 15 million towards the end of the 1840s. See T.J.Cassidy, *British Capital and the Mexican Silver Mining Industry, 1820-50*. Cambridge CLAS, Working Paper No.21 n.d. pp. 10-11.

[38] Orozco y Berra, *Apuntes para la Historia*, p. 141; and Quintana, *Estevan de Antuñano*, Vol. II p. 31.

[39] *Representación a la Exma Asamblea Departamental que hace el Comercio de Puebla sobre acuñación de moneda particular para el Departamento*. Puebla, 1845.

[40] Tamariz, *Pacificación*, p. 10.

to test the validity of such claims. However, the heat of the debate over copper money, and the opposition Bustamante faced in attempting to withdraw copper from circulation, gives them some credence.

Copper money had provoked a mixed response. It was welcomed by the public (it was seen by Liberals as a way of putting purchasing power in the hands of the common people). It was welcomed by retailers who saw copper as an expanding medium of local and regional exchange which would increase demand. Wholesalers, however, would rarely receive it since it was unacceptable internationally, tended to make silver even more scarce (through Gresham's law) and became rapidly devalued (being easy to forge). The government was faced, therefore, with a mounting dilemma. It was obliged to set a good example by accepting copper at face value yet, at the same time, it faced increasing pressure from its creditors, largely wholesale merchants, to return to silver as the exclusive currency. Bustamante ultimately succumbed to this pressure, ordering a stop to the issue of copper coin late in 1836 and proceeding in 1837 to the withdrawal of copper money from circulation.

To manage the redemption of copper, Bustamante established the *National Bank for Copper Redemption.* On 10 March 1837 the copper peso was declared to be worth only 50% of its face value. Holders of copper money were then ordered to exchange their copper for silver. This sparked widespread discontent among holders of copper in cash, credit or bills of exchange. The most serious incident occured in Orizaba where the employees of the Cocolapan textile mill, accustomed to receiving their wages in copper, rioted against their French employers.[41] A combination of popular intransigence and the Bank's failure to raise sufficient funds in silver to reimburse copper money holders, menat that little copper money was redeemed in 1837.[42]

In 1838, Bustamante again attempted to withdraw copper money by shifting the funding of the bank from direct taxes and tobacco revenues to customs revenues and the wealth of the religious orders. This proved no more successful as a result of depressed customs receipts (due to recent import prohibitions and the French blockade) and opposition from the Church.[43] Copper thus remained in circulation for a further three critical years.

During the 1830s, until the final redemption of copper in 1842, copper money gained a special acceptance in Puebla. Copper became an accepted medium with Church loans and rents, as with merchants, shopkeepers and

---

41 Condumex, *Correspondencia de Lucas Alamán*, Hospital de Jesús, Vol. 424 Exp. 12 José María Mendizabal, Orizaba, to Lucas Alamán, July 7 1837.

42 Quintana, *Estevan de Antuñano*, Vol. II, p. 31.

43 AAP, Cabildo, Vol. 105, 27 January 1838; Guillermo Prieto, *Indicaciones sobre el origen, vicisitudes y estado de las rentas generales de la federación mexicana.* Mexico, 1850, p. 116; and Brantz Meyer, *Mexico*, p. 120.

industrialists. By 1840, many workers in Puebla's new factories were receiving their wages in copper. Copper was shown to possess several advantages. It was found to be superior to silver as a medium for day-to-day exchange within the province since the volume in circulation remained fairly constant, nobody desiring to hoard it for export. Indeed, the volume of copper in circulation even expanded slowly, due to forgery. The resulting depreciation did not greatly concern shopkeepers and manufacturers who were anxious to encourage steady and sustained consumer demand to match the more even rhythm of factory production. Copper also possessed the added advantage of deterring importers who sought only silver in exchange for their goods, adding a further margin of protection to the provincial economy. Finally, it was appreciated that copper was a popular and "democratic" currency: it cheapened goods generally and increased demand.[44] It thus served as a balm to soothe the painful first stages of industrialization.

The political and economic consequences of the redemption of copper are examined in Chapters 7 and 10. For the moment, it can be concluded that the circulation of copper currency during the 1830s played an important part in encouraging industrial investment and the development of the internal market. But what other factors helped foster the revival of Puebla's entrepreneurship during the 1830s? International trade recession, the French blockade and copper currency helped to relieve pressure from import competition upon Puebla's industries. But what of Puebla's "natural" locational advantages which accounted for the decision merchants to turn to industry as an attractive field of investment in past times? The most important of these was proximity to the Mexico's principal regions of cotton agriculture. Here, from the early 1830s, commercial prospects began to improve after two decades of decline.

The Revival of Cotton

One of the most important changes in the occupational and productive structure of Puebla over the first half of the nineteenth century was the replacement of hand-spinning of cotton by the mechanized spindle (the Arkwright Water Frame and the Crompton Mule). The economic rationale for this had been obvious, even to Mexican entrepreneurs, from the late eighteenth century . Chapter 1 has already offered an explaination as to why no serious consideration was given to mechanization before Independence. What, then, had changed between 1807 and 1837 to make so many

---

44 Pedro Azcué y Zalvide, *Ligeras observaciones contra el proyecto de la Cámara de diputados sobre la extinción de la moneda de cobre*. Puebla, 1841; and for the Departmental assembly's petition against the withdrawal of copper money, *Proyecto -Santa Anna-Junta Departmental de Puebla*. Puebla, 4 December 1841.

merchants, shopkeepers and professionals choose to invest in modern spinning technology?

The answer lies in five interelated areas: the revival of cotton agriculture in Veracruz, the growing use by cotton weavers of imported factory-spun yarn and the decision by merchants to substitute this; the availability and cheapening of British and United States cotton-spinning machinery; a disposition among Puebla's merchants towards industrial investment and entrepreneurship; and, finally, a more energetic government stance in favor of protecting and encouraging industry.

After thirty years of decline, in spite of every kind of fiscal inducement, from the early 1830s *veracruzano* cotton agriculture began to recover.[45] This was a result of a combination of circumstances: official encouragement to cotton growers from the State government; the securing (in 1836) of an import prohibition on raw cotton (achieved through pressure from the Veracruz and Oaxaca governments); the revival of commercial interest in cotton agriculture from among merchants in Puebla, the port of Veracruz and Tlacotalpan (the commercial hub of the cotton growing region); the willingness of growers to introduce new strains of cotton more acceptable to the cotton gin and the machine spindle; and, finally, the mechanization of the preparation and spinning of cotton itself.[46] The last of these changes - the introduction of the machine - was perhaps the most significant.

The successful introduction of the cotton gin to the Veracruz lowlands enabled merchants to greatly reduce transport costs since bulky raw cotton no longer needed to be transported to Puebla to be stripped. Reduction of bulk was a particularly important consideration given the shortage of draft animals, a problem since long before Independence. The mechanization of the preparing and spinning stage of cloth production removed one entire layer in the commercial hierarchy: the *algodonero*, who had managed the distribution of raw cotton to spinners and spun cotton to weavers. This simplification of the commercial ladder between the field and the factory encouraged a concentration of capital around the growing and trading of raw cotton which would have important consequences for the development of the industry, some of them harmful (it grew easier to monopolize the commodity). Finally, the mechanization of spinning enabled the merchant both to save on labor and to reestablish his links with the weaver by offering a product which could compete with the foreign yarn, to which

---

[45] Raw cotton had been exempted from payment of *alcabala* in 1804 and 1806 and from internal customs in 1821. Raw cotton imports were prohibited in 1821, in 1829 and again in 1836. AGN, Reales Cédulas, 22 April 1804, 1 October 1806; Iñés Herrera Canales, *El Comercio Exterior de México 1821-1875*. Mexico, 1977, pp. 176-9; and Potash, *El Banco de Avío*, pp. 192-3.

[46] Enrique Florescano and Luis Chávez Orozco, *Agricultura e Industria*, p. 192; *Registro Oficial*, Vol. IV, p. 400; and Vol.V, p. 245.

weavers had increasingly turned since Independence.[47] The cost of gins
and modern spinning machinery did not seem to investors to be unduly
expensive. Equipment for a medium-sized textile mill cost around 20,000
pesos in Philadelphia in 1831, no more than a wholesale or retail merchant
might pay for a consignment of imported cloth.[48] And easing the expense
of introducing bulky modern machinery was the widespread availability of
vacant or underused commercial and industrial property. This included
fourteen flour mills, several of them idle due to the depression in the flour
trade and most of them heavily encumbered with transferable Church
mortgages, making their acquisition inexpensive.

Puebla's Merchant Group

The concerted and sustained application of merchant capital and
enterprise to the recovery of industry and the maintenance of protectionism
required a certain disposition among Puebla's merchants. Already
mentioned are the lack of alternative fields of investement in mining or
agriculture, the consciousness of past industrial grandeur and the local
admiration for the "comerciante fomentador" over the dealer in "passive
trade". What else was peculiar about the Puebla environment which made
its merchant body so dedicated to activities which elsewhere in Latin
America only engaged merchants' interest sporadically? This question is
answered more fully through case studies in subsequent chapters. For the
moment, some general features can be sketched out.

Puebla had never attracted a significant number of merchants wholly
dedicated to foreign trade. Before Independence such merchants
congregated around the three *consulados*, in Mexico, Veracruz and
Guadalajara. Possessing neither silver, nor other export staples such as
cochineal (apart from the unstable and ultimately unsuccessful wheat flour),
the city, in spite of its prime location, was surpisingly isolated from the
commercial circuits linked to foreign trade. And after Independence, as has
already been observed, Puebla presented a hostile environment for foreign
merchants, very few choosing to take up residence in a city renowned for
its fanaticism and xenophobia before the 1840s. There were, of course,

---

47 Querétaro's cotton-weavers by 1831 were using imported yarn for weft and national
yarn for warp, permitting them to greatly increase the variety and improve the
quality of their cloth. *Registro Oficial*, Vol. V, 31 May 1831, p. 243.

48 Mexico's strong currency went a long way. In 1831 a cotton gin cost only 180
pesos in Philadelphia. A set of cotton-spinning and weaving machinery (2,400
spindles and 40 power looms - a medium sized factory in Mexico at this time) and
a steam-engine cost less than 20,000 pesos in Philadelphia. A further 7,000 pesos
was required for the cost of transporting the machinery to northern Mexico. AGN,
Banco de Avío, Vol. II, Exp. 72, February 1831, and Exp. 72 July 1831.

several prominent businesses wholesaling imported goods, but as commissioners for houses located elsewhere, chiefly in Jalapa or Veracruz.

Puebla therefore lacked a strong body of foreign import-export merchants. The strength of protectionist sentiment may in part be explained by the absence of the kind of merchants existing in Veracruz, Tampico, Jalapa or Mexico City, who constantly pressured governments for low tariffs, the end of prohibitions, liberal regulations governing the export of specie, and who regularly engaged in contraband.[49] Lacking such businesses, Puebla also had few *agiotistas*: merchants who speculated upon the financial weakness of governments by lending at exhorbitant rates. Most of Puebla's merchants commanded too little liquidity to act as bankers to governments.

Inhospitable terrain for the merchant seeking to engage exclusively in foreign trade, Puebla attracted merchants who had chosen or, more often, had been obliged to diversify out of foreign trade. Recruitment was particularly common from among *veracruzano* merchants who dealt in cotton or wheat, both of which, of course, passed through a production stage in Puebla. These were the merchants most alive to the commercial and industrial potentialities of the highland city. The merchant group in the cotton port of Tlacotalpan had particularly close links with highland interests, since, from their strategic location, they controlled the river and overland transport network linking the cotton producing zone, whose staples they marketed, and which they supplied highland manufactures and flour, as with imported goods. It was these merchants, together with their fellows in Veracruz who, when faced with slump in foreign trade, resulting from commercial recessions, blockades and wars, would seek to intensify their commercial ties with the highlands. Such circumstances led many to migrate inland to take up residence in Puebla. Several of Puebla's leading industrialists during the 1830s and 40s had taken this route from commerce to industry while others relied heavily on credit from *veracruzano* cotton suppliers and import houses.[50]

Puebla thus attracted merchants who sought to intensify the commercial ties between highland and lowland and between the Mexican southeast and the *tierradentro*. They were frequently involved with overseas trade as well but they saw internal trade as a means of compensating for the instability of the external sector. Their commercial success required that the city of Puebla be restored and maintained as a dynamic manufacturing center. This was the vital link in the chain.

---

49 For examples: Barbara A Tennenbaum, "Merchants, money and mischief. The British in Mexico, 1821-1862", The Americas, Vol., 35, 1978-79, pp. 317-339; and John Mayo, "Consuls and Silver Contraband on Mexico's West Coast in the Era os Santa Ana", *JLAS* , Vol. 19, 1987, pp. 389-411; and UG, MSS Wylie Paper (1831-38 Tampico-San Luis Potosí).

50 Estevan de Antuñano and Ciriaco Marrón were the two most prominent.

Puebla held further attractions for *veracruzanos* seeking opportunities inland. It has a cooler and healthier climate than the towns of the *tierra caliente*. There was a gentile, albeit decayed, landowning class which welcomed any addition of mercantile wealth through marriage. Labor was abundant on the plateau, in town and countryside (labor scarcity was a common complaint in Veracruz in this period). Moreover, municipal and state government was open to newcomers and accustomed to defending and advancing regional (including *veracruzano*) interests.

This study has observed two periods of coalescence between mercantile and industrial interests in Veracruz and Puebla. The first developed slowly over the eighteenth century with the growth of lowland cotton production and highland industry, culminating in the short-lived and speculative textile bonanza accompanying the Napoleonic wars. The second occured during the 1830s and early 1840s, accompanying a protracted crisis in Mexico's foreign trade, once more propelling the commercial and industrial interests of the two states together in Mexico's first project of industrial transformation. Later in the century, the manufacturers of Puebla and Veracruz would work together even more closely, in devising common industrial strategies and enforcing harsh labor policies.[51]

Neo-mercantilism and the "Spirit of Association"

The reassertion of Conservative centralism from 1830 brought with it the revival of a mercantilism with its roots in eighteenth-century Bourbon "fomento". In spite of the city's federalist sympathies, many *poblanos* responded energetically to projects devised by Bustamante's Interior Minister, Lucas Alamán, in particular to the *Banco de Avío*. This was a loan bank, funded from customs revenues, with a briefing to favor industrial projects, using modern technology, as well as related agriculture. The board of the bank would also urge the foundation and coordinate the activities of locally organized *companías, sociedades* and *juntas patrióticas*, through which the bank would distribute its funds.[52]

Early in 1831 Puebla became the first city in Mexico to respond to instructions from the *Banco de Avío* by establishing a broadly-based company to promote industrial modernization. The company was formed by the *Sociedad Protectora de las Artes*, established in 1827.[53] In 1830 the

---

51 Leticia Gamboa Ojeda, *Los empresarios de ayer. El grupo dominante en la industria textíl de Puebla, 1906-1929*. Puebla,1985; and Rodney Anderson, *Outcasts in Their Own Land: Mexican Industrial Workers 1906-1911*. Northern Illinois Press, 1976, pp. 137-170.

52 Potash, *El Banco de Avío*, pp. 69-112.

53 *El Poblano*, No.10, 29 April 1827; Quintana, *Estevan de Antuñano*, pp. 61-75.

Sociedad had published a perceptive report on the state of Puebla's industry, listing the reasons for its decline: epidemics reducing consumption, emigration of artisans stimulating industry in other provinces, the return of "capitalists" (merchant-financiers) to Europe, the invasion of the domestic market by imports, undependability of artisans, and declining quality -- all classic features of a declining domestic system which had become evident as early as 1810.[54] The report then proposed the formation of an industrial association to attract capital, to purchase machines, to employ foreign technicians and masters, to buy raw materials and operate a *casa de contratación* which would lend to artisans and market their products. In January 1831 a board of nine directors was elected at a well-attended meting held in the Council building: Cura Antonio María de la Rosa, a renowned theologian and organizer of charities, five wholesale merchants (including Estevan de Antuñano), and the two artisans whose trips to Europe the state government had financed during the 1820s (José Manso and the weaver Vicente Enríquez).[55] The society raised 8,534 pesos from shares to be entrusted to the care of Bishop Pablo Vázquez. This was an impressive subsription for such hard times although it was insufficient to cover the cost (11,050 pesos) of the first consignment of machinery, accompanied by European and American technicians.[56]

It will come as little surprise that the company established by the *Sociedad Protectora* failed for want of funds and the enormity of the task it had set itself. Subscriptions beyond the initial 8,500 pesos were not forthcoming, despite a laudable enthusiasm and the generosity of most patriotic and wealthy *poblanos*. Chief among those who had bought shares were merchants, artisans, bureaucrats, and clerics.[57] Included were many of the the people who would be involved, as entrepreneurs and factory-owners, in Puebla's industrial revival during the 1830s and 1840s, as well as many more humble artisans: potters, iron-founders and weavers. Although the company was dissolved by the Liberal state government in early 1833, it had brought people of like mind together and served as a precedent for the many (generally much smaller) industrial and commercial

---

54 *Registro Oficial*, Vol. III, p. 214-5.

55 Four of the merchants elected - Antuñano, José Cayetano Gallo, José María Pérez Berruecos and Francisco Olaguibel - established modern textile factories late in the 1830s. See Leicht, *Calles*, p. 90; and Quintana, *op. cit.*, pp. 61-75.

56 Two carding machines, three spinning batteries totalling 2,020 spindles, two foot-looms, one indiana (calico) printing machine, one trimming machine, one combing machine, two carpet-looms, valued altogether at 8,750 pesos. Annual salaries of 700 pesos for the directors of spinning, dyeing and calico printing. Quintana, *Ibid.*

57 There were only three contributions of more than 200 pesos (four shares): Antuñano, already setting up a cotton spinning factory, (20 shares/1000 pesos), José María Pérez Berruecos, a merchant, soon to establish a cotton spinning factory, (20 shares/1000 pesos) and Francisco Armenta, operating a specialised weaving factory producing fine rebozos (10 shares/500 pesos). de la Peña , "Notas", p. 154.

companies formed thereafter. It also served as proof to Estevan de Antuñano that a spirit of association and "public conscience" existed, (although later he was to lament that he had carried the burden of Puebla's industrialization alone).[58]

The *Sociedad* was not expected to achieve the transformation of Puebla's industry on its own. It was established partly as an organ through which loans from the *Banco de Avío* could be passed and partly as a pump primer to stimulate private industrial development. Little private capital, however, went into industrial investment before the international commercial crisis of 1837 sent capital, normally invested in foreign trade, scurrying into industrial investment. But what of public funds? How important was the *Banco de Avío* to the onset of Puebla's industrial revival?

The *Banco de Avío* received only eight requests for loans from Puebla before the Liberal revolution of December 1832 commandeered Tampico's customs house, the bank's principal source of revenue.[59] Loans were requested for the funding of cotton growing, sericulture, apiculture and viticulture, the endowment of a prize for industry, and the purchase from abroad of threshing machines, cotton gins, cotton and woollen mechanized spindles and looms. Contrary to the bank's professed interest in funding a broad spectrum of agricultural investments related to industry, loans were granted only to two established industrialists, Francisco Puig and Estevan de Antuñano, for developing their cotton and woollen spinning factories.[60] The six other loan requests, principally for modernising and diversifying agriculture, were turned down.[61] This left considerable bitterness in Puebla.[62] Robert Potash sees, however, the bank's willingness to fund risky investments, often on fragile security, as making a vital contribution to restoring business confidence at a time of great political and economic instability.[63]

From late 1834, conditions in Puebla improved for the reassertion of public and private committment to industrialization. After the stormy Liberal interlude, during which the centralist and neo-mercantilist policies of the Bustamante administration were reversed, the province's exiled Conservative leaders returned to the city. The *Sociedad Protectora* having been dissolved in 1832, the Conservative state admininstration established a new organ for directing industrial revival: the *Sociedad Patriótica para el*

---

58 Charles A Hale, *Mexican Liberalism*, p. 278.

59 *Registro Trimestre*, Vol. I, 1832, pp. 231-64; Potash, *El Banco de Avío*, p. 163.

60 AGN, Banco de Avío, Vol. II, Expedientes 99 and 127; and AGNP, RPP Censos, Vol. 43 f. 284.

61 AGN, Banco de Avío, Vol. II, Expedientes.22, 23, 27, 32, 52, 67.

62 Potash, El Banco, p. 103; and for the bitter reproaches of the Puebla sheep farmer, Manuel Aguado, AGN, Banco de Avío, Vol. II, Exp. 52.

63 Potash, *El Banco*, pp. 185-6.

Fomento de la Industria.[64] Its purpose was to secure import prohibitions on all foreign goods which competed with the state's manufactures, to promote the export of soap and flour (now recognized as the province's staples), and to encourage the revival of the cotton, woollen, glass, pottery, hat, iron, tanning, wood-working, shoe and paper industries. The new society would establish an investment fund which a *junta* of nine, three from each branch of the economy, would administer. Such funds would be spent on attracting European artisans and financing new industrial projects.

The congress was, however, divided on the extent to which the state should intervene directly in the economy, indicating the continuing aversion to special privileges and monopolies, evident in Puebla since Independence. Although in February 1835 a large majority voted for a prohibition on entry to the state of all foreign competitive goods, the more radical motion that these goods be returned their port of origin, was defeated.[65] And in March of the same year the motion that the society should involve itself in the establishment of private industrial companies, the printing of books and the guaranteeing of loans from the Banco de Avío was defeated. This was deemed contrary to the public interest and likely to encourage privileged monopolies. It was argued that the society should do no more than gather and diffuse useful knowledge, pay for the passages of foreign artisans (but not their salaries), and should reserve its funds for improving infrastructure (roads, bridges and canals).[66] Resources were, of course, lacking in 1835 for any of these things. Nothing was heard thereafter of the *Sociedad Patriótica*, which appears to have been dissolved. The interests of industrialists would not receive corporate representation again until the establishment of Puebla's *Junta de Industria* in the early 1840s.

In spite of the weakness of "neo-mercantilist" institutions in Puebla during the 1830s, the political authorities were far from being insensitive to the interests of the widening circle of fledgeling merchant-industrialists. Indeed, throughout the subsequent two decades, merchants involved with industry and industrialists grew to dominate municipal and state government. They would ensure not only a sympathetic hearing for protectionist issues but also vigorous projection in national politics. The confidence this responsiveness gave to entrepreneurs contributed importantly to the resilience of the industrialization process after 1835. But, as the next chapter reveals, the "protectionist" lobby was far from being unified. Critical divisions emerged within it as rival groups of entrepreneurs sought to use institutions, such as the *Junta de Industria,* to further their particular, as opposed to any common, interest. Thus the hostility surrounding Puebla's first *Consulado de Comercio* in 1822-4

64 AAP, Leyes y Decretos, Vol.6, f. 71.

65 *Estrella Poblana*, Vol. II, No.15, 15 February 1835.

66 *Estrella Poblana*, Vol. II, No. 73, 12 March.1835.

continued to be characteristic of attitudes to corporate and para-State institutions throughout the subsequent three decades.

This opposition to attempts to reestablish corporate privileges and colonial "patrimonialism" was an important feature of Puebla's peculiar brand of protectionism, giving it a popular character. Protectionism was no obscurantist illusion about reconstructing a traditional corporate colonial order. It was informed far more by Adam Smith (particularly by his French popularizer,Jean Baptiste Say) than by Colbert, and even less, by Aquinas. The apparent liberal sacrilege of import prohibitions was regarded as a justified intervention in Mexico's external trading relations, necessary to permit the development of a diversified and autonomous regional and national economy. The performance of Puebla's entrepreneurs and the effectiveness of protectionist policies must now be examined.

Chapter 7

THE MODERNIZATION OF PUEBLA'S TEXTILE INDUSTRY, 1832-1852

Traditional hand-spinning and hand-loom weaving took place in poor but independent households, employed a rudimentary and static technology, and involved negligible fixed capital costs. Raw material costs were met through a sophisticated commercial system by merchants who had no involvement in the manufacturing process itself. Incomes and living standards of spinners and weavers, except when war blocked textile imports, did not depart from a low subsistence level consistent with an urban family's basic requirements of food, clothing and housing.

From 1835, the picture changed dramatically. Merchants, shopkeepers, public officials and clerics became directly involved with the manufacturing process. Many chose to apply a far greater proportion of their capital to fixed investment. This was often at the expense of the liquidity which originally had placed them among the merchant body. In fact, they became industrialists, now dependent upon the credit and services of merchants who chose to keep their capital in a more liquid form. These industrial processes were entirely new to Mexico. They represented the application of a new technology (iron and steel machinery), a distinct use of capital (fixed as well as liquid), a novel development in the division and organization of labor (women and children working in large units), a greater differentiation within the ranks of the urban working class with regard to income and occupation (the arrival of the *fabricante* category in the urban census), greater cosmopolitanism and a transformation of attitudes towards the foreigner and the outside world (with the arrival of large numbers of foreign technicians, merchants and industrialists), and, finally, heightened popular political awareness and participation (in the defence of protectionism).

This chapter observes the process of fixed capital formation around cotton and woollen spinning, weaving, bleaching and printing, by tracing the development of particular enterprises. These case studies have been assembled from the records of notarized contracts and from industrial statistics gathered in the 1840s by the *Dirección General de la Industria*.

The chapter also traces developments in the "politics of protectionism" from 1835 until the end of our period.

Case Studies of Puebla's First Water-driven Spinning Factories

Mexico's. first modern operational cotton spinning factory was established by Estevan de Antuñano in company with Gumersindo Saviñon, both born in Veracruz and sons of Spanish immigrants. They acquired the *Molino de Santo Domingo*, Puebla's most valuable flour-mill, along with the rich wheat land around it, late in 1831 with the help of a loan of over 100,000 pesos from the *veracruzano* merchant Pedro Paso y Troncoso. Once Prior of the Veracruz *Consulado*, Paso y Troncoso, like Antuñano, held extensive trading and cotton growing interests in Tlacotalpan.[1] The decision to proceed was made on the understanding that the company would receive loans from the *Banco de Avío* to cover the costs of importing machinery and paying foreign technicians.

In January 1832 the bank granted Antuñano 8,000 pesos, the first part of an anticipated first loan of 30,000 pesos.[2] By August, although this amount had been received from the bank, little progress in building had been made. Over the next three years everything conspired against the enterprise: cholera decimated the labor force constructing the mill, machinery was lost on two occasions in shipwrecks and a third consignment was held up in Veracruz by civil war while eighteen foreign technicians languished in Puebla on large salaries.

In October 1833 Antuñano appealed in desperation to the Bank for a further loan of 60,000 pesos, granted in December.[3] This served for little more than reducing his debts and a visit by Manuel Escandón in March 1834, acting on the Bank's behalf, revealed that while 99,973 pesos had been spent on building work to date, without taking into account advances on the cost of the carding and spinning machinery, a further 108,000 pesos, at least, would be needed before the factory could enter production.[4] Two further loans, amounting to 90,000 pesos, were approved with the return of a Conservative government, enabling Antuñano to commence production of

---

[1] Santo Domingo had been valued at 172,121 pesos in 1827, *El Patriota*, Vol. III, No. 8, p. 29; and Calderón de la Barca, *Life in Mexico*, p. 355. For Atuñano's interest in Tlacotalpan, AGNP, PN, No. 7, 1829, f. 494; and Estevan de Atuñano, *Breve Memorial que guarda la fábrica*. Puebla, 1837. For the Troncoso family in Tlacotalpan in the 1780s: *BAGN*, Ist Series, Vol. XXX, No. 2, 1959, p. 324.

[2] AGN, Banco de Avío, Vol. 1, Expte., 13, 13 January 1832.

[3] AGN, Banco de Avío, Vol. 1, Expte., 13, 14 December 1832.

[4] AGN, Banco de Avío, Vol. 1, Expte., 98, 10 March 1834.

cotton yarn in January 1835.[5] *La Constancia Mexicana* began by producing 1,000-1,200 lbs. of cotton yarn a day on 1,560 of the projected 3,840 Arkwright spindles. In February Antuñano petitioned for a prohibition of yarn imports in defence of "national industry".[6]

During the subsequent seven years most of the fourteen flour mills along the Atoyac and San Francisco rivers were converted to house cotton spinning machinery in a short but impressive wave of industrial investment affecting not only Puebla, but other states -Mexico, Jalisco, Veracruz, Durango, Querétaro, Colima, Yucatán, Guerrero, Coahuila and Sonora - and other parts of Latin America, particularly Central Colombia.[7]

After the inauguration of *La Constancia Mexicana* in 1835, two years elapsed before Gumersindo Saviñon's brother, Estanislao (one of the Conservatives exiled in 1833), in company with Luis Haro y Tamariz and Manuel Martínez del Campo (merchant of Mexico City) formed a company for the conversion of *La Teja* flour mill purchased in 1837 for 20,000 pesos.[8] They chose to invest in modern industry only when the prohibition of cotton yarn and cloth imports had become a certainty with the new customs' law of March 1837.[9] Over three quarters of the value of *La Teja* was in the form of transferable mortgages held with pious works, convents and chaplaincies amounting to 16,500 pesos, upon which the new owners would continue paying interest at 5 percent. Most of the other mills changing hands at this time were similarly encumbered and the existence of such extensive "passive" Church credit, at what was by now considered to be a very low interest rate, undoubtedly eased the decision to invest in modern industry and the ability to assemble the necessary capital.[10]

---

[5] AGN, Banco de Avío, Vol. 1, Expte., 13, 10 January 1835; and Vol. 1, Expte., 98, 19 January 1835. Overall the enterprise absorbed 164,000 pesos of the Bank's funds, 126,000 paid in cash, mostly from the Tampico customs house, and 37,916 pesos worth of machinery supplied by the Bank.

[6] *Estrella Poblana*, Vol. II, No. 30, 2 March 1834.

[7] Potash, *El Banco*, pp. 219-242; and Dawn Keremitsis, *La industria textil mexicana en el siglo XIX*. Mexico, 1973, pp. 9-40. For Colombia see Frank Safford, Commerce and Enterprise in Central Colombia, 1821-1870, unpublished Ph.D. dissertation, Columbia University, 1965.

[8] *La Teja* had fallen in value since Independence having been sold for 31,000 pesos in 1811, 22,900 pesos in 1820, for 32,000 pesos in 1832 after extensive repairs, and for 20,619 pesos in 1837. AGNP, RPP, Vol. 40, f. 73; Vol. 41, f. 379; Vol. 42, f. 66; and PN, No. 1, 1838, fs. 454 and 1415.

[9] Potash, *El Banco*, p. 195.

[10] Interests of over 20 percent might be charged on medium term loans in the 1830s and short term loans could be set at anything from 12 to 24 percent per month. Keremitsis, *La industria*, pp. 19-20; and Shaw, *Poverty and Politics*, p. 78.

242

The company proposed to construct water-driven spinning machinery on the Arkwright principle (1,500 spindles) and to establish forty power-looms in the Calle Real de Señor San José in the old weaving quarter of the city. The mill stream proved inadequate to drive the machinery continuously and so further land was rented in August 1838 for the grazing of oxen and mules to drive a capstan.[11] By October 1838 182,400 pesos had been invested in the enterprise: 104,400 pesos in the cost of the mill and land, 10,000 pesos, the value of 40 power looms, and, 68,000 pesos, the cost of importing and setting up the spinning machinery. Martínez was responsible for supplying raw cotton to the mill and for marketing the yarn and cloth in Mexico City and the interior.

The company, soon after its foundation, decided against vertical integration, selling the power looms in 1838 to that great opponent of mechanization, Pedro de Ascué y Zalvide, who formed a company to operate the factory with the wife of the state governor, La Excelencia Carmen de la Torre Codallos.[12] La Teja continued as an exclusively spinning concern and by 1841 2,500 spindles were in operation, half of them Arkwright, producing warp, half Crompton, producing weft. No further expansion took place. The mill was one of the most successful over the 1840s serving as an important supplier of yarn to Puebla's hand-loom weavers.[13] Estanislao Saviñon, along with Antuñano and Puebla's other leading industrialist, Dionisio José Velasco, became over the 1840s the city's most important dealers in cotton *manta* pieces which hand-loom weavers exchanged for cash and yarn at their factory outlets in the city.[14] Saviñon and Ciriaco Marrón became the principal raw cotton suppliers and creditors to other industrialists.

The *Amatlán-Mayorazgo* mill (belonging to Joaquín de Haro y Tamariz) was the next to be converted to cotton spinning by a company of four: Estevan de Antuñano, Isidro Pérez Toledano (an exiled Conservative in 1833),[15] Fernando Arenas and Lino Romero (formed in July 1837).

11 AGNP, PN, No. 1, 1838, f. 538.
12 AGNP, PN, No. 1, 1838, f. 195, 16 March 1838.
13 Producing both warp and weft, *La Teja* must have been an advantageous enterprise for the handloom weaver to do business with. Both *Constancia* and *Economía* (Antuñano's mills) produced exclusively warp, suitable for power looms which required a strong warp in order to limit yarn breakage but serving only as a very rough weft for the hand loom.
14 Monthly records for *manta* production were included in the *Memorias de Industria* (1841-45).
15 AGNP, PN, No. 1, Vol. 63, f. 119, 2 February 1838. The mill had changed hands on five occasions over the century, its value remaining fairly static: 1800, 36,451 pesos; 1814, 16,000 pesos; 1819, 24,000 pesos; 1834, 21,038 pesos; 1837, 21,046 pesos. AGNP, RPP, Vol. 40, f. 27; Vol. 41, f. 306; Vol. 42, fs. 195, 338, and 343; Vol. 44, f. 67.

Two spinning factories were established on the mill site, the first, *La Benevolencia*, had entered production by late 1837 with 500 spindles (increased to 1,500 by 1841 and to 3,100 in 1843), producing warp and weft. *La Benevolencia* (like *La Teja*), became a very important supplier of yarn to hand-loom weavers over the 1840s. The merchant, Miguel García, (mayor of Puebla in 1838) supplied the factory with machinery and raw cotton and was invited to join the company in 1842 in order to liquidate debts to him. By 1845 García was the principal *manta* dealer in the city, marketing 40,407 *manta* pieces, produced on 60 power-looms established in 1842 by Lino Romero, in company with José Arriaga, or gathered from independent hand-loom weavers.[16] The second mill at Amatlán was established in 1839 by Antuñano's partner, Gumersindo Saviñon, who had withdrawn from Antuñano y Cia. earlier in the year. Gumersindo invested 55,000 pesos in *El Mayorazgo*, bringing by 1843 2,400 spindles into production of yarn, after many financial difficulties.[17]

Antuñano, undeterred by the obstacles he had faced the import prohibition, proceeded with the establishment of three further cotton-spinning enterprises. *La Constancia*'s sister factory, *La Economía*, begun in 1838, located downstream, had entered production with 3,000 spindles by December 1843 after frequent delays accompanying the currency crisis of 1842. Over the long delay while *La Economía* was being built, Antuñano established *La Amistad*, a smaller factory in a two-storey building close to his home in the Barrio del Alto - the woollen weavers' *barrio*.[18]

The purpose seems to have been to use the idle machinery awaiting installation at *La Economía* at a time when demand for domestically produced yarn was growing rapidly and also to produce finer yarn on more modern Arkwright machinery than that installed at *La Constancia*. A further consideration was to take advantage of the rapidly expanding cotton supply from Tlacotalpan, where, since 1836, Antuñano had two gins stripping cotton.

The Tlacotalpan cotton harvest had increased from 2,100 - 2,800 *arrobas* in 1833 to 17,500 *arrobas* in 1836, employing at least 200 families. In return, Antuñano was remitting 20,000 pesos of cloth annually to Tlacotalpan where, until the late 1830s, he faced little competition.[19]

---

16 AGNP, RPP, Vol. 44, f. 291; and Vol. 45, f. 182.

17 AGNP, RPP, Vol. 44, f. 359.

18 AGNP, PN, No. 1, 1837, f. 163, 3 March 1837.

19 Esteban de Antuñano, *Breve Memoria del Estado que guarda la fábrica de hilados de algodón, Constancia Mexicana*. Puebla, 1837. Gins could be acquired for as little as 180 pesos in Philadelphia although it was estimated that to be successfully put into operation, five or six good hands had to be employed and 4,000 pesos invested. AGN, Banco de Avío, Vol. II, 10 May 1831, Thomas McCormick to Lucas Alamán. Antuñano was investing in Tlacotalpan cotton agriculture as early as 1829 when he advanced 1,000 pesos to Miguel Chazaro, a prominent cotton-producing

The third textile enterprise entered by Antuñano was the company for the conversion of the Amatlán mill established in 1837. Thus Antuñano's activities in the late 1830s spanned investment in cotton agriculture and ginning, the running of a wholesale textile business in the Calle de Mercaderes in the center of Puebla, the ownership and management of four cotton-spinning factories, the profits from which left him with sufficient liquidity to lend 80,000 pesos to the British merchant José Welsh towards the building of a spinning mill in Jalapa, to buy shares in the glass, porcelain, paper and iron factories being established in Puebla between 1837 and 1840, and to buy the *Hacienda de la Noria* in 1840 for 62,000 pesos in order to extend his control over access to the valuable water-power of the Atoyac.[20]

La Constancia Mexicana did not serve as the model for the modernization of spinning in Puebla, although plants on a similar scale were established in Mexico and Orizaba and, later, in Atlixco. Most spinning factories established in Puebla between 1835 and 1850 were smaller and less costly to erect. This can be explained by the paucity of water resources of Puebla's two rivers, Atoyac and San Franciso, and the dependence of most smaller units upon either mule-driven capstans or human muscle. Antuñano had chosen the most favored point for water power on the Atoyac and, having purchased the land up and down stream, he jealously guarded his water rights, obliging other prospective industrialists, if they were unable to acquire old flour-mill premises further down the Atoyac, to site factories further afield in Atlixco or Tlaxcala. Antuñano made one exception. In 1837 he allowed Dionisio Velasco, a Spanish import merchant, resident in Veracruz, to lease a site for the construction of an entirely new factory, without existing mill buildings, downstream from *La Constancia*, with water rights sufficient for moving 3,900 spindles. Within a few years, Velasco had overtaken Antuñano to become Puebla's most successful and influential industrialist. His mill, *El Patriotismo Mexicano*, was the only other factory in the Puebla region able to match *La Constancia* in scale of production.[21]

Soon after taking the lease of the 500 yards of the Atoyac river, Velasco persuaded Antuñano to part with the land for 35,000 pesos in silver, a request Puebla's pioneer industrialist, in this period of currency shortage, could not refuse. In 1839, Velasco formed a company with two other merchants: Ciriaco Marrón, with cotton-growing interests in Tlacotalpan, and Andrés Vallarino, a Genoese-born cloth wholesaler who

---

family even as late as the 1870s. Florescano and Chávez Orozco, *Agricultura*, pp. 267-268; and AGNP, PN, No. 7, 1829, f. 494.

20 AGN, Banco de Avío, Vol. II, Expte. 64, 2 July 1838; and AGNP, RPP, Vol. 44, f. 441.

21 For a fuller account of Velasco's career see Carmen Aguirre and Alberto Carabarín, "Proprietarios de la industria textil de Puebla en el siglo XIX: Dionisio de Velasco y Pedro de Zúñiga", in CIHS-ICUAP, *Puebla en el siglo XIX*, pp. 178-186.

had been in partnership with Estevan de Antuñano in Veracruz before moving to Puebla in the early 1820s.[22] The three partners contributed 297,922 pesos to the company, 52,000 pesos of which represented the value of the machinery. Marrón and Velasco were responsible for supplying the factory with raw cotton, Vallarino with operating the factory and with marketing the product (yarn for hand-loom weavers) for which he would receive 60 percent of profits. The company had been so successful by 1849 that its partners renewed their agreement for a further four years.[23] By 1842 *El Patriotismo*'s 6,000 spindles were producing, weekly, 10,800 lbs. of yarn to *La Constancia*'s 15,000 lbs.

La Constancia and *El Patriotismo*, with over 6,000 spindles, and Antuñano's *La Economía*, with 4,000 spindles, were exceptional. Most of the factories established in these years had between 600 and 3,000 spindles, the ten water driven mills generally using the Arkwright principle with around 2,000 spindles, the eight mule-driven urban spinning establishments employing the Crompton mule with around 600 spindles. [24]

Three more flour mills were converted between 1839 and 1842. In 1840 Ignacio Comonfort (future governor of the State and president of the Republic), in partnership with Cayetano Ramírez and Manuel Fernández de las Cuartas, established a company to erect cotton spinning machinery in the *Molino de Santa Cruz* on the Atoyac, across river from *El Patriotismo*.[25] The factory entered production in 1841 with 2,000 spindles. The last two flour mills to be converted were the *Molino del Carmen* and the *Molino de Nuestra Señora de Guadalupe* which Luis Haro y Tamariz acquired in 1842 and 1843. He received *La Carmen* from Bernardo Mier, an exiled Conservative in 1833 and a canon of the cathedral, in exchange for his

---

22 Miguel A. Quintana, *Estevan de Antuñano*, Vol. I, p. 11; and AGNP, PN, No. 5, 1844, 18 March 1844, f. 64 for his will, leaving the estate to his family in the village of Vottei, Genoa.

23 AGNP, RPP, Vol. 46, fs. 10-12.

24 At this stage of the technological development of the industry smallness of scale appears not to have impaired efficiency. Chapman shows that in England, until the invention of Robert's automatic mule in the mid-1830s, there was no particular economy in the concentration in number of spindles; optimum production could be reached with 264-288 spindles, which could fit comfortably into an average sized room. S. D. Chapman, "Fixed capital Formation in the British Cotton Manufacturing Industry", in J. Higgins and S. Pollard (Eds.), *Aspects of Capital Investment in Great Britain, 1750-1850*. London, 1971, pp. 76-81.

25 The company would last for five years, Comonfort would supply the raw cotton, Ramírez would pay for the machinery and operate the factory, Fernández, the owner of the mill (which had increased in value by over 12,000 pesos since he had bought it in 1835 for 24,000 pesos), would be paid 2,000 pesos a year in rent. AGNP, PN, No. 8, 1840-41, f. 140; No. 5, 1840, fs. 115-116; and No. 1, 1838, f. 152.

share in *La Teja*. [26]By March 1843 Haro had established 2,100 spindles and the mill was operating profitably.[27] In April, he acquired the *Molino de Nuestra Señora de Guadalupe*, from the miller-baker, Manuel Caámano, which he exchanged with the Carmen mill, Caámano agreeing to pay Haro half the value of Carmen's spinning machinery (21,000 pesos).[28] By the end of the year, Haro was producing 2,450 lbs. of cotton yarn a week on Guadalupe's 1,090 spindles. He had brought three mills into production within three years.

By 1843, ten flour mills had been converted to cotton spinning on the Atoyac and San Francisco rivers containing between them, 31,994 spindles producing 51,625 lbs.of yarn a week, valued at 24,062 pesos, employing 1197 workers. Three of these mills (*Constancia, Economía* and *Enmedio*) contained power looms (310 in all) producing 1,200 pieces of cloth a week, employing 320 workers.

How did these water-driven mills fare over the 1840s and early 1850s? Taken with the smaller mule-driven urban establishments, shortly to be examined, it is evident that growth of capacity, rapid before 1843, was sluggish thereafter. The city of Puebla's share of national yarn production oscillated between 32 and 38 percent between 1843 and 1852,[29] reaching a peak in 1845 when Puebla possessed 38 percent of the national spinning capacity. If continuity of ownership and remaining in production are taken as indices of success over such unstable times, then Puebla's water-driven mills maintained production and changed hands very rarely over the 1840s. Only two mills were closed down, Antuñano's *La Amistad* in 1841, because of shortage of water and technical difficulties with the steam engine, and the 4,000 spindles erected in the *Molino de Huexotitlan* in 1841, appear never to have commenced production.[30] Continuity of ownership, however, disguises considerable instability in the cotton-spinning business and the disappointment of many entrepreneurs' hopes.

---

[26] Mier had paid 35,000 pesos for *La Carmen*, 27,500 pesos of which was mortgaged to chaplaincies and charities. Haro paid Mier 18,000 pesos taking over mortgages of 20,000 pesos. Haro's share in *La Teja* was valued as 40,000 pesos. AGNP, RPP, Vol. 45, fs. 18 and 46; and PN, No. 2, 1842, f. 307.

[27] *Memoria de Industria*, 1844.

[28] AGNP, RPP, Vol. 45, f. 18. Over the two years under Haro's ownership, the *Carmen* mill had increased in value from 35,000 pesos to 106,962 pesos 7 1/2 reales.

[29] *Memorias de Industria*, 1843-1845; and Keremitsis, *La industria*, p. 57.

[30] AAP, Cabildo, Vol. 105, 20 March 1838; AAP, Aguas, Vol. 50, 30 November 1841; and Leicht, *Calles*, p. 12.

The Problem of Cotton Supply and the Disintegration of the Industrialists' Lobby.

Two obstacles confronting the industry between 1841 and the 1850s go far to explain why, of the 12,240 spindles still under construction in 1843, only 10,000 had entered production by 1852 and why so many hopes were confounded. These were, first, the scarcity and high price of raw cotton, and, secondly, limited demand, the result of the failure to sufficiently reduce the price of ordinary cotton cloth and of currency deficiency. Neither scarcity of capital, nor shortage of labor, nor even contraband imports, were seen by contemporaries as obstacles of comparable gravity to the development of the industry. Capital always seems to have been available when opportunities for expansion appeared, and there were no complaints of labor shortages until the late 1840s.[31] The first labor disputes did not arise until the 1860s. Contraband "floods" occurred only sporadically, and served more to unify industrialists who were effective in pressurizing governments to maintain the policy of import prohibitions until the Revolution of Ayutla in 1854.[32] Much more serious were the problems of bottlenecks in raw cotton supply and demand deficiency. These grew to fashion the entire character of the industry over the 1830s and to create severe divisions within the protectionist lobby:

---

[31] Wolfgang Muller, who has examined the capital market for the textile industry during the entire nineteenth century, found that shortage of capital was the least of the industry's problems, funds always appearing when political and tariff conditions were ripe. He also found that the absence of conventional financial and credit institutions, such as banks, seemed not to have impeded the development of industry and testifies to the importance of "passive" credits on properties in easing their acquisition and transfer. Keremitsis confirms that the high profits obtainable in the cotton industry in some years, served immediately to attract investment from "agiotistas", though when profits slumped they would, just as swiftly, abandon the industry. Wolfgang Muller, "El financiamiento de la industrialización, el caso de la industria textil poblana, 1830-1910", *Comunicaciones*, Vol. XV, 1978; and "Die textil industrie des raunes Puebla (Mexiko) in 19 jahrhundert", unpublished Ph.D. dissertation, University of Bonn, 1977; and Keremitsis, *La industria*, pp. 38-39.

[32] Smugglers used cunning means to stimulate Mexican manufactures, Alamán reporting in October 1843 that the revenue office in Oaxaca had impounded textiles purporting to be from Puebla "y manufacturados en el convento de la Enseñanza de aquella ciudad...resulta que el respectivo artículo no se ha fabricado allí, ni aún existe convento alguno de la Enseñanza." AGN, Banco de Avío, Vol. II, No. 95, 5 October 1843, Luis Alamán to Minister of Justice. The Puebla *Junta de Industria* followed the draconian policy of burning contraband goods-- as did local administrators --Antonio González Gavito of Acatlán being pardoned for any blame for burning 48 pieces of English manta in September 1842. The Department of Industry reported in 1843 that the policy of burning contraband consignments had met with considerable success in deterring contraband imports. AGNP, PN, No. 2, 26 September 1842, f. 1279; and *Memoria de Industria*, 1843, p. 172.

between industrialists and artisans, among the industrialists themselves and between industrialists and cotton growers. The broader political environment also proved unconducive to the maintenance of business confidence with successive Liberal or federalist challenges to the Conservative centralist authority which Bustamante and Santa Anna attempted to impose after the abolition of the 1824 Federal Constitution in 1837, and, to legitimize in 1842 with the constitutional definition of centralist power: *Las Bases Orgánicas.*

The crisis in foreign trade and threatening external circumstances facing Mexico between 1835 and 1839 had created a certain unanimity among diverse regional and sectoral groupings: neo-mercantilist statesmen such as Lucas Alamán, merchant financiers such as Manuel Escandón, Cayetano Rubio, etc. of Mexico City, merchants becoming industrialists (Antuñano, Velasco, and many others), the cotton growers of Veracruz, Oaxaca, Guerrero and Colima and their merchant allies, and the hand-loom weavers. This unanimity began to disintegrate from mid-1839. The fragmentation of the protectionist lobby and the achievements and disappointments of the new industrialists over the 1840s can be traced through the pamphlet literature which issued in ever greater volume during the "protectionist era".

The first division, which has already been touched upon, was between the owners of the new cotton-spinning factories and the hand-loom weavers over the mechanization of weaving. Since the prohibition upon cotton yarn imports in 1837, hand-loom weavers had been kept occupied and politically quiet by the enormous amount of cheap yarn imported over the final year of free trade. During 1837, imports of British yarn had exceeded the combined total quantity imported over the previous five years. This quantity approached the total production of Mexican yarn in 1845, when the new industry had reached the peak of its development. In 1837, yarn imports did little to damage the nascent spinning enterprises, most of which did not enter production until 1839-40. Yarn imports then dropped precipitously and by 1839 Mexican weavers were entirely dependent upon relatively expensive and still scarce yarn produced in Mexico's new factories.[33] Between 1837 and 1839 manta production increased impressively, weavers presumably using stockpiles of imported yarn.[34]

By 1840, however, yarn had become scarce, and hand-loom weavers, unconvinced by the spinning factory owners' promise of the previous year that only a limited number of power looms would be introduced to their factories, called for an absolute prohibition on any further erection of power

---

[33] BL, BPP, Vol. XXXIX, 1842; and *Memoria que sobre el estado de La Hacienda Nacional...* Mexico, 1846, p. 120.

[34] *Representación que los tejedores de algodón, vecinos de Puebla, dirigen al E. S. Gob. del Dept. pidiendo se prohiba a los fabricantes de hilaza tener telares de sus cuenta y que se permita la introducción de hilaza del extranjero, hasta que las fábricas nacionales sean suficientes a proveer los consumos.* Puebla, 1840.

looms and for permission to import yarn. Their request was answered not by the civil government in Mexico City, which generally defended the policy of import prohibitions over the following fifteen years, but by the Minister of War, General Juan Almonte. In September 1840, to forestall a Liberal challenge to the Bustamente regime, the Minister of War permitted General Arista, military commander of Tampico, to allow foreign yarn to be imported, and to use the customs' revenues to finance his campaign.[35] More than two million pounds of yarn entered the country over a few weeks, far exceeding the annual product of Mexican factories. The Arista affair immediately became a "cause célèbre" since it threatened the livelihood of the now numerous and influential cotton spinning factory owners as well as cotton growers and merchants. Any idea the central government may have had of relaxing the import prohibition on yarn, in response to pressure from hand-loom weavers, was immediately abandoned in the face of a broadside of petitions from *Juntas de Industria, Juntas Departmentales*, and associations of cotton growers.[36] The political significance of the Arista affair was that it revealed to the government the strength of protectionist feeling in the country, the speed and directness with which groups concerted pressure upon government, the political complementarity of diverse regional economic interests and the degree to which many of the government's principal financiers had been drawn into the protectionist circle. The government's response to the Arista affair came in the following year. First came the establishment of a new ministry--the *Dirección General de la Industria Mexicana*- to coordinate the activities and attend to the needs of departmental *juntas de industria*. Then Santa Anna incorporated a clause into the ultra-conservative *Bases Orgánicas* stating that no import prohibition might be revoked without the approval of two thirds of departmental (state) assemblies.[37]

This apparent victory for national industry and agriculture over its enemies --foreign merchants, British industry and liberalism-- in fact disguised profound divisions with the protectionist lobby which surfaced between 1840 and 1843. The plight of the hand-loom weaver, appears, however, to have been mitigated, first, by illegal introductions of yarn in 1840 and 41, then by the reluctance of cotton-spinning factory owners to invest further in power looms after 1843, thus removing this threat to their

---

[35] Potash, *El Banco*, p. 198

[36] *La Junta de Industria de esta capital sobre los males que amenazan a este ramo.* Mexico, 1841; and AGN, Industria, Vol. 1, Expte. 29, *Junta de Industria de Jalapa*; Expte. 30, *Junta Departamental de Puebla*, Expte. 32, and *Junta del Departamento de San Luis Potosí*; and AAP, Cabildo, Vol. 108, 13 and 16 February and 5 March 1841.

[37] Potash, *El Banco*, pp. 202, 205, and 208-211.

livelihood.[38] Thereafter, hand-loom weavers would frequently petition alongside spinning factory owners for importation of yarn or for and against the importation of raw cotton but they would never again petition on their own accord for the lifting of the prohibition on yarn imports. This is explained by two changes: the increasing financial dependence of hand-loom weavers upon wholesale merchants and owners of spinning mills and the growing tendency to concentrate large numbers of hand-looms under one roof, both signifying a severe loss in weavers' independence.

Much more serious than the division between the factory spinners and hand-loom weavers was the gulf which opened in the early 1840s between those factory owners favoring the relaxation of the prohibition on raw cotton imports and those who, in league with the cotton growers, favored its maintenance. The cause of the rift was the shortage and high price of raw cotton at a time when most of Puebla's large spinning mills were commencing production for the first time, bringing unprecedented competition to the market for cotton yarn. Costly and scarce cotton is perhaps the main factor explaining the brevity of and limits to this early phase of industrialization.[39] It encouraged factionalism and monopoly among industrialists, it reduced the industry's competitiveness and limited consumption and it undermined the coherence of mercantilist and protectionist policies.

The first request from a factory owner for the lifting of the sacred cow of the import prohibition on raw cotton came in August 1840 from an industrialist: Esteven de Antuñano. He claimed that the price of raw cotton in Veracruz had doubled from 36 reales/arroba in 1838 to 72 reales/arroba in 1840.[40] He received support from Mexico City spinning factory owners although some of his fellow industrialists in Puebla proved reticent to join him in pressuring the national chambers.[41] The Arista affair, in September 1840, temporarily dispelled any further pressure for raising the prohibition on raw cotton imports.

By July 1841, however, with the cotton price reaching an unprecedented 96 reales/arroba. With Alamán's mill in Orizaba having to shut down its night shift and with several of Puebla's mills preparing to do so, Antuñano and Mexico City's industrialists renewed pressure for raw

---

[38] The number of power looms in Puebla increased only by 45 between 1843 and 1852, from 540 to 585.

[39] Lucas Alamán, the Minister of Industry, saw cotton scarcity as "el gran obstáculo que impide el completo desarrollo de este importante ramo de industria, y lo que pone en gran peligro hasta su existencia." *Memoria de Industria*, 1843, p. 169.

[40] Estevan de Antuñano, *Teoría fundamental de la industria de algodones en México*. Puebla, 1840.

[41] *Representación al supremo gobierno de los empresarios de fábricas nacionales de hilados y tejidos de algodón*. Mexico, 1840.

cotton imports.[42] On this occasion the Bustamente government conceded permission for a limited period until the factories were stocked. The response from growers in the *veracruzano* cotton-growing regions was immediate and vociferous, claiming that the harvest had been adequate for the factories and that the shortage was caused by "speculators and monopolists...those ambitious men who offer the Republic the scandalous example of colossal fortunes made suddenly and acquired at the expense of our miserys and toils."[43] By October, Santa Anna had interceded on behalf of his home state and the prohibition of raw cotton imports was renewed.

In spite of the cotton shortage during 1841, Puebla's 21,000 spindles, requiring 91,784 *arrobas* of cotton, were kept moving. Such was not possible, however, in 1842 when a further 29,600 spindles were due to commence production, increasing the factories' demand for cotton to 209,954 arrobas.[44] By July 1842 Antuñano reported that Puebla's industry was being brought to a standstill. Five spinning factories were out of action (*Benevolencia, Soledad, Plazuela de San José, San Roque, Triunfo Poblano*) and half the spindles of *Constancia* and *Economía* were not working. Antuñano and ten other Puebla factory owners, together with the Weavers' Guild of Cholula, Puebla's plumbers, coppersmiths, ironsmiths, carpenters, braziers, architects and oilmakers added their names to a petition to the President of the Republic for a raising of the prohibition on raw cotton imports.[45] As in 1840 and 1841, not all Puebla's factory owners agreed that lifting the prohibition was the answer. Indeed, the *Junta de Industria* of Puebla petitioned for the prohibition to be maintained, arguing that it was not raw cotton which they lacked but access to markets, their warehouses being full of yarn and cloth which they could not sell.[46]

The discord among Puebla's industrialists over the raw cotton prohibition is worth examining more closely since it highlights divergent perceptions of the process of industrialization Mexico was undergoing in these years and illustrates many of its limits. It had become evident as early as 1840 that certain Puebla industrialists were finding it easier than others to gain access to *veracruzano* cotton. In 1841, both the growers and Antuñano had observed that cotton monopolists were in large part

42 Estevan de Antuñano, *Cuatro reflexiones sobre importación de algodón estranjero*, in *Semanario de la Industria Mexicana*. Mexico, 1841, Vol. II, pp. 99-101; and his *Economía política en México*. Puebla, 1841; and AGN, Industria, Vol. I, *Solicitud de la Junta Directora de la fábrica de algodón de Cocolapam*, 26 July 1841.

43 AGN, Industria, Vol. I, *Representación de los labradores y cosecheros de Tlacotalpam*, 20 June 1841; and *Representación a la Junta del Departamento de Veracruz por los labradores y cosecheros de Cosamaloapam*, 26 June 1841.

44 *Semanario de la Industria Mexicana*. Mexico, 1841, p. 51.

45 Estevan de Antuñano, *Economía política. en México*. Puebla, 1842.

46 AGN, Industria, Vol. II, Expte. 7, 18 December 1841.

responsible for cotton shortages. From the late 1830s Antuñano, who had pioneered the recovery of *veracruzano* cotton agriculture for over a decade, no longer exercised financial influence in the cotton growing region. The core of the cotton monopoly was now the Velasco, Marrón and Vallarino company around the *Patriotismo* mill, a monopoly worth, in Antuñano's estimate, 650,000 pesos annually.[47] Scarcity and high price of raw cotton caused Puebla's industrialists and other interests tied to them, to polarize into two groups over 1842-43. The one gathered around Estevan de Antuñano and favored the lifting of the import prohibition. The other, supporting Ciriaco Marrón, president of the *Junta de la Industria de Puebla*, favored its retention.

By 1842 Ciriaco Marrón had become one of the wealthiest and most influential men in Puebla. He owned the city's most opulent wholesaling business in the Calle de Mercaderes, possessed extensive credits and strong family ties in the cotton growing region of Tlacotalpan, enabling him to become the chief raw cotton supplier to many of the city's factories. In 1842, he was chosen to serve as director of Puebla's *Junta de Industria*, a position he exploited to the full in order to oppose any move to raise the prohibition on raw cotton imports which, of course, threatened to undermine his stranglehold over raw cotton supply. An examination of the composition of the group of industrialists making up the *Junta de Industria*, provides some clue to why Puebla's industrialists were so divided at a time when unity would have increased their influence upon issues of more

---

[47] In June 1842 Antuñano was unable to honor a bill of exchange for 2,777 pesos which the wholesale merchant Juan Mugica y Osorio had received from Vesulino Parada (of Tlacotalpan), the value of cotton supplied to Antuñano earleir in the year. The reason Antuñano gave was "la paralización que han tenido sus establecimientos en largo tiempo, provenida de las escaséz y casi absoluta carencia del algodón en rama, ocasionada por la prohibición casi bárbara de la entrada del algodón extranjero, como asi mismo, la suma escaséz de moneda, emanada de providencias gubernativas, no le permite ahora a su pesar cubrir esta libranza." ADNP, PN, No. 2, 1842, 10 June 1842, f. 877. Antuñano was obliged at the same time to sell his share in the Amatlán mill and abandon *La Amistad*, AGNP, PN, No. 2, 1842, 8 July 1842, f. 947.

Other bills presented to Antuñano for payment in 1842:

22 January 1842, for Tomás Carrera, for two bills of 9,897 pesos 2 centavos and 10,169 pesos 60 centavos. Antuñano admits impossibility of paying because of the lack of sales. AGNP, PN, No. 2, 1842, f. 865.

30 May 1842 from Juan Mugica y Osorio for 16,428 pesos 22 centavos (several bills) AGNP, PN, No. 2, 1842, f. 865.

17 November 1843 from José María Gutiérrez on behalf of Alfredo Rashire (New York) for two bills valued at 2,600 pesos and 2,400 pesos. Antuñano was unable to pay due to shortage of circulating medium. AGNP, PN, No. 5, fs. 256-257.

critical long-term significance than the price of cotton, issues such as the shortage of currency or the need for a bank for financing industry.

Of the twenty two members of the *Junta de Industria*, nine were partners in five water-driven spinning factories (*Patriotismo, Teja, Amatlan/Mayorazgo, Carmen and Guadalupe*) established between 1837 and 1841 and in full production by 1842 (Table 7.1). A further ten were owners or directors of eight smaller cotton and woollen spinning factories housed in the core of the city, three of which contained weaving departments, two which had already introduced power looms by 1842. Finally two other members dealt in hand-loom *mantas*, one owning a small weaving factory. Practically all the members of the *Junta* had served as aldermen or mayors on council during the 1820s and 1830s. Most (Puig, Suárez y Peredo, Caballero de Carranza, Arrioja, etc.) had been involved in dealing in cotton *mantas* since the 1820s. Most members of the *junta* resided in the weavers' quarter of Puebla with close and long-established ties among the weaving artisanate.[48] They had chosen to establish small spinning and weaving factories during the 1830s in order to further secure these ties. Apart from the larger water-driven mills, their spinning factories were small 600 spindle enterprises and their weaving factories merely collections of wooden hand-looms brought under one roof. Suárez Peredo and Domingo Ibarra, however, had introduced power looms to their factories. These were working in 1841 with seventy looms, employing 135 men on two eight hour shifts, to produce 1,760 yards of *manta* a day or around 330 pieces a week. Their annual registered production (4,775 pieces in 1842 and 3,946 pieces in 1843) was dwarfed, however, by the *manta* gathered by Velasco, Marrón and Vallarino from hand-loom weavers in exchange for *Patriotismo*'s yarn. In 1841 this company alone gathered and marketed 42,788 pieces of *manta*, almost half the *manta* registered in the entire city and slightly less than the total *manta* registered in Mexico City. Velasco y Cía.'s lead in *manta* dealing persisted during the 1840s, apparently unperturbed by cotton shortages. Here, then, lies the key to understanding the success of this company and the obduracy of the *Junta de Industria*'s opposition to raising the prohibition on raw cotton imports. Conversely, the decline of Antuñano's share of *manta* production, from over two thirds of total production in 1839 (45,416 pieces) to less than 14% in 1843 (15,535 pieces), is evidence of his loss of control over both cotton supply and hand-loom weaving capacity, explaining his militant campaign to break Marrón's cotton monopoly by the removal of the prohibition on cotton imports.[49]

The group of industrialists and artisans who, in July 1842, petitioned with Antuñano for the raising of the prohibition shared a commitment to the

---

[48] They may be traced in the 1830 and 1846 censuses.

[49] *Memorias de Industria*, 1840-1845.

TABLE 7.1 COTTON SPINNING AND WEAVING FACTORIES IN PUEBLA IN 1843

Water Driven Cotton Spinning Factories

	Owner	Spindles	Looms	Workers
La Constancia Mexicana	+Estevan de Antuñano	7680	160	477
La Economía Mexicana	+Estevan de Antuñano	3900	143	243
El Patriotismo Mexicano	*Sres. Velasco,Marróm y Cía	6528	-	250
Triunfo Poblano	+(ceased production in 1842)	1656	30	120
El Enmedio	*Cosme Furlong	2400	20	95
La Benevolencia/Amatlan	+Sres. Romero y Cía	2800	-	90
El Mayorazgo	*Gumersindo Saviñon	2400	-	100
La Teja	*Bernardo Mier y Cía	2500	-	100
Guadalupe (Cholula)	*Luis Haro	1090	-	34
Carmen	*Manuel Caamano	2112	-	65
Santa Cruz	*Sres. Arrioja y Cía	2000	-	63
La Esperanza (Atlixco)	+Francisco Morales	1350	-	-
La Providencia (Atlixco)	Sres. Enciso y Cía	1650	-	-
La Luz del Siglo (Atlixco)	+José Antonio Serrano	1650	-	-
La Beneficencia (Izucar)	+Pedro de los Monteros	1464	-	-
Huexotitla	(never entered production)	4000	-	-

Mule Driven Cotton Spinning Factories

	Owner	Spindles	Looms	Workers
La Amistad, Barrio Alto (shut down by 1843)	+Estevan de Antuñano	1000	-	50
Calle de la Soledad (shut down by 1843)	+Francisco Domínguez	600	-	-
Calle de Cholulteca	+Felipe Codallos	600	36	55
Calle de Belen	+Sres. Fuentes Hermanos	600	10	33
Calle de San Agustín	*Domingo Ibarra	802	60	87
Plazuela de San Javier	*Sres. Ramirez Hermanos	1000	-	32
La Equidad,Clle San Roque	+Francisco Carranza y Cía	600	-	19
Calle de Cholula	*Antonio Uriarte	600	-	19
Plaza de S.S. José	José.M. Pérez Berruecos	600	-	-
Plazuela de San Francisco	Pedro Manzano	600	-	-

Mule Driven Cotton Weaving Factories

	Owner	Spindles	Looms	Workers
Calle de S.S.José	*Velasco, Marrón y Cía	-	58	80
La Buena Fé	+José.M. Suárez Peredo	-	36	45
La Unión	+Joaquín de la Torre y Cía	-	20	26
La Protección	+José de Arteaga	-	60	100

+ – supporters of the Estevan de Antuñano faction during the 1842 cotton famine.
* – supporters of the Ciriaco Marrón/Puebla Junta de Industria faction during the 1842 cotton famine.

Sources: *Semanario de la Industria Mexicana*, Vol. I, p. 340, *Memorias de Industria* 1843-4.

further expansion and modernization of the textile industry.[50] This is in stark contrast to the *Junta de Industria*, whose members with their firmly-established stake in yarn and *manta* production, believed the modernization process has gone far enough. Many of Antuñano's allies had not yet brought their factories into production, hesitating to further involve themselves in a business in which raw material costs were spiralling and the market apparently glutted. Only Domínguez and Carranza belonged to the *Junta de Industria* and both of their spinning factories had been forced to shut down production because of cotton scarcity. Ten of the eighteen enterprises represented in the petition were situated at some distance from the city. The Atlixco and Izucar de Matamoros factories were dependent upon Oaxaca and southern Puebla for their cotton supply where the cotton harvest had declined even more sharply than in Veracruz. Bringing up the rear of the petition were the hand-loom weavers of Cholula, supporting Antuñano perhaps because of their dependence for supply of yarn from the nearby *Constancia*. Finally representatives of various groups of artisans occupied in the construction of new factories added their signatures to Antuñano's petition.

While the struggle over cotton supply provided the occasion for the polarization of Puebla's industrialists into two camps, their differences really went far deeper and involved divergent perceptions about the process of industrialization. The *Junta de Industria* could afford to be complacent with so many of their competitors ceasing production and their own *manta* production keeping up well over 1841-43. They argued that the real reason for the Antuñano group's grievances was not shortage of cotton but:

> las pocas utilidades que recibían sus dueños, por la manera en que eran [las fábricas] dirigidas y por los compromisos, quizás ruinosos, contraidos al tiempo de su erección: otras han cerrado igualmente sus puertas...por no acordarse entre sí los partícipes en ellas, y otras finalmente no las han llegado a abrir o por no estar concluídas sus oficinas... por los continuos y constantes temores de verlas destruídas a consecuencia de la relajación de las leyes protectoras de la industria.[51]

Antuñano, in turn, spared no prose in attacking the members of the *Junta de Industria* as "supinamente ignorante...son precisamente aquellos cuyos establecimientos se hallan más mal economizados, y estos parece que fundan todas sus esperanzas de conservación particular, por la parada o

---

[50] Estevan de Antuñano, *Economía política en México*. Puebla, 1842.

[51] Ciriaco Marrón, et al., *Representación que dirige al... Señor Presidente de la República la Junta de Industria de Puebla combatiendo las razones...* Puebla, 1843, in Miguel A. Quintana, *Estevan de Antuñano*, Vol. II, p. 258.

ruina de otras fábricas, y de los monopolistas".[52] In Antuñano's view, the obstinate defence of the raw cotton import prohibition was imperilling the entire manufacturing sector since cotton shortages had halted any further expansion of production and high *manta* prices had depressed demand and encouraged contraband. Antuñano's perception of the industrialization process, shared implicitly by the group behind him in 1842-43, requires therefore, a brief examination.

Antuñano understood the modernization of the cotton textile industry, which he inaugurated in the early 1830s, to be a dynamic process which would have repercussions throughout the entire economy. First, he anticipated that Puebla would reestablish itself as the workshop of Mexico, recapturing the markets of the north for textiles and other goods, satisfied since Independence by imports. This alone would ensure rapid growth during the 1830s and 1840s. Then a further stage of industrialization would be embarked upon. With highland urban society now restored, and with temperate and tropical agriculture --particularly wheat and cotton-- re-animated as a result of increased urban and industrial demand, general consumer demand would, in turn, increase. The factories, now producing more regularly and in larger volumes, would become more efficient and diversify into finer and more varied cloth. Other branches of industry would follow the example of textiles. The flow of silver abroad would be diverted to lubricate internal exchange which would assume the lead over foreign trade.[53]

Antuñano and his group were to be disappointed. Growth in cotton spinning proved sluggish after 1843. Northern and northwest central Mexico proved particularly vulnerable to contraband, denying Puebla manufacturers this important market, vital to recapture if Puebla was to attract coin to remedy the south-east's currency deficiency.[54] By the mid-1840s, the modern cotton-spinning and weaving capacity of Querétaro, Jalisco and Durango had grown to supply these markets to which Puebla's

---

[52] Estevan de Antuñano, *Economía política en México*. Puebla, 10 July 1845. Evidence from the case studies which follow bear out Antuñano's assertion that many of the smaller factories were badly managed. Manuel Caámano found himself in the hands of his creditors in 1844 and several of the mule-driven spinning factories closed down over the decade.

[53] The most systematic exposition of Antuñano's ideas on industrialization can be found in *Discurso analítico de algunos puntos de moral y economía política de Méjico con relación a sus agricultura cereal o sea pensamientos para un plan para animar la industria mejicana*. Puebla, 1834, in Quintana, *Estevan de Antuñano*, Vol. I, pp. 223-267.

[54] For contraband in northern Mexico in 1843 and the discovery of Sonora's textile factory which had been operating simply as a warehouse for the stamping and transhipment of imported cotton, an accusation also levelled at the Barron and Forbes factory at Tepic, see: AGN, Industria, Vol. II, Expte. 101, 26 September 1843.

manufacturers could now only hope to contribute a small part.[55] Even the market of the south east was not assured, with complaints of contraband imports of yarn and cloth in 1842-43.[56] Thus, Antuñano's hopes of a sustained process of industrialization, with Puebla at its head had, by 1842, foundered in the face of the bad faith and sharp practices of his fellow industrialists, raw cotton famine and high prices, monopoly, contraband and currency deficiency. Although conditions both for his own business and for those of the group petitioning with him were to improve by the mid 1840s, with all of the enterprises which were shut down or not yet started in 1842, commencing production, Puebla's manufacturers failed to recapture their stake in supplying the markets of the interior. Moreover, regional demand was inhibited by the chronic currency deficiency from which Puebla suffered. So, after 1843, the process of industrial modernization and diversification proceeded only haltingly.

In this light, the obstinate position of the Puebla's *Junta de Industria* between 1841 and 1843 appears as a more rational response to the limitations of the domestic market and was perhaps a more realistic appraisal of Mexico's capacity, at this point, to sustain an early industrial revolution. The Junta represented, primarily, the interests of a group of inner-city shopkeepers, merchants and manufacturers who, far from entertaining visions of sustained industrial transformation, saw their role as one of using available modern spinning technology to renew and increase their economic control over the weaving artisanate whom they supplied with yarn and whose cloth they marketed. While they differed from their pre-

---

55 By 1845 Jalisco possessed five spinning factories, reducing the State's dependence upon yarn imports, although manta imports continued to rise during the 1840s, since handloom production was slugglish in comparison to Puebla. Jalisco's imports of yarn decreased from 193,241 lbs. in 1843 to 128,759 lbs. in 1845, while yarn exports from the state iceased from 45,258 lbs. in 1843 to 291,200 lbs. in 1845. Jalisco's *manta* imports increased from 725,515 yards of cloth in 1843, to 1,034,990 yards in 1845, while *manta* exports trebled from 376,487 yards in 1843 to 1,277,397 yards in 1845. (Jalisco's *manta* exports had stood at 1,185,984 yards in 1802.) Jalisco's *manta* production increased from around 480,000 yards in 1844 to 960,000 yards between 1847-54, much reduced fom pre-Independence production of around 7,684,000 yards in 1802. Jalisco's cotton yarn production increased from 101,000 lbs. in 1844 to 175,450 lbs. in 1847. *BSMGE*, Ist Series, Vol. 11, p. 274. Querétaro also became an important cotton-cloth and yarn producer during the 1840s, producing 2,390,176 yards of manta in 1844. *Memoria de Industria*, 1845,

56 Contraband entered the province principally along two routes: from the south, entering by the Pacific coast of Oaxaca and Puebla and from the north, entering by the Gulf coast near Tuxpán whence goods were distributed across the Sierra Madre to Puebla, Mexico and Querétaro. 1843 appears to have been a particularly bad year, Lucas Alamán reporting in August that 40,000 pieces of home-produced *manta* were waiting unsold in Puebla's warehouses, the markets of the interior being glutted with imported textiles. AGN, Banco de Avío, Vol. II, Expte. 101, 28 August 1843, Alamán to Minister of Justice.

Independence counterparts in becoming owners and directors of spinning factories, some employing weavers directly in large weaving establishments, they resembled the "harmonizing merchants" of the late colony in their continued use of credit links with independent weavers as the principal means of controlling and profiting from cotton manufacture. They saw their function, therefore, as essentially mercantile and little changed from the pre-factory spinning era - namely, confined to keeping home weavers supplied with yarn, credit and markets.

For the members of the *Junta de Industria*, the transformation of spinning technology that has occurred in Puebla between 1835 and 1842, with the introduction of the Arkwright throstle and the Crompton mule, was not understood to be the harbinger of an imminent economic revolution but was seen, rather, as a convenient improvement at a specific point in an essentially traditional industrial structure that was not fundamentally altered as a result of this modification. Their principal concern in 1841-43 was not so much with the improvement in the efficiency of their enterprises, even less with the introduction of more modern technology, nor even with the reduction of costs of raw materials but, above all, to retain a steady access to raw material supply in order to keep their enterprises running, maintain the flow of yarn and credit to weavers and conserve their share of manta production and commercialization, while their fellow but rival industrialists, beyond the boundaries of the city, were reducing or stopping production in despair.

The factionalism and rivalry within Puebla were reproduced on the national scale as each state sought to establish its own textile mills, areas of cotton supply, paper factories, iron foundries etc. while erecting from the mid-1840s (and especially after the Revolution of Ayutla) customs barriers to tax and hinder the passage of goods from other states.[57] In the face of the political, geographical and transport realities of the times, these decisions were not irrational. But they combined to frustrate the broader vision of men like Antuñano which, to be realized, required a free flow of goods within a national market and concerted action by state and national governments, to protect the national market from competing imports, to eliminate fiscal and physical obstacles to inter-regional exchange and to ensure an adequate level of circulating medium for the needs of an industrializing society.

The precipitous decline in Veracruz's cotton crop (36,000 quintals in 1841, 30,000 in 1842, 18,000 in 1843 - Puebla's factories needed at least 60,000 quintals to remain in production), and the harm this caused to Lucas Alamán's own industrial interests in Orizaba, brought a coordination of pressure upon the government who finally, in 1843, granted permission to

---

57 Alamán expressed alarm in 1844 at the decision of certain Departmental assemblies to fix tariffs on inter-state trade, in contravention of the federal constitution of 1824, which left commercial relations between the state to the *Congreso General*. *Memoria de Industria*, 1844, pp. 259-261; and Keremitsis, *La industria*, pp. 49-50.

import up to 80,000 quintals of foreign cotton.[58]   This was not before Puebla's *Junta de Industria,* as though to advertise its contempt for its competitors, had publicly burned 6,000 quintals of contraband raw cotton.[59]   Then, late in September 1844, the position of the *Junta de Industria* suddenly changed, Marrón and company petitioning for the first time for raw cotton imports.[60] How can this *volte-face* be explained, particularly in the face of a bumper cotton crop in the lowlands of Veracruz in 1844?[61]

The answer must lie in the overlapping of interests between *veracruzano* cotton monopolists and those merchants in Veracruz standing to gain from importing foreign cotton. Velasco, Marrón and company were ideally placed both in the port and the growing region for this. While the Atlantic coast crop in 1844 had yielded a record harvest, the Pacific coast crop in the states of Oaxaca, Puebla, Guerrero, Michoacán and Jalisco had failed entirely.[62] *Veracruzano* cotton monopolists could therefore extend their control of cotton supply beyond the Mexican southeast by marketing imported raw material to the cotton starved factories of the interior. A further reason why importation of foreign cotton over the winter of 1844-45 served the interests of Puebla and *veracruzano* cotton monopolists was that the availability, but high price, of imported cotton diverted funds from *oaxaqueño* cotton agriculture, whose market in Puebla was now taken by imported foreign cotton. Foreign imports in fact contributed directly to the failure of the crop in southern Oaxaca and Puebla in 1845, precisely where Antuñano and others, in collaboration with *oaxaqueño* merchants and growers, had been attempting to raise production in order to relieve their dependence upon the Velasco-Marrón cotton monopoly.[63] The *Dirección General de la Industria* in its report of 1845, concluded that imports of foreign cotton had served only to increase prices, reduce consumption, increase contraband, reduce customs revenues and tighten the grip of the cotton monopolists in Veracruz who were reported to be paying their own growers 18 reales/arroba, which they then sold for 44-48 pesos/arroba to

---

58   *Memoria de Industria,* 1843, pp. 154-55; and for a lengthy refutation of the *Junta de Industria* of Puebla's arguments in favor of maintaining the prohibition, *Representación dirigida al Supremo Govierno por la Dirección General de la Industria Nacional.* Mexico, 1843. A quintal was roughly 100 lbs.

59   AGN, Industria, Vol. II, Exptes. 77 and 87.

60   AAP, Cabildo, Vol. III, 20 and 28 September 1844.

61   *Memoria de Industria,* 1844, pp. 256-257.

62   *Memoria de Industria,* 1844, p. 256.

63   The dire predicament of cotton agriculture in Oaxaca is described in great historical depth in a letter from the *Junta de Industria de Oaxaca* to the *Junta de Industria de Puebla* of July 1845, published by Antuñano in his *Economía Política* series. Puebla, 1845.

the factory owners.[64] Thus, from Antuñano's point of view, the relaxation of the prohibition on raw cotton imports had unforeseen and unfavorable consequences. It had benefitted the very monopolists it had been designed to combat.

As a result of negative experience of the raising of the import prohibition in 1844, the government returned to a prohibitionist policy, punctuated by the granting of licenses for the importation of determined amounts of cotton for short periods, to merchants who were believed not to be enmeshed in the cotton monopoly. By early 1846 this policy had failed to satisfy many industrialists, faced still with cotton scarcity and erratic prices. On the eve of the American war, the Paredes government conceded freedom to cotton imports, overruling the constitution clause which forbade any relaxation of a prohibition without approval of two thirds of state legislatures.[65] American soldiers then arrived instead of American cotton bales. Ironically, this *de facto* blockade of Mexico's ports served to direct investment into cotton agriculture, Puebla (Tlapa) having bumper cotton harvests in 1849.[66]

Inadequate, irregular and costly raw cotton supply remained the central obstacle preventing the cotton textile industry from cheapening its products. Until the development of cotton agriculture in Northern Mexico, where the drier and calmer weather conditions were more favorable for steady cotton production, Mexico's factories remained dependent upon imported cotton from the United States (meeting over half of the industry's needs by the 1870), and upon cotton grown in the tropical coastlands, particularly Veracruz (Mexico's most important cotton-producing area until the 1870's), despite its unsuitable (excessively humid and windy) climate.[67]

In Veracruz, commercial interests, which had become entrenched in the 1830s, remained dominant as late as the 1870s. Among the names of the principal growers on the "Costa de Sotavento" in 1870 could be found Eustaquio Marrón, Velasco Hermanos, Chazaro Hermanos, Prudencio Escandón, families which had become established as "cotton monopolists" by the early 1840s, with Escandón and Chazaro prominent as cotton dealers since before Independence.[68] While the stranglehold of Marrón, Velasco and Co. over the supply of cotton to Puebla's factories may be held up as one, perhaps the main, obstacle to the further development of the region's textile industry over the decade, accounting for its slow growth after 1843, it should also be remembered that Marrón and Velasco were among Puebla's most successful industrialists, (however critical Antuñano may have been of the poor management of their enterprises). As the city's main

---

64 *Memoria de Industria*, 1845, pp. 361-63.

65 Potash, *El Banco*, pp. 213-218.

66 *Memoria del Estado de Puebla*, 1849.

67 Keremitsis, *La industria*, p. 67; *Memoria de Industria*, 1844.

68 Florescano and Chávez Orozco, *Agricultura e Industria*, pp. 267-68.

cotton suppliers they did not need to be efficient. Indeed, it could be argued that Mexican industry survived over these years because of monopoly not in spite of it.

During 1847-48 prohibitions were relaxed and Mexican industry was exposed directly to foreign competition, "inundados los mercados todos de manufacturas estrangeras, desapareció el verdadero apoyo de su vida."[69] Many factories closed down in 1847-48: the woollen factory in the *Casa de Recogidas* for two months, the cotton spinning factory in the Calle de Cholulteca closed in April 1847, never to reopen, and Joaquín Ramírez closed his spinning factory in August. Leonardo Ramírez, who had taken charge of *La Constancia* after Antuñano's death in 1846, was unable to replace a broken drive wheel, keeping all the spindles inoperative until 1849. The captain of Puebla's industry, Dionisio Velasco, watched his warehouse burnt by American soldiers and suffered thefts of large consignments of yarn in transit to Mexico City.[70] Despite all this, the crisis passed over quickly. The Governor of Puebla was able to report in 1849 that, with the re-establishment of protective tariffs: "La industria fabríl se halla aún más adelantada que la agrícola. Las Artes se cultivan con visibles adelantos, y estendiendo el círculo de sus objetos." He even complained of an unprecedented shortage of labor for the factories.[71]

After the war the industrialists' lobby had to fight for its life against a mounting tide of opposition from a young and vigorous generation of Liberals who pointed at the errors of pre-war governments, and the weaknesses in the structure and organization of the state, which had contributed to Mexico's swift defeat in 1847. They considered that one of the principal errors was the pursuit of industrialization behind prohibitions which had become during the 1840s one of the most potent factors of political instability. Prohibition had deprived governments of 40,000,000 pesos in customs revenues and obliged them to exact innumerable direct taxes, all in favor of a small group of "influential people who became, progressively, the respectable body in society and who in the end could not even secure the bases of their own wealth, many suffering bankruptcies."[72] Several attempts were made between 1847 and 1852 to abolish prohibitions, and the volume of pamphleteering in their defence grew to phenomenal proportions from the departmental assemblies of Puebla, Jalisco, Colima, Oaxaca, Mexico City, as well the smaller towns of the province itself: Cholula, Atlixco, Matamoros, Tlaxcala, Zacapoaxtla, San Juan de los Llanos, Chietla.

---

[69] *Memoria del Estado de Puebla*, 1849, p. 69.

[70] AAP, Hacienda Municipal Varios; and AGNP, Miscellaneous Judicial, 1847.

[71] *Memoria del Estado de Puebla*, 1849, pp. 69-70.

[72] "Varios Mexicanos", *Consideración sobre la situación política y social de la República Mexicana en el año 1847*. Mexico, 1848.

The age of prohibitions was drawing to a close but the partially modernized industrial system in the cities of Central Mexico had acquired such a size and political weight that it could never be ignored in the future. High protective tariffs remained in force throughout the Liberal era, and Mexico's only period of relatively free trade, between 1824 and 1837, was never to be repeated.

Case Studies of Puebla's Smaller Mule-driven Inner-city Spinning Factories.

Eight more factories containing modern spinning machinery, beyond the ten so far.mentioned, were established in Puebla between 1838 and 1843. In contrast to the water driven spinning factories built nearby or within the old flour mills, these eight factories used mule powered capstans to drive hand-operated Crompton mule spindles. They were much smaller establishments, rarely containing more than 600 spindles, and were housed in old domestic quarters in the center of the city, close to the hand-loom weavers.[73]

In February 1838, the governor of the state, General Felipe Codallos (1837-41), in company with Pablo González, a master weaver, established a small factory with 600 Crompton mule spindles and twenty power looms, called *Los Dos Hermanos* in the Calle de Cholulteca.[74] By 1842,

---

[73] Machine-operated self-acting mules were available at this time and were being wisely adopted in Glasgow, but Mexican entrepreneurs chose the hand mule, driven by a mule capstan. There was an enormous difference in productivity between the two processes but water or steam power would have been necessary to drive the self-acting mule. They were also considerably more expensive, 600 hand mule spindles costing only 792 pesos (in England) compared to 2,462 pesos for 1,080 throstle spindles, and self-acting mules were even more expensive than throstles. Hand mules were easily maintained and required only one skilled spinner for a set of 600 spindles. Mexicans therefore selected in the late 1830s an intermediate technology perhaps accepting the advice of the Americans who, themselves, were keeping the hand-operated mules. As one wrote in 1840, "There is considerably more trouble with the self-acting, than with the hand mules, arising from the extra machinery required to perform all the different movements; our spinning master attends upwards of 10,000 spindles, but we find that he has rather too much to do." James Montgomery, *The Cotton Manufacture of the United States contrasted and compared with that of Great Britain.* New York, 1840 (1970 reprint), pp. 75, 79, and 116.

[74] AGNP, PN, No. 1, 1838, 13 February 1838. In 1821, Pablo González was listed in the census as a "maestro de Tejer Lanas", living in the Barrio de los Remedios with his family and 17 *oficiales* and apprentices in wool-weaving, between the ages of 13 and 19, living with them. This "obraje de niños" might well have provided the labor force for *Los Dos Hermanos* in 1838. AAP, Hacienda Municipal, Diversos Años, Vol. 113.

Pablo Gonzalez was no longer managing the factory which was under the same direction of Mariano Villegas, another master weaver, who, in the same year, joined Antuñano in his petition for raw cotton imports. In the following year the factory appears to have picked up, the number of looms being increased to 36, producing 144 pieces of cloth a week, employing a labor force of 55, Codallos registering around 2,000-2,500 pieces of cloth annually during the mid-1840s.[75] Over 1843, profits of 33 pesos a week were being made but Codallos, having fallen ill, chose in 1844 to let the factory for 1,000 pesos per annum to José Mariano Torija.[76] This, however, proved to be an unsatisfactory arrangement, the machinery deteriorating to a point in 1847 that it become necessary to close down the factory indefinitely. The enterprise was finally sold by the Codallos family to Joaquín de Haro y Tamariz in 1852. After the accounts were reviewed, it was declared to have operated so unsuccessfully that it was judged to be worth no more than the value of the machinery: a mere 4,200 pesos.[77]

More successful than the *Dos Hermanos* was the mule-driven, mixed spinning and weaving enterprise established in 1838 by the municipal syndic, Lic. Domingo Ibarra y Ramos, who, in 1846, became governor of the State. This was his reward for supporting Santa Anna's uprising against the Paredes government in favor of restoring the 1824 Constitution.[78] The *Santa Rita*, established in the Calle de San Agustín, and containing 40 power looms and 800 spindles (increased to 1,000 by 1845), was making the highest profits of any inner city factory in 1843: 180 pesos a week. The higher productivity of *Ibarra Hermanos* was perhaps due to the decision to employ French technicians to supervise production: Frederick Maillieu and Charles Carpentier for spinning and Antoine and François Duret for weaving.[79] The business produced the sixth largest amount of cloth registered in the city over the mid-1840s, sending over 14,000 pieces of manta to markets beyond Puebla in 1845, continuing under the same ownership in 1852.

Another small spinning factory was established in 1840 in the Plazuela de San José, costing 13,000 pesos, raised from thirteen share-holders.[80] This was one of the factories whose progress was halted by cotton famine in 1842-43. Production finally commenced in December 1843 under the direction of Jean Haquet, a French mule spinner and textile engineer. The

---

[75] This does not include cloth sold within the city but only cloth sold beyond.

[76] AGNP, PN, No. 7, 1844-45, f. 116.

[77] AGNP, PN, No. 7, 1852, f. 52.

[78] Leicht, *Calles*, pp. 18, 197 and 270; and AGNP, PN, No. 1, 1838, f. 200. As Governor of the State, Ibarra honored Estevan de Antuñano with the title "Benemérito de Estado, Ilustre fundador de la industria fabril en la República".

[79] AGNP, PN, No. 1, 1838, f. 195.

[80] AGNP, PN, No. 1, 1840, f. 69.

owner of the enterprise, José María Pérez Berruecos, landowner and prominent dealer in imported and national cloth since the 1820s, died in this year leaving over 56,000 pesos in debts. His wife was left with the decision of whether to continue the enterprise in order to liquidate the family's liabilities. The family's executors, Gregorio Mujica Elias and Joaquín de Haro y Tamariz, advised Doña Pérez to sell the factory. They argued that it yielded less profit than many of its competitors, because of the high salary of the French mule-spinner (who received 1 real 1 octavo per 1 lb. of yarn produced), and predicted that the age of prohibitions might be drawing to an end. Not accepting their advise, Doña Pérez Berruecos decided to continue operating the factory for a further three years, leaving to posterity some complete factory accounts.[81]

The cotton factory, valued at 12,715 pesos in 1843, was only a small part of the Berruecos estate, the total assets of which amounted to 163,638 pesos against liabilities of 56,804 pesos. The three parts of the business were operated independently under separate managers. The *Hacienda de San Miguel de la Pila* in Tepeaca, valued at 28,845 pesos, producing maize, wheat, chile and beans, yielded an income of 11,120 pesos 71/2 reales between July 1843 and August 1844 against costs of 14,179 pesos 71/4, incurring a loss of 3,059 pesos 11/2 reales.[82] The *Tienda de Ropa*, dealing principally in locally-produced cotton cloth and *rebozos*, but also imported silks, linens and woollens, was valued at 38,227 pesos in 1843 and produced 20,726 pesos 6 reales from sales over the following year. The business was then sold to Francisco de la Torre for 20,087 pesos, representing net profits to the Berruecos family of around 2,500 pesos. Finally, the factory produced 22,969 pesos worth of yarn between 15 April 1843 and 3 January 1844, against labor (19 workers) and raw material costs of 21,788 pesos yielding a profit of 1,180 pesos, or approximately 5 percent (Table 7.2). Profits from the factory and the shop therefore compensated for the losses from the *hacienda*, leaving the family a balance of around 700 pesos, clearly insufficient to sustain the family and repay enormous debts owed to creditors, prompting the decision to liquidate the estate.

Haquet brought his raw cotton principally from Ciriaco Marrón, but also from other wholesalers - José Mariano Benítez, Juan Mujica y Osorio, Estanislao Saviñon, Edward Turnbull, Tagart and Co., and D. J. Guillarmod. He sold yarn to weaving factory owners, cloth dealers and independent weavers: Estanislao Saviñon (who purchased almost one half of the factory's product), Pedro Manzano, Macedonio Arreoja, Pablo González, Domingo Rueda, Francisco Pérez, Fernando Pardo, Luciano Fernández and Mariano Oropeza, all figuring as important *manta* producers

---

[81]   AGNP, Judicial Miscellaneous, 1843 will of José M. Pérez Berruecos.

[82]   Ibid., fs. 125-127.

TABLE 7.2 ACCOUNT OF OPERATION OF PEREZ BERRUECOS' SPINNING FACTORY, 1843-44

COSTS		
42,927 lbs 6 oz.	258 *Tercios* of Raw Ginned Cotton	14,753 pesos 4 reales
	30 *Arrobas* of Yarn	500 pesos 4 reales
	48 *Arrobas* of Yarn	750 pesos 4 reales
	Salary of Juan Haquet, Director (April 15 1843-January 3 1844) + workers wages	5,306 pesos 4 reales
	4 Mules	100 pesos 2 reales
	Rent of house at 30 pesos/month to Convento de la Concepción	280 pesos
	Transport of cotton and yarn	97 pesos 1 real
		21,788 pesos 4 reales
PRODUCT	37,179 lbs. 12 ozs. Cotton Yarn (0.61 ps/lb.)	22,968 pesos 73/8 reales
PROFIT		1,180 pesos 61/2 reales

Source: AGVP, Judicial Miscellaneous Wills, 1843.

during the 1840s.[83] The Berruecos factory remained in production throughout the 1840s and was sold in 1849 to Joaquín de Haro y Tamariz, who had added a further 630 spindles by 1852.

A further inner-city cotton-spinning and weaving factory was established in April 1841 by Lorenzo Fuentes de María, a baker, in company with his brother in the Calle de Belen.[84] The machinery, 600 spindles and ten power looms, ordered from New York, took over a year to arrive, commencing production late in 1842, Fuentes signing Antuñano's petition for the raising of the raw cotton prohibition.[85] In 1844, Enrique Fuentes de María became increasingly indebted to his cotton supplier, Carlos Guillarmod, to the amount of 6,000 pesos. The price of cotton spiralled over this year from 58 reales/arroba in June to 68 reales in November.[86] These debts were repaid finally by March 1849 after the factory had ceased production.[87]

A further inner-city spinning and weaving enterprise, *La Equidad*, was established in the Calle de San Roque late in 1842 by Francisco Carranza, a cloth dealer, founder member of the *Sociedad Patriótica* in 1833, a member of the *Junta de Industria* and alderman in that year.[88] As a latecomer to the industry, in a year of crisis, he subscribed to Antuñano's petition, succeeding in entering production with 600 spindles, costing 8,000 pesos, by 1843. Although labor productivity was high, due probably to Carranza's partnership with Thomas Godden, an English mule-spinner, losses of 130 pesos a week were being incurred in December 1843, as a result of a disproportionately high wage bill (the 19 employees were being paid an average of 10 pesos a week an exceptionally high wage for the times). Like Fuentes, Francisco Carranza became progressively indebted to cotton suppliers, contracting Estanislao Saviñon to supply *La Equidad* with raw cotton on credit of 14,000 pesos over two years at a guaranteed price of 64 reales/arroba - unwise since cotton prices fell in that year.[89] As a result of this imprudent contract, and the loss of the skills of Thomas Godden at the end of his five year contract, Carranza became bankrupt. Saviñon, as principal creditor, gained possession of the factory. Leonardo Collantes, a *montañés* merchant took over the factory in 1849, doubling the number of spindles and setting up 43 looms. But he fared no

---

83   *Memoria de Industria*, 1840-45.

84   AGNP, RPP, Censos, Vol. 45, f. 36.

85   AGNP, PN, No. 2, 1842, fs. 832-33.

86   AGNP, RPP, Censos, Vol. 45, fs. 255 and 277.

87   AGNP, PN, No. 5, 1849, f. 269.

88   AGNP, PN, No. 2, 1842, f. 1840.

89   AGNP, RPP, Censos, Vol. 45, f. 239.

better than Carranza, and the factory was being operated by his creditors in 1852, a year of commercial and financial crisis.[90]

Finally, a more successful inner-city spinning factory was established in 1839, by a father and son partnership in an old pelota court in the Plazuela de San Xavier. By 1843 the 700 spindles of *Ramírez e Hijos* was the most productive factory in the entire city. In 1845 the original company was dissolved and refounded as *'Ramírez Hermanos'* with a capital of 50,000 pesos, made up of five 11,000 peso shares. José Joaquín was charged with the purchase of raw materials and sale of yarn and cloth; Rafael, with employment, book-keeping and the care of machinery; José Ignacio, with "improving the sales of the product in the market place." As salaries, José Joaquín and Rafael would receive 2 percent of the value of the cotton yarn sold and José Ignacio would receive a salary of 600 pesos per annum. In 1846 they increased the capital to 71,000 pesos, investing in 600 more throstle spindles.[91] Production continued steadily and the factory was operating profitably in 1852. It was the only inner-city spinning factory to adopt the Arkwright throstle process and one of the few to remain under ownership of a single company over the decade. Arkwright machinery was more simple to maintain and operate, compared to the Crompton mule. And the power problem, which ruined Antuñano's attempt to establish Arkwright machinery in the Barrio Alto, did not arise as Cristobal Ramírez decided on mule rather than steam power from the start. The factory was vertically integrated, the coarse yarn produced being woven on twenty power looms.

In conclusion, from the available notarial and fiscal sources, the record of the smaller inner-city mule driven cotton-spinning and weaving factories over the 1840s was an uneven one. Of the eight factories established between 1838 and 1843, only three remained in the same hands for more than a decade, three closed indefinitely and two bankrupted, continuing production under the ownership of creditors, in both cases the raw cotton dealers to whom they had been indebted. All but one of the factories that survived doubled their spinning capacity over the decade to between 900 and 1,620 spindles. Five of the eight factories contained power looms totalling 136 in number in 1843 but falling to only 80 in 1852. Most of their yarn product, it must be assumed, went to hand-loom weavers. The skill of foreign mule-spinners, despite the extra labor costs their employment entailed, appears to have been vital to the successful running of these enterprises, although not in itself sufficient to guarantee success. In two instances, companies facing increasing raw material costs and indebtedness to suppliers proved unable to afford the renewal of contracts with foreign mule spinners, to their cost.

---

[90] *Padrón de Fábricas*, 1852.
[91] AGNP, PN, No. 7, 1845, fs. 125 and 147-148.

268

If the record of these smaller inner-city spinning factories was patchy, how did the larger water driven mills fare over the decade? It has already been observed that they enjoyed a higher survival rate and also, that turnover of ownership was less frequent. But this was largely a result of their much greater value, putting their acquisition beyond the means of the kind of retail merchants, bakers, etc. who had chosen to invest in the smaller spinning factories. In general, the performance of the larger factories was similar to, certainly no better than, that of the smaller factories: very few examples of consistent success - Velasco, Marrón and Vallarino being the most notable - many cases of fitful survival, and, several cases of failure.

The most prominent example of "fitful survival" was Esteven de Antuñano and Company. At his death in 1847 the *Constancia/Economía* complex was still the largest spinning enterprise in Puebla, with 11,580 spindles and 115 power looms, closely followed by Velasco y Cía. with 10,800 spindles and 80 power-looms in three factories (*Patriotismo, Santa Cruz* and *Señor San José*). As early as 1840, Antuñano, perhaps as a consequence of over-extending his fixed capital investments, had lost control both of cotton supply and the marketing of the hand-loom weavers' *manta*, and had become increasingly indebted to cotton suppliers and wholesalers over 1841-43. Although Antuñano-registered *manta* production recovered after the famine years, his share of overall *manta* production had become insignificant by 1845, next to Velasco y Cía's dominance of the *manta* business (producing one fifth of all *manta* registered in 1845). Antuñano's inability to profit from dealing in raw cotton or from commercializing *manta* - the two keys to Velasco y Cía's success and clearly where money was made - confined him to being a mere yarn manufacturer, albeit an important one. And yarn production was a highly-competitive business during the 1840s, yielding profits which were insufficient to permit manufacturers, without other lines of business or stout and reliable merchant backers, to keep their heads above water. Thus, Antuñano's business became increasingly indebted to cotton suppliers. Ultimately, the French merchant Pedro Berges de Zúñiga, who had loaned Antuñano 100,000 pesos for buying cotton in 1845, took over the Santa Domingo flour mill, *La Economía* and the *Hacienda de la Noria* from Antuñano's heirs in 1850, acquiring *La Constancia* later in the decade.[92]

Antuñano was not alone in becoming heavily dependent on cotton suppliers. Lino Romero and Miguel García, partners in *La Benevolencia*, were indebted to the amount of 45,045 pesos in 1846 to Ciriaco Marrón and Luis Delhman, a German merchant, for the supply of raw cotton and imported goods. The debts were to be repaid in kind with yarn from the factory as well as with cash from the sales of García's retail outlet in the

92 Aguirre and Cavabarín, *Empresarios de la Industria Textil*, pp. 37-38.

center of the city - *Al Gusto del Día* - at the rate of 1,500 pesos a month.[93] This arrangement clearly proved to be too onerous for Romero and García, *La Benevolencia* passing, by the end of the year, into the possession of Manuel Pérez, owner of *La Teja*, who kept both establishments in production until 1852, and beyond. Even the *Patriotismo* company when it was dissolved in 1849 "to the complete satisfaction of its partners", owed 45,304 pesos, approximately one quarter of the factory's value, to Ciriaco Marrón for supplying raw cotton.[94] Marrón was not the only supplier of cotton who found himself in an unassailable position vis-a-vis spinning factory owners. Manuel Caámano's attempt to combine cotton spinning in the *Molino del Carmen* with flour-milling and baking had failed by 1846 as a result of growing indebtedness to the British commercial house of Robert Smith-Duncan and Co., from whom Caámano had borrowed 30,236 pesos in 1844 (for 4000 quintales of cotton of 60 reales/arroba).[95] In January 1846 Caámano sold his factory and entire business to Juan Mujica y Osorio, wholesaler, shortly to become Governor of the State, for 121,503 pesos. In the notarial protocol, Caámano stated desperately: "to get out of such diverse and numerous undertakings, I sold out -my mill, bakery, sifting shop and machinery."[96]

Cotton Weaving and Innovations in Linen and Woollen Manufacture, Cotton Dyeing, Bleaching and Printing

Emphasis has so far been placed upon investment in modern cotton spinning. This had a revolutionary impact on the previous system of production. Turning to cotton weaving, the most conspicuous characteristic was the survival of many of its more traditional features. In 1852 there remained in Puebla at least 3,000 independent hand-loom weavers working 1,082 looms in their homes.[97] After almost two decades of a precarious existence and, doubtless, long periods of unemployment, the city's weavers had returned to more regular employment from the mid 1830s. This was as

---

[93] AGNP, RPP, Censos, Vol. 45, fs. 415-16 and 458.

[94] AGNP, RPP, Censos, Vol. 46, fs. 10-12.

[95] The conditions of this loan were that Caámano would hand over to Smith-Duncan all the yarn produced by the factory in exchange for 85 *tercios* of cotton a month. In addition, Smith-Duncan was obliged to pay the factory's wages to the tune of 250 pesos a week. AGNP, RPP, Censos, Vol. 45, f. 263.

[96] AGNP, RPP, Censos, Vol. 45, f. 336.

[97] In 1841 there were estimated to be 1,300 handloom weavers working on 1,040 looms producing 16,000 yards of *manta* a day (500 pieces), consuming 3,500 lbs. of cotton yarn. *Memoria de Industria*, 1840; and Juan del Valle, *Guía*, p. 182.

a consequence, first of greatly increased yarn imports, followed by the steady increase of national yarn production. Home weavers appear to have been able to compete with the 1,700 weavers, who, by 1852, had been grouped into 28 weaving factories containing 1,477 looms.[98] This consolidation of weaving into larger units was the most marked change in the organization of cotton-weaving since the introduction of the Castilian loom towards the end of the seventeenth century inaugurated the growth of urban hispano-mestizo cotton weaving in the cities of central Mexico.

In fact, these large weaving factories were merely collections of traditional "Castilian", wooden, hand-looms gathered under a single roof. They remained firmly bedded in traditional technology. They were not costly to set up or acquire. In 1854 one weaving factory, containing 153 looms, was sold for a mere 2,250 pesos. Another, with 117 looms, changed hands in 1857 for only 4,350 pesos.[99]

The amount of ordinary *manta* leaving the city quadrupled between 1837 and 1842, and quadrupled again between 1842 and 1852. Puebla's share of (registered) national production fluctuated between 40 and 55 percent. As had been the case before Independence, the great wholesale businesses, some now·spinning factory owners, marketed the lion's share of Puebla's *manta*, although smaller merchants and the hand-loom weaving factories appear to have maintained their share of production over the 1837-45 period.[100]

The price of Puebla's ordinary cotton cloth fell markedly as a result, first, of imports of cheaper yarn, then of the mechanization of cotton spinning. Before Independence, a thirty two yard piece of *manta* in Puebla could cost between eight and twelve pesos. In remote Chihuahua, Puebla cloth had sold for as much as 20 to 24 pesos.[101] As late as 1834, Puebla cotton cloth was selling at 11 pesos the piece. By 1836, after the opening of *La Constancia*, the price of a piece of hand-woven cloth had fallen to just over 9 pesos and power loom cloth was selling at 10 pesos. Seven years later Puebla's cloth was selling at 7 pesos, 1 peso cheaper than Mexico City cloth. Puebla cloth appears to have maintained this price advantage through to the second half of the nineteenth century, for in 1867 ordinary Puebla *manta* was selling for almost 1 peso less per piece than cloth manufactured in Mexico City, enabling Puebla's *manta* to compete in the markets of the interior (Table 7.3).

---

[98] *Padrón de Industria*, 1852.

[99] AGNP, Judicial Miscellaneous, 1855. Inventory of Cotton Manta Factory, Plazuela de San Agustín; and AGNP, PN, No. 7, f. 314.

[100] *Memorias de Industria*, 1840-45. Reports from departmental *juntas de industria* on *manta* production,.

[101] *Registro Oficial*, Vol. 4, 5 March 1831, p. 53.

TABLE 7.3 MANTA PRICES IN MEXICO, 1777 - 1867

Date	Place	Kind of Loom Hand/Power	Price of Manta Reales/Yard
1777	San Martín Texmelucán (Puebla)	Hand	3.0
1777	Puebla de los Angeles	"	2.0
1777	Cholula	"	1.5
1787	Antequera de Oaxaca	"	1.7
1803	Guadalajara	"	1.6
1810	Puebla	"	2.0
1827	Puebla	"	2.75
1834	Puebla	"	2.75
1836	Puebla	"	2.29
1836	Puebla	Power	2.5
1842	Mexico	"	1.75
1843	Puebla	Hand and Power	1.75
1843	Mexico	" "	2.0
1847-53	Guadalajara	" "	0.25
1867	Mexico (British Cloth)	Power	2.0
1867	Mexico (Mexican high quality)	"	2.13
1867	Mexico (Mexican poor quality)	"	1.56
1867	Puebla	Hand	1.34

Sources: 1777: AGN, Industria y Comercio Vol. 7, f. 305; 1787: Brian
Hamnett, *Politics and Society*, p. 77; 1803: M.L. MSS Add. 17,557;
1810: Robert Potash, *El Banco*, p. 32: 1827: *El Poblano* ,12 March
1827, No. 3; 1836: Miguel Quintana, *Estevan de Antuñano*, Vol II, p.
95; 1842: *Memoria de Industria*, 1843, p. 165; 1843: Estevan de
Antuñano, *Economía Política*, 1843, and *Memoria de Industria* 1843, p.
171; 1847-1853: BSMGE Vol. II, p. 263; Dawn Keremetsis, *La
Industria*, p. 56-7.

The reason for the relative cheapness of Puebla's cloth is impossible to establish beyond mere conjecture. Raw cotton and yarn were certainly no cheaper in Puebla than in Mexico City, so it seems that it was the greater productivity of the Puebla hand-loom weaver which explains the difference, perhaps a result of the consolidation of weaving into larger units.[102]

Rebozo weaving recovered rapidly during the 1840s, but appears to have stagnated thereafter. There were 145 *rebozo* looms in 1841 employing 200 workers. By 1852, 193 looms employed 413 men and women in 23 factories ranging in size from small 3-6 loom establishments to the giant 132 loom factory belonging to Cayetano Aguilar.[103] This is a branch of industry which the mechanization of spinning freed from its traditional region of specialization - the southeast. By the 1840s, Guadalajara, which had depended on Puebla for supplies of *rebozos* before Independence, appears to have reduced its dependence upon other regions.[104]

Attempts at linen manufacture in Puebla over the late 1830s and early 1840s were as unsuccessful as the efforts of the Bourbons to promote the linen industry in the valley of Puebla in the 1770s.[105] Seen as a potential cash crop for reviving agriculture and an alternative occupation for women made redundant by the mechanization of spinning, the Bishop Pablo Vásquez took a great interest in the industry. He planted flax on his own estates and established a factory with fifty benches for preparing linen yarn, taking on fifty young girls late in 1835.[106] While the girls proved apt, earning 3 reales a day working for only eight hours (in contrast to the one

---

[102] The conditions of sale of a weaving factory in a house in the Calle de Iglesias in 1837, containing 30 iron looms, 87 wooden looms and 17 mules to drive a capstan provide some clues to the intensity of production. The factory was sold by Manuel Pérez, owner of two spinning factories (*La Teja* and *Amatlán/Benovolencia*) to Juan Romero for 4,350 pesos. Romero would pay Pérez 100 pesos a month until the debt was paid off on condition that Pérez provide thread sufficient to supply the 117 looms producing 300 pieces of cloth a week. The house belonged to José Calderón y Arroyo who received 400 pesos a year in rent. Ciriaco Marrón, cotton dealer, guaranteed the sale. The anticipated rate of production of three pieces of *manta* (or 32 yards) per loom a week was a marked improvement on the two pieces a week of the handloom weaver before Independence. One assumes that the supervised workplace provided conditions propitious for greater work discipline. AGNP, PN, No. 7, 1857.

[103] Del Valle, *Guía*, pp. 181-182.

[104] Puebla produced 16,484 dozen *rebozos* in 1837 and 27,552 in 1845. Guadalajara imported 12,910 dozen *rebozos* in 1803, 7,083 dozen in 1843, and only 1,980 dozen in 1845. *Memorias de Industria*, 1843-45; and *BSMGE*, Vol. 11, p. 274.

[105] Ramón María Serrera Contreras, *Cultivo y manufactura de Lino y Cáñamo en Nueva España*. Sevilla, 1974.

[106] AGNP, Judicial Miscellaneous, 1835; and for the inventory of the small 50-bench linen factory, which cost only 454 pesos to mount, CONDUMEX, Hospital de Jesús, Vol. 422, Expte. 12.

and a half reales a day they had earned from cotton spinning working from dawn to dusk), problems occurred at the weaving stage. In 1836, Vásquez judged the finished cloth as "fit only for carrying hazelnuts". After failing to attract two German weavers from a colony in the north of the state (Jotutla), the Bishop abandoned the project. A later attempt at linen production by Gumersindo Saviñon and Señor Strybos at San Martín Texmelucan seems also to have failed, a piece of linen cloth "grown, spun and woven in this city" and a bobbin of hemp fibre in the State Museum being all that remained of these ventures in 1852.[107]

The woollen industry retained, in 1850, the small scale to which had been reduced by the end of the colonial period. Modernization did, however, take place in both spinning and weaving. Apart from Francisco Puig's factory in the Parián, established in 1821, a further small spinning and weaving factory, (of 440 spindles and 8 looms brought from New York, costing 6,000 pesos), was established in the Calle de Recogidas by Camilo Campero with two partners, Antonio Rodríguez and Joaquín Moreno, in the early 1840s.[108] Both enterprises appear to have done business in cotton *manta* as well as in woollen yarn and cloth. After Francisco Puig's death, his widow formed a company with a Spanish landowner, Domingo Rueda, which became one of the principal dealers in cotton *manta* over the 1840s. The liquidation of this company in 1850 reveals the woollen factory to be valued only at 1,047 pesos in spite of the many thousands, (including the 10,000 pesos of Banco de Avío money), invested in its since its foundation in 1820. A sign of where most of Puig and Rueda's business had lain during the 1840s was the 32,176 pesos in small debts owed to the company by numerous cotton weavers and yarn customers.[109] By 1852, Puig's factory had closed, Campero's continued under the ownership of Manuel Vidal and another woollen spinning factory, with 800 spindles, had been established by Manuel Morán in the Molino de Cristo to the east of the city.[110]

An altogether more ambitious and significant woollen spinning and weaving enterprise was established by the Puebla merchants Carlos Chávez and Gabriel Rodríguez at Zacatzontetla on the *Hacienda of San Antonio Palula* in Tlaxcala. In 1839 they invested at least 37,000 pesos in modern machinery.[111] By 1840 the French merchant, Agustín Dasque, had joined the company, attracted to Puebla from Mexico City, along with many

---

107 *Memorias de Industria,* 1845, p. 344; and del Valle, *Guía,* p. 160.

108 AAP, Aguas, Vol. 50, p. 193; AGNP, PN, No. 2, 1842, f. 729; and RPP, Censos, Vol. 45, f. 174.

109 AGNP, PN, No. 1, 1850, f. 485.

110 José Manuel Vidal was a French merchant resident in Puebla from the early 1840s, acting as commissioner for the Veracruz-based merchant Pedro Berges y Zúñiga. Del Valle, *Guía,* p. 195.

111 AGNP, PN, No. 5, 1839, fs. 36-37.

foreign merchants, by the city's short and spectacular commercial and industrial revival.[112] By June 1841, Dasque and Rodríguez had invested a further 80,000 pesos in the enterprise, installing spinning machinery capable of producing 30 arrobas of good spun wool daily, (enough to put the woollen hand-spinners of Tlaxcala out of business overnight). The enterprise, called "El Valor", appears to have been clumsily mismanaged. When in 1845, Rodríguez came to sell a share to Charles Guillarmod, a Swiss wholesaler, the factory was found to be "in a veritable state of deterioration." The factory had been out of action since "the last days of Holy Week" of 1843 and the damage to practically all of the cylinders of the spinning mules suggests either neglect or possible physical violence on the part of the local inhabitants.[113] Guillarmod took legal proceedings on what was established, after various visits of inspection from Puebla's immigrant engineering community, to have been a fraudulent sale. They judged that without considerable work requiring steel instruments and the use of an iron foundry and the replacement of many parts accessible only from foreign suppliers, the factory could not re-enter production.[114]

The case illustrates the technical difficulties facing sophisticated factory production at this early stage of industrialization. While the *Memoria de Industria* for 1845 reported the factory to be back in production "with great success", an inventory of the same year shows that the looms and fulling machine had not been brought into use and were kept dismantled in a store.[115] Weaving in Tlaxcala remained the preserve of the independent peasant-artisan until well into the twentieth century, for the weavers of Tlaxcala had always been agriculturalists, working their looms in their spare

---

[112] Dasque had made his fortune in the import trade during the 1830s, the French Consul estimating in 1843 that of the 4,000,000 pesos returned to France during the decade from sales in Mexico City alone, Dasque contributed 7-800,000 pesos. ADF, Documents et Mémoires Amérique. Mexico, California et Oregon, 1843, Vol. 43, Expte. 17, *Proprietés françaises au Méxique*.

[113] Between 1841-44, Dasque and Rodríguez encountered resistance from neighboring villages over access to water and damage caused to crops by the damming of the River Zaguapán, judged necessary to provide a millstream to drive the machinery. They were eventually ordered in 1844 to pull the dam down. This dispute, rather than opposition from hand spinners to power-driven spinning machinery, might have been the cause of the damage to the spinning machinery. For Rodriquez and Dasque's defence see: *Falsedades que contiene el Cuaderno titulado "Despojo a mano armada por el prefecto de Tlaxcala. "* Puebla, 1844. By 1847, Dasque's relations with surrounding villages appear to have stabilised. They agreed to a dam and canal across their land for a rent of 25 pesos per year. AGNP, PN, No. 5, 21 January 1847, f. 4.

[114] AGNP, Judicial Miscellaneous, 22 March 1845, Tribunal Mercantíl, Carlos Guillarmod against Gabriel Rodríguez and Agustín Dasque.

[115] *Memoria de Industria*, 1845, p. 373.

time.[116] Dasque's factory was established to supply them with spun wool in the same way that Puebla's cotton factories were directed at supplying the cotton-weaving artisanate, not at replacing them. Agustín Dasque remained the owner of "El Valor" until 1859 when he sold the heavily indebted business to José Durante for a mere 10,000 pesos. The factory had retained its value - 30,000 pesos - but over 20,000 pesos was owed to creditors in Mexico City and Puebla.[117]

Accompanying investment in spinning and weaving, there was an impressive growth in cotton cloth bleaching, dyeing and printing. Dyeing and printing were not new arts to Puebla. The *rebozeros* would generally have had their own indigo-dye presses in which they would soak their cotton and silk yarn before weaving. *Pintores de Indianas* and *Indianilleros* (calico/*indiana* printers) are evident in the 1791, 1821 and 1830 censuses. However, the modern manufacturing processes introduced during the thirties produced yarn and cloth which required cleaning and bleaching to remove dirt and grease contracted in the manufacture. And, for more perfect dyeing and printing, it was important to remove the natural color of the cotton so as to make the cloth perfectly white (unbleached cotton cloth was yellowish in color).[118] Moreover, dyeing and printing greatly increased the value and attractiveness of the cloth, for Mexicans since Independence had acquired a taste for colorful prints, discarding the often dull livery of the colonial period.[119] With the glutting of the market for ordinary *manta* by the early 1840s, many industrialists saw the printing of cloth as a way of diversifying production and capturing a wider slice of the market from imports.[120]

A Puebla silk-mercer, Joaquín Abaroa, (dealing,one presumes, in imported silk goods) had anticipated the demand for chemical bleaching and dyeing procedures which the new industry would bring in its wake. The technology was already far-advanced in Europe from M. Berthollet's discovery of chemical bleaching in the 1780s. In 1833, Abaroa published the *Memorial Práctico de Químico Manufacturero o Colección de Procedimientos Relativos a las Artes y Manufactura* (Puebla, 1833, 2 Vols.), translated from M. Mackenzie's English translation of the French edition.[121] He added sections of his own, illuminating the merits of certain domestically produced minerals such as *tequesquite* (carbonate of soda)

[116] *Bosquejo Geográfico-económico del Estado de Tlaxcala.* Mexico, 1933, p. 66.

[117] AGNP, PN, No. 5, f. 53.

[118] Edward Barnes, *History of Cotton Manufacture.* Chapter XIII, pp. 245-285.

[119] Keremitsis, *La industria*, p. 29.

[120] *Memoria de Industria*, 1843, p. 174.

[121] A French edition of M. Chaptal's *Química aplicada a las artes* was being used by cotton bleachers and dyers in Mexico in 1808 when its translation was strongly urged by cotton-weavers. *Diario de Mexico*, Vol. VIII, January-June, 1808, No. 957, pp. 438-39.

specifying the quantities to be used in relation to their European counterparts. (*Tequesquite*, of which more will be said in the next chapter, had superior properties to its European equivalent, *Soza de Alicante*, and could be used in measure of 2 oz of the former to 16 oz of the latter.). He added footnotes and comments to encourage the Mexican practitioner ("don't dismay if your first attempts don't work"), inserting a detailed description and diagram of an English steam-engine to complete his manual. In May 1840, he set out to fulfill his ambition to establish a bleaching and printing factory, with a steam engine and rolling machines for stamping and finishing cloth, employing a European master and artisans to bring the factory into production. In the following year he formed a company with Edward Turnbull, an English merchant, and Frederick Vallenburg, named it *La Aurora Industrial, Estampados Poblanos*, and endowed it with a capital of 30,000 pesos.[122] By 1842, production had commenced at 1,009 pieces of cloth, reaching 8,291 pieces by 1845. In October 1843, he petitioned the central government for freedom from new duties (recently increased from 15 to 46 percent) placed on imported chemicals and dyes, of which the factory was consuming 8,150 lbs. a month. This illustrates the conflict of interest between manufacturers adopting modern European chemical and industrial technology and the traditional indigo and cochineal dye producers of Oaxaca and the isthmus, for whose benefit the increase in duties had been granted. Abaroa was granted a dispensation from the new duties and, in 1844, duties on eleven industrial chemicals were removed. By then, government had established its own sulphuric acid factory to supply the industrialists at cost price.[123]

A further cotton printing company was formed in May 1840 when José Guerrero and Joaquín Ochoa solicited a loan of 14,000 pesos from the Banco de Avío to establish a print factory, receiving only 6,000 pesos, one of the last loans administered by the bank before its closure.[124] Later, in 1848, José María Ortega established the largest printing factory in our period. Like the others, this was sited near the San Francisco river, which by now must have compared with the streams running through Stockport, for Ortega was obliged to request (and received) a *merced de agua* from the municipal fishpool in the Paseo Viejo, so filthy had the river become.[125] By 1852 there were 14 stamp factories in Puebla, three large units belonging to Manuel Cardera, José María Contreras and José María Ortega, employing 30, 30 and 60 laborers respectively. The other units were small,

---

122 AAP, Cabildo, Vol. 113, 18 May 1840; and AGNP, PN, No. 1, 1841, p. 262.
123 AGN, Banco de Avío, Vol. II, Expte. 114, 24 October 1843; and *Memoria de Industria*, 1844, p. 308.
124 AGNP, PN, No. 7, 1841, f. 104; and Potash, *El Banco*, p. 172.
125 AAP, Presupuestos y Bienes Municipales, Vol. 201, p. 8.

six of them concentrated in the Calles de Carey and Coro, along the banks of the River San Francisco.[126]

Conclusion

Over fifty textile entrepreneurs have been mentioned in this chapter. All chose between 1832 and 1852 to invest in machinery for the modernization of the cotton, woollen and linen textiles. The investment surge was a very short one. Most of the new enterprises were founded between 1837 and 1842. This was in response to a conjuncture of political and economic circumstances: the re-establishment of relatively stable centralist rule after a short period of intense political instability, and a prolonged monetary crisis and slump in foreign trade, both causing a reawakening of interest in domestic industry. Liberals regarded the official commitment to import prohibitions and industrialization as an attempt by Conservatives, who held government between 1835 and 1846, to add a privileged industrial sector to their traditional ally in the Church. Conservatives justified industrialization as the only means to keep urban society in Central Mexico from falling into complete decay, and as a solution to the problem of public order, the breakdown of which had added an alarming dimension to politics during the late 1820s and early 30s. However, the merchants, who became industrialists invested in industry through simple commercial calculation. They could count a visionary within their ranks: Estevan de Antuñano. But his "Utopia Algodonera", the dream of uniting the tropical lowlands of Veracruz, the industrial emporium of Puebla and the silver rich markets of the interior, and of laying the basis for an indigenous industrial revolution, had been convincingly shattered by the mid-1840s. The rhetoric of the industrialists' lobby, revealed in their pamphlets, obscured the reality of industrial transformation in these years.

In fact, the industrialization which took place in Puebla during the 1830s and 1840s, though appearing superficially as an impressive transformation in the structure of the urban economy, was little more than a qualitative readjustment in the investment of merchant capital. As in the years before the War of Independence, the import warehouse remained in 1850 at the tip of the economic pyramid. Merchant involvement in manufacturing had merely changed in form, not substance. The 'harmonizing merchant' of the pre-war system of independent weavers and spinners had, by 1840, become the merchant manufacturer directly involved in or owning the process of production itself. Nevertheless, their achievement should not be belittled. Most enterprises survived over a decade during which their *raison d'être* in import prohibitions was often threatened, raw materials were very dear, and money always scarce, while

---

126 Del Valle, *Guía*, p. 179.

political instability and foreign intervention in 1847 created a hazardous environment for businesses in which such large amounts of fixed capital were involved. The resilience of these enterprises was therefore remarkable.

These fifty or so entrepreneurs formed joint stock companies, but more often entered into short-term partnerships, generally of three associates (for supplying, financing and managing the businesses), sometimes of the same family, but more often unrelated by blood. Many were *poblanos*, born in the city, who had been engaged in the retail cloth trade, baking, pork-butchering, flour-milling, the businesses which had survived in a depressed state since the crisis of Independence: Haro y Tamariz, Ascué y Zalvide, Ramírez Hermanos, Caámano, Uriarte, etc. A few churchmen became textile entrepreneurs: Bernardo Mier, Luis Haro, and the Bishop, Pablo Vásquez. Merchants from other parts of Mexico made significant contributions; the *veracruzanos* , Antuñano, Paso y Troncoso, Marrón, and Mexicans, Martínez, Romero and García.

Foreigners were vital in industrial investment, technical innovation and management. The Spanish contingent were the most significant: the Saviñon brothers, Velasco, Domingo Rueda, Arteaga, and Olaez, but also French, Genoese, Swiss, English and North Americans: Dasque, Vidal, Berges de Zúñiga, Vallarino, Guillarmod, Archer and Turnbull. And foreign technicians were essential in erecting the factories and in operating them: the skilled mule-spinner, the millwright, the machine specialist. Foreign wholesale and retail merchants, spurned by the city during the 1820s and 1830s, became increasingly important during the 1840s as creditors to the new industry. And their departure was lamented when many left the city as a result of the commercial recession and political instability following the Revolution of Ayutla.

Capital, apart from the initial boost from the funds of the *Banco de Avío*, came from private hands, generally accumulated from dealing in the import trade. This was as much so at the beginning of the 1830s as in 1850. Indeed, perhaps the strongest comment on the nature of industrialization in Puebla in these years was the failure of industrialists as a group to generate autonomous capital formation, form their own enterprises, found a bank and release themselves from an excessive dependence upon the credits of import houses and cotton monopolists.

But industrialists did not form a cohesive or self-conscious social group. To be a factory owner was not automatically to be a member of the social and political elite. Nevertheless five served as state governors over these years and one became President of the Republic in 1855. Industrialists consistently made up a significant proportion of the membership of the city council and the state legislature over the period. But many were men of modest means, and socially were attached to a highly variegated intermediate (plebeian) sector of urban society made up of shopkeepers, artisans and petty officials. Industrial transformation did not create a new class just as it failed to transform the structure of the urban economy. Even Manuel Payno, a most extreme liberal, felt a sympathy for

the industrialists and artisans of Puebla and admired their achievements,
though he despised the 'agiotistas', become industrialists, of Mexico City:

> En cuanto a Puebla, francamente creo que en ningún Departamento mejor que
> en el debe protegerse la industria. El pueblo es vivo, inteligente y de pasiones
> ecsaltadas; se necesita darle pan para que coma, y trabajo para que no este
> ocioso. Dosde el establecimiento de las fábricas en Puebla ha habido
> poquísimas revoluciones y nunca tan sangrientas y terribles como cuando el
> pueblo tenía hambre.[127]

---

[127] Manuel Payno, "Viaje a Puebla en el invierno de 1843", *El Museo Mexicano*, Vol.
III, 1843, pp. 141, 163.

Chapter 8

INNOVATION AND CONTINUITY IN NON-TEXTILE MANUFACTURING

P uebla, of course, was not simply a textile town. The wave of entrepreneurship, innovation and capital formation around mechanized industrial processes swept across the entire industrial structure of the city Glass, pottery, brickmaking, flour milling, soap and oil making, iron and paper were the industries most affected by this. But, whereas mechanization transformed cotton spinning, both technologically as well as socially, it did not affect these other industries with any comparable thoroughness. Indeed, by the 1850s, initiatives involving the modernization of glass, pottery, iron and paper industries had either failed or were encountering severe difficulties.

The Failure of Modernization in Pottery and Glass

Between the industrial censuses of 1794 and 1820, the number of fine (*Talavera-majolica*) potteries fell from 16 to 10 and the number of glass factories, from three to two.[1] The industries appear to have received some protection from the wars, since during the short intervals of peace, the challenge from Spanish imports was substantial. After Independence imports of glass and pottery grew massively. Between 1823 and 1827 imports of pottery increased from 5,406 pesos to 119,256 pesos, and imports of glass from 31,160 pesos to 139,738 pesos.[2] The result was that all but one of Puebla's fine potteries had closed by 1825.[3] Juan Carrillo, master potter and alderman in 1824, spoke of the "deplorable state to which

---

[1] AGN, Historia, "Noticias de Fábricas...1794", Manuel Flon.

[2] Lerdo de Tejada, *Comercio Exterior*, Tables; and BL, State Papers, Returns relating to trade between Great Britain and Mexico, 1820-1841.

[3] AAP, Pensiones Municipales, Vol. 163 (1825 Padrón).

the artisans have been reduced...by the abundance of foreign pottery [which] suffocates the market of this country".[4]

In spite of the high level of glass imports, the glass industry fared better than pottery during the 1820s, the number of factories increasing to four by 1825. In that year Mexico actually exported nine boxes of Puebla glass valued at 309 pesos, the only glass exports recorded during the post-independence period.[5] Moreover, José Manso made the first attempt at transformation of the industry in 1825. He returned from Europe with an oven and rollers for the manufacture of plate-glass, producing twelve sheets before the venture, for want of capital, failed. The machinery and first products were consigned to Manso's "Conservatory of the Arts".[6]

The first Federal Republic came to rescue of Mexico's potters placing a prohibition on imports of ordinary pottery in May 1824.[7] Puebla's finer Talavera and Chinese white pottery and coarser earthenware fell within this category and were therefore, theoretically, protected. However, English and French porcelain was high in estimation among the Mexicans who could afford it, and this newly acquired taste would have been, to some extent, at the expense of Puebla's decorative and handsome, though traditional and clumsy, tableware. Figures for English imports of pottery and glass show a high level of imports to 1827, followed by a sharp decline over 1828 and 1829, after which pottery imports returned to a record level by 1832, retaining a continuing high level through to the late 1840s. By contrast, glass imports from Britain over the 1828-1846 period never returned to the high level attained between 1823 and 1827.[8]

Puebla's potteries did, however, recover. By 1833, ten fine potteries and twenty eight rough earthenware factories were in production. (Table 8.1) After hat-making and cotton-weaving, fine and rough potters led the Puebla artisanate in the value of donations to the annual Corpus Christi procession, contributing 14 pesos and 11 pesos 5 reales respectively, not an insignificant amount considering that the *almaceneros* and mercers provided, between them, only 33 pesos 6 reales. The four glass manufacturers contributed 5 pesos 3 reales.[9]

As with textiles, the second half of the 1830s brought innovations to both the pottery and glass industries. José Manso's experiment in 1825 had not been entirely in vain for in 1836 he was honored with half a share,

---

4   AAP, Tierras y Aguas, Vol. 47, f. 7.

5   Lerdo de Tejada, *Comercio Exterior*, Graph No. 32.

6   *Memoria del Estado de Puebla*, 1830, Graph No. 8.

7   *Prohibición de algunos géneros, frutos y efectos de procedencia*. Mexico, 1824, in R. Flores Caballero, *Protección y libre cambio*. Mexico, 1972, pp. 55-56.

8   Lerdo de Tejada, *Comercio Exterior*; and BL, State Papers, *Reports relating to the trade with Mexico*.

9   AAP, Cuentas, Vol. 83 (1833).

TABLE 8.1 VALUE OF POTTERIES, GLASS FACTORIES AND BRICKWORKS

	Tools, Ovens	Raw Materials *(in pesos/reales)*	Stock of finished goods	Total goods
1) Mayolica pottery (1753)	1,858	1,363.2	1,842.4	5,064.6
2) Mayolica pottery (1795)	269	1,530	2,140.6	3,939.6
3) Mayolica pottery (1832)	-	-	-	5,000
4) Red pottery (1852)		(including buildings)		7,137
5) Glass Factory (1806)	-	-	-	2,842
6) Glass Factory (1827)	-	-	-	2,933
7) Glass Factory (1831)	2,101	1,159.4	781.2	4,042.5
8) Glass Factory (1851)	2,289	2,717	7,000	11,420.7
9) Brick Works (1799)		(including buildings)		3,994.1
10) Brick Works (1821)	-	-	-	1,089

Sources: 1) AAP, Gremios, Vol. 227, fs. 187-8; 2), 3), 4), 9) & 10) AGNP, Miscellaneous Judicial (1795, 1832, 1852, 1799, & 1821); 5) AGNP, RPP, Vol. 39, f. 6; 6) AGNP, PN, No. 4, 29 Jan. 1827; 7) AGNP, PN, No.7 (1831-32); 8) AGNP, PN, No.7, 1851, f. 324.

worth 1,500 pesos, in a new company established for the manufacture of sheet and concave glass of every description "in the European style". The five founding shareholders represented a fair cross-section of the city's elite: José Lang, a German merchant resident in the city since the early 1820s (who may be observed in the frontispiece to this book, exercising his poodle), José María Suárez and Agustín Montiel, also merchants, José María Fernández, secretary of the State government, and Pedro Vázquez, rector of the College of Infants and brother of the Bishop. Between them they amassed 12,000 pesos. The partners shared equal responsibility for acquiring the machinery, for contracting and transporting the director and skilled operatives from Europe, and would receive an equal division of the profits. If the capital should prove insufficient, and the *Banco de Avío* be unwilling to lend, then each partner would increase his share proportionately.[10] Antonio Torres, another merchant, joined the company in 1837, contributing 6,000 pesos to the capital fund, and a French Director, Pierre Quinard, was appointed. No established Puebla glass master was represented on the board of directors [11]and perhaps the untimely failure of the enterprise was due in part to the absence of any continuity in personnel or technique with a local glass-making tradition existing since 1543.[12]

As with the modernization of cotton spinning, investment and enterprise was by men with no direct involvement in the previous manufacturing tradition. Indeed, the substance of their calculation was that the new machines and organization of production would render the old technology and the small workshop obsolete. The intention of partners of the *Companía Empresaria para la Fabricación de Vidrios al Estilo de Europa* was to substitute imports with the help of high tariffs and prohibitions and to supply all the domestic market could absorb. Existing manufacturers might benefit temporarily from protection but eventually, if the new enterprise proved successful, they would face overbearing competition from finer and cheaper goods produced with a superior technology.

The mounting of the factory proceeded very slowly, partly because of technical difficulties but largely through bad luck. The devaluation of currency, the shortage of silver specie and the introduction of an unstable copper currency, greatly hindered the accumulation of share capital and made the salary payments to the French director and artisans particularly burdensome.[13] Suitable clay for lining the high temperature ovens could not be found locally and had, at first, to be imported at great cost. The blockade of the ports by the French during the "Pastry Cook" war held up

---

10 AGNP, PN, No. 8, 6 April 1836.

11 AGNP, PN, No. 7, 1837, fs. 166-167.

12 Mariano Fernández, *Historia*, Vol. I, p. 304.

13 AGNP, RPP, Vol. 44, f. 255.

the clay in Veracruz and, worse, prompted the expulsion of the French population from Mexico, among whom were included Honarato Quinard and his five French employees. A new director and artisans were recruited from Bohemia, practiced in different techniques of glass manufacture from the French. Reporting to the Banco de Avio in 1839, Montiel wrote that "ese complexo de desgracias, nos ha hecho marchar con trabajos imponderables y al través de dificultades que parecían invencibles."[14]

The problem of finance was surmounted, although the factory cost far more to establish than originally estimated. By April 1838 the original 12,000 pesos had been spent and the project remained far from completion. Estevan de Antuñano then joined the company contributing a further 4,480 pesos.[15] In July, Pedro Vázquez succeeded in borrowing a further 10,000 pesos from his brother, Bishop Pablo Vazquez.[16] In the same month, Diego Sánchez Pelaez, director of the orphanage and executor of various pious works, lent the company a further 6,000 pesos.[17]

A year later the factory still had not entered production. Agustín Montiel was forced to ask the *Banco de Avío* for a further loan of 10,000 pesos to help with costs which had now mounted to over 50,000 pesos since 1836.[18] The bank agreed to lend this amount, asking for repayment of 5 percent over seven years, once production commenced.[19] This did the trick. By December 1839 Francisco Javier de la Peña could report that :

después de erogaciones cuantiosas y de algunos ensayos malogrados, han conseguido su objeto. Se hacen y vidrios grandes, medianos y chicos, diafanos y hermosos, y capelos de todos tamaños..suficientes para surtir la República entera...su importe aumentara el poco numerario que circula en nuestros mercados.[20]

Faced with pay arrears amounting to 3,415 pesos demanded by the French artisans, the company commenced production on a weak financial footing.[21] The business did not survive the 1842 commercial crisis accompanying the withdrawal of copper money.

In June 1843 a much more modest glass-making venture was embarked upon (perhaps using the machinery of the *Compañía Empresaria*). This time, two established Puebla glass-manufacturers,

---

14 AGN, Banco de Avío, Vol. 2, October 1839.
15 AGN, PN, No. 7, 1838, fs. 84-95.
16 *Ibid.*, f. 154.
17 AGNP, RPP, Vol. 44, f. 317.
18 AGNP, PN, No. 1, 1839, f. 99.
19 AGNP, RPP, Vol. 44, f. 365.
20 *El Amigo de la Religión*, No. 17, p. 306.
21 AGNP, RPP, Vol. 44, fs. 430 and 435.

Francisco Domínguez and Francisco Alcerrica, in collaboration with Honorato Quinard and his three sons and a lawyer, Lic. Pedro Herrera, formed a company, for five years, of seven 200 peso shares, to be named *Alcerrica y Cía.*[22] The factory, established in the Plazuela de San Agustín, proved no more successful than its predecessor and by January 1844 serious differences between the partners had emerged. The two Puebla glass masters, Domínguez and Alcerrica, then resigned from the company. This was in protest at having their request to buy more shares refused. Their position was taken by Felipe Mateo Gutiérrez, a merchant from Orizaba, who contributed a further 1,000 pesos to the capital fund.[23] Although the company was renewed for a further five years, the factory made serious losses. In January 1846 the company borrowed a further 20,000 pesos from José Dolores Garibay of Mexico City but failed to survive the year, production ceasing in December. Garibay then removed the machinery to the capital, Puebla's ancient competitor in glass-making.[24] Pedro and Honorato Quinard left Puebla to settle in the French agricultural colony of Jicaltepec (north of Papantla, Veracruz), although Honorato later returned to participate in a new glass company formed in 1855 with Manuel Lara and Bernardo Campos.[25]

The specific causes of the failure of these two enterprises do not emerge from the notarial documentation but three likely reasons can be advanced. The first is that Mexican manufacturers did not receive the kind of protection offered to cotton textiles over the 1840s, in spite of pressure from manufacturers.[26] Moderate protection existed, sufficient to protect the cheaper lines produced in Puebla's small traditional factories, but the products of the more ambitious and heavily capitalized ventures - crystal and sheet-glass - faced overbearing competition from European imports. In 1844 alone, foreign glass valued at 32,285 pesos was introduced to Puebla and no exports of glass from the city were reported in 1844 and 1845.[27] With the frequent closure of the new factories resulting from financial, technical and labor problems, the government was unable to concede an

---

22 AGNP, PN, No. 5, 1843, f. 104.

23 AGNP, PN, No. 5, 1844, f. 1.

24 AGNP, PN, No. 5, 1846, f. 8; and AGNP, RPP, Vol. 45, fs. 381-382.

25 ADF, *Mémoires et Documents. Population Française en Méxique*, f. 73; and AGNP, PN, No. 5, 1855, f. 169.

26 Anon, *Industria manufacturera: Prohibición de vidrio plano extranjero*. Mexico, 1842.

27 Lerdo de Tejada, *Comercio Exterior*, Graph No. 46; and *Memoria del Estado de Puebla*, 1849. One of the founding shareholders of the company, Agustín Montiel, is listed as one of the four Puebla merchants retailing fine European glass and crystal in 1846. One must assume that this was where the profits lay. AAP, *Padrón de Comercio*, 1846.

import prohibition on foreign glass.[28] A second possible reason for failure was the onerous cost of fuel (scarce in the central Puebla region) for the high-temperature ovens required for modern crystal and sheet-glass manufacture.[29] Finally, dependence upon costly and, it seems, factious foreign technicians, added to the financial and managerial problems of these enterprises.

The failure of ventures involving modern technology contrasts with the stolid durability of 'traditional' glass factories producing for the lower end of the market. There were still four of these in 1846 and 1852.[30] A new factory was founded in 1848 by José María Narvaéz with a humble capital of 1,300 pesos, lent by Doña Catarina Bueno (who, in 1850, had difficulty in extracting repayment). Debts not withstanding, the factory remained in production in 1852.[31] It appears therefore, that even without protection and in the face of heavy competition from European imports, the small, undercapitalized, traditional and time proven glass factory, producing mugs, bottles and rough tumblers, could survive. Four such factories remained in production in 1885, three in 1896, two in 1907 and two still in 1925.[32]

There remained a place, however, for the manufacture of sheet glass (which the city had exported to Venezuela during the eighteenth century).[33] In 1851, Manuel Lara, the chief retailer stocking European glass since the early 1830s, formed a company with Robert Shultze, a German. Borrowing 9,374 pesos 6 reales from Edward Turnbull and Co., English wholesalers, and recalling Honorato Quinard from Jicaltepec, Lara and Shultze brought the factory into production.[34] By 1852, the diarist Juan de Valle could comment that:

> La fabricación tanto de vidrios planos, como bucosos, ha llegado a toda perfección en esta ciudad teniendo la satisfacción los poblanos de haber visto capelos de vara y cuarta de largo y de una claridad muy hermosa; asi como vidrios planos de vara y octava de largo perfectamente limpios.[35]

Innovation in pottery was as ambitious and as unsuccessful as in glass. Enrique Ventajosa claims that English and North American competition was responsible for the decline of the Puebla pottery industry during the first

---

28   *Memorias de Industria*, 1843, p. 187; and 1845, p. 381.

29   *Memoria de Industria*, 1845, p. 381.

30   AAP, Padrón, 1846; and Juan del Valle, *Guía*, p. 167.

31   AGNP, PN, No. 2, 1858, f. 55.

32   Leicht, *Calles*, p. 189.

33   Arcila Farías, *Comercio entre Venezuela y México*, pp. 101-103.

34   AGNP, PN, No. 7, 1851, fs. 324-325.

35   Juan del Valle, *Guía de Forasteros*, p. 161.

half of the nineteenth century. The number of kilns was reduced from thirty to ten which produced tiles and plates only for common use. The Chinese and the Talavera styles, so prized during the eighteenth century, were abandoned for the Gothic. He concedes, however, that between 1840 and 1850, "there was a momentary resurrection in decorated majolica poblana, limiting itself to reproducing with some skill, pieces imported from Europe: cups, sugar bowls, plates, etc..".[36] This short bubble of prosperity must now examined more closely since it reveals both the ideals as well as the limitations of this early experience of industrialization.

In June 1837, a group of prominent men, representing a cross-section of the Puebla elite, formed a society for the manufacture of fine pottery "in the best European style".[37] Among the original group of nine shareholders were José María Castillo Quintero, lawyer and urban property owner; José María Marin, lawyer, alderman, federal deputy and prominent Conservative; Francisco Morales Clavijero, alderman and baker; Joaquín Vázquez, merchant; Bernardo Mier, cotton mill owner and wholesaler; José Joaquín Reyes, federal deputy in the early 1830s, to become state governor in 1843 and again in 1846.[38] Seven more had joined the company by 1842, among them, Francisco de Paula Reyes, merchant; José María Fernández, secretary to the State government; Pedro de Ascué y Zalvide, merchant and textile entrepreneur; and Joaquín de Haro y Tamariz, textile entrepreneur. Only a member of the clergy, who would usually be found in joint stock ventures at this time, was absent from the company's shareholders. The initial share capital amounted to 40,000 pesos, probably more than the combined value of the tools and stock of the eight traditional potteries. Evidently, the intent was to create an enterprise that would revolutionize the pottery industry.

In April 1838, the Mexican Consul General in Rotterdam, Manuel María Maneyro, invited the Dutch porcelain specialist, Ernest Theodore Biebring, to direct the factory. He would supervise the construction of the ovens, contract two or three skilled workers to help him, and instruct them in the craft. The contract was for three years and the salary, 5,000 pesos a year, unprecedented for the times. The assistants would be payed 2,000 pesos a year and be provided with free accommodation and medical services. The director would bring with him all the books, instruments and machines necessary for mounting a modern porcelain factory, as well as a

---

[36] Enrique Luis Ventosa, "La loza poblana", in Manuel Romero y Terreros (Ed.), *Las artes industriales en la Nueva España*. Mexico, 1923, p. 261.

[37] AGNP, PN, No. 7, 1837, fs. 190-192.

[38] Biographical information has been drawn from Cabildo minutes, commercial and industrial censuses, and from Enrique Cordero y Rorres, *Cronología de Gobernantes del Territorio Poblano*. Puebla, 1970; *Diccionario General de Puebla*. Puebla, 1958, 4 Vols.; and Leicht, *Calles*.

selection of German porcelain to serve as models.[39] The style of the pottery was to be "Gothic", imitating that produced at Meissen in Saxony.[40] On August 16th 1838 Ernest Biebring and his Dutch assistants arrived.[41] By December 1839 Francisco Javier de la Peña could announce that production was ready to commence: "La Fábrica de Sajonia Poblana es magnífica....se ha erigida una fábrica espaciosa, bella y utilísima. Los hornos son muy buenos, las galerías grandes y bien ventiladas, y los depósitos para el barro capaces y cómodos". He reported the clay to be abundant and of excellent quality, brought from a mere nine miles, adding that "Breve saldrá la primera hornada de losa fabricada en esta ciudad, igual a la llamada de Sajonia, y teniendo este ramo de industria nacional, no compraremos la estranjera."[42] Between June 1837 and September 1842, 71,000 pesos was invested in the enterprise, from share capital and loans from Church bodies.[43]

Water was connected to the factory in December 1840 which, it is assumed, then entered production.[44] In the following year Biebring's contract of employment expired and he was replaced by the Englishman, James Brindley.[45] Although no specific evidence of a disagreement among shareholders has been found, it is clear from Brindley's terms of employment, and from the decision to reorganize the company, that matters hitherto had been unsatisfactory. After all, the factory had taken three years to enter production during which 34,000 pesos had been spent on the Dutchmens' salaries, before even a plate had been brought out of the ovens. The large number of shareholders perhaps made the direction of the enterprise unwieldy. In 1841, a *junta menor* was elected to supervise financial as well as practical matters more closely.[46] Brindley was employed on a short, six month, renewable contract at an annual salary of 3,000 pesos. He was charged with selecting skilled potters from England to help him, and with training a Mexican supervisor in all the skills of the art. Apart from his salary he would receive a proportion of the profits, but the salary would be reduced by 600 pesos when, for any reason,

---

39 AGNP, PN, No. 1, 1838, f. 542.

40 Leicht, *Calles*, p. 136.

41 AGNP, PN, No. 1, 16 August 1838.

42 *El Amigo de la Religión*. Puebla, 1839, No. 18, p. 321.

43 AGNP, PN, No. 7, 1849, fs. 49-50; and RPP, Censos, Vol. 45, fs. 34 and 102.

44 AAP, Cabildo, Vol. 107, 7 December 1840.

45 AGNP, PN, No. 2, 1842, f. 1433. Another James Brindley, close friend to Josiah Wedgewood, and engineer of England's first canal (opened in 1761), must surely have been related. Bevis Hillier, *Master Potters of the Industrial Revolution*. London, 1965, p. 75.

46 AGNP, PN, No. 2, 1842, 22 June 1842.

production ceased.[47] The company, thereby, attempted to ensure itself against the losses it had suffered under the Dutch director.

The techniques of manufacture used in the new factory were revolutionary in Mexico (though not in the New World).[48] They differed substantially from the techniques used for centuries in Puebla's traditional *talavera* manufacture. The mixing of the clay, varnishing, and firing in the traditional industry depended for their success on fine judgements of the timing of each process, just as the fashioning and decoration of the objects required great skill and art. In the new industry success was almost guaranteed by the use of chemicals, moulds, high-temperature ovens and copper plate engravings. But raw material costs were much dearer in the modern industry since kaolin, many of the chemicals, the transfers, copper plates, moulds and paints were brought from Europe. In contrast, all the raw materials of the traditional industry were found plentifully locally.

Labor productivity was much greater in the new industry but, in turn, labor costs were much greater. In the *Fábrica de Sajonia Poblana*, the English director and his six skilled technicians (in 1844: Benjamin Haynes, Edward Goodhall, John Mier, Eric Skinner, John Hancock and John Humphrey), received an annual combined salary of 18,000 pesos. A further 100 full time assistants were employed alongside the Europeans.[49] In 1821, the largest traditional *majolica* factory employed 22 workers earning between one to six reales a day. Its annual wage bill would not have exceeded 3,000 pesos, though the workers would have received food rations over their daily wages.[50]

The duration of the production process was perhaps the greatest difference between the modern and traditional industries. In the traditional *mayolica-talavera* manufacture, from the mixing of the clay to the second glazing of the finished object, the process could well last for more than six months. In the new industry, the process could take less than a week. Potential volume of production was thereby incomparably increased. The cramped physical scale of the old *mayolica* works was such that a significant increase in production could take place only with a growth in the number of manufacturing units (accounting, no doubt, for the frequent fluctuation in number of working potteries). In the new industry, the

---

[47] One condition of Brindley's contract was that all pottery should be marked "James Brindley-Compañía Poblana". From examples of Brindley's pottery in the Museo Bello, Puebla, this porcelain, printed in red, blue and black, with pastoral scenes in classical landscapes, was of fine quality. It is clear that the company intended to compete with the finer European porcelain.

[48] A porcelain factory was established on a smaller scale in Bogotá in 1832, operating successfully throughout the middle years of the nineteenth century. Frank Safford, *Commerce and Enterprise*, pp. 164-167.

[49] AAP, Padrones, Vol. 148, f. 13; and Leicht, *Calles*, p. 135.

[50] AAP, Padrones, Vol. 133, fs. 230-234.

TABLE 8.2 ENTRY OF FOREIGN POTTERY TO MEXICO CITY'S CUSTOMS' HOUSE IN 1843, 1844 AND 1845

	1843	1844	1845
White pottery	2,600	67,240	5,660
Stamped pottery	20,050	PROHIBITION	
Fine Porcelain	10,035	33,360	25,920
Total	32,685	100,600	31,580

Source: Miguel Lerdo de Tejada, *El Comercio Exterior*, Graph No. 45

addition of a few extra potters and printers might double or treble production. The directors of the new factory must acted upon this reasoning, believing that their factory might soon supply the whole Republic with porcelain.

Differences in costs and capital investment between the traditional and the modern industries were enormous (both in glass and in pottery). We have seen how at least 70,000 pesos and 50,000 pesos respectively were invested in the modern porcelain and glass factories (with wages absorbing a substantial share of investment). Table 8.2 shows the value of raw materials, stocks, tools and equipment of ten traditional pottery, glass and brick making enterprises. It can be seen that their combined value did not approach the cost of mounting either of the modern factories.

By 1856, the *Fábrica de Sajonia Poblana* had foundered, the buildings in use as an *aguardiente* factory. Pottery-making in Puebla had returned to be the preserve of the traditional coarse red and *mayolica* factories. There were ten *mayolica* factories in 1852 and these ten remained in operation in 1885.[51] Only during the Porfiriato did this ancient industry enter a decline: to 7 units in 1896, to 6 by 1903 , to only 3 in 1930 and 1987. But how can the failure of Puebla's first (and last) modern porcelain factory be explained?

As with the glass companies, the notarial records do not offer explanations for business failure, which only factory accounts, unfortunately lacking, can provide. However, adverse circumstances, similar to those facing modern glass, can be advanced as likely causes for failure. As late as 1845, four years after Brindley's appointment, defects were being found in "el color y la claridad del barníz y en la poca consistencia de las piezas", though, it was reported, this was being remedied.[52] Such problems may well have continued under Mexican management, once Brindley's contract of employment had expired. The principal problem seems, however, to have been the inability to compete with foreign imports, once the "protectionist era" was brought to a close by the Revolution of Ayutla in 1854. By this time, the fiscal privileges- freedom from sales taxes - granted at time of the factory's foundation, had expired.[53]

The most suggestive evidence for the factory's failure comes from a contemporary, a shareholder in the *Fábrica de Sajonia Poblana*. In a communication to the *Dirección General de la Industria* in 1844, he asserted that:

---

[51] Leicht, *Calles*, p. 124.

[52] *Memoria de Industria*, 1845, p. 381.

[53] There is evidence that the exemption from sales tax was hard to enforce even within the State of Puebla. Tehuacán customs house was denounced with charging *alcabala* on Puebla's pottery in 1843. AAP, Cabildo, Vol. 110, 10 May 1843.

> although they [foreigners] remain at a disadvantage with the costs of freight and customs' dues, we still find our markets filled with foreign porcelain and they will always have the edge over us. They bring porcelain made in ancient factories; they have reached their economies, while everything costs its weight in gold to us for we have hardly begun our apprenticeship. Their factories can count on workers who sustain themselves on miserable salaries, but those whom we employ receive enormous salaries, for only with these will they choose to abandon their fatherlands and bring to us their skills and secrets.

An import prohibition on printed porcelain was granted in this year but the response of importers was merely to shift to importing different styles of porcelain not covered by the prohibition. The records of the Mexico City customs' house bear this out. Table 8.3 shows how in the year following the prohibition of printed porcelain imports, the entry of other lines increased.

When the import prohibition was removed in 1851, the Mexican manufacturer was faced with a deluge of imported porcelain. Imports of pottery, porcelain, glass and crystal from France alone were valued at 328,583 pesos in 1851.[54] How could a factory in Puebla survive in the face of this ?

Other Innovations in Puebla: Paper and Iron, 1835-1850.

The most ambitious, yet unsuccessful, modern enterprise springing from the 1830s investment fever was a paper factory: *La Beneficencia Pública*. The manufacture of paper had attracted attention from very soon after Independence. Traditionally, paper for official and legal purposes was sent from Spain and distributed to government departments, notaries and private citizens under a government monopoly. However, there does not appear to have been any restriction on the importation of paper by private citizens. Puebla's main printing company, owned by the De la Rosa family, imported large quantities on its own account over the first quarter of the nineteenth century.[55] The use of paper greatly increased after Independence with the freeing of the press and with the proliferation of representative institutions. Official interest in paper manufacture sprang

---

54 Lerdo y Tejada, *Comercio Exterior*, Graph 39.

55 The source of most paper used in Puebla was Genoa. AGNP, RPP, Censos, Vol..39, fs. 2, 100; Vol. 41, f. 145; Vol. 42, fs. 117, 152, 424.

TABLE 8.3 RETAIL MANUFACTURING UNITS REGISTERED IN TAX CENSUSES, 1820-1852.

	1820	1825	1833	1835	1846	1852
Hatmakers	9	15	-	32	41	71
Wax Chandleries	15	25	10	16	32	33
Iron Forges	8	6	8	-	16	41
Tailors' Shops	-	-	17	-	5	40
Silversmiths	4	12	14	7	7	9
Tanneries	8	12	7	13	8	5
Saddlers	4	4	-	1	1	21
Tinsmiths	-	-	13	-	-	20

Sources: Padrones of 1820 and 1825; Hacienda Municipal, 1833; Padrones of 1835 and 1846; *Guía de Forasteros*, 1852.

from an awareness of its indispensability, as from an appreciation of the dangers of leaving the supply of paper entirely in private hands.[56]

In May 1826 the Puebla state government formed an association of "capitalists both foreign and national" to amass capital for the construction of a paper factory.[57] But not until 1833, when State governor, Cosme Furlong, secured a promise of a loan from the *Banco de Avío*, was anything done to advance the project.[58] A French director and technicians arrived at Veracruz soon after, the State paying their passages and salaries until a loan of 40,000 pesos was received from the Bank in 1835. On May 30 1835, a board of shareholders was formed, comprising members of the State Congress, the *Junta Protectora del Hospicio de Pobres de Puebla* and twenty well-known merchants. It was the largest joint-stock enterprise to be founded during the period. Altogether, 120,000 pesos were assembled.[59]

With the loan from the *Banco de Avío*, the paper factory had a founding capital of 160,000 pesos. In September 1837 the board acquired the *Hacienda de San Miguel Apetlahuca* in the district of Cholula, with water rights on the River Atoyac. These were immediately contested by Estevan de Antuñano, owner of the neighboring *Hacienda de Santo Domingo*. This conflict appears to have been resolved by the time the first reams of paper were produced, (immediately to enter José Manso's industrial museum).[60]

Shortly after the opening, amidst general lamentations and scandal, the factory ceased production. Much of the machinery was declared irredeemably damaged. A complete new set of machinery was ordered from Europe at enormous cost, estimated at between 370,000 and 500,000 pesos, arriving in 1844.[61] This consumed the entire capital fund of Puebla's *Hospicio de Pobres*, a cruel irony since from the 1820s the paper factory, calculated as a commercial certainty because of the captive market, had always been seen as the solution to the funding of the *Hospicio*. Indeed, the experience of *La Benificencia Pública* paper mill stands as one of the clearest examples of how protectionism and state-directed industrialization, at least in the short term, had an adverse impact upon the very public welfare the state claimed to be serving.

---

[56] The chief printing houses were also the principal paper importers. Even before Independence they had acquired a reputation for liberalism and, for obvious commercial reasons, for encouraging free thought.

[57] *Colección de Leyes y Decretos, 1826, 1827, y 1828*. Puebla, 1830, p. 60.

[58] AGN, Banco de Avío, Vol. III, Expte. 196.

[59] For the partners in La Beneficencia: AGNP, PN, No. 7, 1837, 30 May and 15 September 1837; PN, No. 1, 1837, fs. 518 and 536; RPP, Censos, Vol. 44, f. 156; and Leicht, *Calles*, p. 192.

[60] Leicht, *Calles*, p. 192.

[61] Ibid; and *Memoria de Industria*, 1844, pp. 298-301.

The new set of machinery was installed by José María Loustalet, Estevan de Antuñano's nephew. By the end of 1844 it had entered production. The factory operated an eighteen-hour day, employed eighty workers, including twenty children, twenty women and two foreigners. It produced forty reams of paper a day of newspaper size paper (four times the normal foolscap legal document).[62]

The main problem the factory faced was shortage of rag which formed the principal raw material. This was scarce in Mexico and had to be imported at considerable cost. During its first year of operation the mill worked for only 68 days, so scarce was this raw material. During 1845 and 1846, the supply problem was partially resolved with help from Antuñano who set up eight machines in *La Constancia* for processing waste cotton for use in paper making.[63] The State calendar of 1846 was printed on paper from the factory and was reported to be of excellent quality, a view not share by Mexico City consumers.[64] But the factory continued to make large financial losses, further exhausting the funds of the *Hospicio*. It also remained dependent on rags imported from Cuba and Europe. In 1846 Loustalet was obliged to borrow a further 40,000 pesos to keep the factory running. *La Beneficencia* continued until 1853 with no improvement in profitability. In that year Loustalet declared himself insolvent and the factory ceased production. It was converted to cotton-spinning and weaving later in the decade, though, to this day, the factory is called "El Papel".[65]

Puebla was not unique in facing such difficulties in paper-making. Two factories were established in Jalisco in the early 1840s and faced, at first, similar supply problems: inadequacy of water-power and shortage of raw materials. When, by 1844, they finally entered production, demand was found to be insufficient to keep them at a profitable level of production. The Jalisco factories were, however, more successful in responding to these difficulties: by making extensive use of local raw materials (*ixtle* and *maguey* fibres), by diversifying production away from the supply of government and the printing press to producing writing paper for domestic

---

62 *Memoria de Industria*, 1844, p. 300.

63 *Memoria de Industria*, 1845, p. 375.

64 In 1846 the editors of *El Museo Mexicano* had to apologise to their readers for the poor quality of paper offered to them at generously low prices by Señor Loustalet, promising that future editions would be printed on "un excelente papel que nos ha llegado de Nueva York, que aunque sale a mucho mas precio, agradará a los suscritores y satisfará nuestros deseos de que la impresión salga limpia y hermosa." The copy of this review in the BL (Colindale) is, indeed, printed on very inferior paper, varying in color from yellow to brown. *El Museo Mexicano*. Mexico, 1846, Vol. II, p. 2.

65 AGNP, RPP, Censos, Vol. 45, fs. 354-362; and *Periódico Oficial del Departamento de Puebla*, Vol. 1, No. 40, 4 November 1853.

consumption and cigarette paper; by reducing prices, thereby extending the market; and by directing their product at the provinces of *tierradentro* (from which the Puebla was effectively excluded by distance). Moreover, the Jalisco factories were of a considerably smaller-scale than their *poblano* counterpart, were less heavily capitalized, privately owned and, from the official report of 1845, appear to have much more skillfully and flexibly managed.[66]

In its disastrous experience with the paper industry, Puebla was perhaps unfortunate in having been chosen by the *junta* of the *Banco de Avío* to be the recipient for the paper making machinery ordered by the Bank from Europe in 1833. There were costs to be paid as well as advantages to be reaped from the close connections certain prominent *poblanos* enjoyed in the capital during the 1830s.[67] As a result of the Bank's preference for Puebla, the Puebla state goverment, the city's financiers, religious and charitable institutions, merchants and manufacturers were obliged to pay the heavy costs of experimentation and innovation in a new industry which they might otherwise have chosen not introduce, at least not on the scale of *La Benificencia Pública*. An unprecedentedly large fund of capital for a single enterprise was absorbed within its fruitless first seven years. When, in 1844, after a massive re-injection of capital in the new machinery, the factory entered production, it faced overwhelming competition from the Mexico and Jalisco factories in the markets of the *tierradentro*. As with innovation in glass and porcelain, the calculation that the costly new factory would soon enjoy a protected national market, unchallenged by competitors, proved unfounded.[68]

La Beneficencia Pública was not the only paper factory established in Puebla in these years. After *La Benificencia*'s first set of machinery had failed in 1840, a small paper factory named *Los Dos Amigos* was established in the core of the city in the *barrio* de San Pablo, using some of the machinery which had proved unsuccessful in the larger factory.[69] The factory was founded by two of the original shareholders of *La Beneficencia*, Mariano Cao y Varela and Camilo Campero, in company with

66 Memoria de Industria, 1845, pp. 373-379.

67 Estevan de Atuñano's close ties of friendship with Lucas Alamán, the Bank's mentor, are well-known from Robert Potash and Charles Hale's work. During the 1830s and early 1840s, Puebla provided several of Mexico's finance Ministers: Carlos García, Rafael Mangino, and Antonio Haro y Tamariz. Jan Bazant has traced the close ties between the Haro y Tamariz families and General Santa Anna. Bazant, *Antonio Haro y Tamariz*, pp. 15-74.

68 For geographical reasons, Puebla's manufacturers faced foreign competition more directly than the factories of the interior. They claimed in 1850 that *ad valorem* duties of 40% were inadequate protection for the city's paper mill. *Memoria de Colonización e Industria*, 1850, p. 477.

69 AGNP, RPP, Censos, Vol. 45, fs. 12, 208-215.

two others. The whole enterprise, including the purchase of a building, cost only 12,500 pesos to bring into operation. The machinery was driven by mule, and an inventory made in 1846 valued the factory at 5,872 pesos. By 1843, paper was being produced though the factory was reported to be paralyzed in the following year.[70] *Los Dos Amigos* appears to have operated for the rest of the decade but in the 1852 factory census it was again reported to be have been paralyzed since 1850.[71]

Finally we turn to efforts at transformation of the iron industry. A modern iron foundry, established during the late 1830s on the hacienda of Panzacola, ten miles to the north of the city, completed the skeleton of a modern, diversified industrial structure. Puebla's entrepreneurs could now claim, with some justification, that they had introduced the forms of the Industrial Revolution to the Mexican tableland, even if the substance remained wanting.

Although the smelting of imported ingots had existed in Mexico since the sixteenth century, iron smelting from raw ore was not attempted in Mexico before 1808, when the interruption of imports encouraged a Mexican mineralogist, Andrés del Río, to establish a furnace in the forests of Michoacán. The insurgency intervened to bring this initiative to a standstill. After the wars, the mining investment boom inspired a second attempt, this time by Germans, to found the industry. The construction of a high blast furnace had to be abandoned for technical reasons although Catalan forges eventually entered production of iron plates, escutcheons, picks, nails, etc. for supplying the mines. Attempts at making higher-quality iron suited for large castings were, however, unsuccessful. Also unsuccessful was a much more ambitious and costly project, funded by the *Banco de Avío*, to establish a large foundry at Zacualpan de Amilpas for supplying the sugar-milling zone south of Mexico City. Less ambitious ventures at Real del Monte (Mexico), Atotonilco (Jalisco), Chalco (Mexico) and Oaxaca, using the Catalan process and producing for a local market, were more successful.[72]

Of all the foundries established in Mexico during this period, *La Biscaina*, the Puebla plant, was the most ambitious. The directors set out to produce, from tall furnaces, iron ingots to substitute imports, as well as castings required for the new industries being established in the city. Over 90,000 pesos was invested during the foundry's construction, of which 40,000 pesos was borrowed from the *Banco de Avío*, and 40,000 pesos from Estevan de Antuñano.[73] Like the Zacualpan foundry, *La Bizcaina* faced difficulties with the unsuitability of the refractory stone used in

70 *Memoria de Industria*, 1845, p. 374.

71 AAP, Cabildo, Vol. 119; and *Padrón de Fábricas*, 1852.

72 *Memoria de Industria*, 1843, pp. 182-185; and Potash, *El Banco*, p. 102.

73 AGNP, PN, No. 1, 1838, fs. 586-587; and AGN, Banco de Avío, Vol. II, Expte. 65, September 1838.

smelting, insufficient heat intensity and scarcity of coal, as well as from "the incompetence of the operatives who were encharged with its workings". By 1840, with production still not commenced, the company's chief financier, José María Izurrieta, deserted the company. The directors then sacked the apparently incompetent Basque workers, advertising in the United States for workers skilled in iron making. Meanwhile, they borrowed a further 20,000 pesos from the priest and entrepreneur, Bernardo Mier.[74]

After introducing new machinery and adapting the furnace, the American managers and operatives had more success.[75] *La Biscaina* was still directed by an American in 1852, Thomas Marshall, and was an important supplier of spare castings for the textile industry during the vital period of its infancy during the 1840s. Three more iron foundries were established in Puebla during the 1840s, all remaining in operation in 1852: *La Santa Rita*, belonging to the French iron-master Frederick Maillard, which specialized in repairing and replacing textile machinery; *El Refugio*, founded by Bernardo Mier, which Thomas Marshall eventually took over; and a large iron furnace at San Pablo Apetatitlán (Tlaxcala) which became an important supplier of the Mexican artillery during the 1840s.[76] By 1850, although the iron industry in Puebla had not attained the sophistication to be able to produce the capital goods of modern industry, it was certainly sufficiently developed to be able to service the new industry, while fully supplying the regional demand for traditional iron goods (ingots, railings, balconies, spurs, stirrups, etc.). By the 1870s, *La Constancia* textile mill had acquired forty six power looms, made entirely at *La Biscaina*, imitated from British models.[77]

The Traditional Industries of Puebla, 1820-1852

If efforts at technological innovation beyond textiles were often marked by failure during the 1830s and 1840s, how did crafts conserving a traditional organization and technology fare over this period? The absence of guild records after 1820, the small scale and limited fixed capital requirements of most of Puebla's traditional industries, precluding their mention in notarial records, has confined our evidence to censuses, tax records and directories. Tax records must be treated with care since municipal dues were only raised on retail premises. They include,

---

74 AGNP, PN, No. 4, 1840, f. 191.

75 AGNP, PN, No. 2, 1842, f. 1254.

76 *Memoria de Industria*, 1845, p. 380; *Guía de Forasteros*, 1852, p. 166; and Leicht, *Calles*, pp. 373-374.

77 Carmen Aguirre and Alberto Cavabarín, "Proprietarios de la industria textil", p. 218.

therefore, only those craftpersons with a *tienda pública*. Those who did not offer goods directly to the public would not be taxed. It is impossible to calculate the ratio of licensed to unlicensed premises which must have varied between industries depending upon the degree of mercantile intrusion. Thus, while it is likely that most of the city's two thousand, or so, cotton cloth weavers went unregistered in the industrial census, because their cloth was marketed by wholesaler-financiers, it is equally likely that no, or very few, glass and pottery factories went unregistered since these were commercially autonomous, as well as being conspicuous, entities. Table 8.4 is therefore only an approximate guide to the size of certain industries between 1820 and 1852. Only the column for 1852 can be taken as an approximate reflection of the scale of these industries, being drawn from a city directory which claimed to be a comprehensive guide to the city's industry and commerce, regardless of tax status.

The hat industry grew more rapidly than any other over the period after encountering severe competition during the 1820s.[78] The 1829 import tariff prohibited the importation of all types of hats. The impact may be observed in the falling off of hat imports from Britain after 1833, ceasing altogether after 1837.[79] The principal innovation in the hat industry was the rapid growth of palm hat manufacture, a phenomenon shared with other parts of Spanish America at this time, notably Colombia. By 1850, there were 19 palm hat factories concentrated in a single street near the Parián. This industry appears to have migrated to the city from rural areas where it had, historically, been important among the Indian population, especially in the district of Tepeji in the Mixteca Poblana.[80]

Felt hat-making also expanded rapidly after the import prohibition.[81] Established masters opened their outworkers' workshops for retail: José Cadena with two shops in 1820, operated three in 1835 and 1846. Pedro García, Puebla's other leading colonial hat-making family, owned one shop in 1820, five in 1835 and four in 1846. Two Frenchmen from Poissy, Charles Dufat and Antoine Rebouche, established a hat factory in 1842 with 2,000 pesos of capital for the manufacture of hats in the "European style".[82] The enterprise was a success and by 1852 Rebouche owned two shops in the Calle de Mercaderes, by then Puebla's Bond Street, and employed ten men in the factory.[83] In this year hat-making was the city's

---

[78] Lerdo de Tejada, *Comercio Exterior*.

[79] BL, State Papers: *Returns relating to Trade between Britain and Mexico, 1820-1841*.

[80] Leicht, Calles, p. 202.

[81] The effectiveness of the import prohibition may have had something to do with the conspicuousness of this product and "patriotic necessity" of dressing with the products of "national industry" in this troubled period.

[82] AGNP, PN, No. 2, 1842, f. 1260; and Miscellaneous Judicial, 1854.

[83] Juan del Valle, *Guía*, p. 148.

TABLE 8.4 MANUFACTURING UNITS AND EMPLOYMENT IN 1852 (TRADITIONAL INDUSTRIES)

Trade	Number of Workshops	Number of Employees including owner	Average labor force/ unit
TEXTILES			
Handloom cotton weaving factories (looms 519)	24	1700	71
Rebozo weaving factories (looms 118)	26	417	16
Home hand loom weavers	1082	3000	3
Dyeing houses	7	24	3
Cotton print shops	11	11	1
Passamanerist-workshop	6	65	11
Home Passamanerists	65	65	1
Silk spinners	2	13	6
DRESS			
Modistas'	5	5	1
Tailors-shop	40	400	10
Tailors-home	100	100	1
Hatters	68	405	6
Hat borderers	40	40	1
Umbrella makers	2	2	1
Rag doll makers	4	4	1
METALWORK			
Iron foundries (forges)	25	94	4
Silver beaters	2	2	2
Armourers	5	5	1
Tinsmiths	20	77	4
Blacksmiths	15	15	1
Clockmakers	8	8	1
Deadsmiths	1	1	1
Coopers	3	10	3
Silversmiths & Jewellers	25	93	4
LEATHER WORK			
Tanneries	5	55	11
Shoemakers	32	274	8
Saddlers	21	69	3
Mule tackle makers	5	5	1
Bridle & tackle makers	20	20	1
WOODWORK			
Carpenters	146	257	2
Comb makers	5	5	1
Coach makers	19	129	7
Rocket makers	8	29	4
Organ makers	2	9	4
Guitar makers	7	7	1
POTTERY AND GLASS			
White pottery	9	103	11
Coloured pottery	8	8	1
Glass	4	42	10
CONSTRUCTION			
Lime kilns	14	-	-
Brickworks	7	-	-
Bricklayers	6 (masters)	700	117
FOOD AND DRINK			
Tocinería	30	90	3
Mills (flour)	14	-	-
Oil	6	-	-
Aguardiente	3	-	-
Flour sieving plants	6	-	-
Biscuit makers	7	7	1
Soup makers	2	2	1
Wax doll makers	1	-	-
Wax chandlers	16	75	5
Ambulant chandlers	17	17	1
Bakers	24	-	-
ARTS			
Engravers (copper)	4	4	1
Sculptors	5	5	1
Painters	9	9	1
Printers	7		
Binders	4	83	7
TOTAL	2009	8563	4.26

Source: Juan del Valle, *Guía de Forasteros*, Puebla, 1852, pp. 162–199.

largest employer after textiles, tailoring and brickmaking (see Table 8.5), with over 400 workers employed in 68 workshops.

In other 'traditional" industries, production was maintained or increased over the period. Only tanning declined although this was compensated by the growth in number of saddleries. A reflection on changing patterns of employment in these industries is left until the final chapter. For the moment, it can be observed that the families which had become entrenched long before the abolition of the guilds, still remained prominent in these industries in the early 1850s. In hat-making, the Cadena and García families are ubiquitous in the tax records; in tanning: the Roxas and Blanco; in saddlery: the Coronado; in silverware: the Hernández, Ochoa and Patiño; in ironfounding: the Crespin and Ascué. These are the families for whom protectionism and import prohibitions performed as effectively as the old guild ordinances.

Beyond the experiments with modern glass, porcelain, paper and iron manufacture, mentioned earlier in this chapter, innovations were few. The structure of most crafts - in terms of the size of manufacturing unit, the number of workers employed, fixed capital investment, technology, and spatial location in the city - was scarcely altered over the period. The potters, wax chandlers, tanners, ironfounders, glassmakers, hatters, shoemakers were concentrated in the same streets as at the beginning of the century. The growth in number of clothing factories, of which there were 40 in 1852, employing 400 men, with 100 *oficiales* working as outworkers, perhaps represents the major organizational change, akin to the growth in scale of hand-loom textile factories during the 1840s.[84] Shoemaking was also concentrated into larger units, with 8 of the 32 workshops employing more than ten, and three employing more than 20 workers in 1852.[85]

Investments in *aguardiente* distilleries, machinery for brickmaking, brewing, noodle making, a modern tanning factory (*La Curtiduría Francesa*), oil-making machinery, together with the innovations which have been observed in pottery, glass, papermaking and iron, show that industrial modernization was not confined exclusively to the textile industry.[86] However, the majority of the two thousand, or so, manufacturing units remained firmly embedded in a traditional technology, were small in scale and in capital value. The manual skills and inexpensive labor of the *poblano* artisan would ensure that this remained so until well into this century.

---

[84] Ibid, p. 170.

[85] Ibid., pp. 176-177.

[86] AGNP, PN, No. 7, 1852, f. 40; RPP, Vol. 46, f. 119; PN, No. 7, 1853, f.4; and Juan del Valle, *Guía de Forasteros*.

Conclusion

Innovation and entrepreneurship in non-textile manufacturing, apart from the iron industry, was characterized by much more limited success than was the case in cotton-spinning. Whereas modern industrial technology transformed the organization and restored the commercial viability of the cotton textile industry, in the porcelain, glass and paper industries, ambitious ventures were eventually abandoned. This was due principally to market factors and uncompetitiveness, although technical difficulties also plagued all three industries. In pottery and glass, the long-established traditional industries proved much more resilient than the exotic new ventures. Why were attempts to broaden Puebla's "Industrial Revolution" met with so little success ?

Capital does not appear to have been problem. Indeed, the paper-factory absorbed more investment in fixed capital than any other single enterprise over this period. It seems that failure in glass, pottery and paper had far more to do with the "bureaucratic" character of these ventures. The *Banco de Avío* was involved in the original funding of the three principal enterprises. And, in the case of the paper factory, the Bank was responsible for selecting Puebla as the home for Mexico's first major experiment in modern paper-making, a decision which owed more to official patronage than to any consideration of rational industrial location. Moreover, it is notable how many churchmen and government officials figured prominently among the boards of shareholders. Evident also is the dependence of these enterprises on funding from both church and state sources: the *Hospicio de Pobres* in the case of the *Beneficencia* paper mill and the Orphanage and Bishopric in the case of the glass-factory. While any assertion that state or church funding was, by nature, inefficient, should be avoided, it does seem fair to suggest that the failure of these enterprises may have had something to do with the absence from the boards of directors and shareholders, of artisans or specialists in the industries, and with the paucity of merchants on the boards who appeared aware of the limitations of the markets for these products. This last point is central to any understanding failure in the the glass, porcelain and paper enterprises.

In contrast to cotton textiles, the market for all of these products was limited to a relatively small section of the population, scattered thinly over the entire territory. Moreover, it was a market which was more directly exposed to foreign competition, since, at no time was the central government prepared to place import prohibitions upon or guarantee effective protection for these products. Overbearing foreign competition as well as competition from more favorably located, and less ambitious, factories elsewhere in the Republic ultimately doomed Puebla's experiments in large scale production of porcelain, glass and paper, "al estilo de Europa", to failure.

Chapter 9

TRADE, SHOPKEEPING AND MARKETS, 1820-1852

T he study has so far paid more attention to production than to exchange. This chapter examines the structure of Puebla's wholesale and retail trade and its development during the thirty years following Independence. The first part offers, by means of an examination of tax records and business inventories, an analysis of the structure, scale and value of different branches of Puebla's wholesale and retail trade. Then, an account is provided of fluctuations in the size of the different branches of trade and of continuity and discontinuity of ownership. The third section of the chapter examines municipal policy towards market and street-selling focusing upon the affairs of the Parián, one of the principal outlets for the city's artisan manufactures. Finally, an assessment is made of the state of Puebla's commerce by the mid-1840s in the light of the recovery of urban manufacturing.

The Value and Distribution of Puebla's Wholesale and Retail Trade

For the sake of convenience, Puebla's commerce has been divided into four broad categories, (accepting many overlaps between them):

i)   Wholesalers and retailers of foreign and national cloth.
ii) Dealers in food and drink.
iii) Dealers in dry goods (such as rope, pottery, books
     and pictures, hardware and machinery).
iv) Businesses offering services (such as brokers, hotels,
     public baths, coach and cart hire, porterage and transport).

Table 9.1 illustrates the distribution of businesses among these categories in 1852 (with iii) and iv) merged). It also indicates the relative value of selected businesses, estimated from records of a commercial and industrial

TABLE 9.1A WHOLESALE AND RETAIL TRADE IN PUEBLA IN 1852

	Total	Women owned	Foreign owned	BUSINESSES Tax Categories[a] (1947) Total	1	2	3	4	5	6
CLOTH										
Almacenes	15	-	11	13	10	3	-	-	-	-
Tiendas de Ropa Extranjera	30	1	8	34	2	14	3	9	5	-
Tiendas de Ropa del País	12	-	1	-	-	-	-	-	-	-
Tiendas de Manta y Hilaza	11	-	1	30	7	6	8	2	6	
Expendio de Lana	3	1	2	-	-	-	-	-	-	-
Pasamanerías	3	-								
				8	-	-	3	2	3	-
Sederías	4	-	1							
Sombrererías	25	-	-	-	-	-	-	-	-	-
Parián	57	14	-	57	-	2	8	6	22	19
	160	-	-	142	19	25	22	19	37	19
FOOD, DRINK AND DRY GOODS										
Tocinerías	30	-	-	35	-	5	3	10	17	-
Trapiches	63									
Panaderías	24	-	22	2	6	16	-	-	-	-
Cerniderías	-	-	-	10	7	3	-	-	-	-
Carnicerías	36	1	-	42	-	2	9	11	19	2
Cererías	15	2	-	14	1	1	5	5	2	-
Mesones	22	2	2	-	-	-	-	-	-	-
Fondas	6	-	2	-	-	-	-	-	-	-
Figones	84	-	-	-	-	-	-	-	-	-
Cafés	2	-	1	11	2	1	2	1	2	3
Neverías	8	-	-	-	-	-	-	-	-	-
Lecherías (café y Chocolate)	39	-	-	-	-	-	-	-	-	-
Maicerías	52	1	-	-	-	-	-	-	-	-
Pulquerías	120	-	-	68	-	16	36	17	-	-
Cantinas	33	-	-	12	-	1	5	6	-	-
Tiendas Mestizas	60	-	2	90	2	9	10	44	26	-
Tiendas de Cuatros	293	-	-	-	-	-	-	-	-	-
Tabaquerías	14	3	-	-	-	-	-	-	-	-
Casillas de Puros y Cigarros	310	colspan "se mantienen con sus manufacturas mas de cinco mil almas"[b]								
Azucarerías	11	2	-	6	-	2	2	2	-	-
Chocolaterías	15	10	-	-	-	-	-	-	-	-
	1,222	-	-	310	18	56	72	96	64	5

CONTD.

TABLE 9.1CONTD.

	Total	Women owned	Foreign owned	BUSINESSES Total	Tax Categories[a] (1947) 1	2	3	4	5	6
OTHER COMMERCE										
Mercerías y Tlapalerías	21	-	12	14	1	1	3	6	3	-
Jarcierías	15	8	-	17	-	-	-	-	7	10
Loza	9	-	1	-	-	-	-	-	-	-
Máquinas e Instrumentos Agrícolas	1	-	-	-	-	-	-	-	-	-
Librerías	4	-	2	5	-	-	1	2	2	-
Estampas Finas y Marcos	4	1	1	-	-	-	-	-	-	-
Baños	29	14	2	-	-	-	-	-	-	-
Corredores	66	-	-	-	-	-	-	-	-	-
Cargadores	75	-	-	-	-	-	-	-	-	-
Oficina de Diligencias	1	-	1	-	-	-	-	-	-	-
Telégrafo Magnético	1	-	1	-	-	-	-	-	-	-
Coches de Servicio	39	-	-	-	-	-	-	-	-	-
	263	-	36	1	1	4	8	12	10	-

Source: AAP, Padrón de Comercio, 1852.

[a]Tax categories (per month): 1 = 25 pesos; 2 = 12 pesos; 3 = 6 pesos
4 = 3 pesos; 5 = 1 peso; 6 = 4 reales

[b]*Guía* (1852) p. 139

census made in 1847. The census divided businesses into six tax classes according to their monthly turnovers, ranging from Class 1, requiring a payment of 25 pesos a month, to Class 6, requiring only 4 reales a month. Table 9.1 reveals that the trade in cloth,[1] was the smallest yet the most valuable branch of trade with less than 10 percent of the total businesses listed but with the greatest number of first class, as well as a disproportionately large number of second and third class businesses.

In contrast, dealing in "food and drink" occupied almost 75 percent of all businesses and yet possessed only a small number of first class, and a disproportionately large number of fourth and fifth class establishments. If four categories - baking, flour sifting, *tocinería* and wax chandlery - are removed from "food and drink", it becomes evident that businesses in this category were the least valuable. Most of them, indeed, were exempt from taxation because of the limited scale of their turnovers. This said, the *tienda mestiza* (*pulpería*) category contained several highly profitable businesses in the first three tax classes. The ownership of a *pulpería* was good business if managed energetically and located in a part of the city where the local residents had cash to spend (*Tiendas mestizas* and the smaller scale *tiendas de cuatros* were distributed evenly throughout the entire city since they catered for everyday needs).[2]

During the wars of Independence the *tiendas mestizas* were taxed heavily because of their command over the purses of the otherwise untaxable poor population. Tax records over the period of the wars reveal the *pulpería* business to have exceeded that of bread-baking in the value of turnover. The daily retail of Puebla's 73 *tiendas mestizas* in March 1814 was 1,659 pesos amounting to an annual turnover of 517,608 pesos. The 36 bakeries had a daily turnover of 1,333 pesos, retailing 415,896 pesos

---

[1] It should be emphasized that the cloth trade category includes all the Parián businesses, several of which dealt in goods other than cloth, such as leather and ironwork. The "food and drink" category, equally, contains the *tiendas mestizas* which were general neighborhood stores retailing cloth and dry goods as well as fresh food, so the main categories in Table 9.1 are only approximate.

[2] Carlos Sartorius recorded in 1850 that:

The greatest amount of petty traffic is done in the grocers' shops, but it is a wearisome affair. The cooks and kitchen-maids pour in and out, because the requisites of every meal are always fetched in detail. Here it is merely a question of Tlacos and Cuartillas, the smallest coin of the republic [the eight and fourth part of a real], or at the utmost of half a real, and yet this is a most lucrative business, if the shopkeeper understands what he is about. Not only is something flattering said to every female customer, however old and smoke-dried she may be, but she must also have her *algo*, her commission, whenever she buys for more than half a real, when a few cigaritos, or a thimbleful of mistrela (sweet brandy), or something of the sort fall to her share. To attract and retain custom is the business of chandler-shopkeepers.

Carlos Sartorius, *Mexico about 1850*, p. 122.

annually. The smallest *pulpería* retailed 5 pesos daily. The three largest, belonging to Tomás Mantilla, Miguel Briones and José Fernández (all in the main square), retailed 60, 50 and 50 pesos daily, respectively. Daily turnover ranged over a similar scale in 1814 to that revealed by the tax assessment of 1847. Hence, four or five shops enjoyed large turnovers of between 45-60 pesos, ranking with the largest *panaderías* and cloth merchants, all located under the portales of the main square or in neighboring streets. Two thirds of *tiendas mestizas*, however, retailed between 10 and 25 pesos, occupying tax classes 4 and 5. During the wars of Independence, the owners of *tiendas mestizas* never ceased complaining of their tax burden, resenting the exemption cloth dealers enjoyed from the payment of municipal dues. Puebla's *pulperos* insisted, with some exaggeration, that "two of their shops have a turnover the equivalent to all of ours together".[3]

While this comparison is in one sense unfair (since the essence of the *tienda de mestizas'* trade was its continuous sale of items of little value, while a *tienda de ropa* dealt generally in much more valuable items sold much less frequently) it does pinpoint a major difference in the capital value of the two lines of business. Table 9.2 is a synopsis of selected inventories of *tiendas mestizas* and *tiendas de cuatro*. The value of the former always exceeded 3,000 pesos, with stocks generally valued at more than 3,000 pesos, and furnishings valued quite uniformly at around 1,500 pesos. The latter were generally valued at less than 500 pesos, though one example was found valued at 1,125 pesos. It was the nature of credit arrangements which really separated the two types of food shop. The *tenderos de cuatros* served as small pawnbrokers but the total value of their pledges rarely exceeded 20 pesos. They had little access to capital, buying from the market twice a week a sufficient amount of goods for the next three days, financing their purchases with their current takings.

Nevertheless, many stocked imported goods (olives, sardines, etc.) which would have entailed holding credit with importers, probably the larger *tiendas mestizas* in the main square (Table 9.2). Even small companies were formed by *tenderos de cuatros*. Mariano Sánchez de la Vega contributed 240 pesos in capital to Ignacio Mendoza's similar amount in stock and furnishings in a small company.[4] Owners of *tiendas mestizas* took on much larger credit liabilities, as can be seen in Oruño's inventory, made in 1848 after his shop had been sacked by Americans.[5] The difference between the *tienda mestiza* and the *tienda de cuatros* was essentially of scale, not of kind, and there was considerable movement up

---

[3] For requests from owners of *tiendas mestizas* for reduction of tax ratings, see: AAP, Militar, Vol. 118, fs. 129-237.

[4] AGNP, Judicial Miscellaneous, 1847. See Table 9.2.

[5] AGNP, Judicial Miscellaneous, 1848. See Table 9.2.

TABLE 9.2 VALUE OF TIENDAS MESTIZAS AND TIENDAS DE CUATROS

Year	Class of Shop	Owner	Goods sold	Value of goods	Value of furnishings	Owed or Credits	Debts	Value without Debts
1825[a]	Tienda Mestiza	Antonio Miranda	Salt, Beans, Lentils, Ham, Sardines, Wine	2,980p 1rl	1,365p 4 rl	12p 4rl (prendas)	-	4.358p 1 rl
1836[b]	Tienda Mestiza	Manuel Pérez de Oro Peza y Cía	Food	2,296p 3 rl	1,567p 3rl (Capital from partner)	8,000 ps	-	11,863p 6rl
1837[c]	Tienda de Cuatros	Francisco Viguencia	Food, Cochineal, Silk	77p 2rl	456p 7rl	12p 4rl (prendas)		546p 5rl
1845[d]	Tienda de Cuatros	María de la Concepción	Cocoa, Aguardiente, Olives,	334p rl	762p 6rl (prendas)	28p 1rl	-	1,124p 7rl
1847[d]	Tienda de Cuatros	Mariano Sánchez & Ignacio Mendoza	Food, paper	138p 7rl	120p 6rl	18p 5rl +240 pesos capital from Sánchez	-	518p 2rl
1849[d]	Tienda de Cuatros	Francisco Vázquez	Wax, Cigars, Paper, Food	136p 6rl	included with stock	198p 4rl	(Bankruptcy) 753p 2rl	- 418p
1848[d]	Tienda Mestiza	Agustín Ignacio Oruño	Food	1,455p 6rl	1,747p 7rl	5,063p 6"rl	(Bankruptcy) 7,880p 6rl	(liquid) 386p 6rl

Source: [a] AGNP, PN, No. 7, 1836; [b] AGNP, PN, No. 8, 1836; [c] AGNP, PN, No. 8, 1945; [d] AGNP, Miscelanea Judicial

and down the two tiers of trade according to the pressures of taxation and fluctuations in demand.[6]

At the summit of the trade in foodstuffs were altogether much larger concerns. Two inventories, from 1779 and 1842, reveal the breadth of the gulf between the small city foodstore and businesses involved in supplying the regional and extra-regional markets with food products. In 1779, Tomás Méndez de Granilla possessed assets of 237,999 pesos in ten houses containing a flour warehouse, a bakery, a *tocinería*, two dyehouses, a wholesale food store and a *tienda mestiza* (valued at 8,981 pesos with 9,958 pesos in debts).[7] In 1842, a company established between Antonio López and Ana Landeras, specialising in the flour trade, possessed assets of 81,112 pesos, the value of a flour-sieving shop, a warehouse containing modern imported plows and flour sacks, a small sugar-mill, a wheat estate, flour in shipment to Veracruz and Tabasco, various credits in flour-mills and wheat estates and a partnership in the sugar *hacienda* of Atencingo. Over the two years of its life, 46,034 pesos had been invested in the company and profits of 7,128 pesos were divided between the two partners on the company's liquidation.[8] This was an impressive performance over a period of currency instability. These were the kinds of company behind the Puebla region's exports of agricultural products such as flour, soap, sugar, etc..

The value of cloth businesses generally far exceeded the value of *tiendas mestizas*. Wholesale and retail shops dealing in imported and national cloth were concentrated in a small area around the main square and in the streets leading from it to the north and north east. In 1852, Puebla's great commercial houses were located, as in previous centuries, in the Calles de Mercaderes and Mesones, the latter dubbed in 1835 by Francisco Javier de la Peña as "la Calle de la Bolsa de Londres".[9] Wholesalers of imported or domestically-produced cloth stood at the summit of the commercial pyramid. The example of Carlos Chávez's wholesale business in *ropa de tierra* - specialising in Puebla *rebozos* -is illustrative of the generation of merchant capitalists that had sustained Puebla's manufacturing before Independence. The liquidation in 1831 of the business is evidence of the serious decline of this trade over the 1820s. The inventory list credits to 360 individuals in over 50 towns, villages and *haciendas* stretching from Tabasco in the south east to León, Lagos and Silao in the Bajío, varying in size from 2 pesos, the value of yarn supplied to Maestro Vargas, weaver of Puebla, to 6,000 pesos, the value of metal goods and textiles supplied to a

---

[6] A sample of inventories of *tiendas mestizas* in Mexico City shows businesses of a very similar scale and value to their counterparts in Puebla. See John Kicza, *Colonial Entrepreneurs*, pp. 110-115.

[7] AGNP, Judicial Miscellaneous, 1779.

[8] AGNP, Judicial Miscellaneous, 1842.

[9] Javier de la Peña, "Notas", p. 147.

merchant in the fair-town of Lagos in Guanajuato. These credits were valued at 94,891 pesos while his debts to 55 import houses, cotton merchants, brokers, store-keepers and the customs house amounted to 115,486 pesos. A favorable balance of 8,224 pesos resulted when his stock, various pawned items, 32 lengths of *manta* still on the loom, but already paid for in advance, and 2,600 head of cattle, received from the *tierradentro*, were taken into account.[10] The vulnerability of such a dispersed network of credit to civil war and currency crisis in this troubled period is obvious.

Wholesalers in imported goods dealt in goods and extended credit of even greater value. Hube Herklots and Co. and Edward Turnbull and Co.,[11] two of Puebla's principal *almacenistas* of the 1840s and early 1850s (and whose disappearance Eduardo Tamariz lamented in 1858),[12] received 138,961 pesos in cash for goods supplied between 1851 and 1854 to Juan Tamburrel's five *cajones* de ropa.[13] Tamburrel, apart from these shops, owned a sugar-mill in Tepeji and a wheat *hacienda* in Atlixco. His arrangement with the two wholesalers permitted him to sell goods on credit to forty Puebla merchants and shopkeepers valued at 154,664 pesos.[14] This was the kind of business most vulnerable to the crises in commercial confidence occurring so frequently over the decade following the American war. The decision on the part of a wholesaler not to renew supply arrangements with merchants such as Tamburrel and to call in bills of exchange for payment, led to a chain of similar responses down the commercial pyramid. Similar flurries of business anxiety had occurred in 1842, 1844 and 1851-52.[15]

[10] AGNP, Judicial Miscellaneous, Balance of Carlos Chávez, November 1831.

[11] Earlier, Edward Turnbull had formed a company in 1842 with Courtnay Tagart contributing 11,342 pesos 2 reales and 32,656 pesos 7 reales respectively. See AGNP, PN, No. 2, f. 678.

[12] Eduardo Tamariz, *Pacificación*, p. 10.

[13] AGNP, PN, No. 1, 1854, f. 478.

[14] Tamburrel, born in Orizaba in 1827, became a prominent figure in Puebla politics in the 1860s and 1870s, becoming *Jefe Político* of the city and founding the *Casa de Corrección* in 1879. See Leicht, *Calles*, p. 460.

[15] Crises in business confidence had, of course, been a feature of Mexican economic life since the beginning of the nineteenth century. During the 1820s and the early 1830s, wholesale merchants had either been unable or wary to extend credit to retailers, preferring direct cash arrangements. During the late 1830s and 1840s, however, elaborate credit arrangements between wholesalers and retailers became much more common. Commercial crises occurred in 1842 as a result of the withdrawal of copper money; in 1844-45 as a result of the federalist revolution against Santa Anna; in 1848-49 following the American War; in 1851, as a result of the temporary lifting of import prohibitions; and in 1854, accopanying the Revolution of Ayutla. On these occasions wholesalers would call in bills of exchange and demand swift payment of debts. For details for individual periods see:

There was an even greater disparity in the value of businesses in the cloth trade than has been observed for businesses dealing in foodstuffs. The stock of a *tienda de ropa* could vary in value between Diego de Tamizes' 7,578 pesos in linens and silks, to José de Salazar's silk mercery valued at 77,038 pesos, to Francisco Blanco's emporium valued at 100,000 pesos selling cloth of every description alongside a host of other goods: European crystal, porcelain, pianos and furniture.[16] At the bottom end of the trade was the *tienda de cuatros*, selling bed and table-linen, corsetry and undergarments, handkerchiefs and scarves with a stock valued at 127 pesos 7 reales, less than half the value of the pawned goods of a similar nature held by the shop.

Wholesalers and retailers of *ropa de tierra* (national, as opposed to imported cloth) operated generally smaller but not necessarily less valuable businesses. Ambrosio Mier, manufacturer and dealer in Puebla cloth, possessed a stock of 11,488 pesos in 1853 and credits valued at 23,495 pesos with customers throughout the Mexican south-east, including Veracruz and Mexico City. He claimed 7,683 pesos in clear profit after only nine months of owning the business.[17] Santiago Saravia, with a business of a similar nature, though not possessing his own looms, held a stock of 1,506 pesos in 1846 and was owed 1,994 pesos for yarn supplied to 104 weavers resident in towns and villages throughout the province from Zacatlán to Chilapa. He owed more to his creditors than the value he possessed in stock and credits owed to himself, complaining that artisans were deserting their looms to join the army.[18] Finally, José María Ruggiero's Parián *cajón* dealing in *ropa de tierra*, possessed a stock of only 386 pesos, but made a net profit of 113 pesos 61/4 reales between 12 October 1844 and 2 January 1845.[19]

1842: wholesalers withdrawing credit, Juan Mujica y Osorio, Turnbull Tagart y Cía., Agustín Dasque, Francisco Bocarando (Mexico), Diego Moreno (Mexico), Estanislao Saviñon, Carlos Guillarmod: AGNP, PN, No. 2, 1842, fs. 189, 190, 192, 213, 681-682, 865, 877, 880-881, 888, 894, 1400, 1402, 1408-09. 1851: wholesalers withdrawing credit: Edward Turnbull y Cía., Carlos Guillarmod, Nerón y Cía., Señores Smith Duncan y Cía: AGNP, PN, No. 5., 1851, f. 269; No. 7, 1851, fs. 78, 181, 238, 259, and 1852, f. 26.

[16] AGNP, Judicial Miscellaneous, 1761 (Diego Tamizes, Dealer in imported cloth); 1781 (José de Salazar Rendón, dealer in imported cloth); 1852 (Francisco Blanco y Cía., Puebla's first department store).

[17] AGNP, PN, No. 1, 1853, f. 3.

[18] AGNP, Judicial Miscellaneous, Robert Smith Duncan's liquidation of Santiago Saravia's business in 1846.

[19] AGNP, Judicial Miscellaneous, 1845.

Changes in the Size and Composition of the Wholesale and Retail Trade, 1807-1852

If the number of businesses is taken as the sole indicator of size, then the trade in cloth, from a peak in 1803, underwent a marked decline during the late 1800s and 1810s. The cloth trade had recovered modestly by 1825 but remained stagnant over the subsequent decade. From 1835, the cloth trade recovered impressively to attain a level in 1852 comparable to its state at the Peace of Amiens in 1803, after the Napoleonic War boom (Table 9.3).

During the revolutions of Independence and the early 1820s, wholesale dealing in European goods remained fairly stable. Retailing, however, increased significantly. It is fair to assume that the reduction in cloth prices after Independence, when northern European goods for the first time had direct access to the Mexican market (without having first to pass through Cádiz), kept demand for cloth fairly buoyant at a time when poverty and population decline might be expected to have brought an absolute decline in demand. The high level of cloth imports sustained during the first eight years after Independence glutted the market and led to a profusion of dress styles which travellers commented on, contrasting so strongly with the scantily clad ragamuffins of the late colonial period.[20] The increase in wholesaling and retailing of European goods between 1807 and 1820 is not therefore surprising.

The most notable change in the cloth trade over the first twenty years of the century was the sharp decline in number of wholesale and retail merchants dealing in domestically produced cloth (*ropa de tierra*). This was due, of course, to the decline of the textile industry.

The number of shops selling mainly food - *tiendas mestizas* or *tiendas de cuatros* - fluctuated much in unison with population trends, declining between 1803 and 1826 and recovering substantially during the 1840s (Table 9.4). Several bankruptcies accompanied the American war and the financial crisis which followed. This perhaps explains why the number of *tiendas mestizas* had decreased by 1852. However, continuing population growth sustained the increase of *tiendas de cuatros* after the war.[21]

The number of establishments wholesaling and retailing European cloth grew imposingly during the 1840s to a peak of 17 import warehouses and 55 *tiendas de ropa* in 1846 (dropping to 13 *almacenes* and 34 *tiendas* a year later as a result of the American war). *Ropa de tierra* wholesaling and retailing also recovered impressively during the 1840s, numbering 28 businesses in 1852, the same number as in 1803. Tax lists reveal

---

[20] Javier de la Peña, "Notas", p. 165; Ward, *Mexico in 1827*, Vol. I, p. 377; and Basil Hall, *Journal of 1820*, p. 183.

[21] Eighteen *tiendas mestizas* either closed or changed hands in late 1847 and early 1848. AAP, Hacienda Municipal, Vol. 151, "Primera lista de las clasificaciones hechas...conforme al...bando...del 10 de diciembre", 1847.

TABLE 9.3 NUMBER OF CLOTH BUSINESSES IN PUEBLA, 1803-1852

	1803[a]	1807[b]	1820[c]	1825[d]	1835[e]	1846[f]	1852[g]
Warehouses-European goods	52	10	13	11	9	17	14
Retail European cloth stores		24	33	44	45	55	51
Ropa de tierra warehouses	28	5	-	-	-	7	13
Ropa de tierra shops		13	5	11	15	12	15
	101	52	51	66	69	91	93

Sources: [a]Flón, 1803; [b]AGN, AHH, Vol. 663; [c]Padrón, 1820; [d]Padrón, 1825; [e]Padrón,1835; [f]Padrón, 1846; ; [g]*Guía*, 1852.

TABLE 9.4 NUMBER OF TIENDAS MESTIZAS AND TIENDAS DE CUATROS, 1803-1852

	1803[a]	1814[b]	1820[c]	1825[d]	1835[e]	1846[f]	1852[g]
Tiendas Mestizas	-	73	-	-	79	91	60
Tiendas du Cuatros	-	-	-	-	201	255	293
	181	-	158	126	280	346	353

Sources: [a]Flón, 1803; [b]AGN, AHH, Vol. 663; [c]Padrón, 1820; [d]Padrón, 1825; [e]Padrón, 1835; [f]Padrón, 1846; [g]*Guía*, 1852.

considerable stability of ownership among retailers of imported cloth between the 1820s and 1850s. The Abaroa, Vargas, Lara, Villareal, Amador, Cardoso, Buenabad, Berruecos, Puig, Cao y Varela, de la Torre, Villegas, Vidal, Rangel, López and Blanco all remained in business for three decades. Retailing of *ropa de tierra* was less stable, with only the Vargas business surviving from the 1820s to the 1850s. Carranza and Morán, retailers of *ropa de tierra* during the 1820s and early 1830s, had become manufacturers by the 1840s, with Carranza also becoming an important dealer in European cloth. Wholesaling of European cloth was much less stable than retailing, undergoing continual turnover in personnel between 1807 and 1852 with only the Mugica y Osorio family business surviving the entire period.[22] Three wholesale businesses established during the wars of Independence and the 1820s, belonging to Estevan de Antuñano, Andrés Vallarino and José Lang survived the slump in trade over the 1830s. Antuñano and Vallarino switched their speciality from imported to domestically-produced cloth in the 1830s and 1840s and the German, Lang, remained an import wholesaler in 1852. Apart from these businesses, it is clear that wholesalers were fair-weather friends to Puebla's commercial body. The pre-war generation was no longer evident in 1820. The merchants who replaced them during the 1820s were no longer in business by the mid-1830s. Of the new generation attracted to Puebla during the 1840s, very few remained by 1858.[23]

Turnover of personnel in the food trade (*tiendas mestizas* and *tiendas de cuatros*) appears to have been common among the mass of smaller businesses. But impressive continuity is evident among larger concerns with the following families in business in 1814 and still trading in 1852: Anzures, Oropeza, Freiria, Zamudio, and Calderón.[24]

Strong local opposition to foreigners dealing in the retail trade, leading to shortlived prohibitions of foreigners from retailing in the early 1830s and 1840s, appears to have been successful in excluding non-Iberian foreigners from the cloth trade until the late 1840s, when a few foreign names appear, especially in the retailing of European cloth: Abadie, Lanzo, Petriccioli.[25] By 1852 foreigners - particularly the French - were well-represented in the cloth trade though hardly at all in the food trade. Foreigners, of course,

---

[22] Leicht, *Calles*, pp. 262-263.

[23] The information in this paragraph was drawn from municipal tax listings kept in the AAP.

[24] AAP, Militar, Vol. 118, f. 150; and *Guía de Forasteros*, 1852, pp. 134-136.

[25] Foreign merchants and artisans could overcome these restrictions by taking Mexican nationality, something the Italians appeared willing to do but to which the French were averse. The French Minister complained in 1844 of the "sword of Damocles suspended incessantly over the head of our nationals and which President Santa Anna, any fine morning, can wake up with the fantasy of cutting the thread which holds it..." ADF, Correspondence Commerciale, Mexico, 1844-1850, f. 91.

predominated in the wholesaling of European cloth during the 1840s and early 1850s. By the early 1840s, as we have seen, they had taken up a strong position among the artisanry and as technicians to the new industry. As Estevan de Antuñano observed in 1843:

> Hasta el año de '35 no había en Puebla un solo artesano extranjero, porque justamente temían estos la persecución de los que siendo, disculpablemente por la educación colonial, mas fanáticos que católicos, eran crueles é intolerantes, hoy cuenta.Puebla mas de cuatrocientos artesanos extrangeros domiciliados para beneficio de esta afortunada ciudad.[26]

The Spanish, who had traditionally formed the largest contingent of foreigners, were outnumbered by the French in the 1840s. In 1846 there were 54 male Spaniards resident in Puebla, much diminished compared to their number before the expulsion decrees of the late 1820s and early 1830s. Of these, four dealt in *ropa de tierra*, four owned textile factories, and thirty others were involved in baking or other branches of the retail trade. The remaining sixteen were employed in entertainment, the Church, or as craftsmen. All but seven were from the northern provinces of Spain: Galicia, Asturias, Santander, the Basque countries and Catalonia. They were generally young men; 27 of the 38 merchants were in their twenties in 1846.[27]

The French formed the largest immigrant contingent, with 64 male heads of family in 1849. Only nine were employed in trade. The rest involved in diverse activities: Restauranteur (1); Glassmakers (2); Hairdressers (3); Textile Engineers (8); Mechanics (3); Clerks (2); Bakers (3); Joiners (6); Cabinet-makers (2); Gymnastic Artist (1); Tailors (2); Musician (1); Dentists (3); Distiller (1); Iron Founders (4); Tinsmith (1); Jeweller (1); Armorer (1); Pharmacist (1); Cook (1); Wood-Carver (1); Painter (1); Piano maker (1); Confectioner (1); Barrel maker (1); Hatmaker (1).[28] The French Consul reported that this list was incomplete since many Frenchmen had not registered with the consulate. He added that many had left their wives and children in France and were living with Mexican women.[29]

The foreign population of Puebla was small compared to Mexico City where 1,230 foreigners were registered in 1843, comprising almost 10

---

[26] Estevan de Antuñano, *Economía política (en doce cartas) para la historia moderna de algodones en México*. Puebla, 1843, in Miguels A. Quintana, *Estevan de Antuñano*, Vol. II, p. 246. See his Appendix III, Foreigners involved in the textile industry in Puebla, 1843-44.

[27] AEEM, Indice de Matrículas, 1846.

[28] ADF, Mémoires et Documents, México, *Population Française en México*. Paris, 1849.

[29] ADF, Correspondence Commerciale, México, 1844-1850, f. 292.

percent of the population, prompting Santa Anna to briefly ban foreigners from the retail trade in that year. In 1849 foreigners still made up 6 percent of the population of the capital of whom 22 percent were artisans.[30]

Street and Market-Selling, 1800-1850

Street and market selling remained closefully regulated over this period in spite of the granting of formal freedom to selling in 1813. Price assizes on basic goods such as maize, bread, candles, tallow, soap, eggs, cheese, vegetables and fruit were removed in 1813. However, the municipality remained vigilant and frequently reissued and renewed trading regulations. These required dealers in items of basic consumption to erect clearly-written price boards outside their shops and to comply with health standards.

Laws on forestalling and regrating also remained in force after the freedom of trade decree of 1813. It remained illegal for people to buy for resale from any person bringing goods into the city for sale in the public marketplaces. And even in the market places, buying for resale was forbidden before twelve noon "when the public would be well stocked". Heavy fines of fifty pesos for the first offence, 200 for second and imprisonment for third offence were exacted by the Council.[31] From 1815 shopkeepers were permitted to enter the market at 11 a.m. to restock their shops, an hour earlier than the regraters.[32] Shopkeepers (owners of *tiendas mestizas*, *tiendas de cuatros* and *cacahuaterías*) received this privilege in return for quite onerous taxation - the *pensión de algos*. The Council was well aware that these shops acted as great magnets for coin, serving also as important credit institutions for the poorer section of society, for whose needs they purported to provide: "los pobres jornaleros, cargados de familia, las infelices viudas, e impedidos de uno y otro sexo".[33]

The council attempted, more often than not unsuccessfully, to prevent street trade and to confine selling to licensed stalls and spaces in squares designated as public markets. The purpose was not only to protect the interests of the licensed seller from hawkers as well as the consumer from forestallers and regraters, but also to protect municipal revenues, to which market rents would often contribute as much as 15 to 20 percent.[34] Vigilance of the market places was perhaps the Council's principal activity after 1813.

---

[30] Shaw, Poverty and Politics, pp. 36-38.

[31] AAP, Cabildo, Vol. 84, 28 November 1814.

[32] AAP, Mercados, Vol. 88, f. 8.

[33] AAP, Mercados, Vol. 85, f. 287.

[34] AAP, Cuentas, 1800-1850.

Between 1532 and 1801 the Plaza Mayor of Puebla had served as the main market place. In 1798 Manuel Flon drew up plans to remove the market to smaller squares at varying distances from the main square "in the interests of [its] better appearance and beauty".[35] Cloth and vegetables would be sold in a newly constructed Parián in the old Plazuela de San Roque. Pigs and donkeys and livestock could only be sold in the Plazuela de los Zapos. The sale of grain, wood and charcoal was confined to the Plazuelas de Montón, San Francisco, San Antonio and San Agustín. As might be expected, this measure was exceedingly unpopular and the struggle to have the market restored to the central square persisted throughout the first half of the nineteenth century. Owners of stalls feared the loss of security they had received by virtue of their proximity to the municipal palace (and the *guardias serenos*). They insisted that the smaller squares were the prey of robbers and criminals.[36] In 1813 the resentment of the *parianistas*, many of whom were unable to pay their rents (so sparse was trade in this crisis year) came to a head.[37] The Council was obliged to permit the return of a limited number of traders to the main square but only to sell from approved stalls, confined to a small area at one end of the square.[38]

This did not satisfy the food sellers (*tiendas mestizas* and *tiendas de cuatros*) who complained in 1816 that the withdrawal of the market to the peripheral squares had depressed the sales of the *tiendas de cuatros*, which traditionally had served the outer barrios, and had also harmed the *tiendas mestizas* in the center, since without the market, fewer people were attracted to the main square. Such, they claimed sarcastically, was the result of the "inexorable genius of Señor Flon". They appealed to the good sense and domestic responsibilities of the aldermen:

> The market having been scattered among four or five squares, buyers and sellers become confused, some not knowing what is sold in all of them, buy quickly at a high price in order to return to their villages in good time, and others not knowing in which one the best prices are to be found, have to go to one and then to another and like this, the spinning woman, the apprentice and the errand boy spend half the morning buying provisions, and, what is more, they upset the management of the household and the workshop, for even when there is no real need to spend half the morning to find a good buy, the lazy and distracted servant, the restless daughter and the frivolous woman are given a good pretext for their delays.[39]

---

35 AAP, Cabildo, Vol. 70, f. 147.
36 Leicht, *Calles*, pp. 183-184.
37 AAP, Militar, Vol. 118, f. 45.
38 AAP, Mercados, Vol. 86, f. 379.
39 AAP, Cabildo, Vol. 85, f.379.

The Council yielded and permission was granted in 1816 for a full market in the main square to be held on Thursdays and Saturdays only.[40]

After Independence, stalls gradually sprang up beyond the prescribed area of the Plaza Mayor. Providing the market rents were paid, these were only rarely troubled by municipal officials, as in the case of eighteen women market-sellers reproduced in Appendix 2. In 1831, more permanent wooden stalls were constructed in response to a general complaint from merchants and customers that confining trade to the outer squares had led to scarcity, high prices and inconvenience for everyone concerned.[41] Again, in 1841, the Council proposed to clear the market from the central square to the Plazuela de Santo Domingo. However, a commission advised that this was inadvisable and recommended instead that 108 new stalls be constructed in the main square to sell everything except meat which would be sold in the Plazuela de San Luis, cooked food in the Plazuela de la Compañía and pottery and basketwork in the Plazuela de los Zapos. On Thursdays everyone could use the main square. The ash trees planted by Flón were ordered to be cut down for the anticipated flood of sellers back to the market place.[42]

Paintings of the early 1840s (see Frontispiece) show busy, well-constructed, market stalls occupying at least half of the square with soldiers, priests, merchants in top hats conversing, and elegantly dressed women strolling in the other half.[43] In 1854 the Council converted two patios of the Dominican convent into a general market, where it remained until 1986. A photograph made in 1855 shows the central square to be planted up with small trees, the stalls having been removed.[44]

The records of the Parián market, constructed on orders of Manuel Flon, are revealing about street and market-selling after freedom of trade was granted in 1813. The purpose of the Parián was to provide space for the sale of goods produced in the city by independent artisans who could not expect buyers to come to their houses, particularly those from the more distant parts of the city or whose workshops did not front onto the street. The four main branches of trade were:

---

[40] Leicht, *Calles*, p. 471.
[41] AAP, Mercados, Vol. 86, fs. 18 and 43.
[42] AAP, Mercados, Vol. 86, fs. 122, 156, and 157.
[43] Leicht, *Calles*, pp. 475-477.
[44] Ibid, pp. 479-481.

i) Ropa de tierra (*rebozos*, *manta*, woollen cloth and *jorongos* , a type of poncho).

ii) Made-up clothes (shirts, jackets, shawls, napkins, etc.)

iii) Ironwork (from the Barrio de Analco)

iv) Leatherwork and shoes.

Many of the first Parián tenants had previously run businesses from stalls in the main square, often men and women of considerable means, their stocks valued in the hundreds, sometimes thousands, of pesos. Others who took up *cajones* before the war, were established artisans who moved their retail outlets away from their workshops to the Parián, often placing them under the care of their wives. (The tax records show a significant number of women running businesses in the Parián 1833: 17, 1835: 17, 1848: 14.) Indeed, the Parián was intended as a solution to for problems of the independent artisan who did not want, or was unable to find, the marketing services of the wholesale merchant. Until the middle years of the war of Independence the Parián appears to have fulfilled this function satisfactorily and stalls were much in demand. As the *parianistas* later declared (in 1837) when petitioning for a reduction in rents, "it used to be considered a triumph to secure a *cajoncito* in the Parián".[45]

With the collapse of domestic manufacturing during the 1810s and the gradual re-emergence of the old market place in the central square after Independence, it is not surprising that the Parián faced growing problems. Complaints to the Council were voiced at regular intervals, in certain years every few months (1831, 1837, 1843, 1845, 1850), often coinciding with periods of financial or political crisis. The main grievances were: excessive rents; illegal street-selling; physically obstructing or undercutting their trade; the poor siting and inappropriate construction of their brick-built stalls; violence and robberies; and the débris of rubbish and rotting matter which tended to accumulate in these streets near the river. Street-sellers marketing contraband foreign cloth were also a cause for complaint (1815, 1824, 1844).[46]

The 1830s were especially hard for the stall-keepers of the Parián, many *cajones* closing. Indeed, twenty seven had shut down by 1837 (Table 9.5). The Council reduced rents in that years and granted rent exemptions to the shops which had closed temporarily.[47]

During the mid-1840s itinerant sellers became increasingly irksome. It was asserted that they were selling cloth at one half of Parián prices. The

---

45   AAP, Cabildo, Vol. 104, f. 41.

46   AAP, Parián y Mercado, Vol. 117, fs. 154-198.

47   AAP, Cabildo, Vol. 104, f. 41.

TABLE 9.5 PARIAN MARKET OF PUEBLA, 1820-1852

NUMBER OF STALLS	1820[a]	1833[b]	1835[c]	1836[d]	1837[d]	1848[e]
One	54	37	34	-	-	29
Two	27	34	39	-	-	23
Three	-	2	2	-	-	-
Four	3	1	-	-	-	4
Empty stalls	-	5	2	14	27	29
Total	84	79	77	14	27	85

Sources: [a]Padrón de Tiendas, 1820; [b]AAP, Cuentas, Vol.83 ; [c]Padrón de Tiendas, 1835; [d]AAP, Parián y Mercado, Vol. 112; [e]Padrón de Tiendas, 1848

parianistas argued that they faced greater costs and taxes and that the street-sellers molested their customers. They asked for the street-sellers to be confined to one place and taxed.[48] The *parianistas* selling cloth were the most affected, the saddlers and shoe-sellers facing less competition from the street.

During the 1840s the Parián's trade polarized between four successful large concerns, occupying four *cajones* each, and, numerous, marginal one or two *cajón* businesses, as Table 9.5 demonstrates. By 1848, 29 *cajones* had closed down. It is evident that the Council had failed to persuade street-sellers to confine their trade to one place, the minimum condition necessary for the ordinary *parianista* to survive commercially, let alone prosper. The Council had implicitly accepted the plea of an itinerant weaver, hawking his wares, that he be allowed freedom to sell "as we are poor, burdened with family, and will be unable [otherwise] to sell our rebozos".[49] It was perhaps too much to ask of the Council of a manufacturing city to prohibit artisans from selling where they could. After all, street-selling, while perhaps damaging to municipal funds, did not harm the interests of the powerful manufacturing and commercial (largely wholesale) economic interests which prevailed on Puebla city Council. To them, the more independent artisans buying yarn and selling cloth cheaply, the better.

After the Revolution of Ayutla in 1854, particularly during the Three Years War (1858-61), the predicament of the *parianistas* deteriorated further. The liberalization of foreign trade, the increase of foreign goods entering the market, the obstruction of communications with the interior by war and inland tariffs, ("our goods in normal times reached the most remote parts of the national territory", as one *parianista* recalled), all threatened Puebla's trade as a whole. By this time, the relatively protected structure of trade and manufacturing, upon which the city had recovered its prosperity during the 1830s and 1840s, had begun to dissolve. The underlying problem for the *parianistas* was therefore not simply the competition between themselves and the street-sellers, whose antics had become progressively more daring, ("they are selling in the very doors of the Parián stalls"), but the uncertainty of the entire edifice of national manufacturing, facing the greatest onslaught from foreign manufactures since the 1820s.[50] The *pavianistas* found themselves besieged from two sides: on the one hand stood the army of poor artisans hawking their wares or regrating contraband goods and, on the other, a commercial and industrial structure dominated increasingly by large units of production and big firms ruthlessly competing to control the marketing of imported and national goods. There was little that the modest businesses of the Parián could do, without strong

---

48 AAP, Cabildo, Vol. 110, 18 December 1843; Vol. 111, 17 October 1843; Vol. 112.

49 AAP, Parián y Mercado, Vol. 117, fs. 205-214.

50 AAP, Parián y Mercado, Vol. 117, fs. 243-253.

324

municipal intervention, to confront either area of competition. And this was not forthcoming.

Thus, the Parián failed to serve as an adequate replacement for the old cloth market of the main square. *Parianistas* faced competition from the street, from the continuation of the market in the central square, (at first illegally, and then, on a formal basis during the 1840s) and finally, during the 1850s, they faced overbearing competition from the new market in the Plaza de Santo Domingo. The Parián still remains the *mercado de artesanía* of the city, but is dependent for its survival on the itineraries of coach companies carrying tourists from Mexico City.

The influence of the design as well as the location of the Parián might be offered as further reasons for its failure to become the hub of Puebla's commerce. Its architect, Antonio Santa María Incháurrigui, chose a monumental Andalucian style.[51] The *cajones* were given small doors in proportion to the space behind, most of the wares were therefore obscured from the customers' view. For a purchase it was necessary to enter the *cajón*, the *parianistas* being forbidden to hang their wares outside or sell in the street. Thus, the great advantage of a market -the freedom to pass rapidly from one stall to another without compromise- was lost. Moreover, the three terraces of solidly-constructed contiguous stalls with heavy overhanging stone lintels, obstructed any rapid glance from one end of the market to the other, possible in an open market. Thus the tenants of *cajones* on the east side often complained that the *cajones* on the west side did a far better trade. In short, the failure of the Parián serves as an example of how apparently rational, enlightened design went against established custom. It also illustrates how changes in the structure of commerce and manufacturing, which form the substance of much of this book, progressively marginalized the artisans' market.

[51] Leicht, *Calles*, p. 291.

TABLE 9.6 FOREIGN AND NATIONAL GOODS ENTERING AND LEAVING
THE CITY OF PUEBLA, 1844 AND 1845

1844		1845	
Mexican Goods entering Puebla 3,973,721p 3rl	Mexican Goods leaving Puebla 1,686,871p 6rl	Mexican Goods entering Puebla 4,096,495p 3rl	Mexican Goods leaving Puebla 1,753,198p 4rl
Foreign Goods entering Puebla 2,585,204p 6rl (includes 753,487p 4rl of raw cotton)	-	Foreign Goods entering Puebla 1,457,494p 6rl	-
Cotton Goods 362,236p 6rl	Cotton Goods 1,415,249 p 4rl	-	Cotton Goods 1,456,517p
Silks, Linens and Woollens 736,164p 3rl	-	-	-
Metal Goods 89,368p 2rl	Metal Goods 1,656p	-	Metal Goods 2,376p
Foodstuffs 325,911p 4rl	Flour, Aguar-diente, Sugar, Hides & Soap 221,060p	-	Flour, Aguar-diente, Sugar, Hides & Soap 294,495p 3rl

Source: Miguel Lerdo de Tejada, *Comercio Exterior*, Graph No. 46; and *Memoria*,
Puebla, 1849.

Puebla's Commerce in the Mid 1840s

To Manuel Payno in 1843, Puebla presented a surprisingly cosmopolitan aspect which moved him to hyperbole. Walking through the center of the city he observed:

> las casas altas y elegantes, muchas tiendas de comercio iluminadas; multitud de gente y vendedores de dulces y otras cosas, forman un murmullo y confusión bastante agradable...La civilización moderna y el progreso han invadido a Puebla finalmente. Tienen establecidos en la calle de Mercaderes algunos peluqueros, con su vidriera a la Calle, y detrás de ella sus botes de perfumería su agua de colonia, sus trenzas y rizos de pelo, sus cepillos, y sus treinta mil baratijas que venden a peso de oro; tienen en Puebla algunas tiendas con gruesas letras de oro en campo azul o verde, que dicen:
> Madame N. modista de Paris; tienen sombrererías, cafées Oh! No vale la pena este rapido progreso, esta súbita transformación, de pagar 600,000 pesos, y todavía quien sabe cuanto mas? [referring to the cost of import prohibitions] ...el comercio de Puebla es bastante activo, y las calles de los Herreros, Mercaderes y Portales, presentan un aspecto de alegría y actividad durante las primeras horas de la mañana y en la tarde, a la caída del sol, si bien se observa en ellas muy poca gente decente del bello secso.[52]

What a contrast to the impression left upon Poinset and Ward during the 1820's! To what extent is Payno's impression of commercial vibrancy a fair reflection of commercial recovery?

Table 9.6 shows the value of foreign and national goods entering and leaving the city of Puebla in 1844 and 1845.[53] In general, it can be observed that, although in 1844 the value of foreign goods entering the city exceeded that of Mexican goods leaving the city, in the following year, with raw cotton (now prohibited) removed from foreign imports, the trade balance was distinctly in Puebla's favor. Table 9.6 shows that cottons, flour and soap remained Puebla's principal export staples, as they had been before the Wars of Independence. The trading position of the city appears quite favorable, especially in 1845. Foreign imports then made up less than one quarter of Puebla's total registered import and export trade. The details of the goods imported from abroad show the city to have been self-sufficient in printed cottons, ordinary cotton cloth, yarn, soap, most basic food-stuffs, basic metal goods, ordinary pottery and glass. It depended

---

[52] *El Museo Mexicano*, Vol. III, pp. 142-43.

[53] Foreign goods passing through the city and national goods produced beyond the boundaries of the city and destined for markets elsewhere were not taxed and so are not included in the figures. As the greater part of cotton yarn production took place in mills beyond the boundary of the city, direct consignments to other regions would not be included. It can therefore be assumed that the value of the export of cotton yarn and cloth was greater than these figures suggest.

upon the foreign sector to supply, above all: beeswax, cocoa, paper, iron bars for forging, woollen cloth, linen pieces, luxury goods and raw cotton (when tariff laws permitted).

At the very least, it is clear from these figures that the situation of the 1820s and early 1830s, when the city's industrial production had slumped, the circulating medium was being drained abroad and foreign goods dominated the market, had been restrained, if not reversed.

Chapter 10

PUEBLA DE LOS ANGELES ON THE EVE OF THE REFORM

T he last three chapters have focused quite narrowly upon the history of Puebla business and entrepreneurship during the 1830s and 1840s. In this final chapter the focus is broadened to include urban society as a whole. To what extent did the establishment of. a modern industrial sector contribute to the restoration of an urban social and political order seemingly close to dissolution during the 1820s and early 1830s? Did Puebla in 1850 remain a funnel through which migrants from the depressed hacienda districts passed on their route to areas of greater opportunity on the peripheries or beyond the province? Or did the city's population recover and emigration diminish? Were the political divisions, so marked in the city during the 1820s and early 1830s, healed by the re-assertion of more effective political and entrepreneurial leadership? Were the social divisions among artisans, so evident at the end of the colonial period, further accentuated by the onset of industrial modernization? Did the formation of a small factory proletariat substantially modify the social structure of the city? This study can offer only incomplete and speculative answers to these questions.

To visitors from Mexico City (for wealthy *capitalinos* and foreigners during the early 1840s, a visit to Puebla's palaces of modern industry was de rigueur), Puebla seemed a more modern place than the capital. The once proverbially impoverished and lawless city now presented a picture of progress and prosperity which must have reassured the inhabitants of the depressed and politically volatile capital, lately fallen from its colonial grandeur. Puebla offered proof that the future held something in store. Indeed, many Mexico City families (among them the historian Manuel Orozco y Berra), abandoned the capital to reside in the prospering and momentarily more peaceful Puebla of the later 1830s and early 1840s.[1] Contemporaries commented on the improvement of the central area of the

---

[1] Alejandra Moreno Toscano, "Advertencia," in Manuel Orozco y Berra, *Historia de la ciudad de México desde su fundación hasta 1854.* Mexico, 1973, p. 5.

city, with many houses receiving bright neo-classical facades.[2] They also reflected upon the politically calming effect created by the renewal of ties of mutual interest between once divided social sectors.[3] The city's industrial revival had fostered areas of reciprocity, albeit unequal, between merchants and artisans, and between the millowners, factory workers, and the artisans and shopkeepers with whom the factory owners dealt. Together, these groups furnished a social base for the protectionist coalition, perhaps accounting for how forcefully this ideological current was sustained even during the unstable period of the Reform.

However modern superficially, Puebla nevertheless remained, in many respects, a city which had emerged fundamentally unchanged by the introduction of modern industrial technology. Indeed, the well-travelled European, Carlos Sartorius, saw Puebla, even on the surface, as a "pre-industrial" city:

> The manufactories of are not sufficiently extensive to confer a distinctive feature on the population of the respective cities. In Puebla, for instance, there are factories with steam and water-power but the majority of the manufactures are produced by hand and sold to the dealers. The class of factory-laborers is too insignificant to be predominating, as at Manchester, Lyons or Elberfeld; they are lost sight of in the masses...only the mining towns exhibit a spirit peculiar to the inhabitants...[4]

This observation comes as little surprise. Puebla's "modern" textile factories employed only 1372 workers in 1854, barely 1.7 percent of the economically active population.[5] And many of these workers were women and children living in housing constructed by the factory owners, adjoining the mills, or in neighboring villages. Working anything from ten to sixteen hours a day would scarcely have left them time to visit the city, distant by at least an hour's walk. Overall, probably no more than 4,000 men, women and children were employed in the new factories (including the glass, pottery and iron factories and the large weaving shops in the center of the city) in the early 1850s. Puebla's new category of worker, listed as *fabricante* in the census, was therefore almost invisible in a city still populated largely by artisans and men and women employed in services.[6]

The impact of the factories, of course, extended far beyond the private fortunes of the industrialists themselves or the industrial hamlets housing the workers. The reconstruction of a profitable core to the urban economy

---

[2] de la Peña, "Notas", pp. 132-3.

[3] Manuel Payno, "Viaje", pp. 141, 163.

[4] Carlos Sartorius, *Mexico about 1850*, p. 123.

[5] Juan Carlos Grosso "Notas sobre la formación de la fuerza de trabajo fabríl en el municipio de Puebla (1835-1905)", *Boletín de Investigación del Movimiento Obrero*, No. 2, 1981, p. 9.

[6] Contreras and Grosso, "La estructura", pp. 142-46.

reanimated many of the crafts which had long been in decline. Sparse evidence on occupations during the 1840s reveals the persistence or recovery of all the principal occupational categories observable in earlier censuses (1791, 1821 and 1830). The only occupations not to share in this recovery were hand-spinning, which almost disappeared, and the leather related trades - tanning, saddlery and shoemaking - which declined modestly.[7]

Between 1834 and 1844, the main weaving quarters to the north east of the city, (*cuarteles* 4, 6, 7, and 8) experienced imposing population growth. And while the population of the central *cuarteles* of the city (such as 1 and 2) remained static over the same period, the tax value of the same area expanded startlingly in the interval between the property censuses of 1832 and 1854. The growth in property values of the center was in inverse relation to the decline in property values of the peripheral *barrios*, many of them still partially ruined at the end of our period. The south of the city (*cuartel* 2 for instance), once its wealthiest part, did not recover its population during the 1840s while the area to the north of the *zócalo* consolidated its commercial dominance.[8] The demographic and economic decline of the *barrios* to the west of the city was arrested with the recovery of construction related crafts, especially bricklaying. These *barrios* presumably benefitted also from their proximity to the new factories. Finally, the east of the city underwent substantial population recovery between 1830 and 1844, the parish of Santa Cruz (*cuartel* 8) showing a marked recovery in all areas of employment except the leather trades, with the number employed in textiles approaching the level of 1791.[9]

Perhaps the clearest sign that industrial modernization had a wider impact was the overall demographic recovery of the city, at a time when the capital's population remained stagnant. From its lowest ebb of around 40,000 after the cholera epidemic of 1833, Puebla's population rose to 71,631 by 1848 and to an estimated 80,000 by 1850.[10] Stagnant for so much of the eighteenth century, largely due to loss of population through emigration, Puebla's population had doubled within a period of less than twenty years. Thereafter, growth slowed and the 1850 level was not surpassed until the 1890's, a fact probably to be explained by the renewal

---

[7] *Ibid.*, pp. 138-140.

[8] Erdmann Gormsen, "La Zonifación Socio-Económica de la Ciudad de Puebla. Cambios por efecto de la metropolización," *Comunicaciones,* No. 15, 1978, pp. 7-20; Contreras and Grosso, "La estructura" p. 138; AAP, Padrón General de Casas (1832); Padrón General de Casas (1854); "Noticia del valor de las fincas urbanas de la ciudad de Puebla", *El Album Mexicano*, Vol. II, 1849, p. 172.

[9] See Chapter 4.

[10] de la Peña, "Notas" p. 133, *Memoria del Estado de Puebla* (1849), Graph No.3, ADF, Correspondence Comerciales, Veracruz 1838-1850, Vol. II, f. 252, and Richard Morse, *Las Ciudades Latinoamericanas*. Mexico, 1973, Vol. 2, pp. 173-4.

of emigration during the war-torn years of the Reform, the European Intervention and the "Restored Republic". What caused the population surge of the 1830s and 1840s ?

Estevan de Antuñano put the cause down simply to the prosperity brought by the new factories, asserting in 1845 that the city's population had increased by 8,000 over the previous five years.[11] Population recovery must also have been aided by the absence of severe epidemics between the severe cholera epidemic of 1833 and the much milder cholera of 1850. Mass vaccination must be given part of the credit, though 500 people died of smallpox in 1840. As mentioned in Chapter 4, the city possessed a relatively healthy environment, with births exceeding deaths by between 500 and 1,500 in most non-epidemic years between 1831 and 1849.[12] Before research is carried out in parish records, the precise causes of population recovery - whether it was due to increased fertility, diminished mortality, increased immigration or reduced emigration - will elude us.

Were standards of living substantially altered as a result of the city's industrial recovery? In 1845, Lucas Alamán, the Minister of Industry, claimed that in Puebla, "el progreso que han tenido las fábricas, ha producido un cambio muy ventajoso en el bienestar de la generalidad de la población."[13] "Welfare" (*bienestar*) is, however, a relative concept. A group of industrialists and cotton growers in 1841 justified import prohibitions on grounds that industry "se daba ocupación decente a las mujeres, y a las niñas se les proporcionaba un trabajo moderado en que se emplearon todo el día y se las proporcionaba cubierto de la ociosidad, y tal vez de la prostitución".[14] Thus, employment in the new factories was seen by some more as an alternative to urban unemployment and moral decay rather than a possible route from mere "decency" to "respectability". There appears to have been no concern in Puebla for encouraging the kind of genteel female labor force forming at the same time in the mill towns of

---

[11] Miguel Quintana, *Estevan de Antuñano*, Vol. II, p. 246.

[12] Miguel Angel Cuenya, "Puebla en su demografía, 1650-1850. Una aproximación al tema," in CIHS-UAP, *Puebla de la Colonia a la Revolución*, pp. 9-72; and see Chapter 4.

[13] *Memoria de Industria* (1845), p. 321.

[14] *Exposición dirigida al Congreso de la Nación por los Fabricantes y Cultivadores de Algodón*. Mexico, 1841.

Massachusetts.[15] Rather, there was a preference for attracting to the factories hard-working families which had fallen upon hard times.

In a pamphlet published in 1837, Estevan de Antuñano sought to persuade *poblanos* of the virtues of family employment in the new factories.[16] Family labor had, of course, always been a feature of the home-based textile industry. It was, however, a novelty where large units of production were concerned, explaining the need for Antuñano's propaganda. The tobacco factory, founded in the eighteenth century, had been strictly divided between the *Estanco de la Hombres*, employing 990 men, and the *Estanco de la Mujeres*, employing 400 women, with careful attention to keeping the sexes apart (even in the street) by working different shifts and by building the two entrances on opposite sides of the the block.[17] Antuñano believed that a mixed labor-force, far from encouraging promiscuity, would have socially and morally beneficial effects. It should be remembered that the mechanization of spinning had almost entirely undermined one of the principal sources of female and children's employment: cotton preparation (cleaning and caning) and hand-spinning. Nothing, beyond the proliferation of primary schools, had emerged as a morally acceptable alternative.[18]

Antuñano argued that if women and children could work alongside men, the family income would be increased, men would no longer be tempted to abandon their shifts to return home, and, women and children would no longer be left unprotected at home. In fact, he sought to construct a factory labor force made up of family units of the kind suggested by Bartolo Baís' household, as recorded in the 1846 census. Living under the same roof as this sixty year old spinner, were his wife, aged 64, two spinsters aged 50 and 36 respectively, one widow aged 50, one woman of 25 (reported abandoned by her husband), an unrelated *doncella* of 20, and

---

15 In the late 1830s a Durango industrialist, José Ramírez, employed women from Boston, presumably Lowell girls, to instruct Mexican female operatives not simply in machine spinning, but in good manners, urbane dress and civilised habits proper for young ladies. No such experiment was conducted in Puebla, although Antuñano claimed in 1838 that "Constancia girls were setting a fine example on festival days, with their tidy, clean and modern dresses, urbane manners, succeeding in denying the atrocious imputations which have been made of the Mexican character," *El Museo Mexicano*, Mexico, 1843, Vol. I, pp. 121-123; Estevan de Antuñano, *Economía Política de México*, Puebla, 1838.

16 Estevan de Antuñano, *Ventajas políticas, civiles, fabriles, y domesticas que por dar ocupación también a las mujeres en las fábricas de maquinaria moderna que se están levantando en México, deben recibirse.* Puebla, 1837.

17 BL, Add. Mss. 17557, "Noticias de América", f. 66.

18 Mary Kay Vaughan, "Primary Schooling in the City of Puebla," *HAHR*, Vol. 67, 1987, pp. 39-62.

five children, one of whom worked as a cotton weaver.[19] In the traditional textile industry, this was potentially a highly productive household. But with the mechanization of cotton-spinning, such a household presented only a potential social problem. How could it now subsist? What better than to shift such households, in their entirety, to the villages being constructed by the factory owners? At the end of his pamphlet, Antuñano listed a selection of such "ideal" families already employed in *La Constancia*: a widowed flower-seller, now shuttle-winder, with eight children (working as cotton cleaners, rovers, carders, mule-spinners, and speeders), an agricultural laborer, now working as a batter, with five sons working as carders, batters and drawers, and three other smaller families.

To attract and retain such families, Antuñano constructed housing for workers in the first patio of *La Constancia* (the second patio was dedicated to sales and administration and the third contained workshops for repairing machinery and warehouse space, with a small bridge crossing the millstream to the two-storey building housing the machine-rooms). In 1843, Manuel Payno described "the first broad patio...with...a multitude of low, clean and tidy living quarters, with a little garden in front of each door."[20] Two years earlier, Frances Calderón de la Barca, the wife of the Spanish Minister, was delighted by the building which possessed

> ...more the air of a summer palace than a cotton factory. Its order and airiness are delightful, and in the middle of the court, in front of the building, is a large fountain of purest water. [She added that] A Scotchman (sic), who has been there for some time, says he has never seen anything to compare with it, and he worked for six years in the United States."[21]

The census of 1838 for La Constancia suggests that Antuñano succeeded in attracting the kind of family outlined in his pamphlet. Within the gates of the factory lived 32 widows and 129 children in a community numbering only 320 souls.[22] Like the directors of the Scottish industrial settlements at New Lanark and Catrine, Antuñano had followed the maxim that "the ideal inhabitant for every house [was] a poor widow with numerous healthy children."[23] The Constancia model of factory organization, including patios for workers' housing, was also adopted by Antuñano's rival,

---

[19] AAP, Padrones, Vol. 149, f. 246.

[20] Manuel Payno,"Un Viaje", p. 165.

[21] Frances Calderón de la Barca, *Life in Mexico*. London, 1970, p. 336.

[22] AAP, Padrones, Vol. 146, fs. 142-8; Vol. 147, Expte. 1474.

[23] T. C. Smout, *A History of the Scottish People, 1560-1830*. Glasgow, 1969, p. 381.

Dionisio Velasco, for his *Patriotismo* mill, descriptions of which were even more rapturous than those of Payno and Calderón de la Barca.[24]

However pleasant the physical environment around some (by no means all) of the factories, there is little evidence that living standards of the small number of people employed in the new factories were substantially improved. While families benefitted from more regular incomes and salubrious housing, work days were long, extending anything from eleven to sixteen hours, and wages were little better than those received by poorer artisans during the early 1820s. In 1843, the average weekly wage of the 1,622 men, women and children employed in eighteen cotton-spinning factories was 3 pesos 2 reales or 4 reales a day.[25] Wages in fact varied widely with the length of the shift, whether accommodation or rations were provided and according to labor productivity. Thus in Antuñano's *Economía*, the average daily wage was a mere 1.39 reales (less than the standard agricultural peon's wage), with 22.75 lbs of yarn per week produced by each worker. In stark contrast, the average daily wage in *La Pelota* (one of Puebla's best run inner-city spinning factories) was 11.95 reales, with 68 lbs of yarn per week produced by each worker.[26] By 1852, the average weekly wage of 4,000 operatives of the new factories (including the weaving shops) was 2 pesos 6 reales, substantially lower than in 1843.[27] How far could such a wage go? Could a single family live from it?

Jan Bazant argues that a family could live comfortably from a single weekly wage of 3.90 pesos (5 reales a day), slightly more than the average wage in 1843. This, he claims, was sufficient to sustain a family of four persons in comfort (the average family size of the 95 households residing on La Constancia in 1838 was 3.8) He estimated that just over half of this, or 2 pesos, would have been spent on food. For several reasons, Bazant's estimates seem optimistic about the possibility of achieving higher living standards from working in the new factories.

First, Bazant's average wage is probably exaggerated since it was taken from the early 1840s, a period of inflation due to the circulation of copper currency. The average weekly wage was more likely to be less than 3 pesos. Secondly, Bazant underestimates the amount a family of four would have spent on food (he estimates 2 pesos a week). Francisco Javier de la Peña estimated in 1839 that an agricultural laborer would consume around 245 grams of maize a day, while a family of five would consume 700 grams a day. At 45 reales/carga - the median urban maize price for the

---

[24] Federico M. Fusco, "El Patriotismo -fábrica de mantas de los Sres. Velasco Hermanos", *Periodico Oficial*, Puebla, Vol. VII, No. 10, 9 February 1876.

[25] Jan Bazant, "Industria algodonera poblana de 1803-1843 en números," *Historia Mexicana*, Vol. 14, 1964, p. 137.

[26] *Memoria de Industria* (1844).

[27] Juan del Valle, *Guía de Forasteros*, pp. 194-195.

336

1840s - this would imply an outlay of 2 pesos a week on maize alone.[28] In years when maize prices were particularly high (1837, 1841-2 and 1847), reaching at times 80 reales the carga, almost the entire family wage would be consumed on maize alone. Thus, even in normal times, a family of four would have been stretched on 3.90 pesos a week. And in years of high food prices, this wage would have been woefully inadequate.

Only managers and skilled employees, such as textile engineers, machine wrights and mule spinners (often positions held by foreigners), could earn substantially higher than subsistence wages.[29] For the mass of Mexican unskilled factory workers, a solitary income was quite insufficient for supporting a family. Family labor was therefore obligatory if a secure living standard was to be achieved.

Thus, at this stage of Mexico's history, the factory proletariat did not represent the embryo of a new social strata enjoying a higher than subsistence level of consumption. And even the paternalism of such industrialists as Estevan de Antuñano seems to have been accepted as little more than a necessary convenience - because of the remoteness of the factories - rather than a positive inducement. Wages in the factories incorporating planned industrial villages seem generally to have been lower than in less exotic establishments.[30] And later in century, when the streetcar made residence away from the industrial hamlets possible, Juan Carlos Grosso has shown that workers swiftly spurned the putative benefits of factory accommodation for residence in the center of the city.[31]

Industrial modernization and the general economic recovery it brought in its wake, while undoubtedly providing employment to many families and re-animating crafts which had long been in decline, failed to transform living standards or even life styles. But what of the wider political and social impact of this process? Did Puebla become a more peaceful place ? Did protectionism and industrialization engineer a basis for political consensus ? This question has already been partially answered in Chapter 8 when examining the growing divisions within the protectionist lobby from after 1841. In the broader political arena, a similar picture is apparent.

In Chapter 5 it was observed how economic recession, military and political turmoil combined to impel Puebla from being a federalist stronghold, with a radical and vocal artisanry, to becoming a city, by the late 1830s, cowered into consensus and favoring centralism. A similar retreat from radicalism was evident among the working classes of Philadelphia and New York in the same period, as a consequence of

---

28 *El Amigo de la Religión*, Puebla, 1839, Vol. I, No. 4, pp. 51-2.
29 For wage contracts in 1833 with United States masters of spinning, weaving, carding, etc., mostly at the rate of 24 reales (3 pesos) a day: AGN, Banco de Avío, Vol. II Expte. 149, 31 July 1833.
30 *Memoria de Industria* (1844).
31 Juan Carlos Grosso, "Notas sobre la formación," p. 24-25.

commercial recession.[32] Contemporaries, aware of the Puebla's long-established reputation as Mexico's capital for thieves, rogues and sharpsters, commented on the city's sudden change of political temper. The uncharacteristic order and calm they put down to recovery of the city's manufacturing which had reduced unemployment and idleness.[33] This interlude of political tranquility lasted only until the mid 1840s.

From then until to the late 1870s, Puebla returned to the epicenter of the political and ideological conflicts affecting the nation at large: between Liberals and Conservatives, Patriots and Imperialists, Juaristas and Porfiristas, etc..[34] This was, in part, an unavoidable result of the city's strategic location. But it was also due to the presence of still numerous, though increasingly impoverished, religious corporations closely allied with leading elite families. Puebla grew to epitomize, in Mexicans' minds, the Conservative-clerical reaction (a reputation which it has yet to successfully throw off), even though, the city was probably no more "*mocho*" than any other provincial capital in Central Mexico at this time. This reputation was reenforced by the close ties known to exist between certain elite *poblano* families, such as the Haro y Tamariz, and the Conservative dictator, General Santa Anna, recently traced skillfully by Jan Bazant.[35] But while a section of the Puebla elite may have sought Conservative, and ultimately monarchist solutions for Mexico's political deadlock, these were by no means generalized sentiments in a city which provided some notable Liberal leaders during the Reform (Ignacio Comonfort, José María Lafragua, to mention but two) and where artisan radicalism occasionally resurfaced.

During the 1840s, the city continued to provide, as it had done since the wars of Independence, an important source for military recruitment. Large numbers of men were drafted to garrisons elsewhere in Mexico during Santa Anna's centralist republic between 1842 and 1845.[36] But, while military recruitment from the city during the early 1830s had been accomplished by the raising the radical expectations of the artisan soldiers, during the 1840s the *leva* served only to maintain in part an increasingly unpopular Conservative dictator. It was in part the unpopularity of forced recruitment by Conservative administrations which explains why the city

---

[32] Sean Wilentz, *Chants Democratic*, pp. 172-296; Bruce Laurie, *Working People*, pp. 107-133.

[33] *Calendario de Galván*, Mexico, 1842; Manuel Payno, "Viaje", p. 163.

[34] Dawn Keremitsis shows how Puebla's inordinate share of political and military conflict during the wars of Reform and the European intervention caused the textile industry to stagnate with growth occuring only beyond the central states. *La industria textíl*, p. 58.

[35] Jan Bazant, *Antonio Haro y Tamariz*, pp. 29-74.

[36] This would suggest that the recovery of manufacturing contributed only slightly to resolve the city's perennial problem of unemployment. Antonio Carrión, *Historia*, Vol. II, p. 290.

338

had turned against its traditional protagonist by the mid 1840s. When in December 1844, Santa Anna abandoned the capital and marched on Puebla, he hoped to secure a base (as in 1832) from which to rescue the now universally reviled centralist Republic. However, elite and masses in Puebla had also grown disillusioned with centralism, and especially with Santa Anna. Over 8,000 merchants, shopkeepers, artisans and factory operatives took to arms behind General Ignacio Inclán to successfully defend the city.[37]

Subsequent political disorders in the city during the late 1840s suggest at first the revival of a tradition of popular politics evident in the riots and "*barrio* wars" of the late colony and the first decade of Independence. The American invasion was accompanied by widespread disturbances, assassination of American troops and the sacking of American properties.[38] As a result, Puebla's merchants and shopkeepers were obliged, for the first time since the early 1830s, to organize a militia to defend their properties, not against the Americans, but their fellow *poblanos*.[39] Baltazar Furlong, the Prefect of the Department, having permitted the Americans peaceful entry and occupation of the city, was obliged to beseech the population to cease attacks upon Americans:

> No es el patriotismo, sino atentado contra la moral asesinar á traición al enemigo. A los habitantes pacíficos no les toca la guerra, ni esta se ha de hacer ahora en la ciudad.[40]

But contemporaries insisted that the discord of the 1840s was different from the upheavals of the pre-1835 period. As one broadsheet put it:

> los habitantes de Puebla, lejos ya de sus antiguos rencores, de aquellos frequentes levantamientos de unos contra otros barrios, movidos de miserables y vergonzozas pasiones, mesquinas y despreciables intereses; e ilustrados en la actualidad, en el conocimiento de sus derechos y

---

37 Leicht, *Calles*, p. 353, and *Boletín de Noticias*, Puebla, No.10, 30 December 1844. General Ignacio Inclán, military commander of Puebla, was a popular figure among artisans. In July 1844 he was elected as vice-president of the "Junta de Fomento de Artesanos" of Mexico City, whose branch in Puebla was under the presidency of Pablo Carmona, a cotton weaver who has represented Puebla's artisans since before Independence. *Semanario Artístico*, Mexico, No. 24, 9 July 1844.

38 Manuel Covarrubias, "Al Público," Puebla, 29 August 1847; AAP, Cabildo, Vol. 114, 2 September 1847; and Vol. 115, 24 March 1848.

39 AAP, Cabildo, Vol. 114, 17 May 1847; and Dr. N León, *Relación de los sucesos acaecidos en la ciudad de Puebla, del 14 al 27 de Mayo 1847*. Mexico, 1901 [diary of events during the American occupation, written by Manuel Orozco y Berra, mentioning the several attempts made by the "populacho" to free prisoners from the prison].

40 AAP, Cabildo, Vol. 114, 14 October 1847.

prerogativas, formarán UN CUERPO DE CONFIANZA, UN MURO DE BRONCE.[41]

Protectionism and industrial recovery had restored a basis, however fragile, for political consensus. Protectionist pamphlets from the later 1830s, during the 1840s, until the early 1850s, were often accompanied by hundreds of signatures of people grouped by work place, suggesting the considerable political potential of vertical association.[42] But merchants, factory owners, factory workers and artisans were active together far beyond specifically protectionist issues. Such solidarity was demonstrated in 1850 when, reminiscent of the pro-Bishop Pérez uprising of 1821, large numbers of people from the *barrios* gathered and marched to the central square to demand reinstatement of the popular Liberal-federalist governor, textile industrialist and wholesale merchant, Juan Mujica y Osorio.[43] And it is not impossible to imagine a Puebla industrialist leading his operatives into war, as some of his counterparts in Philadelphia did during the 1860s.[44] It was only, perhaps, because Mexican military affairs were less improvised and more centralized than their United States counterparts that such "corporate" formations did not arise.

The political consensus which these vertical ties of mutual economic interest afforded was shattered by the Revolution of Ayutla. For over a decade of civil war and foreign intervention, Conservatives and sections of

---

[41] *Vindicación de los barrios de Puebla sobre las injurias de El Universal.* Puebla, 1850.

[42] *Representación que los artesanos de algodón y algunos ciudadanos de Puebla dirigen al Exmo. Sr. Presidente,* Puebla, 1837; *Representación dirigida al Congreso de la Unión por 6,124 artesanos, pidiendo protección para el trabajo de los nacionales.* Mexico, 1851; *Representación que los que suscriben elevan respetuosamente al Exmo. Ayuntamineto de la Capital de PUEBLA, con motivo del alzamiento que se pretende de las leyes prohibitivas.* Mexico, 1851; *Exposición que varios FABRICANTES de HILAZA y TEJIDOS presentaron al Exmo. AYUNTAMIENTO de esta ciudad para que la eleva a las Cámaras de la Unión.* Puebla, 26 October 1851.

[43] The Conservative press in Mexico City presented this movement as being no more than "catorce ciudadanos de zarape del más bajo pueblo...adictos al Sr. Mujica..." In reply, various lawyers, Justices of the Peace, priests, police officers, priors of convents and numerous artisans claimed that the demonstration was both orderly and massive, involving "Casi la mayor parte de los barrios de la ciudad; entre cuya multitud se enumeraban muchos artesanos conocidos, sin que ocurriese ningún desorden por los parajes donde transito el pueblo." Mujica received petitions from 57 streets requesting that he remain in office, some followed by as many as 400 signatures. Moisés González Navarro, *Anatomía del Poder en México, 1848-1853.* Mexico, 1977, pp. 224-5; "Vindicación de los barrios", *El Universal,* Mexico, 2 February 1850, pp. 2-3.

[44] Philip Scranton, *Proprietory Capitalism: The Textile Manufacture at Philadelphia, 1800-1885.* Cambridge, 1983, pp. 66-68.

340

the clergy sought (ultimately unsuccessfully) to construct a power base in the city, from which liberalism might be combatted nationally.[45] The economic recession and ideological polarization brought about by war provided unsuitable conditions for the vertically organized, single-goal (protectionism-industrialization) politics which had held people together during the later 1830s and 1840s. After 1854, Puebla returned to become a divided city upon which were visited, in the form of repeated sieges, the ideological anguishes of Mexico's first Liberal revolution: La Reforma.

This study must now conclude with a final assessment of the generation of merchants, manufacturers, shopkeepers and artisans, who, through the energetic pursuit of self-interest, succeeded in reconstructing the urban economy during the 1830s and 1840s. Most of those introducing modern industrial processes did not expect to set in motion any miraculous transformation of living standards or life styles. The urban patriciate of Puebla sought, above all, to secure for itself a basis for prosperity, guaranteed by vigorously sustained protectionist policies, strengthened by technological innovations and defended, if necessary, by arms. The state of the city in the early 1830s, dissipated by emigration and disease, beset by crime, poverty and prostitution, was a source of great concern and moral outrage to prominent *poblanos*. There were moments when the entire social order seemed to be threatened, although popular grievances ultimately failed to acquire an articulate or coordinated form. The apparently extreme shifts in the Puebla elite's political allegiance from a general support for the Army of Three Guarantees in 1821, to federalism in 1824, to centralism by 1835, returning to favoring federalism after 1844, can be explained by their consistent search for a satisfactory accord with the national government which would guarantee their interests.

How successful was Puebla's broadly based entrepreneurial class in achieving a reconstruction of the urban economy capable of advancing their interests? In Chapter 7 two groups of industrialists were distinguished. The visionaries, most notably Estevan de Antuñano, sought to encourage a dynamic and autonomous process of industrial development which would eventually transform the entire national economy. The realists, among them the cotton speculators *Velasco, Marrón y Cía* and smaller inner-city factory owners, were satisfied with reaping immediate benefits from a limited adjustment to the traditional structure of the city's trade and manufacturing. Between 1837 and 1842 it was not necessary to be an optimist to share in Antuñano's enthusiasm for a sustained process of industrialization. Thereafter such a vision grew increasingly illusory. By the mid-1840s most people involved with modern industry were concerned more with survival than with further projects of industrial transformation. Their disillusion,

---

[45] Jan Bazant, *Antonio Haro y Tamariz*, pp. 105-56; Miguel Galindo y Galindo, *La Gran Década Nacional*, 3 Vols. Mexico, 1904-06; Laurens Ballard Perry, *Juárez and Díaz, Machine Politics in Mexico*. DeKalb, 1978; Daniel Cosio Villegas, *Historia Moderna de México La Republica Restaurada Vida Política*. Mexico, 1955.

anxiety and sense of betrayal was reflected in the pamphleteering of the period. And, as in the mid-1830s, attitudes crystalized around the currency question.

In 1845 Puebla's main commercial and industrial body (14 textile mill-owners, 35 cloth merchants, 37 grocers and 165 bakers, *tocineros,* millers and farmers) petitioned the Departmental Assembly, requesting permission to establish a company for coining 100,000 pesos in copper. This would be in units valued at one quarter and one eighth of a peso, indicating that it was at the level of small transactions and popular demand that the shortage of coin was most keenly felt. Puebla's merchants and manufacturers contrasted the period when copper money was in circulation (1828-1842), when the city had been alive with activity, with the depressed conditions of the mid-1840s. They asserted that the principal cause for the spate of factory construction, and all the employment and prosperity which it had brought, had been the copious circulation of copper money. Immediately copper money had been withdrawn, recession had set in, bringing a succession of bankruptcies to an extreme at which, they claimed:

> se han dado ya varios casos de que la maquinarias de hilados (que dígase lo que se quiera, han de hacer la felicidad de este departamento) han sido vendidas – a precio de hierro viejo, por no encontrarse ya hombres que tengan un mediano capital para llevarlas adelante.[46]

In response to this petition, the Departmental Assembly formally requested a mint for the coining of a departmental currency, pointing out that both Zacatecas and San Luis Potosí had their own money in circulation.[47] The capital fund of the mint, which would be called the "Casa de Moneda Particular para el Comercio del Departamento de Puebla" to be administered by the *ayuntamiento*, would be secured by outstanding stocks of flour and cotton cloth. This request fell upon deaf ears in the capital during the disordered two years leading up to the American war.[48] Governor Juan Mujica y Osorio, author of the official state *Memoria* of 1849, again blamed currency shortage for the continuing industrial recession:

> todas [las industrias] se resienten todavía del golpe que recibieron en la amortisación del cobre, porque el vacío imenso que esta operación dejó en la

---

[46] *Representación a la Exma Asamblea Departamental que hace el Comercio de Puebla sobre acuñación de moneda particular para el Departamento.* Puebla, 1845, p. 5.

[47] *Exposición que hace a la Excelentísima Junta Departamental de la INVICTA Puebla solicitando el establecimiento de una CASA de MONEDA particular.* Puebla, 1845.

[48] In July 1846 Estevan de Antuñano stressed the urgent need for 2,000,000 pesos in copper", without which factory production would grind to a halt. Miguel Quintana, *Estevan de Antuñano*, Vol. II, pp. 31-2.

masa de numerario circulante, no ha sido suficiente para cubrirlo el decurso de siete años.[49]

In the same year, Puebla's merchants and manufacturers again sought permission to coin 2,000,000 pesos in copper, a measure of the deficit in silver currency following the war.[50] Further petitions for a departmental currency were made in 1858 and 1869, again going unheeded.[51]

The explanation for the central government's refusal to permit the minting of copper by departmental/state governments probably lies with the pervasive influence which *agiotistas*, silver merchants and import merchants exercised upon government policy and the commercial/credit system generally.[52] The release of copper threatened their dominance of Mexico's external and internal trade. Ultimately, however, local manufacturing and commercial interests got what they wanted, not from any concession to coin copper, but from the movement of the United States and most of Europe onto the gold standard, while Mexico retained silver as the basis of it currency. This brought the gradual currency devaluation which protectionists had always sought, while the recovery of silver mining furnished an abundant circulating medium obviating the need for copper coinage.[53] This fact, more than any other, accounts for the ability of Mexico's factories to survive, indeed to modernize, during the second half of the nineteenth century.

The question of whether Puebla's entrepreneurs might have achieved more over these years, had the region been shielded from wider political conflicts, or, had the state possessed greater autonomy from central government (enabling *poblanos* to pursue their own tariff and currency policies), is an intriguing but unanswerable one. This study of these years has shown that a commercial and industrial city in a poor, agricultural country, could rise from the ruins of post-colonial decline to a state of tangible prosperity by the early 1840s, and sustain this recovery thereafter in the face of adverse political circumstances. Contemporaries, however, noticed that the economic recovery and limited industrialization encouraged

---

[49] *Memoria.del Estado de Puebla* (1849), pp. 71-2.

[50] *DOS MILLONES de MONEDA para el Estado de Puebla. Parte espositiva del proyecto que presentaron como ciudadanos el Supremo Gobierno del Estado*. Puebla, 1849.

[51] Leonardo Tamariz, *Pacificación*, p. 10; and Manuel de Ayala, "La Exportación de Dinero," *El Libre Pensador*. Puebla; Vol. III, No. 2, 26 August 1869.

[52] Margarita Urías Hermosillo,"Manuel Escandón: de las Diligencias al Ferrocarril. 1833-1862," in Ciro Cardoso (Ed.), *Formación y desarrollo de la burgesía en México*. Mexico, 1978, pp. 25-56; and David Walker, *Kinship, Business and Politics. The Martínez del Río Family in Mexico 1823-1867*. Austin, 1986, Chapters 5-8.

[53] Juan Carlos Grosso, *Estructura productiva y fuerza de trabajo Puebla, 1830-1890*. Puebla, 1984, p. 15.

by tariff protection, were dialectical processes which, while benefiting certain social groups (merchants, bureaucrats and artisans) in the cities of central Mexico, offered little to, or even harmed the living standards of, rural people, who were obliged to consume expensive national manufactures.[54] Whether the rural population would have done any better from an open tariff policy is of course, quite as debatable.

While the urban or regional economy of Puebla would not again experience, until the 1880s, a period of growth and structural change comparable to the 1835-42 investment flurry, the depression of the mid-1840s was soon overcome and the textile industry continued to expand modestly and to diversify into the early 1850s.[55] Investment opportunities also broadened, with a proliferation of mining companies, and with agriculture, for so long starved of credit, attracting renewed investment as a result of a sudden price rise in the early 1850s.[56] The revolution of Ayutla, however, brought to a halt the renewal of confidence which had followed the American war.

A petition from a city alderman in 1858 to the commander of the Conservative garrison echoed the despair of half a century earlier. He listed the catastrophic moral and economic consequences of the sudden liberalization of trade following the revolution of Ayutla:

> ...ha arruinado nuestras artes y nuestra agricultura...nos ha hecho tributarios en todo, de todos los otros pueblos nos ha prostrado en esa incomprensible y honda miseria que haciendo odioso el matrimonio, graciosa la familia, y lanzando a los hombres al pillaje y las revoluciones, corode la moral, rompe los vínculos sociales, disminuye y degrada nuestra población, y nos lleva precipitadamente a una catastrophe...Miles de extranjeros han vuelto a salir de la República cargados solo de desengaños. En Puebla, círculo que conozco, pueden citarse – los Sres. Lang, Smit [Robert Smith, Duncan y Cía.], Hube [Hube-Herklots y Cía], Trumbult [Edward Turnbull,Courtenay Tagart y Cía], Dasqui [Agustín Dasque] etc., [all leading wholesalers, creditors to industrialists, some becoming factory owners during the 1840s], extranjeros modelos de honradéz, y que contando con los mejores elementos, buenas capacidades, amplias relaciones, y muchas simpatías, se han visto

---

54 Guillermo Prieto, *Indicaciones sobre el origen*. Mexico, 1850, p. 395.

55 The *Memoria de Colonización e Industria* for 1851 observes the further expansion of industry following the American war, Luis Chávez Orozco, *La industria nacional y el comercio exterior, (1842-1851)*. Mexico, pp. 470-71. See also Guillermo Beato, "La Casa Martínez del Río: Del Comercio colonial a la industria fabríl", in Ciro Cardoso (Ed.), *Formación*, p. 105.

56 AGNP, PN, No.5 (1848-49), fs. 34-36; (1850-51), fs. 44-45, 85; PN, No. 7 (1850), f. 341; (1855), f. 63.

marchar, a donde todos en la línea económica marchan en México, a la miseria.[57]

Puebla was, of course, not alone in being deserted by many of its wholesale merchants during the unstable middle years of the century. Recent research on the textile industry during the Reforma show a rentier group taking over factories from indebted manufacturers, the vestiges of the once dynamic entrepreneurial group of the 1830s and 1840s.[58] It was a sure sign that an era of enterprise and business confidence was over.

---

[57] Leonardo Tamariz, *Pacificación*.

[58] Carmen Aguirre y Alberto Carabarán ,"Proprietarios de la industria Textil de Puebla en el siglo XIX: Dionisio José de Velasco y Pedro Berges de Zúñiga," in CIHS-UAP, *Puebla en el Siglo XIX*, pp. 177-224.

Appendix 1

TABLE A.1 WHEAT TITHES, CENTRAL VALLEY OF PUEBLA 1805-1828

	Haciendas	Ranchos	Huertas	Peujaleros	Molinos	1805	1806
TLAXCALA							
San Pablo de Monte	11	-	-	-	1	533.5	464.5
Santa Inés Zacatelco	6	1	-	-	-	658	519.5
Topoyango	-	-	1	-	1	-	167.5
Teolocholco	5	-	-	-	-	34	87
Tetlatlaca	4	-	-	-	-	113	65
Ixtacuixtla	5	2	-	-	1	2191	612
Ponotla	2	-	-	-	-	16	26
Tlaxcala	1	-	-	-	-	103	100
Nativitas	15	1	-	-	-	3891	1784
District of Tlaxcala	49	4	1	-	3	7539.5	3825.5
TEPEACA AND TECALI							
Tepeaca	1	-	-	-	-	70	-
Nopalucan	2	-	-	-	-	974	821
Tecali	2	1	-	-	-	40	-
Zicatlacoya	2	-	-	-	-	-	-
Acaxete	17	3	-	-	-	1199	2226
Districts of Tepeaca and Tecali	24	4	-	-	-	2213	3117
PUEBLA - DISTRICT							
Resurrección	15	-	-	-	-	1465	1651
Huatinchan	7	-	-	-	1	20	140
Amazoque	24	1	-	-	1	169.5	1746.5
Totimehuacán	16	-	-	-	1	281	465
District of Puebla	62	1	-	-	2	2935.5	4002.5
PUEBLA - CITY							
Cathedral	-	2	2	-	3	701	461
San Sebastian	1	6	9	"varios"	4	1415	2260
San Marcos	-	1	10	-	-	239.5	370.5
Senor San José	1	11	5	-	2	587	690
Santa Cruz	-	1	2	-	-	83.5	67
Santo Angel	3	4	2	-	5	299.5	387
City of Puebla	5	25	30	-	14	3325.5	4235.5
CHOLULA AND ATLITXCO							
San Pedro Cholula	11	9	-	-	3	2122.5	3152.5
San Andrés Cholula	5	3	-	-	-	655	1006
Santa Clara Ocoyuca	2	1	-	-	-	965	715
Santa Isabel Cholula	7	-	-	-	-	1129.5	150
Calpan	6	2	-	-	-	205	301
Tianguismanalco	5	1	-	-	-	151	120.5
Curonango	11	1	-	-	-	1566	1533.5
District of Cholula	47	17	-	-	4	5794	6978.5
HUEJOTZINGO							
Huejotzingo	28	1	-	-	-	5404	7811.5
Chaucingo	2	-	-	-	-	-	50
San Martín	3	-	-	-	-	1129	632.5
	33	1	-	-	-	6533	8494
TOTAL	220	52	31	-	23	28340.5	30653

TABLE A.1 *CONTD.*

	1807	1808	1809	1810	1811	1812	1813
TLAXCALA							
San Pablo de Monte	467	248.5	616	370	366	142	204
Santa Inés Zacatelco	519	1050	1028	804.5	828	640	380
Topoyango	45	90	97	45	78	5	10
Teolocholco	114	87	10	20	10	-	-
Tetlatlaca	428	662	560	380	310	21	-
Ixtacuixtla	3201	3361	4104	5352.5	2983	2010	1420
Ponotla	280	101	290	325	-	-	-
Tlaxcala	450	597	240	160	-	-	-
Nativitas	3903	6310	7313	5793	2055	4281	911
District of Tlaxcala	9407	12506.5	14258	13250	6630	7099	2925
TEPEACA AND TECALI							
Tepeaca	58	40	90	160	80	60	140
Nopalucan	30	-	-	-	-	51	-
Tecali	30	-	50	108	60	-	280.5
Zicatlacoya	10	-	-	10	10	-	-
Acaxete	1291	1356	1845.5	1484	1441	963	800
Districts of Tepeaca and Tecali	1419	1396	1985.5	1762	1591	1074	1220.5
PUEBLA - DISTRICT							
Resurrección	1183	1160.5	663	1232	1893.5	1505	384
Huatinchan	188	50	185	180	100	91	170
Amazoque	1423	1388	1779	1514.5	2999	1816	1344.5
Totimehuacán	705	199	931	1146	1264.5	944	428
District of Puebla	3499	2797.5	3558	4132.5	6257	4356	2326.5
PUEBLA - CITY							
Cathedral	725	977.5	733	1216.5	1253	692	397
San Sebastián	2981	2210	3232	3262	3077.5	2827	2002
San Marcos	215.5	157	214.5	182	169	140	173.5
Senor San José	735	741	482.5	1157	1211	1029	973
Santa Cruz	71.5	83.5	78	211.5	268	322	339
Santo Angel	491	606	357	628	594	404	166
City of Puebla	5219	4775	5097	6657	6572.5	5414	4050.5
CHOLULA AND ATLITXCO							
San Pedro Cholula	4099	3656	3651	4099	4551	3092	1849.5
San Andrés Cholula	1356	1883.5	1840.5	2016	1546	1695	651.5
Santa Clara Ocoyuca	260	1020	1505	1543	1080	316	707
Santa Isabel Cholula	96	107.5	49	71.5	78	69	-
Calpan	237	113.5	60	138	157	135	108
Tianguismanalco	110	101	210	141	170	150	170
Curonango	1370	1836	1620	1608	1027	1072.5	506
District of Cholula	7528	8717.5	8935.5	9616.5	8609	6529.5	3992
HUEJOTZINGO							
Huejotzingo	6528	6332.5	5469	6274	3783	4832	2828
Chaucingo	40	75	10	-	-	84	84
San Martín	1521	920	840	770	-	473.5	426
	8089	7327.5	5719	7044	3783	5389.5	3338
TOTAL	35161	37514	39553	42462	33442.5	29862	17852.5

TABLE A.1 *CONTD.*

	1814	1815	1816	1817	1818	1819	1820
TLAXCALA							
San Pablo de Monte	80	144	366	211	301	371.5	629
Santa Inés Zacatelco	77	90	135	144	305	850	375
Topoyango	5	4.5	155	120	171	167	275
Teolocholco	-	5	30	10	-	35	50
Tetlatlaca	60	90	170	165	408	700	295
Ixtacuixtla	1300	970	730	1075	1285	750	616
Ponotla	36	-	50	-	-	78	17.5
Tlaxcala	-	-	-	-	-	-	-
Nativitas	932	1911	1814.5	927	1785	6501	2984
District of Tlaxcala	2490	3214.5	3450.5	2652	4255	9452.5	5001.5
TEPEACA AND TECALI							
Tepeaca	80	45	100	-	30	60	100
Nopalucan	300	300	310	60	100	120	-
Tecali	62.5	269	20	90	40	20	110
Zicatlacoya	-	-	-	-	-	-	-
Acaxete	855	825	1174	1005	977	823	584
Districts of Tepeaca and Tecali	1297.5	1439	1604	1155	1147	1023	794
PUEBLA - DISTRICT							
Resurrección	725	687	745	1146	1281	1247.5	1206.5
Huatinchan	244	145	430	242	393	291	270
Amazoque	1059	888.5	1146.5	883.5	832	486	748
Totimehuacán	503.5	673	838	740.5	1014	714	523
District of Puebla	2531.5	2393.5	3159.5	3012	3520	2738.5	2747.5
PUEBLA - CITY							
Cathedral	493	722	605	1125	1215	1570	1084
San Sebastián	2303.5	3599.5	3190	3658	4467	5135	3402
San Marcos	167	221	179.5	127.5	151.5	144	167
Senor San José	501	588.5	740	1128	1228	1541	910.5
Santa Cruz	384	416	412	207	273	449	230
Santo Angel	405	558	599	636.5	921	627	1008
City of Puebla	4253.5	6105	5725.5	6882	8255.5	9466	6801.5
CHOLULA AND ATLITXCO							
San Pedro Cholula	1215.5	1713.5	1810	2896	3538	3363	3346.5
San Andrés Cholula	678.5	976.5	1213	2774	1708	1633	1394
Santa Clara Ocoyuca	492	912	834	988	803	870	1005
Santa Isabel Cholula	15	-	66	145	8	130	80
Calpan	115	162	100	40	30	44	-
Tianguismanalco	190	156	150	160	160	166	130
Curonango	216	489.5	289	282	676	1299	1002.5
District of Cholula	2922	4409.5	4462	7285	6923	7505	7385.5
HUEJOTZINGO							
Huejotzingo	2537	2663	2733	3852.5	4321	4693	2554
Chaucingo	84	84	84	84	640	110	70
San Martín	1342.5	450	422.5	1080	1063	825	433
	3963.5	3197	3239	5016.5	6024	5773	3057
TOTAL	17458	20758.5	21640.5	26002.5	30124.5	35958	25787

Appendix 2

/f.105r/
Exmo. Sr. [Alcalde]

Con el sincero respeto de buenas hijas a su padre venimos a quejarnos
a V.E. de su acuerdo que dispuso que las que somos llamadas regatonas no
compremos frutas ni otros artículos de plaza a los introductores sino hasta
las once de la mañana, después que hayan comprado los tenderos de
cuatros: y para fundar nuestra queja nos es lícito, por ser indispensable,
representar que ese acuerdo se separa tanto de la justicia cuanto de la
igualdad; es depresivo de las personas miserables; no corresponde a lo que
piden la equidad y humana sensibilidad; no es del día y ahoga al mas
afligido: en suma desdice de las luces y caracter suave de V. E.

Regatón es el que ajusta y porfía sobre el precio de lo que está a /f.
105v. /[la] venta, por que *regatear* no tiene otra significasión que *altercar
porfiar sobre el precio de la cosa puesta en venta* y bajo esta verdad son
regatones todo comerciante, y todo consumidor; y aun en las almonedas
todo licitante es regatón; y no mas a [los] pobres, que hacemos diligencia
por comprar barato se nos ha de llamar regatonas?....Es desgracia que no
apadrina la justicia y   los tenderos de cuatros ? dan al introductor lo que
pide por el huevo, la naranja, granadita y demás artículos? No altercan, no
porfían por ajustar el más comodo precio?....Ah, que animado, de su
mayor dinero en mano, vestido menos pobre que el nuestro comienzan por
tutear al vendedor y así sigue su imperio en el ajuste, y desde que no hay
concurrencia de nosotras y nuestras compañeras hasta que ellos acaban de
proverse, ha debido crecer su señorío su altercasión y su porfía. Y a esos
regatones /f. 106r. /y a tantos que regatean por que pueden y deben regatear
al comprar cargas de maíz, de frijol, de trigo, de arros, de aba, lenteja,
garvanzo, de papa, chile, algodón, azucar, ajonjolí, comino, cebo, papel,
bretañas, pontivi, sábanas, cedas y toda otra mercadería, no se pone taza,
no se señala hora, como tampoco al que negocia en carnes y tantos otros
artículos más necesarios al público que la fruta. ¿Donde está la
igualdad?....y sin ella nada puede ser justo; no por las vocanadas de
igualdad que vierte el siglo mentiroso, sino por que nunca se ha hermanado
la justicia con la acepción de personas. El mercader de ropa, el de licores,
el de abarrotes, el de semillas, el que negocia en carnes compran para
revender, altercan y porfían hasta conseguir el precio que les deje ganancia,
y no tienen taza en lugar ni en tiempo: mas el tendero de cuatros que compra
las frutas en que negociamos; el /f. 106v. / tendero que no vende al sol ni al
aire; el tendero que no paga al tesoro el local en que menudea, ni sufre el
gasto y robos de llevar y traer diariamente; ni que el sol, el aire, las lluvias
le pasmen unas frutas y les fermenten otras, es regatón de chaqueta y
calzado. Nadie negara que si nosotras meresemos ese epiteto, es de ellos
igualmente por que ellos hacen lo que nosotras: compran en la plaza a los
introductores fruta, huevos y algun otro artículo: regatean el precio, esto es,

349

altercan hasta conseguir el más cómodo, y revenden a mayor precio en menudeo lo que compraron. Pues bien que privilegio tienen esos regatones para comprar primero que nosotras? Las diferencias son para que las almas sensibles y equitativas nos dieran preferencia. Ellos tienen buenos lomos, grandes calzones para emplearse en trabajos recios o ir a buscar las frutas /f. 107r. / mas a quien así nos desdeña y nos oprime presentándonos como mas abyectas y obligándonos más en las presentes aflicciones, ahogando nuestra miseria como si esta fuese fuente de daño al público?....El mal que hacemos es comprar en conjunto las frutas de que el rico no se quiere cargar por que no se pudra de su cuenta: el daño que hacemos es tenerla preparada para el día y para las horas de comer que quiere ir a tomarla o mandar por ella el Sr. Alcalde, el Sr. Regidor, los Sres. Eclesiásticos, el comerciante, el artesano, el militar, la señorita y sus niños, cuando ya no parece el introductor, o no quiere menudear por no detenerse según que está con cuidado por las bestias en que trajo sus cargas y por regresar no tarde a su pueblo. Mas, ese introductor cuando a mas no poder menudea, da las mismas o menos piezas al comprador, por /f. 107v. / a Jochimilco, Yautepec, Atlixco, a las Villas, Teocelo y las Mistecas: ellos tienen mayores capitales, ellos revenden a la sombra, no pagan al municipio, revenden a toda hora hasta diez de la noche, y no son pobres mujeres con corto capital tomado aveces a duro premio de Señores duros; nosotras llevamos diariamente en manos del cargador borracho y ladrón las canastas al mercado por cuyo miserable punto que ocupamos cuando más de dos varas en cuadro pagamos al fondo municipal lo que el cobrador ha querido: allí nos cruge el aire, nos abraza el resol, la agua nos penetra, el muchacho hambriento nos roba, el soldado de hoy nos arrebata y en esos puntos que daño hacemos al público para que sus Señores Regidores nos pospongan, nos abatan al tendero de cuartos y al guarda lisongero y chismoso, reduciéndonos a comprar el desecho la resoca la fruta mas procsima a podrirse de pronto? que mal hace /f. 108r. / que todos saben compensarse de la paga del puesto, del mayor trabajo y mayor tiempo, del sol y vientos en frecuentes remolinos y del robo del soldado y del ratero.

Sírvase V. E. meditar que ese acuerdo no solo deprime a infelices mujeres que no hacen mas daño que ser inquilinas de la plaza y tener preparada la mejor fruta para cuando la quieren los habitantes de la Ciudad, sino también deprime al que viene por largas leguas a pié arriando a los pesados y tontos asnos, a introducir las frutas, huevos y otros pobres artículos, pues se les sujeta a mayor dilasión que les hace falta para no vencer a buena hora la jornada de su regreso, y disminuyéndoles la concurrencia simultanea de compradores, se les priva de las ventajas de la competencia, y se les deja bajo la férula del Señor regatón, el tendero de cuatros.

No señor /f. 108v. / déjese libre al vendedor y al comprador: aquel sabe su negocio, dar a quien mejor le pague o a quien ahorre tiempo, gastos y peligros y a quien sabra madrugar si quiere recibir en la plaza al introductor y llegar a tiempo para participar de la vendimia, si se iguala en precio, o llevela quien mejor la pague.

Esto es lo justo, esto lo natural; al vigilante y no al dormido se da en todo la palma: dias hacer que el magistrado sabe que la mejor provisión se consigue bajo la franca libertad sin traba tacsación ni preferencias: cada cual vendedor y comprador saben lo que les conviene, no son nuevos en el mercado, y para su provecho aun el topo es lince. Es violentísima cualquiera preferencia. El magistrado no tiene mas que cuidar del que no se venda gato por liebre, y que los alimentos no esten corrompidos en perjuicio de la salud. /f. 109r. / No permitiesen que dispensen preferencias. ¿Quien mejor las merecía que la clase de mujeres pobres que se ocupan en mantener las frutas y otros rateros artículos para toda hora del mercado, al viento, al sol, a la lluvia; que todo el año son feudatarias a los fondos públicos por un miserable pedasillo de tierra en el mercado, sin el menor abrigo ni comodidad, unas mujeres, cuyo secso está deprimido por que los hombres han sido los legisladores; y cuyos trabajos son servir por tres pesos al mes, o hacer camisas (cuando las hay) en dos días por tres reales, o prostituirse para ser maltratadas y cargar hijos, enfermedades y miserias [?] /f. 109v. /.

Nada tiene Ecsmo Sr. de desmedida nuestra queja: la fuerza del dolor del sentimiento, y de la necesidad habrá traido una que otra frase que desagradará a quien no recuerde la vemencia y fuerza de espresión con que se virtió el Santo Job para con su jus /f. 110r. / tísimo y sobre ecselente Señor, y concluiremos con uno de sus clamores ahora que nos dominan y atormentan altamente los estraños "Tened misericordia de nosotras, tened lástima de estas infelices al menos vosotros Sres. Alcaldes, Regidores y síndicos que sois no solo nuestros amigos sino nuestros protectores y padres, cuya potestad debe ser dulce para todos." Dejadnos comprar libremente por que tenemos iguales derechos en el mercado y por que si somos regatonas, es regatón el tendero de cuatros y todo comerciante, y el mundo se compone de regatones.

A V. E. suplicamos encarecida y rendidamente se nos vuelva a nuestra justa libertad e igualdad con los demás compradores.

Puebla Dic. el once de 1847.

Soledad Romero	Dolores García	Marciada Escobar
Ma. Josefa Rodríguez	Luz Roldán	Trinidad Acevedo
Monica Rosa /f. 110v. /	Soledad Anzares	Cornelia
Aranda Viviana Moral	Nicolasa Quintana	Isidra Pérez
Isabel Domínguez	Guadalupe Leiva	Luz García
Luz Zenteno	Magdalena Islas	Pantaleona Escobar

No saben firmar las mencionadas

Lic. José M[arian]o. Marín.

Bibliography

A. MANUSCRIPT SOURCES.

Archives Diplomatiques Françaises (ADF), Paris
Correspondence Comerciale:
Mexico 1844-1850, Vol. 6.
Veracruz 1838-1850, Vol. 2.
Correspondence Consulaire Commerciale: Mexico Vol. 2, 1830
Mémoires et Documents: Mexique
Population Française au Mexique (1849).
Amérique: Mexico, California et Oregon, Vol. 43 (1843)

Archivo del Ayuntamiento de Puebla (AAP)

Abastos, Vols. 88, 89, 168, 169.

Alhóndiga, Vols. 109, 112, 113, 114.

Asuntos Varios, Vols. 204-209.

Cabildo, Vols. 69-118 (*Actas del Cabildo* 1800-1852).

Cuentas, Vols. 8-160 (corresponding to 1793-1854)

Corredores de Lonja, 1628-1866, Vol. 225.

Expedientes sobre Empedrados y Estadística, Vol. 175.

Fondos Municipales, Vol. 185.

Gremios, Vols. 209, 220, 223, 224, 226, 227, 232, 233, 234..

Hacienda Municipal, Vols. 109, 151, 209.

Matadero, Vol. 226.

Mercados, Vol. 118.

Militar, Vols. 87, 116, 119.

Panaderías, Vols. 82, 84, 87, 230, 231.

Padrones, Vols. 128-148.

Panteones, Vol. 82.

Parián, Vol. 197.

Pensiones Municipales, Vols. 158, 162, 163, 227.

Presupuestos y Bienes Municipales, Vol. 201.

Rastros, Vol. 90.

Sanidad, Vols. 79, 81, 89,

Tierras y Aguas, Vols. 47, 50.

Tocinerías, Vols. 232, 233, 234

Padrón que comprende todas las Casas de Comercio en los 16 Quarteles de la Ciudad, Enero 31 a 31 de Diciembre de 1825. (AAP, Pensiones Municipales, Vol. 163, fs. 1-100).

Noticia de Haciendas de Labor, Ranchos y molinos y Ladrillerías que hay en la demarcación de este Ayuntamiento, de sus dueños, frutos y capitales. (1829) AAP, Estadística, Vol. 175, f. 187.

Padrón General de Casas en que se trata de sus proprietarios, productos y cobradores, Año de 1832, Inventario No. 213.

Padrón de Tiendas y Vendajes formado por D. José Mariano Duarte (1835).

Lista de Fincas Rústicas, comprendida en la Municipalidad de Puebla de los Angeles. (1836). AAP, Vol. 103, f. 223.

Padrón de las fábricas de hilados y texidos de algodón y lana, papel, loza y vidrio que existen en esta capital y su municipalidad. (1852). AAP, Cabildo, Vol. 119, fs. 361-367.

Archivo de la Catedral de Puebla (ACP)

Diezmos de Trigo (1801-1818) 3 vols.

Documentos de Diezmos. Remates 1783-1801.

Libro en que firmen los recibos, 1780.

Archivo de la Embajada Española en México (AEEM)

Indice de Matrículas, 1846

Archivo General de la Nación (AGN), Mexico City

Archivo Histórico de Hacienda (AHH), Vols. 663, 917

Banco de Avío, 3 Vols (1822-1843).

Consulados, Vols. 221, 463.

Epidemias, Vols.13.

Españoles, Vol. 5.

Historia, Vols. 73, 74, 523.

Sección de Industria, 4 Vols (1822-1843)

Industria y Comercio, Vols. 1, 8, 20, 23.

Intendencias, Vols. 13, 40, 48, 59, 61, 734.

Padrones, Vols. 22, 25, 27, 28, 38.

Pasaportes, Vols. 1-9.

Reales Cédulas, Vols. 20, 89, 102, 107, 108, 109, 128, 129, 132, 159, 163.

Archivo General de Notarías de Puebla (AGNP)

Miscellaneous Judicial.

Miscellaneous Wills.

Miscellaneous Guild Affairs. (MGA)

Consulado Papers (1821-1824).

Public Notary
No.1: 1837, 1838, 1839, 1841, 1842, 1850, 1865
No.2: 1842, 1848, 1850.
No.3: 1827, 1835.
No.7: 1829, 1837, 1838, 1839, 1840, 1845, 1849, 1852, 1855.
No.8: 1836.

Registro Público de la Propiedad (RPP), Puebla

Libros de Censos, Vols.38- 46

Archivo de Indias (AGI), Seville

México, Audiencia, Vols. 2485, 2576, 2578.
Indiferente General, Vol. 2438.
México, Vol. 26.

British Library (BL), London

Manuscript Collection (BL. MSS)
9770 K5.
20896, Add. 171,557

British Parliamentary Papers, Vol. XXXIX, 1842

Condumex, Mexico City

Hospital de Jesús, Correspondencia de Lucas Alamán, Vols. 424 & 484.

Instituto Nacional de Antropología e Historia (INAH), Mexico City

Microfilm Collection

Archivo Judicial de Puebla, Roll 38

Museo del Estado de Puebla, Casa de Alfenique, Puebla
Actas del Congreso del Estado. 8 Vols. 1825-1828.

University of Glasgow (UG)
Manuscript collection (UG MSS)
Wylie Papers.

B. PRINTED SOURCES

i) Official Reports, Legislative Debates, Official Actas, Laws,

Acta de la Federación del Estado Libre de la Puebla de los Angeles. Puebla, 1823.

Alamán, Lucas. *The Present State of Mexico.* London, 1825.

Arrillaga, Francisco. *Memoria sobre reformas del arancel mercantil.* Mexico, 1824.

Ayuntamiento de Puebla sobre la amortización de cobre. Puebla, 1841.

Barrio Lorenzot, Francisco de. *Ordenanzas de Gremios de la Nueva España.* Mexico, 1920.

Busto, Emiliano. *Estadística de la República de México.* México, 1880.

Camacho, Sebastián. Exposición de las Rentas del Estado de Veracruz. Jalapa, 1833.

Colección de los Decretos y Ordenes más importantes que espidió el Congreso Constituyente del Estado de Puebla en los años de 1824-25, 1826-28, 1830-31. 3 Vols., Puebla, 1827-1832.

Colección de Leyes y Decretos de la autoridad legislativa del Estado de Puebla correspondiente a la segunda época del sistema federal. Vol. II, Puebla, 1850. Puebla, 1858.

Decretos y acuerdos expedidos por la tercera (y cuarta) legislatura constitucional del estado libre y soberano de Puebla. Vol. I (1832-1835) Puebla, 1850.

Dos Millones de Moneda para el Estado de Puebla. Puebla, 1844.

Estado Instructivo que presenta la Junta de Sanidad. Puebla, October 19, 1813.

Esposición que el Ayuntamiento de la Capital de Puebla dirige a la Excma. Asamblea del Departamento pidiendo su pronta reorganización. Puebla, 1844.

Exposición que hace la Excelentísima Junta Departamental de la Invicta Puebla solicitando el establecimiento de una casa de moneda particular. Puebla, 1845.

Exposición de la Junta Directora del Banco Nacional de Amortización a las Cámaras de Senadores. Mexico, 1841.

García, Carlos. *Manifiesto del Nuevo Consulado de Puebla.* Puebla, 1821.

Iniciativa que la Honorable Legislatura del Estado de Puebla eleva al Congreso General para que no se aprueba la introdución de harina por el puerto de Veracruz. Puebla, 1851.

Lista General de los Sepultados en Santiago Tlatelolco. Mexico, 1833.

Lista de los vecinos honrados que se ha nombrado el ilustre ayuntamiento. Puebla, 1821.

Manifiesto que el Batallón Nacional de Puebla No. 21 hace a toda la Nación sobre la conducta que ha observado al pronunciamiento del ejército de reserva. Puebla, 1830.

Memoria presentada al congreso primero constitucional de Puebla por el Secretario del despacho de Gobierno sobre el estado de la administración pública por el año de 1826. Mexico, 1826.

Memoria...Puebla ..1827. Puebla, 1827.

Memoria...Puebla...1830. Puebla, 1830.

Memoria sobre la administración del Estado de Puebla en 1849, bajo el gobierno del Excelentísimo Señor Don Juan Mugica y Osorio. Mexico, 1849.

Memoria sobre el estado de la agricultura—industria de la República. Mexico, 1843.

Memoria sobre el estado de la agricultura e industria de la república en el año de 1844. Mexico 1845.

Memoria sobre la agricultura e industria de la República en el año de 1845. Mexico, 1846.

Memoria sobre la Dirección de Colonización e Industria. Año de 1849. Mexico, 1850.

Memoria que la Dirección de Colonización e Industria presentó al Ministro de Relaciones en 17 de enero de 1852, sobre el estado de estos ramos. Mexico, 1853.

358

Ofrecimiento de los Señores Eclesiásticos de la Ciudad de Puebla a los Europeos residentes en ella. Mexico, 1821.

Ordenanzas que debe guardar la Muy Noble y Leal Ciudad de Puebla de los Angeles del Reyno de la Nueva España. Puebla, 1787.

Ordenanzas para el nuevo establecimiento de Alcaldes de Quartel de la Ciudad de la Puebla de los Angeles de Nueva España. Puebla, 1796.

Representación que hace a S. M. las Cortes el Ayuntamiento de la Puebla de los Angeles para que en esta ciudad, cabeza de provincia, se establezca Diputación Provincial, como la dispone la Constitución. Puebla, 9 July, 1820.

Representación que hace el soberano congreso de Cortes la junta electoral de la provincia de Puebla.para que en ella se establezca la Diputación Provincial. Puebla, 18 September, 1820.

Representación que la diputación provincial de Puebla hizo al Soberano Congreso en 12 de Agosto de 1823. Mexico, 1823.

Representación dirigida al Excmo. Señor Presidente de la República, por la Junta de Industria de Puebla, a fin de que se queme el algodón introducido clandestinamente. Puebla, 1843.

Representación dirigida al Supremo Gobierno por la Dirección General de la Industria Nacional, contestando a lo que ha expuesto la Junta de Puebla sobre proveer de algodón a las fábricas de la República. Mexico, 1843.

Representación que dirigió al Excmo. Señor Presidente, la Junta de Industria de Puebla, combatiendo las razones con que se ha pretendido la introducción de algodón en rama extranjero. Mexico, 1843.

Representaciones dirigidas por la Exma. Diputación Provincial de Puebla a S.M.I y al Soberano Congreso Constituyente, pidiendo la restricción de la libertad del comercio en los artículos que sostiene a la industria fabríl de esta provincia. Puebla, 1822.

Salazar, Francisco. *Actas del primer Congreso Consituyente de Ecuador.* Quito, 1893.

ii) Printed Documents

Chávez Orozco, Luis "El crédito agrícola en el partido de Cholula, 1790", in *DHCAM*. 24 Vols., 1953-1958.

_____ (ed.) *Industria Nacional y el Comercio Exterior (1842-1851).* Mexico, 1962 (contains the *Memorias de Industria* for the 1840s and early 1850s).

Córdova, Luis (ed.) *Protección y libre cambio: el debate entre 1821 y 1836*. Mexico, 1971.

Del Centralismo Proteccionista al Regimen Liberal, 1837-1872. Mexico, 1976.

Flores Caballero, R. (ed.) *Protección y Libre Cambio*. Mexico, 1972.

Florescano, Enrique and Isabel Gil (eds.) *Descripciones Económicas: Provincias del Sur y Sureste*. Mexico, 1976.

Florescano, Enrique and Rodolfo Pastor (eds.) *La Crísis Agrícola de 1785-86. Selección Documental*. 2 Vols., Mexico, 1981.

Florescano, Enrique and Luis Chávez Orozco. *Agricultura e industria textil de Veracruz: siglo XIX*. Jalapa, 1965

González Sánchez, Isabel. *Haciendas y ranchos de Tlaxcala en 1712*. Mexico, 1969.

Hernández y Dávalos, Juan E. *Colección de Documentos para la Historia de la Guerra de Independencia, 1808-1821*. 8 Vols., Mexico, 1877-1824.

Humphreys, R. A. *British Consular Reports on Latin America, 1824-1826*. London, 1940.

Limosnas y Salarios en la Real Hacienda de Nueva España. Mexico, 1945.

Lockhart, James and Enrique Otte. *Letters and People of the Spanish Indies*. Cambridge, 1976.

"Memorial de Miguel Sánchez de la Parra, 1584", *CDIHE.*, 1892.

Otte, Enrique. "Cartas privadas de Puebla del siglo XVI", *JGSWFL*, Vol. III, 1966, pp. 10-87.

Revillagigedo, Conde de. *Instrucción reservada al Marqués de Branciforte.*Mexico, 1966.

"Notable carta reservada", *BAGN*, Vol. I, 1930, pp. 190- 211; and Vol. II, 1931, pp. 196-211.

Zavala, Silvio. *Ordenanzas del Trabajo: Siglos XVI y XVII*. Mexico, 1947.

iii) Pamphlets

Algunas consideraciones económicas (sobre la protección de la industria). Mexico, 1841.

Alcance al Papel Volante Titulado: Intereses de la Puebla Bien Intendidos. Puebla, 1821.

360

Anon [Presbítero Antonio María de la Rosa]. *Exito del Proceso Formado a Manuel López de Guerrero.* Puebla, 1822.

Anon. *Industria Manufacturera: Prohibición de vidrio plano extranjero.* Mexico, 1842.

Anon. *Noticias Extraordinarias de los últimos sucesos de Puebla.* Mexico, 1833.

Anon. *Para estos lances sirve la imprenta. Dialogo, Un Zapatero y Un Tejedor.* Puebla, 1822.

Anon. *Toma de Puebla y Glorias de la Patria.* Mexico, 1832.

Antunaño, Estevan de. *Ampliación, aclaración y corección a los principales puntos del manifiesto sobre el algodón manufacturado y en greña.* Puebla, 1833 (reprinted in Mexico, 1955).

Breve memoria del estado que guarda la fábrica de hilados de algodón

La Constancia Mexicana y la industria de este ramo. Puebla, 1837.

Comercio exterior de México. Segunda parte. Sistema prohibitivo. Puebla, 1838.

Discurso analítico de algunos puntos de moral y economía política de Méjico con relación a su agricultura cereal o sea pensaminetos para un plan para animar la industria mejicana. Puebla, 1834.

Economía Política en México. Exposición respetuosa que al que suscribe dirige a las augustas cámaras de la nación. Puebla, 1839

Economía Política en México. Cinco documentos para la historia de la industria moderna de algodones, en México. Puebla, 1843.

Economía Política en México. Insurrección para la industria fabril. Puebla, 1845.

Exposición respetuosa que los que suscriben elevan a las soberanas. Cámaras de la Unión sobre la prohibición de artefactos gordos de algodón extranjero. Puebla, 1835.

Primer Asunto de la Patria, el algodón. Manifiesto sobre el algodón manufacturado y en greña. Puebla, 1833.

Reflecsiones sobre el Bloqueo y el Erario de México. Mexico, 1838.

Ventajas políticas civiles, fabriles y domésticas que por dar ocupación también a las mujeres en la fábricas de maquinaria moderna que están levantando en México, deben recibirse. Puebla, 1837

Ascué y Zalvide, Pedro. *Contestación a los Editores del Sol y del Registro Oficial o sea Observaciones sobre el Banco de Avío.* Mexico, 1831.

Ligeras observaciones sobre la extinción de la moneda de cobre. Puebla, 1841.

Observaciones contra la libertad del comercio exterior o sea Contestación al Diario del Gobierno Federal. Puebla, 1835.

Ayuntamiento de Puebla sobre la amortización de Cobre. Puebla, 1841.

"Un Ciudadano" *Carta al Señor Presidente que debe leer toda la Gente.* Puebla, 1832.

"Un Ciudadano de Puebla" *Representación al futuro congreso representativo.* Puebla, 1821.

Consideraciones sobre la situación política y social de la república mexicana en el año 1847. Mexico, 1847.

Crítica del Hombre Libre. *Diálogo entre un religioso y su Pilguanejo.* Mexico, 1821.

Diálogo entre un comerciante y un Tejedor. Puebla, 1833, (Included within Estevan de Antuñano's *Aclaración, ampliación y corrección.*)

Dos Millones de Moneda para el Estado de Puebla. Puebla, 1844.

DOS MILLONES de MONEDA para el Estado de Puebla. Parte espositiva del

proyecto que presentaron como ciudadanos el Supremo Gobierno del Estado. Puebla, 1849.

"E.D.L." *Realizado en Puebla el importante voto de un ciudadano.* Puebla, 13 October, 1821.

Estévez Ravanillo, Lic. Francisco Nepomuceno *Vindicación de Señor de Cortés*

Francisco de Paula Puig por la parte en que lo injuria el Diálogo entre el Tejedor y el Zapatero. Puebla, 6 February, 1822.

Exposición dirigida al Congreso de la Nación por los Fabricantes y Cultivadores de Algodón. Mexico, 1841.

Exposición que varios FABRICANTES de HILAZA y TEJIDOS presentan al Excelentísimo AYUNTAMIENTO de esta Ciudad para que la eleva a las Cámaras de la Unión. Puebla, 1851.

Extraordinaria de Puebla y Temixco. Viva la Federación !! Mexico, 1833.

Extraordinario Violento. Mexico, 1833.

Falsedades que contiene el Cuaderno titulado "Despojo a mano armada por el prefecto de Tlaxcala". Puebla, 1844.

"Filalethes" *Intereses de la Puebla Bien Intendidos.* Puebla, 1821.

Idea de la Sociedad Patriótica formada en esta capital del estado de Puebla para fomento de las artes. Año de 1831. Puebla, 1831.

"J.M.B." *O auxiliamos al gobierno, ó la patria va al infierno.* Mexico, 1832.

Manso, José. *Apuntes Artísticos de un artesano de Puebla.* Mexico, 1835.

Militares a rendirse porque Santa Anna triunfó. Mexico, 1832.

Nueva relación en que se refiere la disputa que tuvo el trigo con el Dinero. Puebla, n.d. [c.1795].

Nueva Siembra de Algodón. Puebla, 1841.

Refutación de la llamada teoría fundamental de la industria de algodones en México, por varios poblanos amantes de la agricultura de su país. Puebla, 1840.

Representación que los comerciantes del giro de tocinería han elevado al Honorable Congreso del Estado de Puebla. Puebla, 1831.

Representación que los artesanos de algodón, y algunos ciudadanos de Puebla, dirigen al Exmo. Sr. Presidente, a efecto, de que no se conceda a Santa Ana de Tamaulipas, el ser puerto de Depósito; sino que antes bien se cierre este al comercio extranejro, para la importación. Puebla, 1837.

Representación que los tejedores de algodón, vecinos de Puebla, dirigen al Exmo. Sr. Gobernador del Departamento, pidiendo se prohiba a los fabricantes de hilazas tener telares des su cuenta y que se permita la introducción de hilazas al extranjero, hasta que las fábricas nacionales sean suficientes a proveer los consumos. Puebla, 1840.

Representación al supremo gobierno de los empresarios de fábricas nacionales de hilados y tejidos de algodón. Mexico, 1840.

Representación a la Excelentísima Asamblea Departamental que hace el comercio sobre acuñación de moneda particular para el departamento. Puebla, 1845.

Representación que los que suscriben elevan respetuosamente al Exmo.

Ayuntamiento de la Capital de PUEBLA, con motivo al alzamiento que se pretende de la leyes prohibitivas. Mexico, 1851.

Representación dirigida al Congreso de la Unión por 6,124 artesanos, pidiendo protección para el trabajo de los nacionales. Mexico, 1851.

Satisfacción que los artesanos de esta Ciudad abajos suscritos dan a Señor su diputado Don Francisco de Paula Puig, por las expresiones que vierte el Diálogo del Tejedor y el Zapatero. Puebla, 1822.

Tamariz, Leornardo. *Pacificación de la República*. Puebla, 1858.

El Tejedor y Su Compadre. *Plática familar entre éstos y un aprendíz. Puebla, Nos. 1-8, 1820*, reprinted in José Miguel Quintana, *Las Artes Gráficas en Puebla*.

Toma de Puebla y Glorias de la Patria. Mexico, 1832.

Triunfo de la Libertad de la Imprenta. Puebla, No. 5, 1821.

Vindicación de los barrios de Puebla sobre las injurias de El Universal. Puebla, 1850.

iv) Contemporary Newspapers and Periodicals.

La Abeja Poblana Nos.1-15. Puebla, 1820-21.

Alzate, J.A. *Gacetas de Literatura de Mexico*. 2 vols., Puebla, 1831.

El Amigo de la Religión, Agricultura, Política, Comercio, Ciencias y Artes. Puebla, 1839.

Boletín de la Sociedad Mexicana de Geografía e Estadística. 1st Series, 1838-1861, Vols. I, II, and X.

El Caduceo. Puebla, 8 Vols., 1824-26.

El Cardillo. Mexico, 1828.

El Cardillo de los Agiotistas. Mexico, 1837.

Correo Semanario Político y mercantil de México. Mexico, 1809, Vols. I-III.

Diario de la Junta Nacional Instituyente del Imperio Mexicano. Vol. I. Mexico, 1823,

Diario de México. Mexico, Vol. IV, 1807.

El Farol. Nos.17 & 19, Puebla, 1822.

Gaceta del Gobierno Imperial de México. Vol. I. Mexico, 1823.

Gacetas de México. Compendio de Noticias de Nueva España desde principios del año de 1794. Mexico, 1784-1797.

La Guirnalda. Semanario de Historia, Geografía, Vol. I, Mexico, 1844.

El Invitador. Puebla, 2 Vols., 1826-1827.

Jornal Económico Mercantil de Veracruz. Vols. I & II, Veracruz, 1806.

El Museo Mexicano. Mexico, 1843-44, Vols. I-IV.

Noticioso Poblano. Puebla, 1821.

El Patriota Puebla, Vol. III, 1827.

El Poblano. Puebla, 1827, Vol. I.

"R. H." *El Tejedor y El Zapatero.* Puebla, 9 February, 1822.

El Registro Oficial. Mexico, Vols. I-IV, 1830-1831.

El Registro Trimestre. Vol. I, Mexico, 1832.

El Semanario Artístico. Mexico, 1944.

El Semanario de la Industria Mexicana. 2 Vols., Mexico, 1841.

El Universal. Mexico, 1850.

La Voz de la Patria. Mexico, Vol. VI, 1830.

v) Travels, Guides, Diaries and Calendars.

Ajofrín, Francisco *Diario de viaje a la América septentrional en el siglo XVII.* Madrid, 1958.

Beaufoy, Mark *Mexican Illustrations.* London, 1828.

Bullock, William *Six Month's Residence and Travels in Mexico.* 2 vols., London, 1825.

Calderón de la Barca, Frances *Life in Mexico.* London, 1970.

Calendario Cumplido. Puebla, 1840.

Calendario Galván. Mexico, 1842.

Calendario de López Mexico, 1844.

Cochelet, Michel "Souvenirs d'un voyage de Mexico a New York par M. Cochelet en 1830", *Extrait d'un Bulletin de la Societé de Geographie.* Paris, 1845.

Clavijero, Francisco "Breve descripción de la Provincia de México de la Compañía de Jesús", in Mariano Cuevas, *Tesoros Documentales de México, Siglo XVIII.* Mexico, 1944, pp. 324-7.

Comyn, Tomás. *Apuntes de un viajero o cartas familiares escritas durante la insurección del reyno de México en 1811, 1812, 1813 y 1814.* Madrid, 1843.

Gage, Thomas *The English American. A New Survey of the West Indies, 1648.* Guatemala City, 1946.

Gemelli Carrerri, Dr. John Francis *A Voyage Round the World.* London, 1752.

Hall, Basil *Extracts from a Journal written on the Coasts of Chile, Peru and Mexico, in the years 1820, 1821, 1822.* 2 vols., Edinburgh, 1824.

Hardy, R.W. *Travels in the Interior of Mexico in 1825, 1826. 1827 and 1828.* London, 1829.

Harvey Gardiner, C. *Mexico, 1825-1828. The Journal and Correspondence of Edward Thornton Tayloe.* Chapel Hill, 1949.

Humboldt, Alejandro *Ensayo Político sobre el Reino de la Nueva España.* Mexico, 1966.

Humboldt, Alexander von *Political Essay on the Kingdom of New Spain.* 5 Vols., London, 1811.

Latrobe, Charles Joseph *The Rambler in Mexico.* New York, 1847.

Mayer, Brantz *Mexico as it was and Mexico as it is.* Philadelphia, 1841.

Payno, Manuel "Un Viaje a Veracruz en el invierno de 1843", *El Museo Mexicano*, Vol. IV, 1843.

Poinsett, Joel *Notes on Mexico made in the autumn of 1822.* London, 1825.

Sartorius, Carlos *Mexico about 1850.* Reprinted New York, 1958.

Thompson, Waddy *Recollections of Mexico.* New York, 1846.

Valle, Juan del *Guía de Forasteros.* Puebla, 1852.

Ward, Henry *Mexico in 1827.* 2 Vols., London, 1829.

vi) Other Contemporary Works, Histories, Chronicles, etc..

Abaroa, Joaquín *Memorial Práctico de Químico Manufacturero o Colección de*

Procedimientos Relativos a las Artes y Manufactura. 2 Vols., Puebla, 1833.

Bermúdez de Castro, Diego Antonio *Theatro Angelopolitano.* Puebla, 1764.

Barnes, Edward *The History of Cotton Manufacture in Great Britain (1835)*

London, 1966 Edition.

Cabrera y Quintero, Cayetano *Escudo de Armas de México.* Mexico, 1746.

Carrión, Antonio *Historia de la Ciudad de Puebla de los Angeles (1898).* 2 Vols., reprinted in Puebla, 1970.

Clavijero, Francisco "Breve descripción de la Provincia de México de la Compañía de Jesús", in Mariano Cuevas, *Tesoros Documentales de México, Siglo XVIII*. Mexico, 1944, pp. 324-37.

De la Peña, Francisco Javier "Notas" [annotations accompanying Fray Juan Villa Sánchez, *Puebla Sagrada y Profana* (1746)]. Reprinted Puebla, 1967.

Fabian y Fuero, Francisco *Colección de Providencias Diocesanos del Obispado de la Puebla de los Angeles*. Puebla, 1770.

Fernández Echeverría y Veytía, Mariano *Historia de la Fundación de la Ciudad de la Puebla de los Angeles*. 2nd edition, 2 Vols., Puebla, 1963.

Galindo y Galindo, Miguel *La Gran Década Nacional*. 3 Vols., Mexico, 1904-1906

García, José María "Apuntes sobre la Ciudad de Puebla", *BSMGE* (lst series) Vol. X, 1861, p. 112.

García Quiñones, José. *Descripción de las demostraciones con que la muy Noble y muy Leal Ciudad de Puebla de los Angeles*. Puebla, 1809.

Hermosa, Jesús *Manual de Geografía y Estadística de la República Mexicana*. Paris, 1857.

León, N. *Relación de los sucesos acaecidos en la ciudad de Puebla, del 14 al 27 de Mayo 1847*. Mexico, 1901.

Lerdo de Tejada, Miguel *Comercio Exterior de México*. Mexico, 1867.

López de Villaseñor, Pedro *Cartilla Vieja de la Nobilísima Ciudad de Puebla*. Mexico, 1961.

Montgomery, J. *The Cotton Manufacture of the United States contrasted and compared with that of Great Britain*. (1840). Reprinted New York, 1970.Navarro y Noriega, Fernando. *Memoria sobre la Población de ueva España*. Mexico, 1820.

Nieto, Vicente *Descripción y Plano de la Provincia de Tehuacán de la Granadas (1791)*. Puebla, 1960.

Orozco y Berra, Manuel *Apuntes para la Historia de la Moneda y Acuñación desde antes la Conquista*. Mexico, 1880.

Paso y Troncoso, Francisco *Epistolario de la Nueva España*. Vol. 16, Mexico, 1939-1942.

Payno, Manuel *Los Bandidos de Río Frío*. Mexico, 1968.

Ponce, Alonso "Relación Breve y Verdadura de algunas cosas de las muchas que sucedían en las Provincias de la Nueva España", *CDIHE*, Vol. MVIII, 1972.

Prieto, Guillermo *Indicaciones sobre el origen, vicisitudes y estado de las rentas generales de la federación mexicana.* Mexico, 1850.

Puebla en el Virreinato. Eighteenth-century document, published in Puebla, 1965.

Revillagigedo, Conde de *Instrucción reservada al Marqués de Branciforte.* Mexico, 1966.

Smith, Adam *The Wealth of Nations.* London, 1970 Edition.

Vázquez de Espinosa *Descripción de la Nueva España en el siglo XVI.* Mexico, 1944.

Vetancurt, Agustín de *Tratado de la Ciudad de México, y las grandezas que la ilustre después que la fundaron Españoles.* Mexico, 1698.

Villa Sánchez, Juan *Puebla sagrada y profana. Informe dado a su muy ilustre ayuntamiento en el año de 1746.* first printed in Puebla, 1835, with annotations by Francisco Javier de la Peña. Reprinted Puebla, 1967.

Villa-Señor y Sánchez, José Antonio de *Teatro Americano. Descripción general de los reynos y provincias de la Nueva España, y sus jurisdicciones.* México, 2 Vols., 1746-48.

Zerón Zapata, Miguel *La Puebla de los Angeles en el siglo XVII.* Mexico, 1945.

SECONDARY WORKS: BOOKS

Abel, Christopher and Colin Lewis (eds.) *Latin America: Economic Imperialism and the State.* London, 1985.

Alvarado Morales, Manuel *La Ciudad de México ante la fundación de la Armada de Barlovento, 1635-1643.* Mexico, 1983.

Anderson, Rodney *Outcasts in Their Own Land: Mexican Industrial Workers, 1906-1911.* DeKalb, 1976.

Archer, Christon *The Army in Bourbon Mexico, 1760-1821.* Albuquerque, 1977.

Arcila Farías, Eduardo *El comercio entre Nueva España y Venezuela.* Mexico, 1950.

368

_____ *Reformas económicas del siglo XVIII en Nueva España.* 2 Vols., Mexico, 1974.

Arrom, Silvia Marina *The Women of Mexico City, 1790-1857.* Stanford, 1985.

Bakewell, Peter. J. *Silver Mining and Society in Colonial Mexico: Zacatecas, 1546- 1700.* Cambridge, 1971.

Barbier, Jacques, and Alan Kuethe (eds.) *The North American Role in the Spanish Imperial Economy, 1760-1819.* Manchester, 1984.

Bazant, Jan *Historia de la deuda exterior de México*, 1823-1946.Mexico, 1968.

_____ *Antonio Haro y Tamariz y sus aventuras políticas, 1811-1869.* Mexico, 1985.

Black's Medical Dictionary. London, 1958.

Borah, Woodrow *Silk Raising in Colonial Mexico.* Berkeley, 1943.

_____ *Early Trade and Navigation between Mexico and Peru.* Berkeley, 1954.

Boxer, Charles *Portuguese Society in the Tropics: the Municipal Councils of Goa, Macao and Luanda, 1500-1800.* Wisconsin, 1965.

Brading, David A. *Haciendas and Ranchos in the Mexican Bajío: León, 1700-1860.* Cambridge, 1978.

_____ *Miners and Merchants in Bourbon Mexico, 1763-1810.* Cambridge, 1971.

Calvo, Thomas *Acatzingo. Demografía de una Parroquia Mexicana.* Mexico, 1973.

Carabarán G., Alberto *El trabajo y los trabajadores del obraje en la ciudad de Puebla, 1700-1710.* Puebla, 1984.

Cardoso, Ciro F. S. (ed.) *Formación y desarrollo de la burguesía en México, siglo XIX.* Mexico, 1978.

Carrera Stampa, Manuel *Los gremios mexicanos. La organización gremial en Nueva España, 1521-1821.* Mexico, 1954.

Castro Gutiérrez, Felipe *La Extinción de la Artesanía Gremial* Mexico, 1986.

Centro de Investigaciones Históricas y Sociales. *Puebla en el siglo XIX. Contribución al estudio de su historia.* Puebla, 1983.

_____ *Puebla, de la Colonia a la Revolución.* Puebla: 1987.

Chance, John K. *Race and Class in Colonial Oaxaca.* Stanford, 1978.

Chapman, S. D. *The Cotton Industry in the Industrial Revolution.* London, 1972.

Chevalier, François *Land and Society in Colonial Mexico.* Berkeley, 1970.

Contreras, Carlos (Ed.). *La ciudad de Puebla. Estancamiento y modernidad de un perfil urbano en el siglo XIX.* Puebla, 1986.

Cordero y Torres, Enrique. *Cronología de Gobernantes del Territorio Poblano.* Puebla, 1970.

_____*Diccionario General de Puebla.* 4 vols., Puebla, 1958.

Cosío Villegas, Daniel *Historia Moderna de México. La República Restaurada. Vida Política.* Mexico, 1955.

_____*La cuestión arancelaria en México.* Mexico, 1932.

Costeloe, Michael *La primera república federal de México, 1824-1835.* Mexico, 1975.

De la Peña, José. *Oligarquía y propiedad en Nueva España 1550-1624.* Mexico, 1983.

Ewald, Ursula *Estudios sobre la hacienda colonial en México. Las propiedades rurales del Colegio Espíritu Santo en Puebla.* Wiesbaden, 1976.

Farriss, Nancy *Crown and Clergy in Colonial Mexico.* London,1968.

Florescano, Enrique (et al.) *La Clase Obrera en la Historia de México, de la colonia al imperio.* Vol. I, Mexico, 1981.

_____*Precios del maíz y crisis agrícolas en México.* Mexico, 1969.

Florescano, Enrique. and Elsa Malvido, (eds.). *Ensayos sobre la Historia de las Epidemias en México.* 2 Vols., Mexico, 1982.

Frost, Elsa Cecilia, (et al.). *El trabajo y los trabajadores en la historia de México.* Mexico, 1979.

Gamboa Ojeda, Leticia *Los empresarios de ayer. El grupo dominante en la industria textil de Puebla, 1906-1929.* Puebla, 1985.

García Bernal, Cristina *La Sociedad en Yucatán, 1700-1750.* Seville, 1972.

Gómez Haro, Eduardo *Puebla y sus Gobernadores.* Puebla, 1915.

_____*La Ciudad de Puebla y la Guerra de Independencia.* Puebla, 1910.

González Angulo Aguirre, Jorge *Artesanado y ciudad a finales del siglo XVIII*. Mexico, 1983.

González Navarro, Moisés *Anatomía del Poder en México, 1848-1853*. Mexico, 1977.

Gootenburg, Paul E. *Artisans and Merchants: the Making of an open Economy in Lima, Peru, 1830 to 1860*. Unpublished M.Phil. dissertation, University of Oxford, 1981.

Greenow, Linda L. *Credit and Socioeconomic Change in Colonial Mexico: Loans and Mortgages in Guadalajara, 1720-1820*. Boulder, 1983.

Grosso, Juan Carlos *Estructura productiva y fuerza de trabajo. Puebla, 1830-1890*. Puebla, 1984.

Hale, Charles. *Mexican Liberalism in the Age of Mora*. New Haven, 1966.

Hamnett, Brian *Politics and Trade in Southern Mexico*. Cambridge, 1971.

_____ *Roots of Insurgency Mexican Regions, 1750-1824*. Cambridge, 1986.

Harris, Charles H. *The Sánchez Navarro: A Socio-Economic Study of a Coahuilan Latifundio, 1846-1853*. Chicago, 1964.

_____ *A Mexican Family Empire: the Latifundio of the Sánchez Navarros*. Austin, 1975.

Herrera, Iñés *El Comercio Exterior de México, 1821-1875*. Mexico, 1977.

Hillier, Bevis *Master Potters of the Industrial Revolution*. London, 1965.

Hoberman, Louisa and Susan Socolow (eds.). *Cities and Society in Colonial Latin America*. Albuquerque, 1986.

Hofstadter, Richard *America at 1750. A Social Portrait*. New York, 1973.

Israel, Jonathan *Race, Class and Politics in Colonial Mexico 1610-1670*. Oxford, 1975.

Jenks, Leland H. *The Migration of British Capital to 1875*. London, 1971.

Jacobsen, Nils and Hans Jurgen Puhle (eds.). *The Economies of Mexico and Peru During the Late Colonial Period*. Berlin, 1986.

Johnson, Lyman L. *The Artisans of Buenos Aires during the Viceroyalty, 1775-1810.* Unpublished Ph.D. dissertation, University of Connecticut, 1974.

Keremitsis, Dawn. *La industria textil mexicana en el siglo XIX.* Mexico, 1973.

Kicza, John E. *Colonial Entrepreneurs. Families and Business in Bourbon Mexico City.* Albuquerque, 1983

Kinsbruner, Jay *Petty Capitalism in Spanish America: The Pulperos of Puebla, Mexico City, Caracas, and Buenos Aires.* Boulder, 1986.

Kreidte, Peter, Hans Medick and Jurgen Schlumbohm *Industry before Industrialisation: Rural Industry and the Genesis of Capitalism.* Cambridge, 1981.

Ladd. Doris M. *The Mexican Nobility at Independence, 1780-1826.* Austin, 1976.

Laurie, Bruce *Working People of Philadelphia, 1800-1850.* Philadelphia, 1980.

Leicht, Hugo. *Las Calles de Puebla.* Barcelona, 1967.

Liehr, Reinhard *Ayuntamiento y oligarquía en Puebla, 1787 - 1810.* Mexico, 2 Vols.,1976.

_____ *Stadtrat und Städtische Oberschicht von Puebla am ende der Kolonialzeit (1787-1810).* Wiesbaden, 1971.

_____ (ed.) *La formación de economías Latino-americanas y los intereses económicas Europeas en la época de Bolívar, 1800-1850.* Berlin, 1988.

Lindley, Richard *Haciendas and Economic Development. Guadalajara, Mexico and Independence.* Austin, 1983.

Marín Tamayo, Fausto *Huexotitla. La Propiedad Privada del Molino Activo Más Ántiguo de América.* Puebla, 1959.

La división racial en Puebla de los Angeles. Puebla, 1960.

McGreevey, William Paul *Economic History of Colombia, 1845-1930.* Cambridge, 1971.

Medina, Aristides *La Iglesia y la producción agrícola en Puebla, 1540-1795.* Mexico, 1984.

Moreno Toscano, Alejandra (ed.). *Ciudad de Mexico. Ensayo de Construcción de una Historia.* Mexico, 1978.

Morin, Claude *Michoacán en la Nueva España del Siglo XVIII Crecimiento y Desigualdad en una Economía Colonial.* Mexico, 1979.

372

_____ *Santa Iñés Zacatelco (1646-1812) Contribución a la Demografía Histórica de México Colonial.* Mexico, 1973.

Müller, Wolfgang *Die textil des raunes Puebla (Mexiko) in 19 jahrundert.* Unpublished Ph.D dissertation, University of Bonn, 1977.

Nash, Gary*The Urban Crucible.Social Change, Political Conciousness and the Origins of the American Revolution.* Cambridge, 1979.

Ortíz de la Tabla, Javier *Comercio exterior de Veracruz 1778-1821 y crisis de dependencia.* Seville, 1978.

Palacios, Enrique Juan.*Puebla y su territorio.* 2 Vols., Puebla, 1917.

Parra Gómez, Roberto *Puebla en Cifras.* Mexico, 1944.

Perry, Laurens Ballard *Juárez and Díaz. Machine Politics in Mexico.* DeKalb, 1978.

Phelan, J. L. *The Kingdom of Quito in the Seventeenth Century.* Madison, 1967.

Platt, D. C. M. *Latin America and British Trade.* London, 1972.

Potash, Robert. *El Banco de Avío de México. El fomento de la industria, 1821-1846.* Mexico, 1959.

Quintana, José Miguel. *Las Artes Gráficas en Puebla.* Mexico, 1960.

Quintana, Miguel A. *Estevan de Antuñano, Fundador de la Industria Textil en Puebla.* 2 vols., Mexico, 1957.

Ramírez Flores, José *Los consulados de comerciantes de Nueva España.* Mexico, 1976.

Randall, Robert *Real del Monte: a British Mining Venture in Mexico.* Austin, 1972.

Real Díaz, Joaquín. *Las Ferias de Jalapa.* Seville, 1959.

Reyes Heroles, Jesús *El Liberalismo Mexicano.* 3 Vols., Mexico, 1974.

Robinson, David J. (ed.) *Social Fabric and Spatial Structure in Colonial Latin America.* Ann Arbor, 1979.

Robinson, David J. and Linda L. Greenow *Catálogo del Archivo del Registro Público de la Propiedad de Guadalajara: Libros de Hipotecas, 1566-1820.* Guadalajara, 1986.

Romero, L. A. *La Sociedad de la Igualdad. Los artesanos de Santiago de Chile y sus primeras experiencias políticas, 1820-1851.* Buenos Aires, 1978.

Safford, Frank, *Commerce and Enterprise in Central Colombia, 1821-1870.* Unpublished Ph.D. dissertation, Columbia University, 1965.

Salvucci, Richard J. *Textiles and Capitalism in Mexico. An Economic History of the Obrajes, 1539-1840*. Princeton, 1987.

Samayoa Guevara, Hector Humberto. *Los Gremios de Artesanos en la Ciudad de Guatemala 1524-1821*. Guatemala City, 1962.

Scardaville, Michael *Crime and the Urban Poor: Mexico City in the Late Colonial Period*. Unpublished Ph.D. dissertation, University of Florida, 1978.

Scranton, Philip *Proprietary capitalism. The textile manufacture at Philadelphia, 1800-1885*. Cambridge, 1983.

Serrera Contreras, Ramón María *Cultivo y Manufactura de Lino y Cáñamo en Nueva España (1777-1800)*. Seville, 1974.

Shaw, Frederick J. *Poverty and Politics in Mexico City, 1824-54*. Unpublished Ph.D dissertation, University of Florida, 1975.

Smout, T.C. *A History of the Scottish People, 1560-1830*. London, 1975.

Stein, Stanley and Barbara Stein *The Colonial Heritage of Latin America*. New York, 1970

Swann, Michael *Tierra Adentro: Settlement and Society in Colonial Durango*. Boulder, 1982.

Telles G., Francisco *De Reales y granos. Las finanzas y el abasto de la Puebla de los Angeles, 1820-1840*. Puebla, 1986.

Thomson, G. P. C. *Economy and Society in Puebla de los Angeles, 1800-1850*. Unpublished D.Phil. dissertation, University of Oxford, 1978.

Torres Ramírez, Bibiano *La Armada de Barlovento*. Seville, 1981.

Trabulse, Elías *Fluctuaciones económicas en Oaxaca durante el siglo XVIII*. Mexico, 1984.

Trautman, Wolfgang *Las transformaciones en el paisaje cultural de Tlaxcala durante la época colonial*. Wiesbaden, 1981.

Van Young, Eric *Hacienda and Market in Eighteenth-Century Mexico: The Rural Economy of the Guadalajara Region, 1675-1820*. Berkeley, 1981.

Walker, David *Kinship, Business and Politics. The Martínez del Río Family in Mexico, 1823-1867*. Austin, 1986.

Whetten, Nathan *Rural Mexico*. Chicago, 1964.

Wilentz, Sean *Chants Democratic New York City and the Rise of the American Working Class, 1788-1850*. New York, 1984.

Secondary Works: Articles and Chapters

Aguirre Anaya, Carmen and Alberto Carabarán Gracia "Formas artesanales y fabriles de los textiles de algodón en la ciudad de Puebla, siglos XVIII y XIX". in CIHS, *Puebla de la Colonia*, pp. 125-54.

"Proprietarios de la industria textil de Puebla en el siglo XIX: Dionisio José de Velasco y Pedro Berges de Zúñiga", *Puebla en el Siglo XIX*, pp. 177-224

Aguareles, Eugenio "Una conmoción popular en el México virreinal", *AEA*, Vol. VIII, 1950, pp. 125-161.

Albi-Romero, Guadalupe "La sociedad de Puebla de los Angeles en el Siglo XVI", *JGSWFL*, 1970, pp. 17-145.

Bazant, Jan "Estudio sobre la productividad de la industria algodonera mexicana en 1843-1845", in Luis Chávez Orozco, *La industria nacional*, pp. 29-85.

_____ "Evolución de la industria textil poblana (1554-1845)", *HMex*, Vol. XIII, 1962, pp. 473-516.

_____ "Industria algodonera poblana de 1803-1843 en números", *HMex*, Vol. XIV, 1964, pp. 131-143.

Beato, Guillermo "La Casa Martínez del Río: del comercio colonial a la industria fabríl", in Ciro Cardoso (ed.), *Formación*, pp. 57-107.

Bieber, Leon E. "Bolivia 1825-1850: Aislamiento internacional y economía nacional", in Reinhard Liehr (ed.), *La formación*, pp. 187-210.

Bronner, Fred "Urban Society in Colonial Spanish America. Research Trends", *LARR*, Vol. XXI, 1986 pp. 7-72.

Bustamante, M. "La situación epidemiológica de México en el siglo XIX", in Enrique Florescano and Elsa Malvido (eds.), *Ensayos*, Vol.II, pp. 417-424

Calvento Martínez, María del Carmen "Intereses particulares y política de abastecimiento en México", *RI*, Vol. XXXVI, 1976, pp. 159-160.

Carabarán Gracia, Alberto "Auge y declinación de los obrajes en Puebla: tres enfoques historiográficos", unpublished paper presented at the LASA conference, Mexico City, 1983.

Carrera Stampa, Manuel "El obraje novo-hispano", *Memorias de la Academia Mexicana de la Historia*, Vol. XX, 1961, pp. 148-171.

_____ "The Evolution of Weights and Measures in New Spain", *HAHR*, Vol. XIX, 1949, pp. 2-24.

Cassidy, T.J. "British Capital and the Mexican Silver Mining Industry, 1820-50", Cambridge University, Centre for Latin American Studies, *Working Paper* No. 21, n.d.

Castro Morales, Efraím "Origen de algunas artistas y artesanos europeos de la Región de Puebla-Tlaxcala", *Comunicaciones*, No.7, 1973, pp. 117-120.

Chance, John K. and William B Taylor "Estate and Class in a Colonial City: Oaxaca in 1792", *CSSH* Vol. XIX, 1977, pp. 454-487.

Chapman, S.D.. "Fixed Capital Formation in the British Cotton Manufacturing Industry", in J. Higgins and S. Pollard (eds.) *Aspects of Capital Investment in Great Britain,1750-1850*. London, 1971.

Chevalier, François "La Signification Sociale de la Fondation de Puebla de los Angeles", *RHA*, Vol. XXIII, June, 1947, pp. 105-130.

Coatsworth, John "American Trade with Euopean colonies in the Caribbean and South America, 1790-1812", *WMQ*, Vol. XXIV, 1967, pp. 243-265.

_____ "Obstacles to Economic Growth in Nineteenth Century Mexico" *AHR*, Vol. LXXXIII, 1978, pp. 80-100.

"The Mexican Mining Industry in the Eighteenth Century." in Jacobsen and Puhle (eds.) *The Economies of Mexico and Peru*, pp. 26-45.

Cook, Sherburne F. "Las Migraciones en la Historia de la Población Mexicana", in Bernardo García (et al.) *Historia y sociedad en el mundo de habla española*. Mexico, 1970.

Cuenya, Miguel Angel "Puebla en su demografía, 1650-1850. Una aproximación al tema", in CIHS-ICUAP, *Puebla de la Colonia*, pp. 9-72

De la Garza, Luis Alberto "Reformismo y Contra Revolución: La Caída de la Primera República Federal en México", unpublished Paper, Mexico, 1987.

Ewald, Ursula "The Von Thünen Principle and Agrcultural Zonation in Colonial Mexico", *Journal of Historical Geography*, Vol. 3, 1977, pp. 122-33.

Garavaglia, Juan Carlos, and Juan Carlos Grosso "La región de Puebla/Tlaxcala y la economía novohispana (1670-1821)", *HMex*, Vol. XXXV, 1986, pp. 549-600.

_____ "Consideraciones sobre las alcabalas de Nueva España", unpublished paper, Mexico, 1984.

Gerhard, Peter "Un Censo de la Diócesis de Puebla en 1681", *HMex*, Vol. XXX, 1980-81, pp. 530-560.

376

Gómez de la Cortina, Conde José "Población en el Departamento de Puebla", *BSMGE*, 1st Series, Vol. I, 1839.

González Angulo, Jorge, and Roberto Sandoval "Los Trabajadores Industriales de Nueva España, 1750-1810", in Enrique Florescano, (ed.) *La Clase Obrera*, pp. 173-238.

González Sánchez, Isabel "Sistemas de trabajo, salarios y situación de los trabajadores agrícolas, 1750-1810", in Enrique Florescano, (ed.), *La clase obrera*, pp. 150-172.

Gootenburg, Paul "The Social Origins of Protectionism and free Trade in Nineteenth-Century Lima", *JLAS*, Vol. XIV, 1982, pp. 329-358.

Gormsen, Erdmann "La Zonificación Socio-económica de la Ciudad de Puebla. Cambios por efecto de la metropolización", *Comunicaciones*, No.15, 1978, pp. 7-20.

Greenleaf, R.E. "The Obraje in the late Mexican Colony", *TAms*, Vol. XXIII, 1967, pp. 227-250.

Greenow, Linda Spatial Dimensions of the Credit Market in Eighteenth-Century New Galicia", in David J Robinson (ed.) *Social Fabric and Spatial Structures in Colonial Latin America*. Ann Arbor, 1979, pp. 227-279.

Grosso, Juan Carlos "Notas sobre la formación de la fuerza de trabajo fabril en el municipio de Puebla (1835-1905)", *Boletín de Investigación del Movimiento Obrero*. (Puebla), No.2, February 1981, pp. 9-31.

Haufe, Hans "El Sueño del progreso. La Arquitectura Poblana del Siglo XIX como Catalizadora", *JGSWGLA*, Vol. XX, 1983, pp. 511-29.

Hirchberg, Julia "La Fundación de Puebla de los Angeles - mito y Realidad", *HMex*, Vol. 38, 1978, pp. 185-223.

_____ "Social Experiment in New Spain: A Prosopographical Study of the Early Settlement at Puebla de los Angeles." *HAHR*, Vol. 59, 1979, pp. 1-33.

Johnson, Lyman L. "The Entrepreneurial Reorganisation of an Artisan Trade: The Bakers of Buenos Aires, 1770-1820." *TAms*, Vol. XXXVII, 1980-81, pp. 139-160.

_____ "The Silversmiths of Buenos Aires: A Case Study in the Failure of Corporate Social Organisation", *JLAS*, Vol. VIII, 1976: 181-213.

Lavrín, Asunción "The Execution of the Laws of Consolidación in New Spain: Economic Aims and Results", *HAHR*, Vol. LIII, 1973, pp. 27-49.

Lewis, James A. "Nueva España y los esfuerzos para abastecer La Habana, 1779-1803", *AEA*, Vol. XXXIII, 1976, pp. 501-526.

_____ "Anglo American entrepreneurs in Havana: the background and significance of the expulsion of 1784-1785." in Barbier and Kuethe (eds.), *The North American Role*, pp.112-126.

Liehr, Reinhard. "Die Soziale Stellung der Indianer von Puebla am ende der Zweiten Hafte der 18 Jahrhunderts", *JGSWGLA*, Vol. VIII, 1971, pp. 74-125.

López Sarrelangue, Delfina E. "Población indígena de la Nueva España en el siglo XVIII", *HMex*, Vol. XII, 1963, pp. 516-530.

MacFarlane, Anthony "The transition from colonialism in Colombia, 1819-1875", in C. Abel and C. Lewis (eds.), *Latin America*, pp. 123-167.

Malvido, Elsa "Factores de la despoblación y de reposición de la población de Cholula (1641-1810)", *HMex*, Vol. XXIII, 1973, pp. 52-110

Mathes, Michael "To Save a City: the *desague* of México-Huehuetoca, 1607", *TAms*, Vol. XXVI, 1970, pp. 419-438.

Mayo, John "Consuls and Silver Contraband on Mexico's West Coast in the Era of Santa Anna", *JLAS*, Vol. XIX, 1987, pp. 389-441.

Miño Grijalva, Manuel "Espacio ecónomico e industria textil, los trabajadores de Nueva España, 1780-1810", *HMex*, Vol. XXXII, 1982-83, pp. 524-553.

_____ "El Camino hacia la Fábrica en Nueva España: El Caso de la "Fábrica de Indianillas" de Francisco de Iglesias, 1801-1810", *HMex*, Vol. XXXXIV, 1984, pp. 135-147.

Montgomery, David "The Working Class of the Pre-Industrial City, 1780-1830", *Labor History*, Vol. IX, 1968, pp. 3-32.

Moreno Toscano, Alejandra. and Carlos Aguirre "Migraciones hacia la ciudad de México durante el siglo XIX, Perspectivas de investigación." INAH-DIH, *Investigaciones sobre la Historia de la Ciudad de México.* Mexico, 1974, Vol. I.

_____ "Migrations to Mexico City in the Nineteenth Century: Research Approaches", *JIAWA*, Vol. XVII, 1975, pp. 27-42.

Müller, Wolfgang "El financiamiento de la industrialización, el caso de la industria textil poblana, 1830-1910", *Comunicaciones*, No. 15, 1978.

Muñóz Pérez, José "Una descripción comparativa de las ciudades americanas en el siglo XVIII", *Estudios Geográficos* (Madrid), Vol. XV, 1954, pp. 89-129.

Navarro García, Luis "La Sociedad Rural de México en el Siglo XVIII", *Anales de la Universidad Hispalense*, Vol. XXIV, 1963, pp. 19-53.

Oliver, Lilia "La pandemia del colera morbum. El caso de Guadalajara, Jalisco, en 1833", in Florescano and Malvido (Eds.), *Ensayos*, Vol. II, pp. 565-582

Ortíz de la Tabla, Javier "El Obraje colonial ecuatoriano. Aproximación a su estudio", *Revista de Indias*, Vol. XXXVII, 1977, pp. 471-541.

Pietschman, Horst. "El comercio de repartimientos de los alcaldes mayores y corregidores en la región de Puebla-Tlaxcala en el siglo XVIII", *Comunicaciones*, Vol. VII, 1973, pp. 127-9.

Quintana, José Miguel "Biografías y Bibliografías de Economistas Mexicanas: Estevan de Antuñano", *Boletín Bibliográfico de la Secretaría de Hacienda y Crédito Público* (Mexico), June, 1955, pp. 1-2.

Riley, James D "Landlords, Labourers and Royal Government: the Administration of Labor in Tlaxcala, 1680-1750." in Elsa Frost (ed.), *El trabajo*, pp. 221-241.

Rosenzweig, Fernando "La economía novohispana al comenzar el siglo XIX", *Ciencias Políticas y Sociales*, Vol. IX, 1963, pp. 455-494.

Safford, Frank "Commercial Crisis and Economic Ideology in New Granada, 1825-1850", in Reinhard Liehr, (ed.), *La Formación*.

Salinger, Sharon V. "Artisans, Journeymen and the Transformation of Labor in Late Eighteenth-Century Philadelphia", *WMQ*, Vol. XL, 1983, pp. 62-84.

Salvucci, Linda K. "Anglo-American merchants and stratagems for success in Spanish imperial markets, 1783-1807", in Barbier and Kuethe, (eds.), *The North American Role*, pp. 127-133.

Seed, Patricia "The Social Dimensions of Race: Mexico City, 1753", *HAHR*, Vol. LXII, 1982, pp. 569-606.

Seele, Enno "Galerias filtrantes en el Estado de Puebla", *Comunicaciones*, Vol. VII, 1973, pp. 141-4.

Smith, Robert S. "The Puebla Consulado, 1821-1824," *RHA*, Vol. XXI, 1946, pp. 150-161.

Super, John "Querétaro Obrajes. Industry and Society in Provincial Mexico, 1600-1810", *HAHR*, Vol. LVI, 1976, pp. 197-216.

Tanck de Estrada, Dorothy "La abolición de los gremios", in Elsa Cecilia Frost (et al.) (eds.), *El trabajo*, pp. 311-331.

Tenenbaum, Barbara A. "Merchants, Money and Mischief. The British in Mexico, 1821-1862", *TAms*, Vol. XXXV, 1978-79, pp. 317-339.

Thomson, G. P. C. "The Americas: Philadelphia and Mexico City", *History Today*, Vol. 34 (May, 1984), pp. 29-35.

_____ "The Cotton Textile Industry in Puebla during the Eighteenth and early Nineteenth Centuries", in Jacobsen and Puhle (eds.), *The Economies of Mexico and Peru*, pp. 169-202.

_____ "Traditional and Modern Manufacturing in Mexico, 1821-50", in Reinhard Liehr (ed.), *La formación de economías Latinoamericanas*.

Urias Hermosillo, Margarita. "Manuel Escandón: De las Diligencias al Ferrocarril", in Ciro Cardoso (ed.), *La formación*. pp. 25-56.

Vaughan, Mary Kay "Primary Schooling in the City of Puebla", *HAHR*, Vol. LXVII, 1987, pp. 39-62.

Vázquez de Warman, Irene "El pósito y la alhóndiga en la Nueva España", *HMex*, XVII, 1968, pp. 395-426.

Vélez Pliego, Roberto "Proprietarios y producción. La economía agrícola del municipio de Puebla a fines del Porfiriato", in CIHS, *Puebla de la Colonia*, pp. 285-326.

_____ "Rentabilidad y productividad en una hacienda mexicana: Hacienda y Molino de Santa Cruz", CIHS, *Puebla en el siglo XIX*, pp. 189-314.

Ventosa, Enrique "La Loza Poblana", in Manuel Romero y Terreros. *Las Artes Industriales en la Nueva España*. Mexico, 1923.

Vollmer, Günter "La evolución cuantitativa de la población indígena en la región de Puebla (1570-1810)", *HMex*, Vol. XXIII, 1973, pp. 43-51.

Warden, G.B. "Inequality and Instability in Eighteenth Century Boston: A Reappraisal", *Journal of Inter-disciplinary History*, Vol. VI, 1976, pp. 585-620.

Index